The German Policy of
Revolutionary France

✄ ——————————————————————————— ✄

VOLUME I

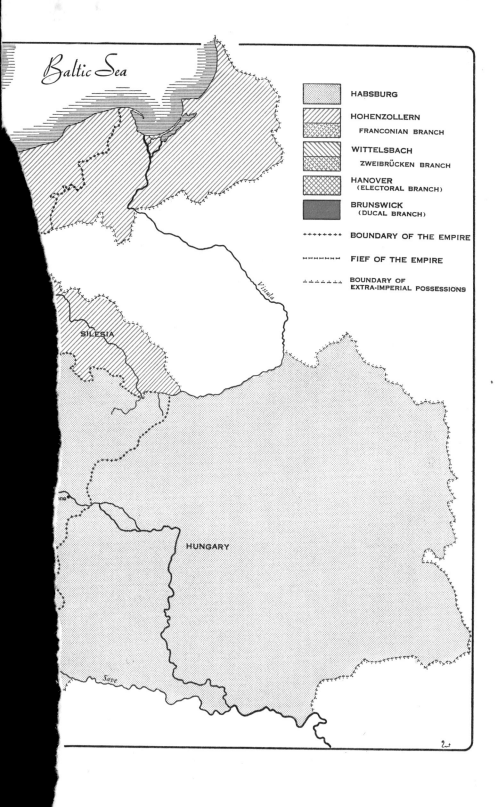

Baltic Sea

HABSBURG

HOHENZOLLERN
FRANCONIAN BRANCH

WITTELSBACH
ZWEIBRÜCKEN BRANCH

HANOVER
(ELECTORAL BRANCH)

BRUNSWICK
(DUCAL BRANCH)

++++++++ BOUNDARY OF THE EMPIRE

H─H─H─H─H─H FIEF OF THE EMPIRE

⌐⌐⌐⌐⌐⌐⌐ BOUNDARY OF
EXTRA-IMPERIAL POSSESSIONS

SILESIA

Vistula

HUNGARY

Save

2

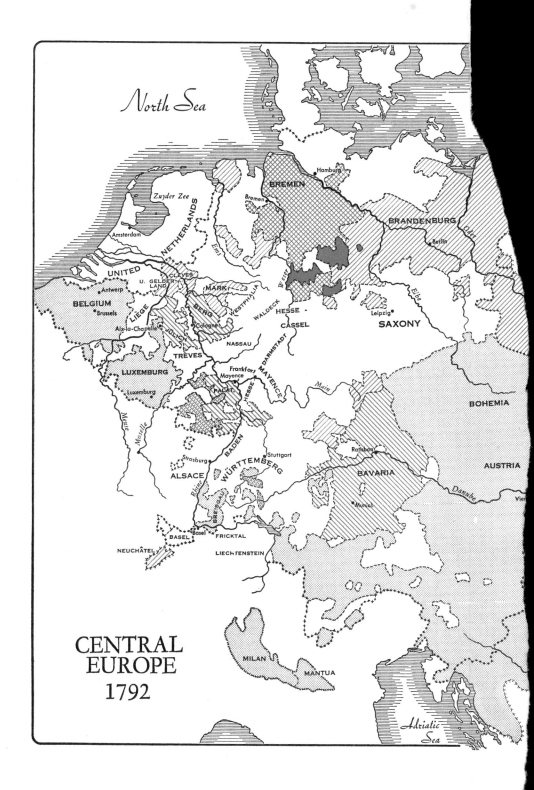

North Sea

Zuyder Zee

Amsterdam

NETHERLANDS

Ems

Hamburg

BREMEN

Bremen

BRANDENBURG

Berlin

Oder

UNITED
GELDER-
LAND

CLEVES

U. GELDER-
LAND

MARK

WESTPHALIA

WALDECK

HESSE-
CASSEL

Weser

SAXONY

Elbe

Leipzig

BELGIUM

Antwerp

Brussels

LIÈGE

Aix-la-Chapelle

JÜLICH

BERG

Cologne

NASSAU

HESSE-DARMSTADT

TREVES

LUXEMBURG

Luxemburg

Frankfort

Mayence

MAYENCE

Main

BOHEMIA

PALAT.

HESSE

Meuse

Moselle

BADEN

BREISGAU

WÜRTTEMBERG

Strasburg

Stuttgart

Ratisbon

ALSACE

Rhine

BAVARIA

AUSTRIA

Danube

Vien

Munich

BASEL

FRICKTAL

NEUCHÂTEL

Basel

LIECHTENSTEIN

MILAN

MANTUA

Adriatic
Sea

CENTRAL
EUROPE
1792

The German Policy of

Revolutionary France

A Study in French Diplomacy
during the War of the First Coalition

1792-1797

Sydney Seymour Biro

VOLUME I

1957

HARVARD UNIVERSITY PRESS

Cambridge, Massachusetts

© *Copyright, 1957*

By the President and Fellows of Harvard College

Distributed in Great Britain by
Oxford University Press
London

Library of Congress Catalog Card Number 56–9370
Printed in the United States of America

Special Acknowledgment

The writer wishes to express his gratitude to the late Robert B. Mowat of Oxford and Bristol Universities, and to Waldemar Westergaard of the University of California at Los Angeles, for invaluable criticisms, and for the kind encouragement without which a work of this nature could never have been written sans fatal results to both writer and reader.

PREFACE

*W*AR, according to General Homer Lea, is the result of the advance of nations along converging lines of self-interest toward a common goal. As the lines approach each other, the points of friction multiply. War results when the lines meet.

This could mean that war is inevitable, and Richard Stockton of the United States Army has published a ponderous monograph to prove that very point. The civilized world refuses to accept such a proposition. We are free agents. Can we not draw the lines over?

The history of western Europe is largely a history of conflict — between the powers holding sway on opposite banks of the Rhine. The question of responsibility for this deplorable situation may be one of great interest to the moralist, but to Man, outraged Man, it is of little moment. To him, the only important, the only vital, question is: How can the national policies of these inveterate combatants be reorientated so that the lines of their ambition should no longer converge but rather run in parallel grooves toward a mutual good?

In order to draw these lines over, we must take as a starting point some era in the past, for direction is controlled by at least two points. The most satisfactory point in the past is the period of the French Revolution, for it was then that modern Europe sprang into being — from soil fertilized with French ideas and watered with French blood. It is the period, also, which beheld the vitalization of a principle officially ignored during the old regime, discarded by Bonaparte, revived in 1919, and essentially involved in early De Gaullist calculations — that of a "natural boundary" between France and Germany.

It is proposed here to make an intensive study of the relations between these two great states during that part of the Revolution when this phoenix principle seemed to be the real obstacle to Franco-German harmony. Except for brief periods, it was such an obstacle until October 1797, when the Emperor agreed to forget his oath to defend the integrity of the Empire in return for

Venetian booty. Prussia and many of the smaller German states had already resigned themselves to France's acquisition of the left bank of the Rhine — for a price. The actual cession of the Rhineland did not take place until March 1798, but its fate was sealed when France and Austria signed the Treaty of Campo-Formio on October 17, 1797.

This book therefore aims to cover the six war years 1792–1797, inclusive. It is the only work in any language which specializes in the policy of Revolutionary France vis-à-vis Germany during these years — or during any years of the Revolution. The writer hopes that the experiences of another generation with problems similar to our own may help us to help the Germans and French compose their differences, and spare them — and us — the indignity of meeting our Maker as a puff of atomic vapor.

A word of definition is necessary here as to the meaning of "Germany" in this work. Technically, there was no Germany from 1792 to 1797. There was only a Holy Roman Empire, and it included many non-Germanic regions. This monograph deals only with the German portion, except where, in a given situation, the German and non-German are inseparably intertwined, or where the non-German throws light upon the German. One German region, Luxemburg, is not treated because it followed the path of the non-Germanic portion of the Austrian Netherlands.

The writer has been careful not to allow America's historic love of France and hatred of Junker despotism in all its forms to influence his judgment of Revolutionary policy. This must often be a severe judgment, for the glorious principles of 1789 were repeatedly prostituted by successive coteries gone mad with fear or freedom or lust for power and profit. Some historians have been content merely to portray, complimenting themselves on their impartiality. "The impartiality of history," says Lamartine aptly, "is not that of the mirror, which merely reflects objects, but of the judge, who sees, listens, and decides." In this work praise and blame are meted out without fear or favor. The aim is a truthful interpretation, no more, no less.

The reader will note in Part I an attempt to glean, from the vast body of printed sources on the Convention, the pertinent and interesting material that others have missed; a new group of archive texts on the Rheno-German Republic; a marshaling of documents to prove that the Montgaillard negotiation was not just a myth; a corrected picture of Robespierre's German policy, and the "policy" of the French people during his hegemony; additional light on the Sorel-von Sybel controversy as to whether Hérault de Séchelles and Barère endeavored to revolutionize Allied territories; new light on Franco-Hamburger relations from both archival and printed sources; the first objective study of the labyrinth of negotiations which ended in the Franco-Prussian Treaty of Basel; a study of that treaty's reception by the

French people according to the Parisian police reports; an archive map of the neutrality line which casts doubt upon the accuracy of von Vivenot's and Putzger's maps; a reappraisal of the documents describing the Hardenberg–Merlin of Thionville "dinner parley"; a virgin treatment from archive texts of Hesse-Cassel's treaty with France; new archive texts on the neutrality of northern Germany in practice, on the question of armistices, good offices, and treaties of separate peace, on the left bank of the Rhine after the Treaty of Basel, on the Théremin and Poteratz missions, etc. The fresh presentation of the entire subject of Franco-Rhinelander relations should be especially noted. In the last chapter of Part I ("Concluding Remarks — Convention") will be found marshaled the Revolutionary period's authorities upon whether the Rhine would make a satisfactory military frontier for France: a study which, for practical purposes, deals with the authorities of both the Convention and Directory without distinction.

In Part II will be found a document from the Austrian archives which seems to clear up the enigma of Carletti's expulsion; a French archival text which shows that Poteratz' mission of revolutionization in Swabia was terminated earlier than heretofore suspected; new light from various archives (French, Prussian, Austrian, English) on France's treatment of the Prussian left bank and of Frankfort-on-the-Main, on the importance of the Solingen region (Ruhr) and Saar Basin to the Directory, on France's interest in Rhine commerce, on the principles governing Directorial warfare, on French attempts to defeat Austria by stirring up revolution in the Habsburg provinces and in non-Habsburg Germany, on the post-Leoben occupation of Austria and the Empire, on the Directory's relations with the Hansa cities, on the influence of Poland on the Directory's German policy, on the contemplated reorganization of the Empire, etc.; corrected versions (by virtue of new material) of Gallo's mission to Basel for *Thugut* and Francis II, of the antecedents of the Treaty of Berlin, of the Directory's supposed renunciation of its renunciation of the left bank early in 1797, of the purpose of Perret's mission to Vienna, of the effect on the negotiations with Austria of the despatch of Barras' secretary, Bottot, to Bonaparte, and of numerous other aspects of the negotiations with Austria. The Paris police reports have contributed to a study of the reaction of the French public to the Treaties of Leoben and Campo-Formio. The difficult lot of the Rhineland under Hoche is here presented for the first time, and Hoche is stripped of the rosy aura in which mistaken historians have for so long enveloped him. In the last chapter of Part II ("Concluding Remarks — Directory") will be found an analysis of the Directory's German policy from the economic standpoint: an analysis which applies equally well, *mutatis mutandis*, to the Convention.

The bibliographical essay serves a threefold purpose: to indicate to the scholar the sources upon which this work is based; to erect signposts for students traveling in the same direction; and to tell the story behind the books which lie at the basis of this, as well as of all other modern studies on the French Revolution.

The appendix contains a chirographical study proving from some two score archive specimens that modern historians have been guilty of mayhem upon the name of that master of backstairs diplomacy, Poteratz.

The writer has endeavored to produce a work of interest not only to those locked within college walls, but to all who read and are concerned with the world in which they live. No heroic measures were necessary, however, to sustain the drama of events. It would require a genius in dullness to produce a dry and insipid product from the throbbing sources upon which this book is based. The author lays no claim to genius.

A personal note: So many people have been of assistance to the author in the gathering of material for this monograph that specific enumeration is impossible. In general terms, they are the archivists or librarians of the Archives Nationales, Archives des Affaires Etrangères, and Bibliothèque Nationale of Paris; the Haus- Hof- und Staatsarchiv and Nationalbibliothek of Vienna; the Geheimes Staatsarchiv and Staatsbibliothek, properly of Berlin; the Public Record Office and British Museum Library of London; the Bodleian Library of Oxford University; the Widener Memorial Library of Harvard University; the Harper Memorial Library of the University of Chicago; and the libraries of the University of California at Berkeley and Los Angeles. The writer wishes to thank them, one and all, for their thousand and one acts of accommodation.

This monograph, completed by chance (or was it by design?) on the birthday of my late mother — to whom it owes more than the world will ever know — is hereby tendered to her as a birthday gift from an ever-grateful son.

SYDNEY SEYMOUR BIRO

September 19, 1954

CONTENTS

PART II. THE DIRECTORY

Berlin and Campo-Formio

MAPS

The German Policy of Revolutionary France

VOLUME I

INTRODUCTION

I. THE NATURAL-BOUNDARY THEORY

*T*HE peace treaties following World War I consecrated the principle of self-determination for the suppressed nationalities of Europe, but that principle was not allowed full sway. Recognizing that strategic considerations are equally important, the Conference of Paris awarded part of the Austrian Tyrol to Italy in order that the Italians should have military control of the ridge of the Alps and especially of the Brenner Pass. Czechoslovakia was given the Sudetenland in order that the Czechs should have the protection of the mountain chain formed by the Sudetes, Erzgebirge, and Böhmer Wald. France demanded the Rhine River as a boundary ostensibly for a similar reason, but her request was denied. Lloyd George did not wish France to become too powerful; and Woodrow Wilson, in his endeavor to be magnanimous to a defeated adversary, saw in France's demand only a resurrection of the old natural-boundary thesis rendered so popular by the Convention and Directory, viz., that Nature had herself determined the boundaries of the French state by placing seas, mountains, and great rivers round about it for its protection.

Indeed, the natural-boundary concept experienced quite a revival in France during the later years of World War I, and following. "It could easily be demonstrated," said one writer — a member of the Institute, "that from the geographic and natural points of view, the Rhine is, for its entire length, the boundary of the French region. . . "[1] And another author, after some misinformatory remarks concerning old-regime policy, spoke quite casually of "the rights of France to her natural frontiers."[2]

[1] E. Babelon, *La Rive gauche du Rhin: Les Revendications françaises dans l'histoire* (Paris, 1917), p. 2. Babelon has written a much larger work, *La grande question d'occident: Le Rhin dans l'histoire*, 2 vols., Paris, 1916–1917, in which he presents at length France's historical claim to the Rhineland. On the title page of the second volume is a quotation from Richelieu: "Jusqu'où allait la Gaule, jusque-là doit aller la France" ("How far Gaul extended, that far should France reach").

[2] E. de Marcère, *La Prusse et la rive gauche du Rhin: Le Traité de Bâle — 1794–1795* (Paris, 1918), pp. 2, 3.

However, as will appear later in the course of this work,[3] rivers afford no real protection from an invading army. President (then General) Eisenhower pointed this out in a United Press interview on February 24, 1945. "In all history," he said, "a river line never has been defended successfully." Yet this aspect of the natural-boundary thesis that exalts the defensive potentialities of a river seems to crop up after every war in which France and Germany are engaged, and France is not the loser. It appeared last toward the end of World War II, and must indeed have provided the occasion for Eisenhower's remarks above.

In the last week of January 1945, De Gaulle told two hundred French and foreign correspondents that "France does not intend to finish this war without assurance that the French army is installed permanently along the length of the Rhine. . . They [*sic*] must be there . . . for French security." Then, apparently remembering the lessons of the Conference of Paris, he added cautiously, "This does not necessarily imply the extension of France's frontier to the Rhine. The determination of the region's political status depends on accords with other nations — but French forces will be installed along the Rhine." [4]

The Free-French hero — anent annexation of the Rhineland — had used the term "not necessarily." His allies soon indicated it would be necessarily not. The De Gaullists thereupon took a page from the history of 1797 and relabeled it 1945. France now affirmatively rejected the thought of burdening herself with a hostile German minority. An autonomous republic on the left bank would answer all France's defense needs, provided she could still maintain her troops along the River *in perpetuum*.[5]

That the Rhine should be France's defensive frontier may have been ordained by Nature, but De Gaulle was apparently of the opinion that even Nature had not foreseen everything. It was essential, he said, for the region separated from Germany to include a twenty- or thirty-mile strip on the right bank of the Rhine, both "to provide an effective defense buffer for France," and to preserve intact the economic unity of the Rhine basin.[6] It would seem, then, that for a modern natural-boundary advocate, as for everyone else, a boundary is the result of the interplay of a number of factors directed upon a certain general expanse of territory. The features of the earth being relatively constant, as the factors vary, the boundary must shift. However, according to the Frenchman of the "natural" age of Rousseau, it was the invariable earth alone which should control the placement of frontiers, and

[3] Pt. I, chap. xvi.
[4] As reported by the Associated Press.
[5] United Press despatch from Paris, Feb. 7, 1945. The Rhineland-autonomy movement following World War I will immediately come to mind in this connection.
[6] *Ibid.*

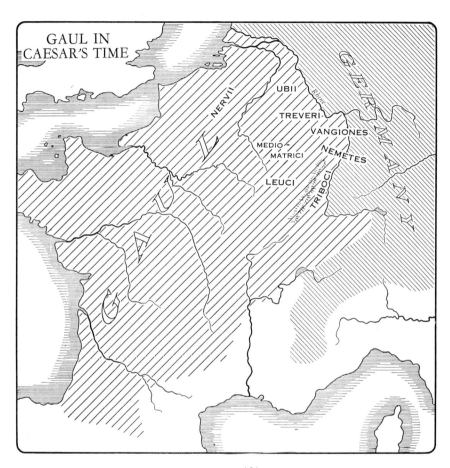

GAUL *c.* 50 B.C., WITH THE GERMAN (?) TRIBES OF GAUL *c.* 100 A.D.
ACCORDING TO TACITUS.

Condorcet, "the philosopher of the Revolution," [7] has contributed the classical expression of the "natural-boundary theory":

The political world tends to take on a solid form. . . . It seems that, in the moral as in the physical, objects seek blindly to range themselves according to their specific gravities.

Since the fall of the Roman Empire, all has been chaos in Europe; feudalism arose, and after a long and hard struggle was crushed by the weight of the throne. The destruction of the barons left the field free to the princes; they are fighting between themselves today. Partitions have been made by fortune and chance, but without appeal to Nature. There is no such thing as prescription; Nature has herself designated the boundary lines of nations: seas, great rivers, [and] mountain chains are the eternal lines with which she has sketched this general map. It can be foreseen that all disputes and claims between nations will end by confining each power within these ramparts which Nature has herself erected; for the successive caprices and punishable passions of men cannot long resist the constant and inflexible law of Nature.

Then invasions will cease; each people, entrenched within its physical and natural boundaries, will occupy itself with its own interests. Nations will be neighbors without being enemies; . . . that is the time when the seeds which philosophy has sown will germinate.[8]

The France of 1789 possessed so-called natural boundaries to the south and west, viz., the Alps, Mediterranean, Pyrenees, and the waters of the Atlantic; but to the east and north its frontier was the artificial product of the age-old conflict between the Emperors and the Most Christian Kings. Here, then, it was necessary to study the will of Nature. Mountains and seas to the east and north there were none, but there were two large rivers, the Meuse and the Rhine. Just which of these had been placed there specially for France's convenience was not known with certainty, but ambition designated the farther one — the Rhine, which had the additional sanction of having been named by Caesar and Strabo as the eastern boundary of Gaul.

The international conflicts of the period of the Revolution were, then,

[7] 1743–1794. Correspondent of Voltaire, Perpetual Secretary of the Academy of Sciences, mathematician, Master of the Mint, authority on finance, and friend of Turgot. Cold externally, but with an ardent soul, and infinite faith in the future — in his case, a strangely sudden death within the shadow of the guillotine — Condorcet was dubbed "a snow-capped volcano" by D'Alembert (J. Michelet, Œuvres complètes [40 vols., Paris, n.d.], XXXIX [Pt. I: Les femmes de la Révolution], 70–73; A. Mathiez, The French Revolution [tr. from the French by C. A. Phillips; New York, 1928], p. 139). It is not unlikely that Condorcet took his own life (F. Uzureau, "A propos de la mort de Condorcet," RF [La Révolution française], LXIX [1916], 510).

[8] Balestrier de Canillac (ed.), Bibliothèque de l'homme public (28 vols. in 14, Paris, 1790–1792), XI, 192–193. Cf. J. G. Fichte, Addresses to the German Nation, no. xii: "The first original and truly natural frontiers of States are unquestionably their spiritual frontiers." — Quoted in J. H. Rose, Nationality in Modern History (New York, 1926), p. 34.

from the point of view of the French people, wars for national security, wars to end war, wars to "make the world safe for democracy." Though the struggle against France was viewed abroad as one against anarchy and usurpation, we must not forget that, whatever the motives of the governors of France may have been, the French masses believed they were fighting for an ideal.

2. ORIGIN AND HISTORY OF THE RHINE PROBLEM

a. The Partition of Mersen the Root of the Problem

The Rhine policy of the Revolution was rooted deep in the past, and was the logical outcome of events of the Carolingian period. After the death of Charlemagne's son, Louis the Pious, the Empire was divided between the three sons of the latter, Charles, Louis, and Lothair (Treaty of Verdun, 843). Charles, known later as "Charles the Bald," received the nucleus of modern France; Louis, henceforth called "Louis the German," obtained the nucleus of modern Germany; and Lothair received a strip of territory wedged in between the two, and extending from the North Sea to the center of Italy.

It is this centrally located state, or rather the portion thereof which lay to the north of the Alps, which must arrest our attention. Called *Lotharii regnum* (whence *Lotharingia*, *Lothringen*, and *Lorraine*), after Lothair's second son, Lothair II, it was partitioned by Charles the Bald and Louis the German in 870.[9] Charles received as his share parts of what we know as the Netherlands, Belgium, and Lorraine, and some territory along the Rhone; Louis obtained the remainder. Thus, the left bank of the Rhine, from Basel to the sea, remained with the Teutonic portion of the former empire of Charlemagne at the dawn of modern history.

That Louis the German had obtained the lion's share in this so-called "Partition of Mersen" admits of no doubt, but is only of academic interest here. What we should like to know is whether any peoples were thus annexed to Germany, who, from a cultural[10] standpoint, seemed intended

---

[9] Robert Minder in his *Allemagnes et Allemands* (Paris, 1948), says (p. 72) that German manuals mention with particular care the date 925, when, after much dispute, the northern part of Lotharingia was regained by Henry the Fowler and attached definitively to Germany. Germany itself was then 14 years old, according to Minder, who sets its birth date at 911. That was the year Ludwig the Child, the last Carolingian, died, and the various German *Stämme*, which seemed about to go their separate ways, decided to remain together.

[10] The word "racial" is avoided here because modern scholarship has a great deal of difficulty defining the term "race." Man has moved about the face of the earth more than any other animal, and his environment, and selective mating, have changed him. To quote a modern authority on anthropology, "Physical anthropology cannot be divorced from cultural and historical associations, and . . . there is no such thing as 'pure' biology, at least in reference to human beings." — C. S. Coon, *The Races of Europe* (New York, 1939), p. vii.

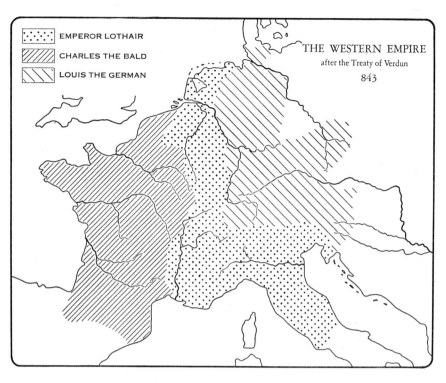

EMPEROR LOTHAIR
CHARLES THE BALD
LOUIS THE GERMAN

THE WESTERN EMPIRE
after the Treaty of Verdun
843

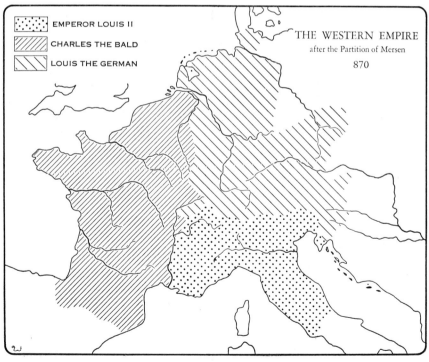

EMPEROR LOUIS II
CHARLES THE BALD
LOUIS THE GERMAN

THE WESTERN EMPIRE
after the Partition of Mersen
870

to become subjects of the nascent French state. In other words, who were these new subjects of Louis the German, and whence did they come?

We must turn back the pages of history — and ponder them well — for this and yet another purpose: The statesmen of the Revolution founded their policies on the ancient history of "France," and Varus, Ariovistus, and the Sequani were as active characters in their minds as were Louis XIV and Louis XVI.

b. Neither Celts nor Germans Indigenous to Gaul

At the dawn of history, we discover two cultural groups, the Celts and the Germans, occupying Gaul.[11] But neither group was indigenous. Both were invaders. Indeed we do not know as much about the Celtic invasion as we do about the posterior German, but we do know that from 1000 to 900 B.C. at the earliest, the use of iron was spreading in central Europe; that the Celts partook of this iron civilization, and brought it across the Rhine some time after 500 B.C. In fact, from 500 B.C. to the beginning of the Christian era, the Celts, from their starting place in southwest Germany, ranged far and wide, from Spain and Ireland to Asia Minor.[12] By the third century B.C., they had occupied, in Europe, the British Isles, half of Spain, most of Gaul, northern Italy, two thirds of present-day Germany, Bohemia, the Danube valley, and the shores of the Black Sea to the Dnieper.[13] It was perhaps the magnitude of this expansion which was responsible for the fact that it did not enter the minds of the Greeks that a wholly unknown and different ethnic group — the German — lay behind the Celts. Thus, Hellenic literature had but one name for the inhabitants of north central Europe: Keltoi, or its equivalent, Galatai. Neither word had any ethnic connotation.[14]

It was the Romans who "discovered" the Germans — in the second century B.C. "German" is not a German word.[15] Indeed, the Germans did not

[11] Who the pre-Celtic inhabitants were is highly problematical. Some persons, arguing from the suffixes of place names in the Rhineland, conjecture that the Ligurians preceded the Celts. No one can say nay, and few dare to say yea (H. Aubin, *Kelten, Römer und Germanen in den Rheinlanden* [Bonn, 1925], p. 3).

[12] Coon, *Races*, pp. 181, 186–187.

[13] F. Lot, *Les invasions germaniques: la pénétration mutuelle du monde barbare et du monde romain* (Paris, 1935), p. 19.

[14] *Ibid.*, p. 13.

[15] It is probably Celtic. Various derivations have been suggested for it, e.g., that the "Ger" has the same root as the German "Gehr" or "Wehr," from which the French have derived "guerre." Hence "German" would mean war-man or warlike man in German (A. Murphy [ed.], *The Works of Cornelius Tacitus* [New York, 1852], p. 532, n. 3). But modern scholars do not think the word is German. Strabo sees the Latin "verus" in "German," making "German" mean true-man or genuine man. In fact, Strabo states categorically that "in the Latin language Germani signifies genuine." — *The Geography of Strabo* (Eng. tr. by H. C. Hamilton and W. Falconer; 3 vols., London, 1854–1857), I, 443. But the consensus of modern opinion is that the word is of Celtic derivation — probably.

possess at all a word to denote the sum total of their tribes. It was the Gauls who dubbed them "Germans," and the Romans followed suit.[16] But the use of this term has given rise to much confusion.

About the end of the fourth century B.C., a group of Celtic tribes, the "Belgae," crossed the Rhine from east to west, and established themselves between the Rhine, Seine, and Marne.[17] They were accompanied by five other tribes with decidedly Celtic-sounding names (Condrusi, Eburones, Caeroesi, Paemani, and Segni), who settled in the central Meuse valley, and to whose descendants has been affixed the appellation "Cisrhenish Germans."[18]

This designation has its roots in the following incident. In 57 B.C., Iccius and Antebrogius, two Rhemi (Belgian) ambassadors, informed Caesar that most of the Belgae were of German origin; that, attracted by the greater fertility of Gaul, they had long before crossed the Rhine to the left bank and expelled the natives.[19] Now, the descendants of the above-mentioned five tribes — the Walloons — possess physical characteristics diametrically opposite to those of the recognized Germanic element of Belgium, the Flemings.[20] Considering the biological law that minority characteristics tend to be destroyed in favor of the predominant type,[21] the belief is necessarily strengthened that these five tribes were not Germanic. It is to be noted also that all the Belgae spoke the same language, by and large, as the rest of the Gauls [22] — despite Caesar ("Gaul is divided into three parts . . . These all differ from each other in tongue"), whom modern scholarship has overruled.[23]

It is the consensus of scholarly opinion today that the word "German" meant, to the Belgae, "neighbor to the east," regardless of ethnic association. A group of Celts, latecomers to Gaul, who also settled along the Meuse, retained this "German" designation.[24] It was only when all [25] the Celts on the right bank of the Rhine had crossed to the left that "German" began to mean German, because there were no more Celts remaining as neighbors to the east.

Of course it was to be expected that such an ambiguous term, in the hands of foreigners, should be subject to a period of stress and strain before general usage should have crystallized it in a certain mold. Thus, all the ancient writers had difficulty deciding its proper connotation. Dion Cassius

---

[16] Lot, *Invasions*, p. 13.

[17] *Ibid.*, p. 20.

[18] *Ibid.*, p. 21.

[19] T. R. Holmes, *Caesar's Conquest of Gaul* (Oxford, 1911), p. 333; *Caesar's Commentaries on the Gallic and Civil Wars* (Eng. tr. by W. A. M'Devitte and W. S. Bohn; London, 1879), p. 45 (Bk. II, chap. iv).

[20] Lot, *Invasions*, p. 21.

[21] *Ibid.*, p. 275.

[22] Holmes, *Caesar's Conquest of Gaul*, p. 320.

[23] *Ibid.*, pp. 211–256; G. Schütte, *Our Forefathers* (Eng. tr. by J. Young; 2 vols., Cambridge, 1929), I, 23. Schütte has been used in this monograph merely as a sort of index.

[24] Lot, *Invasions*, p. 21.

[25] Loosely speaking. "All" never did leave.

Cocceianus — to take a single example — consistently used "Germani" for Celts,[26] "Keltike" for Germany,[27] and "Germania" for the left bank of the Rhine, i.e., Upper and Lower Germany.[28] And, to be sure, what historian can quarrel with him for calling Germany "Keltike"?

In the third and second centuries before Christ, there were still no true Germans on the left bank of the Rhine. In fact, the Celts still occupied much of what we today regard as Germany: Baden, Württemberg, Hesse, Franconia, Bavaria; also Austria and the Sudetenland of Bohemia. Germany was then the area between the lower and middle Rhine, and the Vistula, plus Scandinavia. Indeed, the geographical names in northwestern Germany show that the Celts had preceded the Germans even there. Nor can it be asserted that the Germans were autochthonous to the south shore of the Baltic. (But Scandinavia can be granted to them — it is believed — without reservation. That peninsula appears to have been the cradle of the German race.) [29]

It is possible — but not at all certain — that the Germans may for a time have been subject to the Celts.[30] The French historian Ferdinand Lot says that "it is possible, even certain," that some German bands accompanied the Celts in their "adventurous expeditions" of the third century B.C. — but only as auxiliaries.[31] That the Germans were not always in a subordinate position and required forceful containment is evidenced by the remnants of the line of Celtic forts in the vicinity of the Thüringer Wald [32] — an ancient "Maginot Line" which proved hardly more effective than the modern one.

c. The German Invasions of Gaul to 486 A.D.

The first truly German invasion of Gaul that is based on precise historical data is that of the Cimbri and Teutones in the early years of the second century before Christ. The former tribe issued from northern Jutland, the latter from the region around the mouth of the Elbe and the present Schleswig-Holstein. Under pressure from two powerful Celtic tribes at their rear (the Boii and Scordisci), and accompanied by two small Celtic tribes, they fell upon Gaul. After some initial successes, the two German tribes split up and were separately crushed, the Teutones in 102 B.C., the Cimbri the following year.[33]

A generation passed before another real threat presented itself, and this

---

[26] *Dio's Roman History* (Eng. tr. by E. Cary; 9 vols., New York, 1914–1927), VI, 221 (Bk. LIII, chap. xii, § 6); III, 269 (Bk. XXXVIII, chap. xxxiv, § 1).

[27] *Ibid.*, VI, 221 (Bk. LIII, chap. xii, § 6); VI, 471 (Bk. LV, chap. xxx, § 1).

[28] *Ibid.*, VI, 221 (Bk. LIII, chap. xii, § 6).

[29] Lot, *Invasions*, p. 14.

[30] *Ibid.*, p. 19.

[31] *Ibid.*, p. 321.

[32] G. Poisson, *Le Peuplement de l'Europe* (Paris, 1939), p. 342.

[33] Lot, *Invasions*, p. 23.

one was the creation of two quarreling Celtic tribes located on either side of the Saône — the Sequani and the Aedui. (This was, of course, before the Roman conquest of Gaul.) The Sequani, momentarily subjugated, called in Ariovistus, a Swabian mercenary. It was a fatal error, for the Swabians, recently arrived from the present Brandenburg,[34] had already proved to be infected with the expansionist virus.

Ariovistus was directly in command only of the relatively minor tribe of the Triboci, but he had succeeded in subjugating two closely related other tribes, the Nemetes and Vangiones; moreover, he had attracted to his standard some of the Marcomanni and Quadi, and the Harudi. It was a powerful and well-disciplined host that he led into battle against the Aedui — and, of course, he defeated them (61 B.C.). The Aedui appealed to Rome.[35]

It was a friend of Caesar's, Divitiăcus, who, in tears, presented the cause of his people to Caesar. He said that Gaul was divided into two rival camps, led respectively by the Aedui and Arverni, and that their conflict had been already of long standing when the Arverni and Sequani called in Ariovistus. He told how that German leader had first brought over only 15,000 Germans, but that these were so impressed with the superabundance they found in Gaul that their number soon swelled to 120,000. He asserted that the lot of the Sequani was even worse than that of the Aedui. True, the Aedui had lost all their nobility, their senate, and their cavalry, and had been forced to surrender many of their notables as hostages to the Sequani. But Ariovistus had appropriated a third of all the Sequani's lands, and was demanding a second third to settle 24,000 Harudi. Divitiăcus held out the bleak prospect that within a few years all the Germans might cross into Gaul and its inhabitants would be forced to emigrate.[36]

Caesar did not like the prospect. He saw that it might entail danger even to Rome. He thought to negotiate with Ariovistus, but the latter refused to meet in a neutral third place; Caesar should come to him, he said. And Ariovistus added that it was none of Rome's affair, anyway, how he treated "his" Gaul which he had conquered in battle. The Aedui had nothing to complain of; they had tried the fortune of war, and lost. But they would be quite all right if they observed their agreements and paid their tribute dutifully. And he dared Caesar to oppose him.

This message from Ariovistus was accompanied by news that the Harudi were ravaging the Aedui lands, and that a hundred Swabian cantons were trying to cross the Rhine into Treveri territory. Caesar resolved to act

---

[34] For this point alone, *ibid*.
[35] F. Lot, *La Gaule: les fondements ethniques, sociaux et politiques de la nation française* (Paris, 1947), p. 104.
[36] For this, and the next three paragraphs:

Caesar's Com., pp. 22–42 (Bk. I, chaps. xxxi–liv). *Vide* also *Dio's Roman History*, III, 269–271, 275–307 (Bk. XXXVIII, chaps. xxxiv, xlvii–l).

quickly, lest these new Swabians should succeed in crossing, and reinforce Ariovistus. By forced marches he approached Ariovistus' encampments.

Surprisingly, Ariovistus now agreed to confer. In the meeting, Caesar demanded, among other things, that, if Ariovistus could not send all the Germans back across the Rhine — as Ariovistus had apparently alleged — at least he should allow no more to cross. To this the German leader replied that he did not bring over the Germans to assault Gaul but to secure his position there. He was in Gaul before the Romans, he said; never before had they gone beyond the borders of their Provincia. He offered Caesar a substantial reward if he would allow him a free hand in Gaul, but threatened that, if Caesar refused, he would best the Roman army and put Caesar to death. That, he assured Caesar, "would please many of the nobles and leading men of the Roman people."

No agreement was possible, and the armies came to blows. Ariovistus had tried, apparently with good reason, to put off the actual test of strength until the new moon, according to the advice of the "prophetic women" of his following. But when Caesar learned the reason for the delay, he attacked. It was a hard battle, but decisive, and the surviving Germans raced for the Rhine some fifty miles away. Among those who escaped was Ariovistus (58 B.C.).

When the news spread of Ariovistus' defeat, the Swabians farther north, who had thought to substitute themselves for the Treveri in the valley of the Moselle, likewise fled eastward. And the Ubii,[37] a German tribe whom the Swabians had tried to subjugate, had a field day chasing Swabians in flight.[38] The Romans followed up their victory by crossing to the right bank (55 B.C.).[39] Gaul was saved, at least for the time being.

It is difficult to determine the extent of Gaul's good fortune. It often happens that dominion is a personal matter and dies with a conquering leader. We do not know if a conquest by Ariovistus would have outlived him by many years, if at all. We do know, however, that it was five hundred years before the Franks succeeded where the Swabians had failed, and that these were years of Romanization instead of Germanization.

Caesar was not harsh with the Germans left behind by the flight of Ariovistus and his host. The Roman leader installed the Triboci in Alsace, and the Nemetes and Vangiones in the country they were occupying around Spires and Worms, respectively. This act of seeming generosity should be considered in the light of two facts: (1) All Ariovistus' "Germans" were not German. The very names of the three tribes Triboci, Nemetes, and Vangiones are quite Celtic. Ariovistus' name is not Germanic. And the

[37] The reader will please note these people well. They will appear again in Pt. I, chap. vii. [38] Lot, *Gaule*, pp. 108–109. [39] *Idem, Invasions*, p. 25.

latter's eventual conference with Caesar preliminary to the actual battle was conducted, on Ariovistus' part, in Celtic, of which he was a master.[40] These Germans were already somewhat "westernized." (2) Gaul needed colonists, so much so that, in 38 B.C., Agrippa compelled the Swabian-hating Ubii to migrate to the left bank of the Rhine.[41] Forcible colonization of Gaul with Germans became a custom in the fourth century A.D.,[42] as will be mentioned again presently.

When Tacitus wrote his *Germania* a century and a half after Caesar (probably 98 A.D.), he asserted therein that the Triboci, Nemetes, and Vangiones were "without doubt German tribes," [43] and that "the Ubii (were) not yet ashamed of their German origin." [44] With these two statements there can be no quarrel. But Tacitus also asserted that "the Treveri and the Nervii openly boast[ed] of their claim to German blood." [45] This may be true, but it constitutes no proof that these two peoples were of German blood, as Tacitus seemed to think. The human tongue is, alas! as often used to conceal the truth as to herald it. Moreover, the personal and place names of both the Treveri and Nervii were Celtic.[46]

The centuries following Caesar's victory over Ariovistus were centuries of Roman domination of the right bank of the Rhine as well as the left, so it was no longer possible for the Germans to mount a sudden assault upon Gaul. There were, indeed, revolts in Germany against the new master. The most spectacular of these was that of the Cherusci leader Hermann or Arminius, who cut to pieces three Roman legions under Varus in the Teutoburg Forest in 9 A.D. But that was only a local affair. It did not serve as a signal for Germany to rise.[47]

The next transfusion of German blood into the veins of Gaul was not an incident of war. In the course of the fourth century, as mentioned above, it was the custom of Rome to colonize Gaul forcibly with German laborers and soldiers. These colonists, being small in number in any particular place, soon merged with the Gallo-Romans.[48]

Force was not always necessary to induce colonization. Sometimes the Germans wanted to enter, even requested to enter. The Salian Franks, long

[40] *Idem, Gaule*, pp. 108–109.

[41] *Idem, Invasions*, p. 25. Aubin gives a different interpretation. Says he, in 38 or 19 B.C., Agrippa, Augustus' commander, in order to create an empty space on the right bank of the Rhine so as to relieve pressure against the River frontier, settled the "protection-supplicating" Ubii on the left bank. The same motive, he says, lay behind the establishment of the Sicambri on the left bank by Tiberius in 8 B.C. (Aubin, *Kelten,*

p. 8.)

[42] Lot, *Invasions*, p. 274.

[43] *Germania*, ch. xxviii (the Oxford Translation, Revised; *Handy Literal Translations* series, New York, n.d.).

[44] *Ibid.* (Eng. tr. by W. H. Fyfe; Oxford, 1908.)

[45] *Ibid.*

[46] Holmes, *Caesar's Conquest of Gaul*, p. 332.

[47] Lot, *Invasions*, p. 26.

[48] *Ibid.*, p. 274.

settled along the lower Rhine, were authorized by Emperor Julian to enter the Empire and settle north of the present Brabant as Roman subjects. They were already there in the year 358.[49]

Another peacetime transfusion occurred about the middle of the fourth century. The Burgundians, late of bleak Scandinavia, had recently arrived at the Main River,[50] and were soon knocking at the door of sunny Gaul. Successive Roman governments opened the door; the newcomers streamed across the Rhine, and by *c.* 405 had settled in the neighborhood of Worms and Mayence. This was in the reign of the Emperor Honorius (395–423). In 443, the patrician Aëtius moved them to the area between Yverdon on Lake Neuchâtel and Grenoble, with their center at Geneva.[51] Thus did Gaul (and France) acquire the Burgundians.

In the reign of Honorius, also, the Ripuarian or Hessian Franks began to move peaceably across the Rhine and settle on the left bank: at Cologne, at Coblenz, in the Moselle valley — and at Mayence and Worms after the Burgundians left; but they did not penetrate as far as the Ardennes. They contented themselves with repopulating the left bank of the Rhine and the Moselle valley, "which was just becoming Germanized." [52]

By 450, the Alemanni, who were Swabians like Ariovistus, emulated their kinsman of five centuries earlier, and established themselves in Alsace without invitation or permission. From there they moved against the Ripuarian Franks, seeking to despoil them of Worms and Mayence. And they advanced into what was later to become the Free County of Burgundy. The Burgundians checked them, but that only increased their pressure against the Franks.[53]

The assassination of Aëtius in 454 served as a signal to the Salian Franks to advance farther into Gaul. Following the Roman road from Cologne to Cambrai, and beyond, they reached the Somme. Though they took possession of Cambrai and Tournai, they did not impose their language on them. In fact, the only region they Germanized was that between the Carbonarian Forest and the North Sea.[54]

One more German conquest should be recorded before taking up the conquest par excellence of 486. Trèves (Augusta Treverorum), which had been sacked three [55] times by the Ripuarians, was definitively captured by them *c.* 455. By the time the Empire gasped its last breath, therefore, this magnificent city, once Rome's administrative center for Spain, Gaul, and

---

[49] *Idem, The End of the Ancient World and the Beginnings of the Middle Ages* (Eng. tr. by P. and M. Leon; London, 1931), pp. 214, 249.

[50] *Ibid.*, p. 189.

[51] *Ibid.*, pp. 207, 246.

[52] *Ibid.*, pp. 214, 312.

[53] *Ibid.*, pp. 314–315.

[54] *Ibid.*, pp. 214, 313.

[55] Captured four times previously, according to Aubin (*Kelten*, p. 22).

Britain, and favorite western residence of many Emperors, was definitely a German city.[56]

d. The Regnum Francorum

It has been mentioned that the Salian Franks entered the Empire with Rome's consent, and probably no one, in 481, would have pointed to them as a serious threat, though they did seem bent on conquest. Politically weaker than their Ripuarian brethren, the Salians were divided into several petty and mutually hostile kingdoms,[57] whereas the Ripuarians had a center of authority — so to speak — at Cologne.[58] If anyone had asked an informed Gallo-Roman wherein lay the greatest peril to Roman Gaul — from the side of Germany — he would undoubtedly have replied, "the Alemanni" (discounting for the moment that he loosely called all Germans by that name).

But the year 481 marked the death of Childeric, Salian Frankish "king" of Tournai, and the accession of his fifteen-year-old son, Clovis. In this youth were united those rare traits of great vision, great vigor, great courage, and great ability. At the age of twenty, he attacked and defeated Syagrius, leader of the Roman army (consisting mostly of barbarians, and probably of many Franks).[59] Clovis had succeeded where Ariovistus had failed. A new era was about to begin.

Clovis' first task was to suppress the other petty Salian "kings." That accomplished, he united the Salians and Ripuarians — just how, we do not know, but legend says it was by treason. Then, with a united Frankish army, he faced the Alemanni, who had been contesting the middle, and even the lower, Rhine with the Ripuarians. The Alemanni were decisively defeated (*c.* 496 or 497), and Clovis was master of Roman Gaul.[60] (The Visigoths ruled south of the Loire; the Burgundians, in the Rhone valley.)

Clovis' defeat of the Visigoths does not concern us here except in that it rendered him master of Gaul save for Burgundy, native land of his queen (which his sons conquered after his death). Emperor Anastasius quickly trimmed his sails to the wind, and appointed Clovis consul (508). This imparted a sort of official sanction to his conquest of Gaul — legitimized it, so to speak.[61]

From one point of view, indeed, the victory of 486 was no "conquest." Clovis' father had been in the service of Rome. Syagrius' father, Aëgidus, had been *magister militum* before his death in 464. The incident of 486 was no more than a "'contest of ambition between two chiefs' and not a clash of nationalities" (Lot). It is only with respect to his later victories —

[56] Lot, *Ancient World*, pp. 214, 314.   [59] *Ibid.*, p. 316.
[57] *Ibid.*, p. 316.   [60] *Ibid.*, pp. 316–320.
[58] *Ibid.*, p. 214.   [61] *Ibid.*, p. 250.

over fellow Germans (Salians, Ripuarians, Alemanni, Visigoths, Thuringians) — that Clovis can be considered a conqueror.[62]

Clovis did not pose as a conqueror before the Gallo-Romans. They were neither enslaved nor socially degraded. Franks and Gallo-Romans were regarded as equals before the law. If the Gallo-Romans changed their customs or habits in any way, it was because the political primacy of the Franks gradually created in the Gallo-Romans a desire to be like them. It was a case of imitation, not of oppression. It might be thought that the tendency would have been quite the reverse, for it was the Franks who were submerged in a sea of Gallo-Romans. In such cases, usually, it is the invader who surrenders his identity. But the Franks remained in close contact with the great body of their people on the Scheldt, lower Meuse, Moselle, and Rhine, and so managed to retain their individuality. It was a case — shall we say? — of a constant transfusion of new blood by pipeline from the East.[63]

Ethnically, the Frankish invasion of 486, outside the Rhine and Meuse regions, did not exert an influence at all commensurate with the political primacy of the conquerors. The Gauls were never engulfed, either by the Romans or the Germans. Any Germanic elements in the France of 1792–1797 must be ascribed to the period prior to Clovis' conquest of Gaul. It has been mentioned twice, but will bear repetition, that it was the custom in the fourth century to settle colonies of Germans on Gallic land to enhance the supply of soldiers and laborers.[64] And of course we must remember the Tri-

---

[62] *Ibid.*, pp. 215, 249. Indeed, Babelon regards Clovis as the founder of the French monarchy and upon this view bases the following argument: It was a principle of French law that no lands which belonged to the monarchy could ever be permanently alienated. The left bank formed part of Clovis' domain. *Ergo*, the left bank remained, through the centuries, legally a part of France. And he adds that during the centuries when everyone thought the Rhineland formed part of the Holy Roman Empire, the bond between the left bank and the Empire was only a weak feudal link, having its chief validity on the map. The Rhinelanders were in constant contact with the kings of France, whom they called in to settle quarrels among themselves, and with the Emperor; moreover, most of the left-bank princes were in the pay of France (*Rhin . . . hist.*, II, x–xi).

[63] Lot, *Ancient World*, pp. 321, 405–406.

[64] *Idem, Invasions*, pp. 274–275. The various means by which the Germans entered Gaul (aside from invasion) are listed with commendable detail by Babelon: Many Germans were brought in as slaves purchased from other Germans who had captured them in war. Capture in battle by the Romans was the road by which other large numbers entered. (German prisoners of war were so numerous at times that many who could not be inducted into the army or settled as colonists, were presented as slaves to individuals.) Corps of auxiliaries recruited from beyond the Rhine were permitted to end their days in Gaul; also, corps of German warriors exacted as tribute from defeated German tribes, and simple individuals inducted into the Roman army against their will. German families of low estate were given lands on condition that all able-bodied males of the tribe serve in the army. Fugitive tribes, often famished, were granted asylum in Gaul with the stipulation that they would clear the forests, till the soil, pay rent, and supply soldiers for the Roman legions. Lastly, there were individual Germans who came as colonists or as hired hands to work in city or on farm; and organized bands of

boci, Nemetes, Vangiones, Ubii, and Burgundians; the Salian Franks admitted to the Empire by Julian; the Ripuarians; the Alemanni; not to mention the stragglers of many a defeated German army such as that of the Cimbri.[65] These were all present in Gaul before 486. Some had already been absorbed by the Gallo-Romans, and were no longer distinguishable.

To the Gallo-Romans of the fifth century, the thought of assimilating the barbarian hordes was anathema; people naturally hate whomsoever they fear. However, when Clovis became a Christian, the revulsion inevitably lessened. The melting process was assisted by the realization that the Eastern Emperor was too far away to be of any use, and that the only real sovereign Gaul had was a German sovereign; also, there were the common dependence of both peoples upon the same government, the thousand and one intimate daily contacts, and, eventually, intermarriage. All these worked together to effect the fusion of the two peoples into one by the end of the seventh century. This is true, at any rate, concerning the aristocracy — the only class of any significance then.[66]

In this fusion, the German influence was in many respects the dominant one. Latin names yielded to Frankish. The same was probably true of dress. The German language, however, spread but little beyond the area where it prevailed in 486; moreover, it did not affect the grammatical structure of Latin. But a host of new German words did enter the language of the erstwhile Gaul. And German law proceeded to crowd out the Roman law north of the Loire, and even beyond.[67]

One further point requires mention here. In the division of Clovis' territories among his heirs and their heirs, and the usurpation of power by mayors of the palace, it was the mayor of the palace of the eastern fragment of the *Regnum Francorum*, Pippin II, who succeeded in gaining control of the whole. Now, Duke Pippin did not desert the East, the lower valley of the Meuse, where his family had made its fortune, and from where it could replenish its strength. That region was half Roman, half German, and Pippin's line remained, practically to the end, a line of Germans. When, in 751, the son (Pippin III) of Pippin's illegitimate son (Charles Martel)

brigands who came to loot, but fell in love with sunny Gaul and remained to swell the German population (*Rhin . . . hist.*, I, 436–440).

[65] The Cimbri had left behind, in Belgic Gaul, elements of their army to protect their baggage. When the main army failed to return, these elements settled along the middle Meuse (Aubin, *Kelten*, p. 4).

[66] Lot, *Invasions*, pp. 325–326; *idem*, *Ancient World*, p. 395.

[67] *Ibid.*, pp. 395–396. The German law was personal; it followed the person wherever he went. The Roman law was territorial. (So, also, was the later feudal law.) French law today provides that, in his personal relations, an alien in France shall be ruled by his personal law except where the interest of society would be adversely affected.

brushed aside the last Merovingian *roi fainéant* (Childeric III) and assumed the crown, it was a German sovereign who occupied the throne of the progenitor of France.[68] And when Pippin III's son Karl or Charles was proclaimed emperor by Pope Leo III on Christmas Day, 800, it was a German emperor who ruled in Gaul.

Here we have, then, as near as the historian can give them, the facts necessary to decide whether the Partition of Mersen deprived the future France of lands culturally affiliated with her. If no attempt has been made to define the exact limits of German influence, it is because that influence had no definite starting and stopping place. However, this much is clear from the outline: the left bank of the Rhine was occupied by German people in 870.[69] Some of these German people had settled in Gaul with permission. Others had entered by force of arms. Some, who had entered forcibly, later received explicit authority to remain. Some had merely entered without encountering resistance. Others had been forced to enter and settle. But they were there, all of them.

---

[68] Lot, *Ancient World*, pp. 342, 344. To Babelon, Charlemagne represented Christian Romanism as distinguished from Germanism (*Rhin . . . hist.*, II, xi).

[69] If one sought to determine cultural affiliation by anthropological evidence, rather than historical, he would be certain to have rough sledding. It was from the icebound Baltic basin alone that there issued people with the particular combination of characteristics which stamps them Germans: (1) great height, (2) blond hair, (3) fair skin, (4) blue eyes, and (5) long heads (Lot, *Invasions*, pp. 15–16). Yet contemporaries reportedly had great difficulty in distinguishing them from the Celts (A. Demangeon and L. Febvre, *Le Rhin: problèmes d'histoire et d'économie* [Paris, 1935], p. 327, citing D'Arbois de Jubainville, *Les premiers habitants de l'Europe* [2nd ed.; Paris, 1894]); and Strabo writes that the Germans, though they "differ but little from the Keltic race, except in their being more fierce, of a larger stature, and more ruddy in countenance, . . . in every other respect — their figure, their customs and manners of life — are such as we have related of the Kelts." — *Strabo*, I, 443 (Bk. VII, chap. i, § 2).

Of course, neither the Germans nor the Celts, even before either of them entered Gaul, were of pure stock. The Germans were mixed with some alien dolichocephalic (long-headed) elements (Poisson, *Peuplement*, p. 343). The Celts had received, while yet in their homeland in southwestern Germany, some admixture of brachycephaly left over from Bronze Age inhabitants, and some of dolichocephaly from Nordic invasion. But the Celts were themselves mesocephalic — and not particularly tall (Coon, *Races*, pp. 190–191). Holmes says that the invading Celts, before mixing with the indigenous (?) inhabitants of Gaul, were for the most part tall and fair, and generally dolichocephalic, but he adds that Caesar found a majority of short, dark brachycephali (*Caesar's Conquest of Gaul*, p. 337). Coon maintains that both Romans and Greeks were under a misapprehension as to what was the majority type (*Races*, p. 191). The problem is even more complicated than so far appears, for, especially in the case of the South German tribes, Celts and Germans themselves had become so intermixed that, according to D'Arbois de Jubainville, the Germans had more Celtic blood in their veins than Germanic: "more Celtic blood than we Frenchmen have" (Demangeon and Febvre, *Le Rhin*, p. 20). Lot says the "great resemblance" between Celts and Germans was an "illusion" (*Invasions*, p. 16).

e. Charles the Bold Seeks to Re-create Lothair's "Middle Kingdom"

The five or six centuries following Mersen — or, more accurately, the five or six centuries following 925, when northern Lotharingia became definitively a part of Germany — were dotted with petty skirmishes between the successors of East and West Frankland over a town here, a paltry few acres there. The first really noteworthy action was a product of the fifteenth century.

It will be recalled how the Burgundians, a German tribe, had been permitted by successive Roman governments to settle in the neighborhood of Worms and Mayence, and were moved southward in 443. It is to these same Burgundians — now assimilated by the "more indigenous" populations — that we owe an attempt to "draw over the lines" sketched at Mersen. Philip the Good, Burgundy's duke, aspired to re-create Lothair's "Middle Kingdom," of which the Burgundian territories of 443 had formed part. Philip's ambitions were the source of much worry to Charles VII of France, who did not care to be hemmed in by an expanding power. Accordingly, Charles claimed the heritage of Lothair's as his own, and organized a double expedition — to Lorraine and Alsace — against Philip. Charles's claim of Lothair's heritage necessarily involved a claim of the Rhine as a boundary, and this claim, made in 1444, marks the origin of what the Germans call France's "lust for the Rhine."

Charles VII had no success in discouraging the aspirations of the House of Burgundy, and when Charles the Bold succeeded his father, Philip the Good, in 1467, he started out in earnest to realize the Burgundian plans. Owing to the efforts of his predecessors, Charles the Bold was already the ruler of the rich lowlands from the Somme River to the Zuyder Zee, of Luxemburg, the Duchy and Free County of Burgundy, and the County of Nevers. He wished to acquire Alsace, Lorraine, and Switzerland, so as to render his possessions compact, contiguous, and powerful. But Louis XI, Charles VII's son, was no more compliant than his father. The Swiss and Lorrainers likewise were uncoöperative.

Charles the Bold was killed before the gates of Nancy in 1477 — after only ten years of power — but he had added to his prospective kingdom the Sundgau (Upper Alsace), the Breisgau (across the Rhine), Lorraine, Gelderland (both banks of the lower Rhine), and Eu (along the English Channel).

Charles's heir was his daughter Mary, wife of the future Habsburg emperor Maximilian. Almost before the Bold One had been laid in his grave, Louis XI occupied the Free County and Duchy of Burgundy, and Picardy and Artois; but the Free County of Burgundy and Artois were restored to Mary and her German spouse by Louis XI's successor, who sought thus to ensure his rear while he embarked on an expedition to Naples. In fact, the

interest of France in expansion to the Rhine seems to have slumbered for
three quarters of a century after Charles the Bold's death. Italy and the
Netherlands were the attractions par excellence. In these seventy-five years,
only three texts, so far as is known, even so much as mention the Rhine-
boundary idea.[70]

f. Lorraine and Alsace Change Flags

In 1552, Henry II of France occupied Metz, Toul, and Verdun in a move to
help the German Protestants. Whether France would ever have relinquished
these cities voluntarily, we do not know. Emperor Charles V tried to reconquer Metz, and the brilliant and heroic defense of Francis of Guise so
fired the spirit of France as to render the return of the cities unthinkable.
(It probably was anyway.) Soon the Rhine frontier of Gaul became a quite
general topic of conversation, but the popular interest does not seem to have
influenced the King.

The "natural boundary" theory owes its origin to this period. In 1568,
Jean le Bon, physician to the Cardinal of Guise, published a short treatise
entitled "The Rhine for the King." Therein appeared for the first time the
argument that France was entitled to the Rhine boundary not on historical
but on "natural" grounds. Jean le Bon, incidentally, was not a Frenchman,
but a Lorrainer by birth.

No one took up Le Bon's idea at this time, though he published another
treatise tending to the same end, and using a pseudonym, perhaps to make
it appear that his idea was spreading. The interest of France was focused
upon the rich Flemish lowlands to the northeast, which had been French
for many centuries. They were now under the control of Spain, the Burgundian inheritance having been turned over to that power by Mary of
Burgundy's grandson, Emperor Charles V, when he divided his inheritance
in 1555–1556. Incidentally, the Burgundian inheritance, united with the
Spanish conquests along the eastern frontier of France during the Thirty
Years' War of the next century, might have served as the nucleus for yet
another attempt to re-create the Middle Kingdom. However, before this
war was over, it was France that was in control of a necessary part of that
kingdom — to wit, Alsace — and not vice versa.

Possession of Alsace brought the French frontier up to the Rhine River.
It was a German prince who had helped France deal this body blow to the
Treaty of Mersen. Duke Bernhard of Saxe-Weimar, after an abortive at-
tempt to establish himself as Duke of Franconia, had transferred his ambition

---

[70] For this and the next four paragraphs: G. Zeller, "La Monarchie d'ancien régime et les frontières naturelles," *RHM* (*Revue d'his-toire moderne*), VIII (1933), 307–308, 309–310.

to Alsace. Fortune smiled on his venture, and the troops of the Empire were driven from both the Nordgau and Sundgau. But Bernhard had no money, and soldiers like to be paid. Even Bernhard himself would have liked to be paid if that were possible. Thus did it come about that Bernhard of Saxe-Weimar — a German Protestant — accepted the aid of Catholic France to pay himself and his troops. Bernhard took the precaution, however, of negotiating with the French Crown a compact which recognized his possession of Alsace.

Bernhard's death four years later (1639) afforded Richelieu a golden opportunity. The astute cardinal convinced the troops of the Duke that they belonged more to France than to Bernhard, since the French Crown had been paying them. Thus, France was in possession of Alsace in 1648 at the end of the Thirty Years' War.

The next problem of the French government was to force Europe to acknowledge this possession, but unexpected help came from across the Rhine. The devout Catholic ruler of Bavaria, Maximilian, agreed to further France's designs on Alsace if France would aid him in restricting the amount of territory the Protestant Swedes obtained in northern Germany. Pressure by Bavaria, and France's threats not to evacuate the remainder of the left bank of the Rhine, finally secured from the Empire and the House of Habsburg the cession of their rights in Alsace.

But France received something more valuable even than territory at the end of the Thirty Years' War. The diminution of the Imperial power consequent upon the Peace of Westphalia was equivalent to a gift of relative power to Louis XIV. To perpetuate this advantage, Mazarin induced the princes of western Germany to place themselves under the protection of France (1658). This League of the Rhine could be regarded as the spiritual parent of Napoleon's later Confederation of the Rhine, for the Corsican was a student of history as well as of military science, and cannot but have had the earlier creation in mind.

The Treaty of Münster (1648) and the later Treaty of Nijmwegen (1678) had a strange sequel. Louis XIV of France laid claim to about twenty cities and towns of the Holy Roman Empire on the ground that they had once been dependencies of the districts actually ceded to him by these treaties — and he proceeded to occupy Strasburg, Luxemburg, Saarbrücken, Zweibrücken, Philippsburg, Kehl, Alt-Breisach, and Freiburg-im-Breisgau. The four last-named cities are on the right bank of the Rhine. Some of these twenty purloined towns Louis was later forced to relinquish, but many of the left-bank acquisitions, including Strasburg, he retained.

The Treaty of Münster marked yet another step toward breaking the bonds of the Treaty of Mersen, for it ceded to France Metz, Toul, and

Verdun, which the French had been occupying since 1552. The absorption of these cities was not the start of the absorption process in Lorraine, however. It had been instituted 374 years earlier. The process was already two centuries old when the dreams of Charles the Bold were crushed; it was already one century old when John II of Valois invested his fourth son, Charles the Bold's great-grandfather, with Burgundy. Thus, it need occasion no surprise that the Treaty of the Pyrenees, closing the Franco-Spanish phase of the Thirty Years' War, recognized France as the "Protector" of Lorraine. The process of absorption was completed in 1766 when, upon the death of Stanislas Leszczynski, former King of Poland, Duke of Lorraine, and father-in-law of Louis XV, Lorraine was made an integral part of the French state.

g. D'Argenson and Vergennes versus Rousseau and Montesquieu

The second half of the eighteenth century was a period of governmental pacifism and literary expansionism. D'Argenson, foreign minister of Louis XV, believed — to use his own words — that "France has had enough of aggrandizement and of rounding off to be content. The time has finally arrived for us to commence to govern, after our having occupied ourselves for so long with acquiring what to govern." And Vergennes, foreign minister of Louis XVI, wrote, "France should fear aggrandizements much rather than covet them." [71]

Not that Vergennes did not share the view of Vauban, Louis XIV's great military engineer, that "whatever is on this side of the Rhine suits France," but he did not want to provoke England by occupying the Netherlands, and he did not want to risk losing or weakening France's allies (Sweden, Poland, Turkey, Bavaria, Saxony) by expanding in the German Rhineland. He did express the opinion, however, that any rounding off that the kingdom received should be on the upper Rhine, and we know he agreed with Richelieu that Paris was too near the frontier for safety. It is commonly said that Vergennes' pacifism was due to his conviction that the time was one for circumspection, but his policy formula — "that further expansion of the kingdom would be like a weight placed at the ends, and would weaken the middle" [72] — does not seem to make too much sense, though it was indeed a formula which would not explode in Europe's face, like the natural-boundary formula. It is more than likely that Vergennes was a pacifist largely because he did not see the necessity of conquering by arms when one could secure the same result by paying, or bribing, princes, ministers, councillors, spouses, mistresses. Much of Germany was, already

[71] *Ibid.*, p. 323.

[72] G. Grosjean, *La politique rhénane de Ver-gennes* (Paris, 1925), pp. 7, 8.

for over a century, in the pay of France; the custom of stipending the foreigner was so old it seemed quite natural to all concerned. Rhineland princes dependent upon France's bounty would be useful, too.[73] In the last analysis, as far as results were concerned, was there so much difference between a natural bounty and a natural boundary?

But Rousseau and Montesquieu, in their writings, popularized the natural-boundary program in the face of governmental indifference. For them, Alsace and Lorraine did not suffice to even the score with Louis the German because Louis had had no right to any of the left bank. It was reserved for France since first the Earth cooled and, shrivelling, formed the grooves through which the snows of a later day would wend their way to the sea. In his *Extrait du projet de paix perpétuelle de l'abbé de Saint-Pierre*, Rousseau says:

> The position of mountains, seas, and rivers which serve as limits to the nations which inhabit it [Europe] seems to have determined the number and grandeur of these nations; and one can say that the political order of this part of the world is in a certain sense the work of Nature. . . It is not to be said that the Alps, Rhine, sea, [and] Pyrenees are insurmountable obstacles to ambition; but these obstacles are reinforced by others which fortify them, or lead states back to the same bounds when short-lived efforts have resulted in their deviation therefrom.[74]

h. The Germanic Element of France and the Rhine Frontier

Strangely, it was in large part Germans who, adopting the natural-boundary theory, impressed it upon the French government so that it became — during the 1790's — a living issue, a "policy," if you will. First in point of time was the Paris-domiciled Prussian Cloots, who had advocated French expansion to the Rhine even before the Revolution commenced.[75] Next came a non-German, De Peyssonnel, who, on March 10, 1790, in a speech before the Jacobin Club, called for the "natural boundaries" on all fronts.[76] On January 1, 1792, Cloots called for new squares on the French chessboard (the Rhine and Alps boundaries), also before the Jacobin Club.[77] It was Cloots who managed to reconcile the proposed expansion with the renunciation of conquests of May 22, 1790,[78] by holding out as fairly certain the desire of the

[73] *Ibid.*, pp. 21, 22.
[74] Zeller in *RHM*, VIII, 321.
[75] *Voeux d'un Gallophile* ("Prayers of a Francophile"), Amsterdam, 1786. Background *infra*, Pt. I, chap. iv, § 2f.
[76] J. Hansen (ed.), *Quellen zur Geschichte des Rheinlandes im Zeitalter der französischen Revolution, 1780–1801* (4 vols., Bonn, 1931–1938), I, 637, n. 1.
[77] *Ibid.*, II, 138.
[78] *Ibid.*, I, 628–629. The newspapers in the Rhineland, which region had been the principal scene of France's former expansionism, received the renunciation decree "with a grain of salt." They either did not mention it at all, or limited themselves to a reproduction of the decree without comment (*ibid.*, n. 2).

left-bank populations themselves to unite with France.[79] In this he did yeoman service to Brissot, head of the Girondist party, whose wide-flung projects included the Rhine frontier for France.[80] With the fall of Mayence to the Prussians in the summer of 1793, Cloots was joined in Paris by many German expatriates of like mind, of whom Forster, in Paris already since March, must be singled out for particular mention.[81] Reubell, deputy to the Paris assembly from Colmar, son of France's German-speaking Alsace, also was an early publicist of the Rhine-boundary thesis.[82]

The first official executive intimation that the shade of Charles the Bald was stalking again was supplied by Dumouriez, who became minister of foreign affairs on March 15, 1792. Indeed Dumouriez had not waited until he took office to divulge his tendencies. In the beginning of March, in unfolding a plan of campaign to the Ministry of War, he indicated that he was basing his plan on the fact (to him) that a river such as the Rhine was a natural boundary. About April 18, he stated in the Council of Ministers that "France could have no lasting security without the Rhine as a boundary." He could not announce this publicly, however, because the Republic had renounced wars of conquest, and incorporated the principle of renunciation in its Constitution of September 3, 1791. And indeed the declaration of war of April 20 repeated the renunciation, though it was expected that as soon as French troops appeared on the left bank, all the Germans from Alsace to Nijmwegen would seize the opportunity to embrace the Constitution of 1791 as their very own. On April 30, Dumouriez revealed that whereas it was certainly his intention to slice the Rhineland from the German Empire, he did not intend that France should keep it. He envisaged the left bank as forming several dependent buffer states allied with France.[83]

From the time that war was declared on Austria, the Rhine-boundary concept in some form was never lost to view by the French revolutionists, and by the end of November, Brissot was able to report to Dumouriez — now a general in the field — that the idea was spreading at Paris that the Rhine should form the eastern frontier of the Republic.[84]

i. National Policy Largely a Constant

Thus did it come about that the Revolution took up Charles the Bald's struggle, waging it with ideas as well as with the sword. Under the Conven-

---

[79] *Ibid.*, p. 637, n. 1.

[80] Mathiez, *Fr. Rev.*, p. 285.

[81] *Vide infra*, Pt. I, chap. ii, § 3. Sagnac thinks Forster was the first to advance the natural-boundary theory (P. Sagnac, "Les Limites de la France et la Théorie des Frontières Naturelles du XVIIᵉ au XXᵉ Siècle," *Franco-American Review*, I [1936–1937], 120).

[82] In a letter to the deputies of the Haut-Rhin of Dec. 4, 1791. R. Guyot, *Le Directoire et la paix de l'Europe des traités de Bâle à la deuxième coalition (1795–1799)* (Paris, 1911), p. 118.

[83] Hansen, *Quellen*, II, 32 *, 139, 682. (Asterisk here denotes "of Introduction.")

[84] Zeller in *RHM*, VIII, 330–331.

tion and Directory, the Rhine frontier was conquered, but the Directory found it insufficient. It tried to cross to the right bank, but could not overcome the descendants of Louis the German. Finally, under the Empire, the Rhine was passed, and France, triumphant, set up her creatures on the right bank. However, in 1812 commenced the retreat, which was to end at Waterloo, or, one might say, at Sedan.

But the restless ghost of Charles the Bald cried out in consternation, and the year 1919 found Alsace and Lorraine once more in French hands, with France demanding (in vain) the Rhine frontier — and engaging in annexationist propaganda on the occupied left bank,[85] exactly as in the hoary days of the Revolution. After the fall of France in 1940, the descendants of Louis the German came again into possession of Alsace and Lorraine, and expelled many of the old French families to make room for Germans[86] — thinking in this way to stop the movement of the historical seesaw. But with the defeat of the Nazis, the seesaw has made a partial return. The tricolor today flies proudly over Strasburg and Metz. And for a time after World War II, the words "Rhine boundary" and "Rhineland autonomy" were not expressions drawn from history books, but living things. Especially interesting is it that De Gaulle, like the Directory, wished the boundary between German and French dominion to be located on the right bank — east of that "best" of all frontiers, the river selected by Nature as France's eastern boundary.

Thus, it can be seen that a detailed knowledge of the German policy of the Revolution is essential to a proper understanding of French policy of our own day — for the policy of a state is an astonishingly immutable if intangible thing. It is not the product of chance; neither is it the creation of a given dynasty, or ruler, or minister, or assembly. It is the logical and inevitable result of certain forces and conditions, as location, economic factors, and genius of the people.

The influence of constant factors on the policy of France during the Revolution is well expressed by Sorel. The French, he says,

commenced the war [i.e., the wars of the Revolutionary period] to defend their independence; they continued it to propagate their principles; then by the force of things, by the impulsion of tradition and of the national interest, the spirit of classical magistracy, inbred in the race, overexcited by the revolutionary spirit,

[85] W. C. Langsam, *The World Since 1914* (3rd ed.; New York, 1936), p. 123.

[86] This act, too, has its Revolutionary counterpart. In 1792 or 1793, Mayor Monet of Strasburg, deploring that Strasburg "was not made for liberty — its customs, idiom, and dealings being too closely intertwined with those of the Empire," recommended sending French "patriots" to Alsace, and the Alsatians to the interior of France. And shortly thereafter, the agents of the government at Paris set about proscribing large sections of the population of Alsace (L. Sciout, *Le Directoire* [4 vols., Paris, 1895–1897], II, 533, n. 1).

identified national defense, propaganda, supremacy, the grandeur of France and the happiness of humanity with a single design, that of conquest. Conquest, once commenced, followed the necessary course of conquests. The war absorbed the state. The Revolution realized, to an extraordinary degree . . . , that indistinct state. The Revolution realized, to an extraordinary degree. . . , that indistinct dream of Rome which was lurking in the French imagination: hereditary dream, nourished by the monarchy, suggested ceaselessly to the elite by classical education, [and] to the masses by legend.[87]

[87] A. Sorel, *L'Europe et la Révolution française* (8 vols., Paris, 1885–1904), IV (*Les limites naturelles*, 1892), 462. Query, of course, as to just how true it is that the monarchy nourished a frontiers-of-Gaul concept.

A recent article by P. E. Hübinger attacks, as misleading, the interpretation of Zeller that the old monarchy was not a consistent Rhine-frontier advocate. Says Hübinger: Of course the old monarchy did not strive for the Rhine when it had not yet reached the Meuse. But as soon as the Meuse was reached, and crossed, the Rhine was striven for, reached (and crossed) ("Die Anfänge der französischen Rheinpolitik als histori-sches Problem," *HZ* [*Historische Zeitschrift*], CLXXI [1951], 43). Hübinger's facts cannot be disputed, but because one takes two successive steps does not prove that such was his intention when he took the first step. "None of the kings of France claimed the . . . old boundary of Gaul," says Sagnac; and "the French monarchy never had at its disposal a theory of 'natural bounds.' " But, "without doubt," Sagnac adds, "the history of France presents the spectacle of a constant push toward the north and toward the east. . . " — Sagnac in *Franco-American Review*, I, 118, 120.

The Convention

Valmy and Basel

CHAPTER I

THE SETTING

I. GERMANY AND THE FRENCH REVOLUTION

*T*HE Revolutionary advocates of conquest of the Rhineland did not have to combat a modern unified national state. The Germany whose western dikes were crushed by the flood from Paris was a patchwork of governmental units, large and small, extending from the Vistula to the Meuse. These were ruled by princes (senates, in the free cities) enjoying almost complete sovereignty, for the Treaties of Westphalia had practically nullified the power of the Empire by permitting the individual states to wage war and treat for peace independently.[1] Since 1663, the Imperial Diet had been permanent at Ratisbon, but this permanence was not a source of strength, the princes having ceased to attend in person, and dilatoriness and feebleness having become the order of the day. There was a Supreme Court of the Empire, but it was powerless to punish any but the weakest princes; besides, most of the important cases were reserved for trial at Vienna before the "usurping" Aulic Council. The House of Habsburg had held the Imperial crown, with only five years' intermission, since 1438, but it was so handicapped by the Constitution[2] (if such it may be called) that the power of

[1] More specifically, the Empire consisted of almost 300 practically sovereign princes, and some 1500 lesser territorial lords subject only to the Emperor (Kriegsgeschichtliche Abteilung des k. und k. Kriegsarchivs, *Kreig gegen die französische Revolution, 1792–1797* [2 vols., Vienna, 1905], I, 66).

[2] And yet, German voices could speak very respectfully, very affectionately, about that constitution. When Leopold II was elected Emperor (Sept. 30, 1790), the Neuwieder *Politischen Gespräche der Toten* utilized the occasion to heap praise upon "this lofty indication of our good fortune": "This constitution consists of all three forms of government, monarchical, aristocratic, and democratic, 'combined so that no one of them predominates; each balances the other, each holds the other within bounds. . . Our God . . . has suffered that our neighbors, the French, have made a Babel out of their government; a cutthroat society out of their laws. . . It is the punishment of heaven. . . They have derided, criticized, scorned our form of government. Their writings bulge with exuberant sallies against Germany's constitution. But they have been punished. God has . . . said: . . . I leave the arrogant to destroy themselves with confusion, and you, my children, I leave in the

the Emperor depended more upon his position as hereditary ruler of the Habsburg dominions than upon his Imperial status.

The tiny potentates of Germany, with their paltry acres and few dozen soldiers, are laughable to us today, but they took themselves very seriously. They often established courts in imitation of that of Louis XIV at Versailles; they maintained mistresses and favorites; some of them supported men of letters; and many of them ground down their subjects with their financial exactions. The Habsburgs may have abolished serfdom and decreed religious toleration; the Hohenzollerns may have promulgated a liberal code; the Wettin dukes may have suddenly become virtuous, reformed their courts and their finances, and abolished torture as a punishment for crime; the rulers of Baden, Brunswick, Saxe-Weimar, and Hanover, especially the three former, may have been model administrators, and Baden may even have abolished serfdom; Württemberg may have retained a semblance of constitutional government down through the ages; the princes of the left bank of the Rhine, ecclesiastical and temporal, may have renounced absolutist aspirations since the Cologne elector's sad experience with his estates three generations before;[3] the Archbishop-Elector of Mayence may have taken freethinkers and Protestants into his service; but, on the whole, Germany was in a very sad state.

With the accession of Leopold II in 1790, the Austrian masses had been allowed to sink back into medievalism (only personal freedom and religious toleration remaining of Joseph II's reforms); Prussia had been drifting into bankruptcy and administrative chaos since the death of her philosopher-king; Bavaria was in the throes of obscurantism, religious persecution, immorality, anarchy, and hunger; the hand of the Württemberger Duke weighed heavily on his people, and criticism often led to a dank dungeon for the critic; Mecklenburg was the scene of feudal oppression in its most grievous aspect; the Duke of Zweibrücken had ruined the crops of his people with his devil-may-care hunting parties until the French took over the task; initiative was lacking in the government of Hanover; the Landgrave of Hesse-Cassel sold his subjects to England at £15 per head; the Margrave of Ansbach and Baireuth engaged in the same nefarious traffic in order to obtain funds to squander on his mistresses, and finally even sold his principalities to Prussia at one mistress's behest; the ecclesiastical states were quite regularly the most backward socially and politically of all German states, with a very oppressed peasantry, a lifeless citizenry, a prodigal and carousing

center of Europe as an example . . . of form of government. . .' " — Hansen, *Quellen,* I, 698.

[3] For this item alone, J. Hashagen, *Das*

Rheinland und die französische Herrschaft: Beiträge zur Charakteristik ihres Gegensatzes (Bonn, 1908), pp. 198–199.

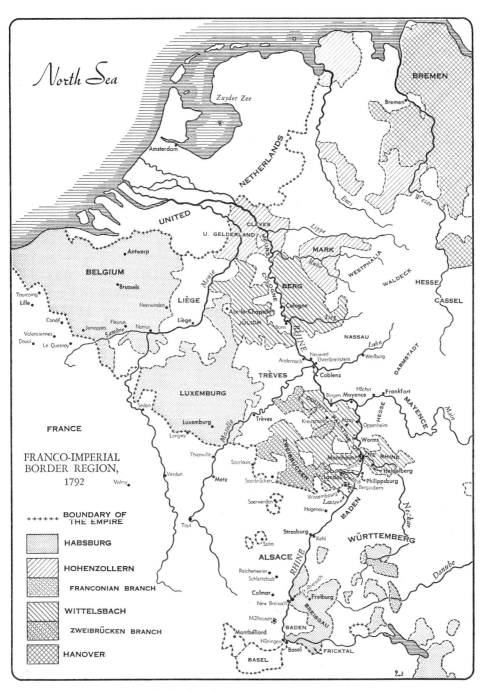

North Sea

Zuyder Zee

BREMEN

Bremen

Amsterdam

NETHERLANDS

Weser

Ems

UNITED

CLEVES

U. GELDERLAND

Lippe

MARK

WESTPHALIA

WALDECK

HESSE

Antwerp

BELGIUM

Brussels

LIÈGE

Neerwinden

Liège

BERG

COLOGNE

Cologne

Rhin

CASSEL

Tourcoing
Lille

Condé

Valenciennes
Douai   Le Quesnoy

Jemappes
Fleurus
Namur

Sambre

Aix-la-Chapelle

JÜLICH

Bonn

RHINE

Sieg

NASSAU

Lahn

Weilburg

DARMSTADT

Meuse

TRÈVES

LUXEMBURG

Luxemburg

Longwy

Moselle

FRANCE

FRANCO-IMPERIAL
BORDER REGION,
1792

Sedan

Thionville

Saarlouis

Metz

Verdun

Valmy

Toul

Trèves

COUNTY PALATINE

Andernach
Neuwied
Ehrenbreitstein

Coblenz

Höchst
Bingen Mayence

Kreuznach

Alzey

Oppenheim

Worms

Frankfort

HESSE

MAYENCE

Main

WEISSENBURG

Saarbrücken

Saarwerden

Hagenau

Mannheim

Landau

THE RHINE

Philippsburg

Bergzabern

Heidelberg

Speier

Neckar

Lauter

++++++ BOUNDARY OF
        THE EMPIRE

HABSBURG

HOHENZOLLERN

FRANCONIAN BRANCH

WITTELSBACH

ZWEIBRÜCKEN BRANCH

HANOVER

Wissembourg

Hagenau

Strasburg

Kehl

Salm

WÜRTTEMBERG

ALSACE

RHINE

Danube

Reichenweier
Schlettstadt

Colmar

New Breisach

Breisach

Freiburg

BREISGAU

BADEN

Mülhausen

Montbéliard

Hüningen

Basel

FRICKTAL

BASEL

Note: The city of Basel lies outside the Bishopric of Basel.

chapter-nobility, and a reckless officialdom; [4] the free cities, except Hamburg and Frankfort-on-the-Main, were lacking in energy, rent by factions, economically and politically decadent, and out of touch with the spirit of the nation; and the domains of the Imperial knights were but sorry remnants of a bygone age, and too often the scene of such tyrannies that the Emperor had to enter and imprison and depose the rulers.[5] Moreover, serfdom in Germany was quite general and quite onerous, some peasants being forced to till their plots by moonlight, so many days each week did they owe to their lords; and where serfdom had been abolished, things were quite as bad, for the peasant did not own the land he tilled, and his personal liberty was subject to various restrictions. Then, taxes were unequally apportioned; justice was often unrecognizable; monopolies, regimentation, and economic cure-all legislation stifled the spirit of enterprise; roads were bad and infested with brigands; canals were lacking; tolls and other artificial barriers were numerous and galling; and the diversity of moneys, weights, and measures hampered the exchange of commodities.[6] In short, economically and politically Germany was still in the Dark Ages, with inveterate particularism and unbridled selfishness bearing it slowly onward to its doom. An expert has diagnosed its disease as "creeping paralysis." [7] A better diagnosis could hardly be given.

In the realm of thought, however, the Germany which came into contact with the Revolution was not the same Germany that had existed even but a few years before. The *Aufklärung* (Enlightenment) [8] had weakened re-

---

[4] The ephemeral nature of the princely office in an ecclesiastical principality rendered the introduction of reforms both useless and inexpedient, so the clerical princes usually gave themselves over to mistresses, balls, and the chase in order to squeeze the last ounce out of their good fortune while it lasted (L. Häusser, *Deutsche Geschichte vom Tode Friedrichs des Grossen bis zur Gründung des deutschen Bundes* [4 vols., Berlin, 1869], I, 101).

[5] One example will suffice. The Count of Leiningen-Guntersblum was deposed for aggravated blasphemy, attempted murder, poisoning, bigamy, lese majesty, oppression of his subjects, and ill treatment of foreigners and clerics. This and other examples: *ibid.,* pp. 113–114.

[6] G. P. Gooch, *Germany and the French Revolution* (London, 1920), chap. i; Häusser, *Deutsche Geschichte*, I, 91 *et seqq.*; E. Denis, *L'Allemagne, 1789–1810* (Paris, 1896), pp. 61–62.

[7] G. P. Gooch, "Germany's Debt to the French Revolution," *Studies in Modern History* (New York, 1931), p. 183. In point of fact, particularism had been elevated to the position of a veritable philosophy of government. The example of Switzerland, and the influence of Rousseau, who extolled the small state, awakened many to its undoubted advantages, and there developed a whole school of German thinkers — among them Herder, Möser, and Johann von Müller; Heeren and Spittler of Göttingen; and Nikolas Vogt of Mayence — who vouchsafed it their allegiance (J. Droz, *L'Allemagne et la Révolution française* [Paris, 1949], p. 7). The *Kleinstaat* concept was furthered by religious division, economic isolation, and the numerous German wars wherein a foreigner was an ally against a fellow German (Hansen, *Quellen*, II, 532–533).

[8] The *Aufklärung*, bursting its dikes in France and England, and early flooding Protestant North Germany, did not even moisten Cath-

spect for all ideas and institutions which could not bear the impact of reason; the expulsion of the Illuminati [9] by the Bavarian government in 1785 had resulted in the dissemination throughout the Empire of the theory that princes had outlived their usefulness; the political, social, and educational ideas of Rousseau, Montesquieu, and Voltaire had met with a lively reception in Germany; Schiller's *Die Räuber* had crystallized the popular hatred of tyranny; and powerful journalists had been waging war for twenty years on the abuses which disgraced most of the states of the Empire. The result was the transformation of Germany by 1789 into a semi-modern state in all respects save the economic and political.[10]

On the eve of the Revolution, many of the noted men of Germany, e.g., Goethe, Schiller, and Lessing, were cosmopolitans. They were citizens of the world, they said; patriotism for a little corner of the earth was narrow-

---

olic South Germany until after the suppression of the Society of Jesus in 1773 by Pope Clement XIV. And from South Germany it flooded over the Rhine into the (Catholic) ecclesiastical electorates, where it encountered some influence coming directly from France. The electoral princes, like their temporal brethren, promoted the movement. Education of the public assumed a new importance in a world where reason was master, and the highest form of culture was to be the eventual lot of all mankind (Hansen, *Quellen*, I, 8*, 9*).

But education did not mean merely schools and universities. The decade preceding the Revolution witnessed the establishment in every city of Germany, and even in the larger villages, of reading circles. Here Kant was discussed, here German and foreign newspapers were eagerly devoured, and here developed hostility to institutions that enslaved the spirit or body of Man. Many of the circles were closely connected with Masonic lodges, which were widely scattered over Germany in this decade. Quite a few Germans who took part later in political events in the Rhineland were members of these circles. The circles themselves had no connection with one another, German particularism militating strongly against such union (Droz, *Allemagne*, pp. 32–33). In the Rhineland there were reading circles in Mayence, Coblenz, Trèves, Bonn, Aix-la-Chapelle, and Cologne (Hansen, *Quellen*, I, 48*).

[9] A secret society founded in 1778 by an ex-Jesuit, Adam Weishaupt, Ingolstadt profes-

sor and canon. Its original purpose was the advancement of reason, science, and morality. It was affiliated to the Freemasons in 1780 through the efforts of one of Weishaupt's friends, Baron von Knigge, an ex-Mason thoroughly steeped in occultism. The new creed of the society, drawn up by "Spartacus" (Weishaupt) and "Philo" (Knigge) was this: The root of all earthly evil is the State, which, by dividing mankind, has sown the seeds of discord. Revolution or reform is of no avail. Destroy the State. Then, with the true religion (whose secrets the Order of course possessed) and proper education, the world would have a golden age. In 1783 a pamphlet revealed the existence in Munich of an antipatriotic and irreligious secret society, and the Order was indicted and (March 2, 1785) expelled from Bavaria (Droz, *Allemagne*, pp. 403–405). The following years were replete with stories about the reconstitution of the society, in part because certain people regarded the French Revolution as its spiritual, if not its actual, handiwork (*ibid.*, pp. 405–406). After their dispersion, some of the Illuminati settled in France. One Dom Pernety established himself in Avignon, made a multitude of converts, and maintained close relations with the Freemason lodges (D. Mornet, *Les origines intellectuelles de la Révolution française* [2nd ed.; Paris, 1934], p. 374).

[10] G. P. Gooch, "Europe and the French Revolution," *Cambridge Modern History* (12 vols., Cambridge, 1902–1912), VIII (*The French Revolution*, 1904), 772–773.

mindedness. "Our object," wrote Goethe, "[is] to get to know Man; we [are] content to let people in general go their own way." "The patriotic interest," affirmed Schiller, ". . . is chiefly . . . for unripe nations. . . . We may excite a different sort of interest if we represent each remarkable occurrence that happened to *men* as being of importance to *Man*. It is a poor and little aim to write for one nation; a philosophic spirit cannot tolerate such . . . arbitrary, fluctuating, accidental [limits]." [11] "The love of country," declared Lessing, "is a sentiment which I do not understand. It is . . . at best a heroic infirmity which I am most happy in not sharing." [12] It is easy to conceive how this attitude facilitated the entrance of foreign ideas into Germany, especially the universal concepts of the French revolutionists. There was no national feeling to resist the invasion. [13]

Perhaps the last assertion should be qualified. There was just springing up in 1789 a desire for German unity. Three plans had been proposed: union of Germany under Austria, union of Germany under Prussia, and a federation of equal states. The first aimed to build a new structure on the existing Imperial foundation, or — in a manner of speaking — to remodel the Imperial Apartments into the Imperial Hotel. The second would tear up the entire foundation as cracked and crumbling — as unable to bear the strain of a structure of any sort, and would build upon the lapsed *Fürstenbund* (League of Princes) of the late Frederick the Great a monument to German unity. The third would also reject the existing foundation as useless, and would erect upon the common historical, cultural, and linguistic background of all Germans a unified national state on the lines of the national states of France, England, and Spain. This third plan had its center of propagation at Weimar; Goethe, as minister, encouraged a German nationalist literature wherein the praises of Germany, of its language, and of its heroes were sung; and in 1787, the Duke of Saxe-Weimar proposed the defense of "the German Rhine" by a league composed of Prussia, Hanover, Saxony, and Baden [14] — that is, of a goodly part of Germany, with no distinction between north and south. [15]

[11] Quoted in Rose, *Nationality*, pp. 37, 39.

[12] Quoted in J. S. Schapiro, *Modern and Contemporary European History* (Cambridge, Mass., 1923), p. 118.

[13] The universal concepts of the Revolution yielded to the doctrine of nationality in France itself as a result of Europe's interference in French affairs. Thereafter, the revolutionists continued to speak as cosmopolitans, but functioned as nationalists.

[14] E. Bourgeois, *Manuel historique de politique étrangère* (4 vols., Paris, 1913–1926), I

(*Les origines*, 6th ed., 1916), 546–547; Gooch, *Stud. Mod. H.*, p. 183.

[15] It has been stated that the proponents of the idea of Fatherland did not have Germany in mind. For the Prussian, the fatherland was Prussia; for the Austrian, Austria. Each looked upon his state as an exalted ideal, materialized, so to speak; and it was this ideal that he — when he thought at all about German unity — visualized as extending over all Germany (*vide* Droz, *Allemagne*, pp. 6–7). Only those who wished to build on

The Revolution was greeted with joy by the mass of cultivated Germans. Georg Forster waxed enthusiastic over "what philosophy has ripened in the brain and realized in the State." Gentz, Wieland, Schubart, Bürger, Voss, Fichte, Herder, Richter, Kant, Hegel, Schelling, Kerner, Schlözer, Müller, Klopstock, Goethe, Schiller, and Prince Henry of Prussia all declared in favor of the French revolutionaries.[16] Schlözer even declared that the angels were assuredly singing *Te Deums* in heaven. However, the chorus of praise was not unanimous, for some noted Germans, e.g., Gleim, Jacobi, Justus Möser, Carsten Niebuhr, Arndt, Zimmermann, Aloýs Hofmann, and Göchhausen looked with disfavor upon the movement.[17]

The courts of Germany, generally speaking, were opposed to the Revolution, though Prussia was at first favorably inclined,[18] hoping, probably, that the upheaval would weaken the Franco-Austrian alliance. The Prussian minister at Paris, von der Goltz, had even fraternized with Jérôme Pétion, the radical, democratic deputy from Chartres in the Constituent Assembly. However, this attitude had changed by July 1790, and the Prussian government, under the influence of Frederick William's confidant, General Bischoffswerder,[19] thought rather of reaction. But it was the petty states of Germany which received the Revolution with the greatest hostility, which were the most indignant that the rights of princes had been infringed.[20]

The attitude of the Rhenish princes is of most interest here. The Elector-Archbishop of Cologne, the brother of Marie Antoinette and of the Emperor

---

the common cultural past of all Germans viewed the Fatherland concept as it is viewed today.

Thus, for the general run of Germans, the following use of the term "fatherland" in the *Bonnisches Intelligenzblatt* of September 28, 1790, seemed quite proper: "Our state, i.e., the one whose subjects we are, and especially the one in which we hold office, is called our fatherland." — Hansen, *Quellen*, I, 694.

[16] Many of these— e.g., Fichte, Klopstock, and Gentz — were cured of their infatuation by the subsequent excesses, principally by the execution of the King. But Kant remained faithful (Gooch, *Stud. Mod. H.*, p. 187). In his *On the Strife of the Faculties*, he affirmed that the Jacobins were not so bad as other tyrants of the past, and that history would proclaim the Revolution a blessing in disguise. (Cf. Forster: "Liberty is worth a certain number of atrocities." — Gooch, *Germ. Fr. Rev.*, p. 305.) And in his *Perpetual Peace* (1795), Kant showed that he

hoped the Republic, "which by its very nature is inclined to perpetual peace," would serve as the nucleus of a federal union which would render obsolete the institution of war.

[17] Gooch, *Germ. Fr. Rev.*, pp. 57–68.
[18] Not spiritually! Frederick William had resolved to suppress the *Aufklärung* in Prussia even before the French Revolution commenced (C. Brinton, *A Decade of Revolution* [New York, 1934], p. 174).
[19] A dull, empty-headed, propertyless nobleman, of doubtful character, but ever anxious to serve his king — this, in essence, is Heinrich von Sybel's none-too-complimentary description of Bischoffswerder (*History of the French Revolution* [tr. from the German by W. C. Perry; 4 vols., London, 1867–1869], I, 328).
[20] G. Blondel, "L'Allemagne," E. Lavisse and A. Rambaud (eds.), *Histoire générale du IVe siècle à nos jours* (12 vols., Paris, 1892–1901), VIII (*La Révolution française, 1789–1799, 1896*), 688–689.

Joseph, referring to the decrees of the French National Assembly, affirmed that France treated Germany like a doll which could be undressed at her pleasure. But he blamed the plight of the royal pair on their own missteps, and did not feel disposed to partake in any monarchical crusade against France.[21] He suggested the imposition of economic sanctions in lieu of war. The Elector of Trèves was far more bellicose, and secretly pressed Prussia and Austria to crush the Revolution.[22] The Elector-Archbishop of Mayence stirred up trouble in Strasburg, and proposed a congress at Mayence to insulate Germany against the new ideas. The Bishop of Spires intrigued against France in the Diet, and — according to a contemporary — would have effected the counterrevolution singlehanded if that had been possible, so violent was he in his hatred of the Revolution.[23]

The peasantry of Germany was also much affected by the news from Paris, but in a different way. Revolts occurred in Rügen, Schönburg (Electoral Saxony), the Upper Rhine region, and the Palatinate. In the two latter districts, the peasants refused service and payments in kind, while in Schönburg, the populace armed itself with clubs and drove out the administrators of justice. The ferment was increased by the warm reception granted by the German princes to the French *émigrés*, whose loudly proclaimed contempt of the lower classes, and whose loose behavior, alienated all who came in contact with them.[24] The principal rendezvous of the *émigrés* was the Rhineland, especially Coblenz, where a virtual little Versailles had been established. The sight of all the strutting Gallic coxcombs disgusted the simple Rhinelanders, hence it was this region which sympathized most with the French radicals.[25]

---

[21] Authority for this sentence only: Gooch, *Germ. Fr. Rev.*, p. 470.

[22] He was the brother of Maria Josepha, Louis XVI's prolific Saxon mother (P. Rain, *La Diplomatie française de Mirabeau à Bonaparte* [Paris, 1950], p. 6).

[23] A. Chuquet, *Les guerres de la Révolution* (11 vols., Paris, 1886–1896), VI (*L'expédition de Custine*), 19–26.

[24] Blondel in Lavisse and Rambaud, *Hist. gén.*, VIII, 690–691.

[25] Chuquet, *Guerres Rév.*, VI, 19–20. The growing abyss between the erstwhile abjectly servile Rhinelanders and their princes is best exemplified by the fact that such an article as the following could appear:

" 'Human society requires states. These cannot subsist without commanders and obeyers. It follows that it is the duty of a subject to obey . . . all commands of the authorities the execution of which does not palpably violate his conscience [Note the influence of Kant] . . .

" 'When we think that the commands of the public authorities are detrimental, or are such commands as should not have been given, and we think . . . that . . . the Regent will change his mind for the better, it is magnanimous to refuse [to obey], to suffer loss of office, even to be placed in danger of life and limb and the loss of one's good name. . .'

" . . . Against tyranny, as Nero, Alba, etc., practiced it, . . . it appears that, under certain circumstances, something may be permitted 'with appropriate restrictions. But the following should be considered: The first fruits of political change are anarchy. . .

" ' . . . One must not help any foreign

2. ORIGIN OF THE FOREIGN WAR

a. General

When the Revolution burst forth, Austria was in the midst of a war with Turkey. Now, as noted above, Prussia at first regarded with favor the revolt in the realm of Austria's ally, the King of France; and in 1790 she allied with Austria's enemy, Turkey.[26] In the mind of the Prussian minister Hertzberg was a grandiose plan which included Austria's renunciation of Galicia to Poland, Poland's cession of Danzig and Thorn to Prussia, and Austria's withdrawal without increase of territory from the Turkish war.[27] Austria thought it best to negotiate, and agreed to Prussia's demand for an armistice, but the remainder of the Hertzberg plan was rendered unworkable by the resistance of Turkey, which did not care to return to the boundaries of Passarowitz; of Poland, which did not care to cede Danzig and Thorn; and of England and Holland, which did not care to see the *status quo* along the Vistula disturbed.[28] The plan was therefore discarded, and Frederick William lent his ear to one who urged him to turn his attention to what was happening in France, and become the "Agamemnon of monarchical Europe." [29]

Bischoffswerder was sent to Vienna to plead for unity of action against France, and he induced Leopold II to transfer his efforts to the West in return for a promise of Prussian friendship. But Bischoffswerder was no namby-pamby sentimentalist, spending his waking hours in commiseration for the unfortunate Bourbon family. In the back of his mind was a plan for Prussia's acquisition of Jülich and Berg, their sovereign to be compensated

---

state to harm the fatherland, and consequently one must commit no treason, i.e., conceal how enemies may harm, and grant them the means therefor. . .

" 'When one has changed fatherlands, one must not utilize to the detriment of his first fatherland those secrets confided to him under a pledge that they will not be revealed. . .

" '. . . One must not reveal . . . through speech, pen, or behavior, that one regards [regents and constituted authorities] . . . as stupid or wicked, nor give others occasion to form such opinions, but much rather must hold their failures secret from the people, and in so far as possible without lying, excuse them.

" '. . . When regents, in an unrighteous [or unjustified] passion, or during insanity

or inebriety, place our lives in apparent danger, no defense is allowed . . . which would place such a high personage (if his life is of great public benefit) in danger. . . The life of a good regent can be worth more than the lives of several thousand citizens. . .' " — *Bonnisches Intelligenzblatt*, Sept. 28, 1790, in Hansen, *Quellen*, I, 692–695.

[26] A. Rambaud, "L'Europe orientale," Lavisse and Rambaud, *Hist. gén.*, VIII, 327–328.

[27] *Ibid.*

[28] O. Browning, "The Foreign Policy of Pitt to the Outbreak of War with France," *C. Mod. H.*, VIII, 293; R. Lodge, "The European Powers and the Eastern Question," *ibid.*, p. 333.

[29] Blondel in Lavisse and Rambaud, *Hist. gén.*, VIII, 692–693.

with Alsace, while Austria might have French Flanders. It was difficult for the Prussian councillors to entertain a purely altruistic thought.[30]

The Austro-Turkish peace was signed at Sistova on August 4, 1791, Austria yielding practically all her conquests.[31] Thus was born the Austro-Prussian concert of 1791–1795 — a concert conceived in high-sounding phrases but dedicated to the proposition that though all Frenchmen might be created equal, they were not bound to remain equal. Not if France could be made into another Poland!

Strangely, it was France which declared war — and on Austria! The reasons were somewhat complex, but yield readily to analysis.

b. The Feudal-Enclave Problem

The Treaty of Münster, as already mentioned, had provided for the cession to France of the rights of the Empire and of the Habsburg dynasty in Alsace,[32] the province to be held by France "without any reservation, with plenary jurisdiction and superiority and sovereignty forever." [33] However, the Imperial cities, seigniories, nobility of lower Alsace, monasteries, etc., were to be left in full enjoyment of their immediateness (immédiateté) to the Holy Roman Empire [34] — an obvious contradiction, and one fruitful of much difficulty.

In August 1789, the Constituent Assembly abolished the feudal system in France. The decree was considered applicable to Alsace because, by the Treaty of Münster, Alsace had been ceded to France. But certain electors, princes, knightly orders, and knights of the Holy Roman Empire still possessed domains in Alsace which the Peace of Westphalia and subsequent treaties had guaranteed to them. These princes opposed application of the law to Alsace, and drew up a protest to the French government in February 1790.[35]

Strictly speaking, this was not the first protest — for that had not been the first transgression. When, in 1787, the Assembly of Notables concerted with Louis XVI concerning reforms which would give France a homogene-

---

[30] Ibid.

[31] To be strictly accurate, by the Treaty of Sistova, Austria returned all her conquests. It was a supplementary treaty which granted her the small gains she did receive (F. Mayer, Geschichte Oesterreichs [2 vols., Vienna, 1874], II, 176).

[32] Treaty of Münster, Art. 75 (H. Vast [ed.], Les grands traités du règne de Louis XIV [3 vols., Paris, 1893–1899], I, 38–39).

[33] Art. 76, ibid., pp. 39–40.

[34] Art. 89, ibid., p. 44.

[35] P. Sagnac, Le Rhin français pendant la Révolution et l'Empire (Paris, 1917), p. 55. The principal temporal princes affected were those of Zweibrücken, Württemberg, Hesse-Darmstadt, and Baden; the principal ecclesiastical princes, those of Strasburg, Spires, Cologne, Trèves, and Basel (P. Muret, "L'affaire des princes possessionés d'Alsace et les origines du conflit entre la Révolution et l'Empire," RHMC [Revue d'histoire moderne et contemporaine], I [1899–1900], 433).

ous government, the first encroachments took place, and the princes then especially affected — the Bishop of Spires, the Landgrave of Hesse-Darmstadt as Count of Lichtenstein, and the Elector of Cologne for his fief of Sulz on the Queich and for his numerous possessions as Grand Master of the Teutonic Order — protested. They protested again after the Constituent Assembly abolished feudalism in France in August 1789, but now they were joined by the Count Palatine of Zweibrücken, the Margrave of Baden, and the Count of Leiningen — for this new decree affected also Lorraine, where the same feudal-enclave situation obtained.[36] The latter protest was referred to the Feudal Committee[37] of the Constituent Assembly. (It should be noted in passing that, perhaps for the sake of brevity, it is the custom among historians to speak loosely of the feudal-enclave problem as if it concerned only Alsace. The context always indicates whether Lorraine must be implicitly included.)

It was not only Germans who looked askance at the abrogation of the time-hallowed feudal laws in Alsace. The city of Strasburg itself had been enjoying certain advantages which it pleaded with the Constituent Assembly not to abolish. It was Reubell, Alsatian deputy from Colmar (whom we have met in his role of Rhine-boundary advocate), who stifled the appeal. He said that the loss of the rights would bind the Alsatians more closely to the French, "and this name ["French"] is the fairest that one can bear." On August 11, the city lost its ancient constitution to boot.[38]

During this year of 1790, there was much discussion in German circles about the possible return of Alsace to the Empire. G. B. von Schirach's *Hamburger politisches Journal* seems to have spread the story that Alsace was about to reunite with the Empire of its own accord, and various other papers followed like sheep. A certain pamphlet took the tack that now was Alsace's great opportunity to rejoin Germany, instead of allowing itself, "contrary to nature," to be merged with France. One writer became quite legalistic: France had herself broken the treaty, he said, by which Alsace had been united with France, so, by all the principles of international law, the province had reverted to Germany. The correspondent of a Cologne paper wrote on June 6, 1790, from Paris that "a tremendous split has become manifest in Alsace, and it is feared that this beautiful province might . . . separate from France." But the death of Joseph II on February 20, 1790, and the inability of the German electors to agree on a successor for seven vital

---

[36] Hansen, *Quellen*, I, 431–432.
[37] Created on August 12, 1789; reconstituted October 9, 1789. This committee consisted of 30 members, and not only prepared laws concerning redemption from feudal dues, but assisted the local authorities in applying them (A. Mathiez, "La Révolution française et la théorie de la dictature," *RH* [*Revue Historique*], CLXI [1929], 314).
[38] Hansen, *Quellen*, I, 432, n. 3.

months, rendered certain that the question would remain purely academic or — should we say? — journalistic.[39]

Meanwhile, however, the French sought to negotiate indemnities for the aggrieved princes, and the Paris minister of foreign affairs, Montmorin, sent De Ternant to Germany to arrange the bases with the principals themselves. However, the Bishop of Spires, who, like the Trèves and Cologne Electors and the Landgrave of Hesse-Darmstadt, did not want an indemnity but only the return of his rights, succeeded in wrecking France's efforts. The Bishop maintained that Imperial law did not permit the individual states to negotiate on a subject pending before the Empire. And directly the negotiations were broken off, the irreconcilable princes turned their attention toward stirring up the Empire to compel France to restore the rights in question.[40]

On October 28, the matter came up again in the Constituent Assembly, and Merlin of Douai propounded the theory that the French people were not bound by treaties made by the French Crown: "There is, between you and your Alsatian brethren no other legitimate deed of union than the social compact formed last year between all Frenchmen, ancient and modern, in this very Assembly. . . Without doubt, a treaty was obligatory for the monarchy. . . But today, when kings are generally recognized . . . only as the delegates . . . of nations . . . , of what importance to the people of Alsace, of what importance to the French people, are the conventions which, in the age of despotism, . . . united the first to the second [?] The Alsatian people is united to the French people because it wants to be; it is its will alone, and not the Treaty of Münster, which has legitimated the union; and as it has not placed on this desire any condition relative to the royal fiefs, no one can claim any idemnity. The German Empire presents [to view] only a composite of independent states . . . ; each of them . . . forms a separate national body. *Ergo* . . . the divers states of which Alsace is composed do not need the Empire's consent to become French. . . The princes of Germany [have] no right to an idemnity." [41]

[39] *Ibid.*, pp. 733–734.

[40] *Ibid.*, p. 734.

[41] *Ibid.*, pp. 735–736. Quaint is the proclamation (1793 or 1794) of Saint-Just and Le Bas, on mission to Alsace, that "the citizenesses of Strasburg are urged to abandon German customs inasmuch as their hearts are French." — Chuquet, *Guerres Rév.*, IX (*Hoche*), 32. And in 1793, we are apprized, the CPS (Committee of Public Safety) dropped the tolerance of former French governments respecting the Germanic tongue of Alsace. German was "little made for free people," the Committee declared (P. Wentzcke, "Die alte Universität Strassburg und das Reich, 1621–1793," *HZ*, CLVIII [1938], 262). But though "the people of Alsace were German in language and tradition, they had . . . become loyal to France," writes R. R. Palmer, who ascribes the persistence of their Germanic attributes to the fact — among other things — that the old monarchy had not availed itself of modern methods of assimilation (*Twelve Who Ruled* [Princeton, 1941], p. 178). Modern Germans admit that Alsatian resistance to in-

Mirabeau, who directed the Diplomatic Committee,[42] saw that such an approach could result only in war, and suggested that the feudal princes be compensated with assignats or some of the national domain. This was decreed by the Assembly, and Montmorin made another attempt to negotiate indemnities. But the princes wanted their rights, and only their rights, and appealed to the Diet of the Empire.[43]

That it was a Herculean task to secure action from the Imperial Diet was common knowledge, so attempts were made to force its hand. A deluge of patriotic pamphlets appeared at Worms, Spires, and Strasburg, calling to mind the century-old War of the League of Augsburg, 1689–1697, in the early days of which Louis XIV, in vindication of the pretended claims of his Palatine sister-in-law, invaded the Palatinate of the Rhine and systematically sacked and burned the right-bank portion. Goertz, the Prussian minister to the Diet, worked on a different tack: He assured the petty feudal lords that the Empire's intervention would result in territorial gains for them at the expense of France, hoping that self-interest would prove a spring of action where nobler motives would probably fail — as they had so often failed in the past.[44]

But the Diet, true to its tradition, refused to act. There was no unity among its members regarding the proper course to be pursued. Prussia, Cologne, Trèves, Darmstadt, and Spires were unwilling to compromise; Hanover and Saxony were conciliatory. So the majority procrastinated, and awaited the Emperor's decision.[45] Leopold let them wait. His interest lay in soothing his ruffled dominions, so sorely shaken by the reforms of Joseph II, and bled of men and money by the war against the Turks. Leopold wished to see agriculture, commerce, and industry flourish, and taxes swell the shrunken Habsburg treasury. Order and productivity were his goal. Of this, war was the antithesis. Therefore, peace was maintained.[46]

c. The Emigré Problem

It was not the feudal princes alone who were anxious for the Empire to take vigorous action against France. Since the Fourteenth of July, a steady

corporation with France soon disappeared, but console themselves that "the people of Alsace . . . , the vastly preponderant majority, have . . . rigidly isolated themselves from French ways in the cultural sphere. Their speech [has] remained German. Alsatian science [has] preserved its German character, as has Alsatian art." — Note of W. W. under "Deutsche Landschaften," *HZ*, CIX (1912), 679.

[42] Created after the Nootka Sound controversy. This committee read the despatches of the ambassadors, and exercised a preponderant influence upon foreign policy (Mathiez in *RH*, CLXI, 313).

[43] Their uncompromising attitude Muret blames on Prussia, which saw in the disordered international situation a chance to play politics (*RHMC*, I, 442 *et seqq*).

[44] Sagnac, *Rhin fr.*, p. 55.

[45] *Ibid.*, p. 56.

[46] L. Leger, *Histoire de l'Autriche-Hongrie depuis les origines jusqu'en 1918* (rev. ed.; Paris, 1920), pp. 386–387.

stream of nobles had been emigrating from France. Most of them had crowded into the Rhineland, especially into Coblenz in the Electorate of Trèves, where the Counts of Provence and Artois, brothers of Louis XVI, were residing; others had settled in Worms, where the Prince of Condé was acting as their leader; still others had taken up their abode in Mayence and other cities on the left bank of the Rhine.[47] These *émigrés* became yet more numerous after the failure of the flight to Varennes, and soon there were twenty thousand at Coblenz alone. "The number of emigrants is indescribably large," says a contemporary account, "and waxes daily. . . All the officers draw half pay, and recently the Princes promised everyone who would enter their service four *Karolin*,[48] an undertaking hard to carry out if it lasts long, though, in addition to Russian financial assistance, the Princes are said to be drawing considerable sums from Holland. . . They [the troops] are practicing with weapons, [and] are laying in a magazine, for which they have already bought 6,000 bales [of hay] and many horses. . . They are providing themselves with saddles, side-arms, [and] munition-wagons, among other things. . . The Prince-Elector of Trèves continues to support the Princes in every way."[49] "Nine wagons laden with small arms passed through this city [Cologne] on their way to Coblenz," ran another contemporary account. "According to all reports, they came from Dutch territory."[50]

Not only did the Princes lay in physical supplies but they struck out for allies in all directions. Of course, those in Germany, by virtue of sheer proximity, bade fair to be the most useful, so Calonne, the old comptroller general, acting as "prime minister of the emigration," sent ambassadors to the various princes of Germany. Specially important for his plans was a request to the Emperor to declare the Count of Provence (later, Louis XVIII) regent of France (on the ground that Louis XVI had shown himself too weak to cope

[47] The right bank of course had its share too. The Diplomatic Committee of the Constituent Assembly reported 500 in the right-bank portion of the Bishopric of Strasburg. What angered the Diplomatic Committee particularly was that the *émigré* leaders were being permitted to recruit troops in these tiny states, whereas the Imperial constitution forbade such a luxury to all but sovereign princes or princes holding "immediately" of the Empire. Thus, the German princes were violating German law to help this scum that France had cast off (Nov. 22, 1791, Hansen, *Quellen*, I, 1024, n. 2).

[48] A gold coin first minted in 1732 by Karl Philipp of the Palatinate, and worth three gold florins (D. Sanders, cont. by I. Schmidt and C. Stoffel, *Muret-Sanders Encyklopädisches englisch-deutsches und deutsch-englisches Wörterbuch* [*Grosse Ausgabe*, rev.; 4 vols., Berlin, 1899], IV, xix, *s.v.* "Karolin").

[49] Monthly report of I. von Hertwich, Office-Director of the Imperial Embassy at Coblenz, end of 1791, Hansen, *Quellen*, II, 11. These "reports" were really a hand-written monthly newspaper put out by one in official position (*ibid.*, I, 28 *).

[50] Imperial Resident in Cologne F. J. von Bossart to Imperial Vice-Chancellor Prince von Colloredo, Jan. 1, 1792, *ibid.*, II, 11, n. 1.

with the forces arraigned against him),[51] and to support this declaration by a movement of troops toward Alsace and Hainault.[52]

The Emperor returned an evasive answer, and further instigation on the part of Artois, uninvited guest of the Prussian and Austrian rulers at Pillnitz, in Saxony, produced only a statement that the predicament of Louis XVI was a matter of common concern to all monarchs. All monarchs were therefore requested to join Prussia and Austria in an invasion of France. But until they should join, Prussia and Austria would initiate no action against their obstreperous western neighbor.[53] Blustering as was this declaration, it was really quite harmless, for there was not the slightest chance that England would join the monarchical crusade,[54] and the participation of *all* the powers was a condition precedent to action by Prussia and Austria. Certainly (as indicated above), Leopold was not eager for war. If it proved absolutely necessary bodily to pluck the Bourbon chestnuts from the revolutionary inferno, he wished Austria's part to be very limited. And when Louis XVI accepted the Constitution of 1791, Leopold decided that the chestnuts themselves had the fire well under control — that the very need for action was past.[55]

That was not, however, the way his sister, the Queen of France, viewed the situation. It was ridiculous, according to her, for Leopold to pretend that the King had "accepted" the Constitution. He was not a free agent, but only simulating agreement for reasons of personal safety, as her brother assuredly knew. And whenever she found herself alone in her room, she dashed off insistent appeals for help to all the powers of Europe, especially to the Emperor, whom she begged "to prove himself to be [her] brother." Marie Antoinette wanted the courts of Europe to assemble a congress which, backed by armed force, would "lay down the law" to the revolutionists.[56] Letters to the same effect were sent by Louis XVI to Prussia, Russia, Sweden, and Spain.[57]

[51] H. M. Stephens, *Revolutionary Europe* (6th ed.; London, 1924), p. 103. It seems that Provence had long had his eye on the regency. That, at least, would seem to follow were we to credit the following story related by Mallet du Pan: In 1787, year of the Assembly of Notables, this little verse was found posted in the streets of Versailles:

"Louis XVI interdit, Antoinette au couvent,
D'Artois à Saint-Lazare, et Provence régent."

— A. Sayous (ed.), *Mémoires et correspondance de Mallet du Pan pour servir à l'histoire de la Révolution française* (2 vols., Paris, 1851), I, 147.

[52] Sagnac, *Rhin fr.*, p. 57.
[53] E. Herrmann (ed.), *Diplomatische Correspondenzen aus der Revolutionszeit, 1791–1797* (Gotha, 1867), p. 88, n. 74.
[54] H. Hüffer, *Europa im Zeitalter der französischen Revolution* (3 vols., Bonn, 1868–1890), I (*Oestreich und Preussen gegenüber der französischen Revolution bis zum Abschluss des Friedens von Campo Formio*), 23–24.
[55] *Ibid.*, p. 24.
[56] Marie Antoinette to Count de Mercy (Aust. ambas. to France), Dec. 16, 1791, Herrmann, *Dipl. Corr.*, pp. 129–133.
[57] King of France to King of Prussia, Dec. 3 (or 2?), 1791, *ibid.*, pp. 127–128. De Mercy

All to no avail. Leopold's attitude was incomprehensible to everyone, and people began to say that perhaps Marie Antoinette herself had written Leopold "to keep his fingers out of our pie." [58]

Rumors of these frantic appeals for foreign aid, the Declaration of Pillnitz, the attempted flight of the royal family, the menaces [59] and intrigues of the *émigrés*, and the protection accorded by the Electors of Trèves and Mayence to the *émigrés* congregated in the Rhineland on France's very doorstep, all created the impression upon the French people that the foreigner was awaiting only an opportunity to pounce upon France. This would have been sufficient to induce the French to be the first to declare war — even over the head of their minister of foreign affairs, De Lessart, who favored peace and the Austrian alliance [60] — had not factors of internal policy reinforced their natural inclinations.

d. Brissot

October 20, 1791, Jacques Pierre Brissot,[61] leader of the Girondist [62] party (who appeared above as a Rhine-boundary advocate), urged in the Legislative

---

blamed De Fersen, a handsome Swedish officer of whom the Queen was rather fond, for Marie Antoinette's discontent with the Emperor's conduct. De Fersen wrote the Queen: "He suspects me of being the cause, and let it be understood that he had proof of it. I think this is only a suspicion, for all my letters have reached you; and if he had developed the writing [they were in sympathetic (i.e., white) ink], he would not have sent them to you." — *Diary and Correspondence of Count Axel Fersen, Grand-Marshal of Sweden, Relating to the Court of France* (tr. from the French by K. P Wormeley; Boston, 1902), p. 310.

Catherine II counselled Louis XVI to make war as a means of crushing the Revolution (*Journal of Khrapovitski* [secretary to Catherine II], p. 35, cited in B. S. Mirkine-Guetzévitch, "La Révolution française et l'idée de renonciation à la guerre," *RF*, LXXXII [1929], 258).

[58] Marie Antoinette to Mercy, Herrmann, *Dipl. Corr.*, p. 130. Paraphrased.

[59] E.g., the uniforms of the Prince of Condé's troops were ornamented with a death's head — gentle hint to the French people what they could expect from at least this group of *émigrés* (Earl Gower [Brit. ambas. to France from June 1790 to August 1792] to Lord Grenville, May 6, 1791, O. Brown-

ing [ed.], *The Despatches of Earl Gower* [Cambridge, 1885], p. 85).

[60] Sagnac, *Rhin fr.*, p. 60. According to the Constitution of 1791, *Titre* III, chap. ii, sec. 4, arts. 1 and 2, the ministers were not responsible to the legislature, but only to the king; nor could they be members of the legislature. There was a complete separation of executive and legislative power (L. G. W. Legg [ed.], *Select Documents Illustrative of the History of the French Revolution* [2 vols., Oxford, 1905], II, 229).

[61] Brissot had once been imprisoned in the Bastille for two months for allegedly attributing the paternity of the Dauphin to a royal prince other than the King (M. de Lescure [ed.], *Mémoires de Brissot* [Paris, 1877], pp. 345, 361). His career included also a scandalous lawsuit incident to the liquidation of a newspaper and reading room which he had founded in England. He has been held morally responsible for the revolt of the negroes in the West Indies (through his Society of Friends of the Negro). Brissot was the leading statesman of the Assembly at this time (Mathiez, *Fr. Rev.*, pp. 138–139).

[62] A group of able deputies coming from the *département* of the Gironde — or, more loosely, from southwestern France in general. They represented the interests of the

Assembly that France solve the problem posed by the assemblages of *émigrés* by attacking directly the Rhineland princes harboring them. It was not that Brissot necessarily regarded the assemblages as such a menace, but he suspected the King of treason and wished to force him to show his true colors.[63]

Brissot's speech made a deep impression on the Assembly, but not on the public, and on the thirtieth, a lawyer, Machenaud, ripped it asunder in the Jacobin Club. The next day, in the Club, Dubois-Crancé assured the members that France's greatest danger lay within her borders, not without. It remained for Carra to blow the bugle for Brissot, but no one rushed to arms.[64] The agitation did, however, prompt action on the part of the Court, to which the Constitution accorded the control of foreign affairs.

On November 14, 1791, Minister of Foreign Affairs De Lessart, in the name of Louis XVI, summoned Klemens Wenzeslaus, Prince-Elector of Trèves, to disperse the *émigrés* organizing into military detachments in his territory. He said the King had heretofore maintained his silence in the hope of inducing the Princes (his brothers) to return home, but now the build-up was becoming a real threat to his kingdom, and the Elector would have to disarm and disperse the *émigrés*. His Majesty did not deny the right of Trèves to grant political asylum, but he did feel that if such asylum did not limit itself to mere hospitality, France had just grounds for complaint.[65] A simultaneous request was directed to the Emperor: to use his good offices to assure that all the states of the Empire observed the laws concerning the maintenance of peace and public tranquillity.[66]

Meanwhile, the Legislative Assembly was attending to other things — or shall we admit that most of the members were not attending at all? It was only on November 27 that the Assembly received for consideration a concrete proposal for action that aroused its interest: Daverhoult had suggested a deputation to the King, plus a fifteen-day ultimatum to the German electors. However, the Assembly adjourned without a vote. Next day, November 28, Dubois-Crancé, in the Jacobins, presented a suggestion of his own — essentially a one-month ultimatum to the German princes.[67]

On this same day, November 28, Robespierre, ex-deputy from Arras, now a public prosecutor, presided over the Jacobin Club. Far from opposing the provocative tone of Dubois-Crancé's draft, he objected only to a detail; and with respect to Daverhoult's plan, he thought the electors were too insignificant to merit France's attention. On the other hand, he said, the

---

merchant class, especially that of Bordeaux. The Girondists favored a federal republic, as distinguished from the united republic favored by the more radical Mountain.

[63] G. Walter, *Robespierre* (Paris, 1946), pp. 223, 239.

[64] *Ibid.*, p. 223; Machenaud's speech, *Moniteur*, X, 456. (Bib. data re *Moniteur* in n. 70, this chapter.)

[65] Hansen, *Quellen*, I, 1012–1014.

[66] *Ibid.*, p. 1013, n. 1.

[67] Walter, *Robespierre*, pp. 225–227.

Emperor might well be threatened with a declaration of war if he did not disperse the *émigrés* in the Austrian Netherlands.[68] The proper formula, according to Robespierre, was "courage, and contempt for tyrants." [69] It would be well to remember that Robespierre started as a fervent member of the war party.

The next day, in the Assembly, Isnard made his oft-quoted proposal, "Let us say to Europe that if the cabinets enlist kings in a war against peoples, we will enlist peoples in a war against kings." The Assembly applauded his speech,[70] and the Jacobins heard nothing from Robespierre. Then, since Klemens Wenzeslaus had not complied with De Lessart's request, the Assembly directed the following message to Louis XVI: "Tell the foreign powers who support the emigrant Frenchmen that in every place where warlike preparations are tolerated, France can distinguish only enemies. . . Tell them . . . that if these German princes continue to favor the preparations against France, the Franks will bring them, not fire and sword, but liberty. . . Set a short time-limit. . . Accompany your declaration with a movement of . . . troops." [71] The King dutifully complied.

Upon Billaud-Varenne devolved the task of analyzing where this war policy would lead. That, he told the Jacobins on December 5, was directly to tyranny, for the instruments sharpened to win the war would be turned on the patriots themselves. The proper course was to defeat the enemy within. Then the foe without, deprived of the ally upon which it had counted to effect a counterrevolution, would melt away. Billaud-Varenne had no confidence in the good faith of the King, and recommended that if the *émigrés* did not disperse at Louis' request, or if France were invaded, it should be regarded as proof that the King had failed to act effectively, and he should be reputed to have abdicated. Robespierre listened intently but said nothing.[72]

e. Robespierre

On December 7, the Count of Narbonne, handsome young lover of Mme. de Staël (daughter of Necker and wife of the Swedish ambassador to France),[73] became minister of war,[74] and Robespierre noted that the follow-

---

[68] This had been done already the previous March, April, and August (1791), for it was the *émigrés* in the Austrian Netherlands that first aroused the solicitude of France (Hansen, *Quellen*, I, 1013, n. 1).

Robespierre was not the first to suggest war on Austria. Lafayette had, in 1790, recommended France's interference in the struggle between Joseph II and his revolting Belgian subjects, on the side of the democratic Vonckists (Rain, *Mir. à Bon.*, pp. 2–3).

[69] Walter, *Robespierre*, pp. 227–228.
[70] *Réimpression de l'ancien Moniteur* (29 vols., Paris, 1858–1863; index, 2 vols., Paris, 1863–1870), X, 504.
[71] Hansen, *Quellen*, I, 1045–1046.
[72] Walter, *Robespierre*, pp. 229–230.
[73] A Mathiez, "Le lendemain du 10 août," *AHRF* (*Annales Historiques de la Révolution française*), XI (1934), 388.
[74] Mme. de Staël had tried to secure the foreign affairs portfolio for Narbonne before De Lessart obtained that post, but the

ing persons presently visited her at the same time: Narbonne, the new minister; Brissot, leading light of the Girondists; Lafayette, associated with the Court and the moderates; and Talleyrand, connected with the directorate of the *département* of Paris. Robespierre remembered immediately Billaud-Varenne's warning of bad faith, and when Carra blew his bugle in the Jacobins on December 11, Robespierre presented a new face. Now the danger from without was not sufficient to excite him. The great danger was from within. External war would only put into the hands of the King the means to crush the Revolution. "Slow and circumspect" was the new formula.[75] A pacifist was born.

On December 14, Danton raised his sonorous voice in the hall of the Club.[76] He would prove, he said, that Lafayette was a conspirator (i.e., conspiring with the Court to crush the Revolution), and he added: "Let those who take delight in stupid confidence prepare to enter the lists against me in the next session." This was of course aimed principally at Brissot. Heretofore, though Robespierre and Brissot had differed, there was no personal antagonism.[77] Henceforth, Robespierre and Brissot would be enemies.

The same day that Danton attacked Lafayette (December 14), the King informed the Assembly that he had tried to induce his brothers to return home and submit to the law of the majority. Furthermore, he had entreated each neighboring German prince not to flatter their hopes. He said the Emperor was behaving toward him like a loyal ally [78] and had forbidden all gatherings in Austrian-ruled territory. Other princes had not, however, given suitable assurances. Louis declared he had given the Prince-Elector of Trèves until January 15, 1792, to disperse the *émigrés* — or be treated as an enemy of France; and he said similar declarations would be sent to other princes if necessary. He said he had asked the Emperor, as head of the Empire, to do his best to secure the compliance of the German princes, for,

---

King had declined through fear of Mme. de Staël's indiscretion. De Lessart, then chosen, had sought to appease the patroness by aiding Narbonne to become minister of war. But Narbonne never forgot his original goal, and continually sought to supplant De Lessart (C. Léon, "Le Comte de Narbonne," *RF*, LXVI [1914], 98).

[75] Walter, *Robespierre*, pp. 231–233.

[76] Danton was seeking to recapture public attention. After the flight of the King, Danton did not divulge his views as to the fate of Monarchy in France, nor did he sign the Champ de Mars petition; yet his arrest was ordered. Escaping to England, he returned to take part in the elections for

the Legislative Assembly, and was seized and thrown into the Abbaye prison. Included in the amnesty voted by the Constituent Assembly, he found his popularity had waned considerably, perhaps because his voice had not been heard for so long in the Jacobin Club (A. Kuscinski, *Dictionnaire des conventionnels* [Paris, 1916], s.v. "Danton").

[77] Walter, *Robespierre*, p. 236.

[78] Brissot ridiculed the idea that the King could have an ally. Only France could have allies, he maintained. Of course, prevailing usage identified a kingdom with its king (L. von Ranke, *Ursprung und Beginn der Revolutionskriege, 1791 und 1792* [Leipzig, 1875], pp. 195–196).

if the Emperor could not succeed either, nothing remained to him, Louis, but to propose a declaration of war.[79]

"How absurd!" wrote Marie Antoinette. "Without an army, without discipline, without money, it is we who want to attack!"[80] But Louis was cheered loudly for several minutes by the Assembly.[81] The French public seemed to be enthusiastically in favor of war.[82]

On December 16, Brissot defended his policy before the Jacobin Club. It would be an error, he maintained, to stop the Court from taking action now when it was at last willing to act. Coblenz was the source of France's ills, within and without. The internal enemy relied on help from Coblenz; Coblenz relied on help from the internal enemy. Destroy Coblenz and France would have both internal and external peace. It was true that the aristocratic generals could commit treason, but not usefully, for their every step would be under scrutiny by loyal troops. And if the King betrayed France, no loss, either. France would soon rid herself of him. (In point of fact, as mentioned, Brissot rather hoped Louis would betray his people. Then Louis could be replaced by the Dauphin, with Orléans regent, and Jacques Pierre his prime minister. But of course Brissot did not announce that.) The speech ended with a plea to support the executive in the performance of its duty. Watch that executive, if necessary, he said, and if it betrayed France — well, "the people are there."[83]

Danton gave his threatened speech the next day. The crowd was there, but not the Danton everyone came to hear. It had been attracted by the prospect of a joust. Instead, Danton ranged himself hesitantly on the side of his announced antagonist. The Tribune of the People commenced with a compliment for "this vigorous athlete of liberty" (Brissot), and then startled everyone with "If the question were to know . . . if we will have war, I would say: Yes, the clarions of war will sound; yes, the exterminating angel of liberty will tumble these satellites of despotism. It is not against energy that I come to speak. But, gentlemen, when ought we to have war?" Here he raised doubts as to the intentions of the executive in proposing war; also, as to the country's readiness. He continued (after some digression): "I want us to have war; it is indispensable. We ought to have war. But we must first exhaust the means which can spare us [from having to fight].

[79] Hansen, *Quellen*, I, 1062–1064. The Prince-Elector of Mayence had, of his own accord, forbidden armed congregations in the Electorate and in his Bishopric of Worms. Condé was the leader in this section (*ibid.*, p. 1071, n. 2).

[80] To Mercy, Dec. 16, M. de la Rocheterie and Marquis de Beaucourt (eds.), *Lettres de Marie-Antoinette: Recueil des lettres authen-* *tiques de la Reine, publié pour la Société d'histoire contemporaine* (2 vols., Paris, 1895), II, 351.

[81] Hansen, *Quellen*, I, 1064, n. 1.

[82] H. A. Goetz-Bernstein, *La diplomatie de la Gironde: Jacques-Pierre Brissot* (Paris, 1912), p. 187.

[83] Walter, *Robespierre*, pp. 237–239.

. . . When I said I was opposed to war, I meant to say that the National Assembly, before embarking on this course, should indicate to the King its desire that he employ all the power of the nation . . . [against the émigrés]."[84]

Much of the speech seems to have been lost. André Fribourg, in the critical edition of Danton's speeches employed above, advises one to regard Danton's recorded remarks as a mere framework. It would seem that, with patently incomplete coverage, it is hazardous to accuse Danton of trimming his sails to the wind, of deserting to the winning side in the middle of a battle — as Mathiez has done.[85] Besides, this assumes that Brissot was winning, which, at that date, was hardly true. Walter points out that Danton's statement of policy varies little from the following statement by Robespierre two days later: "I also want war, but as the nation's interest requires it: let us subjugate our internal foes, and then march against the foreign foes, if any still exist."[86]

On December 18, Robespierre outlined more fully his position to the Club. "The nation does not at all refuse to fight if that be necessary to purchase its liberty; but it rejects every plan for war proposed [with the intent] to annihilate liberty and the constitution itself under the pretext of defending it." He objected to Brissot's seeming indifference to the dangers inherent in his war policy. Brissot's remark that "the people are there" Robespierre interpreted as an appeal to insurrection, and an impudence on the part of one hired by the people to take charge of its protection. He pointed out that the very general, Lafayette, who had given the order to fire on the people at the Champ de Mars, was to lead one of the armies in Brissot's projected war. He said that the trouble was not at Coblenz, as Brissot maintained, but right at home. And Robespierre recommended arming the nation — the troops with guns, the people perhaps merely with pikes; but not to declare war as yet. Try to recoup the finances, he recommended, instead of completing their ruin by a martial adventure. And institute measures for the safety of the state independent of the ministers, so that their nonfeasance or malfeasance should not endanger France. And lastly, be alert — both to sustain the dignity of the people and to discover sedition.[87]

f. Trèves Yields

Louis XVI was certainly not guilty of nonfeasance with respect to the émigrés. It was at his instance that the Emperor wrote personally to Klemens Wenzeslaus — in fact, Leopold wrote to him twice (December 21, and again three weeks later) — pointing out that he, the Emperor, was sworn to protect

---

[84] A. Fribourg (ed.), Discours de Danton (Paris, 1910), pp. 121–123.

[85] A. Mathiez, Danton et la Paix (Paris, 1919),

pp. 6–12.

[86] Walter, Robespierre, p. 241.

[87] Ibid., pp. 243–247.

the Empire from attack, but insisting that the German states must give the French no legitimate grounds therefor. And he directed the expulsion of all armed French nationals.[88]

The same day (December 21), Austrian Chancellor Prince von Kaunitz replied to De Lessart's note of November 14, which had requested the Emperor's good offices. Von Kaunitz said the Prince-Elector of Trèves had promised in writing to adopt the salutary rules promulgated by the Emperor for the *émigrés* in the Netherlands. However, the Elector feared irruptions and violence nevertheless, and had asked the Emperor's assistance should his fears materialize. This, von Kaunitz informed De Lessart, had been promised. "The Emperor . . . hopes . . . one can avert 'this extreme measure [war] and the inevitable results which France would suffer from the direction, not only of the head and states of the German Empire, but likewise from that of the other sovereigns who have united in the common cause of upholding the public peace and the security and honor of crowns.' " [89]

g. Twenty Millions for "the War"

Before the Imperial notes could have come to the attention of the Assembly, Brissot (December 29) defied all Europe and suggested a holy coalition of peoples against kings in general. Condorcet concurred with Brissot, dilating upon the humanity, generosity, and liberty of the French, and proposing "war on kings and peace to peoples." [90] In Brissot's own words, his political philosophy was "to set all Europe ablaze. . . If we push back our frontiers to the Rhine, if in the future the Pyrenees divide none but free peoples, our liberty [will be] firmly established." In this quotation, Brissot showed himself to desire not only the natural boundaries, but republican friends beyond — dependent, of course, upon the Mecca of Liberty. His wild schemes captured the imagination of the Assembly, and it formally adopted Condorcet's proposition of "war on kings and peace to peoples," voting twenty million livres for the war.[91] This, it will be recalled, was the sum requested by Narbonne on December 14.[92]

[88] Hansen, *Quellen*, II, 14, n. 2.

[89] *Ibid.*, I, 1068–1070.

[90] *Moniteur*, X, 755–756. The expression between "quotes" was not used by Condorcet at this time, but that is the sense of what he said. Merlin of Thionville later coined the expression, according to Goetz-Bernstein, *Gironde*, p. 61.

[91] F. Masson, *Le Département des affaires étrangères pendant la Révolution, 1787–1804* (Paris, 1877), p. 128. Before the Jacobin Club, on December 30, Brissot proposed that the French troops entering Germany aid the inhabitants to follow France's example: to overthrow their sovereigns and establish republics according to their own wishes and needs (Goetz-Bernstein, *Gironde*, pp. 60–61).

Reubell wrote later (22 *messidor*, IV; July 10, 1796), "Brissot desired to envelop France with little republics, which he called 'little meat pies.' This term is much more accurate than perhaps he himself realized, for it is with the fat of the meat that little meat pies are made, and it is at the expense of the great Republic that the surrounding little republics would fatten themselves." — Quoted in G. Dejoint, *La Politique économique du Directoire* (Paris, 1951), p. 166.

[92] Walter, *Robespierre*, p. 234.

The Prince-Elector of Trèves was really quite frightened by the French threats — and also by his own estates, which were distressed lest the Elector's conduct should provoke an invasion of the Electorate. "I found myself between a revolt of my subjects, some of whom have absorbed the spirit of the neighborhood, and a hostile invasion by France when the assurances of your Majesty saved me," he wrote on January 1, 1792, to his "very generous protector" (the Emperor).[93] The Elector promptly determined what were the regulations of Austria with respect to the *émigrés* in the Austrian Netherlands, and on January 3, promulgated a decree accordingly. It permitted the *émigrés* sanctuary as unarmed individual civilians, but forbade their congregation in groups, drilling with or without arms, recruiting, and amassing of materials of war. War materials arriving from outside the Electorate would be seized and stored. No *émigrés* could live within four hours' travel of the French frontier.[94]

Louis XVI had given Trèves until January 15 to disperse the *émigrés*, but when von Kaunitz' note of December 21 arrived in Paris announcing that the Emperor had received Klemens Wenzeslaus' written promise to comply, De Lessart thought the occasion one for felicitation, and hastened to inform the Assembly of the good tidings. At least, they were good tidings for De Lessart, who, as indicated, favored peace and the Austrian alliance. Of course, De Lessart tried to deëmphasize von Kaunitz' statement that Trèves had been promised aid if attacked, and read conciliatory letters from German rulers as an antidote.[95]

But there were those in the Assembly who would have no antidote, and of course they fastened upon von Kaunitz' remark about a concert of monarchs to defend the security of crowns. The Girondists of the Diplomatic Committee proposed an ultimatum to Austria: "The Emperor . . . will undertake no measures against [France], its constitution, or its full and entire independence; if it is attacked, he will furnish the aid that he owes by virtue of Article IX of the Treaty of May 17, 1756"; and the Assembly accepted the proposal.[96] It was considered that the Emperor was infringing upon France's "sovereignty, invading its independence, and endangering its security, by concluding alliances and concerts aimed at meddling in its government or changing its constitution by force." [97] The King was asked to give the Emperor until February 10 to explain his transgressions.[98] On January 21, a note to such effect left Paris for Vienna.

On January 2 and 11, Robespierre again tried to stem the tide. He repeated that the veritable Coblenz was in France. He tried ridicule on Bris-

---

[93] Hansen, *Quellen*, II, 9–10.
[94] *Ibid.*, pp. 18–20.
[95] Masson, *Dép. étr.*, p. 129.

[96] Goetz–Bernstein, *Gironde*, p. 66.
[97] Hansen, *Quellen*, II, 69.
[98] *Ibid.*, pp. 32–33.

sot; dubbed his ideas extravagant, his speeches pompous. He parodied Rousseau's "The people always wishes the good, but does not always see it," into "The mandatories of the people often see the good, but do not always wish it." In vain! Though he was assisted by Billaud-Varenne, Machenaud, Doppet, and Desmoulins, and by several newspapers, it was a lost cause.[99]

On January 5, 1792, von Kaunitz, replying to the French note regarding the *émigrés*, informed the French ambassador (Marquis de Noailles) of Klemens Wenzeslaus' action, and asserted he had no reason to doubt the Elector's good faith. The other German princes, he added, were likewise friendly disposed toward France, whatever was the attitude of a couple of thousand *émigrés* concerning whose designs exaggerated alarm has been spread. "And yet," said von Kaunitz, "it [was] under the pretext of this alarm that the Most Christian King sees himself obliged . . . to assemble 150,000 men on the frontier. The generals to command them have been named, the funds voted. . . The national gazettes resound . . . with menaces against all the sovereigns of Europe. . . Such facts present . . . more real occasion for alarm, and cannot but solicit the most serious attention on the part of the foreign powers united in concert with his Imperial Majesty." And von Kaunitz made it clear that any invasion of Trèves or of any other German territory would be regarded as an attack upon the Empire, which the Emperor would have to oppose with all his forces.[100]

"The national assembly [Legislative Assembly] is now absolutely determined upon war," reported the *Mainzer Zeitung* in a message from Paris dated January 15. "To the accompaniment of general, mirthful exultation, a bill was passed branding all Frenchmen who should take part in a congress aiming to propose a settlement [of the enclave question], or a limitation of the French constitution, or a compromise with the emigrated French princes, as infamous, traitors to their fatherland, and criminals . . . and the King was asked to inform all foreign powers of this resolution, and to declare that the French nation would view as an enemy every prince who sought to injure its independence and constitution." [101]

h. Ultimatum to Austria

From January 18 to 25, the Girondists Brissot, Dumas, Vergniaud, Isnard, Condorcet, and Hérault de Séchelles — realizing that, as time went on, the behavior of the Rhineland princes could less and less aptly serve as grounds for a declaration of war, for the *émigrés* were being disarmed and dispersed [102] — swerved to the position that it was not the princelets but the

[99] Walter, *Robespierre*, pp. 248, 251; *Brochures politiques*, "Révolution, 1789–94," LXXXIV, nos. 18, 20.
[100] Hansen, *Quellen*, II, 20–23.
[101] Jan. 23, 1792, *ibid.*, p. 32.
[102] De Lessart's report to Legis. Assem., Jan.

Emperor who was the real enemy all along. The Legislative Assembly (on January 24) gave the Emperor until March 1 to assure France that he renounced all agreements directed against her sovereignty, independence, and security, and it declared that a dilatory or evasive response, as well as silence, on his part would be construed as a declaration of war.[103]

Louis XVI refused to sanction this declaration,[104] but it was despatched nevertheless, apparently without sanction. It could be regarded as especially offensive to the Emperor for two reasons: (1) It was a virtual declaration of war. (2) It set a very short time limit for those days of slow travel. Everyone to whom its content was divulged — it arrived in the midst of a large gathering at Court — felt that the insult could not be tolerated. And of course, with France armed and threatening, there could be no question of yielding to the demands made.[105]

i. The Austro-Prussian Alliance of February 7, 1792

In fact, the Imperial government was at the time engaged in a further activity which the French Assembly was not destined to like. A few days later (February 7, 1792), Austria and Prussia signed an alliance "of friendship and defense" — the product of three months of negotiations. It provided for reciprocal aid in defense against attack from whatever quarter it might come, and the grant of 20,000 men (15,000 infantry, 5,000 cavalry) upon demand. A supplement to the Treaty promised support in combating internal disorder, and the furtherance of a concert of powers to regulate French affairs.[106]

It was only on February 19 that De Lessart's note of January 21 — giving the Emperor until February 10 to explain his transgressions against France's sovereignty, independence, and security — was answered. Von Kaunitz minced no words in his reply. The Emperor had comported himself, he said, like a loyal ally, friend, and relative. And he bluntly blamed the Jacobin party for trying to provoke war by using first the assemblages in Trèves as an excuse, and latterly the explanations that it was demanding. He called the Jacobins "a pernicious sect," [107] and characterized them as the true enemies

16, 1792, based on the reports of Sainte-Croix (Fr. ambas. to Coblenz), *ibid.*, p. 26, n. 2.

[103] Hansen, *Quellen*, II, 33.

[104] *Ibid.*, p. 47, n. 1.

[105] Austrian Ambassador Schlik to Imperial Vice-Chancellor Prince von Colloredo, Feb. 4, 1792, *ibid.*, p. 47.

(Hansen always writes "Schlik"; Vivenot, always "Schlick." The present writer has not himself seen the signature of this diplomat, hence knows not which form is correct. I have decided to use "Schlik" on

the theory that such an unusual spelling could not have inadvertently slipped scores of times into the work of a careful scholar like Hansen.)

[106] *Ibid.*, p. 52. For limitations and qualifications as to the mutual guarantee of internal security, *vide* "Second Article séparé et secret" of the Treaty in Ranke, *Ursprung*, p. 350 (Analects, no. 2).

[107] To this remark, De Lessart replied, through Noailles, that "the King did not think it consonant with the dignity or independence of the nation to enter into

of the Most Christian King, of the Constitution, of peace, and of the general tranquillity.[108] A simultaneous Prussian note, by its context, showed that it had been written in concert with Austria.[109]

On the day that had been set as Leopold's time limit by the Assembly's unsanctioned ultimatum (viz., March 1), Leopold died.[110] The same day, De Lessart, of course ignorant of the death, read the above-mentioned Austrian and Prussian communications to the Assembly, and indicated that his reply would ask the good offices of the Emperor to destroy the concert formed against France.[111]

This was too much for De Lessart's enemies — asking the hated Austrians to intervene in France's behalf. The communications were sent to the Diplomatic Committee, and when that body reported on March 10, Brissot, for the Committee, condemned De Lessart's weak behavior and demanded his indictment for treason and dereliction of duty. Wherein had he failed? The Neuwieder *Geheime Briefwechsel zwischen den Lebendigen und den Toten* (companion to the *Politischen Gespräche der Toten*), in a report from Paris on March 15, explains accurately, if a trifle sarcastically, just how his enemies reasoned, or pretended to reason: "M. De Lessart is a traitor. . . He hesitated in order to give other powers an opportunity to arm, to march, to attack us. Had De Lessart right from the start spoken to the Emperor with the national might . . . O! our decrees would have been oracles respected by all powers." [112]

In a certain sense, of course, De Lessart's indictment was an act of spite against the King. Minister of War Narbonne, as mentioned above, had wanted to control foreign affairs, and his paramour, Germaine de Staël, had tried to induce De Lessart to resign for the good of the state and the Crown. But Narbonne had impudently asked Louis to dismiss the aristocrats from his palace, and Louis, piqued, had thereupon abruptly dismissed Narbonne.[113] So the Girondists — unable (as yet) to venge themselves upon the King directly — vented their spleen on De Lessart, whose policy of peace and friendship for Austria did not accord with their plans.

---

discussion on matters which concerned only the domestic situation of the kingdom." — Hansen, *Quellen*, II, 70, n. 1. On the following April 30, Marie Antoinette wrote to De Mercy that "the national pride is so attached to this idea that it is impossible for the King to deviate therefrom if he wishes to reëstablish his kingdom." — *Lettres Marie-Ant.*, II, 397.

[108] Hansen, *Quellen*, II, 69–70.

[109] *Vide* E. Herrmann, *Die österreichische-preussische Allianz von 7 Februar 1792*

(Gotha, 1861). Prussia did not wish Austria to be able to pose as *the* champion of the Empire and Monarchy.

[110] It was a sudden death — following upon an illness of only two days (Hansen, *Quellen*, II, 83). Smallpox, says Sybel, *Fr. Rev.*, II, 15.

[111] Mathiez, *Fr. Rev.*, p. 146.

[112] March 20, Hansen, *Quellen*, II, 92 and n. 2.

[113] Mathiez, *Fr. Rev.*, p. 146.

j. The War Party Seeks a General

The war party was now rid of the foreign minister who had served as a dam to its bellicose aspirations, and it was soon to have one more to its liking; but it was not to obtain the general in chief it had been seeking for the past several months. When Narbonne, on December 14, had asked the Assembly for 20,000,000 livres, he had scheduled Lafayette, Luckner, and Rochambeau to command armies, but he did not see fit to give any of them the supreme command.

Narbonne was, indeed, a friend [114] of Lafayette's, whose motive in favoring war was the same as Narbonne's. They both thought to provide Louis with a limited war which he could easily win, and to utilize the victory to reëstablish the faded prestige of the Crown and strengthen the executive arm of the government.[115] But this social and political compatibility could not counteract the suspicion with which Lafayette was viewed by Danton and others. Lafayette was an aristocrat, and, as mentioned, it was he who had given the order to fire on the people assembled at the Champ de Mars.

For France to wage a successful war, the spirit of disunity would have to be stilled, and for that a leader was necessary whose reputation and talents placed him above the nation and above the Court. Such a man France did not possess, but there was a foreign prince who had these qualifications. An old general of Frederick the Great, lover of France, and reformer in his own principality, Duke Ferdinand of Brunswick united within himself all the qualities that Narbonne sought. As a foreigner, he would be forgiven his rank; as a famous general, he would arouse enthusiasm and silence dissension; — and what was yet more, if he would consent to lead the armies of Revolutionary France, the forces of reaction would be deprived of their most likely leader. Narbonne convinced the King of the merits of this plan, and young François de Custine, son of the Revolutionary general — not yet

[114] *Idem*, "Frédéric Dietrich," *AR* (*Annales révolutionnaires*), XII (1920), 392.

[115] A. Sorel, "La mission de Custine à Brunswick en 1792," *RH*, I (1876), 156. Lafayette was distrusted by Louis, hated by his (Louis') entourage (Lafayette to Archenholtz, March 27, 1793, *La Vie et les mémoires du général Dumouriez* [4 vols., Paris, 1822–1823], II, 461, "Eclaircissemens historiques et pièces officielles," Note [G], in St. A. Berville and J. F. Barrière [eds.], *Collection des mémoires relatifs à la Révolution française* [55 vols., Paris, 1820–1827]).

As far as Narbonne was concerned, it seems that Marie Antoinette did not trust him. She had tried to induce him not o aspire to the Ministry (Marie Antoinette to Barnave, Sept. 4, 1791, A. Söderhjelm [ed.], *Marie-Antoinette et Barnave, Correspondance secrète (juillet 1791 — janvier 1792)* [Paris, 1934], p. 158 and n. 4). It may be that she feared his ambition. Reputedly natural son of Louis XV, and as such possibly uncle to the King, he was in a favorable position for almost any intrigue (*ibid.*, n. 3).

twenty-three, but precocious — was given the mission to repair to Germany and determine if Brunswick would accept if he received an offer of the supreme command. The post was not offered to him outright to avoid compromising the King should the proposition be refused.[116]

The plan seems chimerical to the modern reader, but France had a precedent in the Marshal de Saxe; it was well known that Brunswick detested Austria; and young Custine's mother-in-law, Madame de Sabran, was an old friend of the Prussian monarch's Francophile uncle, Prince Henry of Prussia, Brunswick's friend. But the Duke refused. He was not sufficiently acquainted with France, he said, and besides, he was not convinced France was in a condition to wage a successful war; the attempt would result only in sullying his reputation. Custine was about to return home when he was ordered to take the place of Ségur, Envoy Extraordinary to Berlin, who had been sent to the Hohenzollern capital to detach Prussia from Austria, but who had found his position there intolerable. Custine's continued presence in Germany enabled him to make another attempt with the Duke of Brunswick — this time by letter. Meanwhile, however, Austria and Prussia had signed the Treaty of Alliance of February 7, 1792, and Brunswick — though not yet appointed Austro-Prussian commander in chief — had been asked to submit a plan of campaign. Naturally, Custine's letter went unanswered. This letter (dated February 27, 1792) constitutes the veritable end of Custine's mission to Brunswick, though the young diplomat remained in Germany until June, as Ségur's successor.[117]

k. *Dumouriez Becomes Foreign Minister*

It has been mentioned that, according to the French Constitution of 1791, the ministers were not responsible to the legislature, but only to the King. However, due to the stormy session of March 10, when De Lessart was indicted, and to pressure from the Jacobins and from the Assembly,[118] the King decided to try out ministers possessing the confidence of the people. To the Ministry of Foreign Affairs he called Charles François Duperrier, at the time commandant of Cherbourg, always an arch-intriguer, and formerly secret agent of Louis XV.[119] Duperrier is no other than the Dumouriez already mentioned.[120]

[116] *Ibid.*, pp. 154 *et seqq.* Wrote Marie Antoinette to De Fersen: "De Narbonne has a silly idea . . . : to invite the Duke of Brunswick to come here and command the army. The idea is so far beyond [the limits of] common sense that I [had] believed nothing further would be said about it. . . I do not doubt that the Duke will refuse, and *that* will likewise be a service to us." — Dec. 28, 1791, facsimile in *Diary . . . Corr. . . Fersen*, p. 223.
Carra would have made Brunswick king of France (J. M. Thompson, *Robespierre* [2 vols., New York, 1936], I, 212).
[117] Sorel in *RH*, I, 154–183.
[118] Hansen, *Quellen*, II, 94 and n. 4; 95, n. 2.
[119] Mathiez, *Fr. Rev.*, p. 146; Hansen, *Quellen*, II, 94, n. 3.
[120] *Supra*, Introduction, § 2h.

The Rhineland papers immediately dubbed the new minister a Jacobin. He was reported to have declared to the members of the Jacobin Club on March 18: "I will conduct the negotiations now confided to me with all the energy of a free people. . . Either these negotiations will presently result in a lasting peace or bring on a decisive war. In the latter case, I shall break my political pen, and again take my place in the army to live victoriously with my fellows or die free."[121] The Neuwieder *Geheime Briefwechsel* said "the entire ministry is Jacobin, the Tuileries are Jacobin — and the first thing you know, the King will be frequenting the Jacobin Club."[122]

One thing was certain. The new foreign minister would have to deal with a greatly aggravated *émigré* problem. Already on February 16, the *Moniteur* reported that the number of *émigrés* was "unbelievable," and that, though they did not wear uniforms at Coblenz, they were divided into companies there. France's ambassador to Coblenz, M. Sainte-Croix, was busy remitting daily or even twice-daily notes concerning violations of Klemens Wenzeslaus' regulations.[123] Yet the situation was not so bad that it could not become worse, which it presently did, for the Austro-Prussian Alliance of February 7 exercised a distinctly emboldening influence both on the *émigrés* and on the Rhineland princes. Sainte-Croix could stand the strain no longer, and was permitted to resign, leaving the now-vain task of checking in other hands.[124]

The worsening of the *émigré* problem cannot have been too unwelcome to Dumouriez, who regarded it as his task to fill in the background of the canvas upon which the war he would provoke would be sketched. For to provoke it he intended, firm believer that he was in the wisdom of the foreign policy of the Girondists. Of course, decency — and practical good sense — required that France retreat from its ultimatum of March 1. Dead men can answer no ultimatums, and the members of the Legislative Assembly must have felt a little silly to admit that there was a Power which could veto their sovereign plans — and they did not even have Its address to send It an ultimatum, too. Louis XVI wrote to Vienna that he was no longer waiting for a *"réponse très prompte,"*[125] and it was not until March 18 that von Kaunitz replied in the name of Emperor Leopold's son and successor, Francis, who (until July 14)[126] was still merely King of Hungary and Bohemia.

[121] The *Aachener Zuschauer*, March 29, 1792, Hansen, *Quellen*, II, 95.
[122] March 27, 1792, Hansen, *Quellen*, II, 95, n. 2.
[123] Of Feb. 24, 1792, *ibid.*, pp. 66–67.
[124] Hansen, *Quellen*, II, 81 *et seqq.*
[125] *Ibid.*, p. 104, n. 1.
[126] This was the date of his coronation at Frankfort (H. von Sybel, *Histoire de l'Europe pendant la Révolution française* [tr. from the German by M. Dosquet; 6 vols., Paris, 1869–1888], I, 476). His actual election was on July 5 (Hansen, *Quellen*, II, 279).

Meanwhile, Dumouriez was busy preparing the groundwork. On the eighteenth, he made his first steps at London and Berlin to see if he could isolate Austria.[127] He offered the yet-vacant Imperial crown to Prussia.[128] He dilated upon the "monstrousness" of a Franco-Prussian conflict, and tried to purchase Frederick William's entourage.[129] He guaranteed Bavaria against Austrian engulfment.[130] He induced the princes of the Empire to renounce

[127] *Ibid.*, p. 104, n. 1. "There is much complaint against the behavior of Prussia, but she is not assailed," wrote Marie Antoinette to Count de Fersen on April 19, 1792 (*Lettres Marie-Ant.*, II, 395).

[128] Sybel, *Fr. Rev.*, I, 441–442.

[129] Goetz-Bernstein, *Gironde*, pp. 202–203. "Millions are consecrated to that end" (i.e., to detaching Prussia from Austria). —Marie Antoinette to Mercy, April 30, 1792, *Lettres Marie-Ant.*, II, 397.

[130] Austria wished to acquire Bavaria, and indemnify the Wittelsbachs with the Austrian Netherlands. Such an exchange would have been disadvantageous to France, for it would have considerably increased the compactness, and hence the power, of the Habsburg patrimony. It would have augmented by fifty leagues the hostile territory which French armies would have to cross to reach Vienna. It would have deprived France of a potential ally in the heart of Germany — close to Austria's capital. It would have relieved Austria of a vulnerable spot where she could be readily attacked, viz., Belgium (A. Rambaud, *La domination française en Allemagne: Les français sur le Rhin, 1792–1804* [Paris, 1883], pp. 72–73). Besides, France was not sure she did not want Belgium herself.

On December 29, 1784 and January 2, 1785, the French ministers of state had remitted to Louis XVI individual memoirs on the question whether the Bavaro-Belgian exchange would benefit or harm French interests. Vergennes, the foreign minister, had outlined six arguments against the exchange, and nine for, and concluded in favor of the exchange. It will be interesting to see what arguments Vergennes conjured up in support of this most unwise of recommendations: (A) 1. The Elector of Bavaria might be a natural ally of France because of his location on Austria's doorstep, but he might not always realize it. The present elector, certainly,

has "the greatest aversion" for France. 2. Bavaria, as an ally, is bound to collapse under an Austrian onslaught, before the French, 100 leagues away, can arrive. Therefore, France would be placed in the position eternally of having to reconquer or ransom her ally. 3. Austria could constantly vex Bavaria, and France's inability to protect her would lower her (France's) credit in international affairs. (B) Bavaria and the Archbishopric of Salzburg do indeed control the passages to Italy, but they could never successfully close them to the Austrians, so Bavaria might, in this respect, just as well not exist. (C) The Emperor's possessions are already in physical contact with Franconia through Bohemia, and with Swabia through the Breisgau; and the Upper Rhenish Circle's princes are too weak to resist him, anyway. (D) The exchange is possible only with Prussia's concurrence, and measures to tranquillize the Hohenzollerns would be concerted. (E) The exchange would free France from the need to divide her forces and always deploy most of her troops in the north, where the frontier is too close to the capital, and the English often land to assist the enemy. Indeed, Belgium serves France as a convenient point of attack against the Emperor, but whenever France seizes it, England and Holland join in the fray, adding a sea war to the land war. France could acquire the Netherlands for herself only as the result of a long and exhausting war — exhausting to France, too. Besides, France's policy should be one of moderation. "Her finest role, the role she ought to play, is to be the guardian of German liberties, the staff of the oppressed, and the arbiter of all differences which may arise in Europe." (F, H) The Bavarian elector, now an uncertain friend, would, in Belgium, be entirely under France's influence. Holland, also, could be more easily held in line, for France could

the thought of fighting for their confiscated possessions, and to accept indemnities instead.[131]

Neutrality of the Empire — i.e., war on the Emperor [132] but peace with the Empire — would not only deprive Austria of resources in men and money but would hamper her military operations. Accordingly, March and the following months witnessed the rush of a veritable flood of diplomats to Germany: Caillard to the Reichstag at Ratisbon; D'Assigny to Bavaria; Villars to Mayence; De Pont to Bonn; Naillac to Zweibrücken; and Maisonneuve to Württemberg and the Swabian Circle. These negotiators were to impress upon the German states that "France is today the only nation which can save German liberty," and to promise that France would confine its prospective war to the Austrian Netherlands and not cross the Rhine if the German states remained neutral and closed their territories to the passage of Austrian troops.[133]

On March 27, Dumouriez appeared before the Assembly and imparted the contents of von Kaunitz' message of March 18, wherein Austria answered once again France's demand for assurances. But there had really been nothing new to say. King Francis, ran the note, knew of no great build-up of Austrian arms which could compare with the armed might amassed by France. He could never consent to tie his hands in advance with respect to measures necessary to maintain order and to stifle Jacobin plots in his territories. The concert of powers could never be dissolved while the conditions still obtained which had provoked its creation. A furious and bloody faction was making a mockery out of France's laws and principles, and Francis was certain the sane part of France viewed as a beacon of hope the very existence of the concert of powers.[134]

Dumouriez characterized this note as "insulting," and asked the Assem-

---

march directly through Belgium and attack the Dutch. (I) If the Wittelsbachs ever died out, Austria would seize Bavaria as a vacant fief, and would then be in possession of both Bavaria and Belgium. A war might then become necessary to undo the seizure. Should the stadholderate of the United Netherlands ever stand vacant, if the Bavaro-Belgian exchange had already taken place, France would be able to exercise the predominant influence there (Dec. 29, 1784, A. Tratchevsky, *La France et l'Allemagne sous Louis XVI, avec un appendice concernant des lettres et des mémoires inédits de Vergennes* [Paris, 1880], pp. 52–56 — "Pièces justificatives," no. 8).

[131] A. Chuquet, "Dumouriez général et ministre," *FH (Feuilles d'histoire du XVIIe au XXe siècle)*, IX (1913), 517. France had never given up its efforts to indemnify the princes. As late as February 25, 1792, the Diplomatic Committee proposed to the Assembly that indemnification be effected. Louis wrote to Leopold to this end (Hansen, *Quellen*, II, 66). Hansen says Leopold did not reply, but — Leopold was dead five days later.

[132] I.e., assuming the probable continuation of the Imperial office in the person of Leopold's son, Francis.

[133] Hansen, *Quellen*, II, 106, n. 2.

[134] To Noailles, *ibid.*, pp. 98–99.

bly to "contain its just indignation" until he was able to read the retort he would send.[135] That retort was an ultimatum, in Louis XVI's own hand, demanding a "categorical reply. . . If that declaration is not very prompt and entirely without reservations, on the courier's return . . . the King will positively regard himself as in a state of war. . . "[136]

The note Noailles delivered to the Austrian vice-chancellor, Philipp Cobenzl, on April 4 demanded peremptorily that Austrian troops be withdrawn from the French frontier;[137] that the suspected Austro-Prussian alliance be dissolved;[138] and that the *émigrés* leave Habsburg territory.[139] Cobenzl said Francis certainly did not wish to interefere in France's internal affairs, and did not intend at all to support the interests of the *émigrés*. It was true that Austrian troops had been sent into the Breisgau, but only to maintain order and justice, and to answer calls for help from neighboring states. The concert could not be dissolved before the three objects to which it owed its creation had been attained: (1) that the aggrieved princes had received back their confiscated possessions; (2) that the Pope had obtained satisfaction for the illegal seizure of Avignon;[140] (3) that France had so set her own house in order that the remainder of the community of nations would no longer be endangered.[141] On April 7, Cobenzl assured Noailles that the note of March 18 constituted Austria's reply to France's continuing demand for explanations, and that it could not be changed, especially since it represented the united views of both Austria and Prussia with respect to France.[142]

l. France Declares War on Austria

On April 20, Dumouriez reported to the Assembly on the state of the negotiations with Austria, and characterized von Kaunitz' note of March 18 as "a virtual declaration of war."[143] Then Louis XVI, who had come to the session with Dumouriez, gravely rose and spoke essentially as follows: You have heard the report. The unanimous opinion of my council, and the wish of the Assembly and of numerous deputations from all over France who have come to see me, is that war should be declared on Austria, and their wish coincides with mine.[144] Therefore, in accordance with the Constitu-

---

[135] Hansen, *Quellen*, II, 104, n. 2.
[136] *Ibid.*
[137] The Austrian forces in the Netherlands and the Breisgau had been strengthened.
[138] Sybel, *Fr. Rev.*, I, 442.
[139] C. J. H. Hayes, *A Political and Social History of Modern Europe* (2 vols., New York, 1917), I, 498–499.
[140] A papal enclave in southern France, annexed by France on Sept. 14, 1791 (Sybel,

Fr. Rev., I, 412).
[141] Noailles to Dumouriez, April 5, 1792, Hansen, *Quellen*, II, 114, n. 2.
[142] *Idem*, April 7, *ibid.*
[143] To the Legislative Assembly, *ibid.*, p. 99, n. 1.
[144] "People here are absolutely bent on war," wrote Marie Antoinette to Count de Fersen (G. Michon, "Robespierre et la guerre," *AR*, XII, 289).

tion, I propose that there be, against the King of Bohemia and Hungary —
here a strange note entered his voice, but he continued — a declaration of
war. He left the chamber. The Assembly deliberated over his proposal, and
at about 10:00 P.M. of the same night a deputation from the Assembly laid
a fateful paper before the King for his signature.[145] Louis signed. The pre-
lude to the War of the First Coalition was in progress.

"Our Parisians are showing nothing but fight now," ran a report of the
twenty-third from Paris. "They are all aflame, ecstatic, and whosoever can
bear arms wants to give battle and die." [146] It is very easy to misconstrue
motives. These people were not just lusting for blood (and tombstones).
They had been led to believe that the foreign monarchs had designs on
their beloved *patrie*. And, indeed, such was the case.

"The French want war," Leopold had declared (after learning of the
incendiary speeches in the Legislative Assembly from January 18–25); "they
shall have it, but they will have to pay the expenses." And negotiations between Austria and Prussia provided that, if war actually came, Alsace and
Lorraine would be divided between Austria, Bavaria, and the princes of
the disputed enclaves. Leopold had died before the conclusion of these
negotiations.[147]

To the French people, then, the war was a matter of ideals, and while
Condorcet's speech of April 20 [148] justifying the declaration of war cannot
have been taken seriously by the great philosopher himself, for he had helped
to instigate the conflict — still that speech accurately characterizes the unselfish abandon and courage of the little man of France as he prepared to
shoulder a gun and sally forth to battle the despots. And that courage is all
the more remarkable when one considers the condition of the country
which was supposed to support his efforts: "France . . . is in a convulsive
state," ran a contemporary account. "Anarchy spreads its horrors, and excess
of liberty engenders crime; factions unsettle the *corps politique*; our armies
are without soldiers and without discipline; our navy is buried under
rubble; our finances are exhausted; public wealth, which rests upon national
credit, is crumbling and in the process of annihilation; the public canals no

---

[145] Hansen, *Quellen*, II, 132–133.
[146] *Kölner Reichsoberpostamtszeitung*, April 28, 1792, *ibid*., p. 133.
[147] Hansen, *Quellen*, II, 69, n. 1. Prussia would get Jülich and Berg, according to the plan (*ibid*).
[148] Every nation, said Condorcet, had the right to adopt whatsoever sort of constitu-tion pleased it. The French nation, true to its oath, was not taking up weapons to conquer any territory, but only to defend its freedom from the unrighteous attack of a king.

Condorcet admitted that on the face of things, it looked as though France had "wilfully provoked or accelerated" the war, but he said the Court of Vienna had insidiously managed to lend a shade of probability to this imputation in order to be able to excite its subjects to the attack it was contemplating (*Moniteur*, XII, 186–188).

longer nourish commerce. . . It is in this terrible situation that France is about to arm against all the powers of Europe." [149]

m. *The Germans of Paris and the Girondists*

One of the reasons why it had been so difficult for Robespierre to resist the martial tide was because the war party was egged on by Germans and German-speaking Frenchmen (Alsatians, Lorrainers), who maintained that the French troops would be welcomed by the oppressed people of Germany. The Prussian Cloots and the Alsatian Reubell have already once been mentioned in this connection.[150]

On December 13, 1791, Deputy Cloots had assured the Legislative Assembly that, one month after the French troops received their marching orders, "the tricolor cockade and the air *Ça ira* [would] be the delight of twenty emancipated nations." [151] Deputy Reubell, on December 4, 1791, had written to certain other Alsatian deputies: "It is at Spires, at Worms, at Coblenz, at Mannheim where the preparations are being made, and where — in consequence — [acts of] hostility are being perpetrated. It is therefore at Worms, at Spires, at Coblenz, at Mannheim that we must make defensive war and thrust back our enemies. . . At Spires, at Mayence, at Trèves, and in the Palatinate the people are entirely on our side. . . A proclamation announcing to these peoples that we wish to treat them as brothers, that we are provoked only with their tyrants, . . . would decide them all to join with us." [152] Robespierre viewed these stories with distinct distrust. Armed missionaries are loved by no one, he said.[153] Moreover, he did not believe that republican institutions, imposed on neighboring peoples, would make them into republicans.[154]

It seems that there was a special affinity between Paris-domiciled Germans and the Girondists, so it may help to understand Girondist foreign policy if

[149] Report from Paris of April 22, in *Gazette de Cologne* of April 27, Hansen, *Quellen*, II, 132, n. 2.

[150] Introduction, § 2h.

[151] Hansen, *Quellen*, I, 1053, n. 1.

[152] *Ibid.*, pp. 1052–1053; Guyot, *Direc.*, p. 118. (If the reader will compare the quotations of these two scholars, he will see that neither scholar has been sufficiently careful to indicate his deletions.) The *Moniteur* of December 13, 1791 reported that a proclamation was being readied. It would say: "Already once before, France conquered liberty for the German Empire; it guaranteed it in the Peace of Westphalia. That liberty was for princes. The liberty that France would conquer today would be

for peoples. Perhaps this year will . . . see the national guard of France embracing its German brethren." — Hansen, *Quellen*, I, 1053, n. 1.

[153] *Vide Brochures pol.*, LXXXIV, no. 18; Michon in *AR*, XII, 265 *et seqq.*

[154] Speech of Jan. 2, 1792: "You will lead your triumphant army among all the neighboring peoples, everywhere you will establish *municipalités* (town councils), directorates, national assemblies, and you will exclaim that this thought is sublime, as if the destiny of empires depended upon figures of speech." — Quoted in Mathiez, *La Révolution et les étrangers: Cosmopolitisme et défense nationale* (Paris, 1919), p. 61.

we seek out the reasons for this affinity. At least four causes can be distinguished. The Girondist idea of universal liberty struck a responsive chord in the oppressed German's breast; the Germans, products of the *Aufklärung*, recognized in the Girondists kindred souls partaking of their predilection for philosophy and their respect for law and order; the Girondists, like the Germans, were bold in speculation, timid in practice; and the Girondists, by favoring federalism for France, seemed to have the same concepts of political organization as the Germans, who could not conceive of a centralized Germany.[155]

Despite the danger of presenting the appearance of a catalog, it were perhaps wise to list here the principal Paris-domiciled Germans who had a more or less direct connection with the Girondists, and to signify wherein lies their noteworthiness. (1) Cloots loudly supported Brissot in his advocacy of war and expansion.[156] (2) Gustav von Schlabrendorff served as guide and inspiration for the German expatriates, and as "contact man" between the Germans, members of the Girondist party, and the English established in Paris. (3) Karl Friedrich Reinhard did his best to impress on Vergniaud, Guadet, Gensonné, and their colleagues the virtues of "German moderation," and was rewarded by the Girondists with a place in the diplomatic service. (4) Georg Kerner enthusiastically supported the Girondists and exercised his influence in combating the excesses of the radicals; he was always ready to risk his life for his idea of what the Revolution should be. "She anticipated us," he exclaimed when Charlotte Corday murdered Marat. (5) Johann Wilhelm von Archenholtz edited a political chronicle (*Minerva, Journal für Politik, Geschichte, und Litteratur*, published first in Berlin and then in Hamburg) which apprized Europe of developments in France. A famous Prussian historian who had little taste for popular excesses, Archenholtz was hounded out of Paris by his fellow Prussian, Cloots. But before he left, he had made the acquaintance of his future collaborators, the Girondist-inclined Reinhard and Œlsner (*infra*), and of the principal Girondists themselves. It seems that Archenholtz favored the Feuillants above the Girondists. (6) Konrad Engelbert Œlsner — at first a Jacobin — powerfully

---

[155] Droz, *Allemagne*, p. 50.
[156] *Vide infra*, Pt. I, chap. iv, § 2d. *Vide* his "Discours d'Anacharsis-Cloots, Orateur du genre humain; prononcé à la Société [des Jacobins] dans la séance du 1er janvier, 1792": "It is because I want peace that I am asking for war. . . The interest of the state orders us to blow the martial trumpet. A disturbing veto agitates us with pain. Well now! let us cross the Rhine and the decree against the priests and the decree against the *émigrés* will be sanctioned by cannon shot. Our victories beyond the kingdom will annihilate the conspirators within the kingdom. The golden age is at the tips of our bayonets. . . Never will there have been a more economical war, for the progress of liberty will spare us the maintenance of a hundred fortresses and a hundred legions. The people will be relieved of a great burden. . . " — *Brochures pol.*, LXXXVII, no. 18 (originals).

reinforced the Girondist stand respecting the desirability of foreign war and the disposition to be made of the King. Œlsner was perhaps the shrewdest foreign observer of the revolutionary scene, and Archenholtz' *Minerva* was the beneficiary for a time.[157] Œlsner's letters from Dumouriez' camp — in the *Minerva* — are particularly famous.[158]

There are historians who would add here — in a sort of textual footnote — a number of German republicans who later made considerable impression upon France's German policy. They were not all Paris-domiciled, though some of them eventually were. However, they were politically attuned to the foreign policy of the Girondists, and have been called "German Girondists." Such were, for example, Forster, Görres, and Geich — three men as far apart as the poles — who all professed a highly exacting moral philosophy which they thought could attain its full bloom only under free institutions. These three will come in for considerable discussion in the course of this monograph.[159] Geich, a Bonn publicist who strove to educate the Rhineland to the advantages of annexation by France, should not, as one historian expresses it, be "mentioned in the same breath" with the truly superior Forster and Görres,[160] yet his influence was great.

The high moral tone of the politics of Forster and Görres does indeed justify the assumption of a bond between them and Brissot, whose politics was based on his concept of morality, and who entered public life only, as he said, to free philosophy, not for politics' sake.[161] But the German hatred of princes had its basis in an entirely different concatenation of circumstances than did Brissot's. Indeed, due regard must be given to French influence, but one should look for the immediate causes rather to the effect of the *Aufklärung* and of the Storm-and-Stress period of German literature. Also, it should be noted that the Rhinelanders did not become, immediately, such confirmed republicans as did Brissot and the other Girondists.[162]

[157] Droz, *Allemagne*, chap. i.

[158] Bavarian Königliche Akademie der Wissenschaften, Historische Commission, *Allgemeine deutsche Biographie* (55 vols. and index, Leipzig, 1875–1912), *s.v.* "Œlsner, Konrad Engelbert."

[159] Pt. I, chap. ii; Pt. II, chaps. xxvii, xxviii; *et passim.*

[160] Hashagen, *Rheinland*, p. 535. But the problem closest to Geich's heart was indeed religion and its relation to the state. (*Vide* Hansen, *Quellen*, III, 571.) Geich considered the development of "individual morality based upon freedom, the combating of selfish impulses, and general morality, as the purposes of the state. . . The ultimate goal of the state is . . . not the happiness

of the citizen . . . but the highest possible degree of morality and of purification of the nation" (Hansen's words, *ibid.*, p. 29). Geich at first preferred an enlightened prince to a republic. He said democracy was "the worst form of government." — "Ueber Demokratie," *Stadtkölnische Kurier*, Oct. 24, 1794, *ibid.*, p. 283.

[161] Hashagen, *Rheinland*, p. 536. *Vide* the very penetrating chapter, "Brissot's General Policy and Character," of E. Ellery, *Brissot de Warville: A Study in the History of the French Revolution* (New York, 1915), pp. 412–427. Brissot, for all his faults and mistakes, was one of the most moral and well-meaning of men.

[162] Hashagen, *Rheinland*, p. 537.

n. The Manifesto of the Duke of Brunswick

The declaration of war did not interrupt the efforts of the royal pair, especially of the Queen, to secure Austrian aid. Both were of course hostile to the thought of a real war. What they wanted was a punitive expedition by the Austrians. The latter, as allies of France, were as interested as was Marie Antoinette in ending a situation which profited only Prussia and England. So ran the Queen's arguments; and she succeeded in enlisting the aid of three members of the Diplomatic Committee. The plan was not to deliver France over to the enemy, but by negotiation with the Emperor and the utilization of his moral support, to quell both superradicals and superconservatives; to restore order and the power of the Crown. The existence of some sort of plot was suspected by Brissot, who accused *all* the members of the Diplomatic Committee of being, in reality, an "Austrian Committee." [163]

Lafayette, though he had promoted the cause of war, does not seem to have intended to fight but only to intrigue; and in this respect his policy resembled that of the Queen.[164] He sought, by negotiation, to keep the Austrians from crossing the frontier while he should descend with his adoring army upon Paris, disperse the Jacobins, recall the *émigrés*, dissolve the National Guard, and establish a bicameral legislature — the *second* chamber to keep the Revolution within bounds.[165] But the Austrians were convinced "that no confidence whatsoever could be placed in the assurances of a man like Lafayette," [166] and when the General deserted (August 14) after the suspension of the King, the Habsburg Court persisted in regarding him as "an abominable man," "one of the most culpable, and doubtless disposed

---

[163] Goetz-Bernstein, *Gironde*, pp. 217–218.

[164] A. Mathiez, "L'intrigue de Lafayette," *AR*, XIII (1921), 91. Marie Antoinette, in fact, had divulged Lafayette's military orders to De Mercy already on March 26. Lafayette was to advance on Liège, she said. Dumouriez had scheduled another column to attack Savoy. The Queen divulged the whole plan then — and again on March 30, to De Fersen (*Lettres Marie-Ant.*, II, 391–392, 393).

[165] Mathiez, *Fr. Rev.*, p. 149. *Vide* also *ibid.*, p. 158; Sybel, *Fr. Rev.*, II, 53.

A letter from Forster to Deforgues, dated November 17, 1793, tells that Forster had been given to read a memoir in the very hand of Lally-Tollendal (of India fame), which memoir, with its supporting documents, "evidently prove that Lafayette, con-

jointly with Luckner, wanted to spirit off Louis XVI in the month of July 1792, and that all was concerted to this end, but that Louis XVI himself refused his adherence to the project." — J. Kaulek, cont. by A. Tausserat-Radel (eds.), *Papiers de Barthélemy* (6 vols., Paris, 1886–1910), III, 228.

[166] Kaunitz to Mercy, May 26, 1792, A. von Vivenot, cont. by H. von Zeissberg (eds.), *Quellen zur Geschichte der deutschen Kaiserpolitik Oesterreichs während der französischen Revolutionskriege* (5 vols., Vienna, 1873–1890), II (*Die Politik des oesterr. Vice-Staatskanzlers Grafen Philipp von Cobenzl unter Franz II*, 1874), 58. Besides, De Mercy knew that Marie Antoinette detested Lafayette (Mathiez in *AR*, XIII, 101).

to do ill where he can, ... to preach insurrection everywhere." [167] William Short, American Minister-Resident at The Hague, wrote of Lafayette on December 7, 1792: "It is certain that he is the individual of all France that both Austrians and Prussians hate the most cordially." [168] (And the Germans put their feelings into deeds. First at Wesel and then at Magdeburg, our Revolutionary hero was subjected to unspeakable horrors — dripping underground dungeons in the first, medieval tortures in the second — until Prussia had had her fill, and turned our beloved fellow citizen over to Austria and the mental constriction of Olmütz.[169] And why all this venom? Because a republican aristocrat was regarded as a renegade, a deserter from the cause to which he had been born; and because, by the very fact of his high birth, he could the more easily become a leader of the revolting rabble.[170] Several times Lafayette was reported dead or insane, but a powerful mind and a true heart brought him safely through the ordeal, and when he emerged from confinement five years later — owing to an agreement outside the Treaty of Campo-Formio — he was still in possession of all his faculties.) [171]

When the French declared war upon Austria on April 20, 1792, they *ipso facto* drew upon themselves the hostility of Prussia by virtue of the Austro-Prussian alliance of the preceding February. But no one in France believed that Prussia would actually fight, though the Berlin cabinet had informed Paris on February 20 that a French attack upon Germany would

[167] Reuss (Aust. ambas. to Berlin) to Saxe-Teschen (Aust. general), Aug. 26, 1792, Vivenot-Zeissberg, *Quellen*, II, 179–180.
[168] B. C. Davenport (ed.), *A Diary of the French Revolution* by Gouverneur Morris (2 vols., Boston, 1939), II, 560.
[169] *Ibid.*, pp. 551–561; "Relation de la détention du général Lafayette par lui-même à madame la princesse d'Hénin," March 15, 1793, dated at Magdeburg, J. Taschereau (ed.), *Revue rétrospective, ou Bibliothèque historique, contenant des mémoires et documens authentiques, inédits et originaux* ... (20 vols. in 3 ser., Paris, 1835–1838), Ser. I, Vol. V (1834), 142–147.
[170] And yet that rabble was demanding his head (Chépy *fils* before the Jacobin Club, July 4, 1792, F. A. Aulard, *La Société des Jacobins* [6 vols., Paris, 1889–1897], IV, 69). The Duke of Saxe-Teschen explained to Lafayette in the following terms the reason for the treatment he was accorded: "You were not arrested, Monsieur, as a prisoner [of war], nor as a member of the Constituent Assembly, nor as an *émigré*.

But inasmuch as it was you who were the abettor of the Revolution which has thrown France into confusion; as it was you who put your king in irons, despoiled him of all his rights and legitimate powers and held him captive; as it was you who were the principal instrument of all the misfortunes which have overwhelmed that ill-starred monarch, it is only too just that those who are laboring to reëstablish his dignity should hold you [captive] until such time as your master, being once more in possession of his liberty and his sovereignty, will be able, according to his justice or his clemency, to decide your fate." — Sept. 8, 1792, Vivenot-Zeissberg, *Quellen*, II, 192.
[171] *Diary* of Gouv. Morris, II, 554–555. Lafayette did not return to France immediately. The conditions of his release forbade it. Also, his name had been inscribed on the list of *émigrés* (A. Dubois-Dilange, "La radiation de Lafayette de la liste des émigrés," *FH*, X [1913], 306–311). *Vide infra*, Pt. II, chap. xxx, § 2.

be regarded as an attack upon Prussia.[172] And when weeks, even months, elapsed and no Prussian army appeared on the horizon, many would-be statesmen congratulated themselves on their astuteness. They were rudely awakened in June, however. Several Prussian columns were observed marching toward the Rhine, and at their head the Prussian King in person.[173] The generals of the Rhine Army were in consternation. "The attack might come tomorrow, even today," they frantically wrote to Paris, "and we are at peace with Prussia!"[174] But the minister of foreign affairs, now the Marquis de Chambonas,[175] hesitated to suggest a declaration of war against the land of the "Philosopher-King" who had been France's ally. De Chambonas thought, no doubt, to continue the fruitless negotiations of Dumouriez. However, his hand was forced by the Assembly, and war was declared upon Prussia on July 6, 1792.[176]

The Duke of Brunswick, who had been appointed Allied commander in chief on April 3,[177] presently removed all doubts that Prussia was an enemy. He, respected general of Frederick the Great that he was, and a lover of philosophy, issued on July 25, 1792, a manifesto of such violent import that many wondered whether he could have been the author.[178] He was indeed — in a certain sense — only the amanuensis, for he truly had not authored the ideas contained therein. June 7, 1792, Baron Johannes Friedrich von Stein, the Prussian chargé d'affaires at Mayence, wrote to his king that Mme. de Chabannes of Mayence had received, through the Archbishop of Aix, a report from the entourage of Marie Antoinette. This report expressed the fear that the King and the entire royal family would be massacred,[179] and asked that the King of Hungary (Francis was not yet Emperor) precede his

---

[172] Mathiez, *Fr. Rev.*, p. 146.

[173] *Ibid.*, p. 173.

[174] *Moniteur*, XIII, 230–231. Dated from Klobsheim, July 1792.

[175] On June 15, Dumouriez had offered to resign, thinking thus to force the King to approve two distasteful measures of the legislature. "I have had thirty-six years of service . . . and twenty-two wounds," wrote Dumouriez to the Assembly. "I would regard myself as extremely fortunate if a cannon ball could unite all [dissentient] opinions." The King thought it might be a good idea to afford some cannon ball a chance, and gave Dumouriez command of an army in the North. (According to Richard M. Brace, it was the Court clique — rather than the King personally — that was disposed to be rid of Dumouriez as foreign minister. ["General Dumouriez and the Girondins, 1792–

1793," *AHR* (*American Historical Review*), LVI (1950–51), 494.] Dumouriez' successor, the Marquis de Chambonas, was peculiarly qualified to manage foreign affairs, his own stormy domestic affairs having provided him with much experience. Other training in diplomacy De Chambonas had none (Masson, *Dép. étr.*, pp. 181, 186).

[176] Goetz-Bernstein, *Gironde*, pp. 232–234.

[177] *Ibid.*, p. 216.

[178] M. Rouff, "Le Manifeste de Brunswick," *RF*, LXIX (1916), 111 *et seq.*

[179] Later, the Queen herself wrote: " . . . the factionists want a republic at any price; to get it, they have resolved to assassinate the King." — To Mercy, July 4, 1792, A. von Arneth (ed.), *Marie Antoinette, Joseph II. und Leopold II. Ihr Briefwechsel* (Leipzig, 1866), p. 265.

declaration of war with a stern threat to the Parisians "that, if they dared to make an attempt on the life of the King or of the royal family, their city would be utterly destroyed, together with all its inhabitants without regard to age or sex." Stein expressed to Frederick William the hope that such a threat might prompt the more moderate Parisians to unite with the party of the middle to avert a common calamity. Stein believed this to be the only way of saving Louis' life. Frederick William replied that he not only approved the idea of such a threat, but had communicated it to Vienna.[180] It was, of course, what Louis and Marie Antoinette had been urging since the end of April, and these unhappy monarchs had pressed the *émigrés* to urge it also. That is how Stein came into the picture.[181]

One De Limon, an *émigré* living in Brussels, drew up the draft upon which the text of the Manifesto was based. The Manifesto was printed in Mayence on the Electoral Court's press, and was signed with Brunswick's name.[182] Addressed to the inhabitants of France, it commenced with a recital of their transgressions against the Empire, the Emperor, Louis XVI, and law and order in general. The King of Prussia and the Emperor, it affirmed, had no designs on French territory, but sought only France's well-being. They did not propose to interfere in the internal government of France, but desired merely to free the King, Queen, and royal family from their chains, and assure them the necessary security so that the King could exercise his functions without danger or interference.

The Manifesto then prescribed the behavior required of all Frenchmen during the invasion. The (French) national guard should maintain order. Troops of the line should remain loyal to the King. All civil officials would answer with their lives and possessions for violence in their respective provinces. The laws of war would immediately be applied to inhabitants who resisted the invading army; their houses would be torn down or burned. The city of Paris should immediately bow to King Louis' authority, set him completely free, and show him proper veneration. Should the Tuileries be attacked or the King or royal family harmed or insulted, the Emperor and King would take an unprecedented, eternally memorable revenge, and subject Paris to military execution, turn it upside down, and sentence the guilty rebels to capital punishment. However, well-disposed subjects, who behaved properly, would be treated with moderation.[183]

Poor Louis. When he received the threat for which he had been yearning so long, he was afraid of the popular reaction. Therefore, when he sent it to

[180] Hansen, *Quellen*, II, 298, n. 3; 265, n. 3.
[181] *Ibid.*, p. 298.
[182] *Ibid.*
[183] Text in P. J. B. Buchez and P. C. Roux, *Histoire parlementaire de la Révolution française* (40 vols., Paris, 1834–1848), XVI, 276.

the Assembly, he tried to divert attention from its contents by questioning its authenticity.[184] Doubt, once planted, spreads wildly, often without inspection of the basis of the original doubt, and presently the *Aachener Zuschauer* observed that "No one could believe in the genuineness of this Manifesto, which was found to be drafted along such singular lines." [185]

The doubts, of course, decreased the poignancy of the warning, but no matter. Its results were bad enough.[186] It enraged the Parisians instead of intimidating them. It resulted in the complete victory of the radical element of the Jacobin Club. It may not have caused, but it certainly accelerated, the dethronement of the King.[187]

A decree was passed to turn the tables on Brunswick. He had practically ordered the French to facilitate his invasion. The Assembly sought to induce *his* troops to desert to France by providing that every deserter should receive French citizenship and a yearly pension. Cloots and other Germans secured official recognition of, and an appropriation for, a German legion to fight the tyrants in this last war of mankind.[188] The Manifesto aroused the "fight" in France, instead of inducing reflection and promoting docility.

"The spirit of political fanaticism . . . is shooting high flames out of the incandescent heads of the French," remarked one journal.[189] "Patriotism everywhere has become more spirited and more fiery," said another.[190] "If one had applied himself to incite the French to resistance," wrote Forster in Mayence, "one could not have begun more cleverly. . . There will be no getting to Paris as quickly as people think, and in no case will France be completely subdued." [191] "The Manifesto of the Duke of Brunswick toppled Louis XVI from his throne," wrote a German observer in Paris on August 21. "If the European princes still hope to work through threats, they will tumble this unfortunate family into its grave." [192]

Dr. Christoph Girtanner, well-known Swiss physician of Göttingen,

[184] Hansen, *Quellen*, II, 306, n. 2.

[185] Aug. 6; report from Paris of Aug. 2: *ibid.*

[186] Bad enough without the *"Declaration additionnelle"* issued on August 27 under pressure from the French princes (Hansen, *Quellen*, II, 299). In this new warning, Brunswick threatened that if the King were expelled by force, every town he (Louis) passed through would share the fate of Paris (Buchez and Roux, *Hist. parlem.*, XVI, 281).

[187] Hansen, *Quellen*, II, 302.

[188] *Ibid.*

[189] Neuwieder *Geheime Briefwechsel zwischen den Lebendigen und den Toten* of July 30, *ibid.*, p. 306, n. 2.

[190] *Gazette de Cologne*, Aug. 9, *ibid.*

[191] To Heyne, Aug. 4, 1792, G. Landauer (ed., tr.), *Briefe aus der französischen Revolution* (tr. principally from the French; 2 vols., Frankfort-on-the-Main, 1919), II, 239–240.

[192] *Ibid.*, p. 302, n. 3. There were, of course, voices in favor of the Manifesto. The *Politischen Gespräche der Toten* likened Brunswick to a hero who was going forth to combat two monsters greater than any that Hercules had ever had to encounter — Insubordination and Anarchy; and it declared that all thinking people the world over were praying for his success (*Beilage*, July 31, *ibid.*, p. 300).

who turned publicist when the Revolution broke out, gives perhaps the most penetrating analysis of the Manifesto's effect. In his *Die Franzosen am Rheinstrome*, he says: "The Manifesto of the Duke of Brunswick was indeed not phrased in insulting language, but it was insulting nevertheless in that it . . . treated [the French] like a pack of rebellious cowards (*Bärenhäuter*) whom he would disperse like timid game. . . This tone, which would have been out of place under the walls of Paris after several victories, was all the more so at thirty hours' distance from the French frontier. . . It was impolitic . . . to excite yet more the fury of the French, who, less than any other people in the world, allow themselves to be trampled under foot. . . The Duke knows the French to be a brave people." [193] This famous — or rather, infamous — Manifesto of the Duke of Brunswick only served to unite France for the coming struggle.

Thus commenced twenty-three years of well-nigh continuous warfare which eventually involved the entire continent of Europe, and which was not to end until the self-styled "Son of the Revolution," who was guilty of patricide with respect to the movement to which he owed his political birth, was safely confined in distant St. Helena. For the time being, however, the Empire itself remained at peace. This was largely the result of the groundwork laid by Dumouriez. "The plan of the ruling party in France," wrote von Kaunitz, "appears to be to lull the German princes to sleep with fair words and fine promises in order that they should neither take an active part in the war nor institute special precautions for the maintenance of internal order. On the other hand, insurrection continues to be preached where only possible, . . . in order that princes who should desire . . . action find resistance in their own provinces." And von Kaunitz announced that the Empire was being flooded with writings issuing from Strasburg, and having such incendiary titles as "Summons to Freedom to Our German Brethren," "Summons to Annihilate Your Despots," "Summons to Suppress the Clergy." [194] The propaganda phase of the war had begun.

3. THE FRENCH ARMY IN JULY 1792

It may not be unprofitable at this juncture to cast a rapid glance over the French army which now found itself at odds, not only with the larger

[193] N.p., 1793, pp. 50–51.
[194] To Lehrbach (Aust. ambas. to Bavaro-Palatinate), etc., June 8, 1792, Vivenot-Zeissberg, *Quellen*, II, 86. Brissot and Dumouriez counted heavily on propaganda to ease the passage of the French troops, and foreign legions of Germans, Belgians, Dutch, and Savoyards were officially established — apparently to supply object lessons to the regions invaded (G. Lefebvre, *La Révolution française* [2nd ed.; Paris, 1951], p. 238, in L. Halphen and P. Sagnac [eds.], *Peuples et Civilisations* [20 vols. Paris, 1928–1939], XIII).

Austrian host, but with the celebrated military machine bequeathed by
Frederick the Great. The French army had been reorganized after the
Seven Years' War into an efficient fighting force, but it still possessed many
of the ills inherent in the system of which it formed a part: Commissioned
officers had to be of noble stock, and military knowledge was not a necessary
prerequisite. Promotion was the result of court influence or gifts of money,
almost never of merit. Except in the artillery and engineers, a nonnoble
could not legally become a commissioned officer — and even in these branches, it was practically impossible to rise from the ranks. Below the dashing,
blue-blooded commissioned officers were the noncommissioned, men who
had grown old in the service of their country without hope of promotion.[195]
What more natural than that these should avidly embrace the new ideas of
liberty, equality, fraternity, and form the nucleus for a revolutionary ferment which would eventually encompass the entire army? [196]

The word "liberty" had special meaning for the rank and file of the
army, which was chafing under the Prussian system of discipline. As the
Revolution progressed, mutinies became an everyday occurrence, and noble
officers were often imprisoned by their troops and even massacred.[197] The
National Assembly looked with favor upon the revolutionary spirit of the
men, and refused to sanction the measures proposed to combat the revolts.
Finally, when the King himself deserted his post, so to speak, and attempted
to flee, the commissioned officers, who had adhered to their duties in the face
of insult and insubordination, considered themselves absolved from their
oaths, and crossed the frontier in large numbers.[198] This was the great
moment for the noncommissioned officers. The National Assembly, with a
war on its hands, and an army denuded of regimental officers, decreed that
one half the vacated commissions should be conferred upon noncommissioned officers.[199] Thus was opened the road for promotion through merit
— a road widened during the latter half of 1793, when the remainder of the
noble officers were cashiered.[200] It was promotion through merit, be it noted,
which gave France that galaxy of illustrious warriors without which the

[195] R. P. Dunn-Pattison, "The General War," C. Mod. H., VIII, 400–402.
[196] Sybel, Fr. Rev., I, 235.
[197] M. Dumolin, Précis d'histoire militaire, Révolution et Empire (2 vols. in 12 fasc., Paris, 1901[06]–1910), I, 60.
[198] Even those of lower rank fled. By March 1792, there were a thousand vacant lieu-tenancies. It is to be noted that the emigra-tion did not restore unity to the army. The officers' corps were rent by discord between constitutional royalists and republicans. In Thionville this resulted in mass duels. The opposing officers rolled dice for the privi-lege of shooting their antagonists unarmed (Krieg g. Rev., I, 310).
[199] Dunn-Pattison in C. Mod. H., VIII, 403–404.
[200] G. Pariset, La Révolution, 1792–1799 (Paris, 1920), pp. 142–143, in E. Lavisse (ed.), Histoire de France contemporaine depuis la Révolution jusqu'à la paix de 1919 (9 vols. and index, Paris, 1920–1922), II,

Revolution would have succumbed in its infancy.[201] Ran a letter from Hamburg, written on November 5, 1793, after a victory by the fledgeling French general Jourdan over the Austrians:

> The Most Serene Prince, the Grand Marshal, the General par excellence, the so-vaunted Austrian, Saxe-Coburg, who has waged war against the Turks with so much glory that the Germans call him the successor of Loudon, [has been] defeated and defeated again by the sans-culotte Jourdan, who, for the first time this year, took it into his head to wage war, who has been a general only a few months. . . Thus perisheth another prejudice.[202]

4. VALMY, AND ITS EFFECT UPON THE INTERNATIONAL SITUATION

a. General

At the commencement of hostilities, both France and Austria [203] were unprepared; while Prussia, though prepared, was unenthusiastic. Thus — unless one pays more attention than they deserve to the "efforts" of Rochambeau and Luckner in Belgium [204] — it was June and even July before the real war

---

[201] It also gave France a fifteen-year-old major, who, after serving in this capacity with quite unhappy results, was nominated for promotion. Father, be it noted, was a general — General Félix Wimpffen. But the heartless Representatives on Mission decided that "the new method of promotion was unable to procure for the 5th Battalion a chief able to command it" and annulled the young man's advancement (Ritter, Rp A. R [Vide Key to Contractions], to CPS, June 19, 1793, F. A. Aulard [ed.], Recueil des Actes du Comité de Salut Public [28 vols., Paris, 1889–1951], V, 21). Strange, that only two months before, the father-General himself had affirmed his dissatisfaction with the mode of nominating officers, stating that it led to lack of discipline (ibid., III, 229). An enlightening commentary on the results of the new system of promotion is afforded by the implications of a sentence in a memoir of the Rhine Army's generals: "High position should be given to the most capable." — Moniteur, XIII, 231.

[202] Ibid., XVIII, 505.

[203] Goetz-Bernstein, Gironde, p. 233.

[204] A. de Ganniers, "La campagne de Luckner en Belgique en juin, 1792," RH, LXVIII (1898), 295. It was Luckner's army to which Minister Dumouriez succeeded. Great hopes had been placed in Luckner's prowess, but he seemed merely to idle — and that, with incredible nonchalance. De Ganniers says he was incompetent, but he certainly had ability during the Seven Years' War. Finally, to repeated urging by Dumouriez that he launch a general attack, Luckner replied: Come yourself and take command of this "pretty army, to which courage and discipline are contraband." This was in the first week on June 1792. Luckner's letter made a deep impression on the Minister, and his ministerial functions commenced to pall on him (Report from Paris of June 6, in the Mainzer Zeitung of June 13, 1792, in Hansen, Quellen, II, 240–241). Soon thereafter, Dumouriez offered to resign, and the King, as mentioned supra, n. 175, was glad to be rid of him, and accepted. But only after Dumouriez had been minister of war for five days (June 13–18). Then Dumouriez went to Belgium as one of Luckner's generals (Hansen, Quellen, II, 241, n. 1). On August 24, 1792, Dumouriez was given command of the Army of the North (Mathiez, Etrangers, p. 68) "in the room of Lafayette." (Sybel, Fr. Rev., II, 54. But Sybel gives the date as August 16.)
Re Luckner's "pretty army," Carnot called it a "bunch of vagabonds." — Car-

began. The Prussians and Austrians agreed that the former would invade Champagne, while the latter would advance on Lille from the Netherlands. The French, on their side, directed four columns, composed largely of untrained recruits, against Belgium.[205]

The first results of the war were unfavorable to the French.[206] They were driven out of Belgium with amazing ease, and in the greatest disorder.[207] Austria immediately concluded that one campaign would be sufficient,[208] that the conflict would be only a punitive expedition "for which two regiments of Hungarian hussars, with whips as their arms, would suffice to terminate the farce." [209] "With 12,000 men," boasted the Duke of Brunswick, "I undertake to enter [France] at Brest and leave by Toulon." [210] The gains that might justly be expected from the war seemed out of all proportion to the insignificance of the risks.

Until this time, Prussia had stoutly resisted every suggestion of the annexation of Bavaria by Austria. However, the particular interest of Prussia in 1792 was a new slice of Poland. To obtain Austria's consent to this acquisition, Prussia now approved with amazing facility Austria's plan of exchanging Belgium for Bavaria. Equality of acquisitions was decreed as the basis of the proposed aggrandizements, so — since an "exchange" is not a complete "gain" — there was question of additional indemnities for Austria: Alsace, the part of Flanders bordering on Belgium, Polish territory, or even Ansbach and Baireuth.[211]

b. Longwy and Verdun

On August 19, the Austro-Prussian army arrived before Longwy, on the northeastern French border, near Luxemburg. The Austrian general Clerfayt summoned the governor of the fortress to surrender, and he refused. A

---

not to Guyton de Morveau, March 28, 1793, reproduced in R. M. Brace, "Carnot and the Treason of Dumouriez," *J. Mod. H. (Journal of Modern History)*, XXI (1949), 315.

[205] Dunn-Pattison in *C. Mod. H.*, VIII, 407–409.

[206] Wrote Lafayette on May 6: "I cannot conceive how, not being ready in any respect, we could have declared war." — Quoted in Chuquet, *Guerres Rév.*, I (*La première invasion prussienne*), 24.

[207] *Vide* Mathiez in *RH*, LXVIII, 295.

[208] Kaunitz to Reuss, May 19, 1792, Vivenot-Zeissberg, *Quellen*, II, 48.

[209] Expression said to have been used by a member of the Imperial War Council, the *Hofkriegsrat* (F. Luckwaldt [ed.] in H.

Hüffer [ed.], *Quellen zur Geschichte des Zeitalters der französischen Revolution*, Pt. II [*Quellen zur Geschichte der diplomatischen Verhandlungen*], Vol. I [*Der Frieden von Campoformio*, Innsbruck, 1907], xviii *et seqq*).

[210] Rouff in *RF*, LXIX, 117.

[211] *Ibid.* Austria's aspirations are outlined in the "Conferenz-Protokoll" of June 17, 1792, Vivenot-Zeissberg, *Quellen*, II, 133–134. *Vide* also the report of Count Philipp Cobenzl (Aust. vice-chancellor) to the Emperor, March 23, 1793, *ibid.*, p. 507. A few months later, part of Lorraine, and the Three Bishoprics (Metz, Toul, Verdun) occupied by Henry II in 1552, were added to the list of possible indemnities (Protokoll, n.d., *ibid.*, p. 350).

second summons the next day was also rejected, and the bombardment of the city commenced, continuing from 10:00 P.M. to 3:00 A.M. during the night of August 21–22. It was resumed at 5:00 A.M. on the twenty-second, continuing until 8:00 A.M. The inhabitants did not enjoy the operation. Some of them were royalists at heart and secretly welcomed the champions of Monarchy. They staged a riot, and demanded that the magistrates compel the governor to capitulate. The magistrates complied — all but one — and the gates were opened on the twenty-third. The populace burned the house of the dissenting magistrate. A few days later, the Prussian commander sentenced the man to be hanged. At the moment of execution, the nails holding the gallows pulled out, the magistrate fell (fifty steps), reached the street, and bounded away — to the French outposts. The French general made him a lieutenant then and there, in recognition of his courage. Thus commenced the Germanic invasion of France — with great cowardice and greater bravery, with high treason and higher patriotism, side by side.[212] The Revolution was a period of extremes.

The story of Verdun was much the same. Invested on May 31, the populace pillaged the military stores, and demanded that the governor surrender — after only nine hours of bombardment. The governor, Beaurepaire, preferred to blow out his brains.[213] His successor yielded Verdun (September 1), the capitulation permitting the garrison freely to withdraw [214] — with the body of its hero-governor. The King of Prussia took possession of the city in the name of the King of France.

The above account is not complete, for an event famed in song and story forms part of this capture. One of the Prussian hussars had been assassinated by the French, and the inhabitants of Verdun were sorely afraid that Frederick William would order the pillage of the city in reprisal. The city officials hastened to the Prussian general to make amends, but he replied that the law of war was strict, and that the Prussian King — who would presently arrive

[212] Société d'écrivains militaires et civils (A. Pilon [ed.]), *Guerres de la Révolution française et du Premier Empire* (12 vols., Paris, 1876), I, 29–31. It can be seen from this account how unjust is the presentation of Mathiez, *Fr. Rev.*, p. 219: "The commandant, Lavergne, surrendered on August 23 after a mere pretense of resistance."

[213] According to Mathiez, he was murdered by royalists, who then spread a suicide rumor (*ibid.*). But when his body was placed in the French Pantheon, on his tomb was inscribed: "He committed suicide rather than capitulate to the tyrants." — *Moniteur*, XIII, 686. *Vide* also *ibid.*, XV, 403. Inasmuch as a murder would have constituted

better propaganda material for the revolutionists than a suicide, the present writer believes we may safely assume that Beaurepaire took his own life. But cf. Sybel, *Fr. Rev.*, II, 126.

[214] It was "confidentially reported" to Paris that the Duke of Brunswick, having encountered "some resistance" from the garrison of Verdun, had put the said garrison to the sword "to the number of four thousand men." So ran the despatch of W. Lindsay (of the British embassy in Paris) to Lord Grenville, Sept. 8, 1792 (*Despatches Gower*, p. 235). Apparently some people believed that Brunswick was as fierce as his proclamations.

at the camp — would decide their fate. Panic-stricken, the inhabitants pondered what they could do to avert the impending disaster. It was finally decided to send a deputation of pretty young women to the King to offer him confectionery and flowers.

Preparations were hastily made. Women gathered together their daughters, nieces, and friends, and without taking the time to tell them anything, dressed them in white, ordered them into a huge basket of flowers, and drove them pell-mell to the Prussian camp. Barbe Henry, only fifteen, and her cousin Sophie were to present the candy, but this had to be delayed a moment until the King recovered from the surpassing beauty of Barbe's older sister, Suzanne. The King accepted the sweets graciously; also the basket of flowers — minus the girls, who had decamped. The women offered purses of money.[215]

The royal wrath was appeased, but when the revolutionists later recaptured the city, they arraigned the "guilty" women and girls before the Revolutionary Tribunal. Of the seven women and seven girls, all were guillotined except Barbe and Sophie,[216] who were so very young. These two were sentenced to exposure on the guillotine for six hours (a fiendish punishment, especially for a mere child!) and twenty years' imprisonment. Release came after Thermidor.

Thus, the celebrated tale of the Virgins of Verdun — a tale unfortunately true.[217] It illustrates perhaps better than anything else the peculiar nature of this struggle, in which feeling ran so high on purely political questions that the bond of blood was relegated to a subordinate position, and the mere suspicion of a different point of view could induce the innately chivalrous Frenchman to forget eight centuries of the worship of Venus. A Frenchwoman who thought like a Prussian was more alien, and hence more despicable, than a Prussian who thought like a Frenchman. Cold, dispassionate logic was king, and the syllogism ruled the temple where once held sway the understanding heart of a generous nation.

[215] A. Chuquet (ed.), *Campagne de France* (Fr. tr. of *Kampagne in Frankreich*) by J. W. Goethe (Paris, n.d.), p. 49, n. 3. This episode is not mentioned in the notes on the campaign taken down by the young Prussian prince royal, later Frederick William III. What he thought worthy of remembrance was this: "As we passed the street which led to the citadel, a young and very pretty girl, fashionably dressed, came out of a house, advanced toward us, gave me her hand with much affability and told me that the Prussians were welcome. — No one else could boast such a reception. . . " — *Documents relatifs aux campagnes en France et sur le Rhin pendant les années 1792 et 1793* (tr. from the German by P. Mérat; Paris, 1848), p. 25. These documents form part of the military papers of Frederick William III (King of Prussia, 1797–1840).

[216] Barbe Henry and Claire Tabouiller, according to J. G. Alger, *Paris in 1789–94* (London, 1902), p. 436.

[217] Chuquet, (Goethe's) *Campagne*, p. 156, n. 4.

c. *Valmy*

The capture of the two important border fortresses of Longwy and Verdun by Prussia appeared to set the seal to the annexations contemplated by Hohenzollern and Habsburg, for the road to Paris was open except for the army of citizens being hastily raised by the Paris Commune and sworn "to make a rampart of their bodies."[218] However, the battle — or rather the cannonade — of Valmy (September 20, 1792) checked the Prussian advance. Not that the Prussian commander, the old Duke of Brunswick, believed himself defeated, for his losses were slight and less than those of the French.[219] True, the enemy guns were tearing holes in his ranks, and he could not silence them. But his failure to silence a voice within himself was probably the real reason for his sudden halt.[220] He, Brunswick, old soldier of Frederick the Great, not only loathed the whole enterprise,[221] but regarded it as contrary to nature for Prussians and Austrians to be fighting on the same side.[222]

The *Courrier français* of June 17, 1793 presents, however, another explanation which is not beyond the range of possibility. An Irish priest who

[218] M. Tourneux (ed.), *Procès-verbaux de la Commune de Paris* (Paris, 1894), pp. 78 et seqq. However, the editor of the *Moniteur* never threatened in his paper that "the Prussians can come to Paris, but they'll not leave." This story has its origin in Goethe's *Kampagne in Frankreich* (*vide* Chuquet's ed., p. 69). Goethe's sovereign, Karl August of Saxe-Weimar, was one of Brunswick's generals during the 1792 invasion, and Goethe accompanied the Prussian army as a civilian, first by carriage and then on horseback (A. Robinet, "Goethe et la Révolution française," *RF*, N.S., 1937, p. 396). On the battlefield Goethe found a *Moniteur* of September 3, in which, under "Extrait d'une lettre de la Haye," a foreign correspondent had written: "Who can prevent the Brunswick column from arriving [at Paris]? It is true that it will not leave. . . The Faubourg Saint-Antoine alone is able to crush . . . 60,000 men." — XIII, 589. Goethe, seeing the dramatic possibilities of these phrases, made use of his poetic license to reconstruct them. Chuquet pointed this out in his French edition, but one still finds writers of learned articles who have not read Chuquet's critical notes (*vide*, e.g., H. Hintze, "Goethe et la Révolution française," *AHRF* [1932], IX, 427).

[219] "[How can we] reconcile the brilliant reputation the Duke of Brunswick has always enjoyed with the unheard-of mistakes which are attributed to him?" — Thugut (Aust. diplomat; later director, then minister, of foreign affairs) to Count Colloredo (Aust. cabinet minister), Nov. 1, 1792, A. von Vivenot (ed.), *Vertrauliche Briefe des Freiherrn von Thugut* (2 vols., Vienna, 1872), I, 4. These mistakes — an even dozen of them — are enumerated by Dumouriez in his *Mém.*, III, 96 et seqq. Wrote Reuss to the Austrian general Hohenlohe-Kirchberg: "The Duke will ever remain a timorous, irresolute leader from whom nothing doughty may longer be expected, especially with an army as democratic as the Prussian is becoming." — Oct. 30, 1792, Vivenot-Zeissberg, *Quellen*, II, 322.

[220] It should be mentioned that the French cries of *Vive la Nation* disconcerted Brunswick, and may have affected his judgment (*Guerres Rév. Emp.*, I, 45–46); also that it had rained and the ground was soaked (J. Calmette, *Trilogie de l'histoire de France* [3 vols., Paris, 1948–1952], III [*Les Révolutions*, 1952], 133).

[221] Sybel, *Europe*, I, 473.

[222] Stephens, *Rev. Eur.*, pp. 115–116.

had accompanied Louis XVI during that monarch's last days was the source of the journal's account, which runs as follows. The mayor and *procureur* of the Commune, fearful lest the mob murder the entire royal family when Brunswick should arrive within ten leagues of the capital, proposed secretly to Louis that he ask Brunswick to halt on condition that the mayor and *procureur* guarantee the safety of Louis and his family. Louis agreed. "I [Louis] sent the letter by the channel of Dumouriez, who placed it in the very hands of the King of Prussia; and it is in consequence of my solicitations that he evacuated Champagne." [223]

This account seems to find corroboration in the memoirs of a French noble of unflinching integrity, Count Roger de Damas. He relates that, after Valmy, Brunswick invited him to his quarters and asked for a point-blank statement as to what people were saying about his conduct. Damas was too refined a man to insult Brunswick to his face, so retailed to him a series of meaningless phrases. Brunswick insisted, however, on the truth, so Damas gave it to him. The Duke listened intently, then confided: "I give you my word of honor that if I were printing [the record of] my conduct and were allowed to publish it, no one would have anything to reproach me for; but I am bound by duty, and cannot. I am not the less unhappy about it." [224]

When the news of Valmy arrived in the Rhineland, the *Aachener Zuschauer* bluntly questioned "from just where the *quid pro quo* for this could have come," for reports from the front had indicated the French would have to capitulate. Several of the Comissioners with Kellermann's army, on the other hand, had reported that "the enemy was hungry, and lacking everything." [225] The *Politischen Gespräche der Toten* tried to explain Valmy thus: It was not intended to risk a decisive battle. The object of the Allies was to reëstablish peace, and military dispositions to this end alone had been made. A murderous battle would have cut down the size of the peace-army, hence might have been improvident. [226] After the battle, Dumouriez and Kellermann reported the success to Paris, but their report failed to make clear exactly what had happened. [227]

The historian Ranke attempts just that: Dumouriez had established his position in the pass at Grandpré, which he called the Thermopylae of France; but he neglected to secure Sainte-Croix, which commanded it. The Prussians thereupon occupied Sainte-Croix, forcing Dumouriez to abandon Grandpré. As the French withdrew, Brunswick could probably have caught

---

[223] Quoted by A. Mathiez in "Louis XVI auteur de la retraite de Brunswick," *AR*, VI (1913), 105.

[224] J. Rambaud (ed.), *Mémoires du comte Roger de Damas* (2 vols., Paris, 1912–1914), I, 206.

[225] Hansen, *Quellen*, II, 359, n. 1.

[226] *Ibid.*, p. 361, n. 1. It had been constituted at the price of too much time and money to endanger it lightly (Lefebvre, *Rév. fr.*, p. 263).

[227] Hansen, *Quellen*, p. 359, n. 1.

up with them and destroyed them as a fighting force. But he did not, perhaps because his troops were exhausted by forced marches, and his food supply was already running low. Dumouriez withdrew to Sainte-Menehould. A considerable body of French troops, under Kellermann, hurried from Metz to join him. The Prussians now advanced by forced marches, thinking to engage Kellermann before his union with Dumouriez. It was confidently expected by the Prussians that the raw levies of the French would flee at the sight of the Prussian armed might, and the road to Paris would lie open. But Kellermann set up his artillery on the heights of Valmy, and the artillery it was which — of all the branches of the French service — had suffered least from the emigration. When the Prussians arrived, they were greeted with a withering artillery barrage. The Prussian lines did not break, but one Prussian brigade which approached too close came off rather the worse for wear. The Duke of Brunswick thought a general attack was impossible so long as the French held the heights. He would have liked to dislodge them with his own artillery, but — at least, so he maintained — he lacked ammunition. Frederick William desired an immediate attack, but Brunswick insisted on postponement, expecting that the French would yet withdraw from their strong position. Such was the engagement at Valmy, indecisive and seemingly insignificant. When Goethe declared after the "battle": "Here and now a new era in world history is commencing," [228] no one echoed his judgment, but the event proved Goethe to have been no mean prophet.

Whatever the cause of Brunswick's mysterious halt, Dumouriez sought to prevent a renewal of the Prussian advance by whispering words of peace. On September 22, he sent Westermann, an agent of the Provisional Executive Council,[229] to the Prussian camp, ostensibly to negotiate the exchange of the captured secretary of the King for the Mayor of Varennes, but in reality to negotiate secretly and separately with Prussia. The French proposition was rejected "with scorn" — at least, so the Prince of Reuss, Austrian Ambassador to Berlin, related. When repetition of the offer failed to change the disposition of the Prussians, Dumouriez decided to inquire what were the terms of the Allies. Inasmuch as General Bischoffswerder, Frederick Wil-

[228] Ranke, *Ursprung*, pp. 306–310; Chuquet, (Goethe's) *Campagne*, p. 93. The Prussians were surprised that the French officers knew how to take advantage of all the potentialities of their very strong position. They had expected to meet tactical novices (Lucchesini [Prus. diplomat in King's entourage] to Prus. Min., Sept. 29, 1792, Ranke, *Ursprung*, p. 369 [Analects, no. 5]).

[229] Danton was the soul of the Council at this time, and Mathiez seems to attribute all the peace efforts of Dumouriez to Danton's influence. Danton, according to Mathiez, believed the time to make peace was after a victory, and that the victor himself should not hesitate to make sacrifices. This sounds like a formula for a just and durable peace, but Mathiez presents it as the most reprehensible of formulas (*Dtn paix*, pp. 48–57).

liam's confidant, was just then ill in bed, the King's aide-de-camp, Manstein, was charged with the negotiation. He presented Dumouriez — and Kellermann, who also was present — with a statement of his king's views respecting the position of Louis XVI and the menace of French propaganda. Dumouriez showed himself willing, almost desirous, that Louis should be freed. At the second meeting, however, Manstein was informed that the monarchy had been abolished in France and a republic proclaimed; but Dumouriez declared that he had not given up hope, and desired the conferences to continue. An armistice had already been agreed upon, and during its entire course, Dumouriez courted the Prussian generals — and Frederick William, to whom he sent some sugar and coffee. The Prussian monarch was sorely in need of these commodities, but they were accompanied by a memoir "which arouses the passions of every honorable man as ever did anything base, vile, and malicious" (Reuss's words). Frederick William, angered, informed Dumouriez that he needn't have troubled to send the sugar and coffee.[230]

d. Dumouriez' Memoir

What was there in this memoir that could be distasteful through a sugar coating? The bitter ingredients were these: The French monarchy had been abolished by the entire nation, hence it was idle to think of restoring it. No choice remained to foreign nations but to recognize the Republic or combat the Republic; there would be nought else. The powers had no legal right to impose laws on such a great nation as France. If they sought their sanction in force instead of in law, they could not complain if they got their fingers burned. "If the king and army that we esteem [the Prussian, of course] do not, by means of a reasonable negotiation, separate themselves from the Austrians and *émigrés* whom we scorn, France will soon change from the defensive to the offensive. It is time that a frank and true explanation terminates our discussions." This threat to his Majesty probably hurt the Hohenzollern pride. Of pleasant ingredients there were many. Frederick William was called the "respectable, if misled, monarch." He was informed that he "has a soul too pure not to be struck by the [following] facts: The Prussians love Royalty because, since the time of the Great Elector, they have had good kings, and because the one who [currently] leads them is doubtless worthy of their love. The French have abolished Royalty because, since the time of the immortal Henry IV, they have constantly had weak kings, or proud, or indolent, governed by mistresses, confessors, [and]

---

[230] Reuss to P. Cobenzl, Sept. 26 and 27, 1792, Vivenot-Zeissberg, *Quellen*, II, 233–235; Mathiez, *Dtn paix*, pp. 48–53; Chu- quet, *Guerres Rév.*, III (*La retraite de Brunswick*), 82 *et seqq.*

insolent or ignorant ministers." "Let us talk about those Austrians! . . . That power [Austria], more formidable to its allies than to its enemies, incites us to make war against a king whom we esteem, against a nation which we love and which loves us. This inversion of all the principles of politics and morals cannot endure." And the "baleful Treaty of 1756" was duly castigated. Lastly, a point was made — twice — that the King was sacrificing his treasure for Austria, for it was well known that Frederick William's principal worry was that he would exhaust the nest egg left him by Frederick the Great.[231] Such was the celebrated Coffee-and-Sugar-Memoir.[232] It is to be noted that Prussia rejected here conditions which she would have been only too glad to accept in 1795.

e. The Prussian Retreat

In response to his memoir, Dumouriez was handed by Manstein another "manifesto" of the Duke of Brunswick. This document presented the French anew with the alternative of restoring to Louis XVI his freedom, his security, and his royal station, or suffering signal vengeance.[233] Dumouriez chided Manstein for submitting a manifesto in response to a memoir "inspired by humanity and reason." He (Dumouriez) said he had sent Brunswick's declaration to the Convention, and would have it read in his camp. He was sure it would cause the same indignation in both places. "One does not treat thus with a great free nation and dictate laws to a sovereign people." Moreover, said the General, since there was no longer a basis for negotiation, "I will inform my advance posts tomorrow morning of the cessation of the truce; do the same on your side." [234]

Manstein was cowed. Dumouriez had not entered into the spirit of the declaration, he said. If they had themselves talked things over, this probably would not have happened. Would Dumouriez meet him tomorrow at the

---

[231] "It is known," wrote Thugut to Count Colloredo on November 1, 1792, "that what causes the King the most disquietude is to see the treasure dwindle that his late uncle left him." — *Briefe Thugut*, I, 5.

[232] Vivenot-Zeissberg, *Quellen*, II, 243–246. This memoir is to be found also in A. F. Bertrand de Moleville, *Histoire de la Révolution de France pendant les dernières années du règne de Louis XVI* (10 vols., Paris, 1801–1802), X, 463–465. There are some twenty differences between these two versions. Some are inconsequential, but a few are important, and inasmuch as Bertrand de Moleville's version makes either

better sense or better French, it is quite probable that his version is the correct one. In Vivenot-Zeissberg, p. 243, l. 30, change "princes" to "crimes"; p. 244, l. 27, change "attira" to "a attiré"; p. 245, l. 8, change "une" to "aucune"; p. 245, l. 11, change "un juste Roi" to "un jour le roi"; p. 245, l. 39, change "n'a pas refuser" to "n'a pas pu refuser"; p. 245, l. 43, change "de défendre" to "de se défendre." Accord: *Mém. Dumouriez*, III, 401–405, "Eclaircissemens historiques et pièces officielles," Note (A).

[233] Ranke, *Ursprung*, pp. 374–376 (Anlage 4 of Analects, no. 5).

[234] *Ibid.*, p. 377 (Anlage 5, *ibid.*).

advance posts, around noon? The Prussian army would not be the first to break the truce.[235] But Dumouriez refused. He had already sent the manifesto to the Convention, he said. Copies had been printed, and distributed among his and Kellermann's army. It was impossible to continue either truce or negotiation with Brunswick's manifesto as a basis. It was now for the sovereign people of France to prescribe the next step. "My good opinion of your honest-man-of-a-king, of your estimable nation, and of you, yourself, makes me regret deeply that one cannot negotiate with manifestoes." [236]

The renewal of the war was expected momentarily. There were many factors, however, which tended to discourage the Prussians from taking the fatal step. To force the heights of Valmy would cost many men, and would really decide very little, for hordes of patriots were flocking to the defense of the capital. There was no longer the possibility of a royal road to Paris.[237] Then the relative strength of Dumouriez' and Frederick William's forces had changed to Prussia's detriment, for reinforcements had arrived for the former but not for the latter. And there were the weather, and illness. Heavy rains had turned the roads into seas of mud. Dysentery had torn greater holes in the Prussian ranks than a dozen Valmys. The French peasants had hidden or burned their crops, upon which the Prussians had relied for sustenance, and supplies had to be hauled all the way from Verdun by a roundabout route.[238] These supplies — of poor quality, to boot [239] — arrived only spasmodically, and hunger forced the troops to comb the countryside for food. But the French peasants had created such a desert [240] that all that the Prussians could find was some unripe [241] grapes [242] — which certainly are

[235] Ibid., pp. 377–378 (Anlage 6, ibid.).

[236] Ibid., pp. 378–379 (Anlage 7, ibid.).

[237] Ibid., p. 322.

[238] Guerres Rév. Emp., I, 64. The Prussians had found 12,000 sacks of grain in Verdun, according to Dumouriez' Mémoires, III, 106. But that did not last long.

[239] The bread, e.g., was orange colored, raising suspicion of sulphur and arsenic. It was also often moldy (Chuquet, [Goethe's] Campagne, p. 118). According to one account, the grain was that stored by Frederick the Great, and "being heated, destroyed, in place of nourishing, [the] . . . troops; and . . . with incessant rains, gave them a dysentery so fatal that it made incredible mortality." — Lady Eglantine (Maxwell) Wallace, The Conduct of the King of Prussia and General Dumourier (London, 1793), p. 38. Lady Wallace says the Prussians only rarely cooked their food,

and when they managed to find a hog, they would skin it alive, cut it up, and eat it (ibid., p. 53). Whether the Lady received this tale from Dumouriez is not indicated. She was in intimate contact with the General — too intimate, the wags said — when he was in England in June 1793. (Vide infra, Pt. I, chap. iii, § 1 and n. 32.)

[240] "[There was] nourishment for no living thing. Amidst the rain, we lacked even water. . . I saw water being scooped out of the hoofprints of horses to slake an unendurable thirst." — Chuquet, (Goethe's) Campagne, pp. 98–99.

[241] Grapes did not ripen at all in 1792. "Everything goes wrong since we invented 'la Nation,'" commented a fruiteress (H. Taine [trans.], Un séjour en France de 1792 à 1795 [Paris, 1872], p. 47).

[242] Buchez and Roux, Hist. parlem., XX, 97–98.

not a cure for dysentery.[243] "A traveling hospital," is the way Goethe described the invincible host bequeathed by Frederick the Great.[244] Under such circumstances, it was the counsel of wisdom to retreat, and retreat is precisely what Brunswick did.

But what a strange withdrawal it was! Dumouriez limited himself to following the Prussians at a respectful distance, yet never for a moment losing them from view. Kellermann wanted to attack their flank and cut off their retreat, but Dumouriez forbade it, and inasmuch as two Commissioners of the Convention were present, Kellermann had to limit himself to protests and complaints. But for the sake of appearances, Dumouriez pretended to be pressing the pursuit with great energy, sending flying columns here and attacking there — but the attacks were timed to catch only the *émigrés*, who constituted the Prussian rear guard, or what was more usual, they were timed to catch no one at all.[245]

When the Prussians reached Verdun, they halted, and under cover of a forest which they occupied, set up some earthworks to defend their left. The French general Dillon's sharpshooters were very successful in harassing the Prussian sentinels guarding these earthworks — so much so, in fact, that the Prussian general Kalkreuth requested a conference with the French leaders. While the Prussian and French sharpshooters imbibed brandy together, Kalkreuth explained that in previous wars, it had been the custom for sentinels of opposing sides to spare each other, and he suggested reestablishment of the custom. Major General Galbaud, who represented Dillon, agreed, provided the Prussians would evacuate the forest. To this, Kalkreuth had no authority to consent, and he called in the Allied commander in chief, the Duke of Brunswick. The Duke professed such love for

---

[243] Mathiez seems to think the grapes caused the dysentery — but that is extremely unlikely (*vide* his *Fr. Rev.*, p. 222).

[244] H. Vast, "La Convention Nationale," Lavisse and Rambaud, *Hist. gén.*, VIII, 233–234.

[245] Buchez and Roux, *Hist. parlem.*, XX, 80–81.

It is difficult to ascertain whether Lady Wallace, in the passage below, intends to insinuate an understanding between Dumouriez and Frederick William: " . . . Whether he had invited the King of Prussia to quit France without resistance, and on his part, promised to spare his [the King's] troops, then totally at his mercy, is a secret known to few besides themselves. I have no doubt that the General, from his soothing manners, found a method

to reconcile his Majesty to his fate." — Lady Wallace, *Conduct . . . Prussia . . . Dumourier*, p. 49.

On the other hand, Dumouriez says in his *Mémoires* that he does not believe that the Prussian army was saved by negotiations, its line of retreat never having been endangered (III, 106). (Note that this does not deny the existence of the negotiations; it merely disputes their necessity from the Prussian point of view. Note also that the Prussians' line of retreat *would* have been endangered if Kellermann had been permitted to attack their flank.) And Dumouriez adds: "It is an error to seek mysterious causes for events which are explainable quite naturally by the simplest precepts of the military art and by good sense." — *Ibid.*, p. 107.

France and such fervent regard for her best interests that Labarolière, Galbaud's associate in the parleys, asked him why he did not evacuate French soil — "the best proof of his favorable disposition toward us." Brunswick said he would refer the two questions, evacuation of the forest, and evacuation of Verdun, to Frederick William; and another meeting was arranged.[246]

But before these conferences were renewed, the French had taken possession of Mt. Saint-Barthélemy, which dominated the citadel at Verdun. Then General Dillon summoned the governor of the fortress to surrender. This demand precipitated another conference between Kalkreuth and the French, now represented by Dillon himself. Each general denied having authority to decide anything, but mutual flattery flowed in torrents. And the "monstrous" Treaty of 1756 was heaped with ignominy. Dillon proposed that Prussia "unite with [France] to humiliate the proud House of Austria, which covets Silesia, and which views with regret that [the House of] Brandenburg is playing one of the premier roles in Europe." Kalkreuth affirmed that this happy union would materialize promptly if it depended upon him.[247]

While Kalkreuth and Dillon vied with each other in tossing verbal bouquets, the capitulation of Verdun was arranged in a meeting between Colonel Manstein for Prussia, and General Kellermann and two Commissioners of the government, for France.[248] On October 12, one of the gates to the citadel was peacefully surrendered by the Prussians. On the twenty-second, a similar arrangement was concluded with respect to Longwy. With the recapture of these two cities by the French, the last enemy soldier had left the soil of France. The *patrie* was saved.[249]

Light beat the heart of France that autumn day — especially light because of the attitude of Prussia. France seemed about to acquire a friend who hated France's hereditary enemy (Austria) even more than did she — if possible. Perhaps nothing so well illustrates the benevolent attitude of the French toward Prussia, which was still at war with the Republic, as a certain popular song which appeared at this time in Paris, and was sung to the tune of "La petite Thérèse":

I

Do you know the pretty story of those famous Prussians?
They were marching on to victory with the allied Austrians.

---

[246] Buchez and Roux, *Hist. parlem.*, XX, 83–88.

[247] *Ibid.*, pp. 89–91.

[248] The text of the capitulation can be found in E. Bonnal de Ganges, *Les représentants du peuple en mission près les armées, 1791–1797* (4 vols., Paris, 1898–1899), IV, 518–519.

[249] Buchez and Roux, *Hist. parlem.*, XX, 93–95.

But instead of palms of glory
They gathered grapes — another story.

II

Grapes are laxative when eaten without bread.[250]
"No more bread than glory is our lot," the Prussians said.
"We sally forth singing of sweet victory.
We draw back hungry as hungry can be."

III

The shortest route great Frederick takes as he flees 'cross French terrain,
But Dumouriez o'ertakes him and sings him this refrain:
"Now don't you nibble at the grapes any more
In the vineyard of those who live next door."

IV

"I'll not be caught at that again," the Prussian hero cries;
"If I escape now I'll surely know how to tell my brave allies:
Go pick the grapes, but by yourself [should it be worth your labor;
I've learned that one should ne'er pick grapes in the vineyard of his neighbor]." [251]

f. Peace Parleys

Many persons in France expected the Prussian retreat to be followed presently
by the withdrawal of Frederick William from the war, but it appears there
was a possibility even of general peace. On October 24, 1792, at the Duke of
Brunswick's request, there met with General Kellermann: the Duke himself; the Prince of Hohenlohe-Kirchberg, the Austrian general; the Prince
of Reuss, the Austrian Ambassador to Berlin; and the Marquis of Lucchesini,
sometime Prussian Ambassador to Warsaw. The purpose was to consider
terms of peace. Kellermann was invited to sketch a basis. He suggested
recognition of the French Republic, and a hands-off policy with respect
to France's king and France's émigrés; and then he added: "I think
that, the Emperor having been the aggressor, . . . France should be given
the Belgian Netherlands as indemnity." The Austrian Ambassador did
not take kindly to this suggestion, but Brunswick said: "General, apprize
the National Convention [elected to formulate a new constitution, but
which became the government of France] that we are strongly disposed
toward peace; and to attest this, we shall repair to any place the National
Convention may suggest. Let it name plenipotentiaries. . ." Kellermann
reported the parley to the Commissioners of the Convention, who sent a
courier to the Convention and the Provisional Executive Council.[252] But five

[250] "Bread" in the sense of "staple food."   98.
[251] Buchez and Roux, *Hist. parlem.*, XX, 97–   [252] *Ibid.*, pp. 95–96.

days later, the Council ordered Kellermann to depart with reinforcements for General Custine, [253] and nothing came of the affair. What is yet stranger is that all mention of the negotiation is missing from the French archives. The Austrian report on the conference says that the ministers had a long discussion, but came to no conclusion.[254]

Equally fruitless were *pourparlers* initiated during the Longwy colloquies by a statement of Dillon's successor, Valence, and subsequently followed up. Valence declared to the Duke of Brunswick that the Convention would be willing to agree to a general peace embodying the following terms: Austria to free Belgium entirely, or surrender it to a less powerful prince; France to set Louis XVI at liberty, and grant an amnesty to the *émigrés*. These terms seemed to tie in with the Bavaro-Belgian exchange plan, so Haugwitz, Prussian minister who specialized in questions of foreign policy, sent the Prince of Reuss and the Marquis of Lucchesini to interview General Kellermann. The meeting took place on the twenty-sixth. Valence, who was also present, announced that France wished to surround herself with free peoples; that if she did not consummate the revolutionization of Belgium, it would be on condition that Austria yielded that choice morsel to the Bavaro-Palatine Elector, who would become only its stadholder with a fixed income. The condition was declared inadmissible. Valence then asked for Prussia's alliance, and Kellermann requested his visitors to initiate peace overtures, to confide their terms to him. The visitors replied that peace parleys involved much preliminary discussion which they would gladly take up with any authorized persons. Lucchesini reported to Haugwitz after the meeting that he saw no present hope of useful negotiations, that the French plan seemed to be to embroil Prussia with Austria, and, by threatening Austria with the loss of Belgium, to force advantageous terms from the Habsburg Court. Lucchesini remained in the environs of Luxemburg to afford the French the opportunity of a second interview should they desire one,[255] but on October 28, Dumouriez forbade Valence to waste his time with "pretended negotiations." [256] Thus ended the parleys — but the spring of Revolutionary ingenuity had not yet run dry.

On October 25, the Prussian minister-resident at Cologne, Baron von Dohm, had written to his king that one Maudillon (i.e., Mandrillon) [257] had made overtures of peace and alliance to him.[258] Nor had Mandrillon been the first to approach von Dohm. The publisher Mettra [259] had pre-

[253] Aulard, *Actes*, I, 208, Oct. 29, 1792.

[254] Clerfayt (Aust. gen.) to Saxe-Teschen, Oct. 26, 1792, Vivenot-Zeissberg, *Quellen*, II, 296. Clerfayt put the date of the conference at October 25.

[255] Lucchesini to Haugwitz, Oct. 26, 1792, Vivenot-Zeissberg, *Quellen*, II, 297–298.

[256] Sybel, *Europe*, I, 594–596.

[257] Editor of the Paris newspaper *Le spectateur américain* (Hansen, *Quellen*, II, 369, n. 1).

[258] Dohm to Frederick William, *ibid.*, p. 369.

[259] Publisher of *Le Nouvelliste politique d'Allemagne* of Cologne; of the *Journal des*

ceded him.[260] And a Count de Géroni [261] had tendered propositions to Lucchesini. Frederick William reacted in the same manner to all these overtures: Inasmuch as the Convention at Paris had announced it would not discuss an armistice or peace so long as there were foreign troops on French soil, his Prussian Majesty decided he would listen to no propositions until Custine's troops had evacuated German soil. In addition, the King wanted, as condition precedent to any parleys, a satisfactory answer to his queries regarding the safety of the royal family. Of interest it is that von Dohm was ordered never to engage in any discussion with the French "without the knowledge and against the interests of the Emperor, my ally." [262]

Some three weeks later (November 23), the Landgrave of Hesse-Homburg declared, in Custine's name, that if Prussia recognized the Republic, France would surrender her conquests and liberate Louis XVI and his family. Soon thereafter, Mandrillon and Mettra renewed their overtures, and Lucchesini repaired to Coblenz to learn from them the French government's plans. These envisaged a Franco-Prussian offensive alliance, and betrayed with crystal clarity that the Republic was not interested in a general peace. "Never will we treat with the House of Austria," Foreign Minister Lebrun's instructions had specified. These proposals were in striking contrast to those tendered by Custine, but neither set possessed a chance of success, for Custine was presently driven back across the Rhine and his bargaining power shrank to nil.[263] It is interesting to note that in these negotiations following Valmy, Mathiez suspects Danton of receiving Prussian gold.[264]

g. The Shadow of Poland

The Prussian King was willing to continue the war, but on his own terms, and he wanted to discuss these with his Habsburg ally. This, Austria refused to do. All efforts should be devoted to the prosecution of the war, she

---

révolutions de l'Europe en 1789 et 1790 of Neuwied and Strasburg; and, with others, of the *Correspondance littéraire et secrète* of Neuwied and Paris. The French foreign minister (Lebrun) had been a newspaper editor in Liège, so was acquainted with Mettra (*ibid.*, I, 30 *, 35 *; II, 365, n. 4).

[260] Dohm to Frederick William, Sept. 30, 1792, *ibid.*, II, 365–368.

[261] Or Gervai, according to Hansen (*ibid.*, p. 369). The Count threatened that if he were not listened to, he would publish the letter which embodied his plan of negotiation (*ibid.*). Just how welcome that would have been to Frederick William may be judged from his annoyance when

Dautzenberg, owner of the *Aachener Zuschauer*, published a report that the King of Prussia was trying to arrange a six weeks' armistice with France. Von Dohm was asked to take up the matter with the Aix-la-Chapelle Senate. But von Dohm was acquainted with Dautzenberg, so personally secured a retraction from him, plus a promise that the King's honor would not again be impugned (*ibid.*, p. 366, n. 1).

[262] Frederick William II to Dohm, Nov. 1, 1792, Vivenot-Zeissberg, *Quellen*, II, 325–326.

[263] Sybel, *Europe*, II, 40–41.

[264] G. Lefebvre, "Sur Danton," *AHRF*, IX (1932), 418.

maintained. However, toward the end of October 1792, Frederick William became too insistent to be longer denied,[265] for the pronounced friendship of France — as attested by the secret offers above mentioned — placed him in a strong position for bargaining. Heretofore, he had demanded only indemnity for the campaign that had just terminated. Now he wanted to be paid for continuing the war. By the Treaty of February 7, 1792, he was bound to furnish only 20,000 men. But if Austria really wished to wage with his aid a full-scale war of conquest, he would consent *if* — and he traced upon a map the least he would accept.[266] It was a piece of Poland double in size what had been agreed upon, and at a time when the conquest of Belgium by Dumouriez, and the invasion of southern Germany by Custine, rendered it impossible for Austria to receive the agreed equivalent. The Habsburg Court pointed this out to Prussia, but the latter power retorted that the principle of equality of acquisition was no longer valid, for Austria was being attacked, while Prussia was not; and that besides it was only right that Prussia, which was in a position to grant aid, should be paid therefor. The Emperor pretended to consent, but appealed to Catherine to put off the actual partition, or at least to cut down the size of the projected Prussian slice. Catherine, anxious perhaps to shake herself free from Austrian influence, decided for Prussia.[267] The Russo-Prussian Partition Treaty was signed on January 23, 1793, and ratified the following March 2.[268]

When Emperor Francis II learned of this treaty, he well-nigh consumed himself with rage. Dismissing his ministers,[269] he created the office of Director-General of the Bureau of Foreign Affairs, and appointed thereto [270] Baron Johann Amadeus Franz de Paula von Thugut,[271] son of an army paymaster,[272] who had risen high in the diplomatic service by sheer ability and downright unscrupulousness.[273]

[265] *Krieg g. Rev.*, II, 284.

[266] Sybel, *Europe*, I, 594–596.

[267] Hüffer-Luckwaldt, *Quellen*, Pt. II, Vol. I, xviii–xxiii.

[268] Text in Vivenot-Zeissberg, *Quellen*, II, 516–519.

[269] *Ibid.*, pp. 541–543.

[270] *Ibid.*, p. 544. According to von Sybel, it was De Mercy who "provoked the nomination of Thugut" (*Europe*, II, 246, n. 1).

[271] His family name originally had the less altruistic and not so complimentary form of Thuenitguth or Thunitguth ("Do-no-good" instead of the later "Do-good"). It was Johann's grandfather who made the change. The historian Matthias Koch affirms that evil names such as Thunitguth, Bauernschelm (Peasant-Rogue), Bauern-feind (Peasant-Enemy) owe their origin to the hatreds incited by the Peasants' Revolt (*Briefe Thugut*, I, 391).

[272] Not the son of a Danube skipper, as von Sybel states (*Fr. Rev.*, II, 469). This is proved by Johann's baptismal certificate, quoted by Vivenot (*Briefe Thugut*, I, 392). For the various legends concerning Thugut's paternity, *vide* the *Allgemeine deutsche Biographie*, *s.v.* "Thugut."

[273] Thugut's father seems to have performed some signal service for the Habsburgs, for Maria Theresa put the son through the Oriental Academy after the father's death. This led later to a diplomatic post at Constantinople. Von Sybel describes Thugut as acute, contemptuous of danger, adept at intrigue, always tactful, imperturbable,

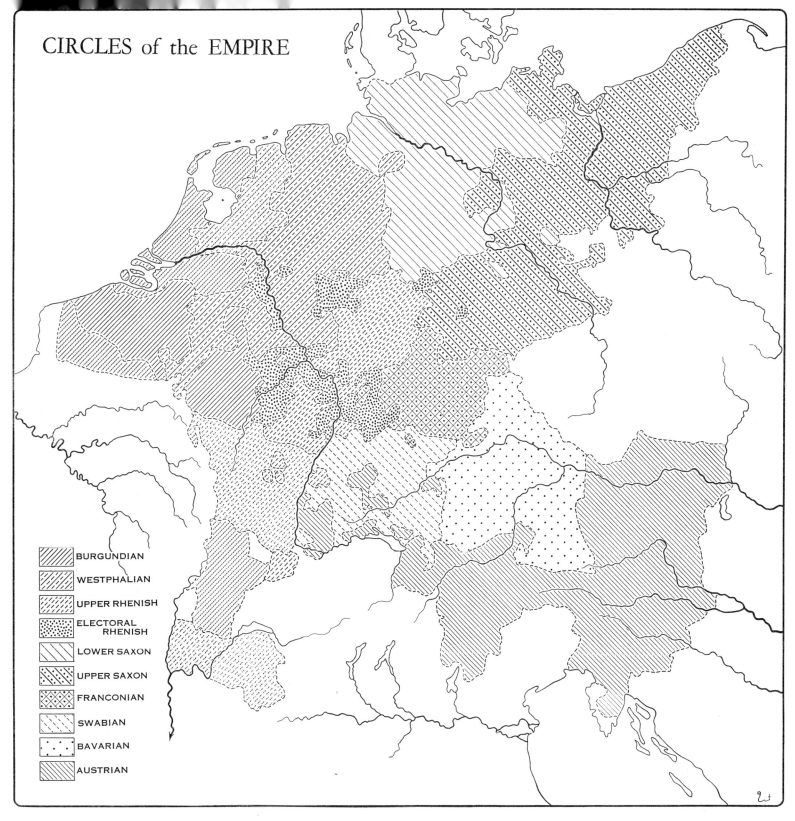

CIRCLES of the EMPIRE

BURGUNDIAN

WESTPHALIAN

UPPER RHENISH

ELECTORAL RHENISH

LOWER SAXON

UPPER SAXON

FRANCONIAN

SWABIAN

BAVARIAN

AUSTRIAN

THE FULL-SHADED AREAS OF THE MAP DESIGNATE THE CIRCLE AS THEY EXISTED IN 1792. THE UNITED NETHERLANDS, FRENCH FLANDERS, LORRAINE, ALSACE, THE FREE COUNTY OF BURGUNDY, AND SAVOY ARE SHADOWED TO SHOW THAT THEY ONCE FORMED PART OF THE SYSTEM OF CIRCLES, BUT NO LONGER.

The historian Aulard declares that "the day that Francis II learned of the treaty of partition of Poland, he saw he had been deceived, he dismissed his ministers, summoned Thugut, demanded [that] Belgium [be] enlarged with French fortresses, and sent Mercy-Argenteau to London to claim compensation."[274] De Mercy was ordered to London on March 18,[275] when the Russo-Prussian pact was yet unknown, but "justly suspected."[276] The purpose, as appears from a memoir of Thugut's before he became Director-General, was to secure England's support for a future Bavaro-Belgian exchange.[277] In a memoir of Thugut's (dated March 18) accompanying the notification to De Mercy of his appointment, no mention was made of French fortresses.[278] This requirement appeared only on March 26,[279] the day after the Viennese Court learned of the Russo-Prussian treaty.[280] But Thugut had not yet been made Director-General, for the instructions to De Mercy of the twenty-fifth and twenty-sixth were written by Philipp von Cobenzl and Spielmann. In Thugut's memoir of March 18, it was specifically stated that the Bavaro-Belgian exchange was not to be regarded as compensating Austria for her losses in the war, and Cobenzl, in his March 25 despatch to De Mercy, treated the exchange only as a "concentration" of Austrian power, and spoke of "acquisitions" besides. Thus, when Thugut was appointed Director-General, the border-fortress and compensation orders had already been issued to De Mercy.[281] Aulard's concatenation of events is plainly misleading.

Be that as it may, some general remarks are in order. Austria had borne the brunt of the war, yet at this time had good reason to fear that she alone would receive no indemnity. Wurmser had been driven from Alsace — as a result principally of Brunswick's failure to support him.[282] Belgium — until Dumouriez' treason – had been lost. The Prussian reconquest of the Palati-

---

frugal (his usual supper consisted of fruit and a glass of water), sober, unreligious, having but one spring of action — self-love. Bonaparte said of him a few years later: "He seems to me to possess but little skill, to see but a little way [ahead of] him." — Sybel, *Fr. Rev.*, II, 469–471.

[274] F. A. Aulard, "La diplomatie du premier Comité de salut public," *RF*, XVIII (1890), 236–237.

[275] Emperor to Mercy, Vivenot-Zeissberg, *Quellen*, II, 503. The order was countermanded on April 17, after Dumouriez' treason had resulted in the Austrian reconquest of Belgium, thus changing the picture in Austria's favor. De Mercy had not started out yet (Thugut to Mercy, May 4, 1793, *ibid.*, III [*Quellen zur Geschichte der Politik*

Oesterreichs während der französischen Revolutionskriege, 1882], 49). Mathiez things De Mercy was already in England (*Dtn paix*, p. 151).

[276] Vivenot-Zeissberg, *Quellen*, II, 504.

[277] *Ibid.*, pp. 498–500.

[278] *Ibid.*, pp. 504–507.

[279] P. Cobenzl to Mercy, *ibid.*, pp. 523–524.

[280] *Ibid.*, p. 516.

[281] Thugut's despatch of April 14 to De Mercy adopts and repeats both orders, however (*ibid.*, III, 24–26).

[282] Aulard in *RF*, XVIII, 238. Several months later, Lord Malmesbury, British special envoy to Prussia, wrote in his diary: "King told me of bad news from Wurmser's army. . . He seemed rather pleased with this bad news." — Dec. 28, 1793,

nate from the French had resulted in close relations between Frederick William and the Bavaro-Palatine Electress, rendering the Bavaro-Belgian exchange more unlikely yet.[283] Under these conditions arrived the news of the Second Partition of Poland. Though Prussia and Russia had agreed in the Treaty of January 23, 1793, to secure for Austria the desired exchange of territory,[284] a bitterness was introduced into Austro-Prussian relations which had much to do with determining France's policy toward Prussia during the remainder of the Convention, and during the entire Directory.

5. THE DIET AND THE WAR

It will be recalled that Dumouriez, as minister of foreign affairs, had sought to localize the war he had personally provoked. "It is only our dear ally, Austria, whom we affirm to be our enemy," he wrote to General Biron, "and we are careful to distinguish it from the other powers which form . . . an infernal league against us." [285] Caillard had been sent as minister plenipotentiary to the Imperial Diet at Ratisbon, with instructions to stir up the Empire against its leaders. He was to point out that Germany fell naturally into two factions, the partisans of Austria and of Prussia, respectively — and that the Alliance of February 7, 1792 was a menace to the small states, the free cities, and especially Bavaria.[286]

The Diet refused to accept Caillard's credentials on the ground that they contained unusual diplomatic expressions,[287] but he clung on, sowing doubts and dissension where he could, in the hope of frustrating the Emperor's appeals that the states enter the lists against France.[288] And though Caillard left Ratisbon on September 15, 1792, his task seems to have been well done, for, instead of working for war, the Circle of Swabia was proposing the formation of a temporary defensive association; the Franconian Circle was fretting at the prospect of having to feed Prussian and Austrian troops passing through the district; the Elector of Hanover was proclaiming his preference for neutrality, and had attracted Saxony and the small states of northern Germany to his standard; and Bavaria was discoursing on her his-

Diaries and Correspondence of James Harris, First Earl of Malmesbury (4 vols., London, 1844–1845), III, 34.
[283] Wurmser to Thugut, April 21, 1793, Vivenot-Zeissberg, Quellen, III, 32–33.
[284] Hüffer-Luckwaldt, Quellen, Pt. II, Vol. I, xviii–xxiii.
[285] Chuquet, Guerres Rév., I, 15.
[286] "Mémoire pour servir d'instruction au sieur Caillard," May 1792, Arch. N., D XXIII,

1, quoted in Aulard, RF, XVIII, 349.
[287] C. Girtanner, Historische Nachrichten und politische Betrachtungen über die französischen Revolution (2nd ed.; 17 vols., Berlin, 1792–1803), VII, 425. Girtanner reproduces the credentials. They are in Latin, and signed by Louis XVI and Dumouriez.
[288] Vivenot-Zeissberg, Quellen, II, 27, 30, 35.

toric friendship for France.[289] Indeed, much of this might have happened without Caillard. The day following France's declaration of war on Austria, Bavaria had given France "the most positive assurances of its invariable determination never to deviate from the policy of perfect neutrality." Saxony had intimated a similar intention, and though the French chargé d'affaires at Dresden was eventually sent home on Austria and Prussia's insistence, and the Saxon chargé d'affaires at Paris tactfully repaired to Bath to take the waters, the secretary of the Saxon legation at Paris had remained at his post. The Duke of Württemberg had spent the winter of 1791 in Paris, trying to reach an understanding with France concerning Montbéliard, whose seizure by France was one of the grievances for which the Diet was being asked to declare war. It was therefore to be expected that when the question of war or peace should arise in the Diet, the Duke of Württemberg would speak words of peace and moderation.[290]

On November 23, 1792, the Diet, after months of wrangling, rendered a *Conclusum* in favor of war with France and "triple contingents," [291] but the long-delayed decision remained practically a dead letter.[292] Truly the Landgrave of Hesse-Cassel did respond loyally with six thousand troops — hoping thereby to receive the electoral cap; [293] and the Emperor did give a hundred ducats to the bearer of the Diet's *Conclusum* — if the *Moniteur* [294] is telling us the truth. But the Landgrave's noble six thousand were only a drop in the ocean, and the Emperor's gesture may have helped the courier but not the war effort. The remainder of the Empire was hopelessly in favor of appeasement. The Duke of Zweibrücken, as indicated above, continued to negotiate with France. The Elector of Bavaria held doggedly to his policy of neutrality. The Circle of Swabia declared itself in favor of the good-neighbor policy in so far as France was concerned; the Swabian contingent, it said, would limit itself to defending the frontiers of the Circle. The Duke of Württemberg engaged in pacific *pourparlers* with France through Doucet, French chargé d'affaires at Munich, and maintained an agent in Paris as long as the Convention permitted.[295]

Austria and Prussia were disgusted with the total lack of patriotism mani-

[289] Sorel, *Europe*, II (*La chute de la royauté*, 1887), 474–475.
[290] Aulard in *RF*, XVIII, 350. But Württemberg's "moderation" availed her nothing, and when, four years later, she still thought to negotiate the question of Montbéliard, she was informed that that province had to be considered as irrevocably united with France (Arch. A. E., *Allemagne* 669, f. 350).
[291] Hansen, *Quellen*, II, 610–611. A "contin-

gent" was the agreed portion of men and money contributed by the individual states to the Emperor so that he could wage an Imperial war. It could be the ordinary portion (*simplum*) or a multiple thereof. *Vide infra*, Pt. I, chap. vi, n. 95.
[292] Aulard in *RF*, XVIII, 350.
[293] Sorel, *Europe*, II, 475.
[294] XIV, 757.
[295] Aulard in *RF*, XVIII, 353–354.

fested by the lesser German states, and endeavored, by means of proclamations, to awaken the German spirit.[296] But it was not until March 22, 1793,
that the Empire took the step of officially declaring war on France.[297] The
Emperor ratified this *Conclusum* immediately,[298] thus adding the last of the
more important states to the Coalition formed against the Revolutionary
Republic — a coalition now consisting of the Empire and the non-Imperial
possessions of Austria and Prussia; of England, Spain, Russia, Holland, and
Piedmont. To meet this coalition, Lebrun proposed the negotiation of a
counterleague composed of France, Sweden, Denmark, Turkey, Bavaria and
the Palatinate, Württemberg, Saxony, Venice, Naples, Tuscany, and
Genoa.[299] And indeed, despite the Empire's declaration of war, negotiations
continued with the states of the Empire, especially with Württemberg, with
which relations were exceptionally cordial. They ceased only under pressure
from Austria and Prussia, and under the influence of the French defeats of
June and July 1793. Or perhaps it would be more correct merely to say that
henceforth the negotiations were more indirect, more tenuous, more elusive
— yet negotiations there were and continued to be, as Chapter III (of Part I)
will indicate. But that is getting too far afield. At present we must return to
1792, and see what the armies of the Republic were doing while the Prussians were busy politicizing with the French.

[296] Examples will be found *ibid.*, pp. 362 *et seqq.*
[297] Probably it was the French invasion of the Rhineland described in the next chapter, rather than the feudal-enclave problem, which finally stung it into action.
[298] Aulard in *RF*, XVIII, 363–364.
[299] *Ibid.*, pp. 346–347.

Catherine's position in the War of the First Coalition is enigmatic. Spiritually, vocally, and economically a belligerent, it was only against the "Jacobins" of Poland that she actually warred. It is questionable whether she should be classed as a nonbelligerent belligerent or as a belligerent nonbelligerent.

CHAPTER II

THE EARLY REVOLUTION AND
THE RHINELAND

I. GENERAL CUSTINE AND THE RHINELAND

a. *General*

IN October 1792, General Custine made a lightning raid on Spires, the base of supplies of the Austrians. At the appearance of the French in the Rhineland, panic seized the petty left-bank states, and rulers [1] and privileged persons fled posthaste across the Rhine. Hardly a hand was raised in defense as General Custine occupied Spires, Worms, and Mayence on the left bank of the Rhine, and Frankfort-on-the-Main on the right.[2] This was at a time when France and the Empire were yet at peace.

Prophetic were the words of the Austrian vice-chancellor, Count Philipp Cobenzl, when this information reached him. "The news coming in from the Empire is very sad," he wrote. "If the French need only push forward . . . to find everyone either unarmed, or being armed, willing . . . supinely to [lay down his weapons and] surrender, conquest will indeed be easy for them, and, like Attila, they will devastate half of Europe."[3]

The rapid and practically unopposed advance of General Custine through the Rhineland does indeed require explanation. Sagnac says that the Elector of Mayence had declared war on France in order to divert a part of the

---

[1] The rulers of the German left-bank states were 9 archbishops and bishops, 2 religious orders, 76 princes and counts, 4 free cities, and many Imperial knights (Gooch, *Germ. Fr. Rev.*, p. 487).

[2] "Our expedition to the right bank of the Rhine [was due] entirely to pecuniary considerations," writes Baron J. L. C. Gay de Vernon, son of Simon François Gay de Vernon, the companion-in-arms and intimate friend of Generals Custine and Hou-

chard. "The treasury of the army was empty. . . . Our incursion into a rich and defenseless country was to procure us the money of which we were in such dire need." — *Mémoire sur les opérations militaires des généraux en chef Custine et Houchard* (Paris, 1844), p. 74.

[3] To Schlik (Aust. ambas. to Electorate of Mayence and to Franconian Circle), Oct. 27, 1792, Vivenot-Zeissberg, *Quellen*, II, 311.

French army, so that the remainder could be caught in a vise formed by the Prussians and Austrians. However, both the Prussian and Austrian hosts had been compelled to retreat, leaving Mayence unprotected. The Elector had pleaded for aid from all his neighbors, but in vain. Thus, Mayence was a sacrifice to the Allied cause. This is all correct except that Sagnac's source, Häusser, does not say that the Elector actually declared war. But that prince's pugnacity is unquestioned, so the effect is not too different.[4]

Another reason for the unparalleled success of the French troops was that for some months past a vigorous propaganda campaign had been conducted in the Rhineland by the Jacobins of Strasburg, Wissembourg, and Landau.[5] In August 1791, there had been broadcast an "Appeal from the Liberated French to the Oppressed Germans." [6] The new ideas had struck root among the intellectual classes of the population,[7] and a small but powerful party, composed principally of university professors, students, doctors, and lawyers, had come to regard Paris as the source of liberty, the Mecca toward which all men yearning for freedom should turn their faces. These men encouraged Custine's advance, convinced that they had nothing to fear from the French, for had not the Constitution of 1791 renounced all idea of conquest? [8] And there was certainly no consciousness of "fatherland" to stand in their way, for the bond of the Holy Roman Empire was especially

[4] Sagnac, *Rhin fr.*, pp. 68–69; Häusser, *Deutsche Geschichte*, I, 405.

[5] On August 5, 1791, the College of Electoral Princes took up the question of French-induced subversion. Special mention was made of the "so-called *Congregation de propaganda*," which was characterized, specifically, as "dangerous" (Hansen, *Quellen*, I, 889–891). The College's action led to the Imperial Censorship Edict of December 3, which dealt with the spread of inflamatory writings and ideas; it provided for severe penalization of the persons involved, and for strictly enforced confiscation of any German or foreign writings; also for suppression of riot and insurrection (*ibid.*, pp. 1049–1050). This decree was sent for execution to the Lower (Electoral) Rhenish-Westphalian Circles, with the following interesting remarks and recommendations: Watch the "Club" at Cologne; many democrats speak very boldly there. Most revolutionary writings are bought in Cologne; should not the Imperial Post refuse to carry them? Someone should be appointed to oversee the literature circulated by Clubs and reading circles. Always have troops on hand, ready to march — cavalry

where possible, as cavalry disperses mobs more easily (*ibid.*, pp. 1050–1052).

[6] Sagnac, *Rhin fr.*, p. 58.

[7] This does not mean to imply that the peasant was not affected. A Dormagen (north of Cologne) news-chronicle editor, reporting on general conditions in his neighborhood at the start of 1792, wrote: "On every side, subjects are rising up against their lords. . . 'For years I was faithful,' observed the man, who, cut to the quick, leans upon his plow and complains to heaven about his hard lot. 'For years I was faithful, he said; 'I never hurt a fly, [and] paid my taxes loyally to the prince. And can I say that one of my good deeds has been rewarded?' Eventually despair enters his heart 'Why should I sweat any more? Do there not live in the cities wealthy people who fatten in indolence on our industry, who spend night and day thinking out how to throw away what we are obliged to give them? Let us burst our bonds and climb *ourselves*, into the lap of luxury.' " — J. P. Delhoven in *Die rheinische Dorfchronik* of Jan. 1, 1792, quoted in Hansen, *Quellen* II, 7–8.

[8] *Titre* VI (Legg, *Select Documents*, II, 242)

weak in the Rhineland, where the numerous petty states had long enjoyed a large measure of independence.[9]

It has been suggested that the fact that Custine was a Freemason may account in large measure for the success of his daring descent into Germany, for it is known that he received repeated invitations from the Freemasons of the western part of the Empire.[10] It is perhaps permissible to speculate whether these invitations were the result of the campaign described below. Mathiez found in the Archives Nationales a letter of one Captain Le Maire to an unnamed general, informing him that he, Le Maire, had ordered the translation "into good German" of a publication of a certain Parisian Masonic lodge; that Dietrich, Mayor of Strasburg, had ordered two thousand copies printed, with a little speech at the end for Freemasons abroad. "This work, especially in German, will do marvels in foreign lands. I have been very fortunate in getting all this quantity to a place of safety on the right bank of the Rhine, and I join here also a list of 44 episcopal cities of Germany and of the Austrian Netherlands where I will have them distributed directly to all the V^{bles} of the Ll ☐ [11] of each of these cities. I will even distribute some of them in the armies, which act will have there a most salutary effect." [12]

In this connection, it would be well to call attention to a story told by Dr. Christoph Girtanner. Girtanner is sometimes wrong and sometimes ironic (or sarcastic), but never deliberately misleading. A tale such as the following should therefore be borne in mind by research workers, so that it may be confirmed or laid honorably to rest. The setting is 1786 — the year following the dispersion of the Illuminati by the Bavarian government; the very year, incidentally, in which Cloots published his appeal for French expansion eastward.[13] In that year, there is supposed to have been founded a secret society — place not indicated, but certainly France — at whose head were Rochefoucauld, Condorcet, and Sieyes,[14] and which functioned under the

---

[9] J. Aulneau, *Le Rhin et la France* (5th ed.: Paris, 1921), p. 64. Hashagen says there were, however, several loyalties which bound the Rhinelanders to their old German institutions: (1) loyalty to their constitutions, princes or senates, and civil servants; (2) loyalty to the Emperor and to Austria; (3) loyalty to Prussia (even in the non-Prussian regions, owing largely to the impression made by Frederick the Great); (4) loyalty to the Church; (5) loyalty to the schools; and (6) loyalty to the German past (*Rheinland*, chap. i).

[10] H. M. Stephens, *A History of the French Revolution* (2 vols., New York, 1886–

1891), II, 193–194.

[11] Masonic lodges.

[12] "Les francs-maçons et la propagande révolutionnaire après Varennes," *AR*, VI (1913), 101–102.

[13] *Vide supra*, Introduction, n. 67.

[14] Or "Sieys." The *abbé* changed his signature to the latter form in 1790, but did not consistently maintain it. On May 24, 1791, and March 23, 1795, he signed "Siéyès." Never did he accent the second *e*. His numerous relatives in Provence used, and still use, the form "Sies," without accent, though pronounced "Siès." " 'Siéyès' is an absurdity," writes A. Mathiez; "it invites a false

descriptive name of "The Propaganda." The society's ramifications soon covered the entire earth, though its membership was limited to devotees of the prevalent philosophy, the politically dissatisfied, and the demented. Its object was to spread propaganda for world revolution, and its creed this: Want and belief are the mainsprings of all human endeavor. If want is made either to rise from belief or to govern belief, the political systems of the world will be shaken to their very foundations. The society had five thousand paying members and over fifty thousand nonpaying, and its treasury, in 1791, held some twenty or thirty million livres in coin.[15]

Intervening years have not betrayed the existence of such a society, and it is difficult to believe that some evidence would not have been found had there been substance in Girtanner's report. It should be realized, however, that, since a conspiracy is necessarily masked, we may not know exactly for what we are looking; and one cannot prove something does not exist until he has identified that something. In the words of a certain philosophy professor: "What is it that ain't?"

It has been the custom to depreciate the part played by secret societies in producing and spreading the great revolutionary movement with which we are dealing. However, Emperor Francis II (Leopold's son) was certain that the upheaval could be attributed in its entirety to ideas sowed by philoso-

pronunciation." — "L'orthographe du nom de Sieys," *AHRF*, II (1925), 487, 583. *Vide* also A. Troux, "L'orthographe du nom de Sieyes," *ibid.*, IX (1932), 66. Also, "Une lettre de Sieyes," *ibid.*, X (1933), 254. The proper pronunciation, according to a letter of Camille Desmoulins to his father, June 3, 1789, is — as to the last syllable — "ess." See-ess (H. Calvert, "Sieys ou Sieyes," *ibid.*, p. 538). It should be borne in mind, however, that, in the writings of the time, the spelling "Sièz" was not unknown — which would indicate a terminal *z* sound (E. Faguet, "La prononciation du nom propre 'Siéyès,' " *Revue Napoléonienne*, Ser. I, Vol. III [1902–3], 359, under "Notules napoléoniennes").

It is interesting to note that in 1777 — eight years before the dispersion of the Illuminati — Mirabeau is supposed to have drawn up a plan of conspiracy based on Freemasonry, where the rank and file of Freemasons would have no idea whither they were tending (C. Jannet, "Les francsmaçons pendant la Révolution," *RR* [*Revue de la Révolution*], I [1883], 273). It should not surprise to find a *grand seigneur* depicted in such a role. It is now the consensus

of scholarly opinion that the French Revolution began as a "predominantly aristocratic revolt against Louis XVI." — R. R. Palmer, "Recent Interpretations" of the Influence of the French Revolution," *J. World H.* (*Journal of World History*), II (1954), 182.
[15] Girtanner, *Histor. Nachrichten*, III, 469–474. Indeed, on November 16, 1793, there appeared on the streets of Strasburg "a number of French-speaking strangers, . . . fierce-looking men with bristling mustaches, wearing red caps and armed with sabres. . . . They called themselves the Propaganda, and . . . set about promoting advanced Revolutionary doctrine." — Palmer, *Twelve*, pp. 187–188.

According to Droz, Girtanner's information, in the text above, is of the same order as that in von Schirach's *Hamburger politisches Journal* of August, September, and October 1790 — which Droz calls "a legend of revolutionary Illuminism" expressly created by German reactionaries to combat the French Revolution by assimilating it to the outlawed Illuminati. Droz leads up to his conclusions in a very convincing chapter entitled "La lutte contre l'Illuminisme" (*Allemagne*, pp. 399 *et seqq*).

phers and Illuminati.[16] Baron von Duminique, Klemens Wenzeslaus' minister, cast his suspicions also upon the "new sect of the Obscurants," and tended to favor the reëstablishment of the Society of Jesus as an antidote.[17] The Imperial *Reichsgutachten* of June 14, 1793, ratified by Francis II in December, forbade secret societies in institutions of learning.[18] The Prince of Neuwied, deposed for alleged incompetence, blamed his ouster on the Illuminati, who, he alleged, were a great force in Neuwied.[19] Von Winckelmann, Cologne's representative to the Diet, wrote on July 16, 1793: "[For twelve years there have been suspicious societies, among them the Illuminati, in Mayence.] How otherwise did this perilous disturbance arise than through the Clubs? Whosoever thinks back ten or twelve years will find that this is the origin of the present fatal wartime. A pity that *Aufklärung*, freedom of the press, abasement of the clergy — Emperor Joseph II's specialties — should not have produced good fruit." [20] On the other hand, J. Venedey, on the basis of his father's notes,[21] deëmphasizes the role of the Illuminati, at least with respect to the Rhineland's almost spontaneous abasement before the expanding Revolution.

It may be true — and may not be — that secret societies, *as* societies, played little part in the spread of the Revolution to the Rhineland. It should give one pause, however, to consider that certain names (Dorsch, Mathias Metternich, Macké) which are about to appear very prominently in the present chapter (as belonging to members of "the Club" of Mayence) could be found on the rolls of the Illuminati between 1782 and 1785, and two others (Forster, Dr. Wedekind) on the register of the Freemasons.[22]

It is the consensus of scholarly opinion today that the Revolution was not a French revolution, but a world revolution — that France merely supplied the leaven to a dough about to rise for reasons of its own.[23] This view

[16] Brinton, *Decade of Rev.*, p. 178.
[17] To Max Franz (prince-elector of Cologne), Hansen, *Quellen*, II, 930.
[18] Hansen, *Quellen*, II, 863. The Emperor later forbade the frequenting of Freemasonic lodges "under whatever name, wherever they exist." — *Allerhöchstes Handbillet*, Vivenot-Zeissberg, *Quellen*, V, 233.
[19] Hansen, *Quellen*, II, 865.
[20] To the Cologne Senate, *ibid.*, p. 887, n. 3. But contra, *vide* the later testimony of M. Metternich, Hansen, *Quellen*, II, 163, n. 3. Re the above-mentioned "Clubs," see § 1b, this chapter.
[21] Michael Venedey was a young Colonais who, after receiving his Bachelor of Arts degree from the University of Cologne, studied law in Bonn but without completing the course. He joined the republican movement when the French occupied Cologne in 1794, became secretary to the cantonal administrator at Andernach, then *garde magasin*. Venedey worked indefatigably for the Cisrhenish-Republic movement and then for annexation of the Rhineland to France (Hansen, *Quellen*, III, 872, n. 3). Venedey's position, given in the text above, will be found in J. Venedey, *Die deutschen Republikaner unter der französischen Republik* (Leipzig, 1870), p. 92.
[22] Hansen, *Quellen*, II, 451, n. 2.
[23] R. R. Palmer, "Reflections on the French Revolution," *Political Science Quarterly*, LXVII (1952), 66 *et passim*. Says Professor Palmer, " . . . In the 1790's, . . . revolutionary aims and sympathies existed through-

may not be quite as modern as some undoubtedly believe it to be,[23a] but it would explain Custine's reception in the Rhineland without the need of bringing in clandestine organizations. What we are seeking, however, is not plausible explanations or rationalizations, but facts, and the pages of Hansen are too filled with references to Masonic connections to permit even a qualified denial of their importance with respect to the Rhineland.

Fear, or rather terror, on the part of the Germans was another element which favored the French advance. As Custine approached Mayence, the nobles and canons of the city determined to flee, and paid 400,000 livres — ten times the ordinary price — to have their furniture and jewelry and other prized possessions transported across the Rhine. Half that sum would have been sufficient to enable the city to defend itself! [24]

The capture of Mayence, the "Key of Germany" and "strongest fort in the world," [25] changed the prevailing fear into panic, particularly at Coblenz. Klemens Wenzeslaus fled from his château at Coblenz to Bonn, followed

---

out Europe. . . They arose everywhere out of local, genuine and specific causes. . . They were not imported from one country to the other. They were not imitated from the French, or at least not imitated blindly. There was one big revolutionary agitation, not simply a French Revolution due to purely French causes, and foolishly favored by giddy people in other countries." Dr. Palmer warns, however, that the emphasis upon local causes must not be carried so far that there is danger that the part of France in arousing Europe (and the world) will be underrated (in *J. World H.*, II, 173–174, 194).

[23a] It can be found in a little book published over a century ago by Cousin d'Avalon (Charles Yves Cousin), *Pradtiana, ou Recueil des pensées, réflexions et opinions politiques de M. l'abbé de Pradt, ex-grand-vicaire de l'archevèque de Rouen, ex-aumônier du dieu Mars, ex-archevèque de Malines, ex-ambassadeur dans le grand-duché de Varsovie* . . . (Paris, 1820), pp. 98–101. De Pradt was, of course, the famous political writer, former member of the States-General, and friend of De Mercy's. Avalon quotes De Pradt's *Petit Catéchisme, à l'usage des Français sur les affaires de leur pays* as follows:

"*Question*: Does France form part of the world?

Answer: That is incontestable.

Q.: Does it form part of Europe?

A.: That is likewise incontestable. . .

Q.: Properly to judge France, one must, then, take account of the state of the world and . . . of Europe?

A.: Just as one must, to evaluate the health of a man, take account of the state of the atmosphere in which he lives. . .

Q.: What is the general state of the world?

A.: A universal perturbation.

Q.: What is the state of Europe?

A.: Completely changed during the last thirty years. . .

Q.: Whence come these great changes?

A.: From three hundred years of innovation and from five principal causes: the 1st, printing, which has changed the course of ideas; 2nd, gunpowder . . . ; 3rd, commerce . . . ; 4th, the Americas, which centupled . . . wealth; and 5th, the Reformation. . .

Q.: Then the Revolution did not just happen, nor is it peculiar to France?

A.: It is the result of the state at which the world arrived in 1789. It could not have been avoided nor advanced nor deferred. The fruit had become ripe. . . "

[24] Sagnac, *Rhin fr.*, p. 68.

[25] Expression used by the Austrian negotiator Louis Cobenzl in the Campo-Formio negotiations, 1797 (*Correspondance de Napoléon Ier* [32 vols., Paris, 1858–1870], XXIX, 377).

by many nobles and ecclesiastics. "Everyone here was busy all night through, packing his effects," runs a contemporary diary. "All night long one could hear only boxes and trunks slamming shut, and wagons and carts rolling along the street." [26] But the common people could not flee, and they were sorely afraid of French vengeance because of Klemens Wenzeslaus' behavior toward France on the *émigré* question. The newspapers had brought news that the Convention had ordered Coblenz completely destroyed, burned to the ground.[27]

The Prince-Elector had left word that if no help was in the vicinity, the city should capitulate on the best terms possible.[28] There appeared to be no aid in sight. The only logical course — the only possible course — seemed to be to seek out Custine and explain to him personally that the people were in no way responsible for their court's policy. Custine had treated Mayence very fairly when it capitulated "on request." They hoped to secure like treatment for Coblenz if they went even further, and practically carried him the keys to the city.[29] Then they heard that it was Kellermann, not Custine, who was approaching. Fear arose that perhaps Kellermann carried with him an order to destroy the city, and that — unless someone got to Custine first so that the order might be countermanded — nothing could avert a disaster.[30]

The estates' syndic, P. E. von Lassaulx, thereupon led a deputation to see Custine in Mayence, but before it left, the chancellor, Hügel, had learned that Prussian troops were arriving. Hügel averred later that he tried to convince von Lassaulx that Kellermann would not be so quick to destroy, but Hügel does not seem to have divulged that help was arriving.[31] What prompted Hügel's silence is of no import here. The fact remains that von Lassaulx did proceed to Mayence. And with him went a seventeen-year-old youth, later married to von Lassaulx's niece.

In point of fact, the presence of this youth may easily be regarded as the most important element in the visit of this deputation.[32] The young man had just entered his last year at the Bonn Gymnasium, where he was absorbing the ideas of the *Aufklärung* with lasting and profound effect. While in Mayence, he visited "the Club" (mentioned above and fully considered shortly) at least once, probably repeatedly, and eagerly quaffed the ideas of

---

[26] Count Boos's *Tagebuch*, Hansen, *Quellen*, II, 464, n. 2.

[27] Hansen, *Quellen*, II, 487, n. 4. Custine himself said the Coblenz operation might be "bloody" if the Coblenzers did not surrender their fortress, "Ermannstein" (Ehrenbreitstein), without a struggle (*ibid.*, p. 501).

[28] *Ibid.*, p. 464, n. 2.

[29] Report of P. E. von Lassaulx (Coblenz syndic), Oct. 25, 1792: *vide* "Exposé," § 36, *ibid.*, p. 499.

[30] Hansen, *Quellen*, p. 485.

[31] *Ibid.*, pp. 486–487.

[32] Unless one considers the execution of General Custine for reasons partly connected with this visit. *Vide infra*, n. 248, this chapter.

other young men there. How he had got into the city is unimportant; there is some evidence that it was by posing as the servant of the deputation. The fact is, he was there, and that alone was destined to have a profound effect on France's relations with the Rhineland. For the young man was Joseph Görres, and he never ceased to nurture the seeds of "liberty" implanted then — seeds fertilized by the subsequent persecution, proscution, and imprisonment, of von Lassaulx for what Klemens Wenzeslaus and von Duminique chose to interpret as treason,[33] but which was probably nothing more than bourgeois panic.[34]

That such fears should assail ordinary citizens is not beyond understanding. But how account for Governor von Gymnich's surrender of the city and fortress of Mayence without serious effort at defense? True, there was not an oversupply of provisions in the city, the garrison was a heterogeneous lot, help was far away, insuccess would have meant a pillaged city, and even a successful defense would have entailed hardship and some destruction; [35] but war is war. When Custine first summoned von Gymnich to surrender, the latter hesitated,[36] and then asked for forty-eight hours to think it over. Meanwhile a few shots were exchanged with the French, mostly for the sake of appearances, it seems. Finally, von Gymnich yielded, and admitted the French.[37] It is interesting to note that the sole member of von Gymnich's council of war who maintained that the fortress could hold off the French — viz., the engineer Rudolf Eickemeyer [38] — requested French citizenship, and offered his services to France, within forty-eight hours after the city fell (or, rather, prostrated itself). This unseemly haste to exchange flags has drawn upon Eickemeyer widespread suspicion of treason, especially as it was he who negotiated the capitulation for the Governor. One of the engineer's apologists, the historian Arthur Chuquet, finds no treason in his conduct, but only indiscretion. He suggests that personal motives probably determined Eickemeyer's actions. The engineer was living with a married woman who had borne him several children, and whom he could not marry so long as the Electoral government subsisted in Mayence.[39]

But treason is none the less treason because prompted by love of woman. And what are we to understand by General Custine's statement on August

---

[33] Hansen, *Quellen*, II, 508–510.

[34] Lassaulx held a long list of offices under France during subsequent years. They are listed *ibid.*, III, 1023, n. 3.

We have come upon Görres once already (*supra*, chap. i, § 2 m), but it will be many chapters before he appears again (Pt. II, chap. xxvii, § 1h *et seqq*).

[35] Custine had threatened to set the city afire with fireballs, and to level it by bombard-

ment (Hansen, *Quellen*, II, 452).

[36] Custine had only 1500 men with him, but he had disposed them cleverly to look like 30,000 (*ibid.*, p. 451).

[37] Chuquet, *Guerres Rév.*, VI, 92–95.

[38] *Vide* G. Six, *Dictionnaire biographique des généraux et amiraux de la Révolution et de l'Empire* (2 vols., Paris, 1934), *s.v.* "Eickemeyer."

[39] Chuquet, *Guerres Rév.*, VI, 95, 103 *et seqq*.

29, 1793 that "I captured Mayence by breaking down open doors, it is true — but with money I had strewn about for that purpose"? [40] With respect to Governor von Gymnich, we may probably say with the old proverb, *Qui s'excuse s'accuse*, for the Governor followed his own craven surrender with a valiant attempt to prove that he could not have done otherwise. According to Venedey, von Gymnich's book only shows that with 3200 citizens aiding his 2800 soldiers, he could have held off the French until help arrived from Germany; [41] but it would be only fair to add that the Prussian Baron von Stein, who was in the city at the time, raised doubts as to the temper of the Mayence *bourgeoisie*, [42] many of whom were donning tri-color cockades. [43]

The terms of the Capitulation of Mayence were honorable, in so far as honor can be said to exist under such circumstances. The troops in the fortress were permitted to go freely wherever they should desire, but were not to serve against France for one year. The inhabitants were guaranteed the possession of their property. The clergy and members of the former government were to be allowed to withdraw with their effects, and were promised the necessary passports. [44]

These terms were so fair, and the promises of the French so enchanting, that hope beat high in the Rhineland's breast. The dawn of a new era, free from oppression, was at hand. Before entering Mayence, Custine had lectured his troops to respect the persons and property of the proletariat, for the masses were their friends, he said. The soldiers should reserve their wrath for the tyrants and tyrants' satellites, for it was they who had oppressed the people, whom the French desired to defend. After the capture of Mayence, Custine proclaimed that the French were angry only with the princes, including the ecclesiastical princes, "who, in the name of God, ravage the earth and enslave the tillers of the soil." [45]

However, these fine phrases soon proved to be but empty bubbles. The

---

[40] *Moniteur*, XVII, 507.

[41] *Deut. Rep.*, p. 92. He had 13,000 troops (Hansen, *Quellen*, II, 450).

[42] Chuquet, *Guerres Rév.*, VI, 94.

[43] Mathiez, *Fr. Rev.*, 276. Hansen believes Wedekind lured Custine to Mayence by representing that the people of Mayence were predisposed in his favor (*Quellen*, II, 450). It is true that the Mayençais were opposed to the pro-*émigré* policy of their prince (*ibid.*, p. 270), but is that the same as being pro-Custine?

[44] Arch. N., F1E 40, d. 1. According to Custine's aide-de-camp, the Capitulation was almost immediately violated by the French military at the instigation of the partisans of the French. Those who wished to leave the city were arrested and searched for coin and objects of gold and silver, and were fortunate to get away with their other possessions. Later, jewels were taken also; and still later, everything except what was graciously accorded them (*Mémoires posthumes du Général François Comte de Custine, rédigés par un de ses aides de camp* [2 pts., i.e., 2 vols. in 1, Hamburg and Frankfort, 1794], I, 84).

[45] Sagnac, *Rhin fr.*, pp. 67, 71-72.

wages of the French army were far in arrears, and the French believed that the Rhinelanders, who had been taxed very heavily by their princes during the year 1791, would not object to paying sums of like enormity to France — for had not the French brought them those priceless possessions "liberty" and "equality"?[46] A contribution of 300,000 livres was therefore imposed on Spires, ostensibly as penalty for having "allowed" the Austrians to violate its neutrality without protest;[47] 600,000 livres was demanded of Worms for having granted hospitality to the *émigrés*;[48] the nobles and clergy of Mayence were taxed 500,000 livres,[49] but no justification was needed for that; and Frankfort was assessed 2,000,000 livres[50] for having "drained off" France's coin by lending money to the *émigré* princes at usurious rates, and for having "tolerated" the manufacture of false assignats.[51] Frankfort's share was later reduced to 1,500,000 livres, and persons with property worth less than 30,000 florins were exempted from contributing thereto. This lifted the burden entirely from the shoulders of the workers and lower *bourgeoisie*.[52]

The speeches made in Frankfort, and in regard to Frankfort, on the occasion of the city's protest against the above-mentioned contributions are a necessary introduction to the policy of France toward the free cities of the Empire. "I have come to Germany," Custine declared, "to offer the people the alliance of the French Republic, and to show the oppressed that liberated Frenchmen have only one wish — to protect the weak, and to convince the iniquitous administrators of wealth that men, equal in rights from their birth, do not have to wear the yoke of the rich."[53] To show his good will, Custine informed the regency of Frankfort that he would willingly agree to the neutralization of the city if Prussia should consent[54] — but that did

[46] *Ibid.*, pp. 83–84.
[47] Gay de Vernon, *Opér. mil.*, p. 58.
[48] Hansen, *Quellen*, II, 42 *. According to Gay de Vernon, *Opér. mil.*, p. 60, Custine exacted 1,400,000 livres from Worms — 220,000 from the bourgeoisie, and 1,180,000 from the magistrates, bishops, abbeys, and noble chapters. The *Kölner Welt- und Staatsboth* gives a total of 1,200,000 livres: 400,000 from the bishop, 600,000 from the city, and 200,000 from the priesthood (Oct. 7–8, Hansen, *Quellen*, II, 382). Of the 600,000 exacted of the city, half was forgiven through the intercession of Custine's German secretary-interpreter, Böhmer. And Custine declared the remaining 300,000 might be paid by the magistrates and not by individuals, for he was warring on palaces, not on cottages (*ibid.*, p. 439, n. 2).

[49] *Kölner Welt- und Staatsboth*, Oct. 25, 1792, *ibid.*, p. 464.
[50] Venedey, *Deut. Rep.*, p. 110.
[51] Report of Lassaulx, Oct. 25, 1792, Hansen, *Quellen*, II, 498. Exacted also as pretended retaliation against three merchants who had supplied some of the *émigrés* with war materiel (*Aachener Zuschauer*, Oct. 27, 1792, *ibid.*, p. 471).
[52] Venedey, *Deut. Rep.*, p. 110; Gay de Vernon, *Opér. mil.*, p. 71. The general statement boldly ventured by Dunn-Pattison, in *C. Mod. H.*, VIII, 414, that General "Custine's heavy exactions . . . had the one merit that they fell on rich and poor alike" must be qualified. *Vide* also Mathiez, *Fr. Rev.*, p. 282.
[53] Venedey, *Deut. Rep.*, pp. 110–111.
[54] Gay de Vernon, *Opér. mil.*, p. 85.

not accord with the plans germinating at Paris. "Frankfort is truly a free state," declared Roland, French Minister of the Interior, to Lebrun, Minister of Foreign Affairs, "but its location, its political connections, and its weakness render it a subject state"; and he recommended the conquest of the hearts of the Frankforters through love, virtue, and the nobility of the French principles.[55]

Whether or no Roland's plan succeeded can best be judged by looking ahead a few months — to December 2, 1792, when Frankfort was retaken by the Germans (Prussians). The French governor of Frankfort had "neglected to take precautions against the inhabitants,"[56] who, "by veritable treason,"[57] seized the gates of the city, delivered them to the Hessians, and massacred part of the French garrison. The Provisional Executive Council was naturally incensed, and suggested to the Convention that it hold as hostages two Frankforters who had come to Paris to request a reduction in the amount of Custine's contributions — the men to be held until Frankfort had paid the entire sum imposed by Custine, or such punitive damages as the Convention might decide upon.[58]

b. Custine Tries to Convert Mayence

Mayence was the most important left-bank city captured by Custine — important both for size and defensive potentialities. It was therefore to be expected that this city should have for Custine a special interest. The Convention had given him no instructions as to administration, so he was free to do as he chose. But his acts represent, nonetheless, the German policy of France as of that date.

It was with great interest that everyone in Mayence awaited Custine's first announcement of policy. It came on October 23, in the form of a proclamation in the French tongue, but translated into German two days later by Böhmer, the General's secretary-interpreter. This proclamation of Custine's, divorced of the usual pretty phrases, contained the following points, all aimed at ingratiating himself with the people and leading them to believe that their fortune lay in union with France. The existing authorities would be maintained until the people had had an opportunity to express their free choice. The customary taxes would remain, but all contributions levied by the French would be directed only against those classes who heretofore had been exempt (nobles, clergy, the Electoral government). France held no grudge against people born with the yoke of despotism about their necks; rather did it offer them fraternity and liberty. (If they accepted liberty, they

[55] Venedey, *Deut. Rep.*, pp. 111–112.
[56] Min. of war to pres. of Conv., Dec. 9, 1792, *Moniteur*, XIV, 699.
[57] Minutes of Dec. 8, 1792 session of PEC (Provisional Executive Council), Aulard, *Actes*, I, 302; Hansen, *Quellen*, II, 621–622.
[58] Aulard, *Actes*, I, 302–303.

would not have to live thenceforth in fear because of the treason [ugly word] committed.) "I will place this city in a most impregnable state, and, despite rumor, I have no intention of abandoning it. I swear to defend it even against all the efforts of our united enemies. The choice is yours. If you prefer slavery to the benefits offered you, I shall leave it to treaties to determine which despot shall restore your fetters." [59]

Convincing speech. It was believed! And Daniel Dumont, president of the merchants, was selected by both merchants' and artisans' guilds to draft a new constitution. Dumont was particularly qualified therefor: originally intended for the ministry, he had received a good education, and was versed in the writings of Montesquieu, Voltaire, and Rousseau.[60] He made so bold as to write to Custine that it seemed to him France's monarchical Constitution of 1791 was the best model for Mayence to follow, considering the city's external relations (i.e., connection with the Empire); the phlegmatic disposition of Germans; the possessions, rights, and privileges of the Mayençais; and their origin. While asking Custine's suggestions, he gave his own: (1) a committee of representatives of the Mayençais "nation," elected by the citizenry and the highborn, to be the receptacle of sovereignty, and to counterbalance the sovereign; (2) the most important offices to be elective, and no non-Mayençais to be permitted to serve in any capacity; (3) a biennially chosen corps of representatives; (4) equal taxes for all citizens, with repeal of the immunity from taxation of nobles and clergy; and (5) confirmation of the Mayençais constitution in the future peace treaty.[61] Many of the guild members would have included also a provision for deposing and pensioning hateful (*gehässig*) princes; [62] but they wanted their princes.

Thirteen of the ninety-seven members of the merchants' guild were in favor of the French republican form of government,[63] so Custine did not have to wait for Dumont's draft to learn he was getting nowhere. On November 4, he announced that "only the representatives of the Frankish nation can determine the rights of those countries which were united to France by the might of her armies and the aid of the citizens." [64] But he did

[59] Oct. 23, 1792, Hansen, *Quellen*, II, 468–469. The German version of this proclamation, dated October 25, contained one new element: "I will maintain all constitutional authorities until the citizens, cottagers and farmers in the cities and villages of the Archbishopric of Mayence, the Bishoprics of Worms and Spires, and in all remaining regions of Germany in which the French flag shall be planted — until, I say, each one of these German peoples has had an opportunity to make its will known." This

is self-determination for the smallest political subdivisions — a concept guaranteed to create confusion (*ibid.*, pp. 510, 511 and n. 2). The principle was carried even further in the Convention's decree of March 14, 1793, *infra*, n. 112, this chapter.
[60] Hansen, *Quellen*, II, 569, n. 1.
[61] Nov. 8, 1792, *ibid.*, pp. 571–572.
[62] Schlik to Imperial Vice-Chancellor Prince von Colloredo, Nov. 2, 1792, *ibid.*, p. 557.
[63] Hansen, *Quellen*, II, 573.
[64] Venedey, *Deut. Rep.*, p. 103.

not give up, at this early date, the hope of converting at least some of the benighted.[65]

Technically, the machinery of conversion was already in existence at Mayence — the "Club" mentioned as having been visited by young Görres, the "Club" whose members were in part Illuminati and Freemasons. Custine, at Böhmer's instigation, had founded this "Society of [German] Friends of the French Constitution" already on October 23. It met in the large festive Academy Hall of the Elector's palace, and was open free of charge to every German who had tired of his chains. But — to be admitted — one had to join, and take an oath to live free or die.[66]

Only twenty members were present at the first meeting. They wrote to the Strasburg Society of Friends of the Constitution of their resolve to live free or die, and asked for a copy of the Strasburg society's rules of procedure. Now, most of the Jacobin societies corresponded, one with the other, and probably all with Paris. On November 4, the *Moniteur*, in reporting on the session of November 3 of the Paris Jacobins, wrote: "A letter from the Friends of Liberty and Equality of Strasburg says that the Mayençais ask to be united with France. . . "[67] Events were moving fast — at least in the minds of some. It is to be noted that the *Moniteur* of November 2 was awake to the potentialities of the situation. It gave space to a letter from Mayence containing the sentence, "The Republic will feel how important it is to recognize brothers in a city which, by its position, is the key of the Empire and the channel of subsistence and of commerce."[68]

Custine founded propaganda clubs in all the three left-bank cities he had conquered — Mayence, Worms (established November 12), and Spires (established November 13).[69] That at Mayence was the most important, probably because most effort was expended upon Mayence owing to its overwhelming strategic importance. When, in the present chapter, "the Club" is spoken of without qualification, the Mayence Club is intended.

The Club numbered several noted men among its members. Georg For-

---

[65] Gooch, *Germ. Fr. Rev.*, p. 477.

[66] Hansen, *Quellen*, II, 469–470. Custine addressed the opening session. He declared that "all people form but a single family, bound together by the eternal principles of reason and virtue." France was making war, it was true, but only in order that there should be no more wars. Besides, German princes were themselves the cause. Deceived by the *émigrés*, "they thought the conquest of France would be child's play." They knew better now. If they should ever dare to attack Mayence, "we would give you an example of the ad-vantage free men enjoy over slaves." And he promised all possible protection and encouragement to the project formed by the Club of instructing the citizens of Mayence in liberty and equality. "Shame eternal to all those who prefer the sinister clanking of their chains to the sweet sounds of the voice of liberty." — *Mém. Custine.* I, 189.

[67] Hansen, *Quellen*, II, 469, nn. 1, 2; p. 470, n. 1.

[68] *Ibid.*, p. 479, n. 1.

[69] *Ibid.*, p. 531, n. 2. Böhmer and Dorsch were the actual instruments in Worms and Spires.

ster has already been mentioned.[70] Born in Poland before the First Partition, of German parents of Scotch lineage, taken to England at the age of twelve, and later to sea on a three-year tour around the world with Captain Cook, Forster became, at the ripe age of twenty-five, Professor of Natural History in the Caroline College of Cassel, and at thirty, professor in the University of Vilna. This last position he found not at all to his liking, but he could not leave because he had inherited from his father an absolute incapacity to remain solvent. Then, suddenly, the unexpected happened. Catherine II of Russia, desiring to arrange a world tour with Forster as scientific guide, paid his debts. Shortly thereafter, war broke out with the Turks, so the trip could not be made. Forster, a free man, returned to Germany — to accumulate some more debts at Mayence, where he became Librarian to the University.[71]

When the French Revolution burst forth, many of the professors of the University of Mayence were converted to the new principles, and joined — come 1792 — Custine's propaganda club. The membership of Forster was much desired by the French and the Mayence "patriots," for the learned librarian was the most distinguished of all the Elector's subjects. Forster hesitated several days before joining the "patriots," and there has been much speculation as to what motives finally decided him. His friend Wilhelm von Humboldt ascribed his act to his usual need of money; his apologist Zincke, to the infidelity of his wife, a daughter of the classical scholar Heyne; others, to the example of his friends, his scorn for the old regime,[72] and his desire to play a role in the world. Whatever the deciding factor, Forster's adherence lent some degree of respectability to the new movement, owing to his profound erudition, and the inimitable clarity and lofty inspiration of his writings.[73] But what would his admirers have said had they known that the Prussian minister Hertzberg had offered the needy librarian money to remain "a good Prussian," and that Forster had accepted it though he was at the time neck-deep in a propaganda campaign in favor of France? "Necessity commands, and my scruples vanish," said he, and that was that. Of course, it could be argued that Forster was a man without a country, inasmuch as Prussia had annexed his birthplace after the Forsters had moved to England. Be that as it may, all Germany was profoundly shocked by his actions, and his own father publicly recommended that he be hanged.[74]

[70] *Supra*, Introduction, § 2h.

[71] A. Chuquet, "Le révolutionnaire George Forster," *Etudes d'histoire* (8 vols., Paris, n.d.), I, 149–155.

[72] And yet he had written to his father-in-law only a few months before: "The Kaiser looks so young, benign, and ingenuous that,

to see him . . . brought tears involuntarily to my eyes and those of others." — Hashagen, *Rheinland*, p. 89, n. 1.

[73] Gooch, *Germ. Fr. Rev.*, pp. 309–310, 314–315.

[74] *Ibid.*, p. 310. In a letter to a Berlin book-dealer, on November 10, Forster sought to

Georg Wilhelm Böhmer, also mentioned above, was a son of the famous Göttingen Professor Böhmer, and himself a professor in the Lutheran Gymnasium at Worms before the Revolution. Having become the object of much ill will because of the trend of a theological review he was publishing, the younger Böhmer transferred his allegiance to France, seeking thus to vent his spleen on his countrymen. His countrymen, however, may have thought it was France's loss and not their own, for, according to Böhmer's sister-in-law, the young professor was a "fool." But fool or no, he proved a useful tool to Custine. Most of the General's proclamations to the Rhineland were translated into German by Böhmer.[75]

Andreas Joseph Hofmann possessed many of the traits of Mirabeau. Corpulent, deep-voiced, rudely frank, brusque, popular, bold, and perspicacious, this Professor of History and Natural Law at the University of Mayence was the idol of his students and of the crowds. A Jacobin at heart,[76] one of his first revolutionary acts was to reveal to Custine the existence of a large store of fodder, which he himself then proceeded to seize for the French at the head of a troop of cavalry.[77]

Georg Christian Wedekind was born in Göttingen, in the Lower Saxon Circle. Son of a Professor of Philosophy and doctor,[78] young Wedekind was himself, in 1792, personal physician to the Elector, and Professor of Medicine at the University of Mayence. On the eve of the siege, he pretended that he had to treat a peasant outside the city, and slipped away, thus leaving the metropolis with one less physician in its hour of need, but insuring the safety of Georg Wedekind.[79] The doughty doctor returned in Custine's baggage with a salary of 500 francs per month.[80] Wedekind was an opportunist, and will always be remembered for his defense of the guillotine. Sömmerring, his old colleague at the University, had written a newspaper

---

justify his conduct: " . . . We live in a rare time when one can hardly judge people aright if one goes only by external circumstances, where the yardsticks with which we used to measure each other must . . . well-nigh be broken, and only the one, that of humanity alone, remains." — *Briefe . . . Rev.*, II, 242.

[75] Chuquet, *Guerres Rév.*, VII, 7. According to Venedey, Böhmer later received a gift of 6,000 francs from France for his services in Mayence (*Deut. Rep.*, p. 106).

[76] "There will come a time," he told his students, "when one will speak publicly and loud of the inherent rights of humanity." — Hansen, *Quellen*, I, 1038, n. 1.

[77] Chuquet, *Guerres Rév.*, VII (*Mayence*), 22–23.

[78] "Declaration" of Wedekind to the Commission of Health, A. R, Aug. 7, 1794, *AHRF*, N. S., I (1924), 450.

[79] This may be unkind and unjust. Wedekind went to Worms, where he met with Böhmer. Hansen says it is "certain" that Wedekind's remarks to Böhmer — probably about the disposition of the Mayençais — brought Custine to Mayence. The Doctor was in Worms on October 18; Custine arrived on the nineteenth (*Quellen*, II, 450). So maybe Wedekind was not looking out for his safety after all, but merely for the unsafety of his fellow Mayençais.

[80] Chuquet, *Guerres Rév.*, VII, 20.

article averring that consciousness continued in the severed head of a guillotined person until sensibility and susceptibility to external stimuli had
ceased; that inasmuch as a severed head often suffered convulsions, which
convulsions could be renewed by irritating the part of the spine remaining
attached to the head, consciousness did not leave the head for quite a prolonged period after execution. This doctrine would have been very unwelcome to the revolutionists, so Wedekind defended death by the guillotine
as the "sweetest known," and accused Sömmerring of "trying to further himself by making a great sensation among the public." [81]

Anton Joseph Dorsch was not a member of the Club at first, but owing
to his later importance, he is included here. Dorsch had been Professor of
Logic and Metaphysics at Mayence until 1791, when he was ousted for
preaching Kant too successfully. His next position was with the Catholic
Academy of Strasburg, as Professor of Morals. But he soon threw off his
holy orders, married, and became an active member of Strasburg's Society of
Friends of the Constitution. Returning to Mayence not long after its capitulation, he allied himself with Custine, sharing the General's favor with
Böhmer. Dorsch was possessed of winning ways, but was crafty and exces-
sively proud — proud not only of his intellectual attainments, but of his
well-molded feet.[82]

The two remaining leading lights of the Club were neither so important
nor so colorful. Mat(t)hias Metternich, before the Revolution, was Professor
of Physics and Mathematics in the University of Mayence; Felix Anton
Blau was Professor of Dogmatic Theology and Under-Regent of the Mayence Seminary.[83] These seven men were the soul of the Club, the spark that
gave it life. Their influence upon Franco-German relations was considerable.

In proportion to the later total membership of the Club (400–450), there
were only a few natives of Mayence. Most of the members were French,
German exiles, or newcomers — all under the immediate control of Custine
and the government at Paris. For the sake of the French members, the
language of the Club was soon changed from German to French *exclusively*,
according to Venedey.[84]

The activities of the Club were very varied. Speeches were made; trees
of liberty were planted; [85] a "Book of Life" bound in red morocco with a

[81] "Sur le supplice de la guillotine; par
Georges Wedekind," *Moniteur*, XXVI, 395–
396.
[82] Gooch, *Germ. Fr. Rev.*, pp. 477–478;
Chuquet, *Guerres Rév.*, VII, 21.
[83] *Ibid.*, pp. 10, n. 7; 20.
[84] *Deut. Rep.*, p. 106.
[85] Sagnac, *Rhin fr.*, p. 86. Trees of liberty
were planted in Worms and Spires also,

and in the following other cities and towns
in the neighborhood: Nackenheim, Wei-
senau, Hallgarten, Oestrich, Niederolm, and
Kleinwinterheim. It required the wishes of
only three inhabitants to secure the planting
of a tree; the French military "took care"
of the rest of the community (Hansen,
Quellen, II, 531, n. 2).

cap of liberty on the cover and tricolor ornamentation along the edge, and a "Book of Slavery" bound in black and surrounded by chains, were opened for signatures; [86] the symbols of feudalism were burned; [87] the iron-sheathed stone standard of measures — which local tradition said the sun would melt when Mayence had regained its ancient liberties — was cleft with a hammer, and the iron sheathing melted into a plaque reading, "The sun of liberty hath melted it"; [88] Pape's German translation of the Constitution of 1791 and Cotta's *Wie gut es jetzt das Volk am Rhein und an der Mosel haben könnte* ("How Fine It Now Could Be for the People along the Rhine and Moselle") were widely circulated; [89] and addresses were sent to the Paris Convention testifying the love of the Mayençais for freedom and France. "Our club is doing famously," Custine wrote to Paris, "but we require men for Frankfort, Worms, and Spires. The Mayençais also require waking up." [90]

The Convention responded to the General's appeal by sending four expert propagandists to Mayence: Dorsch (mentioned above as one of the notables of the Club), Cotta, Pape, and André Meyer. Dorsch, it will be recalled, on arriving in Mayence, formed a species of triumvirate with General Custine and Böhmer. He set up his quarters in the Elector's palace and constituted himself head of the local administration. Cotta, son and brother of the Stuttgart publishers of the same name, had been Professor of Natural and Public Law in the Karlsschule at Stuttgart until 1791, and had then gone to Strasburg. Pape, a Westphalian Benedictine monk, had been Professor of Ecclesiastical Law at Bonn, then Director of the Seminary at Colmar. On arriving in Mayence, he threw off his holy orders, and scathingly denounced the clergy. Pape tried to curry favor with the high-ranking revolutionists at Paris by a rather childish stroke: He composed an "Open Letter to Friedrich Wilhelm Hohenzollern," informing him that soon a meeting of the friends of liberty and equality would be held in the royal palace at Berlin; the letter was signed, "Thine and all kings' enemy, the Republican Pape." André Meyer was a Strasburger, coeditor of the newspaper *Geschichte der gegenwärtigen Zeit,* and secretary of the Jacobin Club of Strasburg. His reputation as a superpropagandist seems to have been considerably enhanced by his showmanship in shattering the Imperial coat of

---

[86] Chuquet, *Guerres Rév.,* VII, 35. A few Mayençais (about 1,000) inscribed their names in the Book of Life, none in the Book of Slavery, and most in neither (Sagnac, *Rhin fr.,* p. 86).

[87] *Ibid.*

[88] Chuquet, *Guerres Rév.,* VII, 34–35.

[89] Venedey, *Deut. Rep.,* pp. 106–107. Hansen gives this title as *Wie gut es die Leute am Rhein und an der Mosel jetzt haben können,* Mayence, 1792. The book declares that union with France would relieve people of the following burdens: serfdom, weregeld, poll taxes, villeinage, tithes, damage caused by game, etc. (Hansen, *Quellen,* II, 531, n. 2.)

[90] Gooch, *Germ. Fr. Rev.,* p. 477.

arms on the post office at Alzey during a French retreat. The most puerile act could make or break a man in those turbulent days.[91]

The Mayence Club, in a letter to the Jacobin Club of Paris, itself set forth the reasons why the Revolution was not popular in Mayence: "(1) difference of race and language; (2) ignorance, and actual weakening of the intelligence through long oppression; (3) superstition; (4) slothfulness and inertia; (5) lack of courage; fearfulness; debilitation of the townspeople under an effeminate, luxury-loving priestly government; (6) distrust of innovation; (7) the burdens of war, which could not readily be borne by the tiller of the soil, and which were actual burdens when the theater of war was so close; (8) complete absence of an enlightened, well-to-do, and effective middle class; (9) the appalling indebtedness of all the emigrant priests and nobles, whose possessions were in large part beyond the city's confines;" and the fact that almost all the public officials depended on Mayence for maintenance, though the city formed but a tenth part of the Mayence state — these "caused, especially in the city, a general exhaustion, penury, and destitution, which were perpetuated by the luxury and fancies of its lords." [92]

But whether the Revolution was popular with the Mayençais or not, the Clubists and the generals were certain that the Rhineland should be annexed by France, and in this they were in accord with the minister of foreign affairs, Lebrun.[93] The Diplomatic Committee of the Convention did not express itself until February, but its opinion then, given by Carnot (the future "Organizer of Victory," and still later, Director), was in consonance therewith.

" . . . The ancient and natural boundaries of France," said Carnot, "are the Rhine, the Alps, and the Pyrenees. The parts thereof which have been dismembered have reached their present status only by usurpation; there would be, then, according to the usual rules, no injustice in resuming possession of them. It would not be ambition to recognize as brothers those who formerly were such. . . But these diplomatic claims, founded upon ancient possession, are as nothing in our eyes compared to those of reason. The immutable right of each state is to live isolated if that pleases it, or to unite with others, if they so wish, for the common interest. We Frenchmen recognize no sovereign but the people themselves; our system is not one of domination at all, but of fraternity. . . " Earlier in his report, Carnot had said: "No annexation, augmentation, diminution, or mutation of territory whatsoever may take place from one end of the Republic to the other unless it can be recognized (1) that this mutation is in no wise contrary to the interest of the state; (2) that the communes . . . concerned have asked for it by

---

[91] *Ibid.*, pp. 477–478; Chuquet, *Guerres Rév.*, VII, 18–19.

[92] Dec. 12, 1792, Hansen, *Quellen*, II, 639.

[93] *Ibid.*, pp. 541–542.

free and formal wish, or that the general safety of the Republic renders it indispensable." [94]

However, everyone in the Convention did not agree with Carnot and the Diplomatic Committee. There were still adherents of Vergennes' policy who preferred that the conquered territories should be transformed into buffer states.[95] The Club itself recognized this double possibility when it wrote to the Convention querying whether that body intended to form the Mayence area into a *département* or into a separate republic.[96] But once Georg Forster got the reins of the Club into his hands, there was no asking of questions. He set himself the task of convincing the world that Mayence and France belonged together.

Forster's speech of November 15 before the Club is one of his most celebrated. Since he believed that the purpose of the state was the moral advancement of the citizen, and that moral advancement was possible only where there was true intellectual freedom,[97] he did not hesitate to point to France as the source of hope for any man, whatever his national origin. However, in his speech, he first mentioned France's frightful devastation of the Palatinate in 1688 (1689) because he knew everyone would be thinking of it; but he insisted that liberty had regenerated the French people. "See, they give us the most touching proof of brotherly love by their willingness to share their so dearly bought liberty with us. . . Thus can liberty work in the heart of Man. . . What were we three weeks ago? . . . Oppressed, maltreated, taciturn slaves of a priest. . . [And now?] free citizens. . . Fellow citizens, brothers, the strength that could change us so can also smelt French and Mayençais into one people. Our languages are different; must our concepts therefore be? . . . Since when has a difference in language rendered it impossible to obey the same laws? Do not Russia's despots rule over a hundred peoples of differing tongues? . . . To me, the freest constitution seems the best. . . We cannot be responsible before God and the world if we reject the opportunity to acquire a constitution. . .

"The Rhine, a great navigable river, is the natural boundary of a great free state which seeks no conquests, but only takes unto itself the nations which voluntarily join themselves to it. [This great free state] is entitled to a just indemnity for the war so wantonly provoked by its enemies. Justice and reason demand that the Rhine remain the boundary of France. . . " [98]

---

[94] Feb. 14, 1793, E. Charavay (ed.), *Correspondance générale de Carnot* (4 vols., Paris, 1892–1907), I, 369–370.

[95] Hansen, *Quellen*, II, 541.

[96] Imperial Ambassador Count von Westphalen to Imperial Vice-Chancellor Prince von Coloredo, Oct. 31, 1792, *ibid.*, p. 550.

[97] Hansen, *Quellen*, II, 534.

[98] *Ibid.*, pp. 584–586. Forster seems somehow to have believed that if Germany were ever to have a constitution, it would necessarily be a foreign importation. On December 21, 1792, he wrote to a bookdealer in Berlin: "Our crude, poor, unlettered people can

The die was cast. From that moment forth, the Club was eloquent and vociferous in its annexationist propaganda. And the voice heard the loudest was that of Forster, who seemed really to believe he was working for a better world. Yet, let it be recorded that, only shortly before (October 25), he had favored a federation of left-bank republics.[99] What caused the change of sentiment, the present author does not know. He only hopes that necessity was not commanding again.

2. THE CONVENTION'S DECREES OF
NOVEMBER 19, AND OF DECEMBER 15 AND 17, 1792

The general plan of campaign of the Provisional Executive Council for late 1792 was as follows: Dumouriez was to conquer Belgium; Kellermann was to thrust past Trèves to Cologne; Custine was to advance from Mayence; and the two latter generals, between them, were to conquer all the German left bank.[100] We have noted the movements of Kellermann and Custine. Now as to those of Dumouriez.

On November 6, 1792, Dumouriez' army, by sheer weight of numbers, and by virtue of the enthusiasm born of the new freedom,[101] defeated the Austrians at Jemappes, and followed them (not drove them) out of Belgium.[102] The "pursuit" occupied only a month, and carried the French until the Roër River. Dumouriez realized that a further advance of ten leagues would compel the Austrian general Clerfayt to flee across the Rhine, but the French army refused to continue the pursuit. A law of December 28, 1791, had authorized volunteers to return home after each campaign, and the troops were deserting en masse. The army of Belgium shrank within a brief period from 100,000 to 45,000 men.[103] This situation was intolerable, for it endangered the victory already won, and on December 14, 1792, the Convention passed a decree which "invite[d] all citizen-soldiers, in the name of their country, not to desert their flags." Furloughs were promised to men with legitimate motives for returning temporarily to their homes.[104] In practice, the Commissioners of the Convention found it necessary to go even further — to grant furloughs to all men seeking them. "It was the only means of preventing them from taking their horses along, in addition." [105] As a further inducement, the Convention offered pensions to those who would serve without interruption till the end of the war.[106]

only fret and fume; they cannot create." — *Briefe . . . Rev.*, II, 243.

[99] Hansen, *Quellen*, II, 518, n. 3.

[100] *Ibid.*, p. 439, n. 2.

[101] Chuquet, *Guerres Rév.*, IV (*Jemappes et la conquête de la Belgique*), 408.

[102] Dumolin, *Précis*, I, 110–115.

[103] *Ibid.*, pp. 115–117.

[104] *Moniteur*, XIV, 745.

[105] L. M. Prudhomme, *Révolutions de Paris* (17 vols., Paris, 1789–1794), XV, 323.

[106] *Moniteur*, XIV, 746.

That happy time was destined to be long delayed, for the Convention had, less than a month before, passed a decree which threw all crowned heads into a panic. The act was not premeditated. It was the result of one of those chance things, little things, that sway the destiny of nations. The twelve villages composing the bailiwick of Bergzabern,[107] in the Duchy of Zweibrücken, emboldened by the proximity of the troops of Republican France, planted trees of liberty, abolished feudal dues, and donned tricolor cockades. The Duke countered with troops, and the rebels sent to the Convention at Paris an address requesting annexation — annexation to France being, in their eyes, the best and only means to render secure their new-won rights. "Legislators," ran the address, "declare to the world that all peoples who shake off the yoke of despotism and desire the protection of the French and union with their Republic will be protected and recognized as Frenchmen. You shall see that it will be the finishing stroke for all tyrants. . . All the piteous subjects of the petty princes of the Holy Roman Empire are awaiting only that longed-for moment to burst their chains."[108] The appeal touched the heart of Rühl, deputy from Alsace, and he moved that the Convention send the appeal to committee for consideration (November 10).[109] Then up spoke Representative Prieur. He said Custine desired to know if the Republic could promise to protect those it had freed from tyrants; the Mayence Clubists had been prodding him (Custine) with respect to this question.[110] On the nineteenth, Rühl returned to the subject, claimed consideration for the bailiwick of Darmstadt — "which should belong to us according to the Treaty of Ryswick"[111] — and announced that the Mayence Club had writ-him, also asking French protection.[112] Revellière, the future Director, proposed that France "accord fraternity and assistance to all people who wish to enjoy liberty."[113] The Convention showed itself sympathetic, and a

---

[107] Bergzabern, Barbelroth, Dierbach, Drusweiler, Ilbesheim, Hergersweiler, Kapellen, Mühlhofen, Niederhorbach, Oberhausen, Volmersweiler, and Winden.

[108] Bonnal de Ganges, *Repré.*, IV, 535–536.

[109] A. Meynier, *Un représentant de la bourgeoisie angevine à l'Assemblée Nationale Constituante et à la Convention Nationale: L. M. Revellière-Lépeaux (1753–1795)* (Angers, 1905), p. 320.

[110] Hansen, *Quellen*, II, 601, n. 4.

[111] *Ibid.*, p. 563, n. 2.

[112] *Ibid.*, p. 601, n. 4. As will appear in § 3 of this chapter, the twelve Bergzabern villages, together with 20 other border localities, were annexed only on March 14, 1793 (after the favorable report of Carnot, of the preceding section). In this action of

March 14, the Convention established the principle that when a portion of a town wanted annexation to France, France would attribute popular sovereignty to that part, and annex it (Decree of March 14, 1793, Hansen, *Quellen*, II, 785–786). Mayence was not annexed until March 30, as will appear also in § 3 *infra*.

[113] Revellière was very sickly and weak since birth, his mother having suffered from intermittent fever while carrying him. He relates in his memoirs how it was thought he would die before he was seven, then before twelve, then before twenty, and how his father had endeavored to strengthen him by physical rigors (*Mémoires de Larevellière-Lépeaux publiés par son fils* [3 vols., Paris, 1895], I, 4–5). The physi-

decree was passed to this effect, with a further provision that French generals should defend citizens who had been vexed or would be vexed in the cause of liberty.[114] The generals were also ordered to print and proclaim the decree in all countries invaded by the French armies.[115]

France had adopted a new role: to set the minds of Europe aflame. Her motto could well have been "Arson — all for democracy!" But who was to pay for this fiery crusade? The French treasury was empty. The Girondists had thought for a time that they could fill it with contributions levied by Custine in the Rhineland.[116] Naïve thought! Custine bled the Rhineland mercilessly,[117] but all he could produce amounted to but a drop in the ocean.[118] Yet the merchant Cambon, financial counsellor to the Convention, convinced that body that it was not at all impossible effectively to shift the expenses of the wars of "liberation" to the "liberated" states.[119]

An interesting debate arose in the Club when the news of the Decree of Novmber 19 arrived in Mayence. The radicals, under Hofmann, chose so to interpret the Decree as to require immediate acceptance of the French constitution, and union with France. Macké, presently to be mayor of Mayence, was less impetuous; he thought a petition should be sent the Convention, but only after the guilds had been polled on the question.[120]

cally handicapped often dream of great and bold deeds, and it may be that it was Revellière's weakness which, in the last analysis, produced the defiant Decree of November 19.

[114] *Moniteur*, XIV, 517.

[115] F. M. Anderson (ed.), *The Constitutions and Other Select Documents Illustrative of the History of France, 1789-1907* (Minneapolis, 1908), p. 133. The provocative proclamation was cancelled in the spring of 1793 when Danton took control of affairs (*vide infra*, Pt. I, chap. iii, § 2); but it had already exercised much influence upon the Rhineland (Gooch, *Germ. Fr. Rev.*, p. 398). Text of repealing instrument in Hansen, *Quellen*, II, 820.

[116] No base motives should be attributed to the Girondists because of this hope. As the *Moniteur* wrote on December 4, 1792, " . . . contributions are, in general, legitimate and proper war." — *Ibid.*, p. 542, n. 1. It is war that is base.

[117] For example, he took *all* the money in the Mayence treasury (Simon and Grégoire to Lebrun, Feb. 11, 1793, *ibid.*, p. 745). The silver of the church and of the University of Mayence was in part melted down and minted, in part transported to France (M.

Metternich's testimony, *ibid.*, p. 890). Four or five hundred French troops swooped down suddenly upon an abbey in Crefeld, blocked the exits, and under severe penalties, demanded all ready money, a contribution of 100,000 livres, and to be feasted on meat, butter, bread, wine, and beer. The abbey did not possess 100,000 livres, so the troops carried off the abbot and steward as hostages (Hansen, *Quellen*, II, 660-661). And Lebrun wrote to Custine on October 20, 1792, in the name of the Provisional Executive Council: "You must sweep up everything before and beside you the length of the Rhine, while treating . . . the people with fraternity." Then he added, as a sort of afterthought, " . . . I believe it would be very nice if you profited by the circumstances to enrich the Bibliothèque Nationale with several great and costly works found in the libraries of the places that you have conquered for liberty." — *Ibid.*, p. 518, n. 3.

[118] Mathiez, *Fr. Rev.*, p. 266.

[119] *Moniteur*, XIV, 760 (Cambon's report is treated more fully in Pt. I, chap, vii, § 1, *infra*).

[120] Hansen, *Quellen*, II, 601, n. 4.

The same day that the Convention passed the provocative decree of November 19, Custine, who had long been provoked with the old administrations he had permitted to continue at Mayence, did some decreeing of his own. It was hardly unexpected. The old officials, contrary to Custine's hopes, had maintained their loyalty to the Electoral regime, and had failed to supply his army properly, perhaps in part because the farmers, believing the French propaganda, had stopped paying feudal dues. Custine had offered the direction of a new simplified regime to Johann von Müller at the start of November, but von Müller had declined.[121] Now, November 19, the General announced abolition of the old administrations of justice, police, and finance, and the appointment of leading republicans in their stead.[122] And he gave it to be understood that he would maintain the old taxes, as he had originally announced. He was not authorized, he said, to abolish them. However, the new administrations would use moderation as their guide.[123]

The farmers were disappointed, for they had counted on relief from feudal dues, and all they had received was additional burdens. The republican propaganda thereby lost much of its charm for them. Mathias Metternich had been laboring strenuously to bring the farmers into the Club, in order that Custine's Mayence republic should include the surrounding territory upon which the city depended economically.[124] The disillusionment of the farmer was a hard blow to Metternich as well.

As far as the constitution of Mayence was concerned, Custine saw his policy had accomplished nothing there, either. Dumont's propositions had been followed by a memorial from the lower clergy, who told the General plainly that there lay a middle ground between absolutism and the extreme republicanism of the French. Custine decided to abolish the governments of Mayence, Worms, and Spires and establish a provisional "General Administration" for that portion of the Rhineland occupied by his army. The new government consisted of six citizens of Mayence, three of Worms, and one of Spires, most of them Clubists. Ex-priest Dorsch was its president, and Forster, his delegate. The dissolution of the three governments created quite a stir, and Custine and the Clubists hastened to assure the people that the popular elections would be soon forthcoming. The magistrates of Mayence, Worms, and Spires were ousted also, in favor of *municipalités*, or city councils.[125]

The promise of popular elections, which the French adherents felt obliged to give, raised in their minds, of course, the fear that perhaps the

---

[121] *Ibid.*, p. 597. Reference is to the Swiss historian who had been in the Elector's service.

[122] *Ibid.*, p. 596.

[123] *Ibid.*, p. 599.

[124] *Ibid.*, p. 598.

[125] *Ibid.*, pp. 599–600.

election results would not prove satisfactory. It were therefore better to hold a sort of trial election, and take no chances. Thus it was that the new General Administration headed by Dorsch and Forster commenced (start of December) to poll Mayence, Worms, and Spires, and the villages between Landau and Bingen. Forster was certain of an overwhelming majority, and had even picked out the name of the new French *département: Bouches du Mein* ("Mouths of the Main [River]").[126] The formulary which was presented to the voters for their signatures read as follows:

In the name of Almighty God, we, inhabitants of —————, declaring ourselves to be weary of our present oppressive constitution, desire to mollify and change it in its entirety. Too weak, however, to defend ourselves during this so necessary improvement in our condition, we implore the protection of our neighbors, the French, and wish henceforth to form but one family with them and to submit ourselves to their laws, so far as these are applicable to our habits and climate. For this reason, delegates will be sent to the legislators of France in order to acquaint them with our views, to convince them of the importance of this union, and to procure from them commissioners to work with us for the improvement of our constitution along French lines. We shall leave the election of these deputies who are to be sent to Paris to our brothers in Mayence if it be that we cannot, within a short space of time, also send members to Mayence to work with them.[127]

But, by and large, no one would sign the formulary; and even in Mayence, seat of the Club, where Mayor Macké, in the name of the city council, summoned the guilds and inhabitants to participate, the results were meager. In fact, the merchants insisted again on their preference for Daniel Dumont's draft. The artisans' guilds preferred, in the main, not to vote. It seems matters in Worms did not advance to the voting stage at all. They might as well not have in Spires, either. There is not available sufficient information regarding hamlets, but there was a preponderance of signers only in Kastel, Nackenheim, Wöllstein, Niederolm, and Klein-Wintersheim. In most of the other towns, the results were negative; and in Finthen and Gonsenheim, Mathias Metternich had to take to his heels. Forster felt constrained to admit that "Here in the city [of Mayence], there is more ill-humor than was to be expected." Still, with magnificent disregard of the truth, he summed up the results: "From Spires to Bingen, there was an almost unanimous vote for acceptance of the French constitution and incorporation into France."[128]

This was indeed an interesting political experience for the French propagandists, but it was of no practical consequence. On December 15 and

[126] *Ibid.*, p. 654.
[127] Venedey, *Deut. Rep.*, pp. 116–117.
[128] Hansen, *Quellen*, II, 654–655.

17, 1792, the Convention, modifying and completing the Decree of November 19 to accord essentially with the desires of the Mountain,[129] established new principles for the handling of the conquered territory, and prescribed new modes of promoting its annexation.

The Decree of December 15 and 17 is popularly known as the "Compulsory Liberty Decree." Its preamble stated that "the Convention, . . . faithful to the principle of the sovereignty of the people which does not permit it to recognize any institutions which violate it," and wishing to establish rules for the generals to follow in conquered territory, decrees as follows . . . There followed provisions of two categories. The first could be called "liberation." In all countries where the French armies had penetrated or would penetrate, the generals should proclaim immediately the sovereignty of the people, the suppression of all the established authorities, and of all existing financial and personal burdens and of all privileges. Among these were, of course, the tithe and the *corvée*. The people should be convoked in primary and communal assemblies to elect provisional administrations and tribunals (their regular authorities having been dissolved). No one serving the former government in any capacity, and no one heretofore privileged, could, "for this time only," vote or be elected to office. This provision was intended to effect a clean sweep of elements whose loyalty to the former government could probably not be shaken. This clean sweep was obligatory. "The French nation," according to the Decree, "declares that it will treat as an enemy of the people everyone who, refusing liberty or renouncing it, wishes to keep, recall, or negotiate with the prince [or] . . . privileged classes. It . . . pledges itself not to sign any treaty or put down its arms until after the consolidation of the sovereignty and independence of the people . . . who have adopted the principles of equality and established a free and popular government."[130]

The second class of provisions of this decree concerned the benefits which should accrue to France from the above "liberation." All the property, real and personal, of the treasury (this was mentioned first), of the prince and his supporters, of public institutions, and of lay and ecclesiastical societies should immediately be taken "under the safeguard and protection" of the Republic, and a detailed list thereof sent to the Provisional Executive Council. The Council should send commissioners to concert with the generals and provisional governments on means of indemnifying France for her past expenditures for mutual defense, and, in case "the common interest" required that French troops remain in the country, on means of feeding and clothing them.[131]

[129] *Ibid.*, p. 646, n. 2.
[130] Arts. 1, 2, 3, 9, 11: *ibid.*, pp. 646–648. The *Moniteur*, XIV, 755–756, gives only the first nine articles, adopted December 15.
[131] Arts. 4, 7, 10: Hansen, *Quellen*, II, 646–648.

The Decree of December 15 and 17 was intended, in part, to deprive the French generals of the power of setting up governments to suit themselves in the territories they had conquered. Chuquet has supplied a very cynical analysis of the purposes of the Convention in passing this decree: "It wanted, by suppressing the taxes and public revenues for a period, to reduce the provisional administrations to impotence, so they would finally be obliged, willy-nilly, to order the circulation of assignats [France's depreciated paper money]. It wanted to establish a species of anarchy during the electoral period, to dispose at its pleasure of the sequestrated properties, to draw all the coin out of the country before its annexation." [132]

Whatever the Convention's purpose, the chances that the Decree would ever be carried out at Mayence were none too rosy. This city was already threatened by the changing fortunes of war. The Prussians were arriving in the vicinity. Frankfort had fallen to them already on December 2.[133] Timid Mayençais were speaking of surrender. (Custine prepared a decree promising the citizens compensation by the Convention in case the city should actually be subjected to siege.) Prices were rising. Meat was unobtainable. The breaking-up of the ice had carried away bridges and mills, and there was no flour. Bread had doubled in price. Firewood was high. But these privations were for the citizens only. The French magazines were full.[134]

3. THE "CLUB" AND THE ELECTIONS

Such were the conditions when there arrived in Mayence, in the beginning of January 1793, three Commissioners of the Convention, to execute the Decree of December 15 and 17. They were Merlin of Thionville,[135] Reubell (whom we have already met), and Haussmann of Strasburg. The Provisional Executive Council sent two more Commissioners to Mayence: Frédéric Simon [136] of Strasburg and Gabriel Grégoire of Thionville. Thus

---

[132] Chuquet, *Guerres Rév.*, IV, 200.

[133] Hansen, *Quellen*, II, 621–622.

[134] Excerpts from private letters, *ibid.*, pp. 679–681.

[135] A contemporary account of Merlin-Th., perhaps the greatest alter ego of the Convention, describes him as "more energetic than adroit, more fit to command a battalion than to head an assembly, more terrible to enemies than formidable to sophists, more brave than eloquent, of a truly martial physiognomy. . . But the love of pleasure is hard to reconcile with that mold of character so necessary to the triumph of a strongly contradictory opinion, and Merlin was a Hercules in whose hands one sometimes detects a distaff instead of a club." — J. J. Dussault, "Fragments pour servir à l'histoire de la Convention nationale depuis le 10 thermidor jusqu'à la dénonciation de Lecointre exclusivement," in C. A. Dauban (ed.), *Paris en 1794 et en 1795* (Paris, 1869), p. 517.

[136] Former Neuwied pedagog, active in the Illuminati (Hansen, *Quellen*, II, 701, n. 1).

it was to Alsatians and Lorrainers that the organization of the Rhineland was confided. Of course this was because they could speak German.

The first report of Reubell, Merlin, and Haussmann betrayed the changed situation: " . . . The people of Mayence and its environs are . . . much inclined to adopt our principles, but let us not deceive ourselves. The occurrence at Frankfort — cruel occurrence, according to all reports [137] — and the presence of the Prussian and Hessian armies have chilled a bit the most ardent patriots. We can succeed in kindling them again, but we will need aid to finish the revolution in this fine part of the Empire. . . " [138] And Merlin spoke out on January 4 and February 4 for the "indispensable" Rhine boundary. In Paris, also, the natural-boundary demand appeared again in a decree of the Convention of January 31, 1793, dealing with the projected annexation of Belgium and Aix-la-Chapelle.[139] Apparently some persons did not care that the tide of war was turning.

Simon and Grégoire reported on February 7 that they had found no elective representatives in the Rhineland; all were Custine's appointees. They had therefore, after consulting with Reubell, Merlin, and Haussmann, and with the local administrators, decided to set February 24 as the date of elections to be held in the territory between Landau, the Moselle, and the Rhine. (Note that this is a larger area than Custine had contemplated: between Landau, Bingen, and the Rhine.) The communes would name some local officials, plus their deputies to the Mayence Convention — which would open its doors at Mayence on March 10, and decide the fate of their country.[140]

Forster could not understand why such a long time was being allowed to elapse between the date of the Convention's decree (December 15) and the elections. But the reason was simple and he, of all persons, should have known it. The Commissioners wanted to prepare public opinion for annexation, and this required time,[141] for the masses were indifferent to revolutionary ideas, and not unfavorable to the old regime, while Custine's arrogance and heavy exactions had intensified their opposition.[142]

Finally, on February 16, 1793, Custine convoked the electors,[143] but informed them that according to a law of December 22 of the previous year, "no one would be permitted to vote in the primary or communal assemblies,

---

[137] As mentioned in § 1a of this chapter, the inhabitants of Frankfort, after opening the gates to the Hessians, murdered some of the French garrison.

[138] To the Conv., Jan. 1, 1793, Hansen, *Quellen*, II, 680, n. 2.

[139] Hansen, *Quellen*, II, 732, 733 and n. 1. It was Danton who brought up the point.

[140] To Lebrun, *ibid.*, pp. 738–739.

[141] Sagnac, *Rhin. fr.*, pp. 81, 88.

[142] R. S. Rait and B. A. Lees, "Plebiscite and Referendum," Great Britain Foreign Office, Historical Section, *Peace Handbooks* (London, 1920), XXV, 20–22.

[143] Each commune was to elect one deputy, though Mayence was to choose six, and Worms and Spires two each (Sagnac, *Rhin fr.*, pp. 88-89).

or be named administrator or provisional judge, without having taken the oath to liberty and equality, and renounced in writing the privileges which he had formerly enjoyed." [144] This renunciation was "to be exacted without delay from formerly privileged persons and their adherents [i.e., "nobles, ecclesiastics, . . . members of the University of Mayence, regents of seminaries, and all civil agents of the former prince"] because of the proximity of the popular elections." [145] Custine threatened, as "the least severe" penalty permissible in a case where "the liberty of the popular elections" was in jeopardy, to deport to the right bank all those who had proved themselves "enemies of France by refusing the present declaration," since their further sojourn would endanger "not only the liberty of the inhabitants of this region, but also the interests of the French Republic." [146]

The philosophy behind this piece of legislation was this: If a means could be found of expelling, before an election, all those who might vote "contra," one could obtain a "pro" majority even if he had but a single "pro" vote. It was not expected that any privileged persons would take the oath and sign; it was not desired that they should. This was an "expulsion-occasioner," not a serious voting regulation. But of course the amenities had to be preserved.

To people who are very certain they are right, this procedure does not seem knavish. Robespierre, the Incorruptible, declared to the Convention on December 27, 1792: "Virtue was always in the minority." Saint-Just argued against referring Louis XVI's fate to the people because, he said, the majority of the French people were against the death penalty. Saint-Just thought it was he who was right.

Custine's proclamation, above, was soon followed (February 18) by a decree of Simon and Grégoire announcing that anyone could vote in the coming elections who had attained the age of twenty, and — being nonprivileged — had taken the simple oath before voting: "I swear to be true to the people and principles of freedom and equality." [147] It was thought that this rather veiled way of swearing allegiance to France would prove less objectionable to the German conscience than the oath prescribed by the General Administration in its trial poll of the previous year, which the Germans

---

[144] The formulary ran: "Ich schwöre der Freiheit und Gleichheit, ich entsage allen Privilegien und dem Römischen Reiche, ich schwöre ab dem Bischofe und schwöre, den Gesetzen der Nation treu zu sein, für dieselben zu leben und zu sterben." — Hansen, *Quellen*, II, 769.

The Decree of December 22 supplanted the provisions of the Decree of December

15 and 17 where the earlier wording had ruled merely that " . . . the heretofore privileged will be, for this time only, inadmissible to vote . . . or . . . be elected . . . " (*ibid.*, p. 647).

[145] Simon and Grégoire to Lebrun, Arch. N., F1E 40, d. 1.

[146] Arch. N., F1E 40, d. 1.

[147] Venedey, *Deut. Rep.*, pp. 117–118.

would not take. But swear allegiance to France the Rhinelanders must, in one form or another, before voting.

The task of inducing the Rhineland to supplicate for annexation to France was no easy one, though it might have been less difficult had the French invaders lived up to the principles they professed. However, such was not the case. "We are going to tell you the truth, the whole truth, and nothing but the truth," wrote Simon and Grégoire to Lebrun on February 20, 1793. "However, we can assure you that we have every reason to hope that the object of our mission will be fulfilled, and that all this country will cast itself into the arms of the French nation, to form a *département* of the Republic, in the course of the next month.

"We confess to you that, the day following our arrival, we found the disposition of the people toward the French nation not only very cold but even very irritated. Malevolence on the one side, clumsiness and imprudence on the other — in general, everything seemed to unite to indispose a people whom it was so important for us to win over. The military agents had assumed so despotic a tone toward the citizens and civil agents that they inspired only terror, and alienated everyone."

Then Simon and Grégoire indicated what they proposed to do to change the disposition of the people. They would hold audiences daily from 8:00 A.M. till night, to hear complaints about abuses. They would concert with Custine to deport every noble, cleric, former official, and university member who would not forthwith take an oath to liberty and equality, and renounce his privileges and his old allegiance.[148] They would publish a grand proclamation in which they would seek to answer doubts and objections. They reported that they had already sent some fifty commissioners to talk to the people personally and prepare them for the elections. But — and here came a surprising confession — they doubted that they could dare to count the votes, for, to find out if one had a majority, one risked finding out that one was in the minority. And that was what they were, they assured Lebrun; according to reports from all sides, they were in the minority. Still, if they could frighten away the contrary-minded, there should always be at least some left to vote (as was desired). Four sentences of the despatch merit quotation: "The Club here is not worth anything. A young man [Böhmer], more ardent than prudent, wanting to be the founder, violated the first rules of prudence when laying its foundations. This Club is highly discredited. If one wants to influence the public, one has to be careful not to make use of the Club."[149]

---

[148] *Vide* Proclamation of Custine, Feb. 16,   [149] Arch. N., F1E 40, d. 1.
1793, Hansen, *Quellen*, II, 751–752.

Nine days earlier, the same Commissioners had supplicated Lebrun to lend the provisional administrations of Mayence 20,000 florins, for "they do not possess a denier, having been obliged to turn over the money they had to the military treasury."[150] In the letter of February 20, of which a part is quoted above, Simon and Grégoire related that in an effort to win over the inhabitants, they had required the military treasury to lend 1,000 crowns to the *municipalité* of Mayence to clean up the city. They said that the French had requisitioned all the city's funds, leaving no money for cleaning the streets, and that it was feared that an epidemic would break out upon the approach of spring, so full of refuse were the streets of this formerly spotless city.[151]

It was inevitable that, with the arrival of Merlin, Reubell, and Haussmann, some latent conflicts of jurisdiction and policy in the administration of the conquered city should come to the surface. It was indeed not long before leadership passed from Custine and his two satellites (Böhmer and Dorsch), and Hofmann became the head of the local administration and Club of Mayence. Then commenced a quarrel among the revolutionists, Hofmann arraigning the French administration of Mayence (in other words, the administration of Custine, Forster, Böhmer, and Dorsch),[152] and Custine threatening to have Hofmann hanged.[153] Of interest it is to note that it was evidence supplied later by Hofmann which helped to send General Custine to the block.[154]

Despite these internal conflicts, the Club continued the good work of propaganda up to the time of the elections, i.e., until February 24.[155] But the people were not responsive to the appeals, and those who could, fled. Forster remarked that Mayence was losing all its population.[156] Report after report flowed into the French Foreign Office attesting that "the Frenchman is not beloved here," "the people do not ask for liberty," "Germans will always remain Germans."[157] A year later (January 8, 1794) Merlin of Thionville declared: "Do not deceive yourselves, my colleagues. Accustomed to the yoke, the inhabitants of Germany prefer its chains, its apathy, to liberty; the

---

[150] Arch. N., F1E 40, d. 1.

[151] Arch. N., F1E 40, d. 1.

[152] Jan. 10, 1793, Gooch, *Germ. Fr. Rev.*, p. 479. Hofmann's bravery was due in part to the fact that Prussian troops were nearing the city.

[153] Jan. 11, 1793, Venedey, *Deut. Rep.*, p. 115.

[154] *Moniteur*, XVII, 507.

[155] Daniel Dumont was banished on the night of February 24-25 because he tried to procure postponement of the elections (he was quite apparently hoping for Prussian rescue); and his property was sequestrated (Hansen, *Quellen*, II, 764, n. 1).

[156] K. G. Bockenheimer, *Die Mainzer Klubisten der Jahre 1792 und 1793* (Mayence, 1896), p. 210. Some merely left the cities, but others fled to the right bank of the Rhine, especially to Frankfort (*ibid.*, p. 356).

[157] Gooch, *Germ. Fr. Rev.*, pp. 478-479.

calm of servitude to the storms of liberty. There are few patriots in Germany, and their fate so far does not induce others to declare themselves." [158]

Custine's proclamation of February 16, 1793, convoking the electors and requiring an oath to liberty and equality, had declared that formerly privileged persons were obliged to take the oath before February 20, if inhabitants of Mayence, and before February 23, if others. But very few persons would swear, either in Mayence or elsewhere, either before the elections commenced, or after.[159]

The merchants' and artisans' guilds of Mayence declared on February 19 and 20 that they would not take the oath, hence would not try to vote on the twenty-fourth. On the twentieth, the officials and ecclesiastics of Mayence affirmed that they would not sign the renunciation required for voting. The magistrates and others drew Custine's attention to the guarantees in the Capitulation of Mayence [160] and the promises in his speeches of October 23 and 25. A handwritten note was presented to the Commissioners, which note — though toned down in its final version — at first read: "It is tyranny, despotism, the most oppressive, insupportable despotism to announce oneself to a people as a liberator, to be well received by them, well treated, to be warmed at their hearths, lodged in their homes, and then, with preponderant force — and contrary to all promises given — to try to force upon this people a formulary of oath, a renunciation within three days under the most terrible threats. . . Free and unfree people on the face of the earth in all parts of the world . . . hear, and, staring into space, exclaim: Thus will we be treated by people who want to free us, to be our brothers. . . Undersigned are prepared to take an oath 'that we will do nothing contrary to the interests of the French nation. . . ' " [161]

But Custine and the Commissioners had already decided to "interpret" the Capitulation, and Lebrun was upholding them,[162] so the appeal was in vain.

Now, in Belgium, the Convention's Decrees of December 15 and 17, and 22, were, at this time, being executed as follows. The people were summoned to meet in the churches. The edifices were then filled with or surrounded by troops, and under the eyes of the military, the people were asked to vote.[163] That, indeed, was the election itself, and not the oath-taking, but the Mayençais developed a sudden aversion to going to mass. They were apparently afraid of being locked in and forced to do the victor's bidding.

[158] Bonnal de Ganges, Repré., II, 36. Quoted at greater length infra, Pt. I, chap. iv, § 2h.
[159] Sagnac, Rhin fr., p. 91.
[160] Arts. 7 and 8 had guaranteed the property of adherents of the former prince-elector.
[161] Hansen, Quellen, II, 762, n. 1.
[162] Lebrun to Simon, March 20, 1793, Arch. N., F1E 40, d. 1.
[163] Chuquet, Guerres Rév., IV, 231 et seqq.

However, they were not at all sure how long they could hold out because of the threat of deportation — without their goods, which would become national (French?) [164] property. The Mayençais sent a messenger to Paris to ask a postponement of the oath-taking until such time as the Prussians would no longer be an immediate threat,[165] but a new Commissioner met the courier and brought him back.[166]

In Worms the citizens vowed among themselves not to take the oath, and were ordered to assemble in a certain place at a stated time. Not a soul appeared. They were threatened soon after with work on the fortifications. At least four hundred persons immediately declared their preference for pick-and-shovel work.[167] In Spires, the citizens refused to assemble, and neither pretty speeches nor threats could budge them.[168] In Bingen, when the people did not assemble after the bells had been rung five separate times, a house-to-house call was made, informing them that if they did not take the oath within the hour, their possessions would be pillaged and their houses burned down. They took the oath.[169]

In Grünstadt, the inhabitants ejected some Mayence partriots who were seeking to obtain oaths, and wounded one of their number. The presence of Forster — with some French troops — was necessary to restore calm. Now, in Grünstadt lived the three Counts of Leiningen — Carl Woldemar, the reigning prince; his son, and his nephew. The counts, especially the nephew, were deeply loved by the local peasantry because of their benevolence and quiet good nature. Forster blamed the counts for the attitude of the people.[170] He demanded that they surrender their titles and privileges, and swear fidelity to France. They showed themselves stubborn, thought to appeal to the Convention at Paris, and were given twenty-four hours to emigrate. They did not leave, and were arrested the next day by order of the Commissioners Reubell and Haussmann. At first they were imprisoned in Landau, but later in Paris.[171] After their arrest and removal, the Grünstädter, cowed, consented to take the oath.[172]

[164] *Vide infra*, this same section.

[165] The Mayençais could see the Prussian guns aimed at the city, and regarded them as a warning not to yield.

[166] Hansen, *Quellen*, II, 762–764.

[167] *Ibid.*, pp. 759–760.

[168] *Ibid.*, p. 759.

[169] *Kölner Reichsoberpostamtszeitung*, March 4, *ibid.*, p. 764, n. 3.

[170] In the French *départements* bordering on the Rhine, the subservience of the people to the aristocracy was also marked (Prudhomme, *Rév. Paris*, XV, 285). The Teutonic respect for constituted authority was doubtless responsible for some of the left-bank resistance to the Revolution. Prudhomme's epigram, "The great appear great to us only when we are on our knees. Let us rise," did not strike a responsive chord in the stolid German's breast.

[171] E. Saulnier, "Une prison révolutionnaire," *RF*, LXVI (1914), 210–212. Saulnier says (p. 211) the Mayence Convention rejected an appeal they made to the Paris Convention; but the Mayence Convention was not yet in existence.

[172] Sagnac, *Rhin fr.*, p. 91.

A rumor had been circulating in the Rhineland that military service in the French armies would be exacted from those who took the oath.[173] To root out this idea, Reubell, Haussmann, and Merlin of Thionville issued a proclamation: "We . . . promise the people of Mayence in the name of our Republic never to require a citizen to serve in our armies."[174] To make sure that everyone knew of the benign dispensation, Commissioners were sent to talk with the people. But the priests of the Rhineland forbade their flocks to read or hear. Thereupon, "the Commissioners of the Convention, in accord with me [Simon], decided to have all these venomous insects deported to the right bank of the Rhine, and wherever this measure has been executed, the remainder [of the people] have taken the oath . . . and elected their municipal offices, as well as their deputies to the Mayence Convention. . . . The villages against which we were obliged to exercise some severity are now undeceived and bless us. I have received several deputations of this sort."[175]

The outstanding characteristics of the elections were intimidation and compulsion. Cavalry patrols escorted the electoral commissioners;[176] soldiers kept "order" in the streets,[177] and proved "patriots" were imposed on the electors.[178] "All the deputies named so far are our friends," wrote Simon to Lebrun, "for I took the precaution of proposing them myself or of having them proposed secretly to the people of the country, who were for the most part deeply in trouble over the task of finding representatives."[179]

That the Rhinelanders experienced difficulty in finding representatives, it is easy to believe. Fear had joined with fidelity to fatherland to dissuade possible candidates from presenting themselves for election. On November 19, 1792, Emperor Francis II had addressed Imperial letters overt to all vassals

---

[173] Bockenheimer, *Mainzer Klubisten*, p. 194. This was due to a suggestion of Custine's that making French citizens of everyone in areas occupied by French troops would be the best means of promoting enlistments (Hansen, *Quellen*, 601, n. 4; 758, n. 3).

[174] Bockenheimer, *Mainzer Klubisten*, pp. 355–356.

[175] Simon to Lebrun, March 9, 1793, Arch. N., F1E 40, d. 1. Less naïve was General Beurnonville, who, in criticism of similar reports (reports of conquered peoples thanking the French for their freedom) wrote on December 18, 1792: "I could have sent you, as did all my colleagues, a thousand journals of proceedings which confirm the planting of trees of liberty and the patriotic magniloquence of the

Laplanders of the state of Trèves. But all that would be an indication only of grimaces in which I do not at all believe — which are dictated solely by fear." — H. Wallon, *Les représentants du peuple en mission* (5 vols., Paris, 1889–1890), IV, 45.

[176] Rait and Lees in *Peace Handbooks*, XXV, 20–22.

[177] S. Wambaugh, *A Monograph on Plebiscites* (New York, 1920), p. 54.

[178] It is to be noted that the virtual director of the elections was the deputy Reubell (Guyot, *Direc.*, p. 117).

[179] March 9, 1793, Arch. N., F1E 40, d. 1. Hansen seems to have missed this little jewel when making his extraordinary compilation.

and subjects of the Empire who had entered the service of France. These announced that the Empire had decided to resist the French aggression by force of arms, and that therefore those who continued to serve France in either a military or a civil capacity would be aiding the enemy of their country. Such service was ordered to cease immediately, and the penalties for disobedience were specified: loss of titles and of property, proscription, and even corporal punishment and death.[180]

This decree, which appeared in all the German-language newspapers, frightened many Germans out of the French service, and threatened to spoil the little drama being staged on the left bank: of representatives elected by Germans begging for annexation to France. Simon and Grégoire were much perturbed. They appealed to the Paris Convention for a decree which would assure the protection of the entire French nation to those who had entered or would enter the service of the Republic, a decree which would promise such persons idemnification if their property were confiscated, and threaten reprisals if the enemy violated the rights of war. "It would be infinitely advantageous if we could announce this decree at the time of the elections, which commence on the twenty-fourth of the current month," urged the Commissioners;[181] and in the meantime they broadcast an antidote to the Emperor's letters overt.[182] This proclamation, translated into German by Hofmann, declared that "if the descendants of these ancient Germans, formerly so jealous of their liberty, are yet animated by that civic ardor, if the same love of liberty still pulsates in their veins, if, wearied of despotism, they prefer to fraternize with a free people, what human power has the right to stand in their way!" If their possessions are confiscated as a result, the Republic can give them in indemnification the former princely possessions in Alsace and Lorraine. If their armorial bearings are taken

---

[180] Certified French translation, enclosed in letter of Simon and Grégoire to Lebrun, Feb. 10, 1793, Arch. N., F1E 40, d. 1. The circles were ordered to prepare triple contingents. It is interesting to note that the city of Cologne declared its neutrality (Hansen, Quellen, II, 671, n. 1). On February 11, 1793, the Emperor ordered the declaration rescinded as unconstitutional; and the city was ordered to supply its contingent and pay its Roman months (Imperial Vice-Chancellor Prince von Colloredo to Imperial Resident F. J. von Bossart in Cologne, ibid., p. 747).

[181] Arch. N., F1E 40, d. 1. On September 15, 1793, several months after the Prussian re-

conquest of Mayence, the Convention belatedly voted to appropriate 50,000 livres to help the Mayence refugees in France who were "in misery" (Moniteur, XVII, 672). This is a far cry from indemnification, but the appeals for assistance were legion, and had started as early as May (vide, e.g., Aulard, Actes, III, 575, 607).

[182] "You did right to combat the dangerous influence," wrote Lebrun to Simon and Grégoire. " . . . Do not forget that public instruction is an important branch of your mission; all people would be French if they knew their true interests." — March 3, 1793, Hansen, Quellen, II, 779–780.

from them, a great loss that would be! Free men surrender such things of their own accord. Lastly, "if, in violation of all the laws of a pure and honorable war, the enemy is so barbarous as to deprive of life a native of Germany who has entered the service of France, we declare in the name of General Custine that he will forthwith hang two captured Austrian or other officers." [183]

Nevertheless, candidates were hard to find. The tide of victory had turned against the French,[184] and their promises were therefore scorned. So noticeable was this change of sentiment, even in that select body of "patriots," the Mayence Club, that Simon and Grégoire had long been speaking [185] of inducing the Club to dissolve itself, and of then reconstituting it. Lebrun approved, but cautioned circumspection.[186] On March 9, one of Simon's [187] friends in the Club proposed to strike out the names of all members who had not attended the primary assemblies of February 24. "This motion was well received," wrote Simon to Lebrun, "and will be executed tomorrow. By this means, several cankered members will be excluded." [188] But there was no purpose in reconstituting the Club at this late date. In fact, the elections ended the next day (March 10) — the day the Club was to have been reconstituted — so it no longer had any *raison d'être*. Merlin therefore dissolved it.[189]

How did the elections turn out? At Mayence, there were but 375 citizens who had both taken the oath [190] and voted (out of 10,000 qualified voters!);[191] at Worms, there were but 427; [192] at Spires, 342.[193] Though but an insignificant fraction of the qualified electors had gone to the polls, and though but few sections were represented at all, the majority of the votes cast was

[183] Feb. 17, 1793, Arch. N., F1E 40, d. 1.
[184] And as the German armies advanced, the "patriots" of the Rhineland fled "to escape the hatred of their petty despots." Ninety-three had fled from Zweibrücken alone, and were being fed by the Representatives on Mission (Rps A. Mo to CPS and Conv., July 7, 1793, Aulard, *Actes*, V, 206).
[185] In a report to Lebrun, Feb. 20, 1793, Arch. N., F1E 40, d. 1.
[186] Lebrun to Simon and Grégoire, March 3, 1793, Arch. N., F1E 40, d. 1.
[187] Grégoire had left Mayence on March 5, 1793, because of ill health.
[188] Simon to Lebrun, March 9, 1793, Arch. N., F1E 40, d. 1.
[189] Gooch, *Germ. Fr. Rev.*, p. 480. It was succeeded by the "Society of Free Germans" (Hansen, *Quellen*, II, 758, n. 3).
[190] Due to the pressure of the siege, and the policy of deportation for refusal, about a hundred more Mayençais took the oath within the succeeding several months (*ibid.*, p. 764, n. 2).
[191] *Ibid.* Not even all the Clubists troubled themselves to cast ballots; in fact, of the approximately 450 members of the Mayence Club, hardly 200 both took the oath and voted. Of these, but little more than half were Mayençais (Venedey, *Deut. Rep.*, 119). In his *Quellen*, II, 80 *, Hansen gives 7,000 as the number of qualified voters of Mayence, but his other figure of 10,000, taken from Klein, is probably right.
[192] Hansen, *Quellen*, II, 760, n. 3.
[193] *Ibid.*, p. 759, n. 3.

in favor of the annexationists,[194] and Forster, brimming with enthusiasm, declared that the vote for incorporation with France was unanimous.[195] "This vote will reëstablish the peace of Europe," he declared. "I do not believe that beyond the Rhine, or elsewhere, the thought of reconquering people who have voluntarily seceded could be entertained." [196]

The Rheno-German National Convention held its first session on March 17, 1793. Practically all of the members [197] were favorable to France. In their ranks were the Clubists Forster, Hofmann, Wedekind, and Metternich; some uncultured peasants; and several professional men (professors, lawyers, physicians, ecclesiastics) and merchants.[198] Hofmann was elected president, and Forster, vice-president.

The next day, March 18, Wedekind explained the necessity of deposing the old sovereigns, and Forster reinforced his arguments. A project of decree in several articles was thereupon proposed and passed, without any discussion whatsoever. Article I declared the territory between Landau, Bingen, and Mayence [199] to be free, independent, and indivisible, and founded upon liberty and equality. Article II proclaimed the sovereignty of the people, and repudiated all connection with the Empire. Article III deposed by name the numerous petty rulers. Article IV threatened with execution those who should try to recover their old privileges.[200]

Some members of the Mayence Convention desired real independence; others thought they should negotiate with France to determine if, and how, France could protect them. But Forster, Hofmann, Dorsch, Wedekind, and Metternich argued that if Mayence formed an independent state, it would be at the mercy of Germany, for alliances do not afford complete security. They said France should be prayed to accept Mayence as part of itself, and they described the brilliant future which this union would bring to the city and to its commerce on the Rhine.[201] After three days of discussion, i.e., on

[194] Rait and Lees in *Peace Handbooks*, XXV, 20–22. As Girtanner pointed out in his *Rheinstrome*, p. 39: "He who forces me to accept a law is already my master; and if he is stronger than I am, it is the counsel of wisdom to yield to all his wishes."

[195] Sagnac, *Rhin fr.*, p. 91.

[196] *Ibid.*

[197] According to Blondel in Lavisse and Rambaud, *Hist. gén.*, VIII, 700, there were a hundred members.

[198] Sagnac, *Rhin fr.*, p. 92.

[199] This is a strip of territory about 30 to 40 kilometers wide, the length of the left bank from Alsace to the large rectangular bend of the Rhine near Mayence. The plan to include up to the Moselle was abandoned.

[200] Hansen, *Quellen*, II, 798–801.

[201] *Ibid.*, p. 801, n. 2. Mayence has often been reproached for its treason, but K. Klein, in his *Geschichte von Mainz während der ersten französischen Okkupation, 1792–1793* (Mayence, 1861), says that the orators for separation were foreigners whom the Elector had called to his court, e.g., Forster, Dorsch (*sic*), Wedekind, and Metternich (Sagnac, *Rhin fr.*, p. 92, n. 1). Klein errs in including Dorsch in his list of foreigners, for Dorsch was born in Mayence (*vide* Chuquet, *Guerres Rév.*, VII, 21).

March 21, it was unanimously decreed that since the left bank between Bingen and Landau owed its independence solely to the victorious arms of the French Republic, gratitude, amity, and reciprocal advantage rendered only natural a union of the two states.[202] A deputation of three — Forster and two others, Adam Lux and Patocki — was thereupon despatched to Paris as bearer of the glad tidings.[203]

Commissioner Haussmann escorted the Mayence deputation to Paris, and to the Convention chamber on March 30. Haussmann delivered himself of a lengthy speech in which he dilated upon the beauty and fertility of the Mayence region. He also took up the military situation there, and pretended it was favorable, though Kreuznach and Bingen had just been lost. He said an attempt had been made at Mayence to repeat the Frankfort "treason" — i.e., that some Mayençais had wanted to open the city gates to the Prussians. But we arrested or deported the leaders, he assured the Convention, and appropriated their property. "Always make good and vigorous laws, and you will find strong men to assure their execution." Then he introduced the deputation "from the free peoples of Germany," and Forster made one of his always-brilliant addresses.[204]

Forster spoke of Charlemagne's empire, of natural bounds, and of the importance of Mayence to France from the economic and military points of view.[205] He declared Mayence to be "impregnable," and urged the Convention to make the entire line of the Rhine an impregnable barrier against which the myrmidons of the despots could strike in vain at the free world behind.[206] Then he presented the bid for annexation prepared by the Mayence Convention,[207] and pleaded, in the name of "the German people on the left bank of the Rhine," for its acceptance.[208]

The Convention, "out of the goodness of its heart, . . . granted the request," [209] but not with respect to the entire territory "from Landau to Bingen," as the Mayence decree had contemplated. Haussmann's address to the Convention had also made use of terms that were much too vast. Only 88 communities were represented by the German delegates voting for annexation; hence that is all France could annex if she wanted to adhere to the pretense of having been asked. There were 890 German communities on

---

[202] Arch. N., F1E 40, d. 1.

[203] Hansen, *Quellen*, II, 801, n. 3. The deputation was the idea of the three Paris Convention's Commissioners.

[204] An abridged English translation can be found in Wambaugh, *Plebiscites*, pp. 355–356. The German text of the speech can be found in Klein's *Die Mainzer Klubisten*.

[205] *Ibid.*

[206] Hansen, *Quellen*, II, 813–814.

[207] *Ibid.*, p. 812. *Vide* the "Décret port aut queles villes de Mayence, Worms, etc. pout partie integrante de la France" [*sic!*] in Bockenheimer, *Mainzer Klubisten*, p. 362.

[208] Hansen, *Quellen*, II, 813.

[209] Girtanner, *Rheinstrome*, p. 40.

that part of the left bank. Thirty-two had been annexed the previous March 14; these were the 12 villages in the Bergzabern bailiwick in which Rühl had interested himself, plus 15 Electoral Palatine communities, and 5 others — all in the neighborhood of Landau and Germersheim.[210] If one subtracted these 32, and the 88 annexed on March 30, there would be left 770 communities unaccounted for.[211] In this 770 were Spires, Bingen, and the domains of the two major princes of the region (the Prince-Elector of Bavaria-Palatinate, and the Duke Palatine of Zweibrücken), plus some possessions of the Landgrave of Hesse-Darmstadt.[212] Though some votes had, as indicated, been garnered at Spires — 342 of them — Spires had sent no deputy to the Mayence Convention, and the Convention, anxious to act quickly, had not waited to find out if the city would eventually be represented. The list of cities not represented by the vote, besides those mentioned (Spires and Bingen), included Kaiserslautern, Zweibrücken, Pirmasens, Neustadt-on-the-Hardt, Frankenthal, and Alzey.[213]

The Convention's decree of *réunion* mentioned specifically each of the 88 communities it was annexing — Mayence and Worms crowning the list. The decree ordered Reubell, Haussmann, and Merlin to take all measures necessary to execute the laws of the Republic in the annexed region.[214] But Prussian troops, at that very moment, had hemmed in Custine near Bretzenheim; and lines were tightening around the city of Mayence.[215] The Prussian locksmith[216] had arrived to turn the Key of Germany and let the owners back in. Forster, Lux, and Patocki found themselves locked out — stranded in Paris.[217]

[210] Hansen, *Quellen*, II, 785.

[211] *Ibid.*, pp. 804–805.

[212] *Ibid.*, p. 800, n. 1.

[213] *Ibid.*, p. 812, n. 2. The author would very much like to know where Rain obtained his information that "the overwhelming majority of the population, rejecting the old regime, wished to constitute a new state, independent" (*Mir. à Bon.*, p. 85). Certainly he did not get it from the documents.

The deputies of Spires and of several other municipalities alleged, as their reason for not appearing, the difficulties of travel in occupied country (Babelon, *Rhin ... hist.*, II, 345).

[214] Hansen, *Quellen*, II, 812–813.

[215] *Ibid.*, p. 816.

[216] The army before Mayence was composed not only of Prussian troops, but of those of Austria, Saxony, Hesse-Cassel, Hesse-Darmstadt, and the Palatinate (A. von

Vivenot, *Herzog Albrecht von Sachsen-Teschen* [2 vols. in 3, Vienna, 1864–1866], II [*Zur Geschichte des Baseler Friedens*], Pt. I, 508).

[217] In reply to their petition for pecuniary assistance, the Convention voted them the same salary — 18 livres per day — that French deputies received (Bonnal de Ganges, *Repré.*, IV, 531–532). Adam Lux was later arrested and executed for writing an *Apologie de Charlotte Corday* and attacking the Jacobins (J. Mathorez, "La pénétration allemande en France au XIXᵉ siècle," *REH* [*Revue des études historiques*], 1923, p. 73). Patocki, dissatisfied with 18 paper livres per day, turned army contractor.

Forster tried to work with the revolutionists, but a glimmer of doubt as to the wisdom of his actions appeared already in his letter of January 28, 1793, to his wife (in Neuchâtel): "Had dreams of

There were those in Mayence who envied them their misfortune. Dorsch, Wedekind, Pape, Blau, and some other erstwhile zealous Clubists and deputies to the Mayence Convention, stole out of Mayence the very day of its annexation by France, and tried to reach Strasburg. Dorsch and Wedekind made it; Blau, Pape, and others fell into Prussian hands. Their colleagues in the Mayence Convention were furious at this desertion.[218] They had been working so earnestly to further the defense of the city. On March 27, they had decreed that all persons who had refused and still refused to vow fidelity to liberty and equality should be expelled with their families; and on the twenty-eighth, they had decreed confiscation of their property.[219] On March 28, they had seized sixteen prominent citizens during the night, and shipped them off in two wagons to Belfort.[220] They had tried to stage a repeat performance the next night, but the city had already been surrounded by the Allies [221] (though the real siege did not start for several weeks because heavy artillery had to be brought in).[222] On March 30, they had expelled four

---

human perfection directed me when I chose what I had to do here, then truly would I have been the fool people take me for. . . It is better to be free, or — shall we say? — to strive for freedom, than . . . to beg for bread under a despot." —*Briefe . . . Rev.*, II, 246.

The desertion of Dumouriez and the advance of the Allied armies produced in their train excesses which alienated the refined soul of Forster, and he wrote, on April 16, 1793, the oft-quoted lines: "Oh, since I know that there is no virtue in the Revolution, I loathe it. Aside from all idealistic dreams, I could march with imperfect Man toward the goal, stumble on the way and rise again and resume the journey; but [to march] with . . . heartless devils like those around me here is to me a sin against humanity, [against our] holy Mother Earth, . . .[against] the light of the sun." Disillusionment was followed by disgust with himself for the part he had played, and this, coupled with actual starvation (Forster to his wife, Nov. 27, 1793, *ibid.*, p. 284), undermined his resistance. His death on January 10, 1794, removed from the political stage the last of the three heralds of Rhenish "freedom" (Bockenheimer, *Mainzer Klubisten*, pp. 303, 306).

In the opinion of Jacques Droz, Forster's bitterness was due to his failure to realize that a revolution is not an abstract prob-

lem to be solved by the application of philosophical maxims, but a flesh-and-blood historical matter (*Allemagne*, p. 48). Still, Forster seemed to have a practical enough mind when he tried to persuade Adam Lux not to publish his *Charlotte Corday*. Argued Forster, one should not despair of the Revolution: The violence and excesses were only storms which would be followed by fair weather. The fact that thunder resounded here or there, or lightning struck some fields, did not justify the belief that the end of the world was at hand. And in his writings, Forster said: "Charlotte Corday turned the head of this fine young man, and he knew no greater bliss than to die for her and for the Girondist party — the only [party] . . . which, according to him, was in the right." To this, Forster added the very practical observation that Lux had so allowed his feelings to rule him that he had eaten almost nothing for a week (A. Chuquet, "Adam Lux," *Etudes*, II, 73).

[218] Hansen, *Quellen*, II, 816, n. 1.

[219] *Ibid.*, p. 815, n. 5.

[220] Bockenheimer, *Mainzer Klubisten*, p. 240. Among the sixteen were a privy councillor, an aulic councillor, a jurist, a professor, an ecclesiastic, and lesser officials and merchants (*ibid.*, p. 363).

[221] *Ibid.*, p. 240.

[222] Wurmser to Thugut, April 21, 1793, Vivenot-Zeissberg, *Quellen*, III, 33.

or five hundred women and children, blindfolded, without even announcing by trumpeter that they were coming. The Prussians thought it was a French sortie, and were about to mow them down when someone picked up a spy-glass.[223]

Of course, these heroic efforts at defense had been going on for some time. Forster had written on March 14 that thirty to forty persons were being shipped across the Rhine each day.[224] But it was found necessary to intensify the efforts. On March 31, the Mayence Convention adjourned after creating a new General Administration of eighteen members, under Hofmann (president) and M. Metternich (vice-president). This body created a Committee of Surveillance to deport troublesome citizens. Hofmann had considerable difficulty with the French military authorities after that. The French would seize for France what was confiscated from the Mayence non-swearers. Hofmann claimed the property for the "Rheno-German Free State," whatever that might mean.[225]

The French were particularly blatant about their seizures because there was serious disagreement in France as to whether an attempt should be made to hold Mayence. Of course, Custine has assured the Mayençais repeatedly that if they would change flags, France would defend Mayence to the bitter end. As late as February 15 he had declared he would answer with his head for the safety of the city.[226] A few days before (February 12), he had ordered — in view of the darkening military situation — that every inhabitant of Mayence should lay in seven months' supplies, and anyone who did not want to comply would have to leave the city.[227] But he reportedly drew heavily on the Mayence garrison to strengthen his troops of the line,[228] and he just did not seem to manifest sufficient solicitude for the defense of the city. Reubell, Haussmann, and Merlin were for holding Mayence at all costs. Merlin was especially eloquent in his arguments: Possession enabled France to feed her armies at the Rhineland's expense. The city held a fine fortress which had been erected at great cost. "Mayence, especially in its present state, is one of the strongest cities in Europe." [229] And it was part of the Rhineland, which, in its entirety, should form France's frontier for reasons of defense.[230]

Beurnonville, minister of war since February 4 (he suceeded Pache), had first favored surrendering the city, but changed his stand early in March.

[223] Hansen, *Quellen*, II, 815.

[224] Bockenheimer, *Mainzer Klubisten*, p. 239.

[225] Hansen, *Quellen*, II, 815, n. 5.

[226] *Ibid.*, p. 758, n. 3. He did.

[227] *Ibid.* The order applied to Kastel and Landau also.

[228] *Ibid.*, p. 816.

[229] Cmrs AA. RVMo to Beurnonville (min. of war), Feb. 10, 1793, J. Reynaud, *Vie et correspondance de Merlin de Thionville* (2 vols. in 1, Paris, 1860), II, 83.

[230] Merlin-Th. to Thirion, Feb. 4, 1793, Bonnal de Ganges, *Repré.*, III, 149–150.

But the way things were going now, militarily speaking, it was no longer so much a question of "will" but of "can," and opinion in the Convention was divided even on the question of "will." [231] Foreign Minister Lebrun ordered Custine to determine adroitly if the Prussians would consent to an armistice in case the city were surrendered. Custine obeyed,[232] and thus gave rise to the general belief in Germany that Mayence would not long resist. Already in April and May, the newspapers beyond the Rhine were proclaiming that the French garrison in Mayence had intimated a willingness to capitulate, and many strange and unbelievable intrigues were conducted by persons seeking personal profit by promoting the anticipated surrender.[233]

One of these plots was engineered by "useless mouths" deported from Mayence, who were anxious to return to their city. These found a willing instrument in a French artillery officer, Corbeau, former page of the Dauphine (in 1766). Corbeau was stationed in the Palatinate, whither Custine had sent him to oversee the Elector's neutrality. There the Mayor of Worms, Winkelmann, visited him and proposed the bases of an "honorable capitulation" for Mayence. Corbeau wrote to Custine, reporting the overture, and asking that one Reibold, Palatine envoy to France, be released from captivity in Mayence so that the Palatine government should cease to detain him, Corbeau, in reprisal — "in order that I can apply myself efficaciously in the preludes of a negotiation . . . [beneficial to] humanity." We do not have Custine's reply, but Reibold was freed, which seems to imply that Custine favored the negotiation. On April 19, Corbeau wrote to Reubell and Merlin of Thionville suggesting that they repair to Oppenheim to renew with the Prussians the negotiations described below. The Representatives [234] ordered him home, and Custine had him arrested to remove suspicion that he, Custine, had authorized the negotiation. Corbeau was not released till the end of 1794.[235]

Another of these plots concerned the Trèves-born French army officer Boos,[236] who was a prisoner in Prussian hands. On April 12, 1793, Boos sent a note to General d'Oyré, in command at Mayence, declaring that Custine had charged him to discuss something with D'Oyré. Would D'Oyré meet him at Hechtsheim? An accompanying letter from Frederick William's aide-de-camp, Major von Zastrow, announced that the King had consented

---

[231] Hansen, *Quellen*, II, 779, n. 1.
[232] Chuquet, *Guerres Rév.*, VII, 177.
[233] Haussmann, Rp A. R to CPS, May 3, 1793, Aulard, *Actes*, III, 588 *et seqq.*
[234] The designation "Representative on Mission" replaced that of "Commissioner" on April 11, 1793. *Vide infra*, Pt. I, chap. iv,

§ 1.
[235] Col. Herlaut, "Les négociations du général Custine avec l'ennemi (décembre 1792– mai 1793)," *AHRF*, IX (1932), 528–531.
[236] This is the "Boze" of the *Moniteur*, XVII, 440.

to the interview provided that he, von Zastrow, and Major von Kleist were present as witnesses. D'Oyré and other French officers repaired to Hechtsheim that very day, with the Representative Reubell. Very softly and haltingly, Boos announced that he had bad news. "Paris is in rebellion. The National Convention has been dissolved. Dumouriez has proclaimed the Dauphin and marched upon Paris to reëstablish order." And he went on to say: "[Custine] has not enough troops to fight the enemy. He wishes the Mayence garrison to rejoin him, and invites you to surrender the fortress." D'Oyré and Reubell would have none of this proposition, and left. But as they departed, Boos managed to slip into D'Oyré's hand a note signed "Custine," declaring that he (Custine) had been deprived of some of his troops to fill up the breaches caused by Dumouriez' treason,[237] that Alsace was in danger, and that it would be very helpful if the Mayence garrison could honorably surrender and join him. The note was of course a forgery — not a very good one; and the scheme failed. Boos had apparently sold his services to Prussia.[238]

Mathiez is troubled by Chuquet's account of the Boos negotiation, but that is because he has not read Chuquet aright. To quote Mathiez: "If M. Chuquet, *Mayence*, page 176, could be believed, the council of war, in its first session on April 12, examined carefully the letter of Custine that Boos had brought, and recognized that 'the signature of the General was counterfeit and too cramped.' It is singular that . . . the council should have even authorized the *pourparlers* if it believed in the falsity of this signature of Custine." [239] But Boos did not bring a letter purporting to be from Custine, and Chuquet does not assert that he did. A trumpeter brought two letters, one from Boos, one from von Zastrow. The letter from Boos asserted that Custine had written to him (Boos); but the letter was still at this time in Boos's hands. Thus, when the council of war authorized the parley, it possessed no document bearing Custine's signature. It was only at the end of the parley that Boos slipped the counterfeit message into D'Oyré's hand. D'Oyré turned the letter over to the council of war, which then scrutinized the signature and found it too cramped.[240]

During Boos's underhanded overture, Reubell expressed the willingness to engage in legitimate negotiations with the King of Prussia. The suggestion soon bore fruit, and several conferences took place between Reubell, Merlin of Thionville, and Simon, on the French side; and General Kalkreuth, Count von Voss, and the Elector of Mayence's jeweler on the German side. The negotiations, at first held at Oppenheim, seemed to lead nowhere,

[237] *Vide* next chapter, § 1.
[238] Chuquet, *Guerres Rév.*, VII, 178–179.
[239] A. Mathiez, "Le Premier Comité de Salut Public et la guerre," *RH*, CLVIII (1928),

263, n. 2.
[240] Chuquet, *Guerres Rév.*, VII, 178–179, and not 176.

but another attempt at the Prussian outposts bade fair to produce a congress at Spires where not only the surrender of Mayence but the bases of a general peace would be discussed. However, the French apparently had no intention of capitulating, nor the Prussians of abandoning the siege; and when the latter intensified their bombardment, the conferences naturally ceased.[241]

The diplomatic breach did not put an end, however, to the camaraderie which had existed from the very beginning of the war between the French and Prussian soldiers. During truces, opposing troops joked together, drank together, broke bread together, pillaged together; in battle they saved each other's lives after wounding each other. It would hardly be an exaggeration to say that the days of chivalry were reënacted during the siege of Mayence.[242] But when the city capitulated on July 23, 1793, the French returned to modern times. Why had the city surrendered when the garrison still had bread?[243] Its defenses had suffered no breach,[244] and two victorious armies — Beauharnais' and Houchard's — were marching to its assistance. Why had General Beauharnais (first husband of the future Empress Josephine) been so lethargic during the siege? Why had General Custine amassed in Mayence much more artillery than he needed — artillery acquired by denuding other cities — and then allowed the Prussians to get it all? Was not Custine secretly playing the game of the foreigner?[245] And Beauharnais,

[241] *Ibid.*, pp. 180–185.

[242] *Ibid.*, pp. 284 *et seqq.*

[243] According to Ruamps (Rp A. R), already a month before the end of the siege, the rations had been reduced to "a small portion of bread, less than a pint of wine, and . . . no matter what Custine says, neither . . . meat nor vegetables." — To CPS, June 19, 1793, Aulard, *Actes*, V, 19. According to the Representatives to the Army of the Moselle, when Mayence surrendered, "it had enough flour for several days, and wheat, wine, and munitions," though the fodder and medical supplies were exhausted (to Conv., July 30, 1793, *ibid.*, pp. 428–429).

The Duke of Zweibrücken, three days after the surrender, wrote: "The King [of Prussia], after the capitulation, gave two field pieces to the [French] commandant as a mark of his esteem. . . Doiré has surrendered a fortress that could yet have defended itself for at least three weeks, which makes me think that money opened the doors. . . The provisions which remain in grain, wheat, wine, and powder are immense. They lacked calibrated bullets and grapeshot." — To Count de Fersen, July 26, 1793, Baron R. M. de Klinckowström (ed.), *Le Comte de Fersen et la Cour de France* (2 vols., Paris, 1877–1878), II, 425.

[244] That is, the defenses of the fortress proper; but the outer works were no longer tenable, and much of the French artillery had been ruined by "forced charging" (Dumolin, *Précis*, I, 192).

[245] Custine was not in Mayence during the siege. He had other armies to command, and occupied his time riding around between his various posts, e.g., Saarlouis, Blieskastel, Zweibrücken, Homburg, and Saarbrücken (Blaux, Rp in Bas-Rhin, Meurthe, and Moselle to CPS, April 19, 1793, Aulard, *Actes*, III, 339). According to the *Mémoires du maréchal-général Soult* (3 vols., Paris, 1854), I, 28, Custine spent his time reviewing his troops, and seeking to win popularity among them at the expense of his officers.

A private letter from Mayence noted, as early as January 9, the unusual behavior of the General. "Custine always sleeps in Kastel now, visits the sentries in their guardhouses, plays cards with the soldiers,

too?[246] The days of chivalry ended with an ultramodern touch — that of the guillotine. France was willing to acquire by "lucky chance,"[247] but not to lose. Custine and Beauharnais would ere long pay with their lives for the surrender of Mayence.[248] All other persons connected with the capitulation

drinks wine or beer with them, the while he smokes his pipe. . ." — Hansen, *Quellen*, II, 682.

Perhaps a bit of public-relations work was a necessity. Custine was "conceited, hard, troublesome, imperious, choleric, and spiteful," says his aide-de-camp; and he was "detested" by both equals and inferiors. He was reprimanded six times in one year for acts of despotism, according to the aide. When fighting in America under Rochambeau, Custine is said to have treated one of his captains — a good man — with such severity that the latter "retired into his tent and blew out his brains. This unfortunate victim forgot that, before ending his existence, he should have rendered a great service to his comrades by ridding them of . . . the author of his despair." — *Mém. Custine*, Preface, pp. xxi–xxiv. The Preface is by the aide, also.

[246] *Moniteur*, XVII, 265–267. Ruamps (Rp A. R, to CPS, June 19, 1793) characterized Beauharnais as one "whose civic virtues are not less doubtful than his military attainments." — Aulard, *Actes*, V, 18. Denzel (Rp A. R, to Conv., July 20, 1793) described the same general as one "who possesses the highest esteem and confidence of his army, which he merits as much by his military talents as by his proved patriotism." — *Ibid.*, p. 317. But as a *ci-devant*, a former noble, Beauharnais was in a precarious position the moment the mills of fate ceased to grind out victories for him. Realizing this, he tried to resign, but the Representatives to the Rhine Army wrote to the Convention: "If good generals were as easy to find as good soldiers . . . , we could readily decide what to do." And the Representatives, bemoaning that "the Republic's choice lay only between treason and ignorance," begged for advice (Aug. 2, 1793, *ibid.*, p. 453). The First Committee did not see how it could dispense with competence, though potentially treasonable; but its successor, the Great Com-

mittee, placed its faith in loyal incompetence — and succeeded magnificently (Mathiez in *RH*, CLVIII, 259).

[247] On August 24, 1793, during his subsequent trial for treason, Custine declared: "Lucky chance rendered me master of Mayence." — *Moniteur*, XVII, 463.

[248] Other factors of course entered. In Custine's case, it was not only his past but his subsequent idleness, and his failure to take possession of Coblenz when it had been offered to him "on a silver platter." He countered that he did not have enough troops to occupy so much territory; that it was Kellermann's place to "capture" Coblenz, anyway, Kellermann being six leagues closer. Custine declared he had renounced with reluctance the two million florins promised him when he should have arrived in the city (Hansen, *Quellen*, II, 908, n. 2). Turning to private crimes, Custine was accused of selling the Elector's furniture and everything else in the palace for his own profit, whereas these articles belonged to France by right of conquest (Prudhomme, *Rév. Paris*, XV, 75; *Moniteur*, XVII, 507).

Even if Custine was guilty of stealing the furniture, it is not true that he despoiled the Electoral palace of "everything else" — unless it was someone else's silver plate that Reubell carted off to Colmar in the dead of night. In the latter robbery, it is not certain that Reubell was not acting for Merlin-Th. as well, for the two men were very close friends. However that may be, people noted that Reubell's carriage, drawn by four horses, was laden heavily though with small bulk on the way to Colmar, and that it soon returned to Mayence very light. Reubell seems later to have removed the stolen treasure to Paris, yet the busybodies would not leave him alone, and his house there was searched. But the sly Reubell had hidden his loot well. A second search revealed it, however, and it was removed to the Mint for coining (A. Mathiez, "Les malles de

were arrested, and their papers placed under seal and sent to Paris. To Paris also was sent a large silver casserole bearing the arms of the Prince of Nassau. This vessel had been found among the effects of one of the French generals responsible for the surrender, and the Representatives to the Moselle Army were convinced it was a bribe.[249]

Some of the Clubists, contrary to the terms of the Capitulation,[250] followed the French army out of the city.[251] Several of these were captured. Goethe, in his *Belagerung von Mainz* ("Siege of Mayence"), describes how the Mayençais ambushed the wagons of the *évacués* and seized those who were Clubists. In one fine carriage drawn by three horses, a beautiful, friendly young lady showed herself conspicuously to fix the roving eyes of the watchers. However, they tore from her side, feet first, a short, fat, pock-marked Clubist. Then "they closed the door of the carriage, and bade the beauty *bon voyage*." But the beast of this tale was beaten so terribly that all (?) his bones were broken and his face was unrecognizable. He was finally rescued from further physical torment by a guard, but the people continued to overwhelm him with abuse.[252]

The Clubists captured at this time were added to the number seized during the previous attempt at escape made several months earlier when the Prussian lines were not yet so tightly drawn. The prisoners — both groups — were incarcerated in Ehrenbreitstein and Königstein (the forts of Coblenz and Mayence) and Erfurt — all except Pape, who was accorded special treatment because of his "Open Letter" to the King of Prussia. The ex-monk was turned over to the tender mercies of Frederick William, who deputed the task of punishment personally to Baron von Stein. Pape's temerity cost him a hundred lashes. Several Clubists later freed by the Prussians were immediately imprisoned by the Mayençais, who consistently proved themselves less lenient than the stern Prussians.[253]

It is surprising that the Capitulation should not have recognized the

---

Reubell," *AR*, XV [1923], 414; IX [1917], 541–543; X [1918], 246–247).

On the score of burglary Custine was no more guilty than Reubell, and Reubell was not executed. Instead, two years later he was elected to the highest office in France. Nor was Custine more guilty than Merlin, who was "more than suspected of having received the price for the capitulation of Mayence" (Report upon Fabre d'Eglantine, quoted by Mathiez, *ibid.*, IX, 543). Regarding the question of Merlin's guilt, *vide* Reynaud's explanations in *Corr. Merlin-Th.*, I, 155–225.

[249] Rps A. Mo to Conv., July 30, 1793, Aulard, *Actes*, V, 429.

[250] *Moniteur*, XVII, 266.

[251] The Representatives to the Rhine Army brought out the Clubists' baggage in the conveyance that carried their own papers (Merlin-Th. to Hérault de Séchelles, Aug. 7, 1793, Aulard, *Actes*, V, 504).

[252] C. Waas (ed.), *Goethe: Belagerung von Mainz, 1793* (Berlin, 1910), pp. 168–169.

[253] Hansen, *Quellen*, II, 888–889; Königstein prisoners to Merlin-Th., Nov. 14, 1794, *Corr. Merlin-Th.*, II, 34–36.

existence of the Clubists by so much as a single word,[254] but that was not the fault of General d'Oyré. He had sought to have them included in the free-departure granted to the French garrison. The King of Prussia had refused. D'Oyré had insisted, arguing that it would be dishonorable for the French nation to hand back its friends and adherents, champions of liberty, to a king.[255] But it was D'Oyré who was capitulating, not Frederick William.

The Capitulation, as finally agreed upon, mentioned only the garrison and "in general, all French persons." Of course, since Mayence had been annexed by France, were not all Mayençais French persons? D'Oyré never thought of that one. He left it to the Clubists themselves to sneak out of the city in disguise.

It seems, indeed, that an agreement outside the Capitulation provided for the possible future exchange of Clubists against German hostages in French hands.[256] Such were the subjects of Zweibrücken arrested in 1792 when the contributions levied on the Duchy were not paid in full; notables of Mayence arrested in March 1793 on the ground of their attachment to the old regime; and presently, additional hostages from Zweibrücken, many of them women, seized when the victorious Germans arrested the wives of the Mayence "patriots." [257] This agreement for exchange does not at all excuse the French for their failure to provide for their friends in the Capitulation, inasmuch as such an arrangement permitted the Clubists to be punished *until* their exchange. And the French government was unbelievably lax in effecting the exchange. Many and frequent were the pleas of the incarcerated for relief,[258] but it was not until February 9, 1795, that action was forthcoming.[259]

Those Clubists whom the Prussians had not imprisoned did not fare any better. The Mayençais were more angry with traitors than with Frenchmen. They seized the Clubists from their beds, and pommeled and imprisoned them. Those who had accepted functions under the French regime, and those who had sworn to be faithful to liberty and equality — and France — were punished. Blau was beaten well-nigh to death.[260] Priests who had taken

[254] Dumolin, *Précis*, I, 193, erroneously states that the Capitulation provided that the French might take the Clubists away with them.

[255] Hansen, *Quellen*, II, 887.

[256] *Corr. Merlin-Th.*, II, 34–49; *AHRF*, N.S., I, 450. Do not confuse the Clubists left in Mayence with the thousand Frenchmen left behind as security for the payment of certain sums due the Prussians, such as hospital and evacuation expenses (*Archives parlementaires de 1787 à 1860*, Ser. I [1789–1794; 82 vols., Paris, 1879–1913], LXXXI, 399).

[257] *Corr. Merlin-Th.*, II, 36–37, note. The wife of the elusive Dr. Wedekind, and the Wedekinder, were among their number (*AHRF*, N.S., I, 453).

[258] *Corr. Merlin-Th.*, II, 34–49.

[259] *Ibid.*, p. 38, note.

[260] Finally the Prussian commandant ordered that punishment of the Clubists be left to the returning Electoral government (Hansen, *Quellen*, II, 888).

the oath were obliged to beg absolution from their bishops and from Rome.[261] The old regime was reëstablished in its entirety.

The populations of the Rhineland greeted their little despots with joy, for the country had been ruined by the requisitions of the French. "The charming ideas of fraternity had taken the form of contributions in florins levied on the inhabitants." [262] General Augereau [263] had been a model of covetousness, and Custine was not without reason accused of having made war on granaries and money-coffers. A swarm of contractors had lit upon the country, devouring everything like locusts. The inhabitants, from desire to exist, had been forced to become antagonists of the invader.[264]

Before the Allied reconquest, one of Forster's friends (a former counsellor to the Elector Palatine), whose harvest had been pillaged by the French, wrote to Custine that "the brigandage of the subordinate employees has already only too well succeeded in alienating the hearts [of the Rhinelanders] and in dissuading them from offering themselves to France. . . The justice and generosity of the Republic are a thousand times compromised. Ah! the inhabitants would have been less cruelly deceived if they had been told right from the start: 'We have come to take everything. We do not care to hear a word concerning your union with us, or your neutrality; we repudiate all connection with you; therefore do not ask that we respect our promises, for we will make use of the rights of war.'" Custine responded that he was ready to give satisfaction to "the friend of Forster," but could not change the system.[265] He also indemnified fully 116 citizens of Spires who had suffered by his invasion, and he left the magistrates of the city 5,000 florins to complete the indemnification of the poor.[266] But such isolated acts of good

[261] Sagnac, *Rhin fr.*, pp. 102–103. Gooch says it was not until after the Peace of Basel, April 5, 1795, that all the Mayence "patriots" were relieved of punishment (*Germ. Fr. Rev.*, p. 480). Not only is the date of relief incorrect — it should be February 9 — but the mention of the Peace of Basel in this connection might lead the incautious to conclude that the release of the Mayençais formed one of the provisions of that treaty, whereas their release resulted from the efforts of Merlin-Th. (*Corr. Merlin-Th.*, II, 49, 38).

Girtanner had been "certain that the German princes were too magnanimous to take reprisals against those of their old citizens who, as mere passive instruments of this violent revolution, could not have done otherwise than swim along with the stream wherever it took them." — *Rheinstrome*, p. 40. But the princes were not so noble.

[262] Blondel in Lavisse and Rambaud, *Hist. gén.*, VIII, 700. If the French regime in the Rhineland "rested largely on the peasantry," as Crane Brinton suggests (*Decade of Rev.*, p. 166), its foundations were certainly very unstable, for though the ownership of the land had been granted to the peasants by the conqueror, practically all of its fruits were being confiscated. Thus, the net result was to the disadvantage of the French new order's "beneficiaries."

[263] This is the Augereau who effected the *coup d'état* of 18 *fructidor*, V (September 4, 1797), for the Directory, *infra*, Pt. II, chap. xxvii, § 2.

[264] Blondel in Lavisse and Rambaud, *Hist. gén.*, VIII, 700.

[265] Sagnac, *Rhin fr.*, p. 83.

[266] Rambaud, *Français sur Rhin*, pp. 181–183.

will could not assuage the woes of the mass of the citizenry for whom the French invasion had spelled economic ruin.

4. AIX-LA-CHAPELLE

The story of Aix-la-Chapelle is the story of Mayence, abbreviated. This former capital of Charlemagne encountered the advance guard of Dumouriez' army on December 15, 1792 — the natal day of the famous Compulsory Liberty Decree. Four days later one Johann Tauzenberg of Aix, a goldsmith's son, hacked to pieces a stone whipping post erected in 1616 as a memorial to a heretical mayor. Then, among the fragments, he planted a tree of liberty. One other person took part in the ceremony, a born Frenchman domiciled in Aix-la-Chapelle. The few natives who gathered to watch emitted no shouts of exultation; they were annoyed, and openly queried what they could get out of such hollow liberty.[267]

On December 26, the Compulsory Liberty Decree was promulgated in Aix, together with a proclamation drafted at the same time as the Decree: "The French people to the ——— people. Brethren and friends! We have conquered liberty and shall maintain it. We offer you the enjoyment of this inestimable benefit which has always been yours, and of which your oppressors could have deprived you only by illegal means. We have driven out your tyrants; show yourselves free men, and we will guarantee you against their vengeance. . . "[268]

Aix's burgomaster responded (to General Desforest) by letter, saying that Aix had no tyrants to expel; that it had been free since 1415; that it would be silly to select temporary officials, as the Decree provided, when the permanent ones were already in office, etc.[269] General Dampierre, commandant of Aix, thereupon appeared before the city authorities and read them part of the December 15 and 17 document, to show them that the Convention had decreed provisional administrations — so they had to have them. And then and there Dampierre convoked "the sovereign people of the city of Aix" in sectional and communal assemblies to elect provisional administrations.[270] Dampierre was not going to disobey.[271] He had already planted a second tree of liberty without any disastrous effects — this time to the accompaniment

[267] *Aachener Chronik*, Hansen, *Quellen*, II, 664–665; *vide* also p. 665, n. 2.
[268] Hansen, *Quellen*, II, 647, n. 1.
[269] Dec. 30, 1792, *ibid.*, pp. 675–676.
[270] Jan. 3, 1793, *ibid.*, pp. 682–683.
[271] Even General Dumouriez, his superior, was obeying, though unwillingly. Dumouriez did not believe in annexing, but in creating buffer states, as mentioned *supra*, Introduction, § 2h. But Danton and Delacroix, two of the Convention's Commissioners, thought an Aix asking for annexation would set a good example to the remainder of the Rhineland. At any rate, so said General Dampierre (Hansen, *Quellen*, II, 776).

of music, exultation, and a speech from the General himself.[272] So why not have a few provisional assemblies? Of course, this was really not a jesting matter. The assemblies were Step One in a settled procedure guaranteed (?) to produce requests for annexation.

The sections met on January 7, each in a neighboring church, and were instructed, on order of the four French Commissioners,[273] to proceed to the election of provisional representatives. At first the sections insisted they would have nothing but their old constitution, so the French arrested the burgomaster and accused him of instigating resistance. And they threatened to deport him and all the magistrates to Paris if resistance to the French-proposed constitution continued. It soon became evident that continued resistance would only bring on unpleasant incidents, so, the next day, seven of the eight sections chose a president, which the French had wanted them to do.[274] (The eighth section would not yield.)

Meanwhile — January 8 — the "Club of Freedom, Equality, and Brotherly Love" was established by General Dampierre. Unlike the Club of Mayence, which was radical Jacobin in tone, the Aix Club was moderate. Its president was the physician Dr. de Vivignis; its vice-president, the French resident who had assisted in the tree-planting ceremony; and its secretary, Johann Dautzenberg, elder brother of the editor of the *Aachener Zuschauer*, and probably the uncle of the tree planter.[275] The Aix Club corresponded with the Jacobin Club of Paris. Speeches were delivered in German and French, and Dampierre often spoke there. We do not know too much about this Club, for although it kept minutes of its proceedings, these were impounded when the French were driven out, and they have since disappeared.[276]

On January 22, the eight sections of the city were ordered to appear in their respective churches and elect a mayor. They did — under compulsion. They also elected the required provisional tribunals.[277] But less than two weeks later (February 4), Dampierre was ordering the new administration to improve the roadways so the French could move about their artillery quickly,[278] for — the enemy was at the gates. However, as in Mayence, such a trifle was not allowed to stop the progress of *"réunion."*

On February 5, Dampierre ordered the sections to assemble and select deputies to a national convention. Some persons came but shrieked: "We don't want to hear anything about any convention or any constitution." The next day, certain leading citizens were arrested, and the city militiamen

[272] *Aachener Zuschauer*, Jan. 3, *ibid.*, pp. 678–679.
[273] Camus, Delacroix (J. F. Lacroix), Gossuin, and Danton (Hansen, *Quellen*, II, 692).
[274] *Ibid.*, p. 693.
[275] Hansen sometimes indicates that the tree-

planter and the Aix Clubist were one and the same person (*vide ibid.*, pp. 692, n. 2, and 821, n. 3; cf. p. 784, n. 3).
[276] *Ibid.*, pp. 694–696.
[277] *Ibid.*, p. 713.
[278] *Ibid.*, p. 735.

were ordered to give up their weapons. But — strangely — no weapons could be found. The French thought they must be in the home of the militia's commander, so swooped down on him. He was gone. So a city-wide search for arms was started. The deputies finally were chosen — on the twelfth. A report of the fifteenth tells us that the burgomaster was ordered to take up the arms of the citizenry, but refused and was imprisoned. Everyone was in a state of great excitement, for the Austrian army was approaching. It was under conditions such as these that the Aix-la-Chapelle National Convention opened (February 25).[279]

We know very little about the work of this Convention. Of course, the goal toward which the French were driving was to have the Aix Convention ask France for annexation. The question of Aix's annexation had come up in the Paris Convention already on January 31, but Belgium — which was being considered along with Liège and the Aix-la-Chapelle territory — was in wild revolt against the Decree of December 15 and 17,[280] and it was decided to prepare the region by a new decree — of January 31. This decree prescribed absolutely the holding of the primary and communal assemblies within a fortnight after promulgation of the Compulsory Liberty Decree and its supplements of December 22 and January 31.[281] The penalty — to be treated as an enemy of liberty and equality — in practice signified to be exiled (or sometimes even slain) and suffer confiscation of property; so only hardy souls would risk suspicion of such a heinous crime. But the Aix-la-Chapelle citizens were exceptionally brave, and cried out: "Our religion is being profaned. . . We are [asked] to become the enemy of Emperor and Empire. It were better for us to die on the spot. Death is better. We prefer death. . . "[282] There was no forcing such people, with the enemy at the gates. This is perhaps why we hear of no last-minute vote of the Aix Convention for annexation.

The French were defeated at Aldenhoven on March 1, and on the second, the Austrians appeared. Some of the French ran right through the city and out on the other side. The streets bore witness to those who did not get away. Part of these owed their untimely demise to the hidden arms of the inhabitants, who fired from windows. Many sick and wounded French soldiers quartered in houses were thrown out of windows onto the streets[283]

[279] Ibid., pp. 736–738, 765.

[280] The Aix people did want liberty, but not the brand they had received. The French decrees of December, they thought, were a violation of the sovereignty of the Aix "nation." And they wanted to maintain the privileges of their nobles and clergy

(ibid., p. 682, n. 1).

[281] Ibid., pp. 732–734.

[282] Ibid., p. 714.

[283] Gillet to the inhabitants of Aix, Sept. 24, 1794, ibid., III, 228, n. 2, for this sentence only.

— a shocking reminder that being a victim does not endow one with virtue where virtue was not before. "[Aix! that's] where we were detested," said a French officer-participant.

Because the Aix inhabitants took an active part in the expulsion of the French, Robespierre "promised" the city that if it ever were recaptured, it would be plundered and burned. It was recaptured in September 1794. That it escaped punishment can be traced directly to the fact that, while the inhabitants were firing on the troops the year before, Freemasons pulled several French soldiers into their lodge for safety, and hid them there until they could escape dressed as monks. One of these soldiers was now attached to the headquarters of the invading army.[284]

It might be queried how it was possible to conceal the Frenchmen from the loyal members (if there were any), but Dautzenberg was one-third owner of the building, and a second third belonged to another Aix Clubist. Both Dautzenberg and Dr. de Vivignis were Freemasons. They left Aix with the French, just like Hofmann of Mayence. Those Clubists remaining were arrested and tried,[285] but not at all with the zeal that some of the citizens and the Imperial regulations (*Reichsgutachten* of February 18) demanded.[286] However, there were no scenes of popular vengeance, as at Mayence.

All this time, while Austria and Prussia were (losing and) reconquering Imperial territory, the clumsy, disjointed machine called the Empire was slowly being fueled and oiled. Measures had been taken against incendiary writings, secret societies in institutions of learning, public or secret declarations of neutrality, service with France, separation from the Empire, the planting of trees of liberty, and the founding of Clubs. Triple contingents had been voted. Finally, in the same month that Aix-la-Chapelle was rescued and Mayence was completely surrounded, came the long-delayed declaration of war against France mentioned in the last chapter (March 22, 1793).[287]

Since the war was now going well, this declaration meant just one thing to the Rhineland — freedom from economic ruin under the cloak of fraternity. The French theory was of course that France supplied the men and management while the Rhineland supplied the money for the mutual defense of common ideals; and that theory, put honestly into practice, makes good

[284] *Ibid.*, II, 775–777; III, 227 and n. 4.
[285] *Ibid.*, II, 776, n. 2; 784, n. 3.
[286] *Ibid.*, p. 821, n. 3.
[287] *Ibid.*, p. 805. Ratified April 30, 1793 (*ibid.*, p. 810). It was Custine's invasion of the Rhineland — German soil — which provided perhaps the most telling argument for the advocates of war. Neither the enclave question nor the plight of the French monarchy had proved to be motives of sufficient strength. Even with the invasion, it took six months for the Diet to make up its mind.

sense and good morals. It seems — does it not? — that to blame the French system because it was so cruel and immoral in practice is like finding fault with Divine Providence because Man corrupts Its kind dispensations. We cannot brook the corruption in either case, but we should know where to assess the blame.

CHAPTER III

FRANCO–GERMAN RELATIONS
UNDER DANTON

I. THE DESERTION OF GENERAL DUMOURIEZ

*T*HE system that Custine "deplored," but could not change, was not a system aimed at the conquered countries. Troops quartered in France itself were quite regularly supported by the same means.[1] Several years later, General Jourdan declared in a speech: "For two years I commanded 150,000 men, . . . and never received more than 10,000 rations per day. I was forced to procure the remainder for my army from the territory it was occupying. However, the treasury has consistently paid for 150,000 rations." [2]

Army supplies lent themselves so readily to "speculation" that they often ended up in private warehouses while soldiers bled and hungered and froze for lack of them. This was the experience of every Revolutionary general. It was the experience of General Dumouriez, the conqueror of Belgium. But certainly it was not Dumouriez' place to criticize, for he had protected the embezzling contractors.[3] And yet it was the failure of supply which contributed largely to his ignominious defeat at Neerwinden on March 18, 1793. The same cause lay behind the shortage of troops of which he complained, for, as soon as French soil had been cleared of the enemy, the hungry and ill-clothed volunteers seized upon their legal right to return to their homes.[4] What else could have been expected of them? If we may believe Bonnal de Ganges, they were quartered out in the open — with nothing over their heads for protection. Their uniforms were in shreds. The shirts with which they had been supplied were made of packing-cloth. Their "new" socks were secondhand and threadbare. Their shoes had been fabricated from cardboard.[5] Neerwinden was due fully as much to the

---

[1] *Vide.*, e.g., *Un séjour en France*, p. 213. Also Sorel, *Europe*, III (*La guerre aux rois, 1792–1793*, 1891), 438.

[2] Sciout, *Direc.*, II, 596.

[3] Mathiez, *Fr. Rev.*, p. 277.

[4] *Ibid.*, p. 296.

[5] Bonnal de Ganges, *Repré.*, IV, 7. Bonnal de Ganges states that he obtained this information from the archives, and there is no reason to question its accuracy beyond that

contractors as to the Austrians, but perhaps most of all to the incompetent Minister of War Pache, the "Disorganizer of Victory." [6]

The Neerwinden reverse had not formed part of Dumouriez' plans. He had expected to march on Paris with a victorious army, disperse the revolutionists, and play Monck with the aid of secret allies in the capital. This idea was not new to him. He had long been planning to restore the Bourbons after a successful campaign against Austria, when his prestige would be at its height.[7] He declared later that he had intended to subdue Holland, use Dutch troops to reinforce his army and conquer Belgium, incorporate Belgium's troops with his own and force the Austrians across the Rhine, then march on Paris, "the Constitution in my hand, exterminate the Republic, . . . reëstablish a king, . . . and dictate peace to the rest of Europe." [8] But the blunders of General Miranda in Holland, the lifting of the siege of Maestricht, and the crowning defeat of Neerwinden of necessity occasioned a change in his *modus operandi*.

Heretofore, Dumouriez had been merely a factionist, one of many such in those hectic days. Now, with but a remnant of his army left to him, and this in retreat, he found it necessary to accept Austrian aid to effect his aim. In enlisting the enemy of the *patrie*, factionism yielded to unvarnished treason, and treason, once entered upon, knows no bounds. When Colonel Mack,[9] sent by the Austrian commander, the Duke of Coburg (more accurately: Prince Friedrich Josias of Coburg-Saalfeld, Duke of Saxony), to discuss a monarchical restoration with Dumouriez, declared that Coburg would enter into no negotiations so long as a single French soldier remained in the Austrian Netherlands, Dumouriez readily agreed to evacuate Belgium.[10] Knowledge of Dumouriez' intrigues had reached the Convention through loyal officers,[11] and the Convention despatched a commission of five mem-

author's chronic untrustworthiness. Shoes were still soled with cardboard in 1796 (A. and J. Bricard [eds.], *Journal du canonnier Bricard, 1792–1802* [2nd ed.; Paris, 1891], p. 211).

[6] Chuquet, *Guerres Rév.*, IV, chap. v; Sorel, *Europe*, III, 77, n. 1.

[7] Dunn-Pattison in *C. Mod. H.*, VIII, 421.

[8] Conversation between Dumouriez and Count von Starhemberg (Aust. min. to The Hague), April 10, 1793, Vivenot-Zeissberg, *Quellen*, III, 7.

[9] Coburg's aide-de-camp. Though only a colonel, Mack was responsible for the success of the Austrians in the spring campaign of 1793 in Belgium; and Coburg threatened to resign if Mack were not promoted to general, and chief of the general

staff (Coburg to Francis II, April 12, 1793, *ibid.*, p. 11). The promotion was denied. Coburg was disgruntled but continued to serve (Mercy to Thugut, May 24, 1793, *ibid.*, p. 76). By the following March, however, the Emperor (or rather, Thugut) was praising the talents of *General* Mack (to Coburg, *ibid.*, IV, 144).

[10] Sorel, *Europe*, III, 354; Goetz-Bernstein, *Gironde*, p. 388.

[11] Also through a commission composed of the Brussels-born financier Proly and his two friends, the Brussels playwright Dubuisson and the Bayonne tobacco manufacturer Pereira, sent by Lebrun to survey Dumouriez. But when the three returned to Paris, they were thrown into jail for their story, so fair were their reputations and so fantastic their

bers,[12] one of which was the minister of war, Beurnonville, to suspend the General from his command, and summon him to Paris for a hearing. The commission arrived at Dumouriez' headquarters the night of April 1. The General exchanged some heated words with its members, took them captive, and next day turned them over to the Austrians — to hold as hostages for the safety of Louis XVI's widow, two children, and sister, imprisoned in the Temple.[13]

The French were indignant with Coburg for accepting the five prisoners, for they had not been captured in war but betrayed by their own countryman.[14] Feeling was at its height, and the Convention took two classes of countermeasures. The first was the arrest of counterhostages. At the outset, it had been intended to transfer to a Paris prison all captured Austrian officers, but the question arose whether this would not lead to reprisals against captive French officers. It was thought wiser, therefore, merely to imprison certain German princes already in French hands. Two of these, the Count of Auersperg and the Count of Leiningen-Westerburg, the Convention mistakenly believed to be relatives of Coburg; another two, the Labarre brothers, were indeed nephews of the Austrian general Clerfayt; and the remaining three, the Counts of Leiningen, will be remembered as the trio arrested in Grünstadt for refusing to swear fidelity to the Republic. To these seven the decree added all German princes in French hands who possessed a deliberative voice at Ratisbon — France's reply to the Empire's declaration of war on March 22. In practice, "in French hands" meant also "or who could be kidnaped." This extension enabled the ill Count of Hatzfeld and the Paris-born Princess of Nassau-Saarbrücken to be added to the

---

story. *Vide* the complete "Procès-verbal des trois conférences que les citoyens Proly, Pereyra et Dubuisson ont eues avec le général Dumouriez à Tournai," *Mém. Dumouriez*, IV, 277–287, "Eclair. hist. et pièces off.," Note (C). Regarding the immediate and eventual lot of the three observers, *vide* Mathiez, *Etrangers*, p. 106, and *Mém. Dumouriez*, IV, 126, n. 1. On April 6, a letter from the minister of foreign affairs commending Proly, Dubuisson, and Pereira was read in the Convention, and that body decreed it was satisfied with their conduct (*Moniteur*, XVI, 76–77).

It is interesting to note that, on March 29, Carnot, then at Lille, had written to a friend that he and six Commissioners were going to meet and decide whether Dumouriez should not be arrested that very day (Brace in *J. Mod. H.*, XXI, 316). This was just one week before the General's desertion.

[12] In reality, of six. Carnot, the sixth member, never arrived (H. Vast in Lavisse and Rambaud, *Hist. gén.*, VIII, 253).

[13] Pariset, *La Rév.*, p. 67; Sorel, *Europe*, III, 359; Sybel, *Fr. Rev.*, II, 459.

[14] Since Coburg had agreed to aid Dumouriez in reëstablishing the monarchy, Coburg was Dumouriez' auxiliary, hence the prisoners in Coburg's hands were constructively in Dumouriez' hands. They were therefore not Imperial prisoners but Dumouriez' prisoners (*Mém. Dumouriez*, IV, 160). However, this legal distinction did not derogate from the reality of their confinement, which lasted until the end of 1795 (*vide infra*, Pt. II, chap. iii, § 3).

list. Except for Clerfayt's nephews, all these persons were incarcerated sooner or later in the somber, humid Abbaye prison in Paris.[15]

The other class of countermeasures taken by the Convention concerned the Bourbons in France. The day following Dumouriez' defection, the arrest of all Bourbons yet at liberty was ordered.[16] This decree of the Convention was implemented on the eighth by a decree of the Provisional Executive Council designating the fort and château of Marseilles as the future home of all Bourbons not currently residing in the Temple.[17] If Dumouriez and Coburg had thought to alleviate the distress of the royal family, they were sadly mistaken. It is to be noted that when Marie Antoinette and Madame Elisabeth were guillotined, the Austrians did not execute their hostages.

After delivering the four deputies and Beurnonville to the Austrians, Dumouriez concerted with Coburg his plans for marching upon Paris to reëstablish the monarchy. The ground had been already prepared by an unsigned *Avis au peuple français*, written in French and German, and distributed throughout France by "the internal enemy." [18] The proclamation invited the French to unite with the invader "who is coming only to break [your] bonds, . . . to arrest the impious regicides . . . , [and] to place at liberty the young King and other unfortunates of the royal family." The utter destruction of Paris was threatened if the royal family were harmed.[19] And on the very day that the march upon Paris commenced, or rather, was scheduled to commence, Coburg published, at Dumouriez' request — and under pressure from Count Tauenzien, who represented the Prussian Court at Coburg's headquarters [20] — a manifesto proclaiming that he, Coburg, concurred in Dumouriez' views, and would coöperate with him "to procure for France a constitutional king, [and] the constitution that France had herself chosen." And then came Coburg's solemn pledge: "I declare . . . upon my word of honor that I will never set foot upon French soil to make conquests there." [21] Dumouriez expected so much from this

---

[15] Saulnier in *RF*, LXVI, 206–217. When, the following year, a relative of the Prussian "tyrant" was captured while in the service of Hesse-Darmstadt, it was decreed that he should constitute an additional hostage (Decree of CPS, Nov. 9, 1794, Aulard, *Actes*, XVIII, 41).

[16] L. Mortimer-Ternaux, *Histoire de la Terreur, 1792–1794* (8 vols., Paris, 1862–1881), VII, 433.

[17] Aulard, *Actes*, III, 157. The Duchess of Bourbon and the Prince of Conti protested vehemently, and petitioned the Convention from every city they passed through on their

way southward. The royal prisoners were taken through Lyons at night to avoid popular demonstrations in their favor (Mortimer-Ternaux, *Terreur*, VII, 441).

[18] Blaux, Cmr in Bas-Rhin, Meurthe, and Moselle, to Conv., April 4, 1793, Aulard, *Actes*, III, 79–80.

[19] *Procès-verbal* of Conv., IX, 91, cited in Aulard, *Actes*, III, 80, n. 1.

[20] Sybel, *Fr. Rev.*, II, 461–462.

[21] Aulard in *RF*, XVIII, 235. Coburg did not want to give his word not to make any conquests at France's expense, but allowed Mack to convince him that the proclama-

pledge that he was willing to purchase it by the "momentary cession" of French border fortresses to the Austrians, the fortresses to be held as a sacred trust.[22]

Alas for Dumouriez! proclamations and pledges were in vain. Though his troops of the line cheered him when he appeared in camp on the morning of April 5, his artillery did not. Imbued with the revolutionary spirit, it had departed during the night for Valenciennes.[23] This placed Dumouriez in a first-class predicament, for it was not at all certain that the troops loyal to him would fire upon their fellows.[24] Dumouriez had told Mack on March 27 that if he had one hundred lives, he would gladly give all of them to end the Jacobin dominion and reëstablish the monarchy. Here was a situation where, by risking his *one* life, he might have won over the remaining troops to decisive action; but he preferred to flee to the Austrian camp (April 5, 1793).[25] Bullets followed him from the guns of the Yonne battalion.[26] The General did not depart alone. With him, or deserting later, were the most compromised of his officers and several hundred soldiers — 883 in all.[27]

Two or three days later, a congress of Allied statesmen and generals met at Antwerp. It had been convoked by Coburg before Dumouriez' desertion, to obtain agreement between the Allies as to what troops and cannon each should contribute to the common cause. Coburg's aide-de-camp, Colonel Mack, outlined to the meeting the history of the Belgian campaign since Neerwinden; showed how, by negotiation with Dumouriez, the subsequent reoccupation of Belgium had cost not a single drop of blood; and finished with a reading of Coburg's no-conquests declaration. The effect of the declaration was like "a clap of thunder." "General indignation" reigned. Austria was accused of deceiving her allies, and threats were voiced to break

---

tion was necessary. (Sorel, *Europe*, III, 364. *Vide* Coburg's manifesto and retraction in *Mém. Dumouriez*, IV, 294–297, "Eclair. hist. et pièces off.," Notes [E], [F].)

[22] Sorel, *Europe*, III, 363.

[23] A. von Witzleben, *Prinz Friedrich Josias von Coburg-Saalfeld, Herzog zu Sachsen* (3 vols., Berlin, 1859), II, 156. Sorel and Sybel both assert it was the volunteers who constituted the recalcitrant element (*Europe*, III, 361; *Fr. Rev.*, II, 456–457). Dumouriez himself says it was the artillery (*Mém.*, IV, 173). However, part of the troops "followed the leader," and departed also (*ibid.*, p. 174).

[24] Dunn-Pattison in *C. Mod. H.*, VIII, 422.

[25] Witzleben, *Coburg*, II, 156–157.

[26] General Chérin ordered his men to fire upon their general in chief (A. Sorel, "Un volontaire de 1792, le général Chérin," *RH*, VI [1878], 369).

[27] Thugut to Count Colloredo, June 2, 1793, *Briefe Thugut*, I, 17. Thugut's official report should end all speculation as to the number of deserters, which was "ten battalions" according to the *Journal de Paris* (Aulard, *Actes*, III, 353); "five thousand men," according to the alleged assertions of the secretary of the King of Prussia (*ibid.*, p. 588, n. 1); "a handful," according to Dunn-Pattison (in *C. Mod. H.*, VIII, 422); "eighteen hundred," according to the Prussian major Tauenzien (Sybel, *Fr. Rev.*, II, 460).

up the Coalition on the spot.[28] "I thought till now," wrote Coburg a few days later, "that the coalesced powers wished to reëstablish Monarchy in France, and order and peace in Europe. . . I see that each is thinking only 'how best to feather his own nest.'"[29]

Count von Metternich, Minister Plenipotentiary of Austria in Belgium,[30] and Count von Starhemberg, Austrian Minister to The Hague, pointed out to the Congress that Coburg had exceeded his authority; and they submitted for approval a revised manifesto which Coburg would be required to issue in his own name.[31] This the Duke most reluctantly did on April 9. He declared his previous proclamation to be merely an expression of his "personal sentiments." He blamed "the stubbornness of highly culpable people who were working for the unhappiness and downfall of their country" for the fact that the sentiments expressed in the first proclamation were no longer applicable. He announced that the armistice had been rescinded, and that a state of unconditional warfare would henceforth prevail.[32]

When Dumouriez learned of Coburg's repudiation of his plighted word, he rushed to see the Duke, a copy of the proclamation in his hand. Dumouriez reproached Coburg for his bad faith; the latter replied that circumstances had changed. He, Coburg, had made his promise when the restoration of the French monarchy was to be effected by Dumouriez' army, with only incidental aid from the Austrians: an auxiliary corps, if necessary. But now that Dumouriez' army had deserted him, the French general, to effect his coup, would need a loan of the entire Austrian army. For that, the Emperor felt the project should be carried out in his own name and for his proper benefit — since he was being asked to take all the chances. Dumouriez retorted that he would have no part of this new arrangement. He had accepted the rank of general of artillery in Coburg's army to be in a position to command the Austrian auxiliary corps to be lent him. That rank he would now slough off — on the spot. And so saying, he hastened from the Austrian camp.[33]

The Count of Starhemberg visited Dumouriez on April 10 at Brussels, whither the General had fled. Starhemberg has penned the following description of Dumouriez: "A very little man of about sixty, already somewhat infirm (cassé), of reddish-brown complexion, with bright and piercing brown eyes, and plenty of hair — gray, but powdered white. . . He often

[28] Starhemberg to Thugut, April 12, 1793, Vivenot-Zeissberg, *Quellen*, III, 9–10.

[29] Sorel, *Europe*, III, 366.

[30] This is the father (1746–1818) of the later Prince Metternich.

[31] Vivenot-Zeissberg, *Quellen*, III, 10.

[32] *Mém. Dumouriez*, IV, 296, "Eclair. hist. et pièces off.," Note (F); Witzleben, *Coburg*, II, 159–161.

[33] *Mémoires et correspondance inédits du général Dumouriez, publiés sur les manuscrits autographes déposés chez l'éditeur* (2 vols. in 1, Paris, 1834), I, 40–42.

looks down at his legs and feet while speaking. . . He has very small, wrinkled hands, with which he gesticulates much. He lacks half the middle finger of his right hand to above the second joint." [34]

In the course of their conversation, the General did his best to convince Starhemberg that Austria should give him a command. Of this, there was little chance. Coburg was indeed willing to incorporate the entire 883 deserters with the Austrian forces, but to this, Thugut was definitely hostile: "[They] could serve only to disorganize our army," he declared, "and indoctrinate our troops in the science *of the rights of Man and of the imprescriptible sovereignty of the people.*" [35] And Thugut uttered the wish that England transport the whole "constitutional horde" to one of the rebellious French provinces, and leave them there to their own devices. [36] Thus it was in vain that Dumouriez vaunted his own talents to the skies, making use of expressions such as, "If they had had my head. . . " And he told Starhemberg that Prussia would attack Austria before a year was up, but that "I will come to fight with you, and I will beat them." The Count's reply is a masterpiece in evasion: "If we ever have the misfortune to become embroiled with his Prussian Majesty, I should believe my country fortunate in having generals who resemble you and who have your military qualifications, . . . so much the more because our soldiers follow well. Our army is good and you know it." To which Dumouriez rejoined: "Monsieur, the Austrian army is the best that I know of. It would, however, be invincible if I commanded it." [37]

Far from employing Dumouriez, Thugut was not even inclined to grant him asylum in Austria. Like-minded was the remainder of Germany. Also Switzerland and Italy. The expatriate offered his services to Czar Paul, but Paul declined with thanks. Dumouriez managed to enter England under an assumed name (Peralta), but was ordered to leave when he disclosed his identity. [38] The hero of Jemappes, the idol of the French army, had become a miserable fugitive. After living at Hamburg by his pen for a time, [39] Dumouriez was permitted to settle in England, was granted an English pension, and engaged as military counsellor to the Duke of Wellington. Follow-

---

[34] Conversation between Dumouriez and Starhemberg, April 10, 1793, Vivenot-Zeissberg, *Quellen*, III, 4.

[35] Underscored in original.

[36] Thugut to Count Colloredo, June 2, 1793, *Briefe Thugut*, I, 17. Coburg had promised Dumouriez that if the latter's scheme failed, he and his officers would be salaried according to their rank, the necessary funds to be drawn from the war-chest. The Emperor — which means Thugut — disallowed this arrangement; but it seems that at least some of the deserting officers were paid, at first out of the Imperial war-chest and later by Austria. In 1806, nine of the deserters were still receiving salaries from Austria (Witzleben, *Coburg*, II, 175 and note).

[37] Vivenot-Zeissberg, *Quellen*, III, 6, 8.

[38] Metternich to Trauttmansdorff, July 7, 1793, *ibid.*, p. 140.

[39] Witzleben, *Coburg*, II, 157, note.

ing the Restoration of the Bourbons, Dumouriez thought to return home, but learned to his dismay that he was still not *persona grata* to France.[40] Louis XVIII perhaps remembered Louis XVI's uncomplimentary evaluation of his (Dumouriez') restless character.[41] It is quite possible that Dumouriez' last years would have been happier if Dumolard's proposal to the French Ministry of Foreign Affairs (May 2, 1793) had been carried into execution. Dumolard had proposed to stab Dumouriez.[42]

2. THE FALL OF THE GIRONDE, AND THE CREATION
OF THE FIRST COMMITTEE OF PUBLIC SAFETY

The desertion of Dumouriez, following upon the disasters in Belgium, produced a veritable panic in the Convention, and the accusing finger was naturally pointed at the Girondists, whose "man" Dumouriez had been.[43] Not that the Girondists as a party had had any part in his treason, but they had been forced by the pressure of the Paris mob to seek a strong arm wherever they could find it, and they thought they had found it in this scheming general who had planned to quell that mob, their enemy, with bullets. Well-nigh a month before Dumouriez took the final plunge, his loyalty was suspected,[44] and the Paris Commune organized what was intended to be a massacre of the Girondists and the suppression of the Provisional Executive Council. Though this riot was successfully suppressed, the defeats following upon the Council's ill-advised order to attack Holland caused a renewal of popular violence. The fact that Dumouriez was the godfather of Civilis Victoire Jemappes Dumouriez Lebrun, infant daughter of the Girondist minister of foreign affairs, and that the General dined with the Lebruns when he was in Paris, were alone sufficient, in Jacobin eyes, to convict not only Lebrun, but the whole Girondist party, of complicity in the treason of Dumouriez.[45]

[40] Six, *Dic. biog.*, *s.v.* "Dumouriez"; Vast in Lavisse and Rambaud, *Hist. gén.*, VIII, 254–255.

[41] Sybel, *Fr. Rev.*, I, 440.

[42] Aulard, *Actes*, I, xxxi. A price was placed on his head (Mercy to Thugut, June 1, 1793, Vivenot-Zeissberg, *Quellen*, III, 105).

[43] Of course, a scapegoat was necessary, since Dumouriez was beyond reach.

[44] Actually, the first traces of suspicion were much older than a month. In October 1792, Dumouriez had ordered the incarceration of two French battalions for murdering four "Prussian deserters." Marat suspected that it was French *émigrés*, arms in hand, who had been slain. Dumouriez was assailed, and Ma-

rat prognosticated that Dumouriez would himself be an *émigré* by March 1793. He proved a shrewd observer (L. R. Gottschalk, *Jean Paul Marat: A Study in Radicalism* [London, 1927], pp. 153–154).

[45] Goetz-Bernstein, *Gironde*, pp. 384, 388–389; Masson, *Dép. étr.*, pp. 278 *et seqq.* Masson erroneously places the date of Dumouriez' desertion at April 1 instead of April 5.

It was to Dumouriez that Lebrun owed his introduction to the Department of Foreign Affairs. Student, soldier, and vagabond in succession, Lebrun had been proscribed by Louis XVI's foreign minister, Vergennes. Lebrun had fled to Liège, and set up a newspaper which enjoyed some currency, the

Robespierre took upon himself to list for the Convention's benefit acts which would tend to indicate that the Girondists were privy to Dumouriez' treason: they had opposed dethronement of Louis XVI; voted for the appeal of Louis' fate to the people; provided for a tutor for the Dauphin, indicating that they expected him to reign, perhaps in his father's place; consistently supported Lafayette and Narbonne; thrust France into war; placed millions in secret funds at Dumouriez' disposal (as minister); controlled the Commission of Twenty-One, which failed properly to supply the troops; tried to turn the Belgian deputies away from union with France; and so forth. The noose was forming and being tried on for size. And of course Dumouriez had not helped the Girondists by his letters to Paris threatening to drive out "the satellites of Marat and Robespierre," and denying the authority of the Convention so long as it should be controlled by "anarchists."[46]

Robespierre's accusations created quite a stir. Naturally the Girondists felt themselves called upon to justify their conduct, and they did so as best they could.[47] But the corn-market section of Paris, already the day following Robespierre's denunciation, commenced to stir. It wanted the guilty deputies arraigned, noble officers cashiered, the administrative system purged.[48] With doubts, suspicions, and recriminations tearing at the nation from within, and treason endangering the state from without, the creation of a stronger executive appeared necessary. Already during the previous January, a Committee of General Defense had been elected by the divers committees of the Convention,[49] but it was now felt that a still greater concentration of power was needed. The Provisional Executive Council could have been strengthened, but the ministers (of which it was composed) were not members of the Convention,[50] and the Convention preferred to strengthen its own position if any strengthening were to be done.[51] Accordingly, it elected twenty-

---

Journal politique et général de l'Europe. Expelled from the Low Countries by the Emperor, in whose pay he is alleged to have been (on this point alone, *vide* Prudhomme, *Rév. Paris,* XV, 438–439; XVI, 207, 257, 436), Lebrun had come to Paris in 1790, and thrown himself with zeal into the revolutionary movement. Dumouriez had noticed his intelligence and indefatigability, and employed him in the Department of Foreign Affairs as senior clerk. By August 1792, the clerk had become minister (W. Miles, *Authentic Correspondence with M. Le Brun* [London, 1796], Appendix, pp. 17, 33, 34).
[46] Gottschalk, *Marat,* pp. 153–154; Walter, *Robespierre,* pp. 362–364.

[47] In his memoirs, Brissot says that the 6,000,000 livres of secret funds, which Robespierre insinuated had been divided up between the Girondists and Dumouriez, were still largely intact; and that Dumouriez' appointment was due to the intrigues of Talon and the Queen, not to the Girondists (*Mém. Brissot,* p. 457).
[48] Walter, *Robespierre,* p. 367.
[49] Stephens, *Rev. Eur.,* p. 127.
[50] Decree of Aug. 10, 1792, of Legislative Assembly, Aulard, *Actes,* I, 1. This was out of deference to the theory of separation of powers (Mathiez, *Fr. Rev.,* p. 166).
[51] Goetz-Bernstein, *Gironde,* p. 389; Masson, *Dép. étr.,* p. 279.

five [52] of its own members as a new Committee of General Defense.[53] The election proved a defeat for the Girondists for, whereas in the former Committee they were in the majority, in the new body they had only nine unquestioned adherents — less than two fifths.[54] But this body was still too large and too limited in power to meet the crisis, and on the proposal of a Girondist, Isnard, a Committee of Public Safety of but nine members was created (April 6).[55] The new Committee, which was renewable monthly, and whose membership was by degrees raised to eighteen,[56] was given charge of defense against enemies of the state, both within and without. It might exercise any power it deemed necessary, even to the extent of suspending decrees of the ministers. All that was required of it was to keep the Convention informed of its acts.[57] It did not, be it noted, have to inform the Convention of acts that it contemplated, but only of the *fait accompli*. During its term of office it was the sovereign power in France. The ministers were really only its clerks, and the Convention presently degenerated into a rubber stamp of approval. And to this all-powerful Committee suggested by a Girondist, there was elected not a single Girondist member,[58] though the Girondists still constituted a majority of the Convention.[59] The Girondists had given themselves the *coup de grâce*.

Danton headed the new Committee of Public Safety, and with Barère, directed foreign affairs. It was not really necessary for the Girondists to have abdicated completely, for Danton was willing to work with them to offset the terrorists. But the Girondists refused to assume a secondary role, and pretended to shudder at the thought of contact with one who had been responsible in large part for the September massacres. Danton, as head of the Committee of Public Safety, persisted for a time in his friendly disposition — even after the Girondists had angered him profoundly by accusing him of conspiracy with Dumouriez.[60] When the Paris Commune tried to arrest the Girondist foreign minister, Lebrun, the Committee of Public Safety ventured a (weak) protest. After the terrorists forced the Convention

[52] Aulard, *Actes*, II, 514; *Moniteur*, XV, 797. Goetz-Bernstein, *Gironde*, p. 389, erroneously gives the membership as 24.

[53] This was its technical designation (Aulard, *Actes*, II, 514), though it presently became known as the Committee of Public Safety (*ibid.*, p. 518, n. 1). Masson gives only the latter name (*Dép. étr.*, p. 279).

[54] Goetz-Bernstein, *Gironde*, p. 389.

[55] *Ibid.*, pp. 389–390. Masson, *Dép. étr.*, p. 280, erroneously gives August 6 as the date of creation of the nine-member Committee of Public Safety.

[56] By the addition of members for specific purposes. Four of the eighteen appear never to have been present at the meetings, for their names do not occur in the minutes (J. Guillaume, "Le personnel du Comité de Salut Public," *Etudes révolutionnaires*, Ser. II [Paris, 1909], no. 4). Guillaume gives the personnel of the CPS during its entire span of existence.

[57] Aulard, *Actes*, III, 115–116.

[58] Goetz-Bernstein, *Gironde*, p. 390; Aulard, *Actes*, III, 116.

[59] Mathiez, *Fr. Rev.*, p. 314.

[60] Of which he may well have been guilty. *Vide* Walter, *Robespierre*, p. 361.

to vote the arrest and trial of the Girondists (June 2), the Committee authorized Lebrun to continue the exercise of his official functions, house-prisoner though he was. On June 7, the Committee, wishing to confer with Lebrun, ordered the Minister of Justice to bring Lebrun and his guard before it. But the Commune won out in the end, and Lebrun was cashiered.[61] Six months later he was executed.[62]

We are not concerned here with the details of the bloody chapter which snuffed out the lives of some of the best elements of the Revolution. Our interest lies in the change of perspective in France's foreign policy caused by the change of leadership. The Girondist draft of a Constitution published by order of the Convention on February 16, 1793 [63] — distinguish from the so-called "Constitution of 1793" [64] — contained provisions inherently dangerous to the peace of Europe: France renounces the annexation of foreign territory unless the majority of the inhabitants thereof requests annexation and such territory does not form part of a state already governed by a constitution freely accepted.[65] (How many such states were there in Europe?) In countries occupied by the French armies, the generals "in no case and under no pretext" may protect customs contrary to liberty, equality, and popular sovereignty.[66] (A hardly veiled summons to occupied territory to rebel.) In its relations with foreign states, the Republic will respect institutions founded upon the consent of the generality of the people.[67] (In other words, it will respect the constitution of practically no nation whatsoever.) [68]

---

[61] Goetz-Bernstein, *Gironde*, p. 391; F. A. Aulard, "Instructions générales aux agents diplomatiques de la République française (1er juin 1793)," *RF*, XIII (1887), 68–70.

[62] Masson, *Dép. étr.*, p. 283. It is interesting to note here that Lebrun had never paid any attention to the Frey brothers (i.e., the Dobruska brothers, ennobled by Joseph II under the name Schönfeld), whom many suspected of being Austrian agents. The brothers had many times submitted memoirs to Lebrun on how to end the war — apparently, by dividing the original allies, Prussia and Austria. (The "Frey" of course had been adopted as a pseudonym because it means "free.") (Mathiez, *Etrangers*, pp. 111–119.) Robespierre characterized the Frey brothers as the "two cleverest scoundrels that Austria has vomited upon us." Needless to say, they were executed under his regime. This they may have richly deserved, for they were in the habit of denouncing others to remove suspicion from themselves, or to curry favor (*ibid.*, p. 180 *et passim*).

Lebrun's correct attitude with respect to the Freys should have indicated to his enemies that here was a man who was determined to stand above suspicion. But Lebrun had associated with Dumouriez and others. Involved in his case, therefore, were two complementary concepts — guilt by association, and innocence by studied nonassociation. Lebrun's enemies naturally failed even to see the second.

[63] L. Duguit and H. Monnier, cont. by R. Bonnard (eds.), *Les constitutions et les principales lois politiques de la France depuis 1789* (5th ed.; Paris, 1932), pp. 36–66. The authorship of this draft should not be ascribed, without qualification, to Condorcet. *Vide* A. Stern, "Condorcet und der Girondistische Verfassungsentwurf," *HZ*, CXLI (1930), 496.

[64] Duguit and Monnier, *Const. et lois*, pp. 67–68. June 24, 1793.

[65] *Titre* XIII, art. 2.

[66] *Titre* XIII, art. 3.

[67] *Titre* XIII, art. 4.

[68] Goetz-Bernstein, *Gironde*, p. 392.

These proposed [69] constitutional provisions, considered together with the propaganda decrees of November 19 and December 15 and 17, 1792, give a fair picture of the system in vogue when Danton and the nine-member Committee of Public Safety came into power on April 6, 1793. And it was a system against which there had been no organized resistance, for though the Mountain had, in April 1792, supported Robespierre's stand respecting the contemplated war on Austria, when once war had been declared, it put its shoulder to the wheel to help defeat the nation's enemy. This was not necessarily pure patriotism. Peace could be purchased from the Allies only at the cost of freeing Louis XVI, and the Mountain was determined that the King should be executed. Moreover, the Mountain's ranks were being swelled by former Girondists (such as Cloots) who brought along with them the expansionist virus.[70] Thus, there was no dam to check the flood of Girondist principles until the advent of the new regime.

It will be recalled that Danton, on April 13, 1793, secured the adoption by the Convention of a decree of nonintervention in the governments of foreign states.[71] The Decrees of November 19 and December 15 and 17, and 22, had rendered all *accommodement* with France impossible. As Wieland's *Neue Deutsche Merkur* expressed it, all peoples had been forced to regard as enemies those "who, through their representatives, had publicly declared that they would never lay down their arms until they had subjected all European states to their newly conceived, nonsensical laws." [72] But with Belgium and the Palatinate lost or almost lost, with Dumouriez a deserter and Custine busy losing his Rhineland conquests, this was no time to leave on the books such provocative legislation.

But the way this conciliatory decree was born is indeed strange. In the fourth section of the present chapter, it will be told that the desertion of Dumouriez was followed by a rash of communications between the Duke of Coburg and the Representatives on Mission to the Army of the North. Some of these letters were read before the Convention, and it was noted that therein could be discerned vague references to peace negotiations. Robespierre thereupon demanded the death penalty for "cowards who proposed to come to an arrangement with enemies of the Republic." That, even, was not enough, he said, and asked that the cowards be outlawed,[73] so that they could be executed without trial, upon mere identification.

At this point, Danton stepped in with his moderating influence: Robespierre had not really meant what he said. What he had intended could be

---

[69] This draft was never adopted by the Convention, but the objections were not to *Titre* XIII.

[70] Mathiez, *Fr. Rev.*, p. 288.

[71] *Vide supra*, chap. ii, n. 115.

[72] Hansen, *Quellen*, II, 646, n. 2.

[73] *Discours de Danton*, p. 398. Explanatory notation.

rendered thus: I demand "the penalty of death against whomsoever should propose to the Republic to come to an arrangement with enemies who would not, as a condition precedent, recognize the sovereignty of the people." And then the same Georges Jacques Danton who, on January 31, 1793, helped to secure enactment of the decree forcing (Belgium and) Aix-la-Chapelle to bow to the Decrees of December 15 and 17, and 22;[74] and whose address to the Convention at that time contained the words, "It is in vain that we are threatened with the anger of kings. You have thrown down the gauntlet. That gauntlet is the head of a king. It is the signal for their imminent extermination"[75] — that same Danton it was who told the Convention on April 13: "In a moment of enthusiasm you rendered a decree of undoubtedly lofty motivation since you obliged yourself to give protection to peoples who desired to resist the oppression of their tyrants. This decree would seem to bind you to come to the aid of patriots who wanted to effect a revolution in China. Citizens, first of all we must think of conserving our own body politic, and establishing *French* grandeur. Let us consolidate the Republic, and France, by its enlightenment and its energy, will attract all peoples. . . Citizens, let us decree that we will not meddle at all in our neighbors' affairs. . ."[76]

This is how the Decree of April 13 was born. Besides declaring that the French people would never interfere in any manner in the government of other powers, it assured Europe that the French would "rather bury themselves under their own ruins than suffer another power to interfere in the internal government of the Republic and influence the creation of the constitution with which it wishes to provide itself."[77] And the death penalty was prescribed for suggesting negotiation "with any enemy who had not first solemnly recognized the independence, sovereignty, indivisibility and unity of the Republic founded on the basis of liberty and equality."[78]

The Decree of April 13, 1793, was implemented seven weeks later by instructions for the guidance of French agents abroad. These instructions, drawn up by Lebrun in the hiding-place whither he had fled to escape the Commune's order of arrest, indicate clearly that a new pilot stood at the helm. Every nation, wrote Lebrun, had the imprescriptible right to choose its own form of government. French representatives abroad should maintain scrupulous neutrality with respect to party in the states to which they were accredited. They should conduct themselves prudently, and avoid provoking the ministers of hostile powers. But if any perfidious insinuations were made concerning France and its Revolution, the representatives should praise the

---

[74] Hansen, *Quellen*, II, 732–733.
[75] Quoted in Rain, *Mir. à Bon.*, p. 78.
[76] *Discours de Danton*, pp. 398–400.
[77] The Constitution of June 24, 1793.
[78] *Discours de Danton*, p. 401.

new principles and point out their advantages "without, however, permitting themselves comparisons which would reanimate the old suspicions and distrust. . . Finally, they should do everything possible to give a favorable impression of their nation, both by their conversation, the channel of newspapers, and the distribution of pamphlets which present in a favorable light the principles, resources, and conduct of the nation." [79]

So thoroughly imbued was Lebrun with the methods of Girondist propagandism that he did not see the obnoxious potentialities of this last suggestion. And Danton does not seem to have noticed them either, for the Committee of Public Safety approved the instructions *in toto*.[80] Danton did not try to terminate the propaganda phase of the *war*, however, for propaganda is a fair and powerful weapon. It is only the indiscriminate revolutionization of the world that was terminated. By abandoning that, it was possible for a sovereign to find some ground upon which a peace with France might be built.

3. THE FIRST COMMITTEE OF PUBLIC SAFETY AND PRUSSIA

As mentioned above, many keen observers expected the Prussian evacuation of France in October 1792 to be followed presently by the withdrawal of Frederick William from the war (and Lebrun offered him Austrian Silesia as a special inducement to withdraw from the Coalition).[81] Some Parisian enthusiasts even envisaged the formation of an offensive and defensive alliance between France and Prussia, aimed at Austria. In point of fact, Lebrun's secretariat began formulating the terms of this alliance the very day Prussia turned the gate at Verdun over to France (October 12, 1792). Ten days later, a letter to Noël, French diplomat in London, betrayed, in its wishful thinking, how much importance was attached to Prussia's alliance: [82]

Next spring, when the moment arrives to commence the campaign, and Austria, confident in the support of Prussia, will be preparing . . . to attack the French on the Rhine, we will suddenly announce that a separate peace between France and Prussia has been concluded. The Prussian army, . . . with 12,000 Hessians,[83] will fall unexpectedly upon Bohemia. Another Prussian army will

[79] RF, XIII, 68–70.
[80] Aulard, *Actes*, IV, 476.
[81] Sorel, *Europe*, III, 296.
[82] Aulard in RF, XVIII, 237.
[83] At the commencement of hostilities, the Landgrave of Hesse-Cassel was very antagonistic to the Revolution (Sybel, *Europe*, I, 472). According to the *Moniteur* (XIV, 757), he promised 12 livres to every Hessian warrior who would bring him the head of a Frenchman — an unlikely tale which profoundly horrified the head-hunters of Paris. (Cf. A. Tuetey, *Répertoire général des sources manuscrites de l'histoire de Paris pendant la Révolution française* [11 vols., Paris, 1890–1914], V, 457, for a similar story concerning the Prussians, and their "custom" of parading the heads of French soldiers on

either invade Silesia or fight the Russians in Poland, assisted by Polish patriots. . .
The Turks will advance [against Russia]. . . The French will oppose the Austrian army on the Rhine, and will soon succeed in driving them [*sic*] completely
from that part of Germany, from the Breisgau, from the frontier cities . . . and
from Lombardy. Our fleet . . . will enter the Black Sea, and enable the Turks
to disembark in the Crimea.[84]

All these bounties, these joys, were within the power of Frederick William to bestow, but he was niggardly. However, if he would not give France
his alliance, his benevolent neutrality could probably be counted upon —
even though he was a belligerent. The Committee was even willing to base
a plan of campaign upon this probability. Prussia would be kept occupied
with negotiations — Prussia and the friendly Rhenish Palatinate [85] — while
General Custine united several of the French armies and crushed Austria.
It was the General's own plan (dated April 9, 1793),[86] and was not based
entirely upon wishful thinking. Custine had engaged in secret negotiations with Prussia the previous December,[87] and personally knew the extent
of Austro-Prussian hostility. For that matter, so did everyone else in a
general sort of way.[88] "The enemy armies touch, yet are a thousand leagues
apart," ran a typical report to the Convention during this very month of
April.[89] With a constantly widening gulf thrusting the two "Allies" ever
farther apart, Custine's plan bade fair to be successful.

Adam Philippe, Count de Custine de Sarreck, was fifty-one years old
in 1793. He had served in the Seven Years' War, and in the American Revolution.[90] Contact with the new ideas had left its imprint on Custine's mind,
and when the French Revolution broke out, he welcomed it and became one
of its leading generals. The acceptance of his plan by the Committee was
Custine's golden opportunity to become a Revolutionary hero but, like Bonaparte later and Dumouriez before, the General was a politician also. The very
day he presented his military plan, he wrote a letter to the Convention demanding in no uncertain terms the establishment of a dictatorship as the
sole means of saving France from the foreign foe — and of course Adam

pikes.) When it appeared, however, that the doughty captain of the Prussian Ship of State was only playing at war, the shrewd land-grave determined to trim his sails to the wind. Accordingly, he affected extreme indulgence toward his French prisoners, returning them to their hearthstones, and offering to dupli-cate this friendly gesture later (A. Sorel, "La paix de Bâle," *RH*, V [1877], 275).

[84] Aulard in *RF*, XVIII, 237–238.
[85] The Rhenish Palatinate had been politically

united with Bavaria since 1777. Zweibrücken or Deux-Ponts was still a distinct segment of the Wittelsbach patrimony.
[86] Aulard in *RF*, XVIII, 238.
[87] Herlaut in *AHRF*, IX, 518.
[88] Du Bois du Bais and Briez, Rps to Valen-ciennes, to Conv., April 20, 1793, Aulard, *Actes*, III, 360; *idem* to CPS, April 29, 1793, *ibid.*, p. 526.
[89] *Idem* to Conv., April 28, 1793, *ibid.*, p. 514.
[90] Six, *Dic. biog., s.v.* "Custine de Sarreck."

Philippe was to be *the* dictator.[91] This letter caused the Committee much alarm, and it ordered Merlin of Thionville and his colleagues to keep a close watch on the General and his entourage.[92] The order was repeated a week later.[93] On the question of Custine's patriotism, Merlin's mind was already made up. Two months before, he had written: "I don't like Custine. He has everything that causes a *ci-devant* to be detested. I have not visited with him three times. I have never eaten there. I am not satisfied with him. I am examining his conduct carefully, and I believe he could have spared us the reverse at Frankfort, and done much better in the last campaign." [94] But another Representative on Mission gave the General a clean bill of health, patriotically speaking. In answer to the Committee's fears that Custine was meeting with royalist agents at some secret rendevous, this Representative wrote: "At Saarlouis, Saarbrücken, and thereabouts, General Custine met only troops, mountains, and dales. I believe his principles are all right." [95]

The Army of the North being without a general, the Provisional Executive Council gave the post to Custine. Barère, in the name of the Committee, proposed that the Convention confirm this appointment. Despite protests, the Convention complied.[96] This gave Custine command of the four armies his plan contemplated: [97] the North (which included the Ardennes); the Rhine, originally his own; and the Moselle, whose command he had secured on April 4 by blaming Major General Ligniville of the Moselle Army for his own shortcomings.[98] The stage being thus set for the diplomatic portion of the plan, a word is necessary concerning the General's German policy.

Authority in central Europe was represented by the Emperor, Archduke of Austria. Prussia was the enemy of Austria. *Ergo*, it was not impossible for a soldier who had distinguished himself at Yorktown to see in the autocratic Hohenzollerns of Brandenburg-Prussia the champions of liberty — or at least nonenemies of freedom. General Custine was one of the warmest advocates of alliance with Prussia.[99] In his advocacy, he was seconded by his son, François, whom, it will be recalled, Minister of War Narbonne had once sent to Germany to offer the supreme command of the French army to Duke Ferdinand of Brunswick, promulgator of undiplomatic manifestoes. That mission had of course failed, but the indirect contact with the Hohenzollerns through Prince Henry, Brunswick's intimate friend — a contact which had become closer when François was appointed, first, special negotiator, and then, minister plenipotentiary to Berlin — had had its part

[91] Mathiez in *RH*, CLVIII, 260.
[92] April 16, Aulard, *Actes*, III, 285.
[93] April 23, *ibid.*, p. 294.
[94] To his colleague Thirion, Feb. 4, 1793, *Corr. Merlin-Th.*, II, 82.
[95] April 24, Aulard, *Actes*, III, 442.
[96] May 13, 1793, *Moniteur*, XVI, 383.
[97] Mathiez in *RH*, CLVIII, 260, 265.
[98] Aulard, *Actes*, III, 60, 205.
[99] *Idem* in *RF*, XVIII, 238.

in framing the General's policy of courting Austria's enemies while striking at Austria herself.

Another enemy of the Habsburgs — not less hostile than the Hohenzollerns, merely weaker — was the Wittelsbach family of Bavaria and the Palatinate. As events arranged themselves, it was the Palatinate which served as the entering wedge for the negotiations contemplated by Custine. It seems that some inhabitants of this region, excited by the rosy vision of liberty so close to their borders, gave expression to "patriotic sentiments" and were murdered by their fellow countrymen. This was yet in 1792. Baron Franz von Wimpffen, a German serving as a French general, thereupon invaded the Palatinate — with which France was at peace — and carried off the assassins, lodging them in Landau, where the General was in command. The Provisional Executive Council at Paris, anxious to humor the Wittelsbachs, rebuked General von Wimpffen for violating the neutrality of the Palatinate — a neutrality guaranteed by the Council on November 9, 1792.[100] The General was ordered to return the murderers to the *locus delicti*, and to content himself with the demand that the Palatine government punish them according to its own laws and customs.[101] This of course created good will toward France, which brings us to the next step — a step involving the Zweibrücken branch of the Wittelsbachs.

It was not France's desire to crush the small states of Germany, particularly not a Wittelsbach-ruled state. So Zweibrücken's neutrality was honored also, and its duke reciprocated by tolerating the presence of a French envoy and the circulation of an extremely democratic newspaper.[102] But here was a problem — a seemingly insoluble one. If all the small German states were to have their neutrality honored, who would feed the French troops? Assuredly not France, for "it is a general principle of war that armies should live at the expense of enemy country."[103] Besides, France did not have sufficient food even for its civilian population. A way was found, to the everlasting credit of French genius, to reconcile the irreconcilable — to enjoy the advantages of neutrality and of a state of war simultaneously. By decree of the Provisional Executive Council, the Duke of Zweibrücken was to be regarded as a neutral on condition that he really observed the rules of strict neutrality, but "that nevertheless there [would] be drawn from his territories provisions for whose value debentures [would] be delivered to him." [104]

This pseudo-neutrality was as ephemeral as it was unsubstantial, which

[100] Arch. A. E., *Allemagne* 669, f. 284.

[101] Dec. 16, 1792 session of PEC, Aulard, *Actes*, I, 336.

[102] Wurmser to Thugut, April 21, 1793, Vivenot-Zeissberg, *Quellen*, III, 32.

[103] CPS to Rps A. RMo, May 15, 1795, *Corr. Merlin-Th.*, II, 190.

[104] Aulard, *Actes*, I, 234. No comment is necessary as to the value of the debentures from an actual-cash standpoint.

brings us to the next step. Urged by Merlin of Thionville, who favored the termination of the neutrality of both the County Palatine and the Duchy of Zweibrücken,[105] the government at Paris took the partial step of occupying the Duchy of Zweibrücken and promulgating therein the "Compulsory Liberty Decree" of December 15 and 17, 1792.[106]

The unrest in Bergzabern had provided the occasion. It is quite likely that this unrest was the work of a small clique, as at Mayence, for Félix Desportes, the French minister at Zweibrücken, had written to Lebrun on December 11, 1792: "The Frenchman is not liked here, as we flatter ourselves. Some people, some cities, may desire liberty, but the mass of the nation, still stupid and superstitious, sees privileged beings in those who govern it. It seems to love the feudal yoke which dulls its perception." [107] And on January 10, 1793, a deputy from the neighboring *département* of the Moselle had declared he "had no desire to bring liberty to men destined to be slaves, and who hate France from the bottoms of their hearts." [108]

The pattern of the Bergzabern uprising is recognizable: an oath to liberty and equality, planting of trees of liberty, wearing of tricolor cockades, formation of town councils, obliteration of the ducal insignia, a club of friends of liberty and equality organized by a Strasburg Club member, and instructions from Landau to associate with neighboring communities, form a republic, and seek annexation to France.[109]

The appeals for annexation have already been noted — they occasioned the Decree of November 19, 1792. The French troops moved in on February 10, 1793. The handle for that was the Decree of January 31. The Duke had been warned that the French had designs upon his duchy, and sent his treasures secretly to Coblenz; but he remained behind. Suddenly, in the middle of the night, he was informed he was going to be arrested directly and transported to France. In a trice he and the Duchess were in disguise, and gone. The flaming torches on their carriage still glimmered in the distance when the French arrived. What is that? they demanded of the servants. A lime kiln, was the reply. And the Duke escaped.[110]

But not so the Duke's minister, Baron Ludwig von Esebeck. And when the French promulgated the Compulsory Liberty Decree, the Baron remonstrated vigorously and was arrested (February 25, 1793). Despite his age and infirmity, he was confined in the military prison at Metz. He protested

[105] To min. of war, Jan. 4, 1793, *Corr. Merlin-Th.*, II, 76. *Vide* also *ibid.*, p. 86, dated March 8, 1793. Bonnal de Ganges, *Repré.*, III, 153, erroneously prints this despatch as part of Merlin's communication of February 10.

[106] Chap. ii, § 2, *supra.*
[107] Bockenheimer, *Mainzer Klubisten*, p. 142.
[108] Hansen, *Quellen*, II, 563, n. 1.
[109] *Ibid.*, p. 563.
[110] *Ibid.*, pp. 740–741.

loudly and so did the Duke; and both offered their services to France in return for the Baron's freedom.[111]

Lebrun found the offer interesting, and sent Dubuisson [112] on secret mission to Metz to chat with von Esebeck and find out how the Baron thought he could be of service to the Republic. What the Baron said we do not know, but it concerned negotiations with some power. That power soon turned out to be Prussia. Félix Desportes, who was forthwith sent to Metz to concert with von Esebeck concerning his plan, applied to the Prussian general Prince von Hohenlohe-Ingelfingen for a passport "to travel in Germany." Hohenlohe complied immediately, but the passport never arrived. Was it intercepted en route? And by whom? We do not know. Desportes eventually received a safe-conduct — a safe-conduct which he never used. But that fact will be considered presently.[113]

Desportes — ostensibly on the basis of his conversations with von Esebeck — wrote to Lebrun that Frederick William's most ardent wish was that France consent to the secularization of the three ecclesiastical electorates — now that the Second Partition of Poland had satisfied him as to his eastern frontier. Desportes suggested that Prussia be offered, as the price of an arrangement with France, the Palatine provinces of Jülich and Berg, half the Electorate of Trèves, and the entire Electorate of Cologne; and that the Wittelsbachs of Bavaria and the Palatinate be offered the other half of Trèves, and the Electorate of Mayence, not including the city of Mayence (which would be a republic). These propositions were communicated to the Prussians by the French chargé d'affaires at Mannheim.[114] After the fall of the Girondists, Deforgues, Lebrun's successor, unable to believe that the conservative Frederick William could contemplate such a blow at the very foundation of the Imperial constitution, ordered Desportes to try to determine if the Prussian Court were truly considering the secularization of the three ecclesiastical electorates. It would be well to bear this talk of secularization in mind when we come to consider later the negotiations which ended in the Treaty of Basel on April 5, 1795.

It appears that a genuine Franco-Prussian *rapprochement* was in the making, for the King of Prussia sent his chamberlain, Baron von Luxburg of Zweibrücken, to visit Desportes in Metz. The Baron was profuse in his expressions of regard. The King of Prussia could "easily" see him at Mayence. If Desportes repaired to Mannheim to visit the Electress of Bavaria,

---

[111] Aulard in *RF*, XVIII, 238.
[112] The Dubuisson who later assisted Proly to survey Dumouriez.
[113] General authority for this and the succeed-

ing paragraphs of this section: Aulard in *RF*, XVIII, 239–247. Particular points have their individual references.
[114] Sybel, *Europe*, II, 298.

it would give the King "pleasure." "The Duke of Zweibrücken has spoken
to him [the King] a good deal about you. The promptitude with which
your passports were accorded demonstrates how favorably you would be
received." Luxburg expressed surprise that Desportes had not made use
of his "passports and safe-conducts," though he had received the latter
already a month before. The Frenchman reminded Luxburg that an Imperial ordinance of May 17 forbade Frenchmen to enter the Empire. To this,
Luxburg blazed: "There is no decree or ordinance which can prevail against
our safe-conducts. . . You will be received with open arms at Mannheim."
Evidently it was contemplated that the Wittelsbachs of the Palatinate and
Bavaria would, as a favor to their Zweibrücken relatives, serve as a channel
for secret Franco-Prussian negotiations behind the back of the Emperor.
The Wittelsbachs were willing to do this because they saw in Prussia and
France their only real protection against Austria's plan for a Bavaro-Belgian
exchange; and it would not do to have one's friends cutting each other's
throats in a time of crisis. And let us assume that the freedom of Baron
von Esebeck was also a consideration. In point of fact, Luxburg informed
Desportes that the Duke of Zweibrücken requested, "in particular," the
liberation of his minister. This unfortunate had been imprisoned already
more than four months now, and the minister of foreign affairs at Paris
was willing that he should be released, for the services he had promised
had been faithfully rendered, and France was currently reaping the reward.[115] But it was the Committee of Public Safety which was the real
master of France, so — though Desportes was sent to Mannheim to follow
up the negotiation instituted by von Esebeck — the Baron himself continued
to languish in prison.

On July 9, 1793, the minister of the interior made a report to the Convention in which he let it be known that peace with Prussia was possible
and perhaps not far distant; and that, during a recent exchange of prisoners
with Prussia, there had been a *de facto* recognition of the French Republic
by the King's agents. Danton's Committee of Public Safety may not have
been an organizer of victory, but it did show a will for peace and a knowledge of the means by which it could be obtained.

The end of the First Committee's life the next day spelled the doom of
the Desportes negotiation. Desportes was recalled, and von Esebeck was
transferred to the Hotel Grange-Batelière in Paris, still a prisoner.[116] Deforgues endeavored, it is true, to save the negotiation from complete collapse, and von Esebeck wrote to his duke asking him to designate a safe
channel of communication. But the Duke had no confidence in the men

[115] Aulard, *Actes*, V, 99.
[116] *Ibid.*, p. 309. He was soon joined by the

three Counts of Leiningen (Mathiez, *Fr.
Rev.*, p. 290). *Vide supra*, chap. ii, § 3.

who had inherited Danton's power. Prussia, however, would not have been unwilling to continue the negotiations, based upon Desportes' propositions.[117]

It is a pleasure to report that in September 1793 von Esebeck was liberated.

4. THE FIRST COMMITTEE OF PUBLIC SAFETY AND AUSTRIA

When Emperor Leopold II passed away on March 1, 1792, it was a bellicose young man who inherited his problems. But Francis II had by degrees lost much of his martial ardor as a result of the cannonade of Valmy, the improvement in Prussia's international situation which followed that "battle," Dumouriez' lightning conquest of Belgium, and Custine's irruption into southern Germany. It was through Francis' mother-in-law, Queen Marie Caroline of Naples, and through the French envoy at Florence, that the Convention received the first intimation of this change of heart. We do not know whether a discussion as to peace terms actually took place, for that question is not answered by the only documentary evidence we have — a retrospective letter of Rivalz,[118] a French secret agent, to Delacroix, later the Directory's first minister of foreign affairs (dated January 16, 1796): "Overtures . . . had been made to me in the name of the Chamberlain, the Count of Säckingen [Sickingen].[119] The Minister [Lebrun] authorized me to facilitate the passage to Paris of all agents of the Emperor. Soon came the defection of Dumouriez, which broke off all my connections with the Chamberlain. . .[120]

The desertion of Dumouriez and his staff, with the resultant confusion in the French army, rekindled the martial flame within Emperor Francis' breast, and held out hope for the conquest of Alsace, part of which had long belonged to Austria.[121] In fact, the desertion of Dumouriez was not yet known to the Emperor when he took steps to turn the Dumouriez intrigue to Austria's account. Unaware that the scheme had failed, and that the French general had taken refuge in Coburg's camp, Francis II wrote to Coburg (April 10): "Dumouriez must have arrived in Paris by now, and the confusion and consternation in France have probably reached their

---

[117] Sybel, *Europe*, II, 300.

[118] This appears to be the proper spelling of his name. At any rate, it is the form to be found in Kaulek's *Papiers de Barthélemy*, published under the auspices of successive French ministers of foreign affairs. Sorel is not consistent in his spelling of Rivalz' name, sometimes writing *Rivalz* (e.g., *Europe*, III, 371, and IV, 359), but generally *Rivals*.

[119] Imperial Minister Extraordinary attached to the Army of the Empire (*Krieg g. Rev.*, I,

122).

[120] Arch. A. E., *M. et D.*, 655, cited in Hüffer-Luckwaldt, *Quellen*, Pt. II, Vol. I, xxi. For Sickingen's further efforts in behalf of peace, some indications may be found in Hügel to Imperial Vice-Chancellor Prince Colloredo, April 23, 1795, Vivenot-Zeissberg, *Quellen*, V, 183; and Dietrichstein to Thugut, July 18, 1795, *ibid.*, p. 297.

[121] Guyot, *Direc.*, pp. 98–99. *Vide supra*, Introduction, § 2e.

zenith. . . On receiving the present [despatch], declare that the armistice is, by my order, forthwith broken." [122] Of course, this iniquitous design had its origin in Thugut's tortuous brain,[123] but the Emperor had ratified it. To Thugut it was immaterial what Dumouriez' intentions were respecting the French throne.[124] The important point was "for the Prince of Saxe-Coburg to favor secretly the party of Dumouriez or any other party whatsoever which will help him to obtain possession of the fortresses and establish himself firmly on French soil. . . What is essential is that there be parties in France who fight and mutually weaken each other, and that we profit by this conflict to render ourselves masters of the fortresses and of as much territory as possible, in order that we can force the party which will finally prevail to buy peace and the Emperor's protection by ceding that part of his [the Emperor's] conquests which his Majesty chooses." [125]

Before hostilities were actually resumed, Dampierre, Dumouriez' successor, foreseeing the rout which would result if his disorganized troops were attacked, asked for a renewal of the truce. He declared that if it were granted, it "would be possible to release the persons whose arrest the executive power has been obliged to order." (These were Germans who had been seized as hostages, as mentioned above.) [126] Dampierre suggested that he could send someone to Paris to propose "the exchange of the four deputies of the National Convention and of the minister Beurnonville, with these same persons at present detained in Paris." [127] And then, as though fearful that sufficient inducement had not been offered for a renewal of the armistice, Dampierre made — "on his own account, without authorization of the regicide Brigands [at Paris]" — "a vague and insignificant proposition" that the royal family might become the basis of an exchange.[128] This was

---

[122] Sorel, *Europe*, III, 368–369.

[123] Thugut to Count Colloredo, undated, but between April 1 and 6, 1793, *Briefe Thugut*, I, 12.

[124] Thugut believed that Dumouriez had not, by his past conduct, earned Allied consideration. On December 13, 1793, the Austrian minister wrote to Count Colloredo: "His disturbed and restless mind makes him a very dangerous man. He has always devoted himself to sowing dissension among the Allies." — *Ibid.*, p. 64.

[125] *Ibid.*, p. 13. Just a year later (March 21, 1794), Robespierre, with his usual clairvoyance, declared before the Jacobin Club: "The foreigner should protect all these factions without adhering to any . . . It is indifferent to [him] . . . which . . . triumphs." — Aulard, *Jacobins*, VI, 8. Thugut had his

equal in the cold, shrewd legislator from Arras.

[126] § 1, this chapter.

[127] Mortimer-Ternaux, *Terreur*, VII, 71.

[128] Coburg to Mercy, May 3, 1793, *ibid.*, p. 72. Count von Metternich-Winneburg (the later Prince Metternich, son of Austria's minister plenipotentiary in Belgium), who had been sent to the Belgian Netherlands with special instructions after Dumouriez' defection, reported this overture of exchange before Coburg did (to the Emperor, April 13, 1793, Taschereau, *Revue rétrospective*, Ser. II, Vol. VI [1836], 438), and so created an interesting situation. Metternich-Winneburg had made mention of the overture on the envelope of his April 13 despatch, and had alleged Coburg as his authority. Trauttmansdorff, answering for the Emperor, replied

the first overture of the exchange which actually took place in 1795, after the death of the Queen, young Louis, and Madame Elisabeth had reduced the Temple's royal occupants to one: Princess Marie Thérèse Charlotte (Madame Royale).[129]

Whether Dampierre's overtures were actually made without authorization from the capital, as he asserted and the Austrians accepted, or whether they were inspired by Danton — as Mathiez believes [130] — is immaterial, for remarkably similar propositions presently emerged from Paris. The above-mentioned [131] Proly, reputedly the natural son of von Kaunitz, the Austrian chancellor, was commissioned — not by the Committee of Public Safety, for that was not created until the next day (April 6), but seemingly by Hérault de Séchelles,[132] probably with Danton's backing [133] — to make known to Austria that France would consent to peace negotiations based on a truce, recognition of France's right to have the government of her choice, and the convocation of a congress to decide the conditions of a general peace. These terms were forwarded by Proly to his mother in Brussels, with instructions to show them "to those who govern Belgium." [134] A few weeks later the Committee, upon the suggestion of Hérault,[135] despatched envoys to Naples, Tuscany, and Venice with oral instructions to say that France would consent to the safety of the Queen and royal children if these three states would continue their old alliances with France.[136] That Danton's young wife was weeping continually over the lot of the unfortunate royal mother [137] is a factor which probably entered into Danton's motives in

---

that "your postscript . . . is very interesting, but inasmuch as Coburg has not said a word about this in his reports . . . , we cannot believe it. It is improbable, anyway, considering the circumstances" (to Metternich-Winneburg, April 23, *ibid.*, p. 447). To which Metternich-Winneburg replied, "[It] is a proven fact [nevertheless], which Coburg confirmed to me when I was at his headquarters. But this proposal was accompanied by the condition of a general armistice, and I suppose the Marshal did not deem it proper to acquiesce in that. It is not my place to judge why he did not inform the Court" (to Trauttmansdorff, May 2, 1793, *ibid.*, p. 452).

[129] Sorel, *Europe*, III, 368–369.
[130] Mathiez, *Dtn paix*, pp. 140–149.
[131] This chapter, n. 11.
[132] E. Dard, *Hérault de Séchelles (1759–1794)* (Paris, 1907), pp. 236–237.
[133] It is not meant to imply here that Hérault was a Dantonist, though Aulard does in-

deed classify him as such. In fact, he calls Hérault the "ornament of the Dantonist party." — A. Aulard, *Les Orateurs de la Révolution: La Législative et la Convention* (2 vols. in 1, Paris, 1906–1907), II, 267. Others agree with Aulard that Hérault supported Danton's policies (e.g., Ellery, *Brissot*, p. 186, n. 1). But *vide* the vigorous protest of A. Mathiez, "Hérault de Séchelles était-il dantoniste?" *AR*, VII (1914), 485 *et seqq.*
[134] Proly's letter is reproduced in Dard, *Hérault*, p. 235, n. 2, with the date April 5. The negotiation failed because Austria refused to recognize the Republic (Mathiez, *Etrangers*, p. 105).
[135] Dard, *Hérault*, p. 237.
[136] Baron A. A. Ernouf, *Maret, duc de Bassano* (Paris, 1884), pp. 152–153; Sorel, *Europe*, III, 424–425. Maret's written instructions spoke only of Naples' neutrality (Ernouf, *Maret*, p. 151).
[137] Sorel, *Europe*, III, 423.

favoring these Italian overtures. The Queen could not just be freed. One had to secure some advantage for France in the process, or the Paris mob might revolt. So the renewal of the old alliances was stipulated.[138]

General Dampierre's overture loosed the gates to a flood of informal communications from Coburg, who seemed determined to bring about an arrangement with France despite the dictum of the Congress of Antwerp.[139] Some of these communications might quite conceivably have led indirectly to Franco-Austrian *rapprochement* had not the Convention and Committee treated them all with such disdain and distrust — as though nothing made in Austria could be genuine. The *Avis au peuple français* had of course preceded the final act of treason. Then came Coburg's *Adresse aux Français*, proclaiming that Austrian troops who pillaged the inhabitants in campaigns on French soil would be executed. It was suspected that this magnanimity was a ruse to dissuade the French farmer from hiding his grain and forage from the invading Austrians, who could then requisition them more readily; [140] and the Convention refused to allow the *Adresse* to be read before it.[141] With the *Adresse* had come a letter for Dampierre that *was* read before the Convention.[142] It was this letter which indirectly provoked Danton to secure the passage of the already-mentioned decree of nonintervention which, while disavowing the intention of France to meddle in the internal affairs of other states, insisted in no uncertain terms that others reciprocate the favor.[143] The next communication was a letter from Coburg to the Representatives on Mission to Valenciennes, wherein the Austrian commander in chief justified Dumouriez' conduct, attributing it to unselfish attachment to the monarchical constitution; and the letter closed with a remark that the fate of the four captured Commissioners depended upon the conduct of the revolutionists in France.[144]

Du Bois du Bais and Briez, Representatives to Valenciennes, in reply

---

[138] It was hoped that, if the overture proved to be abortive, it would at least delay Austria's invasion of France, and so leave more time for military preparations. In Maret's notes, he says that the revolutionists, with the world against them, were seeking friends (Ernouf, *Maret*, p. 153).

[139] Sybel, *Fr. Rev.*, II, 465–466.

[140] Du Bois du Bais and Briez, Rps to Valenciennes, to Conv., April 11, 1793, Aulard, *Actes*, III, 198.

[141] Aulard, *Actes*, III, 199, n. 1.

[142] *Ibid.*

[143] Anderson, *Const's . . . Doc's*, pp. 133–134. But cf. the views of Danton in autumn, 1792: "While it is our duty to give liberty to neighboring peoples, I declare that we have the right to say to them, 'You shall have no more kings, for, so long as you are surrounded by tyrants, a coalition of them may imperil our own liberty.' By sending us here as its deputies, the French nation has created a great, general committee of insurrection of peoples against all the kings in the world." — Quoted in Mathiez, *Fr. Rev.*, p. 278. Mathiez does not believe this was a sincere expression of Danton's opinion even on the date when made, for Danton was secretly negotiating for peace with Prussia at the time (*Dtn paix*, p. 58). Still, he voiced the same sentiments again on January 31, 1793 (*supra*, this chapter, § 2).

[144] Aulard, *Actes*, III, 223, n. 1.

to Coburg, castigated Dumouriez, defended the abolition of the monarchy, and concluded: "You tell us, General, that the fate of our four colleagues is in our own hands. We are not anxious about them, for they are under the protection of the sovereign justice and integrity of our enemies." [145] This was too much for the Convention. Angry exclamations interrupted the reading of a copy of the letter, and the Convention voted that, "indignant at this correspondence which it could not brook to hear to the end, . . . [it] disavows the conduct of Du Bois du Bais and Briez . . . , and censures and recalls them. . ." [146] But the Convention apparently soon realized that the Representatives to Valenciennes had really said no more than international courtesy required — except for their concluding remarks, which were mere wheedling — for Du Bois du Bais and Briez remained at Valenciennes.[147]

On April 13, 1793, Lieutenant Colonel Chérin was sent by Du Bois du Bais and Briez to the Austrian camp with the Representatives' response to another letter of Coburg's,[148] and to try to secure the liberation of Beurnonville and the four Commissioners. Coburg replied that his instructions forbade the prisoners' release.[149] But what was more important, from our point of view, is Chérin's conversation with Coburg and the latter's "intellectual guide," [150] Mack, on the subject of peace. The two Austrians declared that if France should renounce all her conquests, evacuate the Empire, including Mayence, and place a king at the head of her government, peace would be possible; and they suggested sounding Prussia. In fact, preponderant emphasis was placed upon this appeal to Prussia, as though Coburg and Mack were convinced that in Prussia lay the only hope of peace.[151]

The same day (April 13), on the southeastern front, General Wurmser's aide-de-camp declared to Custine that Wurmser desired to see "the cessation of this scourge of war" and so, he was certain, did his Majesty.[152] The historian Aulard declares that "the coincidence of these parleys . . . hardly permits one to doubt that the Court of Vienna had at this moment authorized its generals to commence vague pacific conversations with the French." [153] The present writer submits that this is not a necessary conclusion if one looks a little deeper. On April 5, Lebrun had written to Cus-

[145] *Ibid.*, n. 2.
[146] *Ibid.*, p. 224, n. 1.
[147] *Ibid.*, *passim.*
[148] Coburg was still writing letters to the French sixteen months later. On August 31, 1794, Gillet (Rp A. SMeu) informed the CPS: "I am sending you, dear colleagues, a letter from Coburg . . . We are not in the habit of answering him, though he writes

often." — *Ibid.*, XVI, 442.
[149] Aulard in *RF*, XVIII, 336–338.
[150] Cf. *Briefe Thugut*, I, 17: "The persistence of the Duke of Coburg, or rather, of those who control him . . ." (Thugut to Count Colloredo, June 2, 1793.)
[151] Sybel, *Fr. Rev.*, II, 467.
[152] Aulard in *RF*, XVIII, 338.
[153] *Ibid.*, p. 340.

tine: During negotiations regarding the exchange of prisoners, or other military matters, sound the enemy as to the possibility of a peace based upon the imprescriptible right of France to maintain a republican form of government, and the renunciation of all French conquests.[154] And Custine had been directed to concert, together with the Provisional Executive Council and influential members of the Convention, the steps that circumstances might require.[155] The General had willingly executed Lebrun's order. On April 11, he had sent the Duke of Brunswick and General Wurmser a letter which could well have served as the model for Bonaparte's Klagenfurt letter of 1797.[156] "Whatever glory may be afforded by the vocation of arms," Custine had written, "it is to me a thousand times more agreeable to labor for the consolation of humanity than to aid in shedding the blood of so many brave men." [157] To which Wurmser could do nought but reply: We don't like it any more than you do. But to the Emperor, he wrote: "I was very disinclined to lend myself to anything of that sort. [This is] shown by my answer, in which I told him simply that I had presented his letter to the [proper] authorities." [158] No further proof is necessary that the Imperial Court had not authorized Wurmser to institute negotiations.

As to Coburg's parleys with the French, Francis II wrote to Coburg between April 24 and 29: "My former orders . . . have given you to understand that my intention is that until the minister whom I shall furnish with my full powers for the political part has arrived [at your headquarters] . . . , you will avoid all negotiation with the *nationaux*. . . If we [can] assume the least sincerity . . . in these overtures [of Dampierre], they . . . reveal . . . [the] bad state of [French] affairs, which [is] but one more motive to profit by their distress. I charge you, in consequence, to drop the new negotiation that Dampierre has sought to initiate; whether or no it was concerted with the Commissioners of the self-styled National Convention is immaterial. And if, before the arrival of my minister plenipotentiary for the political part, Dampierre himself repeats new overtures of peace, you will apprize him that you are not authorized in any way to negotiate concerning such subjects. . . If Dampierre again broaches the idea of exchanging the Queen and royal family for Beurnonville and the four Commissioners, you can intimate to him that this project might be acceptable if made in valid form by persons having the power to carry it out." [159] And shortly there-

---

[154] Hüffer-Luckwaldt, *Quellen*, Pt. II, Vol. 1, xxxv.

[155] Herlaut in *AHRF*, IX, 520.

[156] Bonaparte's letter is referred to *infra*, Pt. II, chap. xxi, § 1. The similarity of several phrases is startling.

[157] Hüffer-Luckwaldt, *Quellen*, Pt. II, Vol. 1, xxxv–xxxvi.

[158] May 2, 1793, Vivenot-Zeissberg, *Quellen*, III, 46.

[159] *Ibid.*, p. 39. (A fortnight later, Dampierre was dead, victim of his government's insistence that he fight — in the face of overwhelming odds. A cannon ball laid him low at the head of his troops.)

after, Coburg was informed that the Count de Mercy had been charged with all negotiations and correspondence of a political nature with the French, and that even when Coburg was discussing a purely military matter with the enemy, he should have De Mercy — or an appointee of De Mercy's — with him, "considering that experience has shown that the French ordinarily make use of these occasions to institute overtures upon divers political matters." [160] From all of which it is quite clear that Coburg had never received the Imperial mandate to make peace overtures, vague or otherwise.

It is not unlikely, however, that all the talk of peace prompted the Imperial Court to probe the possibility of an arrangement with France, for peace feelers bearing the mark of official inspiration were presently received from the following places and persons: Naples, Florence, Basel, the Margrave of Baden, and the secretary of the Saxon legation at Paris.[161] The stumbling block to the success of these feelers was, in all likelihood, not the territory conquered by the French, but the form of the French government. The Austrians saw in the reëstablishment of the monarchical form of government in France a guarantee of Marie Antoinette and her children's safety, and the Emperor could not have been indifferent to their fate — despite the stories that he desired the death of the Queen because her degradation humbled all crowned heads, and her execution would legitimate the war.[162] But the general run of Frenchmen regarded the maintenance of the Republic as a point of honor. "Will we have peace? Are you willing to accept a king?" asked a German officer as Chérin left Coburg. " 'No,' I answered in a loud voice, . . . 'the Republic, or war eternal.'" To which the German replied, "That's a pity! The French and we ought to be friends." [163] Or take the story sent in by Du Bois du Bais and Briez: "A French soldier and an Austrian soldier met as friends. We are informed that the Austrians continually seek such occasions. They asked one another why they were fighting. 'For the Republic,' replied the Frenchman. 'And I for a king,' replied the Austrian. 'Well, now,' said the Frenchman, 'step away from me and we shall soon see, pistol in hand, which of us is right.'" But neither of them was an Annie Oakley, so this little tale has a happy ending.[164]

The parleys with Coburg and Mack came, of themselves, to nought. Those with Wurmser were assailed from both sides: The Emperor forbade Wurmser to engage in negotiations — that was Count de Mercy's province. Lebrun wrote to Custine (April 20) that "it is not a question of starting

[160] Francis II to Coburg, n.d., *ibid.*, p. 40.
[161] Aulard in *RF*, XVIII, 341.
[162] Memoir of the Englishman Matthews, to Otto of the French Ministry of Foreign Affairs, August 1793, quoted *ibid.*, p. 251, n. 3.
[163] Quoted by Aulard in *RF*, XVIII, 339.
[164] To CPS, April 17, 1793, Aulard, *Actes*, III, 302.

negotiations, but merely of penetrating the intentions of these two powers [Prussia and Austria]." [165]

The reason for Lebrun's change of attitude can be found in a letter of the Committee of Public Safety, dated April 21: "We have been reassured concerning the military dispositions. . . All our frontiers are about to be covered. . . If the belligerent powers want peace, they will have to explain themselves clearly. Let us place ourselves in a position where we can resist both their armies and their cunning. We must avoid lending to our acts, to our correspondence, an appearance of negotiation and of diplomacy." [166] Two days previously, the Committee had voted to announce to the army that "France neither wishes to have, nor is able to have, a durable peace without victories." [167] And on April 26, Barère drew up a proclamation to the armies which left no doubt as to *his* position with respect to peace: "The Austrians seek to deceive you with honeyed words and hopes of peace. Peace is on their lips, but war is in their hearts. . . It is the peace of the tomb they are offering you; you require the life of liberty. . . Their cry is: Peace and royalty. Yours should be: The Republic and war!" [168]

Two thirds of the Committee members had to agree for the enactment of a decree,[169] but Danton's influence was so great that he was usually able to induce the Committee to view matters as he saw them. And Danton yearned for peace — for peace at any price, according to Mathiez.[170] It has been mentioned that the day before the Committee of Public Safety was created, the Proly negotiation was instituted and Custine was ordered to sound the enemy generals as to peace terms. In Mathiez' opinion, Proly and Custine, and Dampierre, too, acted upon the invitation of Danton; and the machinations of Du Bois du Bais and Briez are certainly not presented as alien to Danton's wishes.[171] But all these overtures had been in vain, and so the aforementioned *démarches* at Naples, Tuscany, and Venice were decided upon.

Noël was sent to Venice, Maret to Naples, and Chauvelin to Florence. Particular stress was laid upon the Florence mission. Chauvelin was advised that the Committee was endeavoring to detach England, Prussia, and Hol-

[165] Hüffer-Luckwaldt, *Quellen*, Pt. II, Vol. I, xxxv–xxxvi. Sorel (*Europe*, III, 401) has "intentions of the Prussians."
[166] To Rps A. RMo, Aulard, *Actes*, III, 371.
[167] Session of April 19, 1793, *ibid.*, p. 327.
[168] Aulard in *RF*, XVIII, 249.
[169] *Idem, Actes*, III, 116; IV, 592.
[170] Mathiez in *RH*, CLVIII, 255. Mathiez says the *Committee* desired peace at any price; but query whether it would not be more correct to say that Danton was anxious for

peace at (shall we say: almost?) any price, and the Committee bowed to his leadership. Certainly Barère's proclamation of April 26, cited in the text, does not bear the aura of a peace-at-any-price advocate; but then, Barère, "clever sophist, knew how to disguise adroitly the versatility of his opinions." — Dussault, quoted in Dauban, *Paris*, p. 515.
[171] Mathiez, *Dtn paix*, pp. 140–142, 144, 145–146, 149.

land from the Coalition, intending then to hurl the unified might of France against Austria. Until the results had become self-evident, Chauvelin should hold his tongue. In case France did negotiate anything with Austria, the first advances would have to come from the Austrians.[172]

Chauvelin's instructions were dated July 7,[173] whereas Noël's were dated May 12,[174] and Maret's,[175] June 17.[176] This does not signify that the Committee of Public Safety had recognized only belatedly the importance of Tuscany. Sémonville, the Committee's new ambassador extraordinary to Constantinople, had been ordered on May 19 to stop over at Florence for a few days to visit with its Habsburger grand duke and his court.[177] Sémonville was to pretend merely to be en route to the Near East, but to be desirous of making, on the way, the acquaintance of Manfredini, the Grand Duke's minister. The latter was sympathetic to the Revolution, and had further endeared himself to France by presenting a memoir to his former pupil, the Emperor, advising recognition of the Republic.[178] Sémonville was to make no propositions, but to listen to any overtures which might be made to him. He was to act in such a manner as to inspire jealousy and uneasiness among the Allied powers, especially Prussia. "To alarm the cabinet of Berlin is what, in effect, Sémonville shall occupy himself with. Our views contemplate thus to disunite the Coalition." [179] Oral instructions ordered Sémonville to discuss the subject of Marie Antoinette's release.[180]

In June, two additional channels were opened for possible peace negotiations. Lebrun had suggested that civil commissioners be named to handle the exchange of prisoners for the Army of the North, and that these commissioners "make or receive conciliatory overtures." The Provisional Executive Council approved on June 8, and decreed that for this purpose men

---

[172] Sorel, *Europe*, III, 424–425; Ernouf, *Maret*, p. 153.

[173] Sorel, *Europe*, III, 425.

[174] *Ibid.*, p. 404.

[175] Maret had been named minister plenipotentiary to Naples (Vivenot-Zeissberg, *Quellen*, III, 154) to replace Mackau, who had made the unpardonable *faux pas* of attending a function to which he had been invited only as a matter of form — it being in honor of a visiting *Austrian* prince (Ernouf, *Maret*, p. 150).

[176] Aulard in *RF*, XVIII, 251.

[177] Session of CPS of May 19, 1793, Aulard, *Actes*, IV, 235. Von Sybel (*Europe*, II, 353) seems to say that both Sémonville and Maret had been assigned to Constantinople ("their mission at Constantinople"), which is of course incorrect. Aulard (in *RF*, XVIII, 251)

thinks Sémonville was accredited to Florence. Duke de Broglie (ed.) (*Mémoires du Prince de Talleyrand* [5 vols., Paris, 1891–1892], I, 174, n. 1) also thinks Sémonville was accredited to Florence. Perroud (in his "A propos des *Mémoires de Talleyrand*" in *RF*, LXI [1911], 59) knows only that Sémonville was accredited to Constantinople, so ridicules De Broglie for mentioning that Sémonville was to discuss the liberation of the French royal family at Florence.

[178] Hüffer-Luckwaldt, *Quellen*, Pt. II, Vol. I, xxxvii–xxxviii; Sorel, *Europe*, III, 403. Francis had grown up in Tuscany, where his father, Emperor Leopold II, had been grand duke from 1765 to 1790.

[179] Session of CPS of May 19, 1793, Aulard, *Actes*, IV, 235; Sorel, *Europe*, III, 403.

[180] Ernouf, *Maret*, p. 157.

of circumspection with political attainments, but unknown in diplomacy, should be employed; and the terms that they should intimate or listen to might concern either a separate peace with England and Holland, or a general pacification with all the powers.[181] The Committee of Public Safety gave its blessing to the plan the same day, and on June 18, the instructions of the new commissioners were drawn up. There was no question yet, they were told, of making serious propositions — at least not to England. The commissioners should listen, but not speak, except in their own names. They were to insinuate that France desired peace, but only if the Republic were recognized and no indemnities were demanded.[182]

The other channel opened in June was through the secret agents under Hérault de Séchelles.[183] One Lafitte [184] was ordered to cross the border as an *émigré* and make contact with Coburg's staff. He did succeed in establishing relations with a certain "G," [185] who may or may not have been the Brabançon priest employed in the chancellery of Metternich, whom Sorel says Lafitte contacted.[186] Dona, another agent, was thereupon sent to facilitate the passage of letters to Lafitte, and a young relative of Hérault de Séchelles (also named Hérault) [187] was ordered to bring matters to a head. This negotiation had produced nothing by the time Danton relinquished power on July 10. In fact, it produced nothing of consequence after that, either, though young Hérault left for Rocroy on August 1 with his pockets bulging with money. The Provisional Executive Council suspended the mission on August 13, under Danton's successor.[188]

Despite all the efforts of Danton with respect to Austria, and all the efforts of the Austrian general Coburg, July 10 found France and Austria in substantially the same relation, diplomatically speaking, as they had been on April 6. Perhaps Danton's colleagues did not feel the time was appropriate for peace when the war was going badly for France. This is indeed what the Committee had announced to the armies on April 19. This is also what Article 121 of the unpromulgated Constitution of 1793 declared — that France would never make peace with a state occupying French soil.[189]

[181] Quoted by Aulard in *RF*, XVIII, 153–154.

[182] Sorel, *Europe*, III, 420. One of the commissioners chosen was the disillusioned Mayençais exile Georg Forster (*ibid.*, p. 421).

[183] Hérault administered the funds earmarked for secret agents by the Committee (Dard, *Hérault*, p. 234). Dard has found among Hérault's private papers some of his official correspondence with these secret agents.

[184] Sorel has "Laffitte" (*Europe*, III, 423).

[185] Dard, *Hérault*, pp. 237–238.

[186] *Europe*, III, 423.

[187] Sorel, *Europe*, III, 423, confuses Hérault with his young relative. A pencil note made by Chuquet in the margin of his personal copy of Sorel says: "Faux. Hérault préside la conv. le 12 août, jour où ce Hérault . . . [illegible] de Rocroy." Dard also corrects Sorel, and points out that "ce Hérault" was a relative of his famous namesake (*Hérault*, p. 239, n. 1).

[188] Dard, *Hérault*, p. 238.

[189] Duguit and Monnier, *Const. et lois*, p. 78. Not Art. 120, as in Sorel, *Europe*, III, 423, n. 3.

Mercier had objected (June 18, 1793)

Official Austria, on the other hand, saw itself in the flood tide of success, and hence for Austria, also, this was not the time to make peace. Danton was destined to go down in history as a blot on France's honor because he sought peace at a time when almost everyone — friend and foe alike — wanted the bloodshed to continue.

that one *could* make advantageous treaties on one's own soil, but he was overruled   (*Moniteur*, XVI, 689).

CHAPTER IV

FRANCO–GERMAN RELATIONS
UNDER ROBESPIERRE

I. THE CREATION OF THE GREAT COMMITTEE OF PUBLIC SAFETY

*I*T will be recalled that the Congress of Antwerp, held soon after Dumouriez' defection, obliged Coburg to withdraw his no-conquests pledge as an expression of his "personal sentiments" (April 9).[1] The Austrians and English thereupon marched south from Belgium into France, and found the road to Paris undefended. Only their stupidity [2] — they were unable to agree on a plan of campaign — saved the capital. To the south, the Prussians invested Mayence. General Wurmser, with a mixed forced of Austrians and Imperials, pushed into Alsace. The Spanish poured through the passes of the Pyrenees. Civil strife rent La Vendée with ever-increasing ferocity.[3] Fire, apparently of incendiary origin, broke out in a cartridge manufactory at Bayonne, an artillery park at Chemille, a sail-loft at the port of L'Orient, and in a half-dozen other places.[4] The high price of bread — it was well-nigh prohibitive in so far as the common man was concerned — was "effect-[ing] the counterrevolution among the very persons who had created the Revolution."[5]

Bread — its high price, poor quality, the difficulty of obtaining it — was indeed the source of much disquietude, and that disquietude was increasing instead of diminishing. One secret agent of the government reported that a man he knew had stood in line for seven hours, commencing at 4:00 A.M., to get bread. The agent suggested that patrols arrest the first person in line at an inordinate hour. There was much grumbling over the mixing of barley-meal with the white flour, and using spoiled wheat. The agents in

---

[1] *Vide supra*, chap. iii, § 1.
[2] A. Merchier, *La bataille de Tourcoing* (Roubaix, 1894), p. 6.
[3] Stephens, *Rev. Eur.*, p. 130.
[4] Barère, for CPS, to Conv., Aug. 1, 1793, *Brochures pol.*, LXIII, no. 7, p. 9.

[5] Saunier (secret agent) to Garat (min. of int.), *c.* Aug. 15, 1793, P. Caron (ed.), *Rapports des agents du ministre de l'intérieur dans les départements (1793–an II)* (2 vols., Paris, 1913–1951), I, 10–11. All food was exorbitant in price, but bread was the highest.

Paris tried to calm the people of the capital by telling them that the *départements* were eating worse bread and paying more for it, and that the Paris bread was "excellent," anyway. Moreover, the inhabitants of the besieged frontier cities were suffering actual famine. The complainers replied that they also would suffer famine when their time came. There was nothing to do but accuse these objectors of counterrevolution — of being in league with the external enemy. And, indeed, hunger was one of the strongest counterrevolutionary forces.[6]

The First Committee of Public Safety, as above mentioned,[7] entrusted the defense of the frontiers to Custine, who spent many precious weeks doing nothing. And when his forces were strengthened by the addition of the Army of the North to his command, he tried to denude the Armies of the Rhine and of the Moselle of vitally necessary elements in order to build up an overwhelming force with which to crush the Austrians in Belgium. But this transfer would have endangered the other frontiers. The generals of the Rhine and Moselle Armies, the Representatives on Mission, and the minister of war all resisted, and on June 19, the Committee revoked its approval of Custine's plan. The revocation prompted no change in Custine's *modus operandi*. He still did nothing [8] — except declaim against his enemies.[9] These included Marat, who had prognosticated that Custine would prove to be "Dumouriez, Volume II"; the minister of war, who had opposed his plan; and Robespierre.[10] And while the patriots of France tore at each other's throats, their common enemy was relentlessly grinding under

---

[6] Perrière (secret agent) to Garat, Aug. 27, 1793 (Perrière's observations are based on the period since his appointment on May 12), P. Caron, *Paris pendant la Terreur: Rapports des agents secrets du ministre de l'intérieur, publiés pour la Société d'histoire contemporaine* (4 vols. of 6 so far, Paris, 1910–1949), I, 4–6.

[7] Chap. iii, § 3.

[8] He was trying, according to Sybel, to reëstablish order and confidence, and that required time; but the patriots of Paris wished him immediately to retake Valenciennes (*Europe*, II, 342). Six months later, their impatience was still manifesting itself — by frequent rumors of its capture or imminent capture (Charmont to min. of int., Dec. 26, 1793, Caron, *Paris*, II, 5; Rolin, Dec. 27, *ibid.*, p. 43; Grivel, Dec. 28, *ibid.*, p. 52; Le Harivel, Dec. 30, *ibid.*, p. 89; Le Breton, Jan. 20, 1794, *ibid.*, III, 62; Le Breton, *s.d.*, probably Jan. 29, *ibid.*, p. 213).

[9] "Custine had committed one capital error — injudicious selection of his parents. He was a noble born." — W. B. Kerr, *The Reign of Terror, 1793–4: the Experiment of the Democratic Republic and the Rise of the Bourgeoisie* (Toronto, 1927), p. 147.

[10] Custine had the unhappy thought of going to Paris to vindicate himself. He was arrested, tried for treason, and condemned to die. But it was not treason, says his aide-de-camp. "The mistakes he had committed . . . were due solely to his lack of talent, the weakness of his spirit and of his character. He had been carried to the clouds when, as a result of chance, he had been successful; he fell into discredit when fortune, which had treated him sometimes as a spoiled child, ceased to favor him." — *Mém. Custine*, II, 252–253. In battle, Custine could think only of his own safety, according to the aide, and that is what doomed him ever to be a mediocre general (*ibid.*, Preface, p. xxiii). The aide was obviously hostile.

foot the soil of their beloved *patrie*. The First Committee of Public Safety had failed signally to accomplish the primary aim for which it had been created — the defense of France.[11]

This was the heartrending situation when, on July 10, 1793, the First Committee of Public Safety was dissolved, and the so-called Great Committee of Public Safety was elected in its place. This Committee owes its designation as "Great" to its accomplishments and not to its size. It was composed of only nine men — that is, originally; subsequent additions raised its membership to fourteen. But from September 20, 1793, to March 15, 1794, it had twelve members, always the same twelve. These included Robespierre, the clear-sighted incorruptible who had resisted the declaration of war on Austria (elected July 27, 1793); Hérault de Séchelles, who (with Barère)[12] took charge of foreign affairs;[13] Carnot, who attended to military matters; and Barère, who served as chairman. Danton had been added on September 6, but had declined on the ninth. Had he accepted, he might have served as a dam to halt or at least to control the flood of extremist principles which was engulfing France,[14] and which was eventually to snuff out the life of Danton himself.

The Great Committee secured obedience to its will by terrorizing every element of the population. A man — or woman — or child could be brought within the purview of the Revolutionary Tribunal and its bloodthirsty handmaiden, the guillotine, by merely giving cause for suspicion of an untoward *thought*.[15] Most everyone, therefore, strove with might and main to prove by his actions that his sympathies were with the Revolution — and thus was attained through fear that unity of effort which would otherwise have been impossible in a state divided against itself by religious, political, economic, personal, and many other considerations.

New armies were raised by conscripting [16] all unmarried men, and child-

[11] Mathiez in *RH*, CLVIII, 266–269.

[12] H. Carnot and R. David d'Angers (eds.), *Memoirs of Bertrand Barère, Chairman of the Committee of Public Safety During the Revolution* (tr. from the French by De V. Payen-Payne; 4 vols., London, 1896), II, 115; Mathiez, *Fr. Rev.*, p. 363. But on II, 117 of his *Memoirs*, Barère declares that "foreign affairs I had but little to do with."

[13] That is, when Robespierre did not have a special reason to interfere.

[14] Guillaume in *Etudes rév.*, Ser. II, pp. 234–236.

[15] As a result, people would "neither speak nor write . . . Not a group dares to form. At night, everyone goes home. People call this withdrawal 'to go sleep their liberty' (*aller coucher sa Liberté*)." — "Résumé d'informations exactes au 25 janvier 1794" (Mallet du Pan), *Despatches Gower*, p. 317.

[16] The new personal freedom to which the Revolution had given birth seemed to allow no logical place for that extreme negation of all personal freedom — compulsory military service. Eberhard Kessel has pointed out that the new spirit of nationality in France, identifying the individual with the nation, rendered the defense of the state the equivalent of self-defense, and so enabled the theory of conscription to be accepted without breach of principle ("Die Wandlung der Kriegskunst im Zeitalter der französischen Revolution," *HZ*, CXLVIII [1938], 248).

less widowers, between the ages of eighteen and twenty-five [17] — constituting Group I of the *levée en masse* of August 23, 1793.[18] Noble officers were cashiered despite past services to the Republic, for it was not known at what moment they might decide to play Dumouriez.[19] The new troops were drilled — and *disciplined!* [20] The new officers were encouraged and tolerated while they passed through their novitiates of bungling [21] and defeat.[22] Deputies of the Convention, imposingly bedecked with sabres, sashes, and round, tricolor-plumed hats,[23] were attached to the armies, with vast discretionary — but not unlimited [24] — power over generals, troops, and supplies. If a general did not win victories, they could order his arrest and trial as an enemy of the Republic.[25] A requirement of daily correspondence between these

[17] The *levée* resulted at first in a flood of enlistments of young men under 18 and over 25, not all of them unmarried — men who saw the mess hall behind the gun ("Informations additionnelles" [Mallet du Pan], *Despatches Gower*, p. 355). Later, the draftable single men protested against the exemption enjoyed by the married. They argued that those who had the greatest stake in the future of the Republic should be singled out to go to the front first (Mathiez, *Fr. Rev.*, p. 307). In Colmar, the levy was resisted — in this sense: The inhabitants wanted to stay and defend their own homes (Adant and Saunier to Paré [min. of int.], Sept. 11, 1793, Caron, *Agents . . . intér.*, I, 23). There was some trouble also in Saarburg (*idem*, Sept. 6, *ibid.*, p. 20).

[18] *Vide Moniteur*, XVII, 474–478 for the report of Barère (speaking for CPS) to the Convention proposing the *levée en masse*.

The decree, in its first article, reads: "From this moment until that when our enemies have been driven from the territory of the Republic, all Frenchmen will be permanently requisitioned for the armed services. Young men will go to fight; married men will forge arms and transport food; women will make tents and clothes, and serve in the hospitals; children will scrape old linen into lint [for dressing wounds]; old men will repair to public places to raise the courage of the fighters, arouse hatred of kings, and promote the unity of the Republic . . ."

The German papers had no confidence that any substantial benefit could accrue to France from this legislation. An earlier decree of the Convention to the same effect (in March) had betrayed serious imperfections. The *Politischen Gespräche der Toten* made the

point, which seems well taken, that the juxtaposition of soldiers, some of whom were fighting under compulsion, and some of whom were inflamed with revolutionary ardor, would not promote order in the ranks even if it did swell the size of the army (Oct. 4, Hansen, *Quellen*, II, 904, n. 1). And wars are won by organization, by teamwork.

[19] Pariset, *La Rév.*, pp. 141–143, 157.

[20] "The soldiers ordered to an advance post do not go there, or do not remain there . . . Does an officer command a soldier? The latter responds proudly that he will not do what he is ordered, and he doesn't do it either. Is a regiment, a battalion, an army, on the march, even in enemy country? The soldiers disband, lag behind, pillage villages, kill and ravish, and rejoin their corps only the next day . . . There is yet another difficulty. If a general or a commander is a stern disciplinarian, the soldiers threaten to denounce him as an aristocrat." — Blaux, Cmr in Meurthe, Moselle, and Bas-Rhin, April 6, 1793, Aulard, *Actes*, III, 130.

[21] Pariset, *La Rév.*, p. 143.

[22] Hoche was very downcast after his defeat at Kaiserslautern, and Carnot wrote to him: "A reverse is not a crime when one has done his best to merit victory . . . You still have our confidence." — Dumolin, *Précis*, I, 206.

[23] Art. 8, Decree of April 4, 1793, Aulard, *Actes*, III, 63–64; reaffirmed by Art. 9, Decree of April 30, 1793, *ibid.*, p. 536.

[24] Bonnal de Ganges, *Repré.*, I, 15. They were subject to recall and punishment for malfeasance, which fact alone destroys the fiction of unlimited power. Cf. Palmer, *Twelve*, pp. 132–133.

[25] Almost every reverse was imputed to treason (Sorel, *Europe*, III, 438). General Hou-

well-nigh omnipotent [26] deputies — or Representatives on Mission, as they were styled [27] — and the Committee of Public Safety, was devised to keep these arms of the central power themselves in line.[28] The system seems to have worked,[29] for presently there followed a series of brilliant successes. The English and Hanoverians were defeated at Hondschoten (September 6–8), and the Austrians at Wattignies (October 16). Hoche overcame Wurmser at the battle of the Geisberg on December 26, despite Pichegru's ill will; and only Brunswick's timely intervention prevented a rout. On the thirtieth, Wurmser abandoned the left bank of the Rhine.[30] Equal success was obtained against the Spaniards, and in La Vendée.[31] It can hence be seen that the creation of the Great Committee of Public Safety is a landmark in the German policy of France. It turned the tide from defeat to victory, thus indicating to the Directory — and to Napoleon — the path of conquest.

2. THE GREAT COMMITTEE AND GERMANY

a. In General

What changes occurred in the German policy of France when the Great Committee of Public Safety succeeded Danton's Committee? It has been averred that the First Committee of Public Safety humiliated France by its "vain attempts" to negotiate with the members of the Coalition; and the Desportes mission is cited as an example of these abortive attempts.[32] It has been pointed out that Prussia was willing to continue the Desportes negotiation, but that the Great Committee, upon its accession to power, recalled Desportes.[33] It would not, therefore, appear that France had been humiliated, but rather that, perhaps just to be different [34] — successor gov-

---

chard, for instance, was executed merely for losing a battle. On ascending the gallows he remarked bitterly: "Shall we fight, then, for these buggers who guillotine us!" — Dumolin, *Précis*, I, 176. Of rare good humor is General Kléber's remark: "Together we will fight, Marceau, and together we will be guillotined." — Bonnal de Ganges, *Repré.*, IV, 3.

[28] A decree of the Convention of August 16, 1793, imposed a penalty of ten years in irons upon administrators who should suspend the decrees of Representatives on Mission (Aulard, *Actes*, VI, 5).

[27] Art. 9, par. 2, decree of Conv. of April 4, 1793, *ibid.*, III, 64, slightly modified by Art. 9, Decree of April 30, 1793, *ibid.*, p. 536. It was on April 11, 1793, that the term "Representative on Mission" replaced that of "Commissioner" in habitual usage (*ibid.*, p. 193,

n. 1), but there were still exceptions for a time (*ibid.*, p. 338).

[28] Conv. decrees of April 8 and 20, 1793, *ibid.*, pp. 158, 533 *et seqq.*

[29] The result is described in glowing terms in Soult's *Mémoires*, I, 198–200.

[30] Dumolin, *Précis*, I, 165–210. Wurmser was an Alsatian by birth, and had invited the natives to join him. Some did so willingly. But he brought in his train all the old exactions of the *ancien régime*, which cannot have been so welcome (Palmer, *Twelve*, p. 179).

[31] Stephens, *Rev. Eur.*, p. 140.

[32] Mathiez, *Fr. Rev.*, p. 341. The entire fifth chapter of Mathiez' *Danton et la paix* is a diatribe against "defeatists."

[33] Chap. iii, § 3, *supra*.

[34] Danton had negotiated with foreign powers, therefore Hérault de Séchelles, of the section

ernments usually think it incumbent upon them to be different — the Great Committee relinquished an opportunity for peace with Prussia.[35]

The Great Committee also did its best to render peace with Austria most unlikely by breaking the key with which Danton had been trying to unlock the door. Reference is intended, of course, to that most dastardly of political murders — that of the Habsburg queen of France, Marie Antoinette.[36] The night that young Hérault de Séchelles left for Rocroy with his pockets bulging with money[37] in pursuance of the secret Lafitte overture, the Great Committee ordered the Queen transferred to the Conciergerie and held for trial. It was a strange accompaniment to a peace negotiation, and one which requires study.

Though we lack definite information on young Hérault's instructions, it has been argued that he must have been charged to promote the exchange of the Queen for the Conventionals in Austrian hands, and that the transfer and order for trial of Marie Antoinette constituted an attempt to put pressure upon Austria to agree to the exchange.[38] But news of a most aggravating nature had recently arrived from Italy. Sémonville and Maret, traveling together to Florence and Naples respectively, had been seized at Novato in the neutral Grisons (Switzerland) by the Austrians, and transported in chains to the Château of Gravedona on the Lake of Como.[39] They had indeed been comporting themselves "with as much clumsiness as indiscretion,"[40] and Austria was perhaps justly fearful not only that they would disseminate revolutionary propaganda in Italy,[41] but that Sémonville's intentions

of foreign affairs of the CPS, shunned all negotiation as smacking of Dantonism (Sorel, *Europe*, III, 524). But, curiously, many of Danton's peace efforts had been prompted by Hérault (Dard, *Hérault*, pp. 234, 237).

[35] It should be realized that Mathiez' bias in favor of Robespierre may have had something to do with his (Mathiez') harsh appraisal of Danton's peace efforts. It would be well to remember also that the French are a warlike and proud people, and regard any peace not dictated at the point of their victorious sword as inglorious — to put it mildly.

[36] The execution of the Queen was quite different from the execution of the King, for he was a born Frenchman and head of the state. But a foreign princess who leaves the protection of her kinsmen to help perpetuate a foreign dynasty is a guest of her adoptive subjects and entitled to plenary protection.

[37] *Vide* chap. iii, § 4, *supra*.

[38] Dard, *Hérault*, p. 239.

[39] Buchez and Roux, *Hist. parlem.*, XXVIII, 461.

[40] Sorel, *Europe*, III, 432.

[41] Sybel, *Europe*, II, 353. In September 1790, a number of German reports declared that Sémonville was one of several secret agents sent to Germany to arouse unrest (Prince-Elector Klemens Wenzeslaus of Trèves to Burgomaster J. W. Reuland of Trèves, Sept. 13, Hansen, *Quellen*, I, 680). On December 18, 1790, it was reported that he had been charged to assure that the Brabant got all the seditious attention that it needed, and while thus engaged, to watch for an occasion to start a revolution in Germany (Prince-Elector Friedrich Karl of Mayence to Prince-Elector Max Franz of Cologne, *ibid.*, p. 749). After Sémonville's Novato capture, a Frankfort-on-the-Main newspaper asserted that on him had been found a book containing the names of all traitors, Clubists, and other French adherents, which book had been sent to Vienna for study. Klemens Wenzeslaus seems to have become quite exercised over this report, but Thugut laughingly dubbed the whole story a fable (*ibid.*, II, 907, n. 2).

respecting Turkey were not at all to Austria's liking.[42] However, the seizure was palpably in violation of international law, the circumstances were aggravated,[43] and the Committee sought to shape its reprisal to fit the misdeed.

There were no Austrians of sufficiently high rank in France who could be thrown into prison on the principle of reciprocity.[44] There was only the hated Austrian Woman, and she was already in prison. To aggravate her lot, it would be necessary to execute her. Her elimination was demanded by

[42] Ernouf, *Maret*, p. 171; Wilczek to Thugut, July 28, 1793, Vivenot-Zeissberg, *Quellen*, III, 155.

[43] The Austrians fell upon the party from ambush. Both the men and the women were despoiled of their money and personal effects. (Cronthal to Thugut, July 27, 1793, Vivenot-Zeissberg, *Quellen*, III, 154). These effects, and personal papers, had occupied four heavily laden wagons of prodigious size. Everything (even the wagons) was sequestered and taken to the château of Milan, pending the Emperor's orders (*idem*, July 7, 1793, *ibid.*, p. 141; Wilczek to Thugut, July 30, 1793, *ibid.*, pp. 158–159). Regarding the money seized, Maret is reported to have departed from Paris empty-handed (Ernouf, *Maret*, pp. 154–155), but it seems that at Sémonville's disposal was a goodly supply of gold (*ibid.*, p. 172) — so much of it that Cronthal had written to Thugut on July 13: "These people must . . . have an unbelievable store of gold along . . . for they appear to value the *louis d'or* no more than a kreuzer . . . The citizens and peasants of Chur know how to comport themselves under such circumstances, and demand for every wagon, every horse, every man, a fourfold price." — Vivenot-Zeissberg, *Quellen*, III, 149.

The French also had along, it seems, a small fortune in jewels — jewels which, with the money, were later contemplated by the Austrians as a partial dowry for Madame Royale. (G. Lenotre [pseud. for L. L. T. Gosselin], *The Daughter of Louis XVI* [tr. from the French by J. L. May; New York, 1908], p. 117. [Regarding the pseudonym, the "G" obviously comes from Gosselin; the "Leno" from the second Christian name, Léon; the "tre" from the two ends of the last Christian name, Théodore.])

Mme. Sémonville and another woman, and the two "very ugly" (Napoleon Bonaparte to Joseph, Aug. 9, 1795, in *FH*, VI [1911], 125) Sémonville girls — both squalling —

were not arrested, but the men of the party, including the envoys, were. They were imprisoned in the unhealthful subterranean vaults beneath the ancient ducal palace of Mantua. (Ernouf, *Maret*, p. 177; Wilczek to Thugut, July 30, 1793, Vivenot-Zeissberg, *Quellen*, III, 158. Not at Milan, as von Sybel has it [*Europe*, III, 353], though that had once been the intention [Ernouf, *Maret*, pp. 176–177]. Mathiez, also, has "Milan" [*Dtn paix*, p. 157].) Chill nights, burning days, and humid air brought on swamp fever, which carried off five of their number within the first six months. Maret might also have succumbed — his health had already been so undermined that he was suffering convulsions daily, and all his hair and part of his teeth had fallen out — had not a deputation from the Academy of Mantua, which remembered his savant-father, come to see how the son was faring. On its recommendation, Sémonville and Maret were transferred to the fortress of Kuffstein in the Tyrol. The others remained at Mantua — to die, with one exception (Ernouf, *Maret*, pp. 176–178).

In sheer justice to Austria, it must be admitted that while the Emperor had ordered the imprisonment of the envoys to be "in the citadel of Mantua or in such other place as you [Archduke Ferdinand, Governor of Milan] may judge most proper to prevent all danger of escape on their part," he had specified: "I believe it meet that they be treated without harshness (*sans rigueur*)." The Emperor's order had been drawn up by Thugut (Aug. 5, 1793, Vivenot-Zeissberg, *Quellen*, III, 172–173). Both Milan and Mantua were Habsburg possessions.

[44] The arrest of all Germans having a deliberative voice at Ratisbon had already been decreed on April 5, 1793 (*Moniteur*, XVI, 70), so there were not too many important Germans left around to imprison.

still another consideration. Knowledge of the projected negotiation had reached the ears of the Paris Commune.[45] If anything spelled political suicide in those chivalrous days, it was to be accused of softness toward the unfortunate queen. Some grand gesture on the part of the Committee was necessary to prove that its heart was really in the wrong place. It met the challenge by securing from the Convention a decree ordering the removal of Marie Antoinette to the Conciergerie, and her trial before the Revolutionary Tribunal.[46] Now no one could accuse it of weakness.

Von Sybel would have us believe that the Committee caused the Queen to be placed on trial because it feared the Austrians would publish that part of the envoys' instructions which dealt with the release of the Queen.[47] Thugut did of course sift the prisoners' instructions. "Send me as soon as possible . . . all the papers found among their baggage," he had ordered (in the Emperor's name) on August 5.[48] And, "I have begun to examine the papers of Sémonville," he wrote to Count von Colloredo the following month; "I believe on first glance that we shall find very curious things there."[49] But Thugut could not publish the portion of the instructions that related to the Queen's release simply because it did not exist. It has been pointed out that that subject formed part of the *oral* instructions.[50] Of course, there was a phrase in letters addressed to Sémonville[51] — "neglect no measures tending to conciliate . . . the Court of Naples"[52] — which the Austrians could have interpreted as referring to Marie Antoinette. However, it was sufficiently vague so that they could not be positive, and neither could anyone else, for that matter. Indeed, that is why the phrase had been used.

A second error in von Sybel's account is his statement that the Committee feared that Austria would betray the secret of the negotiation. That secret had already been compromised before the envoys left France; in fact, the envoys had hurried away to prevent Ysabeau, spokesman of the infuri-

[45] Ernouf, *Maret*, p. 159.

[46] Sybel, *Europe*, II, 353. Other factors of course entered, but none so directly relevant to a work of this nature.

There is some evidence that Danton continued his efforts to save the Queen, even after her transfer to the Conciergerie. In question is a letter purporting to be from Danton to Marie Antoinette, saying: "To Citizeness Marie Antoinette, heretofore queen of France, at the Conciergerie in Paris — Citizeness, you will place these words on your door: Unity indivisibility of the Republic liberty equality fraternity or death.

"Signed DANTON"

(C. Becker, "A Letter from Danton to Marie Antoinette," *AHR*, XXVII [1921–22], 24–46).

[47] Sybel, *Europe*, II, 353.

[48] To Archduke Ferdinand of Milan, Vivenot-Zeissberg, *Quellen*, III, 173.

[49] *Briefe Thugut*, I, 36. Dated Sept. 1, 1793. This letter of Thugut's apparently escaped Lenotre. *Vide* his *Dtr. Louis XVI*, pp. 254–255.

[50] Supra, Pt. I, chap. iii, § 4, with citation Ernouf, *Maret*, p. 152.

[51] The same phrase occurred in Maret's instructions, but Maret had managed to make his instructions vanish (*ibid.*, pp. 174–175).

[52] *Ibid.*, p. 175.

ated Commune, from overtaking them.[53] But whatever the cause of the Queen's trial and condemnation,[54] one thing is certain: This assimilation of an Austrian archduchess to a common criminal could only fortify the war party in Vienna.[55] It was worse than merely ordering her trial by a special court. It was adding insult to injury. The Great Committee had rendered it more certain than ever that peace with Austria would be long delayed.

Political murder was doubtless the creed of some of the members triumphant in the shake-up of July 10. Already, the month before, they had tried to put their ideas into practice, and had hired assassins to murder Frederick William.[56] The plot was discovered through the interception of correspondence at Mayence,[57] and Frederick William continued to grace the planet Earth — but his Majesty's regard for his "natural ally" cannot but have been a little chilled.

Not even dead royalty escaped the revolutionary wrath, for after the

[53] Ibid., p. 159. Ysabeau was a relative of Maret's, and it was Ysabeau himself who had betrayed the secret to the Commune (ibid., and n. 1).

[54] Barère, in his report to the Convention requesting the order for the Queen's removal to the Conciergerie, and trial, made no mention of the Sémonville-Maret mishap. Of course, it would not have been discreet to show the enemy how much importance was attached to his coup at Novato. Barère based his request on the discovery of certain English-language notes and a letter, betraying a connection between England and the French royalists, and suggesting an assortment of ways to harm the Republic. And, indeed, the Convention, in its decree (Article IV), referred to the "cowardly, perfidious, and atrocious conduct of the British government" as though that conduct it was which had motivated the decree — else there was no reason to include the reference to the plot in just this of several decrees. Barère told the Convention "it is necessary . . . to strike England, Austria, the Vendée, the Temple, and the Bourbons on the same day . . . It is necessary that Austria groan, that the very roots of royalty be extirpated . . . All the Tarquins must disappear." — Brochures pol., LXIII, no. 7, pp. 5, 7–10, 27, 34. Tarquin was, of course, the last king of ancient Rome.

[55] Sybel, Europe, II, 353.

[56] This was not the first time his Majesty's life had been in danger. In 1792, the Prussian monarch received several threatening letters,

and about April of that year, a warning arrived from Paris that murderers had left there for Prussia and Russia, to poison Frederick William and Catherine II. Frederick William refused to take precautions. Not that he was so brave; merely, that he was a fatalist. If his hour had not come, he said, all precautions would be superfluous (Morton Eden to Lord Grenville, May 1, 1792, Herrmann, Dipl. Corr., p. 217). On August 26, 1792, Jean Debry, a Girondist who later voted for the death of Louis XVI (Mathiez, Fr. Rev., p. 264), proposed the organization of a special legion of 1200 tyrannicides to assassinate monarchs at war with France, and their generals (Moniteur, XIII, 542). Mathiez, in AHRF, XI, 389, says they were to assassinate enemy generals, without mentioning enemy kings; Bonnal de Ganges, Repré., II, 38, n. 3 says they were to assassinate all kings. Both are of course wrong.

Fear of reprisals against French generals, and solicitude for the fair name of France caused the measure to be rejected. The same arguments defeated (October 8, 1792) a projected decree to place a price of 100,000 livres on the head of the Austrian general Duke Albert of Saxe-Teschen, later (March 17, 1794) Imperial Field Marshal. It is to be noted that Jean Debry thought the latter proposal "would only honor the French nation" (Moniteur, XIV, 152). Bonnal de Ganges (Repré., II, 34, n. 1) unbelievably mistakes the project of decree for a decree.

[57] Sybel, Europe, II, 352.

fall of Mayence and Valenciennes to the Allies, the Convention decreed the destruction of the royal tombs at Saint-Denis and elsewhere. The occasion was the discovery of the conspiracy mentioned above (in the notes).[57a] The object was indeed to vent spleen, and not to obtain lead for cannon balls by melting down the royal coffins, as is often asserted.[58] The date set for the desecration was August 10 — anniversary of the suspension of the King — in the hope of "inspiring" the populace with revolutionary zeal; but the disentombment actually commenced on the sixth, and extended far beyond the tenth.[59] The bodies of fifty-two kings and notables were seized with unholy hands and dumped coffinless into pits in the cemetery, while the lead of their coffins was melted down in a foundry established on the premises. Thus baldly stated, the act does not appear at its best — or worst, and the effect on Europe cannot be rightly gauged. Following are a few brief quotations from John Goldworth Alger's *Paris in 1789–94*:

> The body [of Cardinal Richelieu] was like a mummy. The skin was livid, the cheeks puffy, the lips thin, the hair white. A man cut off the head and carried it away. It passed through several hands, and one owner sawed it in two lengthwise. . .
>
> Three of Du Guesclin's teeth were pulled out and presented to ————.
> The deputation presented the hearts . . . of Louis XVI's parents [to ————].[60]

The attempted assassination of Frederick William, the order for the trial of Marie Antoinette, the fiendish desecration of the dead,[61] and two other

---

[57a] *Vide* n. 54, this chapter.

[58] The search for leaden coffins was a general measure, like the search for bells (J. Guillaume, "La destruction des tombeaux des rois," *Etudes rév.*, Ser. I [1908], no. 21). Said Barère, in his report to the Convention, recommending the destruction: "The royal pride and pomp could not be tempered on this theater of death; and the *porte-sceptres* which have caused so much misfortune for France and humanity seem yet, in the tomb, to plume themselves upon a vanished grandeur. The powerful hand of the Republic should unrelentingly efface these superb epitaphs." — *Brochures pol.*, LXIII, no. 7, p. 28. The destruction of the tombs was ordained by the same decree that sent Marie Antoinette to the Conciergerie and to trial.

[59] Guillaume, *Etudes rév.*, Ser. I, no. 21.

[60] Appendix A of Alger. Let us hope Alger has exaggerated. He is sometimes carried away by his material. Other accounts are in substantial agreement, however. Says Alison:

"The arms and the heads of Louis XII and Francis I were severed and heaped in a corner . . . The body of Henry IV was so entire that it was instantly recognized from . . . prints . . . The venerable remains were at first the object of general respect; but . . . a Jacobin . . . roused the people, [and] they tore the body to pieces . . . The skulls of monarchs and heroes were tossed about like footballs . . ." — A. Alison, *History of Europe from the Commencement of the French Revolution to the Restoration of the Bourbons in MDCCCXV* (7th ed., rev.; 14 vols. and atlas, London, 1849–1850), III, 175–177.

[61] Whereas we shudder, as did Europe, at such gory details, we must — in all justice — realize that these people, through "long communion," had learned to view the dissection of the human body with the equanimity of a veteran surgeon. Thus, when, the previous month, Marat was assassinated, the Jacobins, in all love, voted to cut out his heart and entomb it ceremoniously in a public place.

measures — the arrest of all foreigners in France, and the doubling of the
personnel of the Revolutionary Tribunal to expedite its work — revolted
the spirits of the German governments and people, and rendered peace impossible.[62]

The French, on their own side, did not think of peace but only of defending their native land. Robespierre made a valiant speech before the Jacobin
Club dubbing all traitors and suspected traitors "Englishmen," but laying to
Berlin as well as to London the machinations of the journalists "who conceal
the art of frightening the people 'neath the pretense of zealously guarding
their interests." [63] Robespierre suggested that the forty-eight sections of Paris
send deputies to the Jacobin Club to concert with that society upon means
of saving France. It was from this united group that the idea of the successful *levée en masse* (mentioned in the last section) issued.[64] The *levée* was
aimed at all "tyrants" at war with France.[65] There was no attempt to single
out Prussia for special consideration, either in Robespierre's speech, or in that
of Barère's proposing the law in the name of the Committee of Public Safety.

Robespierre does not seem to have shared with the majority of the revolutionists that preference for Prussia which occupied so large a share in their
calculations.[66] During the early days of the Great Committee — whether
Robespierre was yet nominally a member or not is unimportant — the Desportes negotiations were discontinued. On the first anniversary of Louis
XVI's death (January 21, 1794), portraits of Louis XVI and Frederick William were burned in the Convention, and the ashes stamped under foot.[67]
When Robespierre, toward the end of his virtual reign, decided to institute
negotiations with one of the German powers, it was Austria that he singled
out. And it will be recalled that Robespierre was the one who had most
vehemently protested against the declaration of war on Austria originally.
Not that he would have hesitated if circumstances had rendered it easier or
more desirable to come to terms with Prussia. Among his papers after his

---

This was done, and the memorial speech
contained the phrases: "O holy heart of
Jesus, O holy heart of Marat, you have equal
right to our adoration" (*Kölner Reichsoberpostamtszeitung*, Aug. 13, 1793, quoted in
Hansen, *Quellen*, II, 898). It is intent that
makes an act fiendish or not fiendish — but
of course Europe could not conceive that the
Paris populace should suddenly be composed
exclusively of "surgeons."

[62] Sybel, *Europe*, II, 351–352.

[63] Buchez and Roux, *Hist. parlem.*, XXVIII,
453–458.

[64] *Ibid.*, pp. 466–468.

[65] Text, *ibid.*, pp. 469–471.

[66] That does not mean the Robespierrist Committee favored Austria, but rather that both
Prussia and Austria were viewed indifferent-
ly. When a bust of William Tell was presented to the Jacobin Club (it had been ordered by the Society [Aulard, *Jacobins*, V,
662]), Collot d'Herbois, member of the CPS,
took pains to point out that Tell had been
no friend of the Habsburgs: "I contemplate
with pleasure," he said, "the features of this
old enemy of the House of Austria." — Session of the Jacobin Club of July 7, 1794,
ibid., VI, 207.

[67] Palmer, *Twelve*, p. 278.

death were found two notes. One bore the designation, "Alliance with the Little Powers." [68] The other, entitled "Cursory View of the Policy of the French People with Respect to Foreign Powers," contained the formula, "Levy war vigorously upon the Coalition, but favor secretly the means of detaching Prussia therefrom, and of crushing Austria." [69]

b. Robespierre's "Past"

To understand fully the German policy of Robespierre's Committee of Public Safety, one must first consider the political gyrations of Robespierre, the man. One must remember that he was at first an adherent of the war party when he arrived from Arras at the end of November 1792,[70] and became a pacifist only after Billaud-Varenne had pointed out the dangers to French political liberty inherent in foreign war.[71] One must recall how earnestly he strove to prevent a declaration of war, aided only by a handful of fellow Jacobins and a scattering of journalists. One must realize how unpopular it rendered him to have sponsored the losing side, and how foolish it made him appear when his drear prognostications were viewed against the background of Valmy and Jemappes. His frankness had almost cost him his political life, but he had learned his lesson: Candor is a virtue only in heaven. Down here below, it is the stuff whereof failures are too often made. The pacifist had become a diplomat. Or, as Aulard would have phrased it, the pacifist had become a "hypocrite." [72]

He did not wait for Valmy and Jemappes to change face — and voice. When once war had been declared, he put his shoulder to the wheel, and became an enthusiastic supporter of the war of conquests. Within himself, however, he still nursed the conviction that the greatest danger to France's new-won liberty was victory — more specifically, the victorious general. Himself a cipher in the military art, he ever felt the woeful inability of words to parry the thrust of a blade. Thus, there peer out, through his bellicosity, limiting remarks which would be incomprehensible did one not know the man behind the mask.

[68] Sorel, *Europe*, III, 529, n. 2.

[69] Hüffer-Luckwaldt, *Quellen*, Pt. II, Vol. I, xliii, n. 7. The papers found at Robespierre's home after his death have been published under the title *Papiers inédits trouvés chez Robespierre, Saint-Just* . . . (3 vols., Paris, 1828).

[70] *Vide supra*, chap. i, § 2d. A very bellicose fellow he was, too. On November 28, 1791, he told the Jacobins: "The National Assembly and the Executive Power ought to treat their foreign foes as a free people treats des-

pots. They ought to imitate the Roman who, when commissioned in the name of the Senate to present an ultimatum to an enemy of the Republic, insisted upon an immediate reply. They ought to draw round Leopold the circle that Pompilius drew round Mithridates." — Quoted in Thompson, *Robespierre*, I, 203.

[71] *Vide supra*, chap. i, § 2e.

[72] Says Aulard, "he erected hypocrisy into a system of government." — *Orateurs*, II, 366.

In his speech of April 20, 1792, before the Jacobin Club, Robespierre declared that, since war had been declared, he "also was of the opinion that the Brabant, the [Belgian] Netherlands, Liège, Flanders, etc. should be conquered." [73] In his weekly newspaper, the *Défenseur de la Constitution*, founded the following May 19, he recommended that, since the Belgians seemed favorably disposed toward France,[74] the Republic should precede the arrival of its troops in the Austrian Netherlands with proclamations explaining the French principles and guaranteeing to the Belgians the right to a constitution of their own choosing. He seems, like many Frenchmen of that time, to have had no doubt that Belgium was only awaiting an invitation to incorporate into France, and that such a conquest would be one only in name.[75]

Subsequent events had brought disillusionment, however, and in early 1793, in his *Lettres . . . à ses commettants*,[76] Robespierre bemoaned that the invasion of Belgium had procured for France new enemies instead of a powerful and faithful ally. He recommended that a serious effort be made to end the war, and that — until ended — it be limited in scope to the left bank of the Rhine.[77] But not a word did he breathe about the bounds of Gaul or natural frontiers.

According to Robespierre, the object of the war was not at all to win battles and capture cities. These were means alone. The object was the consolidation of political liberty — France's, primarily, but not exclusively. Universal liberty, no more, no less, was his new goal. "French, Belgians, Germans! unfortunate slaves of tyrants who have partitioned the human race, like lowly herds, among themselves: You shall be free! Have no doubt on that score. I swear it! I swear it! I swear it!" And he recommended that French flags be emblazoned with the inscription: "Peace, universal liberty, war only on despots." According to Robespierre's expressed view, no compromise was possible between the French and kings. Either liberty would triumph "or the last Frenchman [would] vanish from [the face of] the earth." [78]

[73] Aulard, *Jacobins*, III, 518.

[74] During the Belgian revolt against Joseph II in 1789–1790, the Vonckist group sought to establish a connection with the revolutionists in France (Rain, *Mir. à Bon.*, p. 5).

[75] Walter, *Robespierre*, pp. 549–550.

[76] A continuation of his *Défenseur de la Constitution*. The suspension of the King and the summoning of the Convention left no constitution to be defended, so, after no. 12 of the *Défenseur*, its name was changed to *Lettres de Maximilien Robespierre, membre de la Convention nationale, à ses commet-* *tants*. The *Lettres*, of which a second series began about January 11, 1793, appeared periodically until March 15, 1793 (from *Défenseur de la Constitution*, no. 12, contained in C. Vellay, *Discours et rapports de Robespierre* [Paris, 1908], p. 186, n. 1).

[77] C. April 30, 1793. Quoted in D. Guérin, *La lutte de classes sous la première république: Bourgeois et bras nus (1793–1797)* (2 vols. in 1, Paris, 1946), I, 393.

[78] Walter, *Robespierre*, pp. 548–550, for the two preceding paragraphs.

In the second series of his *Lettres . . . à ses commettants*, Robespierre outlined a plan for the proper use of propaganda to secure the downfall of kings. First one had to convince foreign peoples of the perfidy of their rulers, simultaneously imparting to those peoples an exalted concept of the principles of the Revolution. Writings which emphasized love of country and of humanity should be circulated in enemy territory. These writings should be tailored to the customs, beliefs, prejudices, and economic status of the people it was desired to influence. "It is a bad way of attracting the attention of any nation . . . to the cause of liberty to start with placing its pecuniary interest in direct opposition to its political and philosophical ideas." Also, force should not be used; only reason. Force fortifies prejudices; reason dissolves them. France should limit herself to offering conquered peoples the right to give themselves the constitution they themselves want. In this way, one did not violate their prejudices, or derogate from their *amour-propre*, and they would, in gratitude, league with France against the common enemy.

Robespierre foresaw two possible results of this spiritual accord. Either the inhabitants would request union with France, or they would form separate, allied republics. But — and here cropped out again Robespierre's fear of the military: "Let us forbid our generals and our armies to interfere in their political affairs; it is the only means of preventing intrigues which can terminate our glorious revolution. . ."[79]

These were the views expressed by Robespierre between the start of the war and his election to the Great Committee. It will readily be seen that there is at least one contradiction here. If France limited her military enterprises to the left bank of the Rhine, who would revolutionize Germany? — yet he swore it would be revolutionized — swore it three times, in fact. Of course, must one require such unrelenting consistency of a war-to-the-death pacifist?

But seriously, whose program is the above? Is it Robespierre's, or is it essentially that of the Brissotins, with their war against all the kings in the world, and their dependent republics? Apparently Robespierre had decided to drift with the current until he should be strong enough to master it.

c. Soulavie Gives Robespierre a Correspondence Course in Diplomacy

When Robespierre joined the Committee on July 27, 1793, the ex-abbot Soulavie had been French minister resident at Geneva and in the Valais for less than two months (since June 10, 1793). Theoretically minister to Copenhagen for a few months prior thereto,[80] Soulavie (according to his own word) had accepted the Swiss post because Lebrun, who had appointed him,

---

[79] Quoted *ibid.*, pp. 551–552.
[80] He had never actually occupied the post (*La Grande Encyclopédie: Inventaire raisonné des sciences, des lettres et des arts par une Société de Savants et de Gens de Lettres* [31 vols., Paris, 1886–1902], *s.v.* "Soulavie," written by A. Mazon, author of the *Histoire de Soulavie*, 2 vols., Paris, 1893).

promised that he could work in Switzerland for peace. And Soulavie, despite his questionable past — reputedly, pander (*maquereau*) to the Duke de Richelieu,[81] aspired to play a grand diplomatic role.[82]

Soulavie, like Lebrun and Danton, believed compromise was the proper course for France to pursue. To Soulavie's mind, any terms which were honorable and which respected the indivisibility of the Republic were not too bad. In a letter of July 5 to Lebrun's successor, Deforgues, the ex-abbot offered his services as negotiator. Five days later Danton's Committee was no more. The new directors of French policy did not countenance compromise, as had Danton. Soulavie was ordered to mind his own affairs (July 18). But after July 27, when Robespierre joined the Committee, Soulavie found he had a willing audience for his diplomatic reveries, and the ensuing months witnessed what might be called a correspondence course in diplomacy with Robespierre as the student and the ambitious diplomat in Geneva as the tutor.[83]

Let us look in on one of these lessons. Said Soulavie: "We must nationalize the Revolution, consider nothing but France — and return to the traditional policy of the nation. — Our natural enemy is England; our allies, the little powers, — republican for the most part. — [We must] stifle the spirit of propagandism. — [We must] expel without exception all foreigners. — . . . We must arm, not to expand to the Rhine — that would mean war eternal — but in order to dictate peace — a peace without conquests. — . . . Peace is easy to harvest. The King of Prussia is already extending us the olive branch. . . The Coalition is about to dissolve. Let us humor Prussia!" [84]

Soulavie's suggestion regarding foreigners requires certain general remarks. France had always been very open-minded with respect to foreigners.[85] Paris was the "hotel of the world" before 1789, and the French army always had a "notable proportion" of aliens. There were entire regiments of Germans, and, besides Luckner, the following staff officers: Prince Emmanuel of Salm-Salm, Prince Charles of Hesse, and the Saxon Baron von Saiffert.[86]

Luckner, according to one account, was so completely German that when, in the early days of the Revolution, he was ordered to make a patriotic speech to his troops, he found "vivre libre ou mourir" beyond his capacity and could manage only, "Camarades, fifre ou mourir." The commander's aide-de-camp, to tease him, queried: "Marshal, can't you pronounce the word 'libre'?"

[81] Report of Dugas, Dec. 26, Caron, *Paris*, II, 7.
[82] Guérin, *Lutte*, I, 398–399.
[83] *Ibid.*; A. Mathiez, "Une citation apocryphe de Robespierre," *AHRF*, II (1925), 486.
[84] G. Avenel, *Anacharsis Cloots* (2 vols., Paris, 1865), II, 219–220. *Vide* also Buchez and

Roux, *Hist. parlem.*, XXXV, 387.
[85] *Vide* Mathorez in *REH*, 1923, pp. 71 *et seqq.* General Luckner, a Saxon, has been mentioned above (chap. i, § 4a and n. 204).
[86] Mathiez, *Etrangers*, pp. 5, 11.

Luckner, more eager in repartee than in joining battle, shot back: *"Fifre ou mourir* tells the whole story. A Frenchman cannot 'fifre' without being *libre."* [87]

With Germans in their very army, it was natural that the French should have viewed the Germans in their midst without hostility. In fact, the France of 1789 had attained that idyllic state where people were not French or German, but human beings.[88]

The early Revolution not only continued but accentuated this liberal attitude. In August 1792, many foreign notables — among them Priestley, Paine, Bentham, Wilberforce, David Williams, Washington, Hamilton, Madison, Schiller, Pestalozzi, Kosciusko, and Cloots — were granted French citizenship in order that they might be elected deputies. Said Marie Joseph Chénier,[89] in proposing the law: "If the choice of the people were to bring these illustrious men into the National Convention, what an imposing and solemn spectacle would be offered by this assembly, which is about to determine such great destinies! The elite of mankind, brought together from every quarter of the globe — would it not seem to be a congress of the whole world? Priestley, Cloots, and Thomas Paine were elected to the Convention. Priestley declined, but Cloots and Paine accepted.[90]

It was not only to famous foreigners that the French accorded fraternity. Enemy aliens in France were not interned so long as they made a show of loving "liberty." Enemy soldiers were offered employ in the French armies,

[87] Avenel, *Cloots*, I, 350. While this anecdote may be true, Luckner had, notwithstanding, sufficient command of the French language to convey his ideas. Brissot quotes in his memoirs a letter received from one of Luckner's soldiers, as follows: "Yesterday, Luckner went through the camp; he harangued separately all the battalions . . . : 'Let us be united,' he said to us, 'and no traitors whatsoever. I will not betray; if you see that I perform badly, cut me into a million pieces. I am not calling you my soldiers, my regiments, but my brothers, my comrades. Union! I want to live and die with you.' " — C. M. Perroud (ed.), *J. P. Brissot, Mémoires (1754–1793),* (2 vols., Paris, 1911), II, 151, in *Mémoires et Documents relatifs aux XVIIIe et XIXe Siècles* series.

[88] Mathiez, *Etrangers*, p. 12.

[89] His name does not appear in the *Moniteur*, XIII, 525.

[90] Mathiez, *Fr. Rev.*, pp. 216–217. George Monro, British diplomat who stayed on in Paris a short time after Gower's return to England, reported to Lord Grenville (September 20–22, 1792) that Paine was taking part in the debates of the Convention through an interpreter, M. Gonpillian — for Paine "speaks little or no French." — *Despatches Gower*, p. 253. A few days before (September 14–17), Monro had reported: "I have heard nothing of Dr. Priestley; he has perhaps more sense than to come among such fools." — *Ibid.*, p. 250. Cloots made a propitious start. He tried to end the interparty strife with his pamphlet, *Ni Marat ni Roland* (Gottschalk, *Marat*, pp. 139–140). Roland answered in *La Chronique*, calling Cloots a "discontented parasite." ("Parasite" because Cloots was often a dinner guest.) When Cloots presented his rejoinder, "A mon tour la parole. Réponse d'Anacharsis Cloots aux diatribes Rolando-Brissotines," to the *Chronique*, its editor returned the script with the note, "Take your poisons elsewhere." So Cloots had his reply published by the Jacobin Club (*Brochures pol.*, LXXXVII, no. 20).

plus a bounty for their desertion.[91] Exiles from Germany and other states were formed into French foreign legions.[92] France's revolution, in the early days, was the property of the human race. Indeed, it continued to be so for some time. As late as January 1795, Merlin of Douai asserted that "there are still among us people more attached to the *human race* than to their native land." [93] It was Soulavie's desire to stop this unnatural uphill flow of French generosity, to divert it into the more familiar, more human channel of national selfishness.

Soulavie's policy could be summed up thus: no more foreigners, no more internationalism, no more propagandism, no more conquests; Austria to be relieved of her role as chief target of French animosity in favor of England; the little powers to replace Prussia as France's natural ally, while Prussia would be immobilized by kindness.

d. Interimistic Measures

Robespierre did not swallow this policy at a single gulp. In fact, during the early days of the Great Committee, he did not possess a foreign policy at all. Pitiful were the pleas of French agents abroad for instructions. None were given them, for there were none to give.[94] Deforgues directed Grouvelle, French envoy at Copenhagen, in response to the latter's prayer for instructions, to refer to his (the Minister's) preceding letters as a guide "until a general plan has been definitively adopted." [95] This is no criticism of Robespierre. The Great Committee of Public Safety had no time for such things. France was in the position of "a besieged fortress." [96] In this period, one might loosely say the policy of Robespierre's Committee was that of the beast at bay. The beast bares its fangs, and selects its most frightening posture in the hope of scaring away its tormenters. Thus did the Great Committee comport itself with respect to the Allies.

The Decree of September 15, 1793, was proposed by Committee-member Jeanbon Saint-André. Said he to the Convention: ". . . [You see] how barbarous is the war your enemies are waging against you. The audacity of these cannibals is encouraged still more by the philanthropic spirit which animates you. I believe that we should, for a time, renounce our philosophical ideas and use reprisals against these anthropophagites [eaters of human flesh]. I ask you to enjoin upon our generals to follow rigorously the laws of war in the conquered territory." [97]

[91] *Moniteur*, XII, 192–193.
[92] Mathiez in *AHRF*, XI, 391–392.
[93] To Merlin-Th., Aulard, *Actes*, XIX, 260. The italicized phrase was underlined by Merlin-D.
[94] A. Sorel, "La diplomatie secrète du Comité de Salut Public avant le 9 thermidor," *RH*, X (1879), 341, 345.
[95] *Idem, Europe*, III, 528.
[96] Deforgues' expression.
[97] *Moniteur*, XVII, 673.

The Convention dutifully decreed that the generals of the Republic should renounce thenceforth the "philanthropic idea . . . of trying to make foreign nations appreciate the price and advantages of liberty." They were to conduct themselves with respect to members of the Coalition as the Coalition behaved toward France. They were to "exercise the ordinary rights of war toward countries and individuals conquered by French arms." [98] If one looks closely, he will see here a perhaps unconscious renunciation of expansionism, for one of the principal reasons for the French propaganda was to create requests for annexation to France.

The Committee's Decree of September 18 specified, in detail, the measures required of the generals under the Convention's September 15th decree: hostages to be taken; *all* inhabitants to be disarmed; contributions to be levied in coin and kind, principally on the wealthy; the army to be provisioned at the conquered territory's expense; suppplies not immediately needed by the army, whether of foodstuffs, livestock, cloth, fuel, or metals, to be appropriated and stored; church silver and public funds to be seized; "the generals [to] make sure that they . . . destroy the fortresses, fill up the wells, wreck the bridges, canals, and locks, and tear up the road pavements, . . . [and] that contributions be levied regularly, according to the rights of war." [99] Note that all inhabitants were to be disarmed, even those friendly to the French. The purpose of favoring amicably inclined natives in the past had been to foster annexationist or separatist movements, hence here we have, in effect, a further indication of the intention to repudiate expansionism.

But these were really only military dispositions. It was not until the victories of September began to brighten the picture that the lack of an over-all policy was felt. On September 24, the Committee, on the motion of Barère, took a first step toward establishing the bases of its diplomacy. As long as the war should last, it decreed, France would maintain abroad no ministers plenipotentiary or ambassadors, but only (secret) agents, chargés d'affaires, and secretaries of legation — all with unwritten [100] instructions. Only the two democracies, the United States and Switzerland,[101] would be vouchsafed embassies. "The Committee of Public Safety and the Provisional Executive Council will treat with none of the foreign agents and ministers who do not have a positive status with respect to the French Republic." [102] In other words, unless the Republic had been recognized, and a minister had been accredited directly to the Republic, the Committee would ignore him.

[98] Hansen, *Quellen*, II, 904.
[99] Sept. 18, 1793, Aulard, *Actes*, VI, 553–554.
[100] To prevent the seizure of their papers, as in the Sémonville case.
[101] Query, regarding the democracy of some of the Swiss cantons.
[102] Aulard, *Actes*, VII, 28–29.

This, of course, had the effect of bringing to a halt all the semiofficial soundings with which Danton and his followers were still regaling themselves
(*vide infra*).

On their face, the bases of September 24, by cutting off all possible channels of communication with the enemy, seem to mark a determination on
the part of the Committee to negotiate only after complete victory.[103] It is
to be noted, however, that by maintaining embassies in Switzerland and
America, the road was left open for neutral mediation by one of the countries most likely to witness the origin of peace feelers — Switzerland.[104] And
Robespierre was well aware that this road had been left open, for Soulavie
never let him forget it. Officially, however, the roads were blocked and
detour signs posted, so it was quite proper for Deforgues to write to Barthélemy, French Ambassador to the Swiss Cantons,[105] on October 18: "The
French Republic does not wish to make up with its enemies. Powerful, of
itself, it intends to reduce them to supplicating for peace, or to crush them. . .
In this situation, there is no question of entering into negotiations." [106]

Until Robespierre's speech of November 17, the German policy of France
must be gleaned largely from the correspondence and acts of Deforgues,
Barthélemy, Bacher (First Secretary-Interpreter of the French embassy at
Basel),[107] Rivalz, and various agents of the central government — though

---

[103] Mathiez, *Dtn paix*, p. 192.

[104] Guérin, *Lutte*, I, 396.

[105] Nephew of the *abbé* Barthélemy, author of
Le voyage du jeune Anacharsis en Grèce, 4
vols., 1788. The uncle's friendship with the
Duke de Choiseul procured young François
a post as secretary of embassy at Stockholm
when he was only twenty-one. The young
man served subsequently in Vienna and
London, where he worked himself up to
the position of minister plenipotentiary. He
was appointed royal ambassador to the
Swiss Cantons on November 19, 1791, and
the suspension of Louis XVI the following
August 10 should have ended his functions.
He did indeed try to resign, but Lebrun
urged him to remain, and on December 25,
1792, he was formally accredited as Ambassador of the French Republic to the Swiss
Cantons. Trained in the school of Vergennes, Barthélemy practiced his diplomacy
upon his own government as well as upon
the foreigner, toning down the frothy
schemes hatched by the Paris revolutionists,
so that it has truly been said of him that he
was the virtual foreign minister of the Convention (G. Monod and C. Bémont, "Bulletin historique," *RH*, XXXIV, 85–86; A.
Mathiez' review of J. de Dampierre [ed.],
Mémoires de Barthélemy, Paris, 1914, in
AR, VII, 429). Oddly, Sybel's (or rather
Perry's) indexer (*Fr. Rev.*, IV, Index, *s.v.*
"Barthélemy") confuses Adjutant General
Etienne A. Berthelmy or Berthellemy with
Barthélemy (*vide* Six, *Dic. biog.*, *s.v.* "Ber-
thellemy").

Guérin (*Lutte*, I, 396) ascribes noble
birth to Barthélemy, and makes him the
nephew of the Duke de Choiseul. Barthélemy became a marquis only by creation of
Louis XVIII after the Hundred Days (Dr.
J. C. F. Hoefer [ed.], *Nouvelle biographie
générale* [46 vols., Paris, 1852–1864], *s.v.*
"Barthélemy [François, marquis de]").

[106] Quoted by Sorel in *RH*, X, 342.

[107] "Bacher . . . aspires to wealth and honor.
He is adroit and more treacherous than
astute (*geschickt und mehr tückisch als
schlau*) . . . He is jealous of Barthélemy,
timorous, and attached to the ruling party
only because it is the ruling party. That
signalizes his personal character." — Degelmann to Thugut, Sept. 8, 1795, Vivenot-
Zeissberg, *Quellen*, V (*Quellen zur Ge-*

some of the policies these men promoted were later repudiated by Robespierre. Deforgues' letter of October 18 disavowed his intention to negotiate with "any" of the powers leagued against France, but suggested that the dissolution of the Coalition might be accelerated by sowing the seeds of discord and mutual distrust. The instruments of this policy should be — not Frenchmen, for they would have no access to enemy territory! but — foreigners devoted to France.[108] In view of Robespierre's later attitude toward Francophile foreigners, this suggestion is especially interesting.

The idea of employing alien agents was hardly new. On September 13, 1790, Klemens Wenzeslaus of Trèves listed ten French secret agents working in Germany during the previous two weeks, and among them we note a Swedish and a Swiss captain, another Swiss — an exile who was "most dangerous," a German "gentleman," and two surgeons who — judging by their names — were either Germans or of German ancestry. If only one of these surgeons was a German, 50 per cent of these agents were aliens. In passing, let it be noted that one of the nonalien agents was Sémonville.[109]

On November 11, in a letter from Hüningen, Committee-member Hérault de Séchelles (who had been on mission to eastern France) embraced the alien-agent idea. Hérault had seen Barthélemy, and learned that the latter had already amasssed a wealth of information on the subject, and even formulated certain plans.[110] Hérault thought, of course, that he had to preface his advocacy of the idea with the usual revolutionary menaces, so his recommendation to the Committee reads thus: "God forbid that we should even think of commencing any negotiation with the stupid and ferocious despots who merit to receive from us only death . . . , but at least we may desire to be better informed than, up to now, we have been." And he requested permission to authorize Barthélemy to organize for Germany an alien-staffed spy system.[111] The Committee gave its blessing.[112]

Regarding Deforgues' suggestion that an attempt be made to accelerate the collapse of the Coalition, Barthélemy — though certain that the "impious" league would not long endure, "it being much too vast" — scored the practicability of promoting such dissolution by the use of foreign agents of alien origin. If, the Ambassador argued, one would establish contact with ministers and other notables at court, a rare combination of virtues and

---

schichte der Politik Oesterreichs während der französischen Revolution, 1890), 354.

[108] Text quoted by Sorel in RH, X, 342.

[109] To Mayor Reuland of Trèves, Sept. 13, 1790, Hansen, Quellen, I, 680, n. 1.

[110] Sorel, Europe, III, 532.

[111] Report of Hérault de Séchelles, Nov. 11, 1793, Papiers de Barthélemy, III, 215. Mal-

let du Pan suggests that Hérault's exaggerative tendencies were due to a knowledge that, as a member of the old nobility, as the scion of a wealthy family, he would inevitably be suspected of insincerity in his attachment to the Revolution (Mém. corr., II, 40).

[112] Sorel, Europe, III, 532.

abilities was necessary.[113] Barthélemy did indeed know of one foreigner[114] who was eminently qualified: Dorsch — him of the handsome feet. But Dorsch's treason toward Germany, while it would have been a guarantee of his reliability, would also have been a potential threat to the ex-Clubist's life in any mission on German soil.[115]

Though at first doubtful of the practicability of Deforgues' suggestion, Barthélemy discussed with Rivalz the question of accelerating the collapse of the Coalition by means of alien agents, and came to the conclusion that an attempt could well be made to coax the King of Prussia out of the European concert. "Nothing should be easier," he declared, "for the lassitude of this despot is extreme, as is his need to deliver himself peacefully over to his corrupt inclinations. . .[116] All the strength of this power is exhausted." Rivalz suggested breaking the "impious chain of kings leagued against us" by purchasing the Prussian link with cash. "I admit [the benefits] of such an expenditure," wrote Barthélemy to Deforgues, but the same result would follow without it — only "a little later." [117]

Barthélemy, Rivalz, and Bacher assumed the task of finding alien agents. Bacher, really, organized this secret service, Barthélemy retaining responsibility. The agents were given the following duties: to observe what was going on in Germany, both politically and militarily, to make abstracts of the items in German newspapers, and to watch for counterfeiters of the assignat. For the time being, the service was one merely of observation.[118]

e. Robespierre Takes the Reins

As the victories along the frontier continued to brighten the political horizon, Robespierre felt himself called upon (November 17, 1793) to explain his foreign policy; and then appeared frankly for the first time the influence of Soulavie's tutoring. In a report to the Convention made in the name of the Committee of Public Safety, Robespierre betrayed his adherence to Soulavie's expulsion-of-all-foreigners idea; he presented a picture of France as the

[113] To Deforgues, Oct. 28, 1793, *Papiers de Barthélemy*, III, 174–175.

[114] A letter of November 18, 1793, from Deforgues to Barthélemy, tells that Dorsch had become a French citizen (*ibid.*, p. 229).

[115] Barthélemy to Deforgues, Nov. 27, 1793, *ibid.*, p. 253.

[116] A rather harsh designation for poor "Mickie," as she was known. "Her principal merit is youth and a warm constitution," wrote Lord Malmesbury. But there were two other candidates — "for a more substantial degree of favor" than Mary ("Mickie") Doz possessed: Fräulein Bethman, "all sentiment and passion"; and Fräulein Vienk, the unwilling tool of power-hungry politicians (to Lord Grenville, Jan. 9, 1794, *Diar. Corr. Malmesbury*, III, 44). And let us not forget Wilhelmina Rietz, the "longest lasting" of them all (J. F. and L. G. Michaud [eds.], *Biographie universelle ancienne et moderne* [2nd ed.; 45 vols., Paris, 1854], *s.v.* "Lichtenau [Wilhelmina Enke-Rietz]").

[117] Barthélemy to Deforgues, Nov. 6, 1793, *Papiers de Barthélemy*, III, 197–198.

[118] Sorel in *RH*, X, 344.

guarantor of the minor states and free cities of Germany against the encroachments of Austria and Prussia; and he argued that since events had proved
the Republic to be unconquerable — "invincible as reason; immortal as
truth" — common sense dictated the end of attempts to conquer it. "Tyrants,
if you squander your treasure and muster your satellites, you hasten your
own ruin!" Soulavie had said that peace was easy to harvest, and this plea
to the tyrants was most certainly a Jacobin peace feeler. Its only shortcoming
was that it was almost unrecognizable as an overture by anyone accustomed
to the old diplomacy. But what could easily be distinguished as a definite
contribution to peace was the repetition of Soulavie's repudiation of all desire
to convert the world to revolutionary principles by force of arms — Mussel-
man fashion. "It is for the power of reason," Robespierre declared, ". . . to
propagate the principles of our glorious Revolution."[119]

This same repudiation appeared again in Robespierre's speech of December 5. "The French are not afflicted with a mania for rendering any
nation happy and free despite itself. All kings could have vegetated or died
on their bloody thrones had they known to respect the independence of the
French people."[120] It appears to the writer that Robespierre's renunciation
of propagandism on December 5, fitting in as it does with his renunciation
of November 17 and with the Decrees of September 15 and 18, is of great
importance; yet Sorel, in dealing with this speech of December 5, neglects
entirely to mention the renunciation of propagandism, limiting himself to
quoting Robespierre's more colorful remarks: "Kings are the masterpiece of
human corruption. . . The death sentence of tyrants sleeps forgotten in the
faint hearts of timid mortals. We have put it into execution."[121] To quote the
latter passage and omit the other makes it appear as though Robespierre, in
the eighteen days between November 17 and December 5, renounced his
renunciation of propagandism, and it does indeed appear that Sorel believes
this to be the case.[122] To make order out of what, in consequence, appears
chaos, Sorel explains that it was not Robespierre's policy which changed —
that was all along of the world-revolutionizing, king-devouring type. It was
only the tenor of his remarks that changed, and remarks are not important
anyway. It is acts that count. These, we are to believe on Sorel's own authority — for he gives no reference — point indubitably to a resolve to revolutionize, to proselytize, to conquer.[123]

It will appear below how wrong this concept is.[124] Certainly it was not
the view taken by contemporaries. "According to almost all citizens," re-

[119] Buchez and Roux, *Hist. parlem.*, XXX, 224
et seqq. The Decrees of September 15 and
18 had of course foreshadowed this repudiation.
[120] *Ibid.*, p. 317.
[121] *Europe*, III, 531.
[122] *Ibid.*
[123] *Ibid.*, p. 530.
[124] This chapter, § 2k.

ported the secret agent Charmont on January 2, 1794, "we have only to show ourselves to the enemy to be assured of winning. Assuming this to be a correct hypothesis, almost all citizens say we must overturn the crowns which had the audacity to want to enslave us, that consequently we ought to put down our arms only when we have conquered all the territories governed by these despots. But several citizens, partaking Robespierre's opinion, assert that this mode of thinking alone will be our undoing, that it were better to contain ourselves within just bounds, and be able to maintain ourselves there, than to risk . . . the . . . fate . . . [of] last year." [125]

This is not an isolated example. On December 29, 1793, the same agent reported the opinion that moderatism was raising its head in the Convention. "Robespierre himself no longer has the same energy. He has seen his best days." [126] On January 2, 1794, Charmont wrote in, "Robespierre has for some time been accused of being too moderate." [127] On January 19, a citizen in a café was heard to say, "The elder Robespierre is recognized by a large part of the Club of the Cordeliers as the chief of moderatism." [128] The same day, agent Rolin reported, "It is said that the Society of the Cordeliers has passed a by-law in which it declares that it regards Citizen Robespierre as the chief of the moderate party." [129] A few days later, Charmont contributed: "'People say . . . that Robespierre, who has so bold an air in broad daylight, dares no longer to sleep at night, so much he fears to be assassinated.[130] One still reproaches him with being a member of a quite moderate party. . .'" [131]

But we must not allow these examples to carry us progressively further into 1794, for we must still at least make a start toward "expelling all foreigners" — and we shall have to do that in 1793.

f. Fabre d'Eglantine and Anacharsis Cloots

The oft-mentioned Anacharsis Cloots was a native of Clèves, a Hohenzollern possession; but his family tree had its roots in Holland, with four and a half centuries of noble sap in its wide-spreading branches. The Clootses were not only of baronial rank, but millionaires, Great-great-uncle Jean-Baptiste having made the family fortune in Dutch commerce. Anacharsis had been

---

[125] To min. of int., Jan. 2, 1794, Caron, *Paris*, II, 130.

[126] *Ibid.*, p. 68.

[127] *Ibid.*, p. 133.

[128] Charmont to min. of int., *ibid.*, III, 38.

[129] *Ibid.*, p. 48.

[130] Various real or fancied attempts against Robespierre's life dotted his year on the Committee. The two most celebrated attempts(?) — concerning Cécile Renault and Henri Admirat (not Admiral; *vide* R. Schnerb, "A propos d'Admirat et du Baron de Batz," *AHRF*, XXIV [1952], 472 *et seqq.*) — belong to a later period (May 23–24, 1794); but when Cécile and Admirat were executed on June 17, 1794, the heads of fifty-two other "parricides" joined theirs in the basket (Thompson, *Robespierre*, II, 187–188; 208).

[131] Caron, *Paris*, III, 105.

baptized Jean-Baptiste.[132] Whence the "Anacharsis" is a story in itself.[133]

Young Jean-Baptiste was educated in a Brussels grammar school, a Mons Jesuit school, and the Collège du Plessis and the Sorbonne of Paris. He received his military training in Berlin. In each of these schools, French was spoken. In the Berlin military academy the boys were penalized each time they broke into German. As a result, Cloots early developed a great fondness for the French tongue, and never knew German well. Add to this that Clèves had belonged to Prussia for less than two centuries and it will be realized that this young man really had no deep national ties.[134] Moreover, he was endowed with an independent and roving spirit which could not brook the restraints of German military life. Especially cogent for him was the argument supplied by the epidemic of suicides in Frederick II's army. Those fine, straight figures were literally bored to death. Is that what would become of *him*? He decided to flee to the land of philosophy — France.[135]

It was not easy to escape from Prussia, even with an income of a hundred thousand livres. But the young man's father was Frederick the Great's privy councillor, and his uncle was the King's philosopher-friend. Through his uncle — who knew his plans — Jean-Baptiste received permission from the King to clear some of his lands. Repairing to Clèves ostensibly for this purpose, he slipped across the frontier into France. This was in 1776.[136]

The period of Cloots's life between 1776 and 1785 does not concern us. In 1786 he published a treatise recommending that France extend her frontiers to the Rhine, *Vœux d'un gallophile* ("Prayers of a Francophile").[137] Probably, after a decade of exile, Cloots was thinking fondly of his picture-book home — a region called "my paradise" and "my park" by Frederick

---

[132] Avenel, *Cloots*, I, 1–3.

[133] Educated by ecclesiastics, Cloots had grown up antireligious. In the Jacobin Club in 1790, he was so violent in his irreligion that he was asked why he did not debaptize himself. Cloots thought he would if he could find a suitable name. It had to be one which would, in a sense, tell his own history; how he had come from his native land to help fan the fire of liberty burning on a foreign hearth. He found his parallel in the Scythian philosopher Anacharsis, who had come to Athens and assisted in the founding of the Athenian republic. The voyage of Anacharsis was just then on everyone's lips because of the philosophical romance of the *abbé* J. J. Barthélemy, uncle of the French ambassador to the Swiss Cantons. Thus did the world acquire "Ana-

charsis" Cloots (*ibid.*, pp. 208–210).

[134] Mathiez, *Etrangers*, pp. 48–49. The Treaty of Xanten, 1614, ceded the reversion of Clèves to Johann Sigmund, Elector of Brandenberg, whose wife, Anna, was co-heiress of great sweeps of territory along the lower Rhine. (But the Elector had to become a Calvinist to gain the support of the Calvinist princes of West Germany for his acquisitions.) (*The Encyclopaedia Britannica: A New Survey of Universal Knowledge* [24 vols., Chicago, 1952], *s.v.* "Prussia.")

[135] Avenel, *Cloots*, I, 6–18.

[136] *Ibid.*, pp. 28–29. Mathiez says that when his father died, Jean-Baptiste fled to Paris — in 1775 (*Etrangers*, p. 49).

[137] *Supra*, Introduction, n. 75.

the Great.[138] The expatriate's only hope of return lay in a change of sovereignty, and this he never ceased urging to his dying day.[139]

Cloots arrived in Paris after the fall of the Bastille,[140] and cast himself wholeheartedly into the revolutionary movement.[141] He constituted himself Ambassador of Oppressed Sovereigns the world over — the sovereigns being, of course, the people. He advised his "constituents" to "call upon liberty. . . You have a point of support — France. . . The tocsin will sound, the tyrants will pale, and Mankind will be free."[142] He styled himself the Orator of the Human Race,[143] wrote a book on *The Universal Republic*,[144] and presented his work to the Legislative Assembly following a speech replete with phrases such as: "The fate of the human race is in the hands of France. . . God made order out of primeval chaos; the French will make order out of feudal chaos. God is powerful and He has willed it; we are powerful and we will it. . . The citizens of France and the citizens of the world are disposed to make the greatest sacrifices for the success of a cause which vitally concerns all men. Indeed, we shall know how to limit ourselves . . . to the black

[138] Avenel, *Cloots*, I, 2.

[139] A typical pronouncement by Cloots on this subject follows: "Let us precipitate ourselves en masse toward the banks of the great stream [the Rhine] . . . The Romans lost Gaul by leaving the barbarians a toe hold on this side of the Rhine. It would be as impolitic as unconstitutional not to profit by the lessons of history." — Aug. 19, 1793, *Brochures pol.*, LXXXVII, no. 19, p. 8.

[140] On a European tour, July 14 found him in Spain (Mathiez, *Etrangers*, p. 51).

[141] But he did not sign the petition at the Champ de Mars, for he did not believe France was ready for a republic. He argued that as long as the nation was willing to submit to the "sorcery of the mass," it could not be cured of "the dupery of the royal phantom." As will appear presently, this man who thought France was not ripe for a republic, yet desired to republicanize the entire world (*ibid.*, pp. 56–57).

[142] Avenel, *Cloots*, I, 204, 206.

[143] On June 19, 1790, he conducted to the Assembly an "Embassy of the Human Race" purporting to consist of foreigners of every nationality. There were Englishmen, Prussians, Spaniards, Italians, Brabançons, Indians, Arabs, and Chaldeans. The aristocratic press characterized them as streetporters bedecked in strange costumes. Not so, says Mathiez; they were wealthy and sedate individuals, like the Count von Boetzlær, Baron van der Pol, and Abbéma, the banker (*Etrangers*, p. 52). As spokesman for this embassy, Cloots assumed the title — permanently — of Orator of the Human Race (biog. sketch of Cloots in Tuetey, *Rép. gén. sources Paris*, XI, 1).

[144] Willing to recognize only the individual, he proclaimed the "State of United Individuals," wherein states and nations had no existence (B. S. Mirkine-Guetzévitch, "La Révolution française et les projets d'union européenne," *RF*, LXXXIV [1931], 326, n. 1). On April 24 or 26, 1793, he made a speech before the Convention on the "Constitutional Bases of the Republic of the Human Race." He wanted the Convention to decree that its members represented not only France but the entire human family (Aulard in *RF*, XVIII, 133). Ducos interrupted the speech to demand the annexation of the Moon to the Earth (*Le Vieux Cordelier* [crit. ed. by A. Mathiez; Paris, 1936], p. 61, n. 6). In the *Moniteur*, where the session of Friday, April 26, is reproduced, Cloots's speech is mentioned as though made on that day (XVI, 232), yet when it is reproduced on April 30, it is dated Wednesday, April 24 (*ibid.*, p. 251). This explains the different dates given by Aulard and Mathiez in *RF*, XVIII, 133, and *Le Vieux Cordelier*, p. 61, n. 6, respectively.

sauce of the Spartans in order that we may sustain a war which will be followed by perpetual peace." And the erstwhile Baron du Val-de-Grâce [145] — he had sent his armorial bearings back to Prussia [146] — presented the Legislative Assembly with twelve thousand livres to equip and pay soldiers to fight in the war of men against tyrants.[147]

Now, France was in the midst of a financial scandal in the autumn of 1793. Certain deputies, to gain popularity, had challenged the tax-evading schemes of the *Compagnie des Indes* (India Company), and seals had been placed on the Company's offices and papers. A decree of October 8 regulating the disposal of assets permitted the Company to effect its own liquidation under the Taxation Minister's sole supervision. Fabre d'Eglantine, author of an excellent comedy [148] and apologist of the September massacres, ex-secretary to Minister of Justice Danton and dishonest army contractor,[149] succeeded in having carried an amendment to this decree, requiring liquidation of the assets by the government. Three weeks later there appeared in the *Bulletin* a false decree, signed by Fabre, permitting the India Company to liquidate itself. For this consideration, Fabre had received his share of a 500,000-livre bribe (viz., 100,000 livres).[150] Then Fabre enacted a real-life comedy. The faction of Hébert in the Convention numbered several suspicious aliens among its members. It was the Hébertists who were denouncing the dishonest financiers of the Convention. Fabre thereupon attacked the Hébertists by denouncing to Robespierre the Hébertist aliens as secret agents of the enemy. He also denounced Hérault de Séchelles and others as protectors of these aliens. One of these aliens was Cloots, whose policy of war to the bitter end had been adopted by Hérault.[151]

Robespierre was completely taken in by Fabre's "revelations." [152] He saw

[145] Gnadental. His father Gallicized his title before the birth of his son, to be pleasing to Frederick the Great (Avenel, *Cloots*, I, 3).

[146] *Ibid.*, p. 208.

[147] *Moniteur*, XII, 192. Hérault de Séchelles, Cloots's sporting companion, was president of the Assembly at this time, and, anxious to show appreciation of the gift, suggested that it be used to pay bonuses to foreign soldiers who would come over to the French side. Thereupon Briche proposed and secured passage of a measure providing that every foreign deserter should receive 50 livres, French citizenship, and 3 arpents (variously 3 to 4½ acres) of land after the war. Briche's law provided also 200 livres additional bounty if the deserter brought his horse with him, but that item smacked too much of plain theft, and was responsible for

the return of the entire measure to committee (Mathiez, *Etrangers*, p. 63).

[148] S. Mercier (ed.), *Paris pendant la Révolution (1789–1798)* (2 vols., Paris, 1862), II, 2.

[149] Mathiez, *Fr. Rev.*, p. 245.

[150] *Idem*, "Fabre d'Eglantine et la falsification du décret de liquidation de la Compagnie des Indes," *AR*, VI (1913), 613 *et seqq.*

[151] *Idem*, "Fabre d'Eglantine, inventeur de la conspiration de l'étranger," *ibid.*, VIII (1916), 311 *et seqq.*

[152] Robespierre had displayed a cooler head hardly less than two months previously, when Prudhomme (publisher of the *Révolutions de Paris*) sent the Jacobin Club a work entitled *Les crimes des empereurs de l'Allemagne*, with a letter implying that his political antagonists were the agents of the

foreign plots everywhere: Brissot had been an agent of the Anglo-Prussian faction; the recently denounced persons constituted an Austrian faction. "I distrust without distinction all those foreigners," he said, ". . . who endeavor to appear more republican . . . than we. . . They are the agents of alien powers, [which have instructed their emissaries to] affect the most ardent and exaggerated patriotism [the better to mislead us]." [153] And at the meeting of the Jacobin Club on December 12, 1793, Robespierre resolved to purge Anacharsis Cloots from the membership. The Revolution was becoming nationalized, as Soulavie had recommended.[154]

The interrogatory commenced with a query as to the place of Cloots's birth. "I am from Prussia, future *département* of the French Republic," Cloots replied. To which Robespierre [155] retorted: "Can we regard a German

---

"crowned scoundrels." Robespierre, obviously unperturbed, moved that "the sole response should be that the republican Prudhomme be invited to write down — or rather to have printed, for he does not write — the crimes of journalistic writers or printers who are in the pay of foreign powers." — Session of Sept. 8, 1793, Aulard, *Jacobins*, V, 392.

[153] Mathiez, *Fr. Rev.*, p. 419. The tide of sentiment had already been turning against the foreigner for well-nigh half a year when Robespierre joined the Committee. On February 14, 1793, Carnot, in a report to the Convention in the name of the Diplomatic Committee, had expressed hostility to the thought that — "in the system of a universal republic, annexation would exist as a matter of right . . . There would soon sit amongst us our most implacable enemies." — Quoted in "Les annexions de territoires — Principes et vues du Comité Diplomatique de la Convention Nationale," *RF*, LXIX (1916), 68–74. On March 15, the Conventional Duquesnoy, stung by the defeats in Belgium and the loss of Aix and Liège, had suggested that "it is fair to treat foreigners here as the French are treated in Germany, in Prussia, in Spain, and in England," and he had recommended the expulsion within twenty-four hours of all foreigners not vouched for by two good citizens. His proposition had met opposition, however, and had been sent to committee (Mathiez, *Etrangers*, pp. 122–123). At the start of April, a note addressed to the minister of foreign affairs had suggested the expulsion of all suspected aliens (*ibid.*, pp. 126–127).

And on April 24, the bounty allowed to foreign deserters had been suppressed, and foreign legions had been withdrawn from frontier posts (Mathorez in *REH*, 1923, p. 78). As Mallet du Pan observed later, all France, "without distinction of party, ral[ies] everlastingly against foreigners . . ." — July 3, 1795, *Mém. corr. Mallet du Pan*, II, 151.

[154] The present writer suggests that the hostility of Robespierre to foreigners constitutes an argument against the theory that Robespierre was a Freemason (*vide* G. Laurent, "Robespierre franc-maçon," *AHRF*, V [1928], 62–63). It is indeed strange, however, that he should have succeeded in developing such an antipathy to the *étranger* in a family of Freemasonic descent — so to speak — for we *know* that Robespierre's grandfather was a Freemason, and his father too (H. Fleischmann, "Le grand-père de Robespierre franc-maçon," *AR*, IV [1911], 112–114). Of course, Robespierre's was a Fabre-cated hostility, and this is perhaps the explanation we are seeking.

[155] The arguments of Robespierre were "borrowed" from Camille Desmoulins' *Le Vieux Cordelier* [Mathiez' ed.], No. II, pp. 60–66, according to Mathiez. The present writer, basing his position on the report of an Interior Ministry secret agent of December 23, 1793, wishes to suggest that perhaps Robespierre had been himself the inspiration for Desmoulins' article on Cloots (Le Breton to min. of int., Caron, *Paris*, I, 360). Camille and Maximilien had been schoolmates, incidentally.

baron as a patriot? Can we regard a man with more than a hundred thousand livres' income as a sans-culotte? . . . No, citizens, let us be on our guard against foreigners who wish to appear more patriotic than are the French themselves. . . [When] Brissot and Dumourier [*sic*] served the foreign powers and made us declare war, the Prussian Cloots supported their opinions with frenzy. He made patriotic gifts, . . . urged us to attack the entire world. . . His extravagant opinions, his obstinacy in speaking of a universal republic, in inspiring the rage for conquests, succeeded in producing the same effect as the declamations and seditious writings of Brissot. . .[156] Disdaining the title of French citizen, he coveted only that of citizen of the world. Well, if he had been a good Frenchman, would he have wanted us to try to conquer the world? [157] Would he have wanted us to make a French *département* out of Monomotapa? [158] . . . Citizens, I pray you to reflect on the following: When we decreed rigorous laws against nobles, Cloots was excepted; when we decreed the arrest of foreigners, Cloots was again excepted. That's what I said, [citizens,] excepted! At that very moment, even, Cloots was being elected president of the Jacobins.[159] Thus does it follow infallibly that the party of the foreigner dominates in the heart of the Jacobin [Club]. . . Paris is swarming with intriguers — English and Austrian. They

---

[156] It seems that Bonnal de Ganges, *Repré.*, III, 520, accepts implicitly all Robespierre's charges, for he speaks of "the system of the Universal Republic, come from Berlin through the channel of the Prussian baron Clootz [*sic*], secret agent of the Coalition."

[157] Cloots's liberality with French resources for the benefit of Humankind is well exemplified by a speech he made in August 1793. Oddly, this speech was titled "Civic Crusade." Said Cloots:

". . . I have proved, from the tribune of the Convention, that the French people can sustain a perpetual war without tiring or exhausting itself . . . So long as the sun does not tire in spreading abundance over the earth, republicans will not tire fighting for their paternal hearths. We will eat and drink and fight next year like the last, without being concerned about the balance sheets of the financiers. High prices and taxes are dangers for a king, and props for a people. High prices render the rich less rich, and the poor less poor . . . However, our enemies . . . believe high prices will produce a counterrevolution . . .

"France is like a vast forest, which, notwithstanding annual fellings, still exists . . . The war we are waging on cattle does not decimate the pastures, and the war of tyrants against men will not depopulate the one and indivisible Republic. Eight to nine hundred thousand souls die annually in France, and still the population is increasing . . . Unless the earth be struck with sterility, we will sustain the war for centuries on end. We will always have harvests and assignats . . . *Place France in requisition, and you will save the human race.*" — Aug. 19, 1793, *Brochures pol.*, LXXXVII, no. 19, pp. 3–7. Last sentence italicized in original.

Cloots's indifference to finances finds (playful?) echo in De Pradt's "General rule: finances kill only imbeciles and knaves. Another general rule: in [times of] revolution, there are no finances." — *Pradtiana*, pp. 97–98.

[158] A region placed in southeast Africa by old Portuguese and Dutch maps. Some modern historians relegate the region to the realm of myth, but not necessarily correctly so (*Encyc. Brit.*, *s.v.* "Monomotapa").

[159] He was nominated on November 9, 1793.

sit in the midst of us with the agents of Frederick [William]. . . Cloots is a Prussian. . . Let us hear your verdict." [160]

Cloots seems to have been struck dumb, for there was no denying that his blood was a rich Prussian blue. He had thought, however, that, containing as it did the red and white corpuscles of world revolution and perpetual peace, it had become sufficiently tricolored to be acceptable. His failure to defend himself was regarded as a confession of guilt, and he was summarily dismissed from the Jacobin Club.[161] So, also, were all other aliens — plus nobles, priests, and bankers. The nobles were suspected of interest in Monarchy, now a foreign institution. And the international connections of priests and bankers are obvious. So it was thought proper to lump all these together as "alien" elements.[162]

g. No More Philosophy in the Rhineland

Robespierre had always maintained that the internal and external enemies of France presented but two facets of the same problem. Before the Republic could be consolidated, the foreign menace, also, would have to be faced — and definitively ended. The means had been indicated by the Decrees of September 15 and 18. There would be no more philosophy. The generals would fight, with no holds barred. Disarm, appropriate, destroy, tear up — these were the verbs used in the latter decree.

On October 23, Carnot ordered General Jourdan to attack in Belgium with overwhelming force, to publish that he had 200,000 men, to try to frighten the enemy. "Let terror precede you. Spare only humble dwellings. Do not forget to destroy the mills, and to take a great number of hostages." [163] The next day, Minister of War Bouchotte urged Jourdan to render the enemy unable to start another campaign, but the Minister forgot (?) there was to be no more philosophy, and he ordered Jourdan "to prepare the liberation of other peoples and the success of the republican system by making a display of heroic virtues proper to excite their admiration." [164] On October 26, Carnot

---

[160] Buchez and Roux, *Hist. parlem.*, XXX, 335–339.

[161] Cloots answered the reproaches made at the Jacobin Club in his *Appel au genre humain*, which he distributed widely in Paris. Therein, "he persists in preferring the European Republic to the French Republic, the Universal Republic to that of Europe." — Dugas (secret agent) to min. of int., Dec. 23, 1793, Caron, *Paris*, I, 352. A week after this report, Cloots was the subject of conversation in a large Paris cabaret, and a worker defended him, reading part of Cloots's pam-

phlet to his interlocutors. The latter told the worker he was wasting precious time with a — — — — who was a Prussian baron. At this point, some women interjected: "Oh, he's a Prussian? No quarter! . . . We always place our confidence in foreigners who cajole us the better to stab us." — Bacon (secret agent) to min. of int., Dec. 29, *ibid.*, II, 64.

[162] Aulard, *Jacobins*, V, 557.

[163] *Corr. gén. Carnot*, III, 384.

[164] *Ibid.*, p. 397.

became more selective in his terror tactics. The measures of rigor were to be portioned out only as merited, he directed.[165]

Is it not possible that Robespierre did not wish to antagonize the Belgians too much because he thought he might want to annex them some day, despite Soulavie's teaching? It will be recalled that he had displayed annexationist inclinations concerning Belgium in his speech before the Jacobins on April 20, 1792.[166] As to the occupied German territories, certainly there was no thought of mollifying the rigor of the law. There, the winter of 1793–94 acquired the sorrowful name of "the Plunder-Winter." Secret agent Le Breton reported to the minister of the interior on February 5: "It was said today . . . that in the Palatinate, on the left bank of the Rhine, the people rose en masse to reject the French. He was hooted and treated with scorn."[167] But let us permit the Rhineland papers to tell the story in their own words.

You will hear with indignation how the enemy is treating the citizen and the country folk. He does not even conceal the disgraceful intention of having robbery and plunder as his purpose; it is publicly recognized by promulgated decrees. Churches and altars are robbed and defiled; all bells carried away; all cattle, all provisions, beds, linen, furniture and utensils (*Hausrat*) looted; wives and daughters disgraced; young able-bodied men hauled off and forced into [French] service. . . Even the Clubists in Spires and Worms were recently stripped bare by their presumptive rescuers . . .

The writer mentions Dumouriez and Custine, how they deceived people by their talk of "liberty and equality, peace to the cottage [and] war on palaces," but without saying so, he leaves the impression that things were not nearly as bad under them. He continues:

The New Franks speak no longer in the same terms: they are too arrogant to use intrigue and deception against us. Now it is openly a question of liberty to go begging, of equality to make everyone poor and unhappy. Peace to the beggar, who has nothing of which he can be robbed. War on the merchant, war on the baker, war on the steward, war on the miller, war on shoes, war on clothes, war on shirts, draught animals, money, beds, dishes, sheep, geese and ducks, war on produce and on hay. War on everything that can be detached and plundered. . . Dear countrymen, seize your weapons . . .[168]

The above article referred to the Hunsrück in the Palatinate, and its environs. Those directly responsible for this reign of horror felt called upon

[165] *Ibid.*, p. 408. On July 11, 1794, Carnot specified the friendly regions, as he saw them (*ibid.*, IV, 477).

[166] This chapter, § 2b.

[167] Caron, *Paris*, III, 343.

[168] "Ermahnung eines Trierers an seine Landsleute," Coblenz, Jan. 24, 1794, *Kurtrierisches Intelligenzblatt*, Hansen, *Quellen*, III, 11, n. 1.

to justify themselves. They said Mannheim had admitted an Austrian corps forced from Alsace. This is true, but what they did not mention was that Mannheim maintained she had been compelled to admit the force, which is quite probable, for this was, after all, an Imperial war, and Mannheim was a city of the Empire. The *Aachener Zuschauer* asserted on February 10 that "the French generals and Commissioners boasted, 'We left the inhabitants only their eyes — so they could weep.'" Lazare Hoche, who will play an important role later in the Rhineland,[169] was one of these generals.[170]

It is to be noted that Rühl, who patronized the Bergzabern separatists in late 1792,[171] and Merlin of Thionville, whose opposition to Palatine neutrality prompted the invasion of Zweibrucken in early 1793,[172] united in the Convention (January 26, 1794) to justify this harsh handling of the "neutral" Wittelsbach ruler of the Palatinate. Rühl said the time for philosophy was past; France should present the Elector Palatine with a good-sized bill, and not leave the Palatinate until he had paid in full. Merlin contributed the argument that, when the Austrian and Prussian forces surrounded Mayence, the foremost troops were Palatine.[173]

Of course, there was really no such thing as a neutral German state when the Empire was at war. The Imperial constitution forbade it. To France, a neutral German state was one which, for some political reason, she thought should be spared now, for the sake of a greater advantage later. But if a great advantage could be secured now — say, in the form of grain, cattle, shirts, and shoes — well, what prospect more rosy could the dim future hold!

This harsh treatment, it should be noted, was not reserved for German territory. In Strasburg, during the selfsame winter, Saint-Just, in addition to imposing fantastically high monetary levies, requisitioned shoes, beds, and all the overcoats in the city.[174] And in the Jura, Bassal and Lamarque requisitioned 1,200 beds with their bedding, sheets to the value of 5,000 francs and blankets to that of 419,000 francs; and shortly thereafter, all the gold, silver, iron, copper, lead, wood, leather, soap, corn, wine, spirits, vinegar, horses, cattle, forage, and cloth.[175] In Bayonne, all the muslin and lace were requisitioned "to make, as was said, *trowsers* for the troops."[176] Of course, in these areas, the spirit of "fanaticism" or of "aristocracy" was rife. This also was, in a sense, enemy territory whose inhabitants the revolutionists obviously had no desire to indulge.

It would be unjust to the revolutionists if we failed to point out that necessity and long association had developed in them a tolerance for requisi-

---

[169] Pt. II, chap. xxvii; chap. xxviii, § 3.
[170] Hansen, *Quellen*, III, 9, n. 1.
[171] *Vide supra*, chap. ii, § 2.
[172] *Vide supra*, chap. iii, § 3.

[173] Hansen, *Quellen*, III, 9, n. 1.
[174] Sybel, *Fr. Rev.*, III, 231.
[175] *Ibid.*, p. 232.
[176] *Ibid.*, p. 233.

tions, even when applied to themselves. To illustrate: On October 31, 1793, Representative Fouché ordered all inhabitants of the *département* of the Allier to bring in to the committee of surveillance all their coin and all objects of gold and silver except women's jewels.[177] The Convention annulled Fouché's decree, and the central committee ruled that those who had already brought in their valuables, including those who had freely donated them, could have them back. But not one person appeared to reclaim anything.[178]

To people of such a frame of mind, it was certainly not a very heinous sin to requisition the goods of the ideological and foreign enemy. This is not said to excuse, but only to explain, the "Plunder-Winter" of 1793–94.

h. Merlin of Thionville's Foreign-Policy Formula

Merlin of Thionville's activities on mission in the Rhineland have often been mentioned in the foregoing pages. As one who executes a policy often is the real policy-formulator, and Merlin had had so much experience in execution, his opinions were always regarded with great respect. On January 8, 1794, Merlin opened up his heart to the Convention. So closely do the views he expressed parallel those of Robespierre, as modified by Soulavie, that one might almost suspect conscious harmonization. There was the emphasis on the treason of the generals, the antagonism to aliens, the willingness to forego the bounds of Gaul, the emphasis on defensive war unless attacked, and the demand for measures of rigor in conquered territory. Said Merlin: Our conquests last year (1792) were astonishing, but lost not less astonishingly quickly because of the treason of the generals and "our system of universal philanthropy and cosmopolitanism." Let us take a lesson from our foe.

The Prussians are taking everything in the part of the Republic's territory they are occupying. They have left nothing to the cultivator. . . Today we are utilizing the same measures against them, and we are victorious. If we want seriously to be free, we must prevent our enemies from again snatching away our advantages by seizing from them the means of continuing the war. We must destroy their fortresses and forbid rebuilding. Their mines also; let the Rhine flood them and make new lakes which say to tyranny: that is our force and our policy. We must appropriate horses, cattle, iron, gold, silver, food, and ammunition. . .

I want to be French, a free republican and forever free. Before endowing others with liberty, I want to enjoy the constitution, which will be conducive to my happiness only when I can have peace, when the revolutionary laws will be no longer indispensable. I am, indeed, not Anacharsis; I love my country exclusively. Let it be happy before we occupy ourselves with the politics of others.

[177] Garnier to Francqueville (head clerk Bureau of Corr.), Nov. 2, 1793, Caron, *Agents . . . intér.*, I, 451.   [178] *Idem*, Nov. 27, 1793, *ibid.*, p. 461.

Do not deceive yourselves, my colleagues. Accustomed to the yoke, the inhabitants of Germany prefer its chains, its apathy, to liberty; the calm of servitude to the storms of liberty. There are few patriots in Germany, and their fate so far does not induce others to declare themselves. Wisdom forces my veracity to speak to you thus. Be happy at home. That is the means of revolutionizing other peoples — by causing them to envy our lot.[179]

I believe that our present system should therefore be: Let us gather in . . . whatever our enemies can use. . . Horses, cattle, iron, gold, silver, food supplies, and ammunition, . . . all that enables us to take the citadels of our enemies. Let us destroy their fortifications . . . and forbid the reëstablishment. Let us remain steadfast under our arms and at our plows, [the while we] enjoy our advantages — of happiness and of the constitution. And if one dares trouble us, we will carry sword and flame right up to the thrones. . . The inhabitants will complain. Well, let them cast out their kings.

I ask that each of you consider my observations, and if someone proposes that we extend the territory of the Republic, let him present something new [in justification]. . . I wish the Committee . . . would approve my reflections, and that such be its policy. I repeat, experience tells me that this is the only positive means conducive to happiness and public peace.[180]

Merlin's recommendations parallel closely the views expressed three days before by an anonymous sans-culotte in a café near the Convention hall. Said this patriot: "Bread, victories, Toulon taken, the Vendée left without a leg to stand on (à quia) — what more do we want? . . . Let us not pursue our trans-Rhenish enemies too much. . . Let us hold fast, waiting for them [the enemies] to renew the charge if they hanker to do so." [181] And the day before that, a secret agent reported the following concerning Paris opinion: "Others . . . do not want us to cross the frontier because, they say, we know what that cost us last year at Mayence, [and] likewise in Belgium. . ." [182] Robespierre was by no means alone in his policy of cutting the war down to size.

The Committee's only answer to Merlin's speech was to instruct the generals anew in the sense of the Decree of September 18 — to seize everything belonging to cities, towns, and individuals; and to destroy fortresses. Also, it remembered an order of Lebrun's to Custine to abstract "great and costly" books from Rhineland libraries for the benefit of the Bibliothèque Nationale, and on January 25, it ordered the Representatives to the Rhine and Moselle Armies to send to France the "great works of literature and

[179] It will be recalled that in his speech of April 20, 1792, Robespierre did not appeal for annexation of the German left bank (this chapter, § 2b). Neither had Soulavie (ibid., § 2c).

[180] Moniteur, XIX, 162.
[181] Beraud to min. of int., Caron, Paris, II, 186–187.
[182] Charmont to idem, Jan. 4, 1794, ibid., p. 168.

typography" of the conquered country.[183] No attempt was made by Robespierre then, or in the ensuing weeks, to embrace Merlin as a worthy ally, for Robespierre was just then becoming satiated with a vain venture of coöperation with Danton, which also had moderation as its governing principle.

i. Robespierre, Danton, Barère, and Peace

According to the bulletins of English secret agents, Danton and Robespierre collaborated in an attempt to bring peace around the end of November and beginning of December 1793. Danton had had a private interview with one Peter Lewis Robin, a naturalized Englishman of Genevese origin, and had expressed his disinterest in the natural boundaries, his disgust with the excesses of revolution, and his great desire for peace. Whether Danton informed the Committee of this interview, we do not know, but we do know that Danton asked the Committee to name a neutral agent, that one was named, and that Robespierre was on the Committee which named him. Just how peace was to be procured is none too clear. Was it to be by fomenting insurrection in England, or by provoking the fall of Pitt, or by some other means? Fifteen million livres was supposed to be destined to this end, whatever that might be. But the overture failed. Why? Because only a small fraction of the 15,000,000 was forthcoming. Talleyrand, former Bishop of Autun, who had been sent to England early in 1792 to seek its alliance in the proposed crusade against Austria, and who, though later indicted for conspiracy and declared an *émigré*, was yet involved in the financial end of this "deal," declared that he had received only 900,000 livres — only 150,000 personally — and that that was not enough to do great things.[184]

But there were other reasons for failure. Certain elements of the French public did not seem ready for the thought of peace, confusing as they did the success of the Revolution with the success of the war — and the war was not then a pronounced success. Barère wanted to keep fighting "to the bitter end" — until the tyrants had been beaten to the dust — and a large number of former pacifists had gone over to his standard. Many of those in favor of peace were persons with whom it was not politically expedient to be allied in any cause. Then, Robespierre's collaborator, Danton, wanted to go farther along the path of domestic reaction and foreign compromise than did Robespierre. And each of these two men wanted to utilize his position of influence with the mob to be the hero of the peace, and the sole beneficiary thereof, politically speaking.[185] These factors, coupled with the fact that

---

[183] Hansen, *Quellen*, III, 12, n. 1. For Lebrun's order to Custine, *vide supra*, chap. ii, n. 117.
[184] M. Reinhard, "La guerre et la paix à la fin de 1793 — Une interview inédite de Danton," *AHRF*, XXV (1953), 100–102.
[185] Guérin, *Lutte*, I, 394 *et passim*; II, 194.

soundings with respect to Prussia had netted nothing,[186] convinced Robespierre that the time for peace was not favorable, and he approached, for the time being, the "to the bitter end" party of Barère.

Barère's principles, therefore, are of particular interest. In a speech of January 22, 1794, he declared:

> In ordinary wars, after such successes,[187] one would have sought . . . peace. . . . But in the war of liberty, they [successes] are only a means . . . of exterminating despots. . . Neither peace nor truce nor armistice nor any treaty can be made with despots except in the name of a consolidated, triumphant republic . . . dictating the peace. . .

> However, some voices already are raised praising the advantages of peace. . . What sincere patriot . . . would dare to speak of peace without fear of compromising liberty . . . ?

> Who dares, then, speak of peace?

> Aristocrats. . .

> Moderates. . .

> The rich. . .

> Descendants . . . of the hitherto privileged. . .

> Cowardly souls. . .

> Bad citizens. . .

> Pretended patriots. . .

> Who dares speak of peace[!] . . .

> Monarchies need peace; the Republic needs martial energy.

> Slaves need peace; republicans need the ferment of liberty.

> Governments need peace; the French Republic needs . . . revolutionary activity.

> Death were better than a shameful or inadequate peace. . .[188]

What was the attitude of the French people on this question of war and peace? The reports of the secret agents for Paris help to answer this question. Two classes of desire, two classes of rumor, are to be found: One concerns general peace. The other concerns peace with all nations of the Coalition except England.

Between December 23 and January 20, inclusive, the agents reported to the minister of the interior eighteen instances where interest in general peace was openly expressed. A few may be duplications, as the agents were

---

[186] The King had been anxious for peace because of a shortage of funds (Bacher to Deforgues, Jan. 17, 1794, *Papiers de Barthélemy*, III, 354–355), but no longer. He had obtained the 30 million he needed (Burgomaster Kilchsperger to Barthélemy, Jan. 31, 1794, enclosed in letter of Barthélemy to Deforgues, Feb. 1, 1794, *ibid.*, p. 389).

[187] Toulon, night of December 18–19; Frœschwiller, December 24; Geitershof, December 25; the Geisberg, December 26; Wissembourg Lines, December 27; Landau blockade lifted, December 28.

[188] *Moniteur*, XIX, 273–274.

supposed to roam outside their assigned sections; but the total number is great enough to be striking nevertheless.

Two reports mirror pure impatience for peace — one in language not pure enough for the tender eyes of the Ministry.[189] Four reports concern the gaming instinct — peace within six weeks, four months, three months, and "by next *prairial*" being wagered.[190] Six concern the belief or the rumor that peace would soon be made because "the tyrants" or "the monsters" were exhausted, or at bay, or disputing among themselves; or had decided that they might as well recognize the Republic.[191] One mentions France's need for peace — "by spring," or "as soon as we are masters of the left bank."[192] Two express a pious hope for peace.[193] Three betray a universal desire for peace, in one case conditional upon "the complete destruction of the coalesced despots";[194] in another, emphasized by a willingness to sacrifice " 'a thousand crowns,' . . . [or] 'half my property,' to see that happy time arrive."[195] One report, despite Barère's exhortations, speaks of a simple belief "in imminent peace, except on the part of intriguers and aristocrats."[196] Two tell of a rumor that negotiations were already in progress — one, without specification as to the party or parties involved; the second, naming the Circle of Swabia.[197] The last-named report brings us down to the date of Barère's speech of January 22. Truly there were some good citizens who dared speak of peace.

Above have been presented those secret reports not concerned specifically with England. But England was regarded by France as the soul of the Coalition; England's downfall, as the key to general peace. Much wishful thinking concerning England was indulged in by the French, and their rumors were often amusing, such as the one that Pitt's *head* was being borne in effigy through the streets of London.[198] (Apparently the effigy of Pitt had been guillotined in good Parisian fashion.) Many Frenchmen tried to convince themselves that the British Empire was coming apart at the

[189] Le Breton, Mercier, Dec. 23, 1793, Caron, *Paris*, I, 362, 365.

[190] Bacon, Dec. 27; Le Harivel, Dec. 30, 1793; Dugas, Jan. 18, 1794; Le Breton, Jan. 19: *ibid.*, II, 20, 88; III, 24, 43.

[191] Rolin, Dec. 31, 1793; Pourvoyeur, Jan. 2, 1794; Charmont, Jan. 5; *idem*, Jan. 6; Rolin, Jan. 18; Le Breton, Jan. 19: *ibid.*, II, 111, 147, 188, 203; III, 33, 43. Lefebvre attributes the origin of the peace rumors to a speech of Danton's (December 2, 1793) demanding the end of the Terror. The end of the Terror presupposed peace, says Lefebvre, and the rumors started to fly (*Rév. fr.*, p. 372).

[192] Charmont, Jan. 1, 1794, Caron, *Paris*, II, 115.

[193] Pourvoyeur, Dec. 25, 1793; Le Harivel, Dec. 27: *ibid.*, I, 412; II, 29.

[194] Rolin, Jan. 8, 1794, *ibid.*, II, 258.

[195] *Idem*, Jan. 7; *idem*, Jan. 8; Le Breton, Jan. 19: *ibid.*, II, 232, 258; III, 43.

[196] Rolin, Jan. 16, *ibid.*, II, 402.

[197] Le Harivel, Dec. 30, 1793; Latour-Lamontagne, Jan. 20, 1794: *ibid.*, II, 88; III, 61.

[198] Latour-Lamontagne, Jan. 18, 1794, *ibid.*, III, 18. Or the one establishing a national convention in Scotland, apparently to create a sans-kilt republic on the French model (Rolin, Dec. 23, 1794, *ibid.*, I, 369).

seams, and that all they had to do was to show themselves personally to the British people, and not only England but Europe would fall at their feet. Typical are the Paris reports: "Another group wants to invade England as the only means of ending the war." [199] "Some . . . say that before a month is over, we will be in London, and that we must do that to save the Republic." [200] "We must find [rather, seek out] Pitt, and . . . all our enemies will yield." [201] Robespierre's speech at the Jacobins attacking England was read twice in a cabaret and approved. The women said: Robespierre is right that we must occupy ourselves with the crimes of England. "If these dogs of English ministers had not meddled in our affairs, the Austrians would have been overthrown long ago; but before long, all the brigands will be destroyed." [202] "One regards as certain that England is going to retire from the Coalition, and that it will not be long before Prussia follows her example." [203]

It is clear that it was a France yearning for peace upon which Barère had urged war to the death in his who-dares-speak-of-peace speech of January 22. We have seen the attitude of the French people during the month preceding that pronouncement. Now let us seek to determine if any change occurred in the channel of popular thought as a result of Barère's rhetoric. One secret agent's report describes how a group in the "Jardin national" began its discussion with the speech of Barère. "Opinions were divided on the question of the foreign war that he proposed, and not everyone approved equally his brusque sortie against those who lull themselves with the hope of an imminent peace. . ." Someone said, "Let us drive back into their lairs the monsters with which this holy earth is yet defiled; let us finish our Revolution, and confide to each people the charge to make its own [revolution]." [204] This was pure Robespierrist doctrine. It was echoed also in the next report: "Weak minds discredit the measures that Barère has caused to be adopted relative to peace and war. These imbeciles say: 'Well, we are now permanently at war. . . It is desired to ruin us.'" [205] The following report fails to record public horror at the grim prospect of "permanent war": "The public regards it as certain that the tyrants will not be long in asking us for peace, but we will not treat with them, for we want to treat only with peoples and not with kings. The [French] people are inclined very strongly in this direction." [206]

In the Café Payen, someone said a terrible insurrection was about to break out in London against Pitt; that the English people were perhaps

[199] Charmont, Dec. 25, 1793, ibid., I, 390.
[200] Idem, Jan. 4, 1794, ibid., II, 168.
[201] Letassey, Jan. 9, ibid., p. 272.
[202] Bacon, Jan. 11, ibid., p. 296.
[203] Dugas, Jan. 18, ibid., III, 24.
[204] Latour-Lamontagne, Jan. 23, ibid., pp. 107-108.
[205] Charmont, Jan. 26, ibid., p. 155.
[206] Idem, ibid., p. 156.

waiting only for the French to join them in breaking their bonds. "It is in London that we must combat Brunswick and Coburg," the speaker said. "When the tricolor flag waves over the Tower of London, it will not be long before all Europe is free." To which the reply was made: "I would want to employ other means than yours [invasion] to triumph over this obstacle [England]. The discussion that the sagacious Robespierre has opened at the Jacobins is, as I see it, more formidable to Pitt and George than 100,000 bayonets." And it was pointed out that a descent on England would cause the English to rally behind their leaders, and save them from the utter destruction they were believed to be facing.[207]

"Almost everyone approves the views presented several days ago by Barère . . . ," ran another report. "All say that we should never treat with kings, but only with peoples." [208] Thus was public opinion divided, by no means overwhelmingly in favor of Barère, when, on February 1, Barère delivered himself of another "famous" foreign-policy pronouncement.

The occasion for this address was supplied by a letter from Bacher. On January 17, Bacher had informed Deforgues that persons connected with the Habsburgs had inquired of him to whom proposals of peace might be addressed. Bacher had replied that France "had 100,000 negotiators in the Army of the Rhine, and as many more in that of the North. . ." To Deforgues, Bacher ventured the opinion that, for the time being, it was proper to speak only through the cannon's mouth. He regarded the overture as an attempt to sow discord among the French people by holding out hopes for peace.

The peace proposals suggested to him, said Bacher, were these: Provisional recognition of the French Republic and a two-year truce. During the truce, France would put her constitution into effect and organize her government, so that there would exist someone with authority to negotiate. Then peace could be signed and the terms submitted to the French nation for ratification — probably because it was expected the French signatories would soon go the way of the guillotine.[209]

The overture was repeated three days later, with the added items of possible Swiss mediation, and a congress.[210] And on the twenty-second of January, Barthélemy wrote to Deforgues that "an ardent desire for peace" was sweeping Germany.[211]

Barère met the peace offensive head on. He divulged the terms sent in by Bacher, and proceeded to deluge them with ridicule, the most caustic alkali known. "They will recognize the Republic!" he scoffed. "As if the

[207] Latour-Lamontagne, Jan. 27, *ibid.*, pp. 176–177.
[208] Charmont, Jan. 31, *ibid.*, p. 243.
[209] *Papiers de Barthélemy*, III, 354.
[210] *Ibid.*, p. 359.
[211] *Ibid.*, p. 362.

Republic needed them to exist! As if its destiny did not place it in the imposing role of tolerating kings, and recognizing, provisionally, the governments of the coalesced tyrants." He pointed out how stupid it would be for France to paralyze her fifteen armies for two years. The projected dissolution of the Convention (in order to create a permanent government) he characterized as an attempt "to break this principal instrument of the Revolution." Regarding ratification of the peace by the people, he exclaimed, "Baleful shades of Brissot and the federalists . . . !" He dubbed the tyrants "modern Greeks" and urged the people to beware. The people had satirized their government, he confessed; accused it of wanting an impossible peace, of having an exaggerated system. They had demanded if they were never to enjoy the benefits of peace. "Generous friends of peace, beware. The aristocrats applaud you, and the coalition of kings is listening. . . The Committee has prepared a terrible war to arrive at a stable peace. . . The French people can want only a peace dictated by them to Machiavellian governments." [212]

Strangely, the public of Paris received this message quite favorably (or had potential critics merely been rendered speechless?). During the first week after the address, the secret reports of the Interior Ministry recorded nothing but approval. "No peace . . . without the fall of the tyrants" was the substance of "all the versions" on this subject, reported one agent.[213] "Barère's report has exalted all the minds," said another; "people no longer want to hear of peace." [214] A third spoke of the people's admiration for Barère's reply to the crowned brigands and for his words to the Convention, "better a certain death than a shameful peace." Bacher's response likewise was applauded.[215] " 'War! No truce or peace,' said several workers on the Boulevard Montmartre," reported a fourth agent. "We have under arms fifteen to sixteen hundred thousand men. Therewith, we [shall] go plant the tree of liberty in the Grand Turk's [front yard] if he says a word against our laws." [216] Favorable comment on the speech was noted in several cafés by a fifth agent.[217] And a sixth reported these words: "Our enemies the tyrants . . . must exist no more in order that Europe may have peace." [218] Barère had done a good job of selling his idea of war to the death.[219]

[212] Feb. 1, 1794, *Moniteur*, XIX, 356–357.
[213] Pourvoyeur, Feb. 1, Caron, *Paris*, III, 273.
[214] Latour-Lamontagne, Feb. 2, *ibid.*, p. 281.
[215] Pourvoyeur, Feb. 2, *ibid.*, pp. 293–294.
[216] Beraud, Feb. 3, *ibid.*, p. 302.
[217] Charmont, Feb. 3, *ibid.*
[218] *Idem*, Feb. 8, *ibid.*, pp. 391–392.
[219] The spell did not last long, however. "[February 13] was the day of grumbling" about the lack of peace (Rolin, *ibid.*, IV, 93). "Toujours la paix." — *Idem*, Feb. 19, *ibid.*, p. 219. "The public says this campaign will be hard fought." — Le Breton, Feb. 21, *ibid.*, p. 256. "We run the risk of not terminating the war in this campaign." — Charmont, Feb. 22, *ibid.*, p. 272. Evidently war eternal was not so attractive when one thought it over.

After the foregoing, one would expect to read that France was in first-class condition, and well able to take the chances of a war lasting for a number of years. It was only thirty-eight days later that Carnot wrote to General Pichegru: "Do not leave him [the enemy] time to breathe. We want to finish this year. We must wage a war of the most offensive, most vigorous [sort]. All will be lost if we do not . . . crush our enemies . . . within three months from now, for that would mean recommencing the war next year. It would mean dying of hunger and exhaustion. Now, I repeat to you in the name of the Committee and of the *patrie*, we must end it." [220]

j. Robespierre Consolidates His Power

Let us look at the *patrie* and see whether a priest (constitutional, of course) should be summoned on a stand-by basis. The bread famine in the provinces, which was acute at the commencement of the Great Committee's life, was "desolating" by October.[221] In the *département* of the Creuse, where the poor consumed two pounds of grain per day in the form of bread, a mere 31 per cent of that was available.[222] In Paris, when there was bread to be had,[223] it was so bad it was well-nigh impossible to eat it, and the bakers had to reduce its price for fear of losing their shops.[224] But the reduction in price did not render the product healthier, and accounts of bread-poisoning dot the secret reports.[225] The bread seemed to cause diarrhoea. Many were ill from it, and an epidemic malady was feared.[226]

The situation regarding meat can be more briefly described. There usually was none. Indeed many milch cows had been sold to the butcher because there was no fodder; [227] but these too were soon gone. An "ill-intentioned person" maintained that a laborer could not sustain himself without meat. To him were two answers given: that the Pyramids were built by workers fed on leeks and onions; and that one could readily bear for the love of liberty privations which one bore willingly to please deaf and dumb saints.[228]

Butter was "almost no longer found in markets." [229] Farmers bringing in butter (and eggs) to market were so often robbed of their produce, and even

[220] March 11, 1794, *Corr. gén. Carnot*, IV, 303–304.

[221] Desrenaudes to Paré (min. of int.), Oct. 24, 1793, Caron, *Agents . . . intér.*, I, 243.

[222] Diannyére to Paré, Oct. 21, *ibid.*, p. 302.

[223] Grivel reported a bread famine on December 13 (Caron, *Paris*, I, 262). On December 23, he indicated that bread distribution was suspended for days at a time (*ibid.*, p. 353).

[224] Siret, Dec. 19, *ibid.*, p. 294.

[225] Latour-Lamontagne, Dec. 27, *ibid.*, II, 27.

[226] Charmont, Dec. 31, *ibid.*, p. 100.

[227] Monic, Jan. 3, 1794, *ibid.*, p. 162.

[228] Perrière, Feb. 25, *ibid.*, IV, 335. There were no meat substitutes, either, like beans, peas, and rice because of a drought the previous summer (Grivel, Dec. 23, 1793, *ibid.*, I, 353).

[229] Grivel, Dec. 12, *ibid.*, p. 261.

of their coats, that they would not come in again.[230] Butter "lacking," "butter famine," "no butter," and "butter still rare," were the reports on that vital commodity for January and February 1794.[231] And it was not a condition that was going to improve. Three months later the Committee would write to Saint-Just that "the assemblages for butter [were] more numerous and more turbulent than ever. . ."[232] One cause of the butter shortage was that people had eaten many of the milch cows. Another was that tallow for candles was so expensive, people mixed butter with the tallow and burned up their vitamin A.[233]

Above [234] was noted the capture of an English-language letter, which had ordered, among such acts like incendiarism and discrediting of the assignats, the following: "Send up the price of food. Buy up the tallow and candles at any price, and make the public pay for them up to 5 livres per pound." At any rate, this is what Barère told the Convention was the import of the letter.[235] Candles were important to the French war effort because, without them, the hours of labor per day were necessarily reduced.

Candles are made with hard suet or tallow. So is soap. Candles were necessary for light; soap for health. There was keen competition between the manufacturers of these two commodities for the limited supply of suet, and, depending upon which group cornered the suet market,[236] the French were either dirty in the light, or clean in the dark.[237] Perhaps this is painting too rosy a picture. The soap made was of very poor quality and "soils rather than whitens linen." [238] Apparently the people were dirty in either case.

The armies waste suet terribly, reported one agent.[239] A summary of several reports told of the "price-squeeze" to which the candle-maker was subjected. He had to pay 5 per cent "under the table" and to give the butcher boy a triple or quadruple gratuity — yet his selling price could not reflect these very real expenses.[240] Nor could he recoup his losses by volume sales. The shortage of suet forced dealers to limit retail sales of soap and candles to a half pound per customer.[241] It was a hungering, dirty, unilluminated

[230] X, Jan. 6, 1794, *ibid.*, II, 215.
[231] Rolin, Jan. 4; Mercier, Jan. 17; Prevost, Feb. 22; Bacon, Feb. 23: *ibid.*, II, 183; III, 13; IV, 285, 291.
[232] May 25, 1794, G. Michon (ed.), *Correspondance de Maximilien et Augustin Robespierre* (Paris, 1926), p. 288.
[233] Gonchon to Garat (min. of int.), June 11, 1793, Caron, *Agents . . . intér.*, I, 499.
[234] This chapter, n. 54.
[235] Report of Barère, in name of CPS, to Conv., Aug. 1, 1793, *Brochures pol.*, LXIII, no. 7, p. 10.
[236] "A butcher boy told me that he was charged

to buy up all the tallow [or suet]. . . I have never been able to learn his name." — Prevost, Dec. 21, Caron, *Paris*, I, 321.
[237] E.g., Dugas wrote on January 4, 1794 that much soap had arrived (*ibid.*, II, 172). On January 12, Pourvoyeur wrote that merchants say there have been no candles for several days (*ibid.*, p. 327).
[238] Le Harivel, Jan. 2, 1794, *ibid.*, p. 141.
[239] Letassey, Jan. 18, 1794, *ibid.*, III, 28.
[240] "Situation of Paris," Report of min. of int. to CPS, Dec. 18, 1793, *ibid.*, I, 281.
[241] Dugas, Feb. 27, *ibid.*, IV, 367.

existence which Barère wanted to foist indefinitely upon the suffering people of France. Carnot had displayed more perspicacity when he said (March 11) "we must end it."

The powers had shown, however, already several months before, that they had no faith either in the permanence or reliability of the French government. Not in its permanence because of the factions: Robespierrists, Dantonists, Hébertists — it was uncertain as yet which would prevail. Not in its reliability because of the de-Christianization movement sweeping France. Even statesmen who did not themselves believe in God had no confidence whatever in agreements with a nation which could abjure the Almighty, and — on the high altar — replace with a pretty wench [242] the symbols of Man's yearning for the Pure, the Exalted, and the Everlasting. Soulavie and a French agent named Sweitzer had forwarded to Paris a warning by Baron de Staël (then in Switzerland with his father-in-law, Necker) that France was alienating all her friends by her religious attitude.[243] De Staël was referring not only to the worship of a mere human faculty — reason — but to the "antireligious" calendar, which abolished the Lord's Day and disregarded Catholic holidays.[244]

The sovereigns of Europe, perhaps fearful that their own subjects would become infected, and believing, in any event, that here was an opportunity to consolidate neutral opinion against the Republic, had, toward the end of 1793, issued a proclamation in which France was represented as a nation of "abandoned atheists, . . . enemies of God and of man." [245] The Committee had charged Robespierre to prepare a fitting response, which was then adopted by the Convention as its own (December 5, 1793).[246] Therein Robespierre — who, though he believed devoutly in Providence, yet had no objection to de-Christianization but only to the methods of the de-Christianizers [247] — denied that France had abjured the Divinity. France respected the liberty

---

[242] She was probably an actress from the Opéra. Dressed in transparent white crepe (Sybel, Fr. Rev., III, 239), with blue scarf and red bonnet, and sitting on an ivy-bedecked "throne," she received homage as the Goddess of Reason (Kerr, Terror, p. 259).

[243] Soulavie, Dec. 6, 1793, Guérin, Lutte, I, 400; Schweitzer, Dec. 28, ibid., p. 408.

[244] Kerr, Terror, p. 256. The calendar was not only antireligious but, by its very nomenclature — which gave to days such names as hog, horse-radish, spinach, manure, and shovel — imparted the impression that the French were just a trifle under par esthetically. If the innovators had limited their choice of word-symbols to pleasant ones, "nice" ones, they might have been excused.

But "manure" and "spinach" — ! Vide J. H. Stewart (ed.), A Documentary Survey of the French Revolution (New York, 1951), pp. 510–511.

[245] Kerr, Terror, p. 263.

[246] Discours rap. Robespierre, p. 301. Public reaction to the speech was warm. One agent reported that it was "praised to the skies" by the Parisians. "I do not believe there is anyone present in Paris who does not eulogize it. Everyone votes him thanks . . ." — Charmont, Feb. 6, Caron, Paris, III, 352. Another agent quoted a woman to the effect that "this Robespierre has much ability." — Bacon, Feb. 9, ibid., IV, 2.

[247] Kerr, Terror, p. 263.

of all religions, and proscribed none, he declared.[248] Nor was France immoral. "Good heavens, the morality of kings!" he scoffed, and proceeded to castigate royalty for *its* immorality.[249] However, while sloughing off the charges of irreligion as absurd, Robespierre must already then have realized that the atheists would have to go if ever France were to return to normalcy and peace.[250] It was not alone their influence on foreign opinion. A new Vendée in France was threatened. And Robespierre himself, as indicated, was of a deeply religious turn of mind. There was no place for atheists in the virtuous France of his dreams.

One of the de-Christianizers was Cloots, whose expulsion from the Jacobin Club at Robespierre's behest has been treated.[251] Cloots, it will be recalled, was expelled because of his bellicose internationalism; but he was not less extreme as a de-Christianizer. Reared under the influence of his mother's brother, the Franciscan monk and Canon of Xanten, Cornelius de Pauw, whose literary works rank with those of Rousseau and Voltaire,[252] Cloots grew up antireligious. The degree and quality of his hostility appeared early in the Revolution. It was proposed in 1790 that one bishop should be appointed for each of France's eighty-three new *départements*. In the Jacobin Club, Cloots proposed the selection of four circuit bishops instead.[253] "Good heavens!" he exclaimed with indignation, "only twelve apostles were necessary to propagate the Lie, only twelve Spaniards to spread venereal disease [in the Americas?]." [254] Also, Cloots it was who later was instrumental in inducing Gobel, the constitutional bishop of Paris, to resign his functions (November 7, 1793),[255] giving impetus to a great unfrocking movement

---

[248] Freedom of religion was proclaimed three days later — by the Decree of December 8, 1793 (Aulard, *Actes*, IX, 257).

[249] *Discours rap. Robespierre*, pp. 304, 307. Robespierre's full fury was vented upon England, where, he said, patriotism was the monopoly of the opposition party, and therefore a minority characteristic; where the talents of legislators were an article of commerce. "And you dare to speak of morality and liberty!" Then, not to neglect Austria, he promised that the Habsburg line would perish rather than France. "The tyrants . . . and France [had] been weighed in the eternal balance [and] the tyrants [had] been found wanting." — *Ibid.*, p. 309.

[250] Lefebvre says that Carnot, too, "probably" thought a religion was necessary to the people — to prevent social upheaval (*Rév. fr.*, p. 365).

[251] *Vide supra*, this chapter, § 2f.

[252] Mathiez, *Etrangers*, p. 49.

[253] Aulard, *Jacobins*, I, 99.

[254] Avenel, *Cloots*, I, 208.

[255] Camille Demoulins, in his *Le Vieux Cordelier*, No. II, tells that Cloots roused Gobel from sleep one night at 11:00 P.M. to offer him what he called a civic crown if he would unfrock himself at the bar of the Convention on the morrow. But Mathiez points out in his critical notes how wrong it would be to attribute the de-Christianization movement to Cloots (and the Hébertists) alone (*Le Vieux Cordelier* [Mathiez' ed.], p. 62 and n. 2).

Siret, secret agent (of the minister of the interior) for Paris, reported he had found three manuscript copies of "the famous testament of Jean Meslier, who died in 1722. He was the first man to unfrock himself by philosophy. . . " Siret

which filled Robespierre with dismay.[256] "Atheism is aristocratic," the Great Incorruptible averred; "the idea of an Almighty Being, Who watches over injured innocence, is altogether of the people. 'If God did not exist, it would be necessary to invent Him.'"[257] Cloots and the other atheistic Hébertists would indeed have to go.

In his speech "On the Principles of Political Morality Which Should Guide the Convention" (February 5, 1794), Robespierre declared that "to preach atheism is . . . to impeach philosophy; and war declared on the Divinity is but a diversion in favor of Royalty. . ." He carried out this thought further as follows: "If it is necessary to defend our territory, they [the atheists] want to go [and] chastise the tyrants beyond the mountains and the seas; they want to take the churches by storm and scale the heavens. They forget the Austrians to make war on the devout. . . In perfidious hands, all the remedies for our ills become poisons. All that we can do . . . or say, they turn against us. . . They seek to arm fanaticism . . . by the very measures that sound policy — in favor of the freedom of religion — has prescribed for us." Robespierre did not fail to include a thrust at "the hypocritical foreigner, who, for five years, has been proclaiming Paris the capital of the globe. . ."[258]

On the night of March 13–14, the Hébertists were arrested. The occasion therefor they had themselves supplied. At the Cordeliers, they had plotted an insurrection to free the Convention from the influence of the moderates — as they regarded it. But the plot failed because the Commune refused its support.[259] The official charge, as presented to the Convention by Saint-Just, was that there existed a conspiracy, aided and abetted by the aliens in France,[260] to destroy the republican form of government, starve Paris,

said he would have the manuscript printed and distributed at popular prices (Caron, *Paris*, I, 259).

[256] Kerr, *Terror*, pp. 257 *et seqq.* Robespierre had had "clerical teachers and a seminarist training." — Thompson, *Robespierre*, I, 216.

[257] Kerr, *Terror*, p. 265. The sentence "If God did not exist . . . " is from Voltaire's *Epître à l'auteur du livre des Trois imposteurs*, published in 1769.

"There is nothing superstitious in using the name of the Deity. I believe, myself, in those eternal principles. . . The Eternal Being . . . seems to me personally to watch over the French Revolution in a very special way. It is a heartfelt belief; it is a feeling with which I cannot dispense." — Robespierre, March 21, 1792, Thompson, *Robespierre*, I, 215–216.

[258] *Discours rap. Robespierre*, pp. 338–339.

[259] Kerr, *Terror*, pp. 341–348.

[260] A question that could well be the object of further research is the influence of the "conspiracy of the foreigners" upon the internal governmental changes suggested to the Convention by the CPS (speaking through Carnot) on April 1, 1794. Carnot recommended that the system of ministers and Provisional Executive Council be supplanted by one boasting of twelve commissions responsible to the CPS, which (i.e., the CPS) would hold the real power. The reason he adduced for his suggestion was that the former system was an old-regime institution created to perpetuate the division of France into classes; but of course this was nonsense, and Carnot must have laughed at his argument in private. His suggestion was adopted, however, for it

and serve, in yet other ways, the sinister purposes of the Coalition.[261]

By phrasing the charge this way, a number of annoying persons unconnected with the Cordeliers plot could be presented with bids to the execution party, e.g., Chaumette, who had argued that a republic did not need a divinity, but only reason and patriotism;[262] and Gobel, the "unfrocker," who had started the wave of antireligious revolt the previous November. And just to impart some color to the charge of a conspiracy of aliens, several foreign-born persons were included in the roster of guests. Such were Cloots, Proly, Dubuisson, and Pereira.[263] Of course, Cloots's execution was only a matter of time, in any event, and this was as good an occasion as any to punish him for his vision of a universal republic under French hegemony.

Cloots and the other Hébertists, alien and French alike, were arraigned before the Revolutionary Tribunal (March 21 to 24, 1794).[264] Cloots was accused specifically of correspondence with enemy generals. A Prussian deserter, setting himself forth as the adjutant of the Prussian general Kalgstein, claimed to have seen three letters from Cloots to Brunswick in the said Kalgstein's possession.[265] (But the General's name was Kalkreuth, not Kalgstein, and an adjutant of his would certainly have known it!) A voice from the jury-box shouted: "Your system of a universal republic was a profoundly meditated perfidy which supplied the pretext for a coalition of crowned heads against France." The mob cried: "The Prussian to the guillotine."[266]

Cloots understood. The universal republic was dead, and he, the "Don Quixote of freedom,"[267] was to die with it. France had ceased her interest in the world,[268] and would strive henceforth but for her own salvation. Yet Cloots could not resist the temptation to reply to his accusers: "To the

---

was not safe to oppose what Robespierre's Committee suggested, even if it didn't make sense. Twelve commissions therefore succeeded the six ministers, the Commission of Foreign Affairs consisting of a single commissioner reporting daily to the Committee. The result of the change was a greater centralization, not more democracy. Robespierre may have seen in the scheme a means of absorbing all the power of direction in his own hands, but it was not completely carried out until shortly before Thermidor, and then the Thermidorians used it for their own purposes. The system of commissions lasted until November 4, 1795 (Masson, *Dép. étr*, pp. 307–309).

[261] Kerr, *Terror*, p. 348.

[262] *Ibid.*, p. 262.

[263] *Ibid.*, p. 349.

[264] Mathiez, *Fr. Rev.*, pp. 433, 458.

[265] *Vide* this denunciation under "Notes et Glanes" in *AR*, VII (1914), 567–569. By the deserter's own account, he merited anything but credence.

[266] Avenel, *Cloots*, II, 462–463.

[267] Girtanner, *Histor. Nachrichten*, III, 424.

[268] On February 14, 1793, Carnot, in a report to the Convention in the name of the Diplomatic Committee, had declared: "Assuming the possibility of this universal republic, the simplest means of reaching such a goal would doubtless be . . . to establish within the bounds Nature has traced for us [such] prosperity [that] . . . neighboring peoples . . . will be led to imitate [us]. . . The first interest to consult is . . . that of the [French] Republic itself." *RF*, LXIX, 68–74. The *Moniteur*, XV, 455 *et seqq.* gives a lacerated account of this report.

guillotine, then! but you will confess to me, citizens, that it is most extraordinary that the man whom Rome would burn, London would hang, Vienna would break on the wheel, should be guillotined at Paris in the bosom of the Republic."[269] Conviction was a foregone conclusion, for it was not really Cloots who was on trial, but his ideas and his antecedents. He died bravely;[270] in fact, he used his last breath to lecture on materialism to his fellow victims, to prevent them from calling for a priest.[271] Eighteen others died with him.

But Cloots's ideas did not die. They lived on in the heart of the *abbé* Sieyes, future Director of the Republic.[272] The concepts which Cloots had planted in the breast of Hérault de Séchelles, his patron on the Committee, were destined to a much earlier grave, though a trifle delayed. Hérault could not be executed with the Hébertists because he was absent on mission in the Haut-Rhin at the time of their arrest. But he was soon back, and Saint-Just found his handle in Hérault's alleged hospitality to a man accused of emigration — a capital crime. Hérault was arrested on March 17.[273]

The arrest of the ultrarevolutionary Hébertists, with their atheism, their chauvinism, and their wars of conquest, aroused joy in the hearts of many persons with whom Robespierre was not in sympathy. Something had to be done — quickly — to remove the impression that all who applauded were his friends. He had been, all along, advancing the theory that the foreign enemy was behind both the ultrarevolutionaries and the moderates, causing them to combat each other the better to confound the French people. He had destroyed the power of the ultrarevolutionaries; he would now destroy that of the moderates. On March 16, Couthon announced that proofs of the double conspiracy were being gathered, and that the guilty would be liquidated. This was the time for the Dantonists to strike if they did not wish to be next, but they only cringed and awaited their fate.[274]

The framing of a charge against Danton which would justify his execution, after so many services to the Revolutionary cause, was not easy. Indeed, Danton was venal, indulgent to wrongdoers, and coarse, and he believed the Revolution had traveled too far to the left. None of these, however, was a capital offense. It were best to trump up a bit of treason. He was accused of conspiracy with Orléans, Dumouriez, Fabre, and the foreign enemy to reëstablish the monarchy; and a web of inconsequential trifles was spun

[269] Avenel, *Cloots*, II, 463.

[270] *Ibid.*, p. 473.

[271] Mathiez, *Etrangers*, p. 173.

[272] Sieyes, however, had the good sense to keep his ideas to himself until the public was prepared to receive them. "His great art," says von Sybel, "was to advance toward his goal without appearing to; to prepare others for his remote projects — projects which they did not even suspect." — *Europe*, I, 321.

[273] Sybel, *Fr. Rev.*, III, 295.

[274] Kerr, *Terror*, p. 353.

around him.[275] Of course, it was really not necessary at that time to prove any offense. It was sufficient that Robespierre found someone's presence irksome. Danton and his friends were convicted probably because Robespierre wanted to be the one to save France when and as he thought it should be saved.

Robespierre wanted to stop the Revolution when he thought proper, and consolidate its social gains; Danton wanted to stop it immediately, even to retrograde socially. Robespierre had the welfare of the poor sans-culottes at heart; Danton was concerned with the *bourgeoisie*. Robespierre, it will be shown, was willing to make limited concessions to the Coalition to secure peace; Danton was willing to go all the way. Robespierre's moral standard was high, and he wanted to raise France to his level; Danton was corrupt and easygoing, and certainly no elevating influence. But they both wanted to call a halt to the Revolution — to normalize it, so to speak. They both wanted peace. They both objected to atheism, and Danton had been, inconveniently, the first to suggest fêtes "to the Supreme Being, to the Lord of Nature." [276] They both had powerful popular support. And each of them was in the other's way. In such a situation, victory goes to him who strikes first. Robespierre struck first.

The trial commenced on April 3. It was a question-and-answer affair, and conviction was a foregone conclusion. Two days later, Danton and his friends, plus those involved in the India Company liquidation scandal, Hérault, an assortment of aliens (to drive home the foreign-conspiracy theme), a corrupt contractor, and a few others — fifteen in all — paid with their lives for their failure to strike first.[277] There was now but one power in France — the mediocre lawyer from Arras who knew so little about human nature that he thought one could spread virtue — like butter — with a knife.

k. *The Montgaillard Negotiation*

During the de-Christianization campaign, Robespierre had frequently harped on the theme that the de-Christianizers were erecting an insurmountable barrier between France and Europe; and Chaumette was accused, at the time of his arraignment, of propagating atheism in order to convince Europe that France was about to dissolve — as a nation which denies God surely must.[278] In Robespierre's "Report on the Relation between Moral and Religious Ideas and the Republican Principles" (May 7, 1794), he spoke of the necessity of securing for the French character the respect of all peoples, and

[275] *Ibid.*, p. 359.

[276] "We did not seek to annihilate superstition [in order to] establish the reign of atheism." — Danton to Jacobins, Nov. 23,

1793, *Moniteur*, XVIII, 522.

[277] Kerr, *Terror*, pp. 360–361.

[278] Guérin, *Lutte*, I, 409.

of obtaining for France "peace and happiness through wisdom and morality." The road to this goal, he said, lay in recognition of the existence of the Supreme Being and of the immortality of the soul. The new religion should consist, in practice, of carrying out faithfully the duties of Man, and fêtes should be held to call to mind the Supreme Being — and a selected list of "virtues." [279] The report was accepted by the Convention by acclamation.[280] Let it be noted that, in the early part of May, Robespierre was thinking of peace.

It should not surprise, therefore, that in the early days of May, an emissary purporting to be from Robespierre arrived in Belgium with propositions of peace. We have two versions of this incident, and they differ most inconveniently. But they both concern the same person, the self-styled Count de Montgaillard, called Maurice Jacques Roques by those writers who are familiar with Michaud's biography, and Jean Gabriel Maurice Roques by those who have a predilection for Hoefer's product.[281]

According to von Sybel, Roques was a peasant's son from the village of Montgaillard. From his school days, he was known as a worthless fellow. Soldier, speculator, and political adventurer, he served Danton until the latter's fall, spying for him in Belgium. Danton dead, Roques became the tool of Robespierre, and as a recognized, though minor, agent of those in power at Paris, was admitted to an audience with De Mercy. To the latter, Roques declared that Robespierre wished to offer the Emperor a *status quo ante bellum* peace — that, or the dagger that awaited all tyrants. The Emperor took exception to the alternative offered, but Thugut (both Thugut and Francis II were in Belgium) and Belgian Chancellor Trauttmansdorff asked for details. Roques offered the return to Austria and Sardinia of all of France's conquests at Austria's and Sardinia's expense (part of Belgium; Savoy, Nice), on condition that England and Sardinia returned their conquests at France's expense (French West Indies; Corsica). But this would have given England no *quid pro quo* for relinquishing her conquests, arousing Austrian suspicion that the overture was merely an attempt to create dissension between Austria and her English ally. Nevertheless, Roques was sent on to Britain to see how the English would regard the overture.[282]

Roques, Sorel relates, was a former officer of the American Revolution. (He had had six years of service here.) He had long been intriguing in the

[279] Some are not virtues, but no generic name for all of them exists (e.g., Nature, the human race, the martyrs of liberty, infancy, agriculture, misfortune, posterity). Among the virtues designated are justice, amity, courage, good faith, disinterestedness, stoicism (Article VII of the subsequent decree, *Discours rap. Robespierre*, pp. 376–377).

[280] *Ibid.*, pp. 347, 375–377.

[281] These biographies were cited *supra*, this chapter, nn. 116 and 105, respectively. *Vide* also the title cited in n. 285, this chapter.

[282] Sybel, *Fr. Rev.*, III, 422–423.

capitals of the various Allies, trying to play the broker between them and France. The Paris of the Terror was not a healthy atmosphere for him, and he managed to escape to Valenciennes, where the Emperor was staying during his visit to the Netherlands. In Belgium, Roques "tried to play a role and procure some sort of engagement. He had never had, in reality, any connection, either direct or indirect, with any of the members of the Committee of Public Safety, but he spoke of them as if he knew them. . . " He succeeded in conferring with Thugut, De Mercy, Trauttmansdorff, and even the Emperor, and they eagerly extracted from him all the information they could about the state of France and its governors. Roques and the world embroidered this story, and produced a secret negotiation between Robespierre and the Emperor.[283]

What does von Zeissberg say about Montgaillard's visit to Belgium? In the early days of May, Roques arrived in Brussels. He wore a cross of Malta, and described himself as an emigrant army captain who desired to join his family living in Brussels. The famous political writer the Abbé de Pradt gave him a letter of introduction to Metternich, Austrian Minister Plenipotentiary in the Belgian Netherlands; but it is Montgaillard's meeting with Trauttmansdorff concerning which we know most.

Prince August von Aremberg had heard that Montgaillard was noisily claiming to have been initiated into the secrets of the French government, to have attended meetings of the Committees, to have dined several times in Robespierre's home. Von Aremberg arranged a meeting between De Mercy and Montgaillard. After the two men had talked together for some time, the door of the chamber suddenly opened, and Trauttmansdorff entered. De Mercy introduced the "Count." The ensuing conversation is related by De Pradt in his *De la Belgique*[284] as follows:

"[De Mercy to Trauttmansdorff:] The Count de Montgaillard is entirely of my opinion that no peace can be concluded with Robespierre.

"[Trauttmansdorff:] And I am convinced that the time to negotiate has arrived. The government of Robespierre is sufficiently consolidated. It is he who will conclude the Revolution.

"[Montgaillard, replying promptly:] In that case, I advise you to make haste, for in six weeks he will be guillotined.

"[Trauttmansdorff:] Guillotined in six weeks! Where did you get that from, monsieur?

[283] Sorel, *Europe*, IV, 80–81.
[284] *De la Belgique depuis 1789 jusqu'en 1794*, p. 155, quoted in H. von Zeissberg, *Belgien unter der Generalstatthalterschaft Erzherzog Carls (1793, 1794)* (3 vols. called "parts,"

Vienna, 1893–1894), Pt. III, 29–30. The translation given in the text deviates from von Zeissberg's because his translation deviates too greatly from the original. But the general purport is the same.

"[Montgaillard:] From someone who knows it very well — from Barère, who told me two weeks ago, at dinner in his house, that things could not last as they were and that not more than six weeks remained to raise money on the Place de la Révolution.

"[Trauttmansdorff:] Barère can say what he wants; I don't believe it, and don't dine with him.

"[Montgaillard:] That's your misfortune. Unless one dines at Barère's, one does not understand the Revolution and therefore is in no position to combat it."

Von Zeissberg follows De Pradt's account with that in Montgaillard's *Mémoires secrets*,[285] and here he closely parallels Sorel, but gives much more in the way of information about Montgaillard. Von Zeissberg tells that Montgaillard, after his military career, entered the French civil service, and a connection with Minister Delaporte caused him to fear for his life after the Tenth of August. He therefore fled to Belgium, where he stayed with his relative, the *émigré* Archbishop of Bordeaux. But he was back in France in six weeks, thereafter absenting himself only during Robespierre's Reign of Terror.

On the border of Flanders, an Austrian patrol picked him up — man-handled him, it seems, on suspicion that he was a revolutionist, and not a real *émigré*, as he asserted. Montgaillard claimed the intercession of De Mercy, with whom he had had some connection in the past. De Mercy did, in fact, thereafter sponsor him. Montgaillard was allowed to join his family in Brussels, and a conference with the Emperor (which lasted for two hours) was even arranged. Montgaillard also saw Thugut and Trauttmansdorff. These two questioned him about "Robespierre — whose barbarity they could not comprehend, and Barère — whose intelligence they admired." Finally, Trauttmansdorff said: "This Robespierre is a singular person. For six weeks we have not been able to sleep on account of him. Why should he not be recognized? In this way everything could be concluded."

Von Zeissberg repeats, from the *Mémoires secrets*, Montgaillard's denial that he had ever coöperated with Robespierre, or accepted a mission from the Committee, or had any direct or indirect relations with any member thereof. Also the denial that he had gone to Belgium to determine, for General Pichegru, if Austria were inclined to assist in placing the Pretender on the French throne.[286] He (von Zeissberg) is inclined to accept Montgaillard's statements, and put down the Montgaillard negotiation as a myth.

Let us glance back over the accounts of these three authors, von Sybel's,

[285] *Mémoires secrets de J.-G.-M. de Montgaillard, pendant les années de son émigration, contenant de nouvelles informations sur le caractère des Princes français, et sur les intrigues des Agens de l'Angleterre* (Paris, Year XII).

[286] Zeissberg, *Belgien . . . Carls*, Pt. III, 30–31.

Sorel's, and von Zeissberg's. Regarding von Sybel's, the *Mémoires secrets* teach us that Montgaillard's origin was not as humble as von Sybel's statement that he was "a peasant's son" would imply. This is important, as a question of credibility is involved. If he claimed to be what he was not, perhaps his other statements were equally untrustworthy. His father did, indeed, till the soil, but only because the mass of the family property had descended in a collateral line. And he was not a "count." But his paternal ancestors had rendered service to Francis I, Henry III, and Henry IV. And on his mother's side, his claims derived from the very founder of the Order of Malta. Even if his pretensions were exaggerated, he was still not a peasant.[287] Regarding the terms of peace allegedly offered by Montgaillard, these will come in for treatment later.

With respect to Sorel's account, that reflects Montgaillard's *Mémoires secrets*, written in the Year XII, after Montgaillard had deserted the Bourbons for Napoleon. Montgaillard's book is an attempt to whitewash his previous connection with the sans-culottes.[288] Therein will be found the pivotal sentence, "I have never had any connections, direct or indirect, with the members of this Committee,"[289] upon which Sorel bases his position. We may not accept statements written with a purpose.

The same criticism should be directed to von Zeissberg. He lends too much credence to the sentence in question. Indeed his position seems to be well enough supported by four other facts: Montgaillard, according to De Pradt, agreed with De Mercy that peace with Robespierre was impossible; Montgaillard, who went from Belgium to England, published soon after, in London, a pamphlet in which he said: "All peace, all accommodation, all negotiation with their republic [i.e., the republic of Robespierre and his minions] would be the greatest of crimes against the social order";[290] Montgaillard published other pamphlets, in October, in which he recommended the continuation of the war;[291] and one of the Austrian ministers, Rosenberg, denied that there ever were any negotiations.[292]

Montgaillard's October pamphlets do not really constitute a valid argu-

[287] Pp. 7–8. C. de Lacroix, *Souvenirs du Comte de Montgaillard* (Paris, 1895), pp. 2 *et seqq.*, explains that Montgaillard's grand pretensions were not original with him, but were inherited. His father claimed relationship with the Foix and Roquefort families, and traced his genealogy back to 1415. It seems, however, that no document exists to substantiate these pretensions, though "it is certain that the Roques of Montgaillard formed part of the nobility of Languedoc." It was the desire of Mont-

gaillard to be something more than he really was, and the refusal of the upper nobility to admit that he was anything at all, which drove him on to the audacious and not always honorable schemes for which he is notorious.

[288] Zeissberg, *Belgien . . . Carls*, Pt. III, 30.

[289] P. 23.

[290] *Etat de la France au mois de mai 1794*, quoted in Guérin, *Lutte*, II, 418–419.

[291] Zeissberg, *Belgien . . . Carls*, Pt. III, 37.

[292] *Ibid.*, p. 39.

ment, for they were published at a time when Robespierre's policy of a moderate peace had been succeeded by the immoderation of the pugnacious Thermidorians.[293] Rosenberg's denial of negotiations was necessitated by Anglo-Imperial harmony. It is recognized that official denials need have no relation to actual facts.

The pamphlet issued by Montgaillard following his arrival in London is not really an argument for Zeissberg's thesis, but rather — if it is an argument at all — against it. Therein Montgaillard described the inner workings of the Committee with a deftness of touch, a familiarity, which rules out the hypothesis that he was a stranger to that body. Nothing but intimate contact could have produced words such as these:

> The Committee of Public Safety, in which are concentrated all the power, . . . obeys Robespierre; Barère and Saint-Just are his secretaries, rather than his colleagues. They partake of his dangers without participating in his authority. . . The eight other members . . . expedite the work, never direct it. Tyrants under Robespierre, they join him in oppressing France, but they tremble at his approach. . .
>
> It is only by promising each day an imminent peace to the people, and in seeking to persuade them that the victims who glut the scaffolds are . . . [the] enemies [of peace] . . . that the Committee . . . continues to dispose of all the means of France. But lassitude and despair are everywhere. . . Consequently, there is nothing Robespierre would not sacrifice to terminate the war this year.[294]

Can we perhaps assume that Montgaillard's Committee connections were with Barère and those others who resented the primacy of Robespierre, and plotted to be rid of him "in six weeks"? But it was not Barère who was anxious for peace; he was a war-to-the-bitter-ender. It was Robespierre who needed peace as the crowning glory of the ideal society he was trying to create. "What are the other obstacles to the establishment of liberty?" the Great Incorruptible asked in a paper found at his home after Thermidor. And he himself answered, "Foreign war and civil war." (Note that foreign war comes first.) Again he wrote, "Foreign war is a mortal illness so long as the body politic is ill with the Revolution." [295] If Montgaillard was a peace emissary, he was the emissary of Robespierre, not of Barère.

Perhaps Montgaillard, a shrewd individual, was one of those who secure what they desire by advocating its opposite. Shame be unto Man, this is a system that works. We have some evidence that it was practiced on Trauttmansdorff. From the whole performance of Montgaillard, in Belgium and in England, he seems to be saying: I do not think you could make peace

---

[293] Vide supra, Pt. I, chap. vi, § 2.
[294] Etat de France, quoted in Walter, Robespierre, p. 560.

[295] From the Papiers inédits trouvés chez Robespierre . . . , cited in Dauban, Paris, pp. 456–457.

with Robespierre, but he is sitting on a powder keg, and soon will be no more. Then Barère will come into power, and will fight until your bitter end. So, though I, myself, would not do it, you had better negotiate with Robespierre before it is too late.

If this be true, we should be able to find some real evidence of a peace negotiation to offset Montgaillard's and Rosenberg's denials. Such evidence follows, plus some material of value for purposes of corroboration. On May 13, Count Colloredo wrote to Trauttmansdorff: "Regarding your Excellency's postscript, it is desirable that this unfortunate war should be ended by an amicable settlement, and that it may be true that Robespierre also desires nothing more. However, I do not know if we can trust this French 'caracteri.' At best it is adventurers and spurious emissaries . . . who seek to sound our views."[296] Von Zeissberg has himself brought this document to light, but, though admitting that it seems to point directly to Montgaillard, he tries to explain it away. The statement of De Pradt's that Montgaillard regarded peace with Robespierre as impossible, and the denials of Montgaillard in the *Mémoires secrets*, weigh so very heavily on his mind.

But the very year after Von Zeissberg wrote, appeared the *Souvenirs* of Montgaillard. Therein is recorded another statement of De Pradt's, this time quoting De Mercy after Thermidor: "What a misfortune that M. Robespierre did not live a few weeks more. He would have been master of France; the Emperor, my master, would have recognized him as head of the state; and we would all be enjoying peace at this very moment. England and Austria have suffered a great loss there." Also a statement made by Pitt to Montgaillard in August 1794: "The death of Robespierre is a [portentious] event for France and for the world. It disorders [or unsettles] very many things. We'll have to see what happens. I do not believe —" Pitt stopped and would not complete the sentence.[297]

There is much supporting evidence. But it probably should not include the letter written by von Dohm after Robespierre's arrest: "The major offense of which he stands accused is said to be that he secretly engaged in peace negotiations with one of the belligerent powers."[298] Though von Dohm probably thought this a reference to the Montgaillard negotiation, the present author has grave doubts on that score.[299]

[296] Zeissberg, *Belgien . . . Carls*, Pt. III, 33.
[297] Montgaillard, *Souvenirs*, pp. 207–208.
[298] Hansen, *Quellen*, III, 180.
[299] The Englishman Benjamin Vaughn, opposition member of the House of Commons, had fled to France to escape prosecution for taking part in a plan to promote peace with France. Imprisoned as an enemy alien, his good will had been established, and he had been permitted, even helped, to go to Switzerland. From there he had written to Robespierre suggesting a peace of compromise based practically upon the re-creation of Lothair's Middle Kingdom (out of Belgium, Holland, and the left bank of the Rhine). The letter containing this plan arrived in Paris just in time to serve as "proof" that the Great Incorrup-

Von Dohm's dossier on Montgaillard was started on June 15, when he reported "from a source I have found fairly well informed in other cases" that the former Marquis de Montgautier was in Brussels as a representative of Robespierre, and conferring with Metternich and other ministers of the Emperor.[300] Von Finkenstein and von Alvensleben replied that they had heard of it from other sources.[301] On July 4, von Dohm declared that several persons besides Montgaillard had been negotiating on behalf of Robespierre for perhaps two months, and he mentioned General Thouvenot,[302] who was one of the generals who had followed Dumouriez in his desertion.[303] This multiplicity of negotiators is a matter concerning which there seems to be no corroborative evidence at hand.

In August, one Jeanneret, a French agent, wrote to Barthélemy that "it is certain the Court of Vienna has opened negotiations with Robespierre through the Count de Montgaillard."[304] *We* may be certain, however, that Robespierre was not negotiating with Austria at that date; he was probably arranging to guillotine Mephistopheles. Of that, however, we have only circumstantial evidence. In the same class of evidence, though of better quality, is the fact that the Emperor had talked with Montgaillard for two hours.[305] It could be argued that it would have been most unusual for a reigning monarch to spend so much time — or even any time at all — with a simple individual about whom so little was known, and that little not entirely complimentary. The topic of conversation, according to Montgaillard's *Souvenirs*, was the state of Paris and of France.[306] They probably discussed the possibility of peace, but we have no right, without evidence, to affirm this.

General rumor proclaimed loudly that there was a Montgaillard negotiation,[307] but that is not really of great consequence. In fact, the previous April, Robespierre himself had been reported at Valenciennes with propositions of peace.[308] The Montgaillard negotiation seems to have been a very secretive affair, and though De Mercy was one of the principal negotiators, if not *the* Austrian negotiator,[309] he never once mentioned the name of

tible was "conspiring" with the enemy. Whether Vaughn represented Pitt, the opposition, or merely Benjamin Vaughn, is unknown. Probably just himself. But Barère — and Billaud-Varenne — by dint of much distortion, and outright lying, created a heinous plot against the liberty and territorial integrity of France (*Corr. Robespierre*, No. CDLIX; *Mem. Barère*, I, 97, and II, 183–187; A. Mathiez, "Robespierre et Benjamin Vaughn," *AR*, XIX [1917], 1–11; Guérin, *Lutte*, pp. 251–256).

[300] Hansen, *Quellen*, III, 132.

[301] June 24, *ibid.*, n. 3.

[302] To the King, *ibid.*, p. 133.

[303] *Moniteur*, XVI, 78.

[304] *Papiers de Barthélemy*, IV, 279–280. In Montgaillard's *Souvenirs*, p. 26, n 3, this statement is wrongly attributed to Barthélemy himself.

[305] Zeissberg, *Belgien . . . Carls*, Pt. III, 31.

[306] P. 207.

[307] Witzleben, *Coburg*, III, 411.

[308] *Papiers de Barthélemy*, IV, 25.

[309] Hüffer, *Europa*, I, 88. Said von Dohm, "people say openly he is the principal nego-

Montgaillard in all the letters he wrote that summer to his friend Count Louis Starhemberg, Ambassador Extraordinary of the Emperor to the Court of St. James's.[310]

Absolutely certain that there was a Montgaillard negotiation we cannot be. But neither can we be certain of many of the things about us that we daily accept without question. Science, knowledge, is based upon evidence, corroborative evidence. When we think we *know* something, we are deceiving ourselves. All we *know* is that the preponderance of evidence at the moment at our disposal points to a certain conclusion. But it is a tentative conclusion, at best. It will be necessary, however, to find some very excellent new evidence before the Montgaillard negotiation can be relegated to the fairy-tale class, as Sorel and von Zeissberg have sought to do.[311] Above all, we must beware of such historians as Heigel, who do not mention the subject at all.

Now, specifically, as to Robespierre's peace aims: at this point we must pray for divine guidance, for if the evidence so far has been meager, from here on it will be all but negative. Montgaillard has left no written evidence of his master's terms. De Mercy stated to Trauttmansdorff on June 4, "in a long conversation we had concerning . . . peace, that he was convinced that our enemies did not want to hear of peace, that the prerequisite to any negotiation would be the return of all our conquests, and one of the stipulations of the peace would be the extension of the French boundaries to the Rhine."[312]

According to the statesman, doubtless Hardenberg, whose papers form the principal basis of the *Mémoires tirés des papiers d'un homme d'Etat*,[313] "[Robespierre,] more temperate in his views, . . . wanted only to liberate Belgium, and recover all the territories annexed to France by the Conven-

---

tiator." — To the King, July 8, Hansen, *Quellen*, III, 143.

[310] *Vide* A. Count Thürheim (ed.), *Briefe des Grafen Mercy-Argenteau an den Grafen Louis Starhemberg*, Innsbruck, 1884. De Mercy even went far out of his way to remove all possible suspicion of a negotiation from Starhemberg's mind. On May 10, 1794 — in other words, shortly after Montgaillard's appearance — De Mercy wrote Starhemberg: "Now you know by direct channel everything of interest that there is to know in political and military matters . . . " But he had not mentioned Roques (*ibid.*, p. 231). On June 4, De Mercy wrote: "It seems to me that we are suspected in London of a settled plan to abandon the Netherlands, and it would be

well, perhaps, to tender a clear explanation, with frankness and truth" (*ibid.*, p. 241). Evidently it was thought that Starhemberg would be so much more convincing in his denials if he was himself held in the dark.

[311] And — among recent writers — Rain (*Mir. à Bon.*, pp. 101–102). But Rain has not consulted the sources at all.

[312] Quoted in Zeissberg, *Belgien . . . Carls*, Pt. III, 50.

[313] (Anonymous) *Mémoires tirés des papiers d'un homme d'Etat sur les causes secrètes qui ont déterminé la politique des cabinets dans les guerres de la Révolution (depuis 1792 jusqu'en 1815)* (13 vols., Paris, 1828–1838). *Vide infra*, Bibliographical Essay, no. 170.

tion. . . He dreaded war and the ambition of the generals."[314] Assuming that "Hardenberg's" source of information was reliable, this statement is objectionable because it is palpably inexact. Parts of Belgium had been annexed by the Convention in March 1793, and thus are mentioned twice—once as territory to be "liberated," once as territory to be recovered by France. Part of the left bank of the Rhine between Landau, Bingen, and Mayence had also been annexed by the Convention in March 1793, yet it is unlikely that "Hardenberg" had this in mind, or he would not have spoken of Robespierre's willingness to *restrain* his demands to the recovery of "territories annexed by the Convention." And Robespierre certainly did not intend to yield the Alsatian and Lorrain enclaves, yet these were annexed by France long before the advent of the Convention—by the simple act of applying to them the decree abolishing feudalism in France.

Von Sybel's *status quo ante bellum* cannot be accepted because no credible document forms its basis.

Let us see what can be learned from Robespierre's (or the Committee's) past actions and statements, under three headings: (a) conquests in general; (b) annexation of the German left bank; (c) annexation of Belgium.

(*a*) *Conquests in general.* Conquests imply a conqueror—a successful general. Robespierre shuddered at the thought. "The very victories of our generals would be more baleful even than our defeats," he had told the Jacobins on January 11, 1792.[315] His resistance to a declaration of war will be remembered (and his earlier pugnacity[316]—let us hope—forgotten). He eagerly quaffed all reports of defeat, real or imaginary, for they alleviated his fear of the man on horseback—which seems to have been a virtual obsession.[317] To reduce the importance of the military in the scheme of things, he glorified "the laws of Nature, which desire that every man be just and in [a state of] virtue, which is the basis of all society. Better to return to the forest than to dispute honors, reputation, riches. From this contest would result only tyrants and slaves." Then he struck a blow at the glory associated with military victory: "True victory is that . . . against factions; it is this victory which calls forth . . . peace, justice, and happiness. A nation is not illustrious because it has vanquished tyrants or enslaved peoples. . . Our destiny . . . is to found upon Earth the reign of wisdom, justice, virtue."[318] From the insignificance of victory, Robespierre passed to the menace of victory, first elucidated by him on January 11, 1792. Even the day before he learned personally the dangers of victory (8 *thermidor* II, July 26, 1794), he had asked, "What has been done . . . to anticipate the

[314] III, 12.
[315] Buchez and Roux, *Hist. parlem.*, XIII, 153.
[316] *Vide supra*, this chapter, § 2b, and n. 70.
[317] Guérin, *Lutte*, II, 235.
[318] Before Jacobins, July 9, 1794, Aulard, *Jacobins*, VI, 212.

dangers of victory? . . . Without it [i.e., without reason], victory is only a path for ambition and a danger to liberty. . . Without it, what do we care for victory itself? Victory only arms ambition, benumbs patriotism. . . " [319]

It follows inevitably, as the night the day, that if one does not care for victory, he does not care for conquests. It may therefore be recorded that, generally speaking, Robespierre was not interested in conquering blocks of sod or stone. The victories he sought were in the realm of the spirit. (Perhaps that is why he was so assiduous in increasing the population there.)

(b) *Annexation of the German left bank.* At first blush, one might think he has found something indicative in Robespierre's "We must limit our military enterprises to the banks of the Rhine," but on second glance, one sees that this says nothing about annexation or nonannexation. Not more informative is Robespierre's omission of the Rhineland from his list of what he opined should be conquered, viz., "the Brabant, the [Belgian] Netherlands, Liège, Flanders, etc.," because he was only agreeing there with the previous speaker but one (Carra).[320] We do know that Soulavie advised against annexing the Rhineland: "That would mean war eternal." [321] We also have the absolute absence of allusions to natural boundaries and the bounds of Gaul in Robespierre's speeches. Significant, too, is the harsh treatment accorded the Rhineland during his regime. Every effort was made to extract the last ounce of physical wealth, as if "now or never" were the guiding principle. The Plunder-Winter of 1793–94 needs no commentary. Lastly is a letter written by Carnot, in the name of the Committee, to the Representatives to the Rhine and Moselle Armies: "Our intention is not to engage in extensive conquests upon this part of the frontier, considering the . . . difficulty of keeping them." [322] Perhaps it should be noted that a desire was expressed, in the letter just mentioned, to take possession of the region between the Saar and Moselle; but it is not clear whether permanent possession was meant, or merely an opportunity to levy requisitions. Almost certainly the latter, because of this subsequent remark: "It is on victuals, on horses, on provisions of all kinds that we must make war on the Rhine and Moselle frontiers." [323]

(c) *Annexation of Belgium.* We have, for this, Robespierre's declared intention of conquering "the Brabant, the [Belgian] Netherlands, Liège, Flanders, etc." Robespierre did not consider it a matter of conquest. On December 11, 1791, he had told the Jacobin Club that in the Brabant, "the people would unite with us." [324] At Liège "they would mingle with our

[319] Quoted in Guérin, *Lutte*, II, 240.
[320] Session of April 20, 1792, Aulard, *Jacobins*, III, 518.
[321] This chapter, § 2c.
[322] July 18, 1794, *Corr. gén. Carnot*, IV, 508.

[323] *Ibid.*
[324] Says Rain, the clergy of the Brabant opposed itself to the secularizing policies of Joseph II, and the burgomasters to his centralization program (*Mir. à Bon.*, p. 2);

army, and even deliver over to us our enemies."[325] One of Robespierre's accusations against the Girondists after the desertion of Dumouriez was that they had sought to turn the Belgian deputies away from union with France.[326] On November 7, 1793, Robespierre censured Cloots for alienating the devout Belgians with his irreligion.[327] The no-more-philosophy decree was not strictly enforced in Belgium, as it was in the Rhineland. Jourdan was ordered "to prepare [Belgium's] liberation" by displaying "heroic virtues proper to excite [its] admiration," and measures of rigor were no longer to be broadcast there but applied only where merited.[328]

Perhaps the difference in treatment of the two regions can best be indicated by a comparison of two letters, written by Carnot in mid-1794 (July 11) to the Representatives to the Armies in Belgium and in the Rhineland, respectively. *Belgium*: " . . . Take all you can, without permitting pillage or the misconduct which could produce an uprising against us. That is the only rule to follow. We do not want either to excite or to fraternize with this region. . . But wherever you find a body which is friendly, it should be rendered more so by respecting its persons, customs, and usages, and by directing your blows against the rich and enemies of the French name."[329] *The Rhineland* (short and without palliative phrases): "Tear from the enemy all his resources, all his means of existence. It is a great misfortune to have to ravage, still it is better to carry destruction elsewhere than to suffer it on one's own territory."[330]

The next day (July 12), Carnot, in the Committee's name, further elucidated official policy with respect to Belgium: " . . . We reject, *for the present*,[331] union with the territory of the Republic, the system of municipalization (forming of *municipalités*), and everything that would tend anew to render us dupes of the hypocrisy of the numerous enemies of France found in these regions. They are conquered territories, and should be treated as

---

this must lie at the base of Robespierre's belief.

[325] Walter, *Robespierre*, p. 233. Cf. *Corr. gén. Carnot*, IV, 477; "The Brabant, in general, is entirely devoted to the Emperor and . . . has given all imaginable proofs of its hatred for us. It is not, therefore, a country to be spared" (Carnot, for CPS, to Rps A. SMeu, July 11, 1794). Accord: Bentabole to Jacobins, Dec. 12, 1793, Aulard, *Jacobins*, IV, 572.

Robespierre may not have properly gauged the attitude of the Brabant, but during the French invasion of Belgium in 1792, the city of Charleroi had greeted the French troops with cries of "Long live the French nation," and the village "host" of one battalion of seventeen French troopers had refused payment for the "beer, coffee, milk, butter, *schnick* [spirits] and, in a word, the good cheer that he had furnished us . . . Never had a Frenchman received us with such welcome and so much kindness." — *Journal du canonnier Bricard*, pp. 18–19.

[326] *Vide supra*, chap. iii, § 2.

[327] Mathiez, *Fr. Rev.*, p. 412.

[328] *Vide* this chapter, § 2g.

[329] *Corr. gén. Carnot*, IV, 476–477.

[330] *Ibid.*, p. 479.

[331] The italics are the present writer's.

such — *not to cause them useless vexations* [332] but in so far as is necessary to render it absolutely impossible that they should harm us." [333] Less than a week later (July 18), the Committee, in drafting instructions for its agents in the conquered territory, specified: "Remember that the Belgians are attached to their habits and their customs. Never attack these customs, nor their opinions. Never speak of them. . . Scorn cast upon opinions strikes the person. Too much zeal in seeking to instruct others only embitters and irritates." [334]

These remarks betray an interest in the Belgians far beyond that required by the good-neighbor policy. These people were being conditioned for annexation. And, indeed, trees of liberty were being planted.[335] Robespierre maintained an air of hostility toward this activity. He called it a "philanthropic comedy," which merely deprived the victorious Republic of the fruits of victory.[336] But this attitude might well have been assumed to shield himself from the consequences of those plantings should they misfire.[337] Whatever its cause, this much is certain: Robespierre's Committee of Public Safety countenanced — or tolerated, if you wish — the revolutionization of Belgium.

It would seem, then, that Robespierre was not disposed to Rhineland conquests — in fact, he was indisposed to any conquest. But he believed that Belgium really wished to be united with France, and hence the annexation of Belgian territory would constitute no conquest but a natural flowing together of elements that it would require violence to hold apart. If there was some reason to keep Belgium or a part of it, he would not regard his principles as prostituted.

Robespierre undoubtedly asked Carnot's opinion on this — Carnot, who seventeen months before (February 14, 1793) had declared to the Convention in the name of the Diplomatic Committee: "The ancient and natural boundaries of France are the Rhine, the Alps, and the Pyrenees. . . It would not be ambition to recognize as brothers those who formerly were such. . . " [338] However, Carnot was vacillating constantly in his devotion between a wall of fortresses, which he had extolled before the Revolution as the best possible defense for France,[339] and the Rhine frontier, which fired his patriotism; so it cannot have been too hard for Robespierre to impress on Carnot his (Robespierre's) own conviction that any conquest not re-

---

[332] The italics are the present writer's.
[333] *Corr. gén. Carnot*, IV, 481.
[334] *Ibid.*, p. 507. The instructions were not signed until after Thermidor.
[335] Guérin, *Lutte*, II, 237.
[336] *Ibid.*, pp. 237–238.
[337] He had a system which we might call "conscientious objection." He would refuse

to approve orders to which he had no objection in order to be able to attack them if they proved unwise. Thus, he consistently refused to sign military orders (*ibid.*, p. 235).
[338] *Vide supra*, chap. ii, § 1b.
[339] G. Lefebvre, "La Révolution et l'Empire," in *RH*, CLXXXVII (1939), 204.

quired by security was immoral and unwise. Carnot had himself spoken in the same vein on February 14.[340] In a report to the Committee on July 15, 1794, under the title, "Ideas Propounded to the Committee . . . Respecting the Effects upon the Northern Frontier Which Should Follow the Success of the Present Campaign," Carnot declared that "we could, if we wished, plant the tree of liberty on the banks of the Rhine and unite to France all the former lands of the Gauls; but, however seductive this system might be, it might be found wise to renounce it. . . France would only weaken itself and pave the way for an interminable war by an aggrandizement of this nature. Although the Rhine is one of the strongest barriers, in pushing [our conquests] up to it we would extend . . . our frontiers prodigiously, necessitating an extreme dissemination of forces. . . [Only] the most constant vigilance could prevent a clever enemy from managing to sneak across and get behind the armies,[341] [obliging them to retreat. This project of expansion would prolong the war, belie our principle of no-conquests, and add to France a dissentient element — the majority of the inhabitants along the Rhine — which would unite with the foreign foe.]" And Carnot proposed that France limit its conquests to those required by the maximum demands of security.[342]

The report was approved by the Committee, and on July 20, 1794, that body (through Carnot) wrote to the Representatives to the Armies of the North and of the Sambre and Meuse the following: "Hasten, dear colleagues, to send to France all the wealth of Belgium, of which we wish to keep only what can assure the safety of our own frontiers, i.e., to the left, all west Flanders and Dutch Flanders; to the right, the region between the Sambre and Meuse; and in the middle, only everything on this side of the Scheldt and of the Haisne, so that Antwerp and Namur will be the two points of support. . . It is the part to be returned that you should place under contribution."[343]

In the late spring and summer of 1794, a rumor was widely current in Europe that Montgaillard had negotiated with the Austrians a secret agreement for Austria's evacuation of her Netherlands possessions.[344] If such

[340] "It would be odious that it [a nation] should have an intention of harming [the interests] . . . of others without [the justification of] indispensable necessity for itself. These truths, written by Nature in the hearts of all men, compose . . . the foundation of private morality as that of nations. . . Natural law desires that people respect these rights, that they aid each other mutually to defend them. . . " — Corr. gén. Carnot, I, 365.

[341] The meandering Rhine is especially adapted for such a maneuver. Vide the memoir of Boissy d'Anglas to Conv., Sept. 1, 1795, Arch. A. E. Allemagne 669, ff. 236–239.

[342] Mémoires sur Carnot par son fils (2 vols., Paris, 1893), I, 484–487.

[343] Corr. gén. Carnot, IV, 513.

[344] Hoefer, Nouvelle biographie générale, s.v. "Montgaillard (Jean-Gabriel-Maurice Roques, . . . comte de)."

rumor had indeed a basis in fact (and that point will be considered presently), the interest of the Robespierrists in Austria's Belgian provinces would
be still further substantiated. Certainly the Belgian campaign of 1794 is one
of the strangest in military annals, and no account of Franco-Austrian relations can fail to point out its possible implications.

l. The Belgian Campaign of 1794 — Fleurus

In the spring of 1794, the French armies took the offensive on all fronts.
On April 2, the Emperor, though news of a great Polish revolution had
just arrived,[345] repaired in person to the Netherlands to try to inspire his
troops there to great deeds. But his Majesty's presence apparently did not
have the desired effect, for after a few successes, his troops were decisively
defeated at Tourcoing on May 18, 1794.[346] It is true that the Belgian estates
had not given their maximum coöperation. It is true also that many
Austrians felt that England and Holland had a far greater stake in keeping
the French out of Belgium than had Austria, so why should not *they* defend
it?[347] Likewise is it true that the Prussian auxiliary corps, subsidized by the
sea powers specifically to defend Belgium, had not arrived.[348] Lastly, it is
true that Archduke Charles, leader of one of the Austrian columns, had
suffered a bad attack of epilepsy the evening before the battle, and was doz-
ing when a courier arrived with marching orders for the morrow. Charles's
adjutant had refused to wake him, or to allow the next highest officer to
open the despatch. The letter had lain unopened from 1:00 A.M. to 6:00 A.M.;
and as a result, the Archduke's column had not arrived in time to sustain

[345] On March 23, Kosciusko had entered Cracow and raised the standard of rebellion.
The Russians marched against him and
were defeated at Raclawice (April 4, 1794).
On April 18, the triumphant Poles entered
Warsaw. The revolt spread to Prussian
Poland. Certain it was that the Polish
torso would have to be given the *coup de
grâce* (Sorel in *RH*, V, 270).

[346] "Tourcoing is one of the finest battles that
illustrate our military annals. . . It is here
that the *patrie* was saved." — Merchier,
Tourcoing, pp. 42, 45.

[347] Hüffer-Luckwaldt, *Quellen*, Pt. II, Vol. I,
xlvi *et seqq.*

[348] The *Stadtkölnische Reichskurier* of July
9, in a report from Brussels of the sixth,
wrote: "Already for a long time people
have been asking: 'When are the Prussian
auxiliary troops going to turn up, anyway,
and what, indeed, is the reason why they

have not been here already for some
time?'" The report continued: The 62,000
Prussians could indeed have helped. So
would it have helped if the Belgians had
obeyed the oft-repeated summons of the
Emperor to fight for their hearths (Hansen,
Quellen, III, 142, n. 1).

Baron von Dohm wrote on July 4 that
wherever he went, people were blaming
the Austrian reverses on the Prussian
King's failure to help. They were saying
that Prussian aid had been promised and
paid for (to Frederick William, *ibid.*, pp.
133–134).

Two days before Fleurus, De Mercy had
written, "We will not be able to hold
without the help of 40,000-50,000 Prussians; therefore, these must be decided to
rush (*eilen auf Flügeln*) to Flanders." —
To Starhemberg, Zeissberg, *Belgien* . . .
Carls, Pt. III, 111–112.

the Duke of York, as provided in the plans.[349] Whatever the causes of the defeat, the Emperor bestowed the post of Quartermaster General on the talented [350] Prince of Waldeck and returned to Vienna, where he could better keep an eye on the Polish situation — and grant the anxious young Empress the company she craved.[351]

The new appointee was the political and personal enemy of his predecessor, General Mack, who, though unable for reasons of health to take the field, had yet been the "soul of [past] military operations." [352] Waldeck believed it would be more advantageous to Austria to withdraw than to advance, and thought he perceived that the Emperor and Thugut did not care to keep Belgium, it being too difficult to defend and too far removed from the bulk of the Habsburg lands. On June 26, his troops, taking advantage of the level contour of the land, and of the "prodigious body of German cavalry" [353] at their disposal, had practically won the battle of Fleurus when Waldeck suddenly ordered them to retreat.[354]

The battle of Fleurus is one of the enigmas of history. Sorel, like a good Frenchman, merely says: "The French, well commanded, finished in the ascendant" (*finirent par l'emporter*).[355] The very way this is expressed indicates something left unsaid. Louis Cobenzl (Austrian Ambassador to Russia) wrote to Thugut: "Korsakov,[356] who has just arrived, assures [us] . . . that there was not a single chief of column who did not believe he was on the point of reaching his goal when he received the order to retreat." [357] The Count of Langeron, brilliant French *émigré* officer in the Allied service, has written the following explanation of Fleurus — an explanation which, in the last analysis, explains nothing. The Allied right reached its objective successfully, but did not force the French to evacuate Charleroi, which, unknown to Waldeck, the French had captured twenty-four hours previously.

---

[349] L. Pingaud, *L'invasion austro-prussienne, 1792–1794* (Paris, 1895), p. 66 and n. 1.

[350] Thugut to Count Colloredo, Nov. 16, 1793, *Briefe Thugut*, I, 58. But cf. *ibid.*, p. 182, Feb. 11, 1795: "I see more than ever that our good Prince Waldeck with [all his] skill and aptitude has certainly no systematic head. He is a boiling pot."

[351] Pingaud, *Invasion*, p. 69. She was to become a mother (Hüffer-Luckwaldt, *Quellen*, Pt. II, Vol. I, xlix, n. 2).

[352] Mercy to Thugut, May 24, 1793, Vivenot-Zeissberg, *Quellen*, III, 76.

[353] Marquis of Hertford to Lord Grenville, June 26, 1794, Great Britain Historical Manuscripts Commission, *Report on the Manuscripts of J. B. Fortescue, Esq.* — known as *Dropmore Papers* (10 vols., London, 1892–1927), II, 592.

[354] Hüffer–Luckwaldt, *Quellen*, Pt. II, Vol. I, xlvi *et seqq.*

The writer does not know why Coburg's name does not appear at this juncture. We do know that he was suffering from erysipelas of the right foot, and was unable to ride a horse. He retired soon after — in August (A. Beck in *Allgemeine deutsche Biographie*, *s.v.* "Friedrich Josias, Prinz von Sachsen-Coburg-Saalfeld").

[355] *Europe*, IV, 86.

[356] Russian observer serving as a volunteer in the Austrian army of the Netherlands (Thugut to Count Colloredo, Oct. 9, 1793, *Briefe Thugut*, I, 48–49).

[357] Hüffer-Luckwaldt, *Quellen*, Pt. II, Vol. I, l-li.

(How it could be unknown twenty-four hours later in a province under Austrian dominion, where a system of intelligence could so easily have supplied the information, is a question not easy to answer.) [358] In another part of the field of battle, the French used an observation balloon,[359] and were able to hold off the Allies by superior intelligence.[360] When Waldeck learned of these two checks, he lost his head, ordered a local attack which resulted in a defeat of only minor importance — and then a general retreat.[361] "This famous and decisive battle was won by our troops and lost by our general," affirms Langeron.[362]

Waldeck retreated to the farther bank of the Meuse River, and halted. The French pursued him until they too had reached the Meuse — the nearer bank, and then they halted on order of the Committee of Public Safety. Carnot, in his report of July 15, 1794, which sounds very much like the report of one Maximilien Robespierre, had convinced that body that victory was not of itself a goal. It was the beneficial things which came in victory's train for which France was fighting. The counsel of wisdom dictated that the armies should stop at the Meuse — [363] and they stopped.[364] Perhaps another element contributed to the French decision to halt. There were still enemy garrisons in the French fortresses of Landrecies, Le Quesnoy, Valenciennes, and Condé. It was not safe to embark on a sustained offensive with one's rear thus endangered.[365] A decree of the Convention of July 4, 1794, had threatened these garrisons with the sword if they did not surrender within twenty-four hours,[366] but they did not all surrender until August 27. Thus, it is not surprising that the Austrian retreat was followed by a virtual armistice of several weeks' duration — an armistice whose tranquillity was punctured only by the cries of treason on all sides. Austria was accused of pretending that she had been forced out of Belgium.[367]

---

[358] *Vide Guerres Rév. Emp.*, II, 44.

[359] Circumference of balloon, or aerostat, as it was called: 100 ft. Elevation during battle of Fleurus: 500 ft. Time aloft: 9 hrs. Subsequent history: captured by Austrians two years later. Disposition: museum (Palmer, *Twelve*, pp. 355–356).

[360] Comments Mallet du Pan bitterly, "The French raised a balloon . . . from which they made signals; that gave them [the Austrians] the finishing stroke." — *Mém. corr.*, II, 88.

[361] That the retreat was not approved by the troops themselves might be deduced from their "so proud countenances" as they fell back. The retreat, moreover, was in perfect order, without sign of a rout (E. Desbrière and M. Sautai, *La Cavalerie*

pendant la Révolution: La fin de la Convention [Paris, 1908], p. 108).

[362] Pingaud, *Invasion*, pp. 77–78.

[363] *Corr. gén. Carnot*, IV, 496–502.

[364] CPS to Rps A. N, Aug. 4, 1794, *ibid.*, p. 539.

[365] Zeissberg, *Belgien . . . Carls*, Pt. III, 109.

[366] *Corr. gén. Carnot*, IV, 476, n. 1.

[367] Hüffer-Luckwaldt, *Quellen*, Pt. II, Vol. I, li–lii; Zeissberg, *Belgien . . . Carls*, Pt. III, 109–110.

The *Aachener Zuschauer* reported on July 7 that, wherever it had correspondents, the general opinion prevailed that there existed a Franco-Austrian agreement to evacuate Belgium within a specified period (Hansen, *Quellen*, III, 142, n. 1).

Already on June 24 — two days *before* the battle of Fleurus — Harden-berg had written to his court: "The dark rumors that the Court of Vienna [intends] to abandon the [Belgian] Netherlands . . . to their fate are fed by the talk of the Austrian generals. It is known to be the system of the Prince of Waldeck. . . His brother-in-law . . . spoke to me in this strain a fortnight ago."[368] On June 29, Coburg and Waldeck inquired of De Mercy whether the Emperor wanted "to keep or abandon absolutely his Belgian provinces"[369] — a strange question which should supply much food for thought, and which is surpassed in novelty only by the next question, "Shall we evacuate spontaneously the conquered French fortresses [in our possession]?"[370] Wrote the Duke of York on June 28: "From the moment that the Emperor's Determination of quitting the Army, and re-turning to Vienna was known, a visible Dejection has shewn itself among the Austrian Troops, but particularly among the Officers, who have pub-lickly held a language expressive of the most anxious wish to terminate the war, even by abandoning a Country, to the preservation of which, it appears from the Emperor's own Conduct that He was at least indifferent. Before the Prince of Waldeck was named Quarter Master General, He had Him-self held a similar language, which appeared to be dictated by the known sentiments of Baron Thugut[371] whose Creature he is. The Suspicions to which this kind of language could not but give rise, have been in no small degree strengthened by an attentive Observation of the Conduct which the Austrians have pursued of late. Proposed Movements have been desisted from, without any sufficient Cause, Advantages have not been pushed, but have been followed by Retreats. . . Every thing belonging to the Austrian Government has been sent from Brussels to Cologne and from thence to Vienne [Vienna], long before the last Check, or before there was any probability of the Enemy's being able to get possession of that Town. The unfortunate action of the 26th furnishes likewise fresh ground for suspicion as the Army retreated as soon as Intelligence was received of the Surrender of Charleroi, though had it succeeded in defeating the Enemy, Charleroi must have immediately fallen again into our hands."[372] And to the Duke of

---

[368] Quoted in Häusser, *Deutsche Geschichte*, I, 565, n. 2. Indeed, some two months later, Waldeck himself admitted to Thugut that he "had believed for a very long time that his Majesty attached no value to the Netherlands. . . Yes, I fell into this error; I confess it." — Aug. 3 (not 2), 1794, *Briefe Thugut*, I, 389.

[369] Mercy to Thugut, July 3, 1794, Vivenot-Zeissberg, *Quellen*, IV (*Quellen zur Ge-schichte der Politik Oesterreichs während der französischen Revolutionskriege*, 1885),

315.

[370] *Ibid.*

[371] It seems that Thugut, in an effort to coax subsidies out of England, had let fall the remark that perhaps it would be best to leave Belgium to its fate (A. Wahl, *Ge-schichte des europäischen Staatensystems im Zeitalter der französischen Revolution und der Freiheitskriege, 1789–1815* [Berlin, 1912], p. 61).

[372] To Henry Dundas, Witzleben, *Coburg*, III, 472.

Coburg, York wrote the same story in one sentence: "The British nation, whose public opinion is not to be scorned, is unable to reach any other conclusion than that we have been betrayed and 'sold out.'" York's opinion was shared by the generality of English, Dutch, and Prussian diplomats.[373] Contemporary newspapers loudly proclaimed that the Emperor's precipitate departure for Vienna was the first fruit of an agreement to abandon Belgium, the evacuation of which was to be followed immediately by a separate Franco-Austrian peace.[374] Mallet du Pan absolved the Emperor personally, laying the responsibility for the retreat upon Thugut's machinations.[375] But there is no documentary evidence to support either hypothesis.

That the Emperor had not ordered the evacuation is at least indicated by five letters he wrote to his generals, commanding them to stand fast in Belgium or to resume the offensive.[376] If further proof were required, it could be supplied by the tone and content of one of Waldeck's letters to the Emperor, in which Waldeck blamed his "defeat" on the previous surrender of Charleroi, which he declared had been delivered by verified treason.[377] Waldeck promised to do everything in his power to "disengage" the fortresses whose "spontaneous evacuation" he had discussed with De Mercy.[378] And each of the Austrian generals gave his word of honor to the Duke of York that the Emperor had not ordered the evacuation of Belgium.[379] Thugut was furious with the generals for their headlong retreat,[380] and his draft of the Emperor's despatch to Coburg (July 15)

---

[373] K. Heigel, *Deutsche Geschichte vom Tode Friedrichs des Grossen bis zur Auflösung des alten Reiches* (2 vols., Stuttgart, 1899–1911), II, 140.

[374] Starhemberg to Thugut, July 11, 1794, Vivenot-Zeissberg, *Quellen*, IV, 331.

[375] *Mém. corr.*, II, 83.

[376] Emperor to Coburg, July 15 and 30, and Aug. 13, 1794, A. von Vivenot, *Thugut, Clerfayt, und Wurmser* (Vienna, 1869), pp. 5, 9, 13; Emperor to Clerfayt, Aug. 21, 1794, *ibid.*, p. 1; Emperor to Beaulieu, Aug. 21, 1794, *ibid.*, p. 17.

[377] Waldeck to Emperor, July 4, 1794, Vivenot-Zeissberg, *Quellen*, IV, 319. Regarding this charge, *vide* Coburg to Emperor, July 4, 1794, *ibid.*, p. 321; and Waldeck's "Observations on the Present Situation of Affairs," July 1, 1794, Witzleben, *Coburg*, III, 475. In a later letter, Waldeck added a new excuse for his failures: "The two leaders of the Allied armies . . . hate me personally, . . . [and] thinking only of their personal interest, seek but to encircle

. . . the army of your Majesty in order to oblige it to abandon the Meuse . . . to assure the preponderance of the Prussians." — July 18, 1794, Vivenot-Zeissberg, *Quellen*, IV, 343–344. Austria's allies could not accept these explanations, and secured Waldeck's discharge. But to spare the General's sensibilities, he was sent two letters. The first, to show to his friends, "yielded" to his "request" to be recalled. The second really cashiered him (Thugut to Count Colloredo, Aug. 21, 1794, *Briefe Thugut*, I, 126).

[378] Vivenot-Zeissberg, *Quellen*, IV, 319–320. Their Austrian garrisons not having been withdrawn at the time of the retreat, they had virtually become Austrian islands in a French sea.

[379] L. Jouan, *La campagne de 1794–1795 dans les Pays-Bas* (only 1 vol., Paris, 1915), I, 264.

[380] Thugut to Count Colloredo, Aug. 3, 1794, *Briefe Thugut*, I, 118.

ascribed "the deep-rooted, false impression of the Allies concerning my reputed intention to relinquish the [Belgian] Netherlands" to the "thoughtless frivolity . . . with which various officers in the army permit themselves boldly to disseminate their ill-conceived conjectures and judgments." [381]

We are probably safe in assuming that Waldeck had thought to force the hand of his court by presenting it with a *fait accompli* which he thought it really desired but scrupled to effect. And it may well be that Coburg joined in the conspiracy, despite von Zeissberg's well-authenticated assertion that the General in Chief condemned the evacuation in the strongest terms. [382] We know the Austrian generalissimo from of old: how he could not resist deluging the French with negotiations and tokens of his good will.[383] His later disapprobation may have been merely a face-saving measure.

There is some evidence that official Austria was not alien to the evacuation arrangements — but is it credible evidence? On July 8, 1794, von Dohm wrote to his king that a man possessing Count von Metternich's confidence, whom he, von Dohm, had known for years, and with whom he had arranged a secret correspondence, informed him that, some days before Metternich left (Brussels), Metternich had told him (the man) "that the retreat was a matter of agreement or armistice." Though it is unlikely that Metternich should have been so loose-tongued as to disclose such a thing, the informant, von Dohm maintained, was trustworthy. Von Dohm said he was becoming progressively more convinced that the retreat was arranged by De Mercy without Metternich's participation.[384]

Von Dohm carried his suspicions to Bonn, where the Emperor's uncle, Max Franz, Elector of Cologne, was staying. The Elector told von Dohm that he had not thought it necessary to evacuate the Netherlands. It was dissension between the generals and the total lack of a plan which had required the retreat, he said. The rumors of peace negotiations had been planted by the French to sow discord among the Allies. But by October the Emperor would be in possession of Belgium once more. Max Franz was

---

[381] *Thugut, C, W*, p. 7.

[382] Cited by Heigel, *Deutsche Geschichte*, I, 140. H. F. Langwerth von Simmern attributes Coburg's part in the retreat to his inability to reconcile himself to the loss of Mack (*Oesterreich und das Reich im Kampfe mit der französischen Revolution von 1790 bis 1797* [2 vols., Berlin, 1880], II, 74).

[383] It should perhaps be mentioned that Coburg's conduct with respect to the siege of Maubeuge in autumn, 1793, did not seem to Thugut to bear scrutiny. Said the Aus-

trian helmsman at that time: "The Prince of Coburg says that it is because of lack of money that our operations do not have the success to be desired. But doubtless it was not lack of money which . . . [caused him] to flee and raise the siege of Maubeuge after his having had all the advantage in the battle." — To Count Colloredo. Nov. 10, 1793, *Briefe Thugut*, I, 52–53. The similarity of the pattern — both Waldeck and Coburg fleeing from their victories — is striking.

[384] Hansen, *Quellen*, III, 142.

obviously uninitiated or trying to "cover up." [385] Indeed, a few years after Fleurus, an Imperial minister averred that the evacuation of Belgium had probably been the fruit of an agreement with Robespierre. [386] But "probably" is a word which covers a multitude of sins. It enables one to make an assertion without adducing authorities. Ah, if only history could be written thus!

It appears to the writer that Montgaillard must have demanded the cession of at least part of Belgium; that official Austria had refused on grounds of honor; that the Austrian generals, bound by no such scruples, had thought to promote the cause of peace by retreating under feigned compulsion. The only flaw in their plot had been that they were unconvincing actors. "The Austrians are very remarkable. . . They are delighted with their defeats," [387] commented Mallet du Pan shrewdly.

What conclusions can be drawn from the foregoing as to Robespierre's German policy? The details are simple. No annexations on the side of the Rhine — doubtless except for the Alsatian and Lorrain enclaves; annexation of that part of the Austrian Netherlands which would give France a stronger defensive frontier; and noninterference between kings and peoples.[388]

Above are the points concerning which we can perhaps venture to use the word certain. Hansen would have us believe that the formation of a Rhineland republic was contemplated by at least one member of Robespierre's Committee — Carnot; [389] but Hansen's argument cannot be regarded as conclusive.[390] Regarding the attitude of Robespierre himself toward dependent republics, we have his remark in the second series of his *Lettres à ses commettants* that foreign peoples, as a result of French propaganda, might desire

[385] Dohm to the King, July 15, *ibid.*, pp. 146–147.

[386] Hüffer-Luckwaldt, *Quellen*, Pt. II, Vol. I, li.

[387] *Mém. corr.*, II, 88. "The Austrian generals are no longer bothering to conceal the nature of their retreat," von Dohm reported on July 8. "All the strong points occupied by them are left with little or no [means of] defense. At Mons and Tournai, the French entered entirely peacefully by one gate while the Austrians marched out the other." — To the King, Hansen, *Quellen*, III, 143.

[388] Largely in accord: Pariset, *La Rév.*, p. 227. Contra: Palmer, *Twelve*, pp. 277–278.

[389] Hansen, *Quellen*, III, 157, n. 1; 159. He reasons thus: On July 13, Carnot ordered the French army to march north from Trèves, despite the fact that, as a result of the report which he was preparing for

the Committee (Report of July 15, adopted July 16), it was likely that the armies of Jourdan and Pichegru would be halted at the Meuse. Such contradictions, in Hansen's opinion, bespeak an ulterior motive on Carnot's part, and that motive he assumes to be the desire to create an autonomous Rhineland republic.

[390] It was believed that the Austrian armies, after the evacuation of Belgium, might turn south, so Jourdan was ordered to follow them if they did, and Moreaux was sent north to meet them (Carnot, for CPS, to Rps A. SMeu, *Corr. gén. Carnot*, IV, 485; *idem* to Rps A. RMo, *ibid.*, p. 487). Even were this order to Moreaux not merely a military disposition, as the documents prove it to be, it could still have been motivated by something as prosaic as a desire for booty.

to form separate republics allied with France — a remark expressed in language which showed he was not (at least at that time, early 1793) hostile to the idea.[391] It is to be regretted that Benjamin Vaughn's suggestion of a Rhineland, a Dutch, and a Belgian republic, all federated into one, had not reached France before Thermidor.[392] Had it arrived twenty-four hours earlier, we might have received at least a glimmer of light as to Robespierre's position respecting a Rhineland republic in the more sober year of 1794.[393] As matters stand, all we can say is that Robespierre did not desire to *annex* the Rhineland, and that we have no evidence that he would have accepted for his land of virtue a hostile dependency.

In the writer's view, there is little justification for Sorel's presentation of idealistic, melancholy, little [394] Robespierre as an indiscriminate revolutionizer,[395] a war-to-the-death fanatic. It seems that Sorel has permitted himself three unorthodox luxuries: He did not read far enough in Robespierre's speech of December 5 to find the corroboration of his (Robespierre's) previous stand respecting propagandism; he did not properly appreciate the Committee's letter of July 20, 1794, to the Representatives; [396] and he negligently confused incident with essence.

Anent the last point, the measures recommended in the "Mémoire sur un plan de surveillance" ("Memoir concerning a Plan of Supervision") quoted by Sorel do not go to the essence of foreign policy, but only to the means of prosecuting the war, frightful though they may seem: "The foreign agents should occupy themselves with doing harm to our enemies. In short, we must abandon the principles of finesse for a time in dealing with enemies as ferocious as ours. . . We must burn their ports, their arsenals, their factories; . . . entice away at any cost the heads of their great munitions factories, make their people realize the burden and uselessness of the war." [397] The same answer — incident, not essence — could be given

---

[391] *Vide supra,* this chapter, § 2b. It is not intended to imply here that he was later hostile, but only to date the information we have.

[392] *Vide supra,* this chapter, n. 299.

[393] Barère's attitude we know. He was hostile to the idea. He pointed out that it would deprive France of the German left bank and of Belgium (*Mem.,* II, 187).

[394] Robespierre was not over five foot three, says Thompson, *Robespierre,* II, 273. An unhappy childhood and difficulties in his professional career were probably the cause of the melancholy demeanor noted by his friends — which his enemies mistook for arrogance (*ibid.,* p. 276). His mother, having given birth to five children within six years, died from exhaustion at the age of twenty-nine, when Maximilien was six; and he could never recall her without tears. His father, crushed, and apparently demented (?), deserted his family four months later (*ibid.,* I, 3).

[395] In this respect, Sorel's remarks in *RH,* XI (1879), 114–116 are preferable to his account twelve years later in his *Europe,* III, 530 *et seqq.*

[396] This letter he has quoted (in part) in his fourth volume, p. 89, but not in the present connection.

[397] *Europe,* III, 534.

concerning the Agency of Evacuation, which Sorel might have mentioned, but did not. Established on May 13, 1794, its function was to carry off to France everything in the conquered country which France might use.[398] If the Agency's establishment proves anything besides revolutionary penury, revolutionary covetousness, and revolutionary immorality, it is that the Robespierrists were planning to withdraw soon from the conquered territories. It will be noted that when they had decided to relinquish part of Belgium, they ordered that part stripped of all its wealth — by the "Hasten, dear colleagues" letter of July 20, above.

Perhaps one more word should be said about the above-quoted "Mémoire." The archives abound in memoirs of fantastic content to which no one ever paid any attention except their authors. Affirmative proof is necessary that a given memoir exercised influence upon the policy of the Committee. Sorel does say "The Committee decided that agents *of this sort* would be sent etc." [399] The expression is vague and unconvincing.

m. The Importance of the Polish Revolution

What was Prussia doing while Waldeck was busy losing Belgium? In the West, nothing — though England and Holland, by a subsidy agreement of April 19, were paying handsomely for martial activity on its part.[400] But Frederick William was by no means idle. Since the sixth of June, he had been in Poland, making certain that in the inevitable Third Partition, the tricks that he and Catherine had played upon the Emperor should not this time be played upon him. Realizing that the power which put down the Polish revolution would be left in possession of the field, he led fifty thousand men into Poland, defeated the Poles, seized Cracow, and advanced upon Warsaw.[401] With interest centered in Poland, and Austria retreating before the French, Möllendorff — commander in chief of the Prussian forces in Brunswick's stead since January — wished the King to permit his withdrawal also.

The attitude of Marshal Möllendorff had long been an enigma. Before his elevation to the Prussian supreme command on January 12, 1794, he

[398] Pariset, *La Rév.*, p. 227.
[399] Sorel, *Europe*, III, 534. The italics are the present writer's.
[400] Treaty of The Hague; Lord Malmesbury to Duke of York, April 19, 1794, *Diar. Corr. Malmesbury*, III, 92. The Treaty had its origin in a remark by Frederick William to Malmesbury that he would gladly put 100,000 troops on the Rhine if he had the money (*ibid.*, pp. 40–41). The British government offered £2,000,000, two fifths to be paid by England and one fifth each by Austria, Prussia, and Holland — Prussia's share to be repaid later by defeated France. But Prussia did not want even to advance anything, and Austria obected to the principle of paying Prussia. Austria feared, moreover, to see Frederick William at the head of so large a separate army (*ibid.*, pp. 51–68, 76). The result was a compromise army of 62,400 men paid by the maritime powers alone.
[401] Sorel in *RH*, V, 279.

had played the role of a hard-hitting fighting man who realized there was a disagreeable task ahead and was determined to see it through. Wrote Malmesbury to Lord Grenville on January 9, "The first man, undoubtedly, here in every respect is the Marshal Möllendorf[f]; he possesses character and integrity. He thinks and reasons most judiciously. . . It is of the last consequence that he should command the army, if the Prussian army is to act." [402] On the seventeenth, Malmesbury entered in his diary: "Conference with Marshal Möllendorff — his ideas right, and intentions excellent." [403] This coincided with the report sent in to Vienna by Lehrbach, then Austrian Plenipotentiary to Berlin: "Möllendorff, a truly worthy, fair-dealing man, told the Prince of Reuss, 'I have always been against the war, but since it has commenced, I am of the opinion that it should be waged with energy, in order to end it. . . He is a traitor who advises the King to protract matters.' " [404] However, with the passage of time it became evident that the Marshal himself intended to do just that — to protract matters.

Malmesbury's first tendency was to seek excuses for him. On June 17 he wrote to Lord Grenville: "Marshal Möllendorff, against the integrity of whose character there is not a word to say, but whose abilities never were great but in the line of his profession, is now near seventy; his mind has lost its energy, and standing single, he is overruled and led by the crowd of advisers who surround him. . . He is influenced by the most paltry military considerations. His army is still in cantonments, and not a regiment encamped; by these means the tents are saved, provisions are spared, and the troops preserved." [405] It was only gradually that the world realized that the Prussian army was headed by a man who would not fight — an unmartial marshal, so to speak. What Morton Eden, British Envoy Extraordinary to Berlin, wrote in October 1792 with respect to Möllendorff and the monarchical crusade — "Möllendorff has always been antagonistic to the whole undertaking" [406] — was still as true as the day it was written.

Now, in June 1794, Möllendorff cast his eye upon smiling France and beetle-browed Austria, and was overwhelmed by the following considerations. If the bulk of his army remained near the Rhine, that would be sufficient protection against a benign France, especially if steps were taken toward the conclusion of peace. But the twenty thousand Prussians maintained in the West by virtue of the Austro-Prussian agreement of 1792 could well be used in Poland. In their present location, they could serve only a purpose contrary to Möllendorff's wishes — the continuance of the war

[402] *Diar. Corr. Malmesbury*, III, 44.
[403] *Ibid.*, p. 48.
[404] To Prince Colloredo, Jan. 1, 1794, Vivenot-Zeissberg, *Quellen*, IV, 1.
[405] *Ibid.*, p. 115.
[406] To Lord Grenville, Oct. 13, 1792, Herrmann, *Dipl. Corr.*, p. 300.

against France. However, Frederick William feared to send the Treaty Corps to Poland. The distrust existing between Prussia and Austria was so great that the retreating Austrians were viewed at Berlin as a menace to Bavaria and the Prussian possessions in Franconia.[407] The King, moreover, was not inclined to come to any arrangement with the Jacobins — a natural result of the Terror and of the attempt on his life.

Möllendorff, however, and many others, believed the Revolution was drawing to a close.[408] Robespierre was to be the French Cromwell,[409] "the master of France, . . . the chief of state."[410] The Terror was only the means of establishing his hegemony. A French rumor asserted he would marry Madame Royale and mount the throne of the Bourbons.[411] The restoration of the Supreme Being to *His* throne tended to reëstablish confidence. Möllendorff again wrote to the King suggesting peace with France.[412] Several of Frederick William's ministers, moved by Prussia's inability to capture Warsaw, followed suit.[413] But the King, though faced with a two-

[407] Sybel, *Europe*, III, 239–240. In his report of July 4, 1794, von Dohm discussed whether the Emperor, in relinquishing Belgium, would not be strengthened, not only by losing this hard-to-defend distant possession, but by acquiring Bavaria as compensation. The Emperor had coming to him a piece of Poland to compensate for what Prussia and Russia had already taken. This rounding-off of the Austrian possessions would be of great importance to the balance of power in Europe. Von Dohm thought that maybe the Austrian armies returning from Belgium would seize the Emperor's compensation for him. If these were not Austria's plans, reasoned von Dohm, how was it that Austria's best troops were so easily beaten in Belgium? (To the King, Hansen, *Quellen*, III, 133.)

[408] Sorel in *RH*, V, 280.

[409] *Mém. corr. Mallet du Pan*, II, 41.

[410] Montgaillard, *Souvenirs*, p. 207.

[411] A. Mathiez, "Le bruit du mariage de Robespierre avec Madame Royale," *AHRF*, IV (1927), 505. *Vide* also G. Duruy (ed.), *Mémoires de Barras* (4 vols., Paris, 1908), I, 204. In Lenotre, *Dtr. Louis XVI*, pp. 10–12, is told how Robespierre, unaccountably securing admittance to Madame Royale's quarters in the Temple, gazed at her "insolently" — or was it perhaps appraisingly? — and left.

[412] Möllendorff was motivated also by the conviction that Austria was negotiating with

France. Indeed, rumors had been floating about for quite some time that a peace of undefined scope was impending. Some persons "had heard" that a peace congress was about to convene at The Hague; others, that it would assemble in Switzerland (Hüffer-Luckwaldt, *Quellen*, Pt. II, Vol. I, xliii). The Montgaillard negotiation seems not to have been unknown to Möllendorff, for he had requested permission to commence a similar negotiation in behalf of Prussia (Sybel, *Europe*, III, 239). To this, Lucchesini had been directed to reply that the rumors of peace negotiations between Austria and France were groundless (*ibid*). In reality, Möllendorff's request was refused (at least, in large part) for fear of antagonizing Russia with respect to the Polish question (Sorel in *RH*, V, 283).

[413] Sybel, Europe, III, 240. An interesting suggestion, one which would explain much of the inexplainable in Prussian policy, is found in *Diar. Corr. Malmesbury*, III, 45: "Haugwitz . . . is supposed . . . to be an *Illuminé*." Cf. also Lord Holland (ed.), *Foreign Reminiscences* by Richard Henry, Lord Holland (New York, 1851), p. 52: "Of that association of visionaries and imposters (the Illuminati), his favorite, Mr. Bischoffswerder, was a member; and he is much belied if he did not resort to conjuration and apparitions for the purpose of converting the King to his views of

front war, or rather, with two one-front wars,[414] feared to compromise his honor by negotiating with regicides, separately from the Empire,[415] while receiving subsidies to fight. Meanwhile, however, Möllendorff, with magnificent independence, had taken matters into his own hands.[416] Through French prisoners-of-war, he had commenced a negotiation with France, but it was so soon before the *coup d'état* of Thermidor that all the events of significance fall beyond the purview of a chapter on Robespierre's relations with Germany.

policy, which were very versatile and changeable. . . Some odious and many ludicrous instances of the delusions practiced to engage the King in the war, and nearly as many of similar artifices to wean him from the prosecution of it, were circulated and credited throughout Europe. Many, no doubt, were invented; . . . but there could hardly be so much exaggeration without some truth." The King had joined the Rosicrucians in 1781, when still a prince (*Encyc. Brit., s.v.* "Frederick William II").

[414] *Mém. homme d'Etat*, II, 484–485.

[415] Sybel, *Europe*, III, 241–242.

[416] A Prussian officer once likened the Prussian army of this period to a small military republic which, as a sovereign state, was trying to promote peace with France (O. Tschirch, "Knesebeck und Sieyès," *HZ*, CXXVIII [1923], 106). P. Bailleu attributes the pacific inclinations of the Prussian officers — at least in part — to the Prussian custom of denying furlough-money to officers in time of war. This, says Bailleu, was a not-insignificant economic blow ("König Friedrich Wilhem II und die Genesis des Friedens von Basel," *HZ*, LXXV [1895], 239).

CHAPTER V

HAMBURG DURING THE FIRST
TWO YEARS OF THE WAR

HAMBURG was the commercial center of northern Europe, and a convenient post for observing the pulse of Germany. Both these considerations recommended the city to the kind attention of Revolutionary France, and Hamburg reciprocated by tolerating a pro-French party[1] and permitting it to celebrate freely the Fourteenth of July,[2] by legislating[3] against the twelve thousand *émigrés* with their — shall we believe it? — thirteen hundred French prostitutes,[4] and by refusing to heed the appeals of Prussia and Austria for it to join the Coalition. War would have been bad for business, anyway. As a member of the Empire, however, Hamburg could be sucked into the maelstrom despite itself. Truly, the city had certain defenses against involuntary involvement. In 1746, Emperor Francis I had granted Hamburg a diploma permitting the city, in case of wars embracing the Empire, to maintain commercial relations with all countries, even with the enemy, on condition that no contraband were handled. Hamburg had reaped the advantages of this diploma in two wars, during which she had traded freely with the enemy (no contraband, of course). Emperor Francis II had never confirmed his namesake's strange authorization; so when the Empire rendered its *Conclusum* in favor of war with France, Hamburg, continuing to trade with the French Republic (selling everything but the immediate needs of war), applied to the Imperial minister for the confirmation of the diploma.

---

[1] *Moniteur*, XVIII, 317.

[2] *Ibid.*, V, 293.

[3] *Ibid.*, XIV, 617.

[4] J. Godechot's review of P. Rudolf, *Frankreich im Urteil der Hamburger Zeitschriften in den Jahren 1789–1810*, Hamburg, 1933, in *RHM*, X, 74. The *émigrés* had practically taken possession of Hamburg. They had their own papers, their own tutors, their own theaters, their own restaurants — of which thirteen new ones opened during a certain three months to accommodate those who were trying to drown the uncertainties of the future in the sense pleasures of the present (*ibid.*; also anonymous letter of a French republican in Hamburg, July 16, 1798, *FH*, V [1911], 520).

Now, it happens that the Emperor had declared wheat to be contraband,[5] so, though the diploma was confirmed, it did not give Hamburg authority to sell what the French most wanted — wheat.[6] Bread riots were occurring in Paris,[7] and the grain situation was equally critical in Bordeaux,[8] which was horrified at the thought that commerce with the Hansa might be interrupted.[9] The "business as usual" Hamburgers could not bear to see the economic law of supply and demand violated — while profits were crying out to be made. They therefore conspired to violate the Imperial law in order to vindicate the economic law. Specifically, they absolved the captains of ships from the previously required oath not to receive contraband cargoes, and from the need to produce their bills of lading for verification, substituting therefor a wholly ineffectual requirement which permitted the contraband trade to flourish unabated.[10] Not that Hamburg ever admitted it was selling contraband to France, but a treaty draft in the French archives contains the telltale provision: no state may disquiet the Hansa cities for having delivered victuals or any other commodity to the French Republic during the course of the war.[11]

Prussia eventually tired of Hamburg's devices, and threatened to occupy the city with troops unless the magistrates of Hamburg themselves guaranteed that no goods of any nature would be shipped to France, even in neutral bottoms. "Public indignation is at its height," ran a report from Hamburg to the *Moniteur*, "but there is also a general stupor. People are circumspect, they are indignant, [but] they hold their tongues." [12] Some of these tongues were probably anchored firmly in their owners' cheeks, for we learn that one week later a company in Hamburg was willing to sell France 30,000 naval guns.[13] The Committee of Public Safety, on July 1, 1793, authorized the deal, the authorization to be on a separate slip, and filed with the secret papers.[14] And on August 4, the Committee accepted an offer to buy 12,000

[5] *Moniteur*, XVIII, 317. Cloth and skins were also declared contraband (Lagau to CPS, Dec. 13, 1794, Arch. A. E., *Allemagne* 669, f. 83).

[6] Simond, before the Convention, *Moniteur*, XVII, 501. Wheat could not be bought in Switzerland because the Austrians plugged that loophole by refusing to sell wheat to the Swiss unless they guaranteed that it would not be resold to France (Report of Hérault de Séchelles, Nov. 11, 1793, *Papiers de Barthélemy*, III, 214). Basel had cut off the rice trade with France already six months before (Rp in Haut-Rhin and Bas-Rhin to Pres. of Conv., April 28, 1793, Aulard, *Actes*, III, 516).

[7] *Un séjour en France*, p. 53.

[8] Aulard, *Actes*, II, 531.

[9] *Ibid.*, p. 364.

[10] Memoir from Hamburg to the Hanoverian Regency (*Moniteur*, XVIII, 113) and the reply (*ibid.*, p. 317). Both Hanover and Hamburg lay within the jurisdiction of the Lower Saxon Circle.

[11] Memoir of Lagau to CPS, June 26, 1795, Arch. A. E., *Allemagne* 669, ff. 188–189.

[12] *Moniteur*, XVII, 33.

[13] German guns were bought also through Switzerland (Report of Hérault de Séchelles, Nov. 11, 1793, *Papiers de Barthélemy*, III, 214).

[14] Aulard, *Actes*, V, 141.

to 15,000 cwt. of gunpowder in Hamburg.[15] Treason was fast becoming an institution.

Before carrying this tale any farther, a complicating element must be introduced. On May 1, 1792, there had arrived in Hamburg one Lehoc, accredited as minister not only to Hamburg but to the entire Lower Saxon Circle.[16] This arrival coming so soon after the declaration of war upon Austria, it is obvious that the intent of the French government was to preserve existing relations with the Hansa and their environs, and watch over France's wartime interests there. An active agent in the right place at the right time can be worth two divisions. To take one example: A ship was being loaded at Hamburg with munitions for the Prussian army. There arrived at Paris a letter from Hamburg with this information, plus the proposition of a Frenchman to seize the ship. The Provisional Executive Council ordered the purchase of the vessel.[17]

Lehoc seems to have fared well at Hamburg until the execution of Louis XVI, though in the meantime (November 23, 1792), the Diet of the Empire had rendered its *Conclusum* in favor of war. The death of the King revolted many thinking Hamburgers, and rendered them more susceptible to the pressure of the Coalition. On February 1, the Senate of the city informed Lehoc that it could no longer recognize him.[18] But the Coalition wanted more. It wished the expulsion of the French envoy. The Hamburgers attempted to defend Lehoc. He was alleged to be indispensable to commerce with France. However, inasmuch as commerce with France surreptitiously included contraband, this argument did not carry much weight. Finally, the Empire, through the King of Prussia and Brunswick, the latter in his capacity as Director of the Lower Saxon Circle,[19] ordered Hamburg to expel Lehoc

[15] *Ibid.*, p. 470. This list could be extended almost indefinitely. On December 17, 1793, the CPS arranged for the payment of 800,-000 silver marks to a Hamburg merchant for irons (*fers*), hemp, masts, and 200,000 cwt. of wheat (*ibid.*, IX, 460). *Vide* G. Lefebvre, "Le commerce extérieur en l'an II," *RF*, LXXVIII (1925), 229, n. 3.

[16] *Moniteur*, XII, 397.

[17] Session of Sept. 2, 1792, Aulard, *Actes*, I, 44–45.

[18] The *Moniteur*, XV, 616, says the Senate had not recognized Lehoc since January 21, date of the King's execution. The discrepancy is due probably to the length of time necessary for the news to have reached Hamburg.

This step was a brave act for Hamburg, which usually brooked anything for the sake of gain. For example: Six years later the French demanded a loan from the city. The chances of repayment were practically nil. Prussia offered to protect Hamburg in its refusal. But there was no refusal. The traders feared France would retaliate with an embargo, which would cause them more loss than the amount of the loan. The question of right or wrong did not enter into their calculations (Elgin to Lord Grenville, April 5, 1798, P. R. O., F. O. 64, 48).

[19] A word about the Imperial organization is necessary here. One or two of the most important princes of each circle were entrusted with the function of convoking and presiding over the Kreistag or Diet of the Circle, and of carrying out the resolutions passed. They were known as *kreisausschreibende Fürsten* (convoking princes)

within twice twenty-four hours. The Senate tried to soften the blow by informing Lehoc confidentially and amicably what was in store for him. The Minister decided to safeguard his dignity and that of the Republic by leaving the same day. The news soon became public property, and a great tumult swept over the city. The Bourse ceased its operations. The Senate was asked to prevent Lehoc's departure. The Chamber of Commerce sent a farewell deputation to the envoy, and secretly filled his ship with provisions of all kinds. The Senate forwarded its regrets to Paris, and protested its lack of power to resist; it declared to the Provisional Executive Council that it had good reason to believe that the Empire would not interfere with the shipment of wheat to France — a statement which was guaranteed to please the starving French.[20]

What was the source of this extreme regard for French sensibilities and French interests? Was it solely the desire not to antagonize a good customer? That is the usual view, but let us look farther. The French had developed a plan to invade Hamburg.[21] Considering that France was honeycombed with enemies of the Revolution, it is not impossible that the news had penetrated beyond the frontiers. Only a motive as powerful as the fear of invasion can excuse — or rather explain — Hamburg's perfidy with respect to the shipment of contraband to France. Perhaps the city was acting under duress. Its behavior was indeed regarded as inexplicable. "The conduct of the city of Hamburg . . . has revolted all Germany," wrote the Regency of Hanover, "and the very manner in which you seek to justify it is such that it confirms these reproaches and fortifies them." [22]

As soon as the Provisional Executive Council heard of Lehoc's expulsion, it decreed that the minister of the navy should order an immediate embargo upon ships of all the Hanseatic cities, and that privateers be informed that Hansa ships were fair prizes (March 1, 1793).[23] But the Committee of General Defense was not sure this was the proper course to pursue, for five days later it was still debating "the help that we could expect from them [the Hansa], . . . and if it is in our interest to make war on them." [24]

---

and *Kreisdirektoren* (Directors of the Circle). In the Lower Saxon Circle, the Kreistag had not met since 1682, yet the King of Prussia as Duke of Magdeburg, and the Elector of Hanover and King of England as Duke of Bremen, were *kreisausschreibende Fürsten*, alternating the Directorship between themselves. The oldest Duke of Brunswick was co-Director of the Circle, and it was in fulfilment of his function as such that Brunswick ordered Hamburg to expel Lehoc (*Krieg g. Rev.*, I, 88,

93).
[20] "Précis historique de la conduite du sénat de Hambourg depuis le 21 janvier de cette année [1793], a l'égard de la République française," quoted by Aulard in *RF*, XVIII, 357–358.
[21] Jan. 18, 1793 session of PEC, Aulard, *Actes*, I, 482.
[22] To the city of Hamburg, *Moniteur*, XVIII, 317.
[23] Aulard, *Actes*, II, 227.
[24] *Ibid.*, p. 270.

Meanwhile, however, the Convention had (March 4) given the force of law to the embargo and privateering decree of the Council,[25] and the attack upon Hamburg's commerce began.

When the Senate of Hamburg ousted Lehoc under pressure, it did not intend that there should be any consequences. That was one reason why the sensibilities of the Minister had been so spared. Hamburg therefore continued surreptitiously to sell contraband to the French — and the French continued to seize Hamburger ships. When the Paris government realized the anomaly of the situation, it repealed the Decree of March 4 (on March 29).[26] The Hansa's minister thereupon requested the restoration of the several vessels already seized by French warships and privateers. The Provisional Executive Council was baffled. The claims of both sides were equally good, in its opinion. It finally thought out a compromise: the ships and cargoes could be returned to the Hansa, which itself should indemnify the captors in proportion to the value of said ships and cargoes. Unwilling, however, to take the responsibility for its Solomonic solution, it threw the whole problem into the lap of the Convention.[27] The Convention did not wish to make the Hamburgers pay for the return of their own property, for Hamburg's good will was important. It therefore suspended the execution of judgments of prize courts with respect to Hanseatic ships (Decree of May 9, 1793).[28]

It was at this point that Prussia threatened to occupy Hamburg if *all* trade with France did not cease. Not long thereafter, two members of the French Naval Committee appeared before the Commitee of Public Safety, and asked for a renewal of the embargo (May 25). Undecided, the Committee adjourned the question to another session, and summoned the minister of foreign affairs to attend.[29] But the Naval Committee seems to have carried its point, for it was on the basis of *its* report that the Convention decreed, on June 9, that privateering against the Hansa should be resumed. If the Committee of Public Safety was not a party to this decree, its indecision on May 25 shows that it certainly was not hostile. On August 16, the Convention aggravated its previous decree. It decided that the owners of Hanseatic ships could not appeal to the regular courts from the decisions of the prize courts; and that ships belonging to states having a deliberative voice at Ratisbon were enemy ships.[30] Some persons would have gone even further. Simond proposed in the Convention that since the Hansa cities were prohibited from exporting grain to France, and since they had furnished their contingents to the Army of the Empire, they should be declared en-

[25] *Ibid.*, III, 531, n. 2. Aulard, in *RF*, XVIII, 359, l. 11, has March 5 instead of 4.

[26] *Idem* in *RF*, XVIII, 359.

[27] Session of April 30, 1793, *idem, Actes,* III, 531–532.

[28] *Idem* in *RF*, XVIII, 359.

[29] *Idem, Actes,* IV, 320.

[30] *Idem* in *RF*, XVIII, 360 and n. 2.

emies.[31] Now, a secret article of the Franco-Hanseatic commercial treaty of 1716 had provided that in future wars between France and the Empire, these cities should be reputed to be neutral.[32] What was annoying Simond was that, at the time, Hansa ships had ceased to call at French ports. Just how he expected them to call when they had been declared lawful prizes is difficult to comprehend. Not that they would necessarily have called had there been no seizure decrees, but they certainly could not call with those decrees on the books — even had they been willing to brave the wrath of the Empire. Rühl spoke in the same sense as Simond. He said that the Hansa cities, not forming a state controlling its own destinies, did not have it in their power to remain neutral, and never should have entered into a neutrality agreement. Replied Mailhe: Without doubt, the Hanseatic cities are our enemies, since they have participated in the measures taken by the Diet, but one does not rush blindly into something like this. There are consequences which must be considered. Saint-André concurred. We have too many enemies already, he said, and besides, "the Hanseatic cities . . . are the granary of Europe." The matter was shelved for the time being by referring it to the Diplomatic Committee.[33] It was recalled to life by the case of the good ship *La Christine*, which braved Empire and Republic for Mammon's sake.

A decree of the Convention of July 28, 1793, forbade the exportation from France of articles of prime necessity. Carnot, on mission to the Army of the North, hearing that huge quantities of prohibited merchandise were on their way to Dunkirk for shipment to Hamburg before the government should have had an opportunity to promulgate the above law, ordered the municipal officers of Dunkirk to prevent the loading of such goods, and to sequester what had already been loaded.[34]

The Hamburger ship *La Christine*, having delivered a cargo of soap and coal at Dunkirk on July 13, was planning to return on the thirtieth with a cargo of rum, tea, sugar, coffee, tobacco, etc., *purchased and loaded before the Decree of July 28 was passed*, and certainly before it was known at Dunkirk. The civil authorities would not allow the ship to sail, and the Hansa protested.[35] Thus was the question raised as to the status of Hamburg, for by the Decree of August 16 mentioned above, the entire ship and cargo could be regarded as a lawful prize of war if the city had a deliberative voice at Ratisbon.

Deforgues, Minister of Foreign Affairs, rendered his opinion to the Com-

---

[31] *Moniteur*, XVII, 501.
[32] Lagau to CPS, Sept. 4, 1795, Arch. A. E., *Allemagne* 669, f. 291.
[33] *Moniteur*, XVII, 501–502. Session of Aug.

26, 1793.
[34] Aug. 1, 1793, *Corr. gén. Carnot*, II, 436–437.
[35] *Ibid.*, III, 429, n. 1.

mittee on October 21. Therein he declared that "such is the vice of the German constitution that the college of Imperial cities is not admitted to the conference of electors and princes. . . It counts for nothing. . . Thus, in principle, the city of Hamburg and the other free and Imperial cities did not at all contribute to the Empire's declaration of war." [36] The Minister was mistaken, probably knowingly, but the error permitted a thriving if surreptitious traffic to continue. The *La Christine*, however, was forced to disgorge her epicurean delights. [37]

On April 23, 1794, the Committee, certainly on the basis of the above fiction, decreed that "citizens of the Hanseatic cities residing in France [should] be treated as citizens of neutral or allied countries." [38] Thus, there would not be applied to them the Law of April 16, 1794, whose sixth article forbade the residence of enemy aliens in seaports, in Paris, and in fortified cities. [39]

The war was destined to weigh lightly on the Hansa merchants, and they waxed fat. Their prosperity aroused the resentment of the lean and hungering Republic. Jealousy is a human trait which possesses governments as well as individuals, and causes them to plot even against those whose well-being is necessary to their own welfare. But the "great rage" against Hamburg belongs, properly, to Part II of this work. [40]

[36] *Ibid.*

[37] CPS to Deforgues, Oct. 29, 1793, *ibid.*, pp. 428–430.

[38] Aulard, *Actes*, XIII, 3.

[39] *Ibid.*, XII, 620.

[40] Pt. II, chap. xxv.

CHAPTER VI

THE EARLY THERMIDORIANS AND GERMANY

1. THE *Coup d'état* of 9 *thermidor*

*T*HE ninth day of *thermidor* in the Year II (July 27, 1794) marked the end of Robespierre's virtual reign. Under him and his two friends, the dynamic Saint-Just and the hard-working though physically handicapped Couthon, the Committee of Public Safety had grown steadily in power at the expense of the Convention. The necessities of the foreign war, the demands of the cities and the armies — which were faced with "permanent famine"[1] — and other factors, had gradually concentrated in the Committee all the power of the French state. Robespierre leaned heavily upon the popular clubs throughout France for aid in administration and supervision. According to Mathiez, he tried to bind their members more closely to his cause by effecting a social revolution — and that revolution Mathiez blames largely for the revolt of 8 and 9 *thermidor*.[2] Another view, however — and this is perhaps the best view — is that Robespierre had little to do with social revolution; that his fall was the result of personal antagonisms and conflicting aims of a less noble order.[3]

Carnot regarded the armies as his own preserve. Robespierre's plans, whatever they may have been, could recognize no boundaries. Saint-Just, who really had military ability, was sent to the armies to counteract Carnot's influence there. In one meeting of the Committee, Saint-Just entered on a long tirade against the members charged with the direction of the war, and Robespierre drew in question the conduct of several Representatives on

[1] A. Mathiez, *La réaction thermidorienne* (Paris, 1929), p. 1.
[2] *Ibid.*, pp. 1–4. As early as December 2, 1792, Robespierre had declared: "Everything that is necessary for preserving life is common property. Only the surplus belongs to the individual." — Mathiez, *Fr. Rev.*, p. 272.
[3] R. R. Palmer, "Fifty Years of the Committee of Public Safety," *J. Mod. H.*, XIII (1941), 382.

Mission to the Armies. In another Committee session, Robespierre, who knew nothing about strategy, attacked Carnot's plans of campaign and accused him of being in league with the enemy; Carnot put his hands to his face, and cried — so angry was he. Robespierre went so far as to cashier two of Carnot's own clerks, and this poaching soon led to other lines of attack. Persons — apparently agents of Robespierre — with and without credentials from the Committee, did a great deal of enigmatic traveling in the north of France, and one of their functions seems to have been to declaim against Carnot and Barère, his friend.[4]

Whether Robespierre's aim was to promote peace, and he saw in Carnot the leader of the war party, as has been maintained (by De Héricault),[5] or whether Robespierre merely regarded Carnot's hold on the armies as a barrier to his personal ambitions and so sought Carnot's abasement, cannot be answered. The conflict between the adherents of the two men was long and bitter, and on June 28 or 29, Saint-Just, after the above tirade against those of the Committee who directed the war, threatened Carnot with the guillotine. Carnot turned to Couthon and Robespierre. Without the trace of a tear, he said coldly: "Triumvirs, you will disappear." And there are indications that he assisted his prophecy to fulfill itself.[6] Robespierre himself helped. His speech before the Convention on 8 *thermidor* in which he demanded a personal dictatorship for the security of France, was a threat to the lives of all yet-unguillotined members of the Convention,[7] and the latter banded together against their prospective executioner. His arrest was ordered by the Convention the next day, along with that of Saint-Just and Couthon. Escaping, the three were outlawed.[8] The day following witnessed their execution.[9] The Reign of Terror was over.

Many Thermidorians intended the ousting of Robespierre to be only a "palace revolution." "Revolutionary government, which is feared alone by knaves and intriguers, . . . which accelerates the movement of armies and conserves victory," was recommended to the Convention by Barère, and loudly applauded. "Yes, yes, we all want it," the assembled deputies cried.[10]

---

[4] Guérin, *Lutte*, II, 260–263.

[5] *La Révolution de Thermidor*, cited *ibid.*, p. 259.

[6] Before Thermidor, Carnot sent to armies far from the capital those cannoneers of the national guard of Paris who were favorable to Robespierre. Whether or not Carnot sent them away precisely because they were pro-Robespierre, the fact remains that their absence contributed materially to the swift success of the *coup d'état* (Gen. Herlaut, "Carnot et les compagnies de canonniers des

Sections de Paris au 9 Thermidor," *AHRF*, XXIII [1951], 9–16).

[7] *Moniteur*, XXI, 329–331.

[8] Aulard, *Actes*, XV, 467.

[9] *Ibid.*, p. 487. Robespierre's epitaph, translated, would read:

"Bewail not, friend, my tragic lot,

Were I still living, thou wert not." —

L. Jacob, *Robespierre vu par ses contemporains* (Paris, 1938), p. 194.

[10] Aug. 11, 1794, *Moniteur*, XXI, 476.

Barère proposed merely to add three new members to the Committee to replace those executed,[11] but other deputies detected an opportunity to recover the independence of the Convention.[12] Cambon proposed that each of the twelve executive commissions of the Convention be attached to a distinct committee, and that each of these committees select one of its members to form, together, a new Committee of Public Safety. According to this arrangement, the Committee of Public Safety would have become a mere technical adjunct to regulate the relations of the twelve committees, and it was protested that this was not the time, with fourteen armies in the field, to disorganize the government.[13]

The Law of 7 fructidor, Year II (August 24, 1794), incorporated much of Cambon's proposition. The functions of the Committee of Public Safety were divided among three committees: the Committee of Public Safety, still in charge of foreign affairs, war and related matters, the manufacture of munitions, mines, the importation and domestic movement of food, requisitions, and (in concert with the Committee on Finances) coin; and the Committees on Legislation and General Security. It is to be noted that the new Committee of Public Safety could not arrest a civilian. This was to guard against resumption of the Terror. There were thirteen other committees, ten with executive commissions under their supervision. All committees, including that of Public Safety, were to be renewed monthly by fourths to prevent any possible recurrence of Robespierrism.[14]

This law, which formed the constitution, so to speak, of the Thermidorian Convention, remained in effect until the Directory took over the reins. August 24, therefore, marks the end of governmental centralization and the disappearance of that concentration of potential force which was able to produce unity through terror, and victory through unity.[15] The victories continued for a time, however, owing largely to inertia.[16] Certainly they were not the result of the Committee's power — or rather, of the Three Committees' power, for henceforth the government of the later Convention is properly styled the Three Committees.[17] Its plurality gives the clue to its degree of absolutism. The Convention had again come into its own.

---

[11] F. A. Aulard, *Histoire politique de la Révolution française* (Paris, 1901), p. 504. In reality, the guillotine had created four vacancies on the Committee. It will be recalled that Hérault de Séchelles had been guillotined on April 5, during Robespierre's pontificate.

[12] Mathiez, *Réac. ther.*, pp. 10, 13.

[13] *Ibid.*, pp. 13–14.

[14] Aulard, *Actes*, XVI, 310–320.

[15] Mathiez, *Réac. ther.*, pp. 20–22.

[16] It is strange that they should have continued, for the troops were bewildered by the *coup d'état*, not knowing whom to follow, and sometimes following no one at all — as was the case with the two armies encamped before Mayence (Vivenot, *Bas. Fried.*, Pt. I, 14–15).

[17] Mathiez, *Réac. ther.*, p. 21.

2. THE EARLY THERMIDORIANS AND THE WAR

It was not known just how far Saint-Just had succeeded in attaching the armies personally to his master; and the possible displeasure of the armed forces was the source of much perturbation to the victors of Thermidor. "The enemy will certainly try, by his lies, to draw advantage from a crisis which is entirely to the profit of liberty," wrote the Committee to the Representatives to the Armies on July 28 — the day following the coup. "Instruct the generals to redouble their vigilance so that a reverse will not furnish new weapons to the malevolent. . . [Let them] maintain strict discipline." [18] In another letter, Carnot, above his own signature and not anonymously as a member of the Committee, pretended to the army that the Robespierrists had been trying to "calumniate" it. "Infamous tyrants who had usurped the name of patriots wished to disorganize the victory which . . . has become the order of the day," ran the communication. "Private letters apprize us, dear colleagues, that the Army of the North has concluded an armistice, that French troops are forbidden to fire upon the enemy, and that the volunteers are about to drink with the satellites of the tyrants. These facts appear so absurd to us that we refuse to believe them, and attribute this news to the profound villainy of the . . . culprits who have just been delivered over to the avenging sword." [19] The Sambre and Meuse Army, to demonstrate its approval of the *coup d'état*, sent in a grandiloquent paean of praise to the Convention, with thirty pages of signatures.[20] The Rhine and Moselle Armies do not seem to have done likewise, but they, and two of their Representatives on Mission, were just then occupied in capturing Trèves,[21] and the Representative who might have busied himself with rousing the soldiers to some dramatic act had been summoned to Paris to explain himself.[22] On August 12, two Representatives to the Rhine and Moselle Armies reported that the Prussians were procuring desertions by crossing over daily to the French lines and chatting with officers and men; that it was the Prussian custom to praise certain corps exclusively, thus rendering those corps suspect to their fellows — a situation fraught with ominous potentialities. The Representatives ordered the colloquies to cease, and the French sentries were directed to fire upon all comers.[23] It was a nervous and suspicious France that faced Europe after Thermidor.

[13] *Corr. gén. Carnot*, IV, 523.

[19] To Rps AA. NSMeu, July 28, 1794, Aulard, *Actes*, XV, 486–487.

[20] *Ibid.*, p. 797, n. 1.

[21] Rp AA. RMo to CPS, Aug. 7, 1794, *ibid.*, p. 752.

[22] *Ibid.*, p. 776.

[23] To CPS, *ibid.*, XVI, 62. That did not stop the Prussian efforts to speak with the French. Four months later, Merlin-Th. informed the Prussian general Rüchel, who had repeatedly asked to see General Kléber, that if he had information to impart, he should ask General in Chief Möllendorff to

It must have been a suspicious Europe that faced France when, on December 8, 1794, and March 8, 1795, the surviving Girondists were recalled, and restored to their seats in the Convention. It was the Girondists who had declared the war, who had wanted to revolutionize the world. But suffering had tamed their spirits. Some of them had even become royalists.[24] They were rather an element conducive to peace and order.

Internal conditions in France were certainly favorable to the development of a desire for peace. The winter of 1794–95 was the harshest since 1709,[25] and to make matters worse, the Seine had frozen over from bank to bank, halting the already insufficient traffic in coal and wood. There was nothing to do but hew down the trees at Boulogne, Vincennes, and Saint-Cloud, and unscrupulous persons plied a lucrative trade in this wood — at four hundred francs per cord! [26] Of course the poor could not pay such prices. They sawed up their wooden bedsteads and burned them to keep warm. When they had no more to burn, they perished from the cold. The government found itself obliged to ration candles as well as meat and bread. The rationing of candles cut down the number of hours per day that the poor could work, and increased their already-overwhelming hardships; but the most serious problem, as under Robespierre, was the shortage of bread and meat.[27]

The legal bread ration was theoretically a half pound per person per day. In practice, however, several days would often elapse during which no bread was distributed at all, either because there was no wheat, or because wheat could not be bought with the worthless assignats.[28] When a few loaves would become available, long lines of shivering people would stand for hours, even all night,[29] outside the bakeries, where each person received — if he was fortunate — four ounces or less at an exorbitant price. This was especially hard on the poor, who often had nothing to eat but

transmit it through regular diplomatic channels (Merlin-Th. to CPS, Jan. 2, 1795, ibid., XIX, 235 and n. 1).

[24] Aulard, Hist. pol. Rév. fr., p. 524.

[25] Sorel, Europe, IV, 217. On the winter of 1709, vide A. de Boislisle, "Le grand hiver et la disette de 1709," RQH (Revue des questions historiques), LXXIII (1903), 442–509; LXXIV (1903), 486–542. Hunger and cold being the same in any generation, these two winters produced much the same repercussions — even down to the organized raids on the farms, mentioned in the text below.

[26] Even five hundred francs (F. A. Aulard [ed.], Paris pendant la réaction thermidorienne et sous le Directoire [5 vols., Paris, 1898–1902], I, 423). The franc replaced the livre during this winter of 1794–95 (Moniteur, XXIV, 195).

[27] Mercier, Paris . . . Rév., I, 355–357.

[28] "Memorandum on the State of France, founded on the Reports of British Diplomatic Agents," Dropmore Papers, III, 82–83.

[29] Scandalous immorality during these all-night vigils posed a difficult problem for the police. Finally bakers were forbidden to sell bread before 5:00 A.M. Vide Mercier, Paris . . . Rév., I, 353–354.

bread, and habitually consumed two pounds daily per person.[30] One father with a hungry child tried to buy some wheat direct from a farmer, and received such a beating from the latter that he could barely work afterwards.[31] Probably the farmer had hungry children too, for the Commissioners of the government seized most of every crop for the army and the cities and the speculators — or perhaps one should say for the speculators and the army and the cities. This discouraged the planting of crops, with resultant bankruptcy for the farmer and misery for the nation.

The meat situation was equally tragic. Requisitions of cattle to feed the army had created such a shortage of meat that many of the few remaining milch cows were slaughtered. When these were gone, there were no milch cows and no milk. As the supply of milk dwindled, there developed a shortage of butter, which caused people to abstain from purchasing fish till the milch cows had been consumed.[32] When that time came, the catch was already so tainted that grave illness resulted. Those who survived purchased what they could of lamb — at fifteen francs a pound! [33] Fortunately the meat ration was only one tenth of a pound per person per day, but to the workman, that tenth of a pound represented almost his entire wages, sometimes more. It was the speculators in national lands, contractors, and jobbers alone who could meet such prices. They bought up all the lamb — and the poultry. Followed also a famine in eggs. The government had "frozen" the sale of beans, lentils, and peas for army use, so there were no substitute protein foods. There was only one course open: band together and raid the farms. It was tried. Some raiders, after glutting themselves, even sold the farmers' goods to speculators before their owners' very eyes. The result was the complete disappearance of protein foods from the French market.[34]

This shortage was, in its inception, not wholly an "act of God." Human covetousness had contributed to give it life. The police report of December 16, 1794, said: "The meat market [had] less stock [today than usual]." On December 21, the report ran: "No butter or eggs at all." On December 24: "The meat market was poorly stocked." But on that selfsame day, December 24, the Law of the Maximum, the Revolution's ceiling-price law, was repealed. On December 26, the police report announced that there had "arrived on the floor of the market 2,300 pounds of butter and 20,500 eggs."

[30] On March 15, 1795, the Convention decreed that those who worked with their hands should receive at least 1.5 lb. of bread per day, reducing if necessary the portions of those nonlaborers who could afford to buy substitute foods at whatever price was demanded (*Moniteur*, XXIII, 699).
[31] *Un séjour en France*, p. 264.
[32] The author knows not the connection between butter and fish.
[33] Some women announced vociferously that they preferred to pay more for meat, and to be able to buy it at their pleasure, than to pay less and have none at all (Dauban, *Paris*, p. 185). The meat famine seems to have been particularly acute at Paris (*ibid.*, p. 167).
[34] Mercier, *Paris . . . Rév.*, I, 350-353.

The next day it stated that "the [meat] market was fairly well stocked. Sales were without disturbance, but at exorbitant prices." [35] Apparently there was still enough to eat — for those who could pay fantastic prices. On December 29, the police report commented that "laborers, and citizens who have modest positions, are no longer able to obtain the necessities of life." [36] And on January 5, it related that people were complaining that prices in Paris had doubled since the repeal of the Maximum only eleven days before.[37] Thus, though succeeding police reports affirmed that the markets were well stocked except for the vegetable market,[38] there was an actual dearth of available food as far as the common man was concerned.[39] Although the famine was partly an artificially created famine, it was no less real to the starving populace. And after the victuals coaxed out of hiding by the repeal of the Maximum were exhausted, the famine became very real indeed.

Now, without meat, fish, eggs, butter, milk, legumes, candles, and fuel, revolt brewed in the hearts of many Frenchmen. And since the needs of the army were largely responsible for the famine, the revolt took the form of opposition to the Convention's foreign policy. One actual example will suffice — that of the father who had been beaten for trying to obtain bread for his little daughter.

This morning I asked a man who was sawing wood for us why the church bells had pealed all night.

"I've been told," he replied, "that it was for some city captured by a general of the Republic. That will help us stupendously, won't it! Peace and bread would do us a lot more good than all these conquests."

I told him he ought to observe more prudence in his speech.

"To die or to die," he said almost gaily. "I'd just as lief die on the guillotine as from hunger. My little girl hasn't had any bread for the last two days. . ." [40]

A dangerous attitude, this! Yet what was still more dangerous were the rumors of impending peace sweeping the army, and undermining its will

---

[35] Aulard, *Paris*, I, 320, 327–328, 336, 341.

[36] *Ibid.*, p. 349.

[37] *Ibid.*, p. 367.

[38] *Ibid.*, pp. 345, 361, 362, 423, 429, 450, 454, 456, 469.

[39] *Ibid.*, p. 477; *vide* also pp. 351, 365.

[40] *Un séjour en France*, pp. 264–265. Examples could be multiplied ad infinitum. Following is an interesting one from the Paris police reports: "Goupilleau announces that order reigns in his *arrondissement*, but he adds that, wherever he goes, he hears only murmurs against the constituted authorities, even against the national representation and the present government, because of the reputed lack of everything; that, when an attempt is made to console and encourage the discontented, they respond: 'Yes, but we have to pay six times more than under the old regime. . . Formerly, I got these sabots for 12 sous; today I must pay 3 livres 10 sous for them. . . I have just paid 70 livres for a load of wood, and you talk to me of the Republic! Give me the means of keeping alive and of enabling my family to live, and I will love the Republic.' " — Aulard, *Paris*, I, 357–358.

to fight.[41] No fighting, no war, is axiomatic if the enemy is of kindred disposition. "We noted with some anxiety," wrote the Committee of Public Safety to Merlin of Thionville, "that . . . you spoke of the desire of the army [for peace]. . . You know how vexatious it could be if it were suspected that the desires of the army decided the question of war or peace." [42]

Was there any justification for the peace rumors? A categorical "no" would be misleading. There were secret negotiations going on between Austria and France, or rather, between individuals in behalf of the two countries, with official connivance. Augeard, formerly Marie Antoinette's private secretary, chatted with Bacher at the end of 1794, and informed the Vienna Court that France preferred peace with Austria to peace with Prussia. Augeard suggested a negotiation based upon the exchange of Belgium for Alsace. Thugut did not regard this suggestion seriously, but he did authorize Augeard to continue supplying information to the Court, and cautioned "absolute silence concerning the divers facts and ideas contained in these letters." Another contact seems to have been established through the channel of one Pellenc, whom Wickham, British agent in Switzerland, later characterized as "the principal agent of these negotiations." [43] "People are talking a good deal about peace, about negotiations commenced," wrote Queen Caroline of Naples to her daughter, the Empress. "I do not meddle in such things at all, and shall not; but this is of too great interest and importance to us. . . Ask your dear husband, in our name, not to let us learn about it through the newspapers." [44]

It was the rumors of peace which prompted Merlin of Douai on December 4 to outline to the Convention the foreign policy of the Thermidorian Committee of Public Safety. Merlin denied that France was averse to making peace with nonrepublican states, and rejected upon Robespierre all responsibility for the credit such an idea might have acquired. France was willing to conclude peace, he said, "but we want [a peace] guaranteed by our own power and the powerlessness of our enemies ever to harm us." And he then declared that it was not the proper time to make peace: "No, Frenchmen, no! You . . . have not advanced so rapidly in this glorious career to halt at the moment when the goal is in sight. . . Soon we will prove, by

[41] Merlin-Th., to CPS, Dec. 12, 1794, *idem*, *Actes*, XVIII, 668.

[42] Dec. 15, 1794, *ibid.*, p. 730.

[43] A. Sorel, "L'Autriche et le Comité de Salut Public, avril 1795," *RH*, XVII (1881), 51–53. Pellenc had been the secretary of Mirabeau and was now in the employ of Austria. The *Mém. homme d'Etat* states that, at the end of the campaign of 1794, the French intriguer Poteratz was sent on a secret mission to Thugut (III, 201). Poteratz, whose name is well-nigh universally misspelled "Poterat" (*vide* Appendix A *infra*, "Poteratz vs. Poterat, with the Archives as Umpire"), is dealt with at length in Pt. I, chap. xv, and in Pt. II, chaps iii, vi, viii, ix, *et passim*.

[44] Aug. 9, 1794, Vivenot-Zeissberg, *Quellen*, IV, 384.

new efforts and new triumphs, that we also desire peace, but a peace worthy of our intrepid defenders. . . In a word, when the French people no longer regard the war as necessary either to appease their wounded dignity or to guarantee themselves against new perfidies, then only will they rein in the steeds of victory, then only will they command peace." [45]

The next day, on André Dumont's motion, the Convention ordered Merlin's speech translated into "every tongue" and sent to all the armies [46] and all the communes, in order that the French people might say with the Convention: "Peace, but a durable and glorious peace." Dumont ascribed the rumors of peace to Robespierrists.[47]

If this attitude needed verification, that was not long in forthcoming. In August 1794, Greiffenegg, President of the Imperial Administration of the Breisgau, had sent an agent across the Rhine to learn what he could about the attitude and resources of Thermidorian France. The agent was at Paris from October 3 to December 21, 1794. His report declared that the majority of the Convention was in favor of continuing the war, and that its war aims were of such a nature that France's enemies could not possibly subscribe thereto.[48]

Yet further verification was provided by a remark issuing from Bourdon, a member of the Convention, in reply to a speech made by Boissy d'Anglas in the Committee's name. Boissy's speech, delivered before the Convention on January 30, 1795, declared that the need for indemnities and for a just and durable peace guaranteeing France from "all invasion . . . for a long series of centuries," obliged the Republic to extend its frontiers to those designated by Nature. To this, Bourdon added: "I . . . applaud . . . my colleague, who has had the courage to come, in the midst of the prosperity of our arms, . . . to say that we have fought only for our liberty, that we will confine ourselves within the limits that Nature has prescribed." [49] Apparently victory had advanced some minds in the Convention beyond the natural-boundary stage, else it would not have required courage to suggest the natural boundaries as a frontier.

[45] Dec. 4, 1794, Moniteur, XXII, 667–668. This extended quotation shows how misleading is the statement in Stephens, Rev. Eur., pp. 148–149 that "Merlin . . . read a report . . . declaring that the Republic did not wish to be at war with Europe for ever." There is nothing in Merlin's speech which could conceivably serve as the basis for so general a statement, though, had Mr. Stephens spoken alone of peace with Prussia, he could not be criticized.
[46] There it would find itself in good company.

On November 14, Carnot had written, in the name of the Committee, to the Representatives to the Rhine and Moselle Armies: "Let it not be said, dear colleagues, that you suffer the enemy to keep a foot of our territory, for we regard as such all that is on this side of the Rhine. Victory . . . gives us the deed to it." — Corr. gén. Carnot, IV, 709.
[47] Moniteur, XXII, 671.
[48] Sorel in RH, XVII, 51.
[49] Moniteur, XXIII, 343.

3. THE EARLY THERMIDORIANS AND AUSTRIA

The early Thermidorians, then, were not pining for peace. The trend of battle was too much in their favor. The Austrians, on the other hand, being on the receiving end of the French muskets, were surfeited with the conflict. Some generals asseverated that they would not fight another campaign, and that no one could induce them to cross the Rhine. Civil authorities were protesting against the extraordinary taxes. The Hungarian harvest was exceptionally insufficient that season.[50] The young Grand Duke of Tuscany, the Emperor's brother, who had signed a treaty with France on February 9, 1795,[51] wrote to the Austrian ruler that he also could conclude peace with facility, "for the whole French nation wants and needs it and is only waiting for the other powers to make an overture."[52] Lastly, an unsigned memoir, "How Can Austria Withdraw from the War of the French Revolution with Honor and Advantage?" which advocated peace with France and war on Prussia for the recovery of Silesia,[53] was read "with gusto" by the Emperor and sent to Thugut for his remarks. The latter, it seems, did not like the document's pro-French flavor.[54]

Thugut was not unwilling, however, to bring the French war to a close — if that could be done without violating Austria's obligations to her allies, or enabling the revolutionary principles to blanket Europe. Though the *Reichsfriedensgutachten* (Decision Concerning the Peace of the Empire)[55] of December 22, 1794, which expressed the hope of peace with France through the concurrent mediation of the Emperor and of the King of Prussia,[56] was disagreeable to Austria in so far as the coöperation of Prussia was concerned, it struck a note which resounded throughout the Habsburg dominions[57] — and all of Germany,[58] where general discouragement prevailed.[59]

---

[50] Authority for this point alone: T. Grenville to Lord Grenville, Sept. 15, 1794, *Dropmore Papers*, II, 631.

[51] Thugut had long been watching what he called the "Florentine intrigues. . . The very culpable . . . cabinet of Tuscany . . . has never ceased to be in collusion with the French." But Thugut had not expected the "intrigues" to lead to peace. "The Convention wants to keep its hands free," he had written to Count Colloredo as late as November 20, 1794 (*Briefe Thugut*, I, 153–154).

[52] Feb. 10 and April 7, 1795, Vivenot-Zeissberg, *Quellen*, V, 99, 156. Rumor at Basel said that Tuscany had been charged to

negotiate peace for Austria (Degelmann to Thugut, Feb. 18, 1795, *ibid.*, p. 105).

[53] Cf. Lebrun's early offer of Austrian Silesia to Prussia, to induce Frederick William to desert the Coalition (*supra*, chap. iii, § 3).

[54] Hüffer-Luckwaldt, *Quellen*, Pt. II, Vol. I, lv-lvii; Emperor to Thugut, March 6, 1795, Vivenot-Zeissberg, *Quellen*, V, 125.

[55] Vivenot, *Bas. Fried.*, Pt. I, 246. *Vide* next section.

[56] Art. 4.

[57] Hüffer-Luckwaldt, *Quellen*, Pt. II, Vol. I, lv *et seqq.*

[58] Sybel, *Europe*, III, 366.

[59] Emperor to Saxe-Teschen, Dec. 31, 1794, Vivenot, *Bas. Fried.*, Pt. I, 133, n. 1.

For political reasons, also, it was desirable that Austria should come to terms with France. The Russo-Prussian Treaty of January 23, 1793, the Second Polish Partition treaty, had excluded Austria from all share, the wily Catherine having realized that Austria was already so immersed in the war that she could not withdraw, so there was no need of bribing her to continue — with territory which Catherine might herself want some day.[60] Thugut, when he came to the helm, had renounced Austria's claims against Russia in order to gain Catherine's support against Prussia.[61] Russia charged herself to restrain Prussia as long as the war in the West continued,[62] and by the Treaty of January 3, 1795, the Czarina solemnly promised Austria the Palatinates of Cracow and Sandomir,[63] which had already been occupied by Prussia,[64] and the aid of the entirety of Russia's forces if Prussia should attack Austria for any reason whatsoever.[65] It was this possibility of war with Prussia which rendered a Franco-Austrian composition desirable — even vital, for time brought to light the startling fact that, in case of an Austro-Prussian conflict, Catherine expected Austria to bear the major share of the burden.[66] This was, however, quite foreign to the obvious intention of the Treaty, and hence unsuspected as yet.

The Treaty of January 3, 1795 appeared the triumph of Thugut's statesmanship, for it forced Prussia to the wall, as Austria had been forced to the wall in 1793.[67] However, it deprived Austria of her freedom of action, for the concessions from Catherine had been purchased at the expense of a promise to continue with vigor the war against "the French Jacobins." [68]

---

[60] Sorel in *RH*, V, 267.

[61] *Vide* R. Lodge, "The Extinction of Poland, 1788–97," *C. Mod. H.*, VIII, 549.

[62] Thugut to Count Colloredo, Dec. 4, 1793, *Briefe Thugut*, I, 61.

[63] This is the form in Sorel's *Europe*, the *Dropmore Papers*, and F. W. Putzger, *Historischer Schul-Atlas zur alten, mittleren und neuen Geschichte* (28th ed., Leipzig, 1904), Plate 25. Variants are Sendomir, Sendomiers, and Sandomierz.

[64] Catherine had the choice of giving the Emperor some of the Polish territory she had occupied, or some that Frederick William had occupied. She chose the latter. The Hohenzollern king did not like the rules of the new game, and refused to play. Thus arose the Cracow-Sandomir controversy (Whitworth [Brit. ambas. to Russia] to Lord Grenville, Nov. 4, 1794, and Feb. 6, 1795, Herrmann, *Dipl. Corr.*, pp. 502, 509).

[65] Hüffer-Luckwaldt, *Quellen*, Pt. II, Vol. 1, lvii–lix. The Czarina also recognized in the

Treaty the claims of Austria to Bavaria, and to supplementary indemnity at the expense of the Venetian possessions in case a slice of France could not be obtained. It was to take care of this contingency that Thugut refused to recognize Louis XVIII. In compensation for the Second Polish Partition, Catherine dangled before Austria's eyes the expectation of Turkish territory (*ibid.*; Guyot, *Direc.*, pp. 98–99; Häusser, *Deutsche Geschichte*, I, 583–584).

[66] Thugut to L. Cobenzl, Sept. 30, 1795, Vivenot-Zeissberg, *Quellen*, V, 402.

[67] Thugut to Count Colloredo, Jan. 22, 1795: "The King of Prussia has been foiled quite in the same manner as we were two years ago by the famous Convention of January 23, 1793." — *Briefe Thugut*, I, 175.

[68] Sybel, *Europe*, III, 370. Russia knew that she was asking not a little, that Austria wanted "to have her hands free to apply herself to an object which interested her much more intimately, viz., to secure an adequate in-

Moreover, as will appear later, it helped to drive Prussia out of the Coalition, and threatened for a time to cause the Hohenzollern ruler to ally with France to resist by force of arms the pretensions of Austria and Russia.[69] But more of this anon. What concerns us here is only the attitude of Austria regarding peace with France during the closing days of 1794 and the early part of 1795. It appears that she was not averse to peace, but that her hands were bound — bound by the clanking chains of the ghost of Poland. Perhaps it was just as well, for peace is a reciprocal affair, and the Thermidorians, flushed with victory, could not readily have brought themselves to halt their conquering legions, especially when their antagonist was Austria.[70]

4. THE EARLY THERMIDORIANS AND PRUSSIA

It will be recalled that the Prussian field marshal Möllendorff, despite the repugnance of his monarch to treat with regicides or to negotiate with the Empire's enemy while receiving subsidies to fight, had opened with France negotiations which he hoped would lead to peace. The mechanics of Möllendorff's overture was simple. The Marshal asked one of Brunswick's lieutenants to write a letter in the French tongue, affirming his, Möllendorff's, desire for an exchange of prisoners, and his willingness to do anything to that end which would not compromise himself or the interests of his court. This letter Möllendorff turned over to some French officers who were prisoners, with the request that they inform the Convention of his friendly disposition. The officers wrote the following note of their own: Möllendorff's letter indicates his prime motive, "but he has told us verbally many other things. . . The Prussians desire to institute negotiations with France. When they know her intentions in the matter, they will send a delegate. . . Until the final conclusion, they request that their overture remain covert." [71]

The combined messages were delivered to Barthélemy at his sumptuous residence in Baden, Switzerland, on July 31, 1794, by a Kreuznach wine

---

demnity, and to check the too rapid growth of her rival." The Russian chancellor, Count Ostermann, declared to Charles Whitworth, as fact, that if Prussia refused to yield a part of the Palatinates of Cracow and Sandomir to Austria, the Emperor would make peace with France on the best terms possible, and attend to Prussia himself; and Whitworth lent a good deal of credence to this statement (Whitworth to Lord Grenville, Feb. 6, 1795, Herrmann, *Dipl. Corr.*, p. 509; *vide* Thugut to L. Cobenzl, Sept. 30, 1795, Vivenot-Zeissberg, *Quellen*, V, 402). It was owing to Prussia's stubbornness in the Cracow-Sandomir

controversy, and to the intrigues of the French agent Descorches de Sainte-Croix at Constantinople, that Catherine was afraid to weaken her forces by contributing concrete military aid to the war against France (Whitworth to Lord Grenville, Feb. 6, 1795, Herrmann, *Dipl. Corr.*, p. 509; Sorel, *Europe*, III, 527).

[69] Sybel, *Europe*, III, 518.
[70] Jordis to Saxe-Teschen, Nov. 25 and 27, 1794, Vivenot, *Bas. Fried.*, Pt. II, 51. *Vide* also Clerfayt to Saxe-Teschen, Oct. 19, 1792, Vivenot-Zeissberg, *Quellen*, II, 279.
[71] Sorel in *RH*, V, 284.

merchant named Schmerz. Barthélemy was busy with visitors when Schmerz arrived, and the messages were handed to an employee. When presently it was desired to speak personally with the messenger, he could not be found, despite a thorough search of the house and gardens; yet he had not been seen to leave. All that was known of him was what the servant who took the packet could remember: a poorly dressed German civilian speaking an atrocious French.[72]

But the elusive visitor appeared again, only this time at Basel, at the home of the burgomaster, Ochs. Ochs was on very friendly terms with the French delegation, especially with Bacher, and Schmerz was soon able to confide personally to Bacher the purpose of his mission. This, according to Bacher's report, included the negotiation of an armistice to become effective as soon as the subsidy treaty with England had expired (December 1, 1794) — the Prussians meanwhile to "act only weakly." Bacher was convinced of the great importance of this negotiation, but the Thermidorians were too immersed in their *coup d'état* to have a taste for anything else.[73] Perhaps it was better so, for Möllendorff was supported by not a shred of authority when he offered to "act weakly" and proposed an armistice. How the King would have received his meddling, had he known, may be judged from Frederick William's reply to his former minister Hertzberg's unsolicited suggestion that Prussia "offer . . . an armistice to the belligerent powers, and even definitive peace upon the basis of the *status quo ante bellum*." [74] Follows the King's reply:

I had counted on your discretion to spare me advice which I value only in so far as I seek it. Leave it to the ministers whom my confidence has placed at the head of affairs . . . to receive my orders and execute them. I can appreciate patriotism, and I should like to believe that it alone has inspired your offers. But it may be that self-love has taken the form of patriotism in your eyes, and deceived you as to your true motives. I should be charmed if this idea placed you sufficiently on guard against yourself as to confine you henceforth within the circle of your actual duties.[75]

It is not that Frederick William was opposed to a cessation of hostilities against France. The Polish expedition was going too badly for him to be so foolish as that. What plagued him was his honor. He was determined not

[72] A. J. F. Fain, *Manuscrit de l'an trois* (Paris, 1828), p. 21; Sorel in *RH*, V, 284–285.
[73] *Ibid.*, pp. 286–287. A glance through Vols. XV–XIX of Aulard's *Actes* will emphasize to what extent the *coup d'état* of Thermidor colored the remainder of the year 1794.
[74] *Mém. homme d'Etat*, II, 490.

[75] *Ibid.*, p. 494. Sorel in *RH*, V, 283, n. 1 gives this reference erroneously as p. 498. On December 29, 1793, Lord Malmesbury wrote in his diary: "Dined at Hertzberg's — found him shewing three Poles, on a map, how *he* would have divided Poland, if he had been consulted." — *Diar. Corr.*, III, 35.

to be the first to broach the subject of peace — to desert the Empire.[76] But whereas the stubborn King would not yield in the face of adversity, his ministers were more realistic, and commenced to bombard him with suggestions not so different from Hertzberg's.[77] Wrote Hardenberg to the King's headquarters in Poland: "Our forces are exhausted. A prompt peace is indispensable. Public opinion is hostile to the war; especially is the army opposed." And Hardenberg suggested a general peace on the basis of the *status quo ante bellum*.[78] Lucchesini insisted — with eventual success — that the King allow him to go to Vienna [79] to sow the seeds of a general peace,[80] but the King exacted that all propositions should appear to emanate from Lucchesini himself. This was progress nevertheless.[81] Möllendorff sent his adjutant general, Meyerink,[82] to Frederick William with the suggestion — not of a separate peace, to which the King, he knew, would never agree, but — of mediation by Prussia of a Franco-Imperial peace. The means suggested were the means of which Möllendorff had already availed himself, viz., negotiations for the exchange of prisoners. And since Prussia possessed more French prisoners than France did Prussian, it was intimated that Prussia might be able to obtain, in compensation, a truce for its Rhenish provinces.[83]

The King was favorably impressed with Möllendorff's suggestion, for such mediation would permit him to withdraw his forces from the Rhine without incurring the odium of deserting the Empire. And the services of the twenty thousand troops held in the West by virtue of the Treaty of February 7, 1792, were desperately needed in the East, considering Austria's

---

[76] He was certainly not so squeamish about his honor in early 1794, when he threatened "to withdraw his army into his own territory and leave the Empire to its fate" unless he received financial succor (Imperial Ambassador Count von Westphalen to Imperial Vice-Chancellor Prince von Colloredo, Feb. 5, 1794, Hansen, *Quellen*, III, 70).

[77] Sybel, *Europe*, III, 240, 242.

[78] Sorel in *RH*, V, 290–291.

[79] Lucchesini was, of course, ambassador to . Vienna (since 1793), but he was what might be called an ambassador *in absentia* — he spent most of his time with the King.

The pacific maneuvers were not confined to Vienna (Thugut to Mercy, Aug. 30, 1794, Vivenot-Zeissberg, *Quellen*, IV, 414).

[80] Lucchesini argued that just because the King was averse to a separate peace was no reason for believing he would object to a general peace (Sorel in *RH*, V, 290).

[81] Sybel, *Europe*, III, 242–243. The degree of success to be expected from Lucchesini's mission was of course directly proportional to Lucchesini's credit at Vienna. Said Thugut of him with manifest sarcasm about a year before: "The virtuous Lucchesini . . . [has] the purest intentions, the most unsullied loyalty, the tenderest affection" (to Count Colloredo, Dec. 1, 1793, *Briefe Thugut*, I, 61). And a few months later: "Lucchesini never ceases to invent malicious tricks to stir up the King [of Prussia] more and more against us" (*idem*, March 1, 1794, *ibid.*, p. 80). It appears that Lucchesini's credit at Vienna was of the negative sort. According to Lord Malmesbury, Lucchesini was "harsh and not cordial; . . . Italian and shabby." — *Diar. Corr.*, III, 34, dated Dec. 28, 1793.

[82] Rumor had it that Meyerink was Möllendorff's illegitimate son (Barthélemy to CPS, Feb. 18, 1795, *Papiers de Barthélemy*, V, 82).

[83] Sorel in *RH*, V, 291.

refusal to send help against the Poles (who, the Hohenzollern monarch maintained, were threatening Prussia itself). It should be pointed out that Frederick William, in approving the principle of mediation, did not necessarily favor the conclusion of *peace* with the regicides of France. He hoped rather for a long-term truce. He did not even wish to communicate with Paris, but rather with some French diplomat abroad, such as Barthélemy.[84] Yet, while taking all possible precautions against contamination by the revolutionists, he decided definitively to withdraw from the Coalition. Möllendorff was ordered to avail himself of all opportunities to make or receive preliminary overtures.[85]

Möllendorff of course had the machinery for such a negotiation already in running order. Apparently determined to keep one step ahead of his instructions, the Marshal thereupon proposed to the Elector of Mayence that he induce the Diet to make peace overtures to France.[86] It will be recalled that the Elector had been very hostile to the Revolution in the early days of the upheaval;[87] but the requisitions, contributions, destruction, and bloodletting of the war had afflicted the Rhineland first and foremost, and given birth to unconcealed pacifism throughout the length and breadth of the German left bank.[88] Möllendorff had intended that the Diet should ask the King of Prussia to serve as mediator. Instead, that body, acting on the recommendation of the Elector of Mayence, sought the mediation of Sweden and Denmark.[89] Von Sybel suggests that this choice may have been the result of an agreement with Vienna — to diminish the role Prussia might play.[90] This is unlikely, for the two northern countries were not on good terms with the Imperial government. They had failed to send their contingents to the army of the Empire — Sweden for Pomerania, and Denmark for Holstein — and answered the Imperial summons with subterfuge and procrastination.[91] Their past history had, for a long succession of years, been one of alliance with France to the detriment of the Empire, and everyone, including the Emperor, knew that it was only fear of the English fleet which kept them from recognizing the Republic. Moreover, the diplomacy of the two northern states was closely leagued with that of Prussia. Thugut viewed the entire mediation plan of the Prince-Elector as "a great, hard-to-remedy political blunder," and his answer took the form of measures intended to

[84] Sybel, *Europe*, III, 258–259.
[85] *Mém. homme d'Etat*, II, 506.
[86] Sorel in *RH*, V, 303. Thugut attributed the *démarche* to the "artifices of the Court of Berlin" (*Briefe Thugut*, I, 145).
The Elector of Mayence was ex officio archchancellor of Germany, by virtue of the Golden Bull of 1356.
[87] *Vide* chap. i, § 1, *supra*.

[88] *Mém. homme d'Etat*, II, 506.
[89] The Hohenzollerns were more successful in the diet of the Upper Rhenish Circle, where, on the recommendation of the Palatine government, Prussia was designated as mediator (Vivenot, *Bas. Fried.*, Pt. I, 166).
[90] Sybel, *Europe*, III, 261.
[91] *Vide* the note of the Imperial vice-chancellor in Vivenot, *Bas. Fried.*, Pt. I, 138.

compel negligent or unwilling states to fulfil their Imperial obligations.[92] Peace, according to the Emperor, meant a just, honorable, and acceptable peace. The best way, in his eyes, to secure such a peace was by a more vigorous prosecution of the war, by the states' furnishing promptly quintuple contingents[93] for the next campaign. Thus did the Emperor, by the simple use of a few definitions, nullify the effect of the Diet's *Conclusum*.[94]

What the Empire needed, indeed, was less peace proposals and more earnestness in carrying on the war; less Frederick Williams and Möllendorffs, and more Karl Friedrichs. Karl Friedrich, Margrave of Baden, had put his finger on one important reason why the war was going badly. The old system of Roman months[95] was ineffective against a country fighting a total war, such as France. In concert with Hesse-Cassel,[96] he had proposed (summer, 1794) that the prominent princes of Germany league together in an unselfish, "all-out" effort to win the war[97] — and he had asked Catherine II for her moral support.[98] (There was no use asking for more.) If he had hoped Prussia could be drawn out of her treasonable inclinations by his own patriotism, Karl Friedrich was destined to be disappointed. Frederick William "applauded with all [his] heart, [but] circumstances . . . and past sacrifices obliged [him] to limit [him]self to ardent wishes." [99] The proposal reminded Austria too much of Frederick the Great's League of Princes, and all Habsburg officials in the Empire were ordered to conduct the suggestion of a league into the channel of association-of-the-circles.[100] Several of the lesser German princes announced their acceptance in principle of Karl Friedrich's proposal, but neglected to implement their consent with actual deeds.[101] Thus the Margrave's so-called Wilhelmsbader Conferences

---

[92] *Ibid.*, pp. 143–148, *et passim.*

[93] Voted, October 13; ratified by Francis, October 24 (Hansen, *Quellen*, III, 268).

[94] Fain, *Ms. l'an III*, pp. 83–84.

[95] The extraordinary contributions granted by the states of the Empire to the Emperor to support an Imperial war. Their designation as "Roman months" goes back to the Middle Ages — to the progress of the Emperor to Rome for coronation by the Pope. An army accompanied him as a guard of honor and as a measure of safety, and this army was contributed by the states of the Empire. It consisted of a certain number of horsemen and foot soldiers, their pay supplied. The same army, or a multiple thereof, was levied for service in time of war — hence the extension of the term. In 1681, the size of the single unit (*Simplum*) was raised to 12,000 horse and 28,000 foot soldiers, with their pay — though actually the figure always fell far short of that (*Der Grosse Brockhaus* [15th, rev. ed.; 21 vols., Leipzig, 1928–1935], *s.v.* "Römermonate").

[96] Hesse-Cassel's patriotism was undoubtedly fed by her desire for electoral status. *Vide* Kaunitz to Bartenstein, June 20, 1792, Vivenot-Zeissberg, *Quellen*, II, 96–97.

[97] The documents on this subject are all in Chap. IV of B. Erdmannsdörffer, cont. by K. Obser (eds.), *Politische Correspondenz Karl Friedrichs von Baden, 1783–1806* (5 vols., Heidelberg, 1888–1901), II, 157 *et seqq.*

[98] Memoir of Karl Friedrich to Catherine II, Oct. 6, 1794, *ibid.*, pp. 202–204. *Vide* Catherine's reply *ibid.*, pp. 245–246.

[99] Frederick William to Wilhelm of Hesse-Cassel, Oct. 24, 1794, *ibid.*, p. 227.

[100] Divers letters, *ibid.*, pp. 291–307.

[101] *Ibid.*, p. xxv.

failed to accomplish anything,[102] and presently succumbed to the interest aroused by the Mayençais peace proposals.

An idea akin to the Margrave's in potential result, but antithetic in form, had been Austria's proposal to the Diet on January 20, 1794, of a German *levée en masse*.[103] Very attractive to the Emperor in that it would have enabled the raising of a sufficiently large army despite Prussia's virtual withdrawal from the war, this proposition was loudly condemned by Frederick William. The Hohenzollern monarch was afraid to arm his masses for fear the French principles would seduce them,[104] and he was too money-minded to think of supporting so many soldiers.[105] In fact, he was trying to induce the circles to support what troops he already had.[106] He therefore stirred up the petty princes to resist the measure, and it was defeated.[107] Thus, two measures looking toward a more vigorous prosecution of the war failed of success during this year of 1794. Let us see now how the *peace* proposal of Mayence fared.

The three colleges of the Ratisbon Diet wrangled for months over the Prince-Elector's suggestion. The friends of Austria argued that it was not the time, when the military situation was unfavorable, to talk of peace, but that, in any event, the question of peace could best be entrusted to the head of the Empire, and to him alone. The adherents of Prussia maintained that since the Empire had little power without Prussian assistance, Prussia should at least participate in the making of peace. And that the time was ripe for peace negotiations was the opinion not only of Prussia but of most of the Empire. A compromise cut the Gordian knot. By the aforementioned *Reichsfriedensgutachten* of December 22, 1794, it was decided that while prosecuting the war unremittingly, the Emperor should favor an armistice as the first step toward peace with France. The hope — or rather trust — was expressed that the French nation and government were also peace-minded. The Diet ordered military preparations continued to guard against "inscrutable fate." The Emperor was directed to consult, without delay, with the Prussian King, to prepare a peace with France which should be consonant to the Peace of Westphalia, reasonable, and acceptable.[108]

Vivenot declares that the hope that France was also peace-minded

---

[102] So the Margrave suggested that Russia mediate peace. Russia's mediation was acceptable to Karl Friedrich probably because a Badenese princess was the wife of the Russian heir apparent (Vivenot, *Bas. Fried.*, Pt. I, 173). But it was surely not to Frederick William's liking. Prussia and Russia were just then very much at odds over the Polish question (Häusser, *Deutsche Geschichte*, I, 583).

[103] Beroldingen to Botzheim, July 30, 1794, *Pol. Corr. Karl Fr.*, II, 158.

[104] Berlin did indeed have a serious riot the following year (*Mém. homme d'Etat*, III, 186).

[105] "Déclaration de S. M. Prussienne," March 13, 1794, *Papiers de Barthélemy*, IV, 18.

[106] Hansen, *Quellen*, III, 75.

[107] Sybel, *Europe*, III, 46.

[108] Vivenot, *Bas. Fried.*, Pt. I, 233–246.

stemmed from a speech of Tallien's in the Convention, in which Tallien is supposed to have said, "France is not waging a war of conquest." [109] That does not seem to be the spirit of Tallien's policy, as reported in the *Moniteur*.[110] According to this journal, Tallien said on November 14: "Let the government take discreet measures to make an honorable peace with some of our enemies." Also "the tricolor flies over the Rhine[land], of which [we] are masters." [111] On December 4, Tallien recommended humoring those states which had not joined the Coalition. "We should leave it to time to destroy the thrones which still encumber the Earth." [112] But unless the *Moniteur* has been guilty of distortion or omission — crimes of which it has sometimes been convicted — Tallien made no remark which could have given hope that France would consent to a *status quo ante bellum* peace.[113]

When Frederick William ordered Möllendorff to make and receive preliminary overtures, Möllendorff placed his own interpretation on the order, and sent Schmerz to Basel to betray to the French — in Möllendorff's name — the successive steps of the Allied plan of campaign.[114] Möllendorff's plan involved, besides this betrayal of plans, a promise not to coöperate with the Austrian forces except when absolutely necessary for the sake of appearances, in which case the minimum of coöperation would be accorded. An interesting situation arose when the (Prussian) Prince of Hohelohe-Ingelfingen, uninitiated in the treacherous designs of Möllendorff, attacked *before* the time Schmerz had said he would, and helped the Austrians win a brilliant victory (Kaiserslautern, September 20, 1794). Möllendorff was

[109] *Ibid.*, p. 246, n. 1.

[110] Or as sketched by Fain, *Ms. l'an III*, pp. 41–42.

[111] *Moniteur*, XXII, 506.

[112] *Ibid.*, p. 672.

[113] Unfortunately, the *Archives parlementaires* does not reach this period, or we should be able, from the best journals of the time, to decide this question with ease.

[114] "The movements that the Austrian armies will attempt are even predicted." — Fain, *Ms. l'an III*, p. 22. "Predicted" sounds so much better than "betrayed." Thugut knew with whom he had to deal. Already the previous year (May 11, 1793), he had written to Count Colloredo: "I confess to your Excellency that I have so little confidence in our dear Prussian ally that I wish it were possible not to be in too much of a hurry to communicate to it all our plans. [We should] say to it simply that his [Imperial] Majesty has ordered the Prince of Saxe-Coburg to draw up a plan of operations, . . . of which the King will be informed as soon as possible." — *Briefe Thugut*, I, 16. On September 30, 1793, Thugut wrote to Count Colloredo: "The conduct of the Prussians is the acme of perfidy," and "Our good allies are truly an infernal race." — *Ibid.*, p. 46. Early in 1795, Möllendorff asked to be informed of the Allied plan of campaign for that year. The Duke of Saxe-Teschen, the Imperial field marshal (*vide* Vivenot, *Sachsen-Teschen*, I, 51; cf. Witzleben, *Coburg*, III, 46–47), replied that the plan yet lacked the ratification of his court, but that he would impart it to Möllendorff if the latter promised to take part therein (Thugut to Count Colloredo, Jan. 30, 1795, *Briefe Thugut*, I, 178). Of this, Möllendorff had no intention. "Winter was made for negotiating, not for fighting," he wrote to his adjutant (A. Sorel, "La paix de Bâle," *RH*, VI [1878], 57).

incensed. So were the French. Meyerink explained to Bacher that until the treaty of subsidies expired, Prussia's hands were tied. As mentioned above, that treaty was due to expire only on December 1.[115]

England eventually tired of Prussian duplicity, and in the latter days of September, informed Frederick William that if his troops did not forthwith march to the defense of Holland and Belgium, the sums payable on October 1 would be withheld. At this time the Russians were victoriously overruning Poland; Austria and Russia were secretly planning the Third Partition, and Prussia was fully cognizant of Austria's intent to exclude her from all share therein. This was not the time to become involved in the West, Frederick William reasoned. The October 1 payment was therefore never made, and within the course of October, the subsidy treaty was formally denounced by both Prussians and English.[116]

England's refusal to continue the subsidies without an honest *quid pro quo*, and Austria's refusal to send Prussia the twenty thousand troops she had requested for help against the Poles, freed Frederick William from his inhibitions, and he ordered Möllendorff to lead his army to the right bank of the Rhine, and to send the treaty force of twenty thousand to Poland.[117] Möllendorff was delighted. Peace seemed closer now than ever. Meyerink communicated to Schmerz the pacific disposition of the King, and ordered him to arrange with the French that the retreating Prussians should not be harassed. If they were attacked, they would fight. Now the Committee did not believe it to be in France's interest for the French army to know anything about Franco-Prussian diplomatic relations. Bacher had (November 22, 1794) informed General Michaud that Prussia was suing for peace, and so caused that general to slow down his already slothlike movements.[118] "A general should fight, and not mix in politics," Bacher was informed. And all the Representatives on Mission were apprized "how important it is that the army have no knowledge of our diplomatic situation with respect to Prussia." [119] Obviously the Committee was of the opinion that the harder it hit Prussia, and kept on hitting her — even after she cried *Kamerad*, the more the interests of peace would be served. It was not an ethical philosophy, but it worked.

Not only was the Committee averse to holding its armies in check, but it desired not even to discuss the subject. In fact, it was loath to discuss anything with the Prussians — the exchange of prisoners included. Not that it was so very hostile to Prussia, for it wasn't. The rub was of a political nature. The Committee did not know the exact extent of its powers, and

[115] *Ibid.*, V, 293–296.
[116] *Ibid.*, pp. 296–299.
[117] Sybel, *Europe*, III, 261.
[118] Sorel in *RH*, VI, 39.
[119] *Ibid.*, p. 78.

was afraid to invite the intermeddling of the Convention. As long as it limited itself to war and diplomacy, it was the undisputed master of its own decisions.[120] Thus did it come about that the Prussians evacuated the left bank on October 22 without any agreement having been reached either as to the exchange of prisoners or as to the behavior which might be expected of the French troops during the Prussian retreat.[121]

In leaving the Rhineland, the Prussians abandoned the defense of Mayence to the Austrians.[122] The French, of course, would have liked to inherit the mighty fortress, but Prussia felt a species of fatherly care for the stronghold it had helped to capture from Custine. In early December, Merlin of Thionville suggested to the Committee the burning of Mannheim on the right bank if Mayence were not "returned" to France.[123] This was apparently not the first time Mannheim had been confronted with a fiery fate, for Schmerz, in October, had pleaded with Bacher: "Are you willing to treat Mannheim with consideration? . . . Why burn cities if you want to make peace with us and with the Empire?" [124] On December 8, 1794, Carnot suggested that a few shells tossed into Mannheim might prompt the surrender of Mayence as well as Mannheim.[125] Obviously Mannheim was viewed by the French largely as the key to the Key of Germany.[126] To the Prussians, however, it was a possession of the friendly Wittelsbach family, and they did not desire that the first fruit of their retreat should be the destruction of a friendly city. This concern for both Mayence and Mannheim must be kept in mind as we turn to the next stage of the Franco-Prussian negotiations.

When the Prussians retreated to the right bank of the Rhine, Merlin of Thionville became curious as to what was going on there, and commissioned one Schmitz of Kreuznach[127] to do a little spying. Fully aware of the precarious nature of the mission, Merlin suggested to Schmitz that if he were suspected, he should demand to be conducted before the nearest Prussian general, and say: "The Representatives on Mission offer to ask their government to make peace with Prussia if the Prussians are willing to withdraw openly from the Coalition." Schmitz, after gathering a wealth of valuable information, was duly arrested and taken before the Prussian general Kalkreuth.[128] He said his little piece and was escorted back across the Rhine

[120] Ibid., p. 49.
[121] Ibid., V, 302.
[122] Mém. corr. Mallet du Pan, II, 132.
[123] Aulard, Actes, XVIII, 518, Dec. 4, 1794.
[124] Sorel in RH, V, 302.
[125] To Rps AA. RMo, Corr. gén. Carnot, IV, 736.
[126] Though not entirely. Cf. Merlin-D. of CPS to Merlin-Th., Dec. 3, 1794: "I need not

tell you that to arrive at a prompt and glorious peace with a portion of the powers, it is indispensable for us to have Mayence and Mannheim." — Aulard, Actes, XVIII, 491.
[127] Do not confuse with Schmerz of Kreuznach.
[128] It was Kalkreuth to whom Mayence had been surrendered in 1793.

with the following reply: "Before peace can be discussed, the French attack on Mannheim and Mayence must cease; then an agreement can be reached." Merlin's rejoinder was to order increased pressure on Mannheim and Mayence.[129]

On November 22, Field Marshal Möllendorff, who could be counted upon not to let pass any opportunity for negotiation, authorized or unauthorized, wrote to one of his agents in Basel: "The Representative Merlin requested an interview of General Kalkreuth. The latter approved, but his reply has remained unanswered. Since then nothing has been seen or heard of Merlin. Such procedure does not tend to inspire confidence." The Prussian agent gave a copy of Möllendorff's letter to Bacher, and Bacher sent it in to the Committee. The Committee was in consternation, for it feared that another Dumouriez coup might be brewing. "We don't know what all this means," it wrote to Merlin. "It seems very strange to us that you took upon yourself to ask an enemy general for a diplomatic interview, and yet stranger that after making such a request, you did not inform us." [130]

Bacher had written also to Merlin of Thionville. The latter, not knowing whether Bacher were freely avowed by the Committee, replied with a letter of such content that it could be shown to the Prussians.[131] Then Merlin queried of the Committee if he should not send a similar letter to Möllendorff, "in order to mask a new trip of my man behind the lines of the enemy army. . . To know what the enemy does and thinks is half of war." [132] It is clear that the Schmitz overture bears little resemblance to the Schmerz overture with which it is likely to be confused. Merlin of Thionville was certainly not trying to prepare the peace.

Meanwhile, Möllendorff was puzzling why the Schmerz negotiation appeared to be leading nowhere. The French government seemed merely to ignore it. Perhaps, thought Möllendorff, the rank of secret agent did not sufficiently impress the French. Accordingly, on November 3, he gave Meyerink full powers to treat in the King's name respecting not only the exchange of prisoners, but also any related matter. Meyerink forthwith established contact with Bacher, and poured out to him a touching tale of Prussia's gratitude to France for singling out the Hohenzollern possessions for better treatment than other German states. This consideration, according to the Prussian envoy, had so touched Frederick William's heart that he had decided to withdraw his forces from the neighborhood of the Rhine, and to allow his subsidy treaty with England to lapse. But the withdrawal

[129] Merlin-Th. to CPS, Dec. 4 and 12, 1794, Aulard, *Actes*, XVIII, 516–517, 667.
[130] Merlin-D. of CPS to Merlin-Th., Dec. 3, 1794, *ibid.*, p. 491; CPS to Merlin-Th., Dec. 5, 1794, *ibid.*, p. 530.
[131] Merlin-Th. to CPS, Dec. 4, 1794, *ibid.*, pp. 516, 519.
[132] *Ibid.*, p. 519.

from the Rhine had to be very gradual, the envoy explained, to avoid a
charge of defection. Regarding the Empire, Meyerink declared that the
King preferred to see it neutralized — that is, neutralized with respect to
France. With respect to Prussia, however, Frederick William was asserted
to have rallied to the system of Frederick the Great, who had sought, by
his League of Princes, to attach the Empire to Prussia under the guise of
hostility to Austria. Meyerink knew that would please Bacher, and Bacher
was pleased, for he reported to the Committee that Meyerink was "sweet,
honest, . . . and with a touching tenderness, like a man who cherishes
liberty." To this liberty-loving man, Bacher then divulged that France
desired to deprive of its liberty the left bank of the Rhine, from Alsace to
Holland.[133]

Bacher received his answer from the Committee on November 16: "According to the decrees of the National Convention, the Committee of
Public Safety is the sole power which is authorized to listen to [these
agents]. Let them address [their] propositions directly to [us]." Accordingly, Meyerink composed a letter for Bacher to forward to Paris. This letter,
dated November 22, 1794, suggested an exchange of prisoners, an armistice,
the neutralization of Mayence, and the relief of the Prussian left bank from
the charges of war. It offered that Prussia would withdraw from the Coalition pending the conclusion of a separate Franco-Prussian treaty. Three
days later, Meyerink confided to Bacher that Prussia "has a pressing need
of peace" and would do almost anything to obtain its blessings. The same
day (November 25), Meyerink's plenary powers were confirmed by the
Prussian Ministry. He was authorized to treat in the name both of Prussia
and of those German states that wished to make common cause with her.[134]

The next day, Baron von Luxburg — he of the abortive Desportes negotiation[135] — arrived in Basel to sound Barthélemy.[136] It was evident to
some, including Bacher, that Prussia earnestly desired peace. Barthélemy,
however, was not too sure that these demonstrations of pacific intentions
were not poses to frighten fresh subsidies out of the Coalition.[137] Merlin of
Thionville's attitude is important here because of his close friendship with
Merlin of Douai of the Committee. Merlin of Thionville, veritable fire-
eater that he was wherever a tyrant[138] was concerned, saw only Prussian

---

[133] Sorel in *RH*, VI, 36–37. Newspapers and
letters were soon humming with the news
that France and Prussia were negotiating
peace. On November 18, 1794, the Prussian
court newspaper formally dubbed the rumors unfounded (Reuss to Thugut, Nov.
18, 1794, Vivenot-Zeissberg, *Quellen*, V,
27).

[134] Sorel in *RH*, VI, 38, 43.

[135] *Vide supra*, chap. iii, § 3.

[136] Sorel in *RH*, VI, 46.

[137] *Ibid.*, pp. 39, 47, 59–60.

[138] When, on Aug. 26, 1792, Jean Debry had
suggested the formation of a corps of tyrannicides, Merlin-Th. announced he would
join as soon as his term of office expired. He
suggested the name "Avenger of Humanity" for the corps — which, however, was

deceit in Möllendorff's honeyed letters, and recommended an irreconcilable attitude.[139] Many members of the Convention, particularly the remnants of the old Mountain, believed in war to the death as essential to the perpetuation of revolutionary government.

The Committee really desired to negotiate, for it saw in a separate peace with Prussia a guarantee of its continued dominance, owing to the increased respect it would necessarily command. But it wished to appear to negotiate reluctantly, so as to disarm the fire-eaters. Meyerink's propositions were dubbed "unimportant," but Bacher was nevertheless empowered to grant him a passport to explain them verbally to the Committee.[140] And Merlin of Douai, while relieving himself of the fierce speech of December 4, managed to sandwich in between the dire imprecations addressed to Europe in general, a very conciliatory paragraph concerning Prussia and peace.[141] As he wrote later to Merlin of Thionville, he (Merlin of Douai) was convinced that Prussia sincerely desired the end of hostilities.[142]

The granting of full powers to Meyerink, and their ratification by the Prussian Ministry, did not end the era of covert negotiation by agents of lesser stamp. The reason is not far to seek. Prussia, fully conscious that she was acting underhandedly in making a separate peace, instinctively favored indirection; and intrigue was Möllendorff's specialty.[143] France, too, was hesitant to work out in the open, for so far, the history of revolutionary diplomacy had been the history of the machinations of secret agents, and the Committee felt at home with nothing else. Some of the men who prepared the approaching Franco-Prussian peace were not of the highest character or station in life. Others were wealthy or held positions of trust. Together they formed a steady stream, sometimes rather muddy, winding its way through devious channels from Switzerland to Germany and back again. Many of these instruments have left no name. Others have left only a name. Still others, nothing.

The most important of this group was perhaps the Frankforter merchant and banker Jordis, husband of a native of Nantes (France). Bound by marriage to the French cause, Jordis became an agent of the Republic, and an active worker for the French separate-peace system. But he talked too

---

never formed (*Moniteur*, XIII, 542). In 1795, Merlin had not yet grown out of the stage of desiring "to break the chains of all peoples . . . and establish the happiness of the world." — Speech before the Conv., Jan. 14, 1795, *Moniteur*, XXIII, 211. *Vide* also the revolutionary "Propositions de paix" presented by Merlin-Th. to a Prussian minister in Frankfort, and which, though purporting to be from the CPS, are yet charged

with a Merlinian flavor (Vivenot, *Bas. Fried.*, Pt. I, 253, n. 1).

[139] Merlin-Th. to Bacher, n.d., *Corr. Merlin-Th.*, II, 131; Rp AA. RMo to CPS, Dec. 12, 1794, *Actes*, XVIII, 667–668.

[140] Sorel in *RH*, VI, 48, 50.

[141] *Moniteur*, XXII, 667–668.

[142] *Corr. Merlin-Th.*, II, 141, Dec. 15, 1794.

[143] Sorel in *RH*, V, 281.

much, and the Austrians threw him into prison. He was released at Prussia's behest, with the result that he became an agent of Prussia and avowed enemy of Austria. It is interesting to note that the contraband trade between Prussia and France via Switzerland was reputed to pass through his hands. Jordis the banker must not be confused with Jordis the Austrian general, who had been sent to Basel to watch the goings-on of the swarm of French secret agents there. The two Jordises knew each other well, though we do not know that they were related.[144] The banker told the general everything he knew — perhaps more; and the general faithfully reported all to the Imperial authorities.[145]

Next in importance, but of higher rank and different function, was Marval, Prussian minister at Neuchâtel. Couriers were constantly rushing between Marval and Möllendorff, and one of these couriers, a hunter whom Möllendorff had sent to Marval, and Marval in turn had despatched to Basel, disclosed that he was going next to Frankfort, then on to Berlin, and finally back to Neuchâtel. The Berne newspapers referred to Möllendorff and Marval as *Friedensstifter* (peacemakers, mediators), and there is little room for doubt that Marval had something to do with the peace. The same can be said of the Palatine major Potzheim; of Frederick the Great's old banker, Ephraim; of the coadjutor Dalberg; and of two agents appointed by the Convention to receive Meyerink, viz., Bossé and Richard.[146]

Vivenot sees in these lowly and clandestine efforts at negotiation an earnest of the character of the peace which was destined to result therefrom.[147] To him, that peace was merely a defection and an attempt to deprive the Emperor of his rightful control over the Empire by taking advantage of the general desire for the cessation of hostilities. Vivenot quotes a Prussian agent of the time to the effect that an armistice and peace might be expected from France as soon as the Prussian King had established himself as "head of the Germanic League." [148] There is much in what this Austrian historian says, and yet Prussia did have a most desperate need for peace.

5. PROBST

The mention above of the swarm of secret agents in Basel brings inevitably to mind Deforgues' alien-agent plan.[149] It will be recalled that his dream agents, like griffins, were to breathe fire and reduce the Coalition to cinders,

---

[144] According to the General, the banker was only "a good friend" (Vivenot, *Bas. Fried.*, Pt. II, 50). Thugut asserted that the two were brothers "or at least cousins" (to Count Colloredo, Dec. 7, 1794, *Briefe Thugut*, I, 161–162).

[145] Vivenot, *Bas. Fried.*, Pt. II, 49–52.
[146] *Ibid.*, pp. 46–48.
[147] *Ibid.*, p. 48.
[148] *Ibid.*, pp. 57–58.
[149] *Vide supra*, chap. iv, § 2d.

but that only a watered-down information service had resulted. The matter had not ended there, however. The Committee had ordered Deforgues to prepare a plan for despatching propagandist-spies into enemy territory. Before the end of 1793, there were almost fifty of these. Their function seems to have been to enlist the active aid of native Germans in creating demonstrations to hamper the prosecution of the war.[150]

Their activities did not end at Thermidor,[151] and it is for this reason that we should have, at this point, a closer look at their operations. Citizen Probst, one of the most prominent of them, will serve very well as an example. His principal connections were originally with Stuttgart and Nuremberg, but toward the end of September 1794 he took up his abode in Augsburg. His reports to Paris traveled by way of Schaffhausen and Basel. His correspondence with other French agents, both within the Empire and without, bore the superscription "Jean Tobias Kiesling, Nuremberg." [152]

Justus Christian Kiesling paid the expenses of Probst during a six weeks' sojourn of the latter at Nuremberg. These expenses, totaling 3,449 ducats, were incurred principally for the translation, printing, and dissemination of French propaganda designed to "educate" the Germans; and for postage on letters to and from Basel, Baden (Switzerland), Schaffhausen, Hamburg, Altona, Gothenburg, Leipzig, Ratisbon, Amberg, Passau, Salzburg, Linz, Augsburg, Munich, Stuttgart, etc. For short trips that Kiesling made to Ansbach, Erlangen, Lichtenau, etc. in the company of Probst, an additional sum of 1,014 ducats was paid by Kiesling. This German patriot was of course compensated by France.

Justus Christian Kiesling also served as the instrument whereby Probst maneuvered the escape of French prisoners in Germany, but Kiesling's principal function was that intimated above: to represent to the Imperial cities that the Emperor's demands incident to the prosecution of the war were peculiarly burdensome to them and to their commerce, and thereby to foster the formation of a French party, and to incite riots. The aim in view was not really the revolutionization of Germany, but rather the crippling of the German war effort; and those not in the plot may not have looked farther than their profits. In consideration of this criminal blindness — for the law imputes criminal intent where negligence is too patent — France exempted four Nuremberg merchants from a July 18 decree hindering German tradesmen from vindicating claims against their French brothers.

---

[150] Sorel, *Europe*, III, 534.
[151] Nor with the Convention. *Vide infra*, Pt. II, chap. xxi, § 6.
[152] Thugut to Lehrbach, Oct. 20, 1794, Vivenot-Zeissberg, *Quellen*, V, 6–8. This citation applies to the next two paragraphs of the text also. Probst was eventually arrested by the Austrians (Thugut to Emperor, Sept. 2, 1795, *ibid.*, p. 344). His German accomplices were placed under surveillance (*ibid.*).

One of these Nuremberg merchants was named Karl Gottlieb Kiesling. It seems that in those days, "Quisling" began with a K.[153]

[153] The document containing the foregoing information — the above-cited letter from Thugut to Lehrbach, Austrian ambassador to the Wittelsbachs — seems to settle the question so bitterly debated between von Sybel and Sorel as to whether Hérault de Séchelles and Barère of the Robespierrist Committee endeavored through secret agents to revolutionize Allied territories. Von Sybel maintained the affirmative; Sorel, the negative (H. von Sybel, "La propagande révolutionnaire en 1793 et 1794," *RH*, XI (1879), 103–114; A. Sorel, "Réponse," *ibid.*, pp. 114–116). In reality, both were probably right, for the revolutionary activity of agents like Probst and their German partisans was not, we see, aimed specifically at the overthrow of the Germanic constitution, but rather at smoothing France's road to victory, hence was not revolutionization in the thoroughgoing sense of the Decrees of November 19 and December 15 and 17, 1792.

CHAPTER VII

THE EARLY THERMIDORIANS AND
THE LEFT BANK

I. REVOLUTIONARY FINANCE

*E*VER since the conquest of Belgium and a strip of the Rhineland in the autumn of 1792, the idea had been gaining ground in France that Belgium and the German left bank could be utilized to redeem the depreciated assignats.[1] Perhaps this subject requires a few words of explanation. The "assignats" were, of course, paper money secured by the confiscated lands of the French church. Legally, no more assignats could have been issued than the lands were worth, but poverty and the temptation of easy money had rendered the check inoperative, and as the volume of assignats had swelled, their value had declined. This value was not the same everywhere at a given moment, and it was especially low near the frontier and across the frontier, where it suffered from comparison with "hard cash." Yet it was in these regions that the French armies were quartered and provisioned.

The situation reached a critical stage soon after the desertion of Dumouriez in April 1793. The traitor had been very prodigal with France's slender resources, the service of the army rising to thirty million livres in coin per month. This coin had been bought from money-jobbers at a constantly increasing price in assignats, and the burden threatened to ruin France.[2]

It had been the intention of the Convention that Belgium and the other "liberated" regions should pay the expenses of their own "liberation." Cambon had been repeatedly cheered when, on December 15, 1792, he proposed the following principles in the name of the Finance, Military, and Diplomatic Committees: "Upon invading a country, what should be our first care? To take the goods of our enemies as a guarantee of the expenses of

[1] *Vide supra*, chap. ii, § 2, Chuquet's remarks on the purpose of the Decree of December 15 and 17, 1792.

[2] Circular of CPS to Rps, April 14, 1793, Aulard, *Actes*, III, 242.

the war. . . [But since the abolition of feudal dues and other impositions will leave the conquered lands without revenues] it is necessary to open the [French] public treasury to all people who desire to be free. What are our treasures? They are our territorial possessions, which we have converted into assignats. . . In entering a country, in suppressing its taxes and offering it a part of our resources to aid it in the reconquest of its liberty, we are offering it our revolutionary money. This money will become its own. We shall not then have to buy coin at great expense in order to find clothing and food in the country itself. From that moment we shall increase our own power, since we shall have a channel to diminish the mass of assignats circulating in France; and the security furnished by the [alien] property in the custody of the Republic will increase the credit of these very assignats." [3]

But Dumouriez, for reasons that are none too clear, refused to drain the lifeblood from the Belgian territories he conquered.[4] Wherever possible, he contracted for supplies and paid for them in coin, instead of commandeering them. He levied no contributions. He scrupulously paid the customary local tolls. He even ordered the return of church plate which had been confiscated by others.[5] Perhaps his motive was to keep the Belgians satisfied so that they should not rise up and threaten his rear.[6] Or he may have thought to create a little principality for his very own, like Bonaparte's later Cisalpine Republic, and Hoche's short-lived Cisrhenish Republic. Whatever the motive, the fact remains that Dumouriez' conquest of Belgium was an expense instead of a source of income, as contemplated by Cambon and the Convention. Result: further depreciation of the assignat, and the impending ruin of France.

Such were the circumstances when the Convention decided upon a bold stroke. On April 8, 1793, it decreed that all purchases made by the Republic

[3] *Moniteur*, XIV, 760; or Wambaugh, *Plebiscites*, p. 305.

[4] But he wrote to General Kellermann, in urging him to seize Trèves and Coblenz: "We must have 150,000 men beyond the frontier this winter, primarily to procure us coin and to utter (*placer*) our assignats." — Sybel, *Europe*, I, 597. Dumouriez added: ". . . and then in order that the armies should not exhaust all the provisions of our own country." Dumouriez should not be judged too harshly for his suggestion to live at the enemies' expense, despite von Sybel's indignation (*ibid.*). It has always been a practice of war to sit uninvited at the enemy's table. Austria herself followed this practice in the neighborhood of Metz (*vide* Bonnal de Gan-

ges, *Repré.*, II, Appendix, no. iv). And the Austrian vice-chancellor, Philipp Cobenzl, wrote to Spielmann, the *Staatsreferendarius*, on September 20, 1792, "It will be necessary that at least the largest part of the united armies spend the winter on French soil." — Vivenot-Zeissberg, *Quellen*, II, 216.

[5] *Moniteur*, XIV, 759; Mathiez, *Fr. Rev.*, pp. 283, 300.

[6] He was very considerate, also, of the people of Aix-la-Chapelle. His ill-nourished and ill-clothed troops perpetrated many thefts and robberies in the neighborhood of Aix and of Liège. Dumouriez ordered full respect for persons and property under penalty of death for disobedience (Hansen, *Quellen*, II, 650, n. 1).

should henceforth be paid for in assignats, and that soldiers and officers, heretofore paid partly in coin, should receive all their remuneration in assignats — with a paper bonus. On the eleventh, it decreed that in all commercial transactions, acquittal should be made in assignats, and that coin could be given and received in payment only on the same basis as assignats. The government did not anticipate trouble from these decrees within the interior of France, where coin had practically disappeared, but it was extremely nervous about the frontier regions and the armies. "Make use . . . of all measures . . . to prevent murmurs, to dissipate distrust," the Committee wrote to the Representatives on Mission. "The patriotism of the armies is a sure guarantee of the success of this measure with respect to it [sic]. He who fights for liberty naturally does not compute like the slave of despotism." [7]

But arithmetic is arithmetic for slaves and freedmen alike, and the troops could not cash their patriotism at the corner grocery. In the neighborhood of Saarbrücken, one hundred livres in assignats had a market value of less than forty-five, and in the environs of Wissembourg and Strasburg, it was twenty-five. The Decree of April 8 caused the Army of the Moselle "great emotion" [8] and "ill humor." [9] In fact, it refused to believe that such a decree existed, "because, in point of fact, assignats are not accepted in this region." [10] Around Wissembourg, too, the paper promises had well-nigh disappeared from circulation as a medium of exchange, and the troops of the Army of the Rhine were accustomed to make use of them only to buy coin, which in its turn was used to buy goods. But of course the money-jobber had intervened in the process, giving less coin even than the market dictated, and threatening not to accept the paper at all. [11]

The Decree of April 8 was fruitless, [12] though it may have had in some places a momentary effect. [13] "Selfish and greedy" merchants in the Rhineland refused to accept the paper, [14] and the government had to supply, in

[7] Aulard, Actes, III, 241–243.

[8] Blaux, Rp in Bas-Rhin, Meurthe, and Moselle, to CPS, April 16, 1793, ibid., p. 294.

[9] Idem, April 19, 1793, ibid., p. 339.

[10] Ibid.

[11] Rps A. R to CPS, April 15, 1793, ibid., p. 274.

[12] S. A. Falkner, Das Papiergeld der französischen Revolution, 1789–1797, pp. 47–48, quoted in L. R. Gottschalk, The Era of the French Revolution (New York, 1929), p. 165. Vide also ibid., p. 164.

[13] Rps A. R to Pres. of CPS, April 18, 1793, Aulard, Actes, III, 319.

[14] The attitude of the Rhineland toward the forced acceptance of the assignat is well portrayed by the following remarks of the Politischen Gespräche der Toten (published in Neuwied, but widely circulated on both banks of the Rhine) when the first laws on this subject appeared in France in 1790: "Finally the National Assembly has decreed that the nation would be under compulsion to accept the assignats as hard money. What did you say? under compulsion? Yes, under compulsion. But that is a crime against . . . national liberty. Liberty here, liberty there. The assignats are the last resource of the state, and must be accepted. Goodness gracious, who would ever have thought that the

kind, articles of prime necessity to the troops.[15] An entrepreneur of fortifications demanded to be paid 180,000 livres in coin, and the Committee feared
to deny the claim, for his services were needed for other works of defense.
The Committee therefore ordered the Representatives to the Rhine and
Moselle Armies to "do what will not retard the works," and authorized them
to draw on the tax collectors for the necessary funds.[16] In France itself, some
départements "totally rejected" the assignats, and inasmuch as there were
millions of counterfeit bills in circulation,[17] the government could do nought
but establish "verifiers." [18] The Representatives on Mission in the Ardennes
felt constrained to continue a meat contract providing for payment half in
coin, half in paper, lest the troops starve[19] — for those with goods to sell
could not find it in their hearts to exchange them for what they knew to
be printing-press money.

Something was badly needed to reëstablish confidence in the assignat.
It was supplied by the success of French arms in the summer and autumn of
1794. After the Austrian evacuation of Belgium, General Jourdan had
turned east, and occupied Aix-la-Chapelle (September 23, 1794), Cologne
(October 6), Bonn (October 8), Crefeld (October 9), Clèves (October 19),
and Coblenz (October 23); while in the south, General René Moreaux had
occupied the Palatinate and the Electorate of Trèves, including the city of
Trèves itself (August 8).[20]

Of course, the brilliance of these victories was due in part to the with-

---

Rights of Man would sink to the forced acceptance of assignats! O unfailing wisdom of
the 1200 Lycurguses, O unfailing folly of
the 24 million inhabitants. . . O holy flame
of philosophy!" (Oct. 2, Hansen, *Quellen*, I,
659–660.)

[15] Rps A. R to CPS, April 26, 1793, Aulard
Actes, III, 478.

[16] CPS to AA. RMo, April 21, 1793, *ibid.*, pp.
372–373.

[17] The importance of the false-assignat problem can be gauged by the following despatch
from Bacher to Deforgues, February 3, 1794:
"The French Republic has two enemies much
harder to combat than all the coalesced powers: famine, and the introduction of counterfeit assignats." — *RH*, X, 345–346. At the
end of 1792, Baron Bréteuil, *émigré* in Frederick William's camp, had proposed that
Austria and Prussia manufacture 150,000,000
livres' worth of false assignats (Vivenot-
Zeissberg, *Quellen*, II, 440–444). To the
credit of Emperor Francis was his reply:
"Such an infamous project is unacceptable."

— *Ibid.*, p. 437.

False assignats were manufactured, among
other places, in Luxemburg and Frankfort-
on-the-Main. The town of Kusel in the Saar
Valley — not in the Electorate of Trèves, as
Representative Hentz thought — was burned
on Hentz's order on July 26, 1793, allegedly
for harboring a counterfeit-assignat printery
(Hentz, Rp AA. RMo, to CPS, Aulard, *Actes*,
XV, 492 and n. 3). But Hentz wrote the
CPS on July 28 that the generals had asked
for authorization to burn Kusel because it
interfered with their operations. So he burned
it but gave therefor a reason which he
thought would "serve as an example to this
wicked country, where the people are arming against us." For a long period, the 2,000
inhabitants of Kusel had no shelter whatsoever over their heads (Hansen, *Quellen*, III,
157, n. 2).

[18] Rps in Mont-Blanc to Conv., April 21, 1793,
Aulard, *Actes*, III, 377–378.

[19] April 24, 1793, *ibid.*, p. 441.

[20] Hansen, *Quellen*, III, 173, 226, 254, 275.

drawal by Prussia and Austria of their best troops because of the menacing aspect of the Polish question.[21] Prussia, in fact — as stated above — withdrew all her troops behind the Rhine in October. Coburg, deprived of Prussia's help long before October, had appealed to the patriotism of the Rhinelanders for troops and supplies, and against the "corruption" of the French.[22] The response could be described almost as negative.[23] Left to their own resources, the weary Austrian troops were no match for the zealous French. On November 2, 1794, the fort of Rheinfels was lost to the Allies; [24] on December 25, the bridgehead of Mannheim.[25] With the exception of Mayence, the entire German left bank of the Rhine was in French hands by the end of 1794.[26] And so much did it appear that that, too, would soon fall, that the Mayençais were instructed by their government how to comport themselves with respect to the "conqueror." [27]

Here now, with Belgium and almost all the left bank in French hands, was the opportunity to put into practice a theory of finance which would be painless to France and to — well, painless to France, anyway. The Habsburg and ecclesiastical possessions of Belgium and Liège alone would serve as sufficient security for over two thirds of the French paper.[28] And in addition, there was all the coin that could be obtained there and on the left bank in forced exchange for assignats, plus what could be secured by levy (contributions). On August 3, 1794, the Committee had written to the Representatives to the Armies of the North and of the Sambre and Meuse:

. . . Several times . . . we have told you very categorically: (1) to treat these countries as conquered territory, not to fraternize with them, nor to municipalize them [i.e., not to create *municipalités*], not to concern yourselves with annexation; . . . (3) to overwhelm the rich, to take hostages, [but]contrariwise, to respect the people . . . ; (4) to strip Belgium of provisions, horses, copper, cloth, of everything conducive to our end . . . ; to utter the assignats, establish contributions, take all the money you can. . .[29]

[21] Stephens, *Rev, Eur.*, pp. 149–150.

[22] Bonnal de Ganges, *Repré.*, III, 610–612. Coburg even threatened to requisition everything the French might find of value for maintaining themselves, and to withdraw over the Rhine, leaving the left bank to the "fury" of the enemy (*ibid.*).

[23] Hansen, *Quellen*, III, 171, n. 2 gives the details. A few thousand troops, and some arming of the inhabitants, was the meager result. And, of course, the threats were not appreciated.

[24] *Guerres Rév. Emp.*, II, 171.

[25] *Moniteur*, XXIII, 91.

[26] Dumolin (*Précis*, I, 268) is a little too enthusiastic when he says, in italics: "Every-

where the Rhine boundary was attained." He himself recognizes on p. 276 that Mayence had not yet been captured. For that matter, neither had Luxemburg (*Guerres Rév. Emp.*, II, 314), which did not fall until June 1795 (*ibid.*, p. 331). Luxemburg is, however, beyond the purview of the present work, though forming part of the Empire.

[27] Hansen, *Quellen*, III, 295, n. 2. E.g., they might take the French oath under compulsion, so long as they remained faithful in their hearts.

[28] Merlin-D., before Conv., Sept. 30–Oct. 1, 1795, Hansen, *Quellen*, III, 652.

[29] Signed by Carnot, Barère, and Tallien among others. Aulard, *Actes*, XV, 640.

Carnot, in the name of the Committee, had written three weeks earlier, "Remember, the infamous Dumouriez left a thousand millions of our coin there."[30] As the Sambre and Meuse Army swept southward along the Rhine, the above rules gradually became applicable also to the northern Rhineland, and on August 17, they were rendered applicable to all the Rhineland by their imposition on the Rhine and Moselle Armies.[31]

How did this new system of finance work in practice? One of the first acts of the French, in entering the cities of the Rhineland, was to order merchants to accept assignats in return for their goods,[32] and to prohibit the raising of prices to offset the worthlessness of the paper.[33] (To this end, they imposed the established maximum prices of Lille upon the left bank.)[34] Then they ordered statements rendered of moneys on deposit in public and private institutions,[35] and, under penalty of death,[36] effected the exchange of the coin there for paper.[37] And they imposed coin contributions, usually so excessive that payment was beyond the range of possibility. Sometimes, one or the other of these steps would be delayed for a purpose, but it was potentially always there, as part of the system.[38]

Naturally, the merchants of the left bank hesitated to dispose of their goods in return for worthless paper, and closed their shops. But the French forced them open, and seized their stocks in return for assignats.[39] And they "bought" up all the farmers' products for paper. But when the farmer came to town, he discovered that he could buy nothing with the paper[40] unless he also had a gun and could speak French. "Here one neither offers nor accepts assignats any more," said a left-bank newspaper, "for neither

[30] To Rps A. SMeu, July 13, 1794, *ibid.*, p. 142.

[31] Hansen, *Quellen*, III, 151, n. 1.

[32] *Ibid.*, pp. 256, 278, 381.

[33] *Ibid.*, pp. 235, n. 1; 311.

[34] *Ibid.*, pp. 290, n. 1; 311, n. 1. France still had its Law of the Maximum. For France, this law was repealed on December 24, 1794, but it was maintained on the left bank until February 10, 1795. The obligatory acceptance of the assignats was continued on the left bank until April 25 (*ibid.*, p. 328, n. 6).

[35] *Ibid.*, pp. 212, n. 4; 260. The Cologne Senate, awake to what was happening (Rp A. SMeu to "city council" of Cologne, Oct. 8, 1794, *ibid.*, p. 260), saw to it that the municipal coffers contained only 14,000 silver livres, 708 new taler, and 82 bars of silver. At least, so says Venedey (*Deut. Rep.*, p. 175).

[36] Hansen, *Quellen*, III, 323, n. 5.

[37] *Ibid.*, p. 330.

[38] Thus, Representative Bourbotte did not ask for coin (contributions) during the first days of the conquest of Trèves, but only for grain, fodder, mattresses, linen, and supplies and merchandise of every kind, minutely detailed — in other words, requisitions (*ibid.*, p. 215, n. 1). These other demands he thought stood a better chance of fulfillment if the people were led to believe that that was all which would be asked of them. "But tomorrow or [the day] after I shall make them open their coffers and [I shall] order the restitution of our coin [i.e., coin spent by the French *émigrés* in Trèves]." — *Ibid.*, p. 212, n. 4.

[39] *Aachener Zuschauer*, Aug. 14, 1794, *ibid.*, p. 167, n. 2.

[40] Delhoven in *Die rheinische Dorfchronik*, Jan. 1-7, 1795, Hansen, *Quellen*, III, 347.

beer nor anything else is sold openly." [41] The effect on commerce may easily be imagined.

Besides acceptance of assignats, Law of the Maximum, and coin contributions, there was yet a fourth aspect of the above-described new system of finance. True, it was but a reflection of France's own laws respecting émigrés. As the French approached a town, all sovereigns, nobles, clergy, and wealthy bourgeois who were able fled in panic with what possessions they could. When the French arrived, they gave all fugitives (the erstwhile princes excepted) two weeks to return on pain of confiscation of whatever property they had been unable to take along — usually furniture and real estate.[42] A number did return.[43] But sometimes persons were absent because they had business elsewhere, and they did not even know they had been ordered to return; or they could not manage to return within such a short period; or they were prevented from returning by a German army order not to cross the Rhine. The property of these, also, was confiscated and sold, until their complaints became so deafening that it was no longer possible to pretend not to hear.[44] Then a new two weeks' limit was set on their return.[45]

The property of emigrants was put up for sale to the highest bidder. This property may have belonged to the former reigning prince, or some respected and wealthy fellow member of the community, and the Germans refused to bid.[46] Suddenly the French officials discovered that, unless a person can use something himself, only that is valuable which someone else wants. Here they were encumbered with more castles and goods than they could possibly embezzle — and to what end? They solved their problem in part by threatening to tear down every house they could not auction off.[47] Since failure to bid would not save the "emigrants'" property for them, there was no reason for people not to bid. But because only a very doubtful title could be passed, sales were at prices far below actual value.[48] This fact, combined with maladministration and the aforementioned embezzlements,[49] rendered this aspect of France's financial system hardly worth the violent hatreds it induced. Interesting it is to note that one of the first acts of Klemens Wenzeslaus, when the French were ousted in the

[41] *Ibid.*, p. 348.
[42] Gillet, Rp A. SMeu, to inhabitants on right bank of Meuse, Sept. 24, 1794, Hansen, *Quellen*, III, 234.
[43] Dohm to Frederick William, Nov. 28, 1794, *ibid.*, p. 324.
[44] Hansen, *Quellen*, III, 450, n. 1; 457.
[45] *Ibid.*, pp. 451–452.

[46] "Honorable men will not buy these properties." — From the later *Gegenaufruf an die Bewohner des linken Rheinufers* of Privy Councillor J. P. Weckbecker of Electoral Trèves. (*Vide infra*, Pt. II, chap. xxvii, § 1j.)
[47] Hansen, *Quellen*, III, 324.
[48] *Ibid.*, p. 450, n. 1.
[49] *Ibid.*, p. 457.

autumn of 1795, was to invalidate the auctions.[50] The law of the conqueror did not extend to private property, he said.[51]

Not only was the property of emigrants regarded by France as its national domain, but also *all* factories, mines, and smelters. The administration of the national domain will come in for consideration later in this chapter. The details of the contributions — and the requisitions — bound up together, as they were, must be considered more fully if one is truly to understand the Rhine policy of the early Thermidorians.

2. THE LEFT BANK SOUTH OF THE MOSELLE

It will be remembered that on May 13, 1794, the Robespierrist Committee of Public Safety had secured the passage of a law establishing an Agency of Evacuation. This law, still on the books, required the removal to France, through the Agency, of everything in conquered territory which France could use. Trèves was the first Rhineland city to fall to the French in the campaign of 1794. It was a very wealthy city, a city with a present and a past. Situated in the lush Moselle valley, and drawing unto itself the threads of commerce of a wide and productive region, it was a prize for any conqueror. But above all, it was one of the jewels of Klemens Wenzeslaus, who had harbored the French *émigrés.*

Barère announced the capture of Trèves to the Convention by reading a despatch from Bourbotte, Representative to the Rhine and Moselle Armies. It was an enthusiastic despatch. Trèves would be "a true milch cow to the French Republic, . . ." Bourbotte said. "The Moselle, the Saar, the numerous boats in port, will serve well to evacuate everything that embarrasses this country and which the Republic needs. I am going . . . to apply my thoughts . . . to a new mode of contribution to be imposed on the Electorate. I think that three to four millions in coin . . . can easily be paid . . . within forty-eight hours." [52]

The despatch caused Barère himself to wax dramatic: "Trèves has swallowed our coin for four years; she shall return it. Trèves has disparaged our assignats for four years; she shall accept them. Trèves has welcomed *émigrés,* that dross of the nation; Trèves shall nourish the victorious troops of the Republic." [53]

The same day, Bourbotte and his colleague Goujon wrote further that not only had they found in the city a vast store of supplies, both munitions and articles of subsistence, but "everywhere we find cellars, granaries of

[50] That is, judging by the regulations drawn up in summer, 1795, to govern the Prince-Elector's projected return (*ibid.*, p. 548).

[51] *Ibid.*
[52] *Ibid.*, p. 174.
[53] Aug. 12, 1794, *ibid.*, p. 173, n. 2.

abundance, which we have left under the guard of a sentinel at each door. The civil magistrates appear to lend themselves with the best of grace to our searchings . . . , and the care that we have exercised to establish order has reassured the inhabitant that his house will not be pillaged, and will doubtless decide him to bring from his vaults the provisions and effects he has hidden. . . [The] ecclesiastical foundations, established as they are upon the principle of charity, will doubtless not refuse to share with the Republic a portion of their abundant provisions, and we shall not be surprised to hear . . . that all the silver saints . . . have emigrated [to France]. . . Today we are examining public coffers. . . We have ordered the collection [of taxes] to continue, but disbursements to cease provisionally. We shall endeavor to stimulate the activities of the agents charged with evacuating every object . . . useful to the French Republic, which will, according to a first estimate, draw from the Electorate almost a thousand millions in coin and provisions." [54]

The previous day, Carnot, on hearing of the fall of Trèves, had written to the above Representatives: "Now we must profit by the victory. Send promptly [to France] . . . all . . . articles of consumption. Levy contributions on the rich exclusively, . . . spare the poor in their property, customs, and usages. Maintain the discipline and disinterestedness of the troops." [55] From all of which it appears that we are about to witness the sack of another Rome.

It was Bourbotte who was the Nemesis of Trèves. Above was mentioned that he planned to draw three or four million francs from the Electorate. That figure had been arbitrarily arrived at. Bourbotte knew that all those who had any possessions of value had emigrated, taking their treasures with them, for on August 29 he had written to the Committee, "The more they [the people of Trèves] have allowed their émigrés, nobles, and priestly riffraff to carry their property away . . . , the more those who remain will be obliged to contribute, because — in a word — the Republic should not lose anything on that account." [56] But the Committee, through Carnot, had ordered him to spare the poor, as mentioned. To these orders Bourbotte gave merely lip service: the one and a half million livres that he demanded of the city of Trèves on October 11 (of the three million asked of the occupied part of the Electorate and Luxemburg) he stipulated should be apportioned only among the wealthy, especially among the nobles and clergy; [57] but he threatened to burn the city and even to execute the city councilmen if the money were not forthcoming in short order.[58]

---

[54] To CPS, Aug. 12, 1794, Aulard, *Actes*, XVI, 63–64.

[55] *Corr. gén. Carnot*, IV, 564.

[56] Aug. 29, Hansen, *Quellen*, III, 212, n. 4.

[57] *Ibid.*

[58] *Ibid.*, p. 215, n. 1.

The sum was raised, but later the citizens of Trèves "could not recall without shuddering those days of desolation and of terror." The city council, crushed with requisitions, outraged by insolence, and menaced with fire and sword, extorted coin, assignats, and ornaments from the inhabitants — rousing them in the middle of the night, so short was the time allowed.[59] And the merchants, faced with the death penalty if they refused to sell their goods for assignats at face value, saw their stocks wiped out by troops and others,[60] who, for pieces of paper, "bought" everything up and sent it to France. Some persons even had the brazen effrontery to buy trifles with large-denomination assignats and demand change in coin.[61]

It will be noted that "coin, assignats, and ornaments" were extorted for remission to Bourbotte. One might well be puzzled at the mention of assignats here, for it was partly to raise *their* value that the coin was being exacted. Let us allow Bourbotte to explain: "The city council's having asked me if assignats . . . could be received in payment, I answered affirmatively in order not to discredit our paper money . . .; but if the amount of the assignats given in payment exceeds a quarter of this contribution, then, to effect the restitution of our coin [spent by the *émigrés* in Trèves], I shall establish, by way of supplement to the first [contribution], a second . . . of 400,000 or 500,000 livres which will be payable only in coin. I shall set forth the reasons in the preamble of my decree in such a way as to sound very plausible."[62] But on September 17, Bourbotte found another way out. No more assignats would be accepted, he said, because many counterfeit notes had been found among them.[63]

The same problem — would not France herself discredit the assignats if she refused to accept them?[64] — was thrown into the lap of the Committee by Merlin of Thionville three months later. The Committee's reply was frank and simple. " . . . In Belgium, your colleagues . . . require payment in assignats, hence nothing stands in the way of your doing likewise in the Palatinate, Trèves, etc. We invite you, however, to urge the payment of contributions in coin. The government needs coin most imperatively."[65]

The contribution of October 11 was applicable only to the country then in the hands of the Rhine and Moselle Armies. On November 5, Bourbotte announced another contribution — for territory subsequently occupied (viz.,

[59] The urgency of these trying days vibrates in the *Trierer Tagebuch* of L. Müller, *ibid.*, pp. 213–218.

[60] I.e., other Frenchmen or their adherents. Between themselves, the Germans discounted the assignats drastically, despite the heavy penalty involved (*ibid.*, p. 332, n. 1).

[61] *Mémoire justificatif* of the Trèves town council, of 1794, published July 16, 1802,

ibid., p. 215, n. 1.

[62] To CPS, Sept. 2, Aulard, *Actes*, XVI, 481.

[63] Müller's *Tagebuch*, Hansen, *Quellen*, III, 217.

[64] Merlin-Th. to CPS, Dec. 12, 1794, Aulard, *Actes*, XVIII, 669.

[65] CPS to Merlin-Th., Dec. 18, 1794, *ibid.*, pp. 790–791.

Coblenz and its environs). Coblenz was assessed 1,500,000 livres for its 8,000 inhabitants![66] but required to pay 4,000,000; the 2,500,000-livre difference it was to collect from the surrounding communities.[67] The contribution was to be acquitted solely in coin because — and here Bourbotte proved his ingenuity — if France did not recover the French coin poured into enemy territory, principally Coblenz, that coin might reach the right bank and repair the finances of the Coalition. But such a use could not be made of assignats. Therefore, though assignats were worth "at least as much as metallic money," only coin would be acceptable in this contribution.[68]

In Trèves, the contributions had been postponed until after the initial heavy requisitions had been levied. In Coblenz it was the same. Almost simultaneously with the routine order for the acceptance of the assignat at face value, another, issuing from the *Agence d'Armement*, commanded the surrender in exchange for assignats of some forty specified materials: cannon, gun carriages, mortars, shells, howitzers, grenades, bullets, small arms of all kinds, iron of every description, wire, nails, files, anvils, bellows, hammers, tongs, workbenches, hatchets, spades, hoes, pickaxes, chains of all sizes, hemp, anchors, copper, calamine, tin, lead, sheet metal, gunpowder, saltpetre, potash, sulphur, charcoal, pit-coal, peat, and building lumber of all kinds. The penalty for concealing any of the above-named materials, or for making a false declaration regarding possession thereof, was specified as death.[69]

Such treatment was not likely to inculcate love for France in the hearts of the Coblenzers, but this was war, and people everywhere have always recognized that one must bow to the exigencies of warfare. But the very code of war is usually a guarantee that one will be fleeced with dignity. This was not, however, the experience of Coblenz: The French troops in Coblenz were in need of shoes. The chairman of the *Agence de Commerce et des Approvisionnements* (Alexandre) suggested that a public meeting be called. The curious Coblenzers flocked in throngs to the castle square. The exits were closed; the people were required to take off their shoes and give them to the soldiers. Home they then were free to go — in their stockinged feet.[70]

This treatment, so derisive, requires a word of explanation. It will be recalled that Coblenz had harbored the largest concentration of *émigrés* in the Rhineland in the early Revolution. Human nature being what it is, the

[66] Hansen, *Quellen*, III, 292.
[67] The area upon which this second contribution was imposed contained 18,270 families or 103,338 souls. The entire left-bank section of the Electorate contained 160,000 souls (Coblenz District deputies to Rp Gillet, Sept. 10, 1795, *ibid.*, p. 622).
[68] Hansen, *Quellen*, III, 291.
[69] Venedey, *Deut. Rep.*, p. 183.
[70] *Ibid.*, pp. 184–185.

city could now hardly expect to be treated with finesse. But, fundamentally, Coblenz was not treated more harshly than Lyons, where Fouché commandeered all the boots of the civil population; or Marseilles, where Barras exacted two shirts from each of twenty thousand wealthy citizens;[71] or Strasburg, where Saint Just — as mentioned above sans details — exacted five thousand pairs of shoes and fifteen thousand shirts, and a fortnight later, ten thousand additional pairs of shoes and every overcoat.[72] It seems, indeed, that Coblenz was not so much the victim of anti-Germanism as — in common with Lyons, Marseilles, and Strasburg — of anti-anti-Revolutionism.

So much for money contributions and requisitions in the former Electorate of Trèves. Now for the "Evacuation," an operation also organized by Bourbotte, Hentz, and Goujon, Representatives on Mission to the Rhine and Moselle Armies. In some respects it is difficult to distinguish requisitions from "evacuation." It is largely a matter of extent and purpose, the character of the article, and the identity of the authority making the levy. Requisitions are, as above recognized, a legitimate wartime measure, sad but necessary, born of the need to support and outfit troops in the field. Evacuation is statutory brigandage on a grand scale. Contemporary accounts written from the victims' viewpoint often couple the two together without distinction. Thus:

> Today everything in the shops made of copper was seized. (Another) day, 30,000 pairs of shoes and boots were requisitioned. One day 60 horses were taken from a little bailiwick, without making payment, and without even furnishing the proprietors with a receipt . . . ; and later a number of vehicles were demanded — vehicles which could not be moved except by those selfsame horses. . . One day . . . all existing wheat was seized; . . . the next day several thousand rations of bread were demanded.[73]

L. Müller's *Trierer Tagebuch* gives a close look into one phase of the "Evacuation." On September 10 the stoves were taken from the rooms of the fathers in several churches. At one monastery, all beds, all stoves, were seized; also all tinware, only earthernware being left. On the twelfth, a nunnery was stripped, even the nuns' handkerchiefs and underwear being taken. And work was begun on removing the leaden roof of St. Simeon's Church. At another church, all the lamps were taken; also all the chalices and all the stoles but one of each. Taken, also, were the ciborium and monstrance.[74]

The Agency of Evacuation had just the effect that might have been

[71] L. Madelin, *The French Revolution* (tr. from the French; London, 1918), p. 362.

[72] Palmer, *Twelve*, p. 184. *Vide* chap. iv, § 2g.

[73] Coblenz District deputies to Gillet, Sept. 10, 1795, Hansen, *Quellen*, III, 618.

[74] In Hansen, *Quellen*, III, 215–216.

expected — economic disaster. He who had not, could not be robbed; therefore destitution suddenly assumed an aspect of bliss. The merchants sold not, the farmer produced not — and soon the French troops ate not. They died like flies; their bodies were stacked up like cord wood until a sufficient number had accumulated, and then they were hauled to a nearby sandpit and dumped. Twenty, thirty, forty a day succumbed; seven hundred in one place in the week preceding Christmas week.[75] Only then did a voice presume to question this revolutionary measure which shone like a beacon of hope to a nation which had "gone without" for so long.

It was in the name of the subsistence of the occupying French forces that Merlin of Thionville warned the Committee of Public Safety: "The army still needs clothes, shoes, hats. How do you expect it to get them if the merchant is stripped of all he has? How do you expect bread to be sent to the armies if the farmer has neither horses nor oxen? The Agency of Evacuation would be excellent if we were only raiders. In the present circumstances it is disastrous. . . Take, I pray you, the measures that I indicate relative to this Agency of Evacuation. [But] before you do anything, listen to Bourbotte. He has seen it operate!"[76] Merlin was really asking only for ratification, for already on December 19 — one week before the date of his letter — he and his colleague Féraud had themselves suppressed the Agency and appealed to the inhabitants of the conquered territory not to resist the requisitioning of food needed by the army and "not absolutely essential to you." For such foods, it was promised, the French would henceforth pay. "Have confidence in us. We will redress abuses. . . Peace and fraternity to the friends of the Republic; implacable hate to its enemies!"[77] But fair measures could not undo what had already been done. The army was living in a desert. This desert was the work not only of the Agency of Evacuation. The army itself had contributed. For months it had drawn its subsistence from its immediate vicinity until the region had been bled white. Now it was reduced to seeking its very bread from localities sixty leagues distant.[78] If ever economic rehabilitation were a crying need, such was it at this epoch in the region ruled by the Rhine and Moselle Armies.

There was one incident of the occupation which tended to foster commerce. That was the repair of existing roads and the building of new ones. Though this amelioration in the conditions of travel might appear as an attempt at economic betterment, Merlin of Thionville, its author, was

[75] *Ibid.*, p. 365, n. 1.

[76] Nov. 26, 1794, Aulard, *Actes*, XVIII, 357–358. As if Bourbotte were not the arch culprit!

[77] *Corr. Merlin-Th.*, II, 142–143.

[78] Merlin-Th. to CPS, Dec. 4, 1794, Aulard, *Actes*, XVIII, 515.

probably motivated by the loss of six hundred horses during the previous campaign. Merlin forced the peasants to construct a Trèves-to-Saarburg road, and a Saarburg-to-Perl road. The peasants were obliged also to repair the roads from Trarbach to Mayence, and from Mühlheim to Kirchberg. "It is the local peasant who does all that by *corvée*," wrote Merlin to the Committee, "and he does it ungrudgingly, because I assure him in your name that he will remain French, and that he will not be despoiled; and the peasant has confidence in me."[79] That the French Revolution was supposed to stand for the abolition of such feudal duties as the *corvée* apparently did not trouble Merlin's conscience. However, in fairness, it should be pointed out that the French themselves were subjected to similar burdens. In the neighborhood of Saint-Quentin, workers were requisitioned to dig gravel to repair the roads. At Port-Malo, masons, stone-cutters, and carpenters were required to erect fortifications without compensation.[80] A person was reputed to desire affirmatively to help his *patrie*. That was part of the privilege of being free. The Rhineland was to become an integral portion of the *patrie* some day, and Merlin saw no reason why the inhabitants should not share its burdens. Viewed in this light Merlin's remarks do not seem quite so artful.

3. THE LEFT BANK NORTH OF THE MOSELLE

North of the Moselle, the story was much the same, only different, there being but one Bourbotte. The Agency of Evacuation evacuated here too, but with — shall we say? — more finesse — though that finesse did not prevent its removing the leaden roofs from churches, as in the south.[81] Similarly, the requisitions were "enormous" and included "every conceivable object" from metals and grain to tools and garden seeds, not excluding the usual cattle and forage, and cloth. The article requisitioned was not always immediately removed by the French, but if one failed to declare his possession thereof, he was, or might be, executed, the same as if he had refused to accept an assignat at its face value.[82]

The Maximum was not promptly introduced north of the Moselle, and the cloth-manufacturing industry in Aix-la-Chapelle, Montjoie, Eupen, and Monschau[83] enjoyed a momentary prosperity. Large orders were received from the French military; prices and wages were raised to compensate for the cheapness of the new medium of exchange; and everyone was happy

[79] *Idem*, Nov. 26, 1794, *ibid.*, pp. 357–358.
[80] *Ibid.*, pp. 190–191.
[81] Prof. B. Oberthür, Jan. 1, 1795, Hansen, *Quellen*, III, 385, n. 2.
[82] Dohm to Frederick William, Nov. 28, 1794, *ibid.*, p. 323 and n. 5.
[83] Re Monschau alone: Hansen, *Quellen*, III, 290, n. 3.

until the "Guillotine of Business" [84] (the Maximum) interposed its lugubrious form. Then Aix and the other manufacturing cities became as Cologne had been all along—dead. And why was Cologne dead? Because her economic life depended principally upon the forwarding of freight, upon shipping;[85] and businessmen ship only when they can sell at a profit. Of Cologne and Bonn at this time, an *émigré* professor wrote, "The people stalk along like phantoms, . . . impoverished and careworn people . . . who formerly lived in comfortable circumstances. The merchant has no stock; what he did have, he had to surrender for assignats. Cologne, the erstwhile so-rich city, has become very poor." [86]

With the stimulus to produce gone, actual want soon raised its grim head, not only among the inhabitants but also among the French military. Wrote Joubert and Portiez of the Oise, Representatives on Mission, to the Committee on December 24: "You, at Paris, are being deceived as to the amount of provisions in these regions, especially [the region] between the Meuse and the Rhine. . . It seems to be forgotten that for six months and more, the most numerous army of the Republic has been sustained by the grain of the country. . . Several causes have concurred to produce this painful state of affairs: bad military administration, the crossing of [different] requisitions made at the same time in the same communes, the discredit of the assignats, the preference everywhere accorded coin, . . . personal interest, . . . the hid[ing] of grain, . . . [and] the absence of means of transport. . . We have only one enemy to fear here; it is famine. We shall endeavor to effect the disappearance of coin, and to accredit the assignats." [87]

The Representatives, two days before, had decreed the long-expected general contribution.[88] It was apparently with this that they hoped to effect the disappearance of coin. This levy, a 25,000,000-livre blow to the economy, was to be paid in specie by the occupied territory north of the Moselle. It will be explained later how the northern left bank had been divided into several administrative districts, with a Central Administration at Aix. Of the 25,000,000-livre total of the contribution, the Aix District was expected to pay 5,000,000; the Bonn District, 8,000,000; and the Geldern District, 4,000,000. The district administrators were given the task of distributing the burden over their districts.[89]

[84] *Aachener Zuschauer*, Dec. 27, 1794, *ibid.*, p. 328, n. 6.

[85] Dohm to Frederick William, Nov. 28, 1794, Hansen, *Quellen*, III, 323.

[86] Oberthür, Jan. 1, 1795, on conditions in October, *ibid.*, p. 385, n. 2.

[87] Aulard, *Actes*, XIX, 69.

[88] Soon after the conquest of Cologne (pop., 45,500 [Hansen, *Quellen*, III, 355, n. 2]), a

local contribution of 5,000,000 livres had been announced; also 5,000,000 for the Duchy of Jülich. However, before these had been put into effect, they yielded to the system of an over-all contribution for the entire left bank north of the Moselle (*ibid.*, pp. 229; 312, n. 2). Joubert and Portiez' decree had been expected since Nov. 15 (*ibid.*).

[89] *Ibid.*, p. 337, n. 1.

No milk and honey flowed on the left bank as a result of this contribution, and soon it was necessary to assure the people that "only the malevolent, and aristocrats, paint the future dark and speak of impending famine." [90] Yet the army itself was admittedly out of food, clothes, shoes. On January 29, the threat was voiced to take fifty hostages unless the inhabitants supplied shoes to the soldiers, who "are marching barefoot and dying of cold and fatigue, . . . they, who are suffering only for the happiness of the inhabitants of the conquered region!" [91] It was recognized that most of the farmers were in a sorry state, but they were castigated nevertheless for "their paucity of gratitude and humanity. What baleful consequences would result if the troops themselves were obliged to forage!" [92]

On January 12, the Representatives on Mission Haussmann, Roberjot, and Briez, in a letter to the Convention, ascribed the distressed condition of the occupied regions to a veritable system of fraud on the part of agents of the military, and begged the Convention to "deliver the army, deliver the people, from this accursed race." [93] The day after — not as a consequence of the Representatives' letter, for sufficient time had not elapsed for that — the Central Administration at Aix-la-Chapelle announced to the inhabitants the end of requisitions by the military. Henceforth, the people were told, the civil authorities "would invite them to do their duty as good citizens." [94] But the impositions themselves continued,[95] and, during the succeeding weeks, numerous burgomasters were imprisoned as hostages for the delivery of supplies to the army.[96]

On February 10, 1795, the Committee decreed that there would be no more requisitions in the conquered region except to provision the army, and those requisitions would be made through the constituted authorities; it provided that the remainder of all contributions might be paid half in coin, half in assignats; it ordered the remission of fines levied, and the release of hostages taken, for nonpayment of contributions; and it abolished the Maximum in the conquered territory.[97] (This law had already been abolished in France.) [98]

This was a start in the right direction, but it failed to recognize frankly

---

[90] Central Administration to inhabitants between Meuse and Rhine, Jan. 13, 1795, *ibid.*, p. 354.

[91] Lamotze, National Agent to Central Administration, to Malmaison, National Agent to District of Geldern, Jan. 29, 30, 1794, *ibid.*, pp. 364–365.

[92] Descamps, substitute of Lamotze, to Malmaison, Feb. 9, 14, *ibid.*, p. 365, n. 1.

[93] Aulard, *Actes*, XIX, 441.

[94] Jan. 13, 1795, Hansen, *Quellen*, III, 354.

[95] E.g., agriculture of the District of Bonn was facing ruin because of a daily requisition of 100 horned cattle. On urgent plea, this number was cut to a third (February 10). But on April 22, 6000 cows were demanded, immediately, from the region between the Meuse and Rhine (*ibid.*, p. 402, nn. 1, 2).

[96] *Ibid.*, p. 365, n. 2.

[97] *Ibid.*, p. 396.

[98] On Dec. 24, 1794. *Ibid.*, p. 167, n. 3.

that Portiez and Joubert's 25,000,000-livre tonic had only made the patient worse. Four days later, however, another doctor was called in — a really good doctor. He (Representative Gillet) declared that 8,000,000 units was all the patient could tolerate; that there were not 25,000,000 livres in coin on the whole left bank; that unless that bloated figure were cut, the patient would be reduced to despair. He said the country was in "a violent state" and something had to be done to calm it. Gillet reduced the 25,000,000 to 8,000,000,[99] and the Committee approved. It decreed, further, that no more contributions should be imposed.[100]

Toward the end of the winter of 1794–95 (i.e., *ventôse*, Year III),[101] the Convention sent Representative Roberjot on an inspection tour of the Rhineland. He was surprised with what he saw at Aix. Excessive provisions were being exacted at low prices, and even these greatly reduced prices were not being honestly paid. The French officials were comporting themselves as though they had been given office only for their personal gain. The country was in a sort of stupor. Many inhabitants had emigrated. Roberjot and his colleague Dubois made some changes in the personnel of the administration, and tried to make some sense and justice out of the sorry mess into which the left bank had been thrown by the planless creation of *émigrés*.

In point of fact, the French laws respecting emigration had never been extended by legislation to the conquered territory. There was no reason why they should have been. These laws were aimed at those who, theoretically at least, had borne arms against their French fatherland.[102] Those who had fled the Rhineland had never borne arms against either their own country or France. Moreover, residence was not a requirement of the Rhinelander's law. However, these fine legalistic points did not bother those who, when in France, could make *émigrés* out of people who had never left the country, nor even Paris, nor sometimes even their beds,[103] or who had crossed the frontier for a time to seek health at some mineral spring.[104] The day after the capture of Aix, Representative Gillet was threatening to regard all

---

[99] Feb. 14, 1795, Aulard, *Actes*, XX, 276–277.
[100] Decree of CPS, Feb. 25, 1795, Hansen, *Quellen*, III, 425.
[101] *Ventôse* extended from February 19 to March 20, inclusive.
[102] "Theoretically," because only a handful of the *émigrés* — less than 10,000 — had borne arms against the revolutionary government of France (Sciout, *Direc.*, I, 430).
[103] *Ibid.*, pp. 430–431, 527.
[104] This was the case of the Marquise de B., who, being ill, had gone to Germany before the Revolution to take the waters. While she was away, the Revolution burst

forth, and the revolutionists set a time limit upon residence abroad. Those not returning within the designated period would be reputed to have emigrated, said the law, and of course their property would be confiscated. When the old lady wished to return, the time limit had already expired, but a 100,000 livres' bribe paid to the deputy Chabot obtained for her a passport from the Provisional Executive Council. Returning, she was executed as an *émigré* despite her passport; and her tenants became suddenly quite enamored of her property (*Un séjour en France*, pp. 249–250).

absent persons as *émigrés* and to confiscate their property.[105] From then on, it was open season on *émigrés* and their possessions.

Roberjot and Dubois decided to define an *émigré* so as to remove many of the crying injustices, and still not deprive the French *fiscus* of the opportunity of hypothecating at least a goodly share of its assignats on property belonging to someone else. They decreed that the term *"émigré"* included: First, all those who were absent from the territory ruled by the Central Administration of Aix-la-Chapelle, and who had borne arms against the French Republic, or assisted the enemy armies in person or by furnishing them men, arms, or other things necessary to levy war. Second, all absent persons who formerly constituted part of any of the following groups — archbishops, bishops, princes, abbots, lords, and nobles, and their retainers; priests and ecclesiastics of all classes, and, in general, all persons bound by vows; agents, customs officials, employees, and receivers of the chapters, abbeys, and secular and regular corporations and communities. Third, those who, exercising public functions of any kind when the said countries were evacuated by the enemy armies, deserted their posts to follow them. And, last, those who, at the time of the retreat of the French in the year 1793, betrayed by their violence their hatred of liberty. No other persons would be reputed to have emigrated, even if absent from the territory between the Meuse and the Rhine, provided they reëntered the said territory within four *décades* (i.e., forty days), counting from the date of promulgation of the decree.[106]

This decree exercised much effect upon the *émigré* situation north of the Moselle, but that effect took place principally after the Treaty of Basel, i.e., after April 5, so its consideration will be postponed at this time.[107] With respect to the region between the Moselle and Rhine, no attempt was made to mollify the rigors of the decrees in force, and only a few *émigrés* were allowed to return.

The *Tagebuch* of L. Müller tells of two who returned via the "greased-palm route," and the palm was that of Representative Neveu.[108]

4. CULTURE THROUGH PLUNDER

There is an aspect of French policy which is certainly not deserving of the dignity of a separate section; yet it is said that even the Devil is entitled to his day in court. The comparison is apt, for the subject to be discussed here

[105] Gillet to inhabitants on right bank of Meuse, Sept. 24, 1794, Hansen, *Quellen,* III, 234. But it should be recognized that it was the system which was bad. Gillet's good intentions toward the left bank of the Rhine during his entire sojourn there were never disputed (*ibid.,* p. 619, n. 1).

[106] Arch. N., AF III 76, d. 314, March 24, 1795.

[107] *Vide infra,* Pt. I, chap. xiv, § 2.

[108] Hansen, *Quellen,* III, 452, n. 1.

is the systematic plunder of France's neighbors for — yes! — educational and cultural purposes.

The background is simple. French mobs had destroyed many of the great artistic and cultural treasures of Paris in 1792. That loss had been realized, and the revolutionists began casting covetous eyes at the Rubens paintings, the incunabula, the ancient implements, the Cologne mummy, even the marble columns of Charlemagne's tomb — all in the Rhineland at the very doorstep of the Republic. Now, the Convention, on September 15, 1793, had repudiated philosophical warfare. On September 17, it had ordered its troops to strip the enemy bare. And on December 19, it had created a Temporary Commission of the Arts "to inventory and collect in proper warehouses the books, instruments . . . and other objects of the sciences and arts appropriate to public instruction" which would be found in occupied enemy territory. On May 13, 1794, the Committee had created Agencies, one for each army, to execute the task of transporting to Paris the cultural treasures of France's neighbors.[109]

However this may sound, the revolutionists knew how to endow it with a holy mien: "This right of conquest of a new species would honor exceedingly the victors, since it would have instruction — which belongs to all men — as its goal. [Also], thereby, objects would be preserved, which, in wars of tyranny, are often abandoned to deterioration or annihilation." [110]

In Aix-la-Chapelle, all thirty-eight of the ancient porphyry columns of the Carolingian Münster Church were ripped out and sent to Paris.[111] Seven of the thirty-eight columns, each worth 300,000 livres,[112] had supported the tomb of Charlemagne, and were too large for the ordinary carts of that day, so the arsenal of Maestricht was asked to supply the necessary transportation to Paris.[113] With the columns went a bronze statue of Charlemagne and other valuable pieces.[114] The work of removing the columns had begun soon after the capture of Aix (September 1794), and continued for four months beyond the Treaty of Basel.[115]

In Cologne, the pastor of Peter's Church was informed on October 9 that a famous oil painting of Rubens' was going to be removed from his church, and he was told to close the edifice at a certain time "in order that I be not interfered with in my operations. Also, some one will have to be at the door with the keys. Kind wishes and fraternity." [116] Starting with the end of October, the libraries of Cologne's churches and religious houses

[109] Ibid., p. 150.
[110] Faujas and De Wailly (of the Temporary Commission of the Arts) to Rps Frécine and Joubert, Nov. 22, 1794, ibid., p. 308.
[111] Hansen, Quellen, III, 262.
[112] Die Aachener Chronik, Aug. 4, 1795, ibid., p. 546, n. 2.
[113] Hansen, Quellen, III, 546, n. 2.
[114] Ibid., p. 262. It was returned in 1804 (ibid., p. 230, n. 3).
[115] Ibid., pp. 262; 546, n. 2.
[116] Ibid., p. 262.

were painstakingly searched for books "worthy of . . . Paris." Eventually, all libraries were ransacked for manuscripts, incunabula, and copper engravings. The Cologne armory was relieved of its mummy, its Roman antiquities, its sepulchral monuments, and its collection of Middle Ages artillery. Some of these ancient cannon were eighteen feet long, capable of shooting forty-pound balls, and their removal posed a problem. (But revolutionary genius triumphed.) The city was relieved also of its valuable stamp collection — a loss which it took very hard.[117]

J. N. Dumont, one of the two burgomasters of Cologne, wrote to Representative Gillet: "Ah, if some rare and valuable pieces can serve to augment the luster of your museum, of your collection of masterpieces of the arts and of human industry, we would be happy, we would be proud, to offer you something worthy of the attention of France. But leave us the rest, representatives of a generous people." [118]

After Cologne came Bonn and Coblenz and Trèves.[119] But the story was the same everywhere, and is not so pleasant as to bear repeating for its own sake. Suffice it to say that this is one of the least defensible aspects of the German [120] policy of the Convention.

5. THE ADMINISTRATIVE ORGANIZATION OF THE LEFT BANK

It is desired at this point to take up the attitude of the early Thermidorians toward annexation of the left bank, but first the administrative organization of the left bank by the French must be made clear, for French policy was often uttered through the mouths of administrative organs. On November 14, 1794, the Representatives Haussmann, Frécine, and Joubert created a Central Administration at Aix-la-Chapelle for the region between the Meuse and Rhine.[121] The choice of Aix was probably due to an attempt to give the new government borrowed esteem — borrowed from Charlemagne, whose capital Aix was.[122]

The general regulations of the new administration provided for the con-

---

[117] Ibid., pp. 305–308. The stamp collection consisted of 26,949 stamps in 208 volumes, and Cologne had refused 100,000 livres for it a few years before ("Senate of the Ubii or of the Free City of Cologne to the National Convention," enclosed in letter of Cologne Senate to Lamotze, Jan. 25, 1795, ibid., p. 370 [the "Ubii" letter was, intrinsically, an appeal to France to honor Cologne's ancient institutions]).
[118] To Gillet, Dec. 10, 1794, ibid., p. 329, n. 3.
[119] Hansen, Quellen, III, 262.

[120] The rape of Belgium's art treasures also forms part of France's German policy in a sense, because Belgium belonged to Austria. But, by definition, Belgium is excluded from this monograph.
[121] This superseded the central administration of the District of Aix-la-Chapelle, created November 4 (ibid., p. 286).
[122] The French were very historical-minded, and even did some excavating in Münster in the hope of finding the grave of Charlemagne (ibid., p. 230, n. 3).

tinuance of all laws and customs not contrary to decrees of Representatives on Mission; the preservation of all existing taxes and levies for the benefit of the French treasury; the exchange of all moneys in public treasuries for assignats; the acceptance of assignats by public authorities and in commercial transactions; and the Maximum.[123]

The first members of the new government — the decree set the number of members at eighteen [124] — were not all Frenchmen, as has sometimes been asserted.[125] There would be slight purpose in naming them, as probably the only name that would be recognized at this point would be that of A. J. "Handsome Feet" Dorsch, its first president.[126] The National Agent representing the French Government, who constituted the nineteenth member, was J. Lamotze until the end of January 1795, then N. J. Descamps to March 1795, and then L. P. Caselli.[127]

The country was divided into seven districts, each with a managing committee (*Verwaltungsrat*) of fourteen members, plus a National Agent representing France. The four German districts were Geldern for Gelderland, Meurs, and Clèves; Aix-la-Chapelle for the Duchy of Jülich, Aix, and Burtscheid; Bonn for the Electorate and city of Cologne; [128] and Blankenheim for the Eifel region.[129] Each district was divided into seven cantons, and of the above-mentioned fourteen members of the managing committee, seven were to exercise their functions locally — one in each canton.[130]

The new central government was ceremoniously installed on December 20, 1794, simultaneously with the dedication of a temple to the Supreme

[123] *Ibid.*, p. 310.

[124] *Ibid.*, p. 332.

[125] E.g., C. Schmidt, *Les sources de l'histoire des territoires rhénans de 1792 à 1814 dans les archives rhénanes et à Paris* (Paris 1921), p. 5.

[126] Two other members, Vossen and Cromm, will appear in the next section.

[127] Hansen, *Quellen*, III, 333, n. 4.

[128] It is difficult to describe the violence of the tempest in a teapot that this subordination of Cologne to Bonn induced. Bonn had been governed by a prince; Cologne (the Ubii) had been free for 2,000 years. Caesar had mentioned the senate of the Ubii and their conventions. So had Tacitus. The Franks and the Holy Roman Empire had recognized Cologne's freedom. Through the centuries, lawsuits innumerable had been instituted by Cologne to resist the encroachments of Bonn. What could the French have meant by subjecting a free people to slaves! And when Bonn apportioned a contribution laid upon the conquered country by the French, loud were the cries (not entirely groundless, by any means) of "prejudiced," "unfair," from the "Senate of the Ubii." Letters innumerable, and J. N. Dumont, one of the two Cologne burgomasters, were despatched to Paris. It was all in vain, but it must be admitted that it was a magnificent effort, and shows clearly why Cologne had been able to maintain its freedom through the centuries. Only the French revolutionists — masters of the well-turned phrase themselves — had proved able to withstand such a barrage of words (*ibid.*, pp. 313, 328, 355, 360, 366, 382, 392, 404, 423, 445, 452, 464, 516, 607). It is interesting to reflect that all this hostility between Cologne and Bonn blazed while the national enemy was within the gates.

[129] *Ibid.*, p. 311.

[130] Schmidt, *Sources rhénans*, p. 5.

Being. Portiez of the Oise, lawyer and journalist, who succeeded Gillet, delivered the first oration, and Dorsch the second. What they said was indicative of a trend, and will be considered presently.

For the country between the Rhine and Moselle, the first French organization — the author is tempted to say "disorganization" — introduced was the execrable Agency of Evacuation.[131] This institution, as has been seen, created in the newly conquered Electorate of Trèves such intolerable conditions from the local viewpoint, and abuses from the French viewpoint [132] — and gave rise to such a flood of complaints against both the Agency and Bourbotte, its local organizer [133] — that it was abolished (January 1795).

To fill the void, a General Direction of National Domains for the entire region between the Rhine and Moselle was formed at Trèves (January 27, 1795), with ten (later seven) [134] district directions. The functions of the General Direction were to make an inventory of the sequestrated property of emigrated or absent persons, and of mines, smelters, and factories, and to collect their respective incomes; to collect taxes and customs; and to requisition grain, fodder, and livestock.[135] From what has been said — and left unsaid — the fact emerges that the southern Rhineland was not given a civil government such as was the north. The Armies of the Rhine and of the Moselle [136] still ruled the region. As Representative on Mission Dubois wrote later, "it was abandoned to itself and to the vacuity of an isolated march." [137]

It was soon realized, however, that centralization of all the administrative authorities of the conquered left bank would present undoubted advantages, so on March 10, the General Direction of Trèves was placed under the Central Administration of Aix-la-Chapelle.[138] A district administration was thereupon set up at Trèves,[139] and installed with great ceremony on April 29.[140] Complaints followed, mostly, it seems, because Germans were included in the government; but that was in line with Paris' orders: that at least three quarters of the personnel should be natives. Representative Dubois said that "natives, when one knew how to choose them, were worth more

[131] *Supra*, chap. iv, § 2l.
[132] Aulard, *Actes*, XVI, 64; Lassaulx, etc. to Gillet, Sept. 10, 1795; Hansen, *Quellen*, III, 617–618. "Everybody from the trooper to the general in chief complains against the Agency," wailed an Agency inspector arraigned before the Revolutionary Tribunal. "Never was an administration so calumniated as is the Agency" (*ibid.*, p. 449, n. 4).
[133] Hansen, *Quellen*, III, 174, 448, 541.
[134] *Ibid.*, p. 6 *.
[135] *Ibid.*, pp. 379–380.

[136] These were distinct armies, but, since April 4, 1793, under one and the same general (Aulard, *Actes*, III, 60). They became one army (Rhine and Moselle) only in early March, 1795 (*ibid.*, XX, 695); March 3, says Hansen (*Quellen*, III, 403).
[137] Dubois to CPS, May 21, 1795, *ibid.*, p. 489, n. 4.
[138] By Rp Neveu, *ibid.*, p. 440. The French were very conscious that Aix had been Charlemagne's capital (*ibid.*, p. 230, n. 3).
[139] By Dubois, *ibid.*, p. 481.
[140] *Ibid.*, p. 482, n. 1.

than the legion of knaves who pride themselves on their French origin." It was the latter group, he said, which was making France detested in many regions. Dubois outlined how he had tried to inspire confidence among the original administrators of the region. "I guarantee they will serve us yet, and actively, when the French government feels the time has finally come to occupy itself with the fate of this region." [141]

But the complaints continued. The Plunder-Winter of 1793–94 in the Palatinate, and the Plunder Summer and Autumn and Winter of Bourbotte and the Agency of Evacuation,[142] rendered imperative the use of extraordinary measures, and Aix-la-Chapelle was too far away and too disinterested. Or, at any rate, Aix did not have the confidence of the southern populations.[143] Another reorganization must therefore be expected — within the month, in fact — but, for Cronus' sake, that must be dealt with in another chapter.[144]

6. THE PSYCHOLOGICAL CRUSADE

The Committee's instructions of August 3, 1794, to the Sambre and Meuse Army, extended on August 17 to the Rhine and Moselle Armies, had ordered a "conquered-territory treatment" for the left bank, to include nonfraternization, nonmunicipalization, nonconcern with annexation — and stripping of the conquered regions of all their worldly goods.[145] It can probably be stated with assurance that, on August 17, there was no affirmative plan in the mind of the Committee to keep the left bank. It should be noted, however, that the left bank was not being treated as enemy country, which is what the conquered territory really was. The strictest order was maintained by the conquering French troops. There was no plundering. "All reports agree," wrote von Dohm, "that the French everywhere are observing an uncommonly strict discipline. The slightest offense is severely punished, and no one's property rights are being encroached upon." [146] "Only robbers plunder," Representative Gillet told the Sambre and Meuse Army just before the conquest of Aix-la-Chapelle, "and whosoever is guilty of such [conduct] de-

---

[141] Aulard, *Actes*, XXIII, 413.

[142] At least passing mention should be made of Rougemaître, who "evacuated" the houses of *émigrés* in the Palatinate from September 5 to October 16, 1794. He was a "barbarous man, ferocious and terrible, whose every order was under penalty of death." So ran a report on him to the Convention by Rp Becker, June 13, 1795 (Hansen, *Quellen*, III, 448, n. 3).

[143] *Ibid.*, p. 583, n. 2.

[144] *Infra*, Pt. I, chap. xiv, § 7. If Cronus was not the god of time, as mythologists now tell us, he is hereby officially appointed to that post. We need a god of time to watch over our chronology.

[145] *Vide* § 1, this chapter.

[146] To Frederick William, Nov. 28, 1794, Hansen, *Quellen*, III, 322.

serves death. . . Plundering and every other excess will . . . be punished,
in this city as elsewhere." [147]

The emphasis on "this city" carries the mind back to the ousting of the
French from Aix on March 3, 1793, when the inhabitants shot at the fleeing
French from their windows, or utilized those windows to send wounded
soldiers plummeting to the street below. Robespierre had "promised" that
if France ever returned to Aix as a victor, the city would be plundered and
burned.[148] Now, on September 23, 1794, the French were on the outskirts,
but Gillet was telling the troops: "Leave the task of punishing the guilty
to me. They shall receive the wages of their misdeeds, and I shall know,
on the other hand, how to recognize the services of those who assisted our
brothers." [149]

Of course, some of Gillet's moderation must have been due (aside from
the quieting effect of Thermidor) to the influence of a deputation sent that
very morning by the Cologne Senate to French army headquarters at Herve.
Of the two deputies, Dr. jur. J. J. Vossen and N. Cromm, the former was a
member of the Masonic lodge that had rescued a group of French soldiers
during the debacle of March 3, 1793, and one of those very French soldiers
was now *Colonel* Mariète at French headquarters.[150]

We have seen some indication that the French invaders were not going
to take literally the instructions of August 3. But that is not the end of our
evidence. Trees of liberty sprang up everywhere: at Trèves (October 3),[151]
Cologne (October 9),[152] Coblenz (October 26),[153] Monschau (November
14),[154] Clèves (November 15),[155] and Aix-la-Chapelle (March 10, 1795).[156]
Certainly they could not have sprung up in the face of army disapproval.
Of course, there could have been mere army indifference, but that is unlikely.

There was also some founding of Clubs. This is all the more remarkable
when one considers that Clubs had fallen into disfavor in France because of
their connection with the Terror.[157] There was strong Club membership
at Cologne.[158] The president of the Central Administration at Aix, Dorsch's
successor Simeon, on March 28, 1795, summoned a secret "Association of
Friends of Freedom on the Banks of the Rhine" to divulge the location of

---

[147] Sept. 23, 1794, Hansen, *Quellen*, III, 226,
n. 3.
[148] *Supra*, chap. ii, § 4.
[149] Hansen, *Quellen*, III, 226, n. 3.
[150] *Ibid.*, pp. 226, n. 3; 227 and n. 4.
[151] *Ibid.*, p. 217, n. 2.
[152] *Ibid.*, p. 261.
[153] *Ibid.*, p. 278.
[154] *Ibid.*, p. 290, n. 2.
[155] *Ibid.*, p. 256.

[156] *Ibid.*, p. 229. And the stone whipping-post
monument, destroyed by Johann Tauzenberg in 1792 and reërected in 1793, was
again destroyed (*ibid.*, p. 232, n. 2).
[157] Prohibition of the association of clubs and
of correspondence between clubs, and the
closing of the Jacobin Club of Paris, had
followed close upon one another in the
autumn of 1794 (*ibid.*, p. 271, n. 3).
[158] *Ibid.*, p. 220.

its meeting-place.[159] Biergans, the publisher of *Brutus*, in a speech in Düren, seventeen miles east of Aix-la-Chapelle, mentioned that he had spoken before a secret society a few months before.[160] And at Saarbrücken, which the French had been occupying since 1792, a certain dozen persons founded a Club, drew up a petition for annexation to France, and tried to induce their fellow townsmen to sign it.[161]

Municipalités or town councils were set up in Spires, Worms,[162] Aix[163] — in fact, in every city of the left bank but Cologne.[164] The preservation of Cologne's Senate was due to its persistence, its eloquence, its logic, its pleading, and its reminding France that the latter still owed it 3,000,000 livres expended to assist France in 1756.[165]

When a normal school was founded at Paris (October 30, 1794) to teach "not only the sciences but the art of teaching the sciences," it was provided that each district might send one pupil for each 20,000 inhabitants, that the pupils should arrive in Paris by the end of December and remain four months, and that the expenses of the trip and of the sojourn in Paris would be borne by the state.[166] But there was no indication in the decree that the normal school was not for France alone. It was two months later that the surprise came.

On January 6, 1795, the Representatives to the Sambre and Meuse Army released the following order: "Convinced that public education is one of the surest means to consolidate the dominion of liberty and equality, to accustom a person's mind to virtue, and to render him receptive to republican customs; and likewise zealously eager to permit the inhabitants of the conquered lands to participate in the advantages [of the normal-school decree, it is ordained that] . . . every district administration shall within 3 days . . . send . . . to Paris [one pupil for each 20,000 of population], — in its choice only those citizens to be considered who are of clean habits [and] proved patriotism . . . and possess the necessary foundation to receive and give instruction."[167]

---

[159] *Ibid.*, p. 462.

[160] *Ibid.*, p. 431.

[161] *Ibid.*, pp. 210–212. No one would, even though the Clubists procured the arrest of several persons in a valiant effort to put through their plan. The Club was finally dissolved in February 1795 (*ibid.*).

[162] *Ibid.*, p. 231, n. 1.

[163] *Ibid.*, p. 229.

[164] *Ibid.*, p. 577, n. 2.

[165] *Ibid.*, pp. 355, 359, 360, 366, 392, 445, 452, *et passim*. During the Seven Years' War, Cologne — when France's credit was insufficient to purchase needed supplies —

borrowed 3,000,000 livres to help outfit the French. Cologne was still paying interest on that 3,000,000, for France, despite repeated requests, had refused reimbursement (*ibid.*, p. 383).

[166] *Ibid.*, pp. 232–233.

[167] *Ibid.*, p. 350, n. 1. There seems to have been little response to the glowing offer, for on March 16, 1795, Representatives Roberjot and Dubois were decreeing the "execution without delay" of the January 6 order. Students were then chosen, and one of them was J. B. Geich, publisher of the *Dekadenschrift*, etc. But already

It is hardly necessary to comment on the extent to which this order deviates from the Committee's instructions of August 3, 1794. Apparently a change of policy gradually effected itself as the armies advanced and consolidated their positions, and the enemy failed to recoup his losses.

It will be recalled that, on July 16, Carnot had recommended the Meuse frontier for France. Remembered, also, will be the position taken by Hansen: that Carnot did not intend that France should renounce all connection with the left bank, but only that a buffer state should be formed between the Meuse and Rhine.[168] But it would seem — would it not? — that if Carnot had been thinking seriously of a buffer state in the middle of July, the instructions of August 3 would have contained no ban on fraternization or municipalization.

Be that as it may, Carnot's attitude now was that of the enthusiastic victor anxious to gather in the spoils, and on November 14 he wrote to the Representatives in the name of the Committee the words quoted above [169] that the left bank was legally French, for victory gave title. And on November 26, Merlin of Thionville echoed the same thought: "It has doubtless been decided that the Rhine will remain the barrier of France." [170] On December 4, in the speech mentioned above,[171] Merlin of Douai implied, without saying so, that France would not agree to peace without the Rhine boundary.[172] Merlin of Douai had not been so coy the previous October 7 when he declared: "In a few days the Rhine will be our limit; the nation has never been greater." [173] In February of 1795, Cambacérès, speaking for the Committee, declared that the Rhine frontier was essential to France if she would destroy the germ of future wars.[174]

Not all voices, however, bowed to the fickle present. Several memorials appeared in the latter part of 1794 arguing that annexation of the Rhineland would lead to a long war, that the large armies such expansion would necessitate would endanger French liberties and end in despotism; and that England, and Europe in general, would never permit France to enjoy her conquests in peace.[175] In February of 1795, there appeared in Paris an anonymous treatise (by General Miranda) [176] which created quite a stir. It maintained that France's best defense was its line of forts, and it frowned upon the absorption of peoples of different languages, passions, and opinions.[177] In

the school was failing, and it was abolished after its first four months' course, January–May 1795 (*ibid.*, pp. 443–445).
[168] *Vide supra*, chap. iv, § 21, and nn. 389–390.
[169] Chap. vi, n. 46.
[170] To CPS, Aulard, *Actes*, XVIII, 357.
[171] Chap. vi, § 2.
[172] *Moniteur*, XXII, 667–668.
[173] Hansen, *Quellen*, III, 271.
[174] *Ibid.*, p. 471.
[175] *Ibid.*, p. 271.
[176] *Ibid.*, p. 574, n. 2.
[177] *Ibid.*, p. 471. This treatise later appeared in a pamphlet entitled: *Les frontières de la France considerées sous un point de vue politique et militaire; ouvrage dédié à la Convention nationale* (Paris, 1795).

March, from Hamburg, appeared Dumouriez' *Coup d'œil politique sur l'avenir de la France* ("Hasty Political View of the Future of France"), in which he asserted that Belgium could be amalgamated with France because of identity of tongue, but the German Rhineland — never. And in a letter to the translator of the history of his life, Dumouriez made the point that though Caesar had found a Gaul extending to the Rhine, Alps, and Pyrenees, it was not a unified country like France that so extended; it was composed of hostile republics always at swords' points.[178] It seemed to be generally agreed that the key to an early peace was the renunciation of conquests, and indeed many in the Rhineland believed that was France's intention. As *émigré* Professor Oberthür wrote, "Now they are starting to remove the lead, brass, and iron from [our] churches. Truly from this one can conclude that the French have no intention of keeping these territories, since they treat them thus." [179] Both the *Aachener Zuschauer* [180] and Merlin of Douai [181] mentioned the widespread rumors of impending peace current in Paris — rumors which would indicate that, in Paris, too, renunciation would not have been unexpected.

But from the Rhineland itself came a long list of inspired statements so jumbled with pleas of an "economic" nature as to be almost unrecognizable, but which certainly should have cast doubt upon France's intention to renounce. The short-lived District of Aix-la-Chapelle, whose jurisdiction extended from the Meuse to the Roer, proclaimed to the people on November 4, 1794: "The most magnanimous nation of the earth . . . embraces us fraternally. She calls to us: Become our brothers and free people. . . We have received the command from the Representatives on Mission . . . to break the ice. However, fellow citizens, . . . consider, and forget not, that no undertaking can be begun without effort and sacrifices." Then came a plea to accept the assignats and to obey the soon-to-be-established Maximum, followed by threats of death for violators. And the appeal ended with a wish that the people "might be worthy of a nation which has treated [them] . . . so magnanimously." [182]

"Your hearts have secretly reached out for freedom," Representative Frécine informed "the Cologne people" on December 10, "but to possess it, you must be worthy thereof. It will cost you only small sacrifices. . . Requisitions will, in the future, be directed only to the administration. . . All abuses will . . . be punished severely. . . Finally, there is the Maximum, based on the need of establishing a healthy balance between necessi-

[178] Hansen, *Quellen*, III, 471 and n. 7. *Vide supra*, Introduction, § 2c.
[179] Hansen, *Quellen*, III, 385, n. 2.
[180] Of Oct. 23, 1794, *ibid.*, p. 271, n. 3.
[181] In his report of Dec. 4, 1794. *Vide supra*, Pt. II, ch. vi, § 2.
[182] Hansen, *Quellen*, III, 286–290.

ties and the means of the . . . people. In order, however, that you might
enjoy all these advantages to the fullest, it is required that the circulation
and credit of the assignats be maintained. They are the coin of the Republic;
their security is the integrity of the French people. This gives you an inestimable advantage over vile coin. . . People of the Cologne region! do not
cease to be good, sensible, and righteous. The happiest fate awaits you. . .
The day is no longer far distant when, . . . with rapture, the inhabitant
and the wanderer . . . will . . . find protection from the heat of day in
the hospitable shade of the tree of liberty." [183]

When the new Central Administration at Aix ceremoniously supplanted
the District of Aix, Representative Portiez of the Oise spoke thus: "You,
inhabitants of the conquered territory, you can contribute to the triumph
of liberty through sacrifice to it. . . You aspire to the glory of becoming
French. Then show yourselves worthy of this great people by your submission to its laws. In the future, requisitions will be paid within a short period.
Therefore, hasten to fulfill them. . . Provide the example of honoring the
value of the assignats. . . The privation of which you complain has its
origin only in the refusal shown by the country people with respect to the
assignats." [184]

Dorsch, president of the Central Administration, followed Portiez on the
platform. Said he, "How can the inhabitants of these territories be so blind
as not to perceive that their happiness lies in union with the French Republic? . . . We are a conquered land, so we must bear the cost of the war. But
do not the French pay for everything delivered to them . . . ? Yes, but in
assignats, some of you say. . . Was it not assignats which saved America
and France, and have they not already earned, on that account, preference
over every other mintage?" [185]

On January 6, 1795, the Representatives to the armies occupying the left
bank north of the Moselle issued a proclamation applicable to both Belgian
and German territory. It declared that if the inhabitants supplied the French
troops, paid their contributions, and accepted the assignats, they would be
participating in the fame and success of the French, and would be "united
with the great family of the French Republic." "If you want to hasten the
time of your union with France, hasten to pay the arrears in your contributions. . . The Representatives of the French People to the Armies have
been authorized to promise you explicitly that annexation will follow as
soon as, by your sacrifices, . . . you have proved yourself worthy thereof." [186]

Just one week later, the Central Administration in Aix extended its sympathy to the inhabitants: "You were distressed, good citizens, over the un-

[183] Ibid., pp. 331–332.
[184] Dec. 20, 1794, ibid., p. 336.
[185] Ibid., pp. 338–340.
[186] Ibid., pp. 348–350.

certainty of your fate. You stretched your hands out to liberty and asked the same of the French. Your wish, citizens, shall be heard. . . Make yourselves worthy of the great and happy lot which the Republic has destined for you. . . We shall divide everything with our French brethren." [187]

On January 29, Simeon, the new president of the Central Administration at Aix, told "the citizens to rejoice, your freedom is established. . . The malevolent intimated that the invincible republicans were unwilling or too weak to maintain themselves in this region. . . Thence, the lack of confidence in the honorable French nation; thence, the serious discredit of the assignats; thence, the slowness and unwillingness to fulfill the requisitions; thence, the fear to express true patriotism, to dedicate oneself to the service of the Republic, to accept public office, . . . to supply necessary sustenance to the gigantic armies of the Republic, and to solicit annexation of these territories by the foremost Republic in the world! But now the panicky fears must have subsided since republican heroes have conquered Holland. . . Have a better opinion of the most magnanimous and mightiest nation on earth. It will not only preserve your liberty, of which you are so worthy, but will fully replace everything of yours that you have had to share with its army. . . The conquest of Holland will restore the true value of the assignat. Soon there will no longer be any difference between assignats and specie. . ." [188]

The contents of these declarations would lead one to expect that if a request for annexation had been forthcoming from the Rhineland, it would at least have formed the subject of serious consideration. On February 20, 1795, the Central Administration of Aix, in a letter to the Convention thanking it for lifting the Maximum, freeing hostages, and granting other boons on February 10, asked for annexation on the basis of sacrifices made and to be made, as promised by the Representatives on Mission.[189] But the Convention merely turned the request over to the Committee of Public Safety.[190] Roberjot and Dubois, on an inspection tour of the Rhineland, had diagnosed many economic ills as springing from a lack of popular knowledge as to the eventual fate of the region. In their report of March 15 to the Committee, they announced that they would "present . . . annexation as the inflexible wish of the French people" in order "to raise a little the value of the assignats," and they urged the Committee to represent, in its reports to the Convention, that France could make peace only on the basis of the Rhine frontier.[191] The Committee did not reply to their suggestion.[192]

[187] *Ibid.*, pp. 353–354.
[188] *Ibid.*, pp. 380–382.
  Dorsch had accepted employment in the foreign affairs department at Paris.
[189] *Ibid.*, p. 399.
[190] *Ibid.*, p. 398, n. 3.
[191] *Ibid.*, p. 441.
[192] *Ibid.*, p. 441, n. 2.

From the foregoing, it seems that we may draw the following conclusions. The government at Paris did not know for certain what attitude toward annexation would finally be adopted, so wanted to postpone decision on the matter, but it reasoned that if its indecision were realized, not only would the Rhinelanders lag behind in their contributions and requisitions payments, but they would try not to accept any more assignats. This would cause a further decline in the value of the assignat. It was thus necessary to dangle annexation constantly before the people's eyes. Roberjot and Dubois say plainly that that was what they contemplated doing, and why. It was also desirable to keep the subject of annexation "warm" in case it should eventuate that France did want to annex. This seems to be the only explanation of that strange medley of the sublime and the ridiculous which constitutes the subject matter of the above harangues.

It might be suggested that in these numerous addresses, two psychological principles were being applied to the Rhinelanders: (1) that of the repeated affirmation — one is expected to believe eventually what he has heard a sufficient number of times; (2) that of the desirability of the unattainable — perverse humanity is reputed to want what it cannot have, or can have only with difficulty. So the French and their German adherents repeated again and again: You want (or crave) annexation but you cannot have it — until you pay this or that (better, this *and* that). This was supposed to have the double advantage of maintaining and whetting local appetite for annexation, and of shifting some of France's economic burden to the enemy of the *patrie*.

Perhaps this sounds a bit too hard and calculating. Voices — earnest and honest voices — were raised in the Paris Convention that the French Revolution should be rendered less tempestuous so it should not be objectionable to the peoples of the left bank.[193] Prudhomme pointed out in his *Révolutions de Paris* that it was not necessary to "sacrifice ourselves [on the battlefield] for the happiness of the human race. . . The spectacle of *our* happiness, . . . [of] the order and harmony which reigns among *us*, as well as between all the branches of our government, will conquer more peoples for liberty than our armies. . . If you want to render [a] people free, conquer its soul before conquering its soil."[194] And Metternich, the Mayence Clubist, published in the *Brutus, der Freund seines Vaterlandes* ("Brutus, the Friend of his Fatherland"), a fictitious address of a peasant of Jülich to his prince. The peasant compared the old regime with the new, and remarked in conclusion: "We are glad that the French have delivered us from such

[193] Aulard, *Jacobins*, VI, 580–581.
[194] "Faut-il poursuivre nos conquètes?" ("Is it necessary to continue our conquests?") XV, 68. The italics are the present writer's.

brigands. We are more satisfied now. Justice is rendered gratis; cases are decided in an instant and without lawyers. . . We are men as much as the clergy, the rich, and the noble." [195]

[195] Sagnac, *Rhin fr.*, p. 115. More complete text in Hansen, *Quellen*, III, 521–524, under the title "Sendschreiben eines jülichschen Bauersmanns an seinen Kurfürsten Karl Theodor von Pfalzbayern, Herzog von Jülich-Berg." Karl Theodor was probably singled out for attack because, septuagenarian that he was, he took unto himself a nineteen-year-old bride — while his Rhineland possessions were being ground under the conqueror's heel. The bride, incidentally, was a Habsburg princess.

CHAPTER VIII

THE FRANCO–PRUSSIAN TREATY OF BASEL, APRIL 5, 1795

I. FIRST PRINCIPLES AND FIRST PARLEYS

a. General

THE Austro-Russian Convention of January 3, 1795, was at first held secret, but Prussia suspected its existence.[1] The Hohenzollern king considered Austria's claims to the Palatinates of Cracow and Sandomir as "utterly incompatible with the safety of his dominions,"[2] and he was not inclined to relinquish possession of the provinces. However, if he were to defy both the Czarina and the Emperor, prudence demanded that he should at least terminate the war with the Convention.

Another factor may also have entered into his calculations, viz., fear that Austria would make a separate peace with France on the basis of the Bavaro-Belgian exchange.[3] Such an arrangement would have amounted to virtual encirclement of Prussia by three hostile powers—a predicament which it was essential for Prussia to avoid by making peace with France before Austria should. And indeed, the danger was not chimeric, for the *abbé* Sieyes was not averse to Austria's acquisition of Bavaria (with the

---

[1] Lodge in *C. Mod. H.*, VIII, 551.

[2] Lord Henry Spencer (British Envoy Extraordinary and Plenipotentiary to Prussia) to Lord Grenville, March 30, 1795, *Dropmore Papers*, III, 561.

[3] Merlin-Th. to CPS, Dec. 4, 1794, Aulard, *Actes*, XVIII, 517. The rumor was current that Carletti, minister of the Grand Duke of Tuscany, was about to repair to Paris to negotiate a Franco-Austrian peace (Sorel in *RH*, VI, 332). And, indeed, Thugut was thinking of peace. He wrote to Cobenzl on February 4 that the possibility that Russia would not overawe Prussia into yielding on the Palatinates question was "one motive more to hasten the moment of our peace with France."—A. von Vivenot (ed.), *Thugut und sein politisches System. Urkundliche Beiträge zur Geschichte der deutschen Politik des österreichischen Kaiserhauses während der Kriege gegen die französische Revolution* (2 parts, Vienna, 1870), Pt. II, 9, reprinted from the Kaiserliche Akademie der Wissenschaften (ed.), *Archiv für Kunde österreichischer Geschichtsquellen*, XLII, XLIII.

qualifications explained below);[4] Sieyes became a member of the Committee on March 5;[5] and the *abbé* was making arrangements through Gérard de Rayneval, one of Louis XVI's councillors of state, for the despatch of an Austrian negotiator to Paris when, or shortly after, the Franco-Prussian peace was finally signed.[6]

Cessation of the western war was necessary for still another reason. The suppression of the Polish revolution of 1794 and the necessities of the struggle against France had exhausted the finances of barren little Prussia.[7] According to the negotiator who finally signed the treaty of peace with France (Hardenberg), there would have been uprisings in Prussia if the conflict with France had continued, so discontented were both army and populace with the war.[8]

The attitude of the King's advisers was also not without weight. Foreign affairs were under the control — after the King — of Alvensleben, bitter enemy of the Austro-Prussian concert; of the aged Finkenstein, who perpetuated in his every word the anti-Habsburg tendencies of Frederick the Great; and of Haugwitz, originally Austria's friend but now weakening in his allegiance. Lucchesini, former reader to Frederick the Great, though not a cabinet minister like the three other statesmen, was yet of great influence in foreign affairs, and he too was hostile to the western war. And of course the finance ministers, Struensee, Werder, and Blumenthal, deprecated the outflowing of so much treasure. In his council, the King had often been the sole advocate of his foreign policy, and now he too was weakening under the pressure of men and events.[9] It is true that he could no longer pretend to be the champion of Louis XVI, but he could still pose as the champion of the Empire. Polish territory was, however, so much more concrete than glory, and there would be a sort of glory — would there not? — in extending Prussia's boundaries. Besides, after France had defeated Austria, Prussia could put France in her place.[10]

It was, then, not love of France or sympathy with the Revolution, but prudence, poverty, Polish territory, and perhaps also the hope that peace

[4] Chap. x, § 3.

[5] Guillaume, *Etudes rév.*, Ser. II, p. 241.

[6] Sorel in *RH*, XVII, 53. The overture was abortive (A. Sorel, "Les frontières constitutionnelles, 1795," *ibid.*, XIX [1882], 26). Hüffer is too certain that fear of a Franco-Austrian accord had no influence upon the signature of the Treaty of Basel (*Europa*, I, 143).

[7] Caillard to Delacroix, Dec. 5, 1795, P. Bailleu (ed.), *Preussen und Frankreich von 1795 bis 1807, Diplomatische Korresponden-*

zen (2 vols., Leipzig, 1881–1887), I, 431.

[8] Barthélemy to CPS, Oct. 27, 1795, *Papiers de Barthélemy*, V, 490. There was indeed a revolt *after* the signing of the Peace of Basel and the supplementary Convention of May 17, 1795. It was attributed to the contagion of French principles. For several days, Berlin was in an uproar (*Mém. homme d'Etat*, III, 186).

[9] Bailleu in *HZ*, LXXV, 238–239.

[10] Wahl, *Staatensystems*, p. 67, for this last sentence only.

would prove more disastrous to the Republic than war [11] which induced the Prussian King to commence unvarnished overtures for peace with France.[12] That his overtures would be kindly received he was certain, not only from the general course of past Franco-Prussian relations, but from the reports of Mallet du Pan. "The Convention is lost if it cannot produce a signed peace treaty before spring," wrote Mallet on November 1, 1794. "No longer does there prevail a strong desire for peace, but a thirst." [13]

On December 1, 1794, Frederick William II summoned Count von der Goltz, Frederick the Great's ambassador to France, into conference. The choice of von der Goltz, who hated Russia, despised Austria, and esteemed France, was due to the King's uncle, Prince Henry, who, it will be recalled, was a decided partisan of Prussia's great western neighbor.[14] The instructions of the envoy bore the date of December 8, 1794. He was to repair to Switzerland and declare to whomsoever the Committee might appoint to negotiate with him that the fall of the Jacobin party in July had raised hopes of peace; [15] that the King of Prussia coveted the role of pacificator of Europe, and would be glad to mediate peace, not only for his coprinces of Germany, but for Austria, England, Sardinia, and Holland; that Prussia could not make a definitive peace with France (that was possible only for the Empire), much less an alliance, but desired an armistice which would include Mayence and grant the benefits of neutrality until the pacification of the Empire; that the King preferred not to recognize the Republic, but would do so if France evacuated the Prussian left-bank possessions; and that a peace on the basis of the *status quo ante bellum*, which would renew the "integrity of the Empire" guarantee of the Peace of Westphalia, was desired.[16]

b. Harnier

To prepare this negotiation,[17] Harnier, secretary to the Prussian legation at Basel, was ordered to return to Basel and proceed from there to Paris.[18]

---

[11] Because the factions would combat each other the instant external danger ceased (Sorel, *Europe*, IV, 195).

[12] They were not avowed before the world, however. On December 26, 1794, Jacobi, Prussian Ambassador to London, officially informed Starhemberg, Austrian Ambassador to London, "that he had received an order from his court to protest openly against the scurrilous rumors of a separate peace which were current with respect to the King his master." — Starhemberg to Thugut, Dec. 26, 1794, Vivenot-Zeissberg, *Quellen*, V, 73. Degelmann, Austrian Minister to Basel, was ordered to observe von der Goltz (*vide* text, next paragraph) to ascertain whether the latter's actions coincided with his court's declarations (Thugut to Degelmann, Jan. 14, 1795, *ibid.*, p. 85).

[13] *Mém. corr. Mallet du Pan*, II, 133. Cf. the reserved official tone in Aulard, *Paris*, I, 425.

[14] Sorel in *RH*, VI, 65.

[15] *Vide* Art. 2 of these instructions in *Papiers de Barthélemy*, IV, 582.

[16] Sorel, *Europe*, IV, 195–196.

[17] *Ibid.*, p. 197.

[18] Sybel, *Europe*, III, 367.

Harnier was the son of a Hessian official, yet he was not unfriendly to the Republic. Quite the contrary. On crossing the frontier into France, he shouted, "Long live the King of Prussia! Long live the French Republic!" and donned a tricolor cockade.[19] Thus bedecked, he proceeded to Paris.[20] Bacher described him to the Committee as "a zealous patriot . . . charged with a desire to serve the cause of liberty." [21] It is clear that Harnier had resolved to do everything in his power to negate the thought that he was hostile to the Revolution. It was a diplomatic way to institute negotiations, but it was neither very patriotic nor very dignified.

Harnier conferred with the Committee of Public Safety from January 7 to 9. He found that the ignominious failure of the Allied campaign of 1794, which had ended with the French conquest of Holland at approximately the same time that the Mannheim bridgehead fell to the French, was visible in every word and gesture of the Committee.[22] The Committee knew the importance of the Dutch conquest. Europe had united in the seventeenth century to check the designs of France upon the United Netherlands. If Prussia was willing to close her eyes to Louis XIV's sans-cullotish successors, the Committee knew that the power to resist had left Frederick William's breast. "Do what you will, but rid me of the war with France," that monarch is said to have told his ministers.[23] The French did not know the words, but they were aware of the gist. It was to be a peace at (almost) any price, and they immediately hoisted the price. Had not someone — without authority — clamped a ceiling on that price, all accord would have been impossible. But let us not anticipate.

Harnier's first effort was expended in conveying the pacific wishes expressed in von der Goltz's instructions. The Committee responded with an offer of immediate alliance against Russia and Austria — an alliance to be reinforced later by the accession of Sweden, Denmark, Turkey, and Poland.[24] When Harnier interposed that the King would never take up arms against his old allies, but desired only to mediate a general peace, the Committee declared that it would never consent to mediation, for that implied authority in the mediator, and the Republic had conquered a position in Europe where it did not need to recognize any foreign authority.[25] The most that the Committee would agree to accept was good offices, and it reserved the right to treat, unhampered, separately, with any state.[26] This reservation betrays the French reluctance, which later appeared, to honor the Prussian good offices.[27] Regarding an armistice, that was definitely out of the question.

[19] Vivenot, *Bas. Fried.*, Pt. II, 59.
[20] *Ibid.*, p. 60, n. 1.
[21] Sorel in *RH*, VI, 37–38.
[22] Häusser, *Deutsche Geschichte*, I, 588.
[23] *Mém. homme d'Etat*, II, 580.

[24] Sybel, *Europe*, III, 374.
[25] Sorel, *Europe*, IV, 224.
[26] Häusser, *Deutsche Geschichte*, I, 589; Sybel, *Europe*, III, 375.
[27] Sorel is misleading when he says the Com-

Then the Committee divulged its conditions of peace: the Rhine boundary,[28] and the surrender of Mayence. Harnier protested that Prussia could consent to no terms which were not honorable; that she had a mission to fulfill: to become the leading power of Germany, and could not commence by agreeing to the dismemberment of the Empire.[29] The Committee remained inflexible. Harnier thereupon decided to utilize the storm to drive the Prussian ship of state, and declared that if the King should consent to renounce his trans-Rhenish possessions, he would certainly require adequate indemnification therefor. The Committee affirmed that it was not adversely disposed to Prussia's acquisition of Austrian or ecclesiastical territory on the right bank, and that it would have even offered Hanover to Prussia had Harnier not declared that alliance was out of the question. At this juncture the conversations ended.[30]

c. The Committee Outlines Its German Policy

The Committee recapitulated the points discussed, and sent a copy to Barthélemy, with a note announcing that he had been chosen to treat with von der Goltz, or any other Prussian minister, at Basel.[31] The recapitulatory document is very important, for it lays bare the German policy of the Convention, which, by and large, was later to be that of the Directory also:

The government of France . . . is decidedly disposed to make peace with Prussia.

It will not at all insist on the immediate establishment of an . . . offensive and defensive alliance. . .[32]

The recognition of the Republic should not enter into the articles of the treaty of peace, since it [the Republic] exists in fact. . .[33]

The Rhine will be the new boundary of France. . . The [cession] of the

mittee declared it would *willingly* accept good offices (*Europe*, IV, 224). If this were true, the Committee's later reluctance would represent a change of policy, of which there is no evidence.

[28] This requirement had already been intimated to Prussia through Merlin-Th. and Bacher, and through Möllendorff's Swiss agent, according to Merlin-Th.'s letter of Dec. 12, 1794, to CPS, Aulard, *Actes*, XVIII, 667.

[29] Häusser, *Deutsche Geschichte*, I, 589. Vivenot, with the hostility of the Austrian of 1866 for Prussia, tries to throw doubt upon Harnier's reluctance to violate the integrity of the Empire (*Bas. Fried.*, Pt. II, 60, n. 1), inasmuch as Harnier presently agreed to the spoliation. But Harnier was in a

difficult position — in consequence, of course, of Prussia's studied inactivity during the period of supposedly active hostilities.

[30] Sorel, *Europe*, IV, 225.

[31] Jan. 15, 1795, *Papiers de Barthélemy*, V, 47–48, 57.

[32] Cf. CPS to Barthélemy, Jan. 15, *ibid.*, p. 48: "While reflecting on the state of Europe, you have surely realized that the two nations ought to unite against the common enemy. It is the principal object of the negotiation."

[33] *Vide* instructions of CPS to Barthélemy, Jan. 15, 1795: "The Republic, the existence of which could not be prevented, is recognized the moment one treats with it." — *Ibid.*, p. 52.

Prussian states on the left bank . . . will form the principal object of negotiation between the two powers. France . . . will not oppose his Majesty's . . . acquisition of an equivalent portion of territory beyond the Rhine. It can even concur to procure it for him. . .

To promote and abridge this principal negotiation, the Committee prefers that the seat thereof should be established at Paris.[34]

Concerning the German Empire. — France is equally disposed to conclude definitive peace with the [individual] states of the German Empire.

It establishes the principle that all those who have interests on this side of the Rhine will sacrifice them. It is disposed to allow them to have such equivalents or indemnities as the circumstances permit.

The negotiation may commence simultaneously with that of Prussia, or follow closely its conclusion.

The French government, while refusing all mediation in the strict sense of the term, understands that his Prussian Majesty will offer his good offices for the pacification of his German co-states, and particularly in favor of those who attach themselves to the system in regard to which there is a conformity of interests and of views between France and Prussia.[35]

Armistice. — No suspension of hostilities, no armistice, no neutrality of the states of the Empire before the definitive pacification, accords with the interests of France.

Neutralization of Mayence. — The occupation of Mayence is an object from which France cannot depart under any circumstances whatsoever. . .[36]

d. Barthélemy's Instructions

The same day that the above document was despatched to Barthélemy, the Committee drew up its plenipotentiary's formal instructions. These speculated as to the causes which had prompted Prussia to open negotiations for peace, and then put the rhetorical question whether Prussia would treat solely as an independent kingdom (which would leave the Prussian contingent with the army of the Empire), or in the double capacity of independent kingdom and state of the Empire. The Committee declared that peace in both characters was the desire of France, and expressed the belief that this was also the intention of Frederick William. In regard to Holland, the Committee asserted that if the Prussian King were of good faith,

[34] The Committee had ordered Barthélemy, on January 1, 1795, to repair to Basel to hear the propositions of the Minister Plenipotentiary of Prussia, whose arrival was then momentarily expected (*ibid.*, p. 40). The instructions of Barthélemy, January 15, 1795, declared that "Citizen Barthélemy will enter into conference with these plenipotentiaries [of the King of Prussia], either at Basel, or at such other place as he judges most fitting for the negotiations. He will insinuate that to abridge the course thereof, the Committee of Public Safety would prefer that their seat should be established at Paris." — *Ibid.*, p. 50.

[35] That is, particularly in favor of those antagonistic to Austria.

[36] Jan. 8, 1795, *Papiers de Barthélemy*, V, 48–49.

he surely viewed with satisfaction that France had wrested that country from the hands of the English, even though the Hohenzollerns and Nassau-Orangists were united by ties of marriage; and that if the King were not of good faith, any guarantee on his part not to attack Holland would be due to his belief that he was powerless to do so, and hence valueless. Barthélemy was instructed to say that Germany had been too long the prey of Austria, and that the time had come for a remolding of the Empire at the expense of Habsburg influence, on the lines set down by the Peace of Westphalia. The Committee affirmed its determination not to permit Russia to immolate Poland, though it confessed its inability to take immediate countermeasures. Barthélemy was to report to Paris the Prussian viewpoint regarding Polish affairs.[37]

A supplement of instructions of the same date authorized Barthélemy to make use of the secret agents of the Republic to sound the governments of Germany as to their intentions. "They must be drawn from their timorous incertitude," the instructions said, "by enlightening them as to our intentions. A means that could be usefully employed with precaution and the necessary discrimination would be to prepare public opinion, especially in Germany, by writings which would have a more or less direct relation to the great matters which are about to become the order of the day. Discussions upon the danger with which the alliance of Austria and Russia threatens Europe, upon the interests of Prussia and of the German states, upon the absurdities of the Treaty of Westphalia and its incompatibility with the spirit of the century,[38] upon the nature of ecclesiastical property in Germany, even upon the system of the boundary of the Rhine, could produce very beneficial effects." [39]

Three other articles of the instructions require mention: "If, in the course of the negotiations, . . . Barthélemy finds a favorable occasion to engage the King of Prussia to sell or give to the Republic horses with which he believes he could dispense, he is charged to do so." [40] This attempt of the Republic to recoup itself for its loss of horses through the benevolence of Prussia soon developed into a regular system whereby the Convention, and later the Directory, restocked its cavalry at the expense of those other German states which had found themselves obliged to solicit France for armis-

---

[37] *Ibid.*, pp. 50–55.
[38] Notice that the instructions proper had expressed a desire to remold the Empire on the lines set down at Westphalia.
[39] *Papiers de Barthélemy*, V, 56–57.
[40] Glanders had made great ravages among the horses requisitioned in France (Desbrière and Sautai, *La Cavalerie . . . Rév.*, p. 241). Barthélemy, in his memoirs, p.

134, declares that (several months later) a French traveler carried the "Regent" diamond to Berlin to serve as security for a loan of coin which the French needed to buy horses for their army. It was hardly to be expected that the money-conscious Frederick William would care to play Santa Claus to his erstwhile antagonists.

tices or treaties of separate peace. The second article was an order to Bar-thélemy to concert with the Prussian negotiators on means of establishing a trade route for France across Westphalia and Lower Saxony to the Baltic. This order was the Committee's answer to the combined land and sea blockade by Austria and England.[41] The third article concerned the Danish minister of foreign affairs, von Bernstorff.

e. A. P. von Bernstorff

Count Andreas Peter von Bernstorff was a German, one of a line of von Bernstorffs who had served the Danish Crown as ministers of state for many years, though it is said that up to this time none of them had ever identified himself with the country he ruled to the extent of purchasing Danish realty.[42] A. P. von Bernstorff fostered the commerce of Denmark, and maintained friendly relations with all nations.[43] "A man of enlightened understanding, agreeable manners, and benevolent disposition," [44] a philoso-pher of the vintage of 1789, von Bernstorff bared his heart and his official secrets to Grouvelle, envoy of the French Republic at Copenhagen. France, in declaring war upon practically every great nation but Turkey and the United States, had cut herself off from her natural channels of information. Von Bernstorff filled the void, and paraded his partiality for France and for French victory.[45]

The Danish minister's partiality did not end there. He was also partial to the personal ambitions of Herrn von Bernstorff. Burning with the desire to play a great role in the world by serving as mediator between the Con-vention and the divers states of the Empire, the Minister averred his belief that the acquisition of the Rhine boundary by France was in conformity with the interests of the Republic and compatible with those of Germany; and he declared that he would willingly concur to obtain the left bank for the Republic.

The Committee was inclined to encourage von Bernstorff, for it saw an advantage in negotiating directly with the small states of Germany through the medium of another small state.[46] It therefore wrote to its agent at Copen-hagen: "Say to Herrn von Bernstorff that we do not believe *mediation* . . . is in the interest of the Republic. But though the word appears inappropriate to us, we really want its essence. We would be pleased to see the little secular states rally about Prussia. At the same time we are disposed to treat *sepa-rately* with them, and it is especially through the channel of Herrn von Bernstorff that we would most willingly receive their propositions." [47] The

[41] *Papiers de Barthélemy*, V, 56–57.
[42] Lord Holland, *For. Reminis.*, p. 45.
[43] Sorel in *RH*, V, 272.
[44] Lord Holland, *For. Reminis.*, p. 45.
[45] Sorel in *RH*, V, 271–272.
[46] *Idem, Europe*, IV, 227.
[47] Fain, *Ms. l'an III*, p. 49.

Committee informed the Danish minister of the Franco-Prussian negotiations, and authorized Barthélemy to correspond with him, sending the Ambassador a cipher for the purpose.[48]

Von Bernstorff's son was the Danish minister to Berlin, and the father had long thought of utilizing this relationship to mediate peace between France and Prussia. The year 1794 was filled with the importunities of the elder von Bernstorff that France commence negotiations with Prussia before it was too late: "There is not a moment to lose. . . Hardly three weeks remain for the first steps." Haste was represented as so necessary because England was offering Prussia subsidies to remain in the Coalition. But the three weeks came and went without any attempt at negotiation on the part of the Committee.[49] Not that Robespierre was indifferent to peace. This was shortly before the Montgaillard parleys with Austria, and the Great Incorruptible perhaps did not believe in negotiating with opposite sides at the same time.

On April 19, 1794, England and Holland, as stated, pledged themselves to support a Prussian army of 62,400 men,[50] and Prussia became once more an active member of the Coalition — at least theoretically. The news of the Polish revolution arrived in Berlin soon after the subsidy treaty had been agreed upon (though not yet signed). Von Bernstorff assured Grouvelle "very affirmatively . . . that if [Frederick William] had foreseen the great Polish insurrection, . . . Prussia would have persisted in its defection." "We have been assured," Grouvelle wrote to Paris on June 3, that "an arrangement with France had been much favored at Berlin. All the ministers were for it. . . Certainly, the tendencies of the Berlin cabinet continue to be the same." [51]

After the *coup d'état* of 9 *thermidor*, von Bernstorff immediately expressed the wish that "this change be conducive to general peace." When Russian troops defeated Kosciusko and threatened to engulf the remaining shreds of Poland, when the Prussians in consequence withdrew behind the Rhine and denounced the subsidy treaty,[52] von Bernstorff returned to the charge. He declared that Prussia's interest "counselled her to reconstitute the Germanic confederation, and to sustain against Austria the cause of the princes of the Empire who . . . aspired to peace." And of course he intimated that Herr von Bernstorff was the one and only person fitted to bring about this peace.[53]

It will be recalled that on October 24, 1794, the Elector of Mayence had

[48] *Papiers de Barthélemy*, V, 56–57.
[49] Sorel in *RH*, V, 276–277.
[50] Chap. iv, n. 400.
[51] Sorel in *RH*, V, 278–279.
[52] The agreement had already been denounced by Britain (October 17, 1794) because the

Prussians had "completely failed in fulfilling the intention of the treaty." — George III to Lord Grenville, April 9, 1795, *Dropmore Papers*, III, 50.
[53] Sorel in *RH*, V, 302–303.

proposed to the Diet at Ratisbon that Denmark and Sweden be requested to mediate a peace for the Empire. Frederick William had approved in principle, but objected to the choice of mediators, desiring to be himself the mediator. The Emperor had protested that it was passing strange not first to have consulted him as head of the Empire; that besides, it was not the time to talk peace while French boots were grinding to dust the German sod. But von Bernstorff could not honor these objections when his heart's desire seemed so near fulfilment. He thereupon announced that he was willing to mediate for a majority of the states, regardless of their size. This declaration prompted Prussia to accelerate her preparations for negotiation with France, lest tiny Denmark carry off the honor of restoring peace to the Empire.[54] One may well imagine how enthusiastically von Bernstorff received the news that Prussia was negotiating with France. The crop he had so carefully nurtured was to be reaped by another.

Presently — as contemplated by the Elector of Mayence — there appeared on the scene a representative of Sweden. He was Baron de Staël-Holstein, husband of the brilliant and amorous Germaine. The Baron talked matters over with von Bernstorff in Copenhagen, then dropped in on Barthélemy at the latter's home in Baden, Switzerland. De Staël cast aspersions upon Prussia and von der Goltz, and told doubtful tales about Austria's vast military preparations, about an English frigate laden with subsidies for Prussia, about hirelings of Pitt in Paris. He declared himself willing to work for the general pacification, and claimed to have the widest powers. According to Barthélemy, who had to listen to him, he managed to talk at length without really saying anything, from which the conclusion was inescapable that he was authorized only to listen, and to preach peace in general terms.[55]

[51] Ibid., pp. 303–305.
[55] Barthélemy to CPS, Jan. 3, 1795, Papiers de Barthélemy, IV, 528–529. Sweden attached great importance to the opportunity to mediate, which opportunity part of the Ratisbon Diet had voted to accord her. Prussia, however, wanted to monopolize the honor (ibid.). This accounts for De Staël's bitterness toward Prussia.

Guérin, citing Lefebvre (Thermidoriens, p. 143), credits De Staël with rather too much influence upon the negotiations which resulted in the Treaty of Basel. De Staël had told Barthélemy that he possessed extended powers to work for general peace, and would repair to Paris if assured he would be welcome there (Papiers de Barthélemy, IV, 528). The fact that De Staël subsequently arrived in Paris and was accepted, with impressive ceremony, as Ambassador of the King of Sweden to the French Republic (Moniteur, XXIV, 292–293) does not prove his influence upon the negotiations with Prussia. We know that Prussia begrudged the interference of anyone, and France was an apostle of the separate negotiation. Moreover, De Staël was not recognized as ambassador until eighteen days after the treaty was actually signed. Undoubtedly some influence must be ascribed to him as to every other advocate of peace, but does it not give a false impression to say, as Guérin does, that De Staël served as intermediary between the King of Prussia and France at the end of 1794, and that "he will come to Paris to negotiate with the Thermidorians"? (Lutte, I, 400, note.)

f. Armistice a Prussian Sine Qua Non

Barthélemy arrived in Basel on January 12, and immediately entered into conference with von der Goltz, who had been there already since December 28. The Prussian envoy requested an armistice as a means of stopping unnecessary bloodshed, but Barthélemy insisted that discussion of the treaty of peace itself should be forthwith commenced. Von der Goltz declared that his instructions categorically prescribed an armistice as a preliminary to the negotiation proper, so it was agreed that the ministers would refer to their respective governments.[56] In the meantime, the envoys discussed general principles, especially Mayence, the evacuation of which the Committee regarded as a *sine qua non.*

g. Mayence, the French Sine Qua Non

France, it will be recalled, had lost Mayence to the besieging Prussians on July 23, 1793. By the end of the year, however, due to the heroic efforts of the Robespierrist Committee, the neighboring Palatinate was again filling with the ragged champions of liberty and equality. So rosy seemed the hopes that Mayence also would soon be French again that the Mayençais patriots in Paris began to agitate for positions in the new government. On January 4, 1794, Merlin of Thionville presented to the Convention the offer of thirty penniless exiles to serve "their new country . . . by propagating . . . republicanism among their fellow citizens [in Mayence] . . . , by exposing aristocrats, . . . by [serving] as commissioners of victuals and forage, etc." Merlin proposed that the exiles be supplied with money to go to the front to assist in the reconquest, and that the Representatives to the Armies employ them according to their talents. This, the Convention decreed.[57] But the progress of the French army was slow owing to a multiplicity of factors, and it was not until October 1794 that the French commenced the investment of the city.[58]

At first the siege was hardly more than a parade. The French seem to have expected the gates to open presently, as they had done on October 21, 1792. But that was, in common parlance, an "inside job," and now all the traitors were outside, looking in — that is, all who were not in German prisons. By December 1794, after two months of siege, the French were beginning to realize that "lucky chance" had lost its efficacy. Wrote Merlin of Thionville to the Committee on December 4: "Kléber will take Mayence." [59] But later in the same letter, Merlin suggested — as mentioned above

[56] *Papiers de Barthélemy*, IV, 578–579.

[57] *Arch. parlem.*, LXXXII, 688–689.

[58] Heigel, *Deutsche Geschichte*, II, 197.

[59] Aulard, *Actes*, XVIII, 515.

—that the surrender be procured by a threat to burn Mannheim (possession of a prince friendly not only to Prussia but, potentially, to France herself).[60]

The next day the Committee sent the following note to Merlin: "Möllendorff appears to find it undesirable that we should continue the siege of Mayence. He must be either jesting or setting a trap into which we shall not fall. If Prussia sincerely wishes to make, with France, the treaty which conforms with the interest of our two nations, Mayence should be ours. . . It is important to [Prussia] that we take possession of it. . . Her interest even exacts that we soon become its master, for that would mean just so much [strength] pared from the powers of the second order which are strongly attached to the House of Habsburg, veritable common enemy of France and Prussia. Press then, dear colleague, press with all your means, with all your energy, the siege of this fortress, so that, in a few days, we can proclaim this . . . precious advantage."[61] On December 6, Carnot began to seek excuses. "It is always difficult to capture a position which you cannot completely surround,"[62] he wrote to Merlin of Thionville. "You should be able to cross the Rhine, but that operation would perhaps be more difficult than the siege itself."[63] On December 12, Merlin informed the Committee that, in an effort to spur the army on to great deeds, he had announced to the men that "peace . . . lies in [the capture of] Mayence. . . It is essential for the Republic to dictate peace from one bank to the other." But those in command before Mayence were "apathetic." "I burn, as you do," Merlin wrote to the government, "with the desire to end matters quickly, but too much time was lost arriving before the fortress, and the enemy was permitted to seize the islands [in the Rhine]. In spite of that, in spite of the season and the devil, Mayence must burst."[64]

But Mayence did not burst. In fact, it did not even bulge, and on the fifteenth, at two o'clock in the morning, Merlin of Douai, member of the Committee of Public Safety, wrote to Merlin of Thionville: "[The Prussians] continue to insist that we suspend the siege of Mayence. We have just replied that we are willing provided that Mayence be provisionally abandoned to us with the understanding that we hold it as a neutral city until the peace treaty grants it to us definitively. You can see by this that it is essential to

[60] *Ibid.*, p. 518.
[61] *Ibid.*, pp. 530-531.
[62] Encirclement was accomplished only on September 26, 1795 (*Guerres Rév. Emp.*, II, 483). But the advantage was quite ephemeral (Heigel, *Deutsche Geschichte*, II, 200).
[63] *Corr. gén. Carnot*, IV, 732. According to Bacher, Merlin-Th. aspired to enter Mayence in triumph. Merlin's ambitions mattered little to the Republic, said Bacher; but it *was* important that France should have Mayence as a point of commercial communication with Germany, especially with Frankfort (Sorel in *RH*, VI, 63).
[64] Aulard, *Actes*, XVIII, 668.

press the siege more vigorously. Peace will be decided the day we enter the city as victors." [65]

But that day was destined not to arrive for three years, and on December 20, 1794, a new note — an ominous note — crept into the Committee's letter to its Rhine army Representatives. This note had already appeared in Carnot's private correspondence with Merlin,[66] but had apparently required a fortnight to make its dismal rounds and become the voice of the Committee: "When this siege operation was undertaken, we had reason to believe it would be a matter of only a few days. . . Today the capture of Mayence appears to us very difficult, and potentially even bloody. . . Since trenches have not yet been dug before Mayence (at least, such we believe to be the case), if we abandoned operations now, it could not be said that we had raised the siege — for the siege has not yet really begun. But if we pursue this enterprise farther, we shall no longer be able to conceal the fact that the Army of the Rhine has suffered a reverse." The Committee left it to Merlin and his associate to decide whether or no the siege should be abandoned. If they decided in the affirmative, the Representatives should pretend to the Prussians that the abandonment was in deference to Prussian wishes.[67] Merlin of Douai, in a special despatch to Merlin of Thionville, laid stress upon the political advantage which France might draw by pretending to Möllendorff that "it was the confidence with which he inspired the Committee that brought about the termination of the siege operations." [68]

On December 29, the Representatives to the Rhine army received another invitation from the Committee to abandon the siege,[69] but they had probably already despatched their decision to Paris, for two days later the Committee approved their resolution to hold on.[70] As one of the Representatives wrote not long after, "we all feel that one step backward would embolden the enemy." [71]

"How's your siege going?" queried Merlin of Douai on January 4. "It would be a fine stroke if you could end it within a few days. I fear that Mayence trammels our negotiations with Prussia, or at least, draws them out. If we were its master, I wager that the treaty would be signed in ten days." [72]

Mayence was indeed the stumbling block in the path of a quick settlement. Von der Goltz regarded the defense of the city as a matter of honor. His Prussian Majesty, von der Goltz insisted, could not stand idly by while the French were attacking it. However, the Prussian King's honor was apparently of an off-brand sort, for his envoy suggested — off the record, let us

[65] *Ibid.*, p. 731.
[66] *Corr. gén. Carnot*, IV, 732.
[67] Aulard, *Actes*, XVIII, 811–813.
[68] Same date, *ibid.*, pp. 813–814.
[69] *Ibid.*, XIX, 158.

[70] CPS to Rps AA. RMo, Dec. 31, *ibid.*, pp. 192–193.
[71] Féraud to CPS, Jan. 20, 1795, *ibid.*, p. 589.
[72] To Merlin-Th., *ibid.*, p. 259.

assume — a sort of stratagem whereby France could gain possession of Mayence without, as he said, Prussia's being compromised: The King of Prussia could send a courier to Vienna inviting the Austrian government to withdraw its troops from the fortress in order to assure the neutralization of Mayence during the negotiations at Basel.[73] The courier could announce that the Prussian King was about to withdraw his own troops from the banks of the Rhine. If Austria refused, and she would refuse,[74] France could attack and capture Mayence. This would not compromise Prussia, for the blame would fall on Austria for her refusal. If the Court of Vienna consented to recall its forces from Mayence, the troops of the circle would replace the Austrian soldiers until the end of the conferences at Basel.[75] When the parleys ended, the fortress would be turned over to France by the troops of the circle.[76] In either case, France would obtain possession of Mayence.[77]

h. Miscellaneous Questions

The location of the Franco-Prussian parleys was also discussed by the envoys. The Committee was anxious that the negotiations should be held at Paris, where it was possible to bargain orally and without intermediary. It would be interesting to know whether any misgivings fleeted across the mind of the old-regime Prussian diplomat as he contemplated himself opposing the wills of twelve regicide rebels in the heart of Rebeland. The objections he raised were indeed sufficiently numerous definitely to rule out the suggestion of negotiations at Paris. Briefly, they were: the impossibility of isolating oneself in so large a city; the prevalence there of the factional intrigues inseparable from a capital; the existence of a pro-Austrian party at Paris; and the necessity for his remaining at Basel, where he was serving as informant of Field Marshal Möllendorff and the Prussian Court.[78] The Committee yielded the point without further argument,[79] and the conversations therefore remained at Basel. This is important, as it is unlikely that anyone but

---

[73] On December 27, 1794, Bacher had written from Basel that, according to what he had heard, Prussia was not averse to the neutralization of Mayence until the peace by installing therein a mixed Prussian and French garrison — half of each nationality. Merlin-D. wrote to Merlin-Th. that the members of the Committee could not agree among themselves as to whether this proposition were acceptable. The CPS, he said, was still awaiting Möllendorff's reply to its proposal that he abandon Mayence to France with the understanding that the Republic would regard the city as neutral until peace had been concluded (Dec. 27, 1794, ibid., p. 123).

[74] Vide Thugut to Count Colloredo, Jan. 8, 1795, Briefe Thugut, I, 169: "People are not ashamed to talk of . . . abandoning it [Mayence]."

[75] This suggestion appeared later on the tongue of Merlin-Th. (Merlin-Th. to CPS, May 20, 1795, Corr. Merlin-Th., II, 193.)

[76] In other words, France could easily seize Mayence from the troops of the circle. This is the only interpretation possible, for nothing agreed upon between France and Prussia could affect the legal status of Mayence.

[77] Papiers de Barthélemy, IV, 579.

[78] Ibid., p. 581.

[79] Mém. homme d'Etat, II, 563.

the conciliatory and tactful Barthélemy could have reconciled the stubborn Frederick William and the hotheaded revolutionists.

Von der Goltz broached the subject of Prussian mediation between France and the states of Germany, thinking of course to increase the importance of his king. Barthélemy responded that the Republic was as much disposed to make peace with the small states as with the King of Prussia, and that it would treat with them either conjointly with Prussia or separately, as equal with equal, on the same conditions as with Prussia. Von der Goltz should have seen the rebuff contained within this statement, but he was delighted with what appeared to him an opportunity for Prussia to play a role among her co-states.[80] Subsequent events were to bring out the full significance of Barthélemy's words.

The Committee of Public Safety, on January 29, informed Barthélemy that in its opinion Prussia was asking for an armistice as much from political motives as from humanitarian. The Hohenzollern king was in need of time to induce the Emperor to withdraw his troops from Mayence, and Frederick William wanted this withdrawal to precede the Prussian retreat from the banks of the Rhine in order that the responsibility for the future loss of the Key of Germany should be laid to the Austrians. The Committee did not propose to yield to the Prussian request, but was not anxious to antagonize a potential ally. It therefore instructed Barthélemy to offer, as if spontaneously, that though the French felt obliged to insist on the immediate discussion of the treaty itself, the parleys could be held secret until the Prussians had succeeded in their proposed negotiation with the Austrians. Then an armistice could be agreed upon.[81]

i. The Demise of von der Goltz

In the meantime, however, von der Goltz, who had brought his gout with him from Berlin, contracted in addition a bilious fever.[82] Obliged to take to his bed, he died at midnight on February 5, the very day that there arrived in Basel the Prussian answer to the Committee's refusal of an armistice.[83]

The suddenness of von der Goltz's illness and death puzzled the attending physicians, and gave rise to suspicions of poisoning by Austrian agents. The deceased was given a post-mortem examination, but everything within was found in perfect order.[84] It seems that the Prussian diplomat

[80] Barthélemy to CPS, Jan. 24, 1795, *Papiers de Barthélemy*, IV, 580. This desire to play a grand role in Germany, to pose as the real leader of the Empire, sometimes caused Prussia flagrantly to overstep the bounds of propriety. In 1793, Thugut complained that the Prussians were attracting to their own standard the contingents of the Empire (to Count Colloredo, May 4, 1793, *Briefe Thugut*, I, 15).
[81] *Papiers de Barthélemy*, V, 60.
[82] Barthélemy to CPS, Feb. 3, 1795, *ibid.*, p. 61.
[83] *Idem*, Feb. 6, 1795, *ibid.*, p. 66.
[84] Sorel in *RH*, VI, 353-354.

had been toasting the Republic with excessive food and drink. Not that von der Goltz was such a Francophile — Pichegru's invasion of Holland had cured him of his former tendency in that direction. This invasion, during the negotiations, seemed to the Prussian envoy "the greatest infamy that France could have perpetrated," and he worried a good deal about its implications. But as a negotiator, he believed it incumbent upon him to continue smiling — and drinking healths.[85] Toward the end of January, when the conquest of Holland was well under way, Thugut received the following letter from the Austrian colonel of engineers and observer Count Dietrichstein: "Monsieur von [der] Goltz has uselessly troubled himself to drink to the Republic's health at Barthélemy's house, for a member of the Committee of Public Safety has said: 'The toasts of Goltz will not hinder us from dictating peace in the town hall of Amsterdam.'"[86]

Here we have, then, excessive food and drink heaped into a stomach whose normal functioning had been slowed down by worry. And when illness supervened as a natural consequence, the element of worry was yet aggravated. Von der Goltz feared that, should he lapse into delirium, he might blurt out what he thought of the French, and so destroy all hope of a pacification. His servant was given strict instructions that if he became delirious, no one but his most intimate friends should be admitted to the sick-chamber.[87] Von der Goltz did become delirious before he died, but apparently his words never reached French ears, for cordial relations continued between the two states, though, considering the circumstances, it was the cordiality of a cat playing with a mouse — or, should we say, with the mouse's Orange tail?

2. THE HARNIER NEGOTIATION

Harnier, though without any powers, had taken charge of the negotiations during von der Goltz's illness,[88] hence upon him devolved the task of informing Barthélemy of the contents of the latest royal despatch. The Prussian Ministry, he announced, was very irritated at France's refusal to grant an armistice, and at the harshness of the French proposals, but took comfort in the thought that the Committee was as anxious for peace as was the King, so would probably modify its conditions.[89]

A new question, also, was broached by Harnier at this time. Wesel, a

[85] Vivenot, *Bas. Fried.*, Pt. II, 70–71.
[86] *Thugut, C, W*, p. 69.
[87] Vivenot, *Bas. Fried.*, Pt. II, 71.
[88] *Vide* Barthélemy's account to the CPS of

his conversation of February 5 with Harnier, *Papiers de Barthélemy*, V, 62–66.
[89] Barthélemy to CPS, Feb. 6, 1795, *ibid.*, pp. 65–66; Feb. 9, *ibid.*, pp. 68–70.

Prussian fortress on the right bank of the Rhine, was menaced by the French occupation of Holland, and the King of Prussia wished France to agree not to attack the fortress in return for a Prussian guarantee that Austrian troops would neither be requested nor permitted[90] to reinforce its insufficient Prussian garrison. It was in France's interest, Harnier argued, that Prussia alone should guard Wesel.[91] Barthélemy referred the Prussian request to the Committee of Public Safety. The Committee decided that to engage itself not to attack Wesel would be equivalent to agreeing to an armistice, and as such was inadmissible.[92] Such a reply was evidently not unexpected, for the *Moniteur's* correspondent at Bremen wrote on February 15: "The generals in command there [Wesel] are hastening to place that city in a position to withstand a siege. Foreigners have left. The inhabitants have been provided with victuals for three months. The garrison has been augmented."[93] And Möllendorff had despatched a strong force to cover Westphalia.[94]

Incidentally, Möllendorff, at the same time, transferred his own head-quarters to a position two leagues from Frankfort, thus leaving Mayence exposed to French attack. Barthélemy suggested that the Marshal might have utilized the danger to Wesel as an "honorable pretext" for doing this very thing.[95]

On February 16, there arrived from Berlin a despatch for von der Goltz. The vicissitudes of the war in Holland and the consequent danger to north-ern Germany, it declared, had augmented the King's desire to conclude directly a separate peace without losing precious time negotiating an armis-tice which would become superfluous the moment the peace was signed.[96] Von der Goltz was instructed to direct his attention to the peace itself, and to inform the French that the despatch of Prussian troops to the vicinity of Wesel was not only for the purpose of protecting Westphalia, but also of facilitating the rapid reëntry of the troops into Prussian territory as soon as peace should have been concluded. The King renounced the idea of media-tion, and declared himself content with the opportunity of offering his good

[90] The Austrians were insisting that they should be allowed to reinforce the Prussian garrison. Cf. Barthélemy to CPS, Feb. 16, 1795, *ibid.*, p. 76.

[91] *Idem*, Feb. 9, 1795, *ibid.*, pp. 68–69, *et passim*.

[92] CPS to Barthélemy, Feb. 16, 1795, *ibid.*, pp. 74–75.

[93] *Moniteur*, XXIII, 577.

[94] Barthélemy to CPS, Feb. 5, 11, 14, *Papiers de Barthélemy*, V, 65, 71, 73.

[95] *Idem*, Feb. 11, 14, *ibid.*, pp. 71, 73.

[96] The despatch spoke very strangely regard-ing von der Goltz's insistence on an armis-tice, so much so that it appeared to Barthélemy that the armistice was the Prus-sian envoy's own idea. Said the despatch: "You have been determined by very laud-able motives to insist upon the conclusion of an armistice even before the pacification, and we cannot disapprove of your conduct in this respect." The instructions of von der Goltz, it will be recalled, prescribed an armistice. Evidently the King was trying to withdraw gracefully from the position first assumed.

offices to those of his coprinces who did not desire to treat directly with France.[97]

When the Committee learned of this despatch to von der Goltz, it believed that peace was assured, and decided to yield regarding the question of Wesel. On February 16, Barthélemy, instructed by Meyerink, had informed the Committee of a plan conceived by Möllendorff: If the French should agree not to disquiet Wesel, the Prussians would consent to stand idly by should the French cross the Rhine either above or below the Prussian states.[98] "Would it not be better," Möllendorff had written to his adjutant on February 13, "to agree amicably in advance on a line of neutrality than to expose ourselves to the danger of fighting at the very moment when everything indicates intentions favorable to peace?"[99] The Committee decided on February 22 to accept Möllendorff's proposal, and even to facilitate its execution by sending a corps to invade Westphalia. If Möllendorff utilized this invasion as a pretext to leave even the neighborhood of Mayence, Wesel was to be respected, but if he did not, it was to be assumed that the Marshal begrudged Mayence to France, in which case the corps was to storm Wesel.[100] This would of course have forced Möllendorff to fly to the aid of Wesel. The matter was settled by Möllendorff's decision to station his troops between the Lippe and the Weser, and a promise by the Marshal not to leave this position whatever the French armies did in northern Germany, so long as they respected Prussian territory.[101]

On February 17, Barthélemy affirmed that the French government, now that the Prussian troops were leaving the neighborhood of Mayence, would insist on but one point as the basis of the peace negotiation, viz., the cession of the left bank. Harnier protested that this cession could be made only by the Empire, but affirmed his belief that the renunciation of the Prussian left-bank states would not entail much difficulty. Regarding indemnification of those princes who had lost their territories to the west of the Rhine, the Secretary of Legation foresaw much bickering; he himself firmly believed in the necessity of making a new Peace of Westphalia, and of secularizing "more than one" ecclesiastical state.[102]

This accommodating attitude of Harnier lasted only until February 23, when there arrived a royal despatch dated February 15. This message, which reflected the ideas of the King as distinguished from those of his ministers,

[97] Annex (dated Feb. 6) to Barthélemy's despatch of Feb. 16, 1795, *Papiers de Barthélemy*, V, 77–78.

[98] *Ibid.*, pp. 75–76.

[99] Quoted by A. Sorel, "La paix de Bâle," *RH*, VII (1878), 35.

[100] CPS to Barthélemy, *Papiers de Barthélemy*, V, 84.

[101] Bacher to CPS, Feb. 16, 1795, *ibid.*, p. 79.

[102] Barthélemy to CPS, Feb. 17, 1795, *ibid.*, p. 81.

expressed "surprise" and "extreme vexation" at Barthélemy's insistence that Prussia should renounce her left-bank possessions. The King protested that he was not anxious for the stigma of having been the first to agree to the dismemberment of the Empire. Even if it were possible to compensate him for the loss of his left-bank territories at the expense of his coprinces, such indemnities were repugnant to him, he affirmed. Moreover, he was unable to see how France could desire him to do something so detrimental to his prestige if she really sought in him a useful friend. On the ground that only the Empire could cede a part of the Empire, he ordered Harnier to demand of Barthélemy that the entire question of the cession of the left bank should be postponed until the general Franco-Imperial peace, and that no mention of the matter should be made in the Franco-Prussian separate convention. He insisted, moreover, that until the general peace, France should evacuate his left-bank states.[103]

Had Barthélemy held to the letter of his instructions, he would have been obliged to break off the negotiations forthwith, since Prussia was refusing the immediate cession of her left-bank possessions. However, the French plenipotentiary had too high a sense of duty to permit a rupture to occur on a point not essential to France's welfare, so attempted to cajole the Committee of Public Safety into a more conciliatory attitude:[104] "It appears that if we manifest for the King of Prussia the consideration which he requests, the separate peace with him will be immediately concluded; the bonds of the Coalition will be forthwith broken; the acquisition of the left bank of the Rhine will be assured. It seems to us,[105] as well as to Harnier, that this article of the peace could declare simply that the territories of Clèves and Meurs should share the fate of the entire left bank of the Rhine at the general pacification of Germany."[106]

At a meeting between Barthélemy and Harnier on February 23, there was sketched out for the first time part of the future treaty of peace. With the question of the cession of the Prussian left bank to France as the first article, Bathélemy suggested that by the second, Prussia should renounce her adherence to the armed coalition against France. This the French ambassador had been formally instructed to demand; a similar provision had made part of the Franco-Tuscan treaty signed on February 9. Harnier

---

[103] Extract from the King's letter, annexed to Barthélemy's despatch to CPS, Feb. 23, 1795, *ibid.*, pp. 88–89.

[104] Harnier, also, showed himself more accommodating than his government. According to Barthélemy, he declared his vexation at the King's demand that the French evacuate the Prussian left bank, and his belief that the demand was not meant seriously, even in Berlin (Barthélemy to CPS, Feb. 23, 1795, *ibid.*, p. 87).

[105] Barthélemy and Bacher.

[106] Barthélemy to CPS, Feb. 23, 1795, *Papiers de Barthélemy*, V, 87–88.

denounced the Prussian participation in the war as meriting public castiga-
tion, but appealed to French magnanimity not to recall Prussia's errors in
such a conspicuous and humiliating way. For the third article, Harnier
proposed an agreement whereby the King would offer, and France accept,
the good offices of Prussia for the pacification, successively, of the states of
the Empire. It was suggested that articles four and five should concern the
exchange of prisoners and the reëstablishment of commercial relations.[107]

When the Committee learned of Prussia's refusal to cede forthwith its
left-bank possessions and to renounce adherence to the Coalition, it concluded that the Prussians were not honestly desirous of peace with France.
It therefore revoked its promise respecting Wesel, and announced its intention to prosecute the operations of war despite the negotiations for peace
(March 1).[108]

The very next day two important letters were despatched from Basel to
the Committee. The first, from the pen of Barthélemy, declared that Möllendorff was about to take up a certain position in Westphalia which, in
accordance with the Committee's plan, would prevent all clash between the
Prussians and French.[109] The second, of Bacher's composition, announced
that Möllendorff would depart for Westphalia on the eighth of March,
described the exact positions which the Prussians would assume, expressed
the assurance that they would remain on the defensive, and declared that
Möllendorff had sworn on his word of honor not only to observe his promise
but also to oblige the English troops to embark and the Hanoverians to
return to their firesides. Prince Hohenlohe-Ingelfingen, commander of the
Prussian treaty force fighting with the Austrians,[110] was to be ordered to
descend the Rhine at the first opportunity in order to break off all contact
with the Imperial forces; and the Prussian contingent was to be withdrawn
from the army of the Empire. The possibility was also intimated of allowing
French merchants to open immediate communication with northern
Europe via Wesel.[111]

Soon there arrived from Berlin (March 4) a most conciliatory despatch.
The King's letter of February 15, refusing to yield his left-bank possessions,
had been, as above stated, written under the personal influence of the King.
It was not long, however, before the Ministry had succeeded in inducing the
Hohenzollern monarch that concessions were indispensable. The new despatch interpreted the note of February 15 to mean that the King would
consent to yield his left-bank states, but desired that the cession should be

[107] *Ibid.*, p. 88.
[108] CPS to Barthélemy, *ibid.*, p. 92.
[109] *Ibid.*, pp. 92–93.
[110] This was the force of 20,000 men provided for by the Treaty of February 7,
1792. *Vide supra*, chap. i, § 2i.
[111] *Papiers de Barthélemy*, V, 93–94.

negotiated in the way least compromising to Prussia.[112] Harnier, after informing Barthélemy of this despatch, announced that Hesse-Cassel and Brunswick were soliciting the good offices of Prussia, and that the King would be glad to allow the French to trade with Germany by way of Wesel. Barthélemy, in reporting these concessions to his government, discoursed on the immense service which the resumption of the German trade would render to France, and expressed his confidence in the sincerity of the King.[113]

A word of comment on Franco-German trade during the was is necessary here. This trade had never really ceased. It will be recalled how the King of Prussia and the Duke of Brunswick drove Hamburg's commerce with France under cover. There it found itself in good company. Much of the prewar German trade with France had slunk into surreptitious channels. Even the Habsburg dominions, which were making the greatest effort in the war, took part in this treasonable traffic [114] — Vivenot to the contrary notwithstanding.[115] Francis II would have instituted an Imperial embargo by decree, but was apprized that such a measure would be a dead letter because of general resistance. Prussia and the Hansa cities did not hide their hostility to such a measure. Prussia was plying a lively trade in cloth with France via Switzerland — with the assistance, it was said, of the Frankforter Jordis.[116] Hamburg's machinations have of course been treated *in extenso* in the fifth chapter above. In Augsburg, Max Christoph Graf, one of Probst's partisans, engaged to send to France by way of Basel: barley and flour labelled as hair-powder, and potash and saltpetre designated as alum. Graf had the rashness to route these goods through Austrian territory, and they were seized.[117] In October 1794, the Convention voted that the outstanding claims of Nuremberg should be paid because that city "had proved its attachment for the French Republic" — which speaks for itself. Bremen, Lübeck, Danzig, Elberfeld, and Solingen were also trafficking with the enemy.[118]

On March 6 arrived at Basel the Committee's letter declaring that the war against Prussia would be prosecuted until peace had been signed. Barthélemy was much perturbed. He felt himself obliged to inform Harnier, since orders had probably been given to the French army to attack the Prussians while the latter were expecting a neutrality agreement. However,

[112] Sorel in *RH*, VII, 318.
[113] Barthélemy to CPS, March 4, 1795, *Papiers de Barthélemy*, V, 96.
[114] Hungarian copper reached France by way of Switzerland (Palmer, *Twelve*, p. 237).
[115] Vivenot, *Bas. Fried.*, Pt. I, 178.
[116] On Jordis, *vide supra*, chap. vi, § 4.
[117] Authority re Augsburg: Thugut to Lehrbach, Oct. 20, 1794, Vivenot-Zeissberg,

Quellen, V, 8. Mallet du Pan reported to Lord Elgin the previous March that Swabia, in company with Lombardy, had sent 60,000 horned cattle and horses through Switzerland into Alsace; also grain, cloth, and hides ("Informations additionnelles," *Despatches Gower*, p. 358).
[118] Vivenot, *Bas. Fried.*, Pt. I, 177–180; Pt. II, 52.

he did not choose to allow the Committee to precipitate a rupture. He introduced the conversation with the statement that Harnier "knew too well the exaggerative tendencies which the expiring Revolution had bequeathed to most people to be astonished at finding them manifested even in a letter from the Committee." [119] Then he read the despatch of March 1.

Harnier was surprised and grieved. He declared that Prussia was willing to detach herself from the Coalition, but did not care to have this breach of her plighted word consecrated in a solemn public act. He insisted that it was not in Prussia's power to cede a part of the Empire, and that to force her to pretend to cede what did not belong to her would be to dishonor her uselessly before her co-states. Lastly, he pointed out that France seemed to forget that Frederick William's army was sixty thousand strong, and would be obliged to resume hostilities as soon as the first shot came from the French lines.[120]

Harnier reported to his government (March 6) that Barthélemy and Bacher seemed to share his point of view, and that they had given him to understand that a minority of the Committee was like-minded, as was a goodly proportion of the Convention and of the French public at large.[121] To provoke a change of sentiment on the part of the majority of the Committee, Barthélemy drew up a project of treaty which would reconcile the opposing opinions, and sent it in to Paris.[122] He also forwarded Bacher's "Reflections Concerning the Present State of the Negotiation of a Separate Peace with the King of Prussia": "The King of Prussia offers to remain . . . on the defensive with the Hessians, Saxons, and Hanoverians, and to oblige the English to embark. [If we accept his proposition,] . . . 100,000 men [will be] neutralized, northern Germany will be opened to commerce, the example of Prussia will draw along the [other] German states, the Coalition will be dissolved, the Austrians will remain alone. . . If we refuse: the war will continue with Prussia, the 100,000 men at her disposal will endeavor to penetrate into Holland, the Austrians will try to cross the Rhine and menace Alsace, [and] we shall have to renounce pressing the siege of Mayence." [123]

These despatches had the desired effect on the Committee. It wrote to its plenipotentiary at Basel (March 10) [124] that though the Prussian offer to open Wesel unconditionally to French commerce was unacceptable because it could be interpreted as an armistice, the desire of the Committee to augment the consideration and influence of the King in Germany, and to cement

---

[119] Harnier to the King, March 6, 1795. Quoted from Ranke by Sorel in *RH*, VII, 47.
[120] Barthélemy to CPS, March 6, 1795, *Papiers de Barthélemy*, V, 99–100.
[121] Sorel in *RH*, VII, 49.

[122] Annexed to Barthélemy's despatch of March 6 to CPS, *Papiers de Barthélemy*, V, 102–103.
[123] Reproduced by Sorel in *RH*, VII, 50, n. 1.
[124] Sorel gives this date erroneously as March 11 (*ibid.*, p. 52).

the bonds of amity between the two states, were inducing it to offer advantageous terms.

Then followed a nine-article project of treaty, of which Articles IV, VI, and IX must be examined closely.[125] Article IV required the Prussian King to reduce to prewar proportions the armed forces he was maintaining in his right-bank states. This the Hohenzollern monarch hesitated to do for two reasons: he did not trust the Republicans; and he was a deserter from the army of the Empire, and might yet need to defend himself against Imperial punishment. Article VI provided that the French should continue to occupy the Prussian states on the left bank of the Rhine, and that the said states should share the fate of the remainder of the left bank at the general Franco-Imperial peace. It is to be noted that by this wording, the duration of the French occupation of the Prussian lands was not specified. Article IX announced the willingness of the Republic to accept the good offices of Prussia in favor of those German princes who should desire to negotiate treaties of separate peace with France. This was calculated to satisfy the *amour-propre* of Frederick William, who, disrupter of Imperial unity that he was, wished to pose as the pacificator of the Empire.

The Committee's project concluded: "In order to coördinate our Franco-Prussian relations with our general system of diplomacy, we desire to insert a secret article: an urgent invitation, or better still, a sort of engagement on the part of Prussia to adhere to a plan either of armed neutrality, or, preferably, of offensive and defensive alliance, between Sweden, Denmark, and *perhaps*[126] Holland. We do not doubt that this is the veritable intention as well as the real and pressing interest of Prussia."[127]

The day the Committee sent this project of treaty to Barthélemy, it announced to the Representatives to the Armies of the North and of the Sambre and Meuse "that the misunderstandings which had clouded the negotiations between the Republic and the King of Prussia appeared to have been dissipated," and that the arrangement concerning Wesel and the Prussian army, which the French government had revoked on March 1, was to be reëstablished. The Representatives were ordered so to apprize Möllendorff.[128]

---

[125] An English translation of the entire project will be found, in slightly abridged form, in Appendix B of this work.

[126] Underscored in original.

[127] *Papiers de Barthélemy*, V, 105–107. When Barthélemy suggested to Harnier the formation of this league, the latter declared he believed his court would be favorably disposed thereto, but that the necessary negotiations would delay the signing of the peace treaty. Harnier proposed that the alliance should constitute the subject of a second public act (Barthélemy to CPS, March 16, 1795, *ibid.*, p. 115). The Committee, on March 22, declared that it approved of Harnier's proposal to postpone the question of a league (CPS to Barthélemy, *ibid.*, p. 124).

[128] Quoted by Sorel in *RH*, VII, 53.

That the Committee eventually agreed to respect Prussian sensibilities of course does not mean that it renounced one iota of its plan to acquire the left bank. The speech of its presiding officer, Cambacérès, before the Convention on March 3, 1795, leaves no doubt in this regard — for he spoke in the name of the Committee when he said:

It is ambition which arms kings; justice which arms peoples. . .

In listening to the voice of justice, in guarding ourselves against the illusions of ambition and instigations to vengeance, we must not forget our obligation to the prosperity [129] of our country, to the consolidation of the Republic. Peace should destroy the germs of future war. . . It is by the experience of past centuries and in foresight of the future that we must weigh the conditions of our treaties. The present generation has not suffered so many trials and made so many sacrifices without the certitude that posterity will gather the fruits. . .

We are not fighting for [pride or pettiness] . . . or for some distant possessions. . . When an entire nation has risen in arms against invasion, treason, famine, civil war, the partition of its territory, [and] the annihilation of its existence, it . . . should use its power to ensure that [its rights] will be respected forever. . . If there existed in Europe . . . a guarantee for the security of weak states, the terms of peace could be easily dictated and [easily] accepted; [but there does not] . . .

The Republic possesses natural boundaries in the Alps and the Pyrenees, in the two oceans and in a free country [Switzerland] . . . [but has none to the northeast at present]. The counsel of Nature and the experience of the ages [demand that this lacuna should be filled. However,] Europe must know that you are not directed by designs of aggrandizement but by the thought of your tranquillity, that twenty-five million men associated for liberty and happiness do not covet a few hundred square leagues [of territory] because of that lust for conquest which can guide a despot, or an aristocracy concentrated in a senate.[130]

At the renewal of the Committee on March 5, Reubell and Sieyes entered that select body.[131] Reubell, who was adjoined to Merlin of Douai to attend to the correspondence concerning Prussia, drew up on March 16 a letter to Barthélemy, which, after changes and corrections by Merlin, was approved by the Committee and despatched.[132] It announced that the note of March 10 was to be considered as the Committee's ultimatum, and urged a rapid termination of the negotiations. It declared that the desire expressed by Prussia that the treaty should "*avoid everything tending to weaken* Prussia

---

[129] The present author queries whether Cambacérès did not mean to say "posterity," or perhaps did say it. The context of the paragraph seems to render "posterity" the more appropriate word. Sorel (*RH*, VII, 55) accepts "prosperity." Sorel also has the word "justice" instead of "the Republic" at the end of the sentence — which is incorrect.

[130] *Moniteur*, XXIII, 597.

[131] Aulard, *Actes*, XX, 659.

[132] Sorel in *RH*, VII, 59–60.

in any way [133] [was] . . . very strange . . . , especially when one reflects on the aggrandizement which Prussia herself has procured elsewhere." [134] A postscript stated that the treaty should bind Prussia not to proceed hostilely against the United Provinces, or any other countries occupied by French troops. [135]

Three days later (March 19), the Committee again invited Barthélemy to bring the negotiations to a conclusion, adding that the French troops could already have taken Wesel and entered into a country where there were yet resources. [136] But it was not until the very day the Committee was writing this despatch that there arrived in Basel the long-awaited successor of von der Goltz — Karl August, Baron von Hardenberg, Prussian cabinet minister. [137]

[133] Underscored in the original.

[134] The draft of Reubell contains here: "A yet stranger proposition is the one which tends to reject every equivalent [which is] at the expense of someone else. . . The Republic would gladly concert with the cabinet of Berlin to establish, beyond the Rhine, such a system that Prussia could oppose a solid dike to the devouring ambition of its natural enemies." Quoted by Sorel, in *RH*, VII, 60, n. 2.

[135] CPS to Barthélemy, *Papiers de Barthélemy*, V, 111.

[136] March 19, 1795, *ibid.*, p. 116.

[137] This is not what the Anglo-Saxon understands by "member of the cabinet." The Prussian cabinet ministers were private advisers. For the intricate but instructive subject of Prussian governmental organization in the 18th century, *vide* Königliche Akademie der Wissenschaften, *Acta Borussica* (Berlin, 1894–), Vol. VI[1].

CHAPTER IX

THE TREATY OF BASEL — *Continued*

I. THE COMMITTEE'S PEACE POWERS DETERMINED

*F*ROM a strictly legal point of view, it was well that Hardenberg had tarried on his way, for only two days before, the Convention had brought to a close a prolonged and fiery debate on the highly relevant subject: what are the powers of the Committee of Public Safety with respect to armistices; truces; treaties of peace, alliance, neutrality, and commerce; secret articles; and the ratification of the patent and secret portions of treaties? Up to this time the Committee did not know the extent of its own powers, for the Law of 7 *fructidor*, II (August 24, 1794) had specified only that "The Committee of Public Safety shall have the direction of foreign affairs in their political aspects, and shall supervise the administrative aspects." [1]

The debate had commenced on March 12. The Convention agreed without much difficulty that the Committee, as a corollary of the above-quoted provision of the Law of 7 *fructidor*, could legally negotiate treaties of peace, alliance, neutrality, and commerce, or could depute someone to negotiate them in its stead; and that these agreements would be binding only after ratification by the Convention. Whether the Committee could negotiate armistices and truces, and whether they would require ratification by the Convention, caused a certain amount of trouble. It was agreed after some argument that since a general in the field absolutely must possess the power to make an armistice, if only to afford him the opportunity to bury his dead, the Committee should be able to order him to make one, provided

---

[1] Aulard, *Actes*, XVI, 311. Some people queried whether there existed any person or body in France possessing the power to make international agreements, seeing that all the constituted authorities were of revolutionary origin. These doubts were of course most unwelcome to the Convention, which regarded itself as the temporary depositary of the nation's sovereignty. Declared Boissy d'Anglas in a speech before the Convention (January 30, 1795): "Our government is the plenipotentiary named by the totality of the French people to terminate the Revolution and the war; and I doubt whether one has ever seen an ambassador clothed with more ample power and with a more august character. . . . A nation which knows how to conquer has the power to negotiate." — *Moniteur*, XXIII, 343.

it were limited in time to the requirements of the purpose to be accomplished. But fears were expressed that, if a truce did not require the Convention's approval, some ill-willed Committee of the future might make a truce for years and so circumvent the requirement that peace treaties must be ratified to be valid.[2]

It was, however, the question of the ratification to be required of secret articles that raised the greatest storm. Cambacérès, who was fathering the proposed legislation for the Committee, did not dare to hope that the Convention would dispense with every form of ratification whatsoever, so proposed that the Convention appoint a commission of twelve to pass upon secret articles, or that the Committee on Legislation should be ordered to fulfil this function. But the argument presently degenerated into a discussion whether secret provisions were necessary at all. Were not the motives of free men so pure that the universe could well be witness to their every thought and act? This obstruction finally hurdled, it was argued that if a treaty contained secret articles, it would be in those articles that the peace really lay; and unless the Convention could itself pass on them, the Constitution (what constitution?) — which required that peace be made by the Convention — would be violated. It was suggested that the Convention constitute itself a committee of the whole, to consider, behind locked doors, the secret articles of treaties. To this it was protested that if so many people knew a secret, it would not long be secret. Replied the brilliant author of the suggestion: The secret will finally come out anyway. "It was acknowledged in the old diplomacy that the best-guarded secret was no longer a secret on the fortieth day. And yet there were then only one or two depositaries." A wiser head pointed out that no foreign state would confide its secrets to 750 confidants, and that if the Republic really wished for peace, it would have to make other provisions. Cambacérès' commission to approve secret articles was rejected on divers grounds, and it was argued that since the Convention controlled the personnel of the Committee of Public Safety, the latter body could really be trusted. Besides, how did the Convention expect Europe to have faith in the Committee if it (the Convention) demonstrated that it had none itself?[3] By limiting the content of prospective secret articles to what "assured the defense of the Republic or increased its means of prosperity," by providing that "these articles must neither contradict the patent articles nor attenuate them," and by requiring that they should be imparted to the Convention as soon as secrecy was no longer necessary, the various viewpoints were finally reconciled, and the result was crystallized into law on March 17, 1795.[4]

---

[2] *Ibid.*, pp. 674–676.

[3] *Ibid.*, pp. 676–677, 679–684, 709 *et seqq.*

[4] Aulard, *Actes*, XXI, 128–129.

An interesting situation had presented itself four days before the final decision. Rühl, an Alsatian, had proposed that the Convention define the boundaries of the French state. At this suggestion, according to the *Moniteur*, murmurs filled the hall, and several voices cried, "You don't want peace." Rühl continued: "Then the secret articles can apply only to the indemnities. I demand, therefore, that we first determine our boundaries, which are naturally the Pyrenees, Mediterranean, Rhine, and Ocean; and that we decree that we will make no peace with the powers before they recognize these boundaries." No one seconded Rühl's motion, and it was moved that the discussion be terminated.[5] Apparently on March 13, 1795, there were doubts in a good many minds as to the advisability of annexing the Rhineland to France. This fact might well be kept in mind as we take up the remainder of the discussions at Basel.

2. HARDENBERG AND THE SIGNING OF THE TREATY

Hardenberg was a Hanoverian by birth, and hence enjoyed a wider vista than the other Prussian cabinet ministers, who distrusted him precisely because of his non-Prussian origin. Hardenberg claims in his memoirs that he was one of the first to suggest peace with France. But not a separate peace! That, he declared, would be "a veritable misfortune." It was a general peace for which he yearned — a peace including the entire Empire, and procured by the mediation of Prussia. He would have nought to do with the machinations of Möllendorff and Kalkreuth, though he did correspond with Schmerz and Meyerink. And he engaged in long and heated conversations with Haugwitz and von der Goltz.[6] Mallet du Pan sent him, at his request, four letters — all of them appealing for a more vigorous prosecution of the war, and emphasizing the unwisdom of a separate peace; and Hardenberg had appeared to appreciate the potency of the arguments. And when Mallet refused to continue the correspondence after Hardenberg's appointment to negotiate with "the bandits of the Tuileries," the new negotiator protested.[7]

It appears to the present writer that Frederick William selected Hardenberg as von der Goltz's successor because he knew Hardenberg was opposed to a separate peace, and he (the King) had begun to doubt the wisdom of his own negotiation — which is not strange, considering the advance of the French armies in Holland, revolutionizing as they went. Or it may be that the French activity in the north merely lent accent to what the King had been thinking all along, for on January 5, 1794, his Prussian Majesty had

[5] *Moniteur*, XXIII, 684.
[6] Heigel, *Deutsche Geschichte*, II, 175.
[7] Mallet du Pan to Gen. Heyman; to Marshal de Castries: *Mém. corr. Mallet du Pan*, II, 136–139.

expressed to Lord Malmesbury his "invariable abhorrence of the French principles, and his thorough conviction that if they were not checked, all government and order would be overthrown. [He affirmed] that he had in [no] degree altered his sentiments on these points, . . . that it was necessity and necessity alone which governed his conduct, and that if he was not certain that another campaign would completely exhaust his treasure, . . . he should not hesitate a moment as to the line of conduct he should observe." [8] When Hardenberg arrived in Berlin to receive his instructions, he broached the subject of subsidies to Lord Spencer, British Envoy Extraordinary and Minister Plenipotentiary to Prussia. Wrote the latter to Lord Grenville: "Hardenberg is, I believe, the only one of the King of Prussia's ministers who agrees with the wishes of his Majesty to continue the war. However, he is completely convinced of the manifest necessity of an immediate peace if England does not come forward with subsidy offers. I believe he is empowered to sign the treaty, but has been directed to protract matters so as to [permit us an opportunity to make known] our intentions." [9] And two weeks later: "Herr Hardenberg, who is still hoping for help from England, has prolonged his trip. . . He will comport himself similarly during the early days of the Conferences. But if, after this delay, he is convinced that no offers will be made to the Prussian ministers, he will . . . conclude peace with the French on the best possible conditions." [10] Hardenberg stopped at Brunswick on his way to Basel. There he saw Lord Malmesbury, and obtained from him a promise to propose to the English government the renewal of subsidy payments. [11]

It looks very much as if the King were playing with France to frighten subsidies out of England. Mallet du Pan had much the same idea when he suggested that perhaps the Basel negotiations were "a comedy staged to clip off some palatinates from the Court of Vienna." [12] Was not the march of Möllendorff's troops back toward Westphalia [13] — reported by Malmes-

---

[8] Malmesbury to Lord Grenville, *Diar. Corr. Malmesbury*, III, 40. Note also, that when von der Goltz was sent to Paris the previous December 1, the King, at the same time, ordered the Prussian troops to remain on the Rhine despite a previous command (in October) to be ready to leave (*vide infra*, n. 13); also, that, a few days thereafter, Frederick William, in the face of remonstrances from all his ministers, authorized Hardenberg to continue with energy the subsidy negotiations with England (Bailleu in *HZ*, LXXV, 253, 275).

[9] March 10, 1795, Herrmann, *Dipl. Corr.*, p. 513.

[10] March 24, 1795, *ibid.*, pp. 513–514.

[11] Malmesbury to Gen. Harcourt, March 16, 1795, *Diar. Corr. Malmesbury*, III, 253.

[12] *Mém. corr. Mallet du Pan*, II, 138.

[13] In October 1794, because of the explosive nature of the Polish situation, Frederick William had ordered Möllendorff to prepare the entire Prussian army for withdrawal into Westphalia and Ansbach, but Möllendorff, fearful for the safety of Mayence, Frankfort, and the Empire in general, had induced the King to content himself with the treaty force of 20,000 men (Bailleu in *HZ*, LXXV, 265–266). The remainder of Möllendorff's troops had remained on the

bury on February 16 [14] — timed most conveniently to fit into the general scheme of things? [15] Certain it is that Hardenberg's actions do not indicate an earnest desire to conclude a treaty. First came the long delays: in reaching Berlin, and in attaining Basel. Second was the urgent request for English subsidies. Third was Hardenberg's attitude with respect to the negotiations: as will appear below, he treated them as virgin soil about to be broken for the first time, whereas the French considered that Hardenberg's function was to sign what von der Goltz and Harnier had negotiated.[16] Fourth was the way the new negotiator held Harnier aside — Harnier, who had done so much to promote the peace.[17] Fifth was not so much a physical act, as the exercise of that elusive function called cerebration: Hardenberg wrote in his notes that his predecessors in the negotiation had feared a rupture overmuch; that the French invasion of Holland should have stiffened their attitude instead of melting it.[18] Apparently Hardenberg would have viewed a rupture with more equanimity than either von der Goltz or Harnier. An additional point — the last — concerns the thought processes of Hardenberg's royal master, and for this we must look ahead to April 21, sixteen days after Hardenberg, almost despite himself, successfully concluded the negotiation. On that date Lord Spencer reported, "I know that the King is at heart extremely vexed at the success of the negotiation." [19]

If his Majesty was indeed enmeshed in the toils of his own plot, and preferred subsidized war to peace, his vexation must have been great indeed, for on April 9, only four days after the signature of the Treaty of Basel, George III, fearful for his Hanover because the Austrians were retiring to the Rhine, proposed to Lord Grenville the renewal of the subsidy agreement with Prussia.[20] Favorable action followed on the part of the English Ministry, and on April 21, Spencer reported to Lord Grenville:

---

right bank within reach of possible danger points (*ibid.*, p. 267). It was the treaty force which was returning.

[14] To Lord H. Spencer, *Diar. Corr. Malmesbury*, III, 243.

[15] It appears to the writer that Möllendorff's movements were designed to whet the taste for Prussian assistance — for a price. When Malmesbury first learned of the marching orders given to Möllendorff, he was inclined to believe that Frederick William had resolved "to pursue the war with vigor and in earnest." — To Lord Grenville, Feb. 3, 1795, *ibid.*, p. 240. But on February 8 he wrote to Gen. Harcourt that as a result of information "through a private channel . . . on which I can rely: I am very much afraid that we must not look upon them

[the King's intentions] as sincere." — *Ibid.*, p. 241. Nevertheless, Malmesbury did consent to present Hardenberg's request for subsidies to his government (Malmesbury to Gen. Harcourt, March 16, 1795, *ibid.*, p. 253).

[16] *Vide* Fain, *Ms. l'an III*, p. 119: "The question was at such a point of maturity that the new negotiator seem[ed] to [have] come to Basel less to discuss than to sign or to break."

[17] Sorel in *RH*, VII, 325, 329.

[18] Häusser, *Deutsche Geschichte*, I, 593–594.

[19] To Lord Grenville, Herrmann, *Dipl. Corr.*, p. 514; accord: Dietrichstein to Thugut, April 30, 1795, Vivenot-Zeissberg, *Quellen*, V, 192.

[20] *Dropmore Papers*, III, 50.

"Colonel Calvert arrived here yesterday with three despatches for me. . .
Had I received them a few days sooner, I may venture to assert that England
would [now] have at her disposal the best-appointed army in Europe,
perfectly experienced and admirably well situated for the most active
operations." [21] Poor Frederick William, when the subsidies came, it was too
late! [22] But perhaps it was just as well, for his resistance probably would not
have lasted through the first campaign. As Malmesbury wrote, "Those who
direct the King of Prussia (and he is always directed) [23] are bent on peace
on any terms." [24] But let not the tragicomedy of the subsidy question cause
us further to neglect Hardenberg — waiting at Basel for our attention.

Hardenberg commenced the parleys by requesting that France should
make further concessions to Prussian consideration in the Empire. He
declared Article IV of the Committee's project to be somewhat (un peu)
humiliating. The circumstances of the war, he said, and even the interest of
France, necessitated the maintenance of more troops on Prussia's western
frontiers than before the war. He intimated that his government would
favor the neutralization of northern Germany, the neutrality to be guaranteed by an armed force established by common agreement. Barthélemy
replied that neutralization did not enter into the Committee's intentions,
that it could, he believed, form no part of the pacification, but would have
to be arranged between the French and Prussian generals by military convention. Hardenberg then objected to Article VI of the Committee's project.
He declared that if France were seeking to prepare future arrangements
beneficial to her policy, it was strange to commence by despoiling Prussia
of a part of its ancient domain, and dishonoring it before its co-states. He
asserted that all Germany would consider the cession of Clèves as prejudic-
ing the question of the Rhine frontier for the Empire. Hardenberg requested
that the French evacuate the Prussian left bank until its absolute cession at
the general peace. Barthélemy refused. Hardenberg proposed that neither
French nor Prussians should occupy Clèves, i.e., that it should be neutralized.
Barthélemy again refused. Hardenberg asked that the cession should not be
mentioned in the patent articles, but relegated in very modified form to the
secret provisions. Barthélemy protested than an article of such import could
not be omitted from the patent treaty, and that its further modification was

[21] Herrmann, Dipl. Corr., p. 514 and n. 343.
[22] The next subsidy offer was not made until
January 11, 1797, and was applicable to a
case where "France shall involve him into
a fresh war by his defending the north of
Germany." — Geo. III to Lord Grenville,
Dropmore Papers, III, 293.
[23] Vide supra, chap. iv, n. 413.

[24] To Gen. Harcourt, Feb. 8, 1795, Diar. Corr.
Malmesbury, III, 241. Bischoffswerder was
surprisingly enthusiastic for a peace at any
price, and did not exclude from his calculations the possibility of alliance with France
at some future date (Heigel, Deutsche Geschichte, II, 172).

impossible. However, though the French plenipotentiary refused all concession to his Prussian interlocutor, he wrote home to the Committee that "perhaps, while conserving the military possession in question, we could allow the King of Prussia to maintain there a shadow of civil administration." [25]

If the civil administration of his left-bank lands were returned to the Prussian King, it was certain that he would lay claim to the taxes he collected. Article VI of the Committee's project did not make it clear whether the civil administration would be confided to Prussia or not. The opening words, "The French Republic will continue to occupy . . . ," seem to imply only military occupation. Barthélemy foresaw the difficulties which would arise later on this score, and, already on March 16, he wrote to the Committee: "Will not the Prussian Ministry protest that in virtue of this article, you are to occupy only provisionally and militarily the state of Clèves, etc. . . . ; [that] it would in consequence be just that, although occupied by French troops, the Prussian administration there should be provisionally maintained, and the public funds placed in reserve, until the general pacification with Germany had pronounced upon the fate of the frontier of the Rhine?" [26] The Committee's answer, dated March 22, could leave no doubt as to its principles: "Our object . . . in proposing . . . this article . . . is obviously to assimilate these lands to the others similarly occupied by Republican troops. Now, these [other] territories are provisionally governed by the Republic, and it is to the Republic that they are paying their taxes." The Committee declared, furthermore, that any demand on the part of Berlin to recover the civil administration of its left-bank territories was absolutely inadmissible, especially as the Convention would never ratify such an arrangement.[27]

The Committee's despatch of March 22 discussed also the tantalizing question of indemnities. "If it were possible to make him [the King of Prussia] accept our guarantee for any . . . territory whatsoever to be ceded to him — some bishopric, for example — and to insert a secret article to that effect, we would be very pleased for two reasons: first, this article would prove to us the veritable good faith of the King of Prussia in the present negotiation, and his intention not to abrogate the treaty at his first opportunity; second, the Prussian government would thereby bind itself to our cause against the Coalition. . . But if this would delay the progress of the negotiations, we renounce it." [28] The first version of this despatch had gone more into detail regarding the indemnities: "It is for him [the King of

[25] Barthélemy to CPS, March 20, 1795, Papiers de Barthélemy, V, 117–118.
[26] Ibid., pp. 114–115.
[27] Ibid., p. 124.
[28] Ibid.

Prussia] to choose them beyond the Rhine. Let him take them in the ecclesiastical states or in Hanover; let him even arrange with the Duke of Brunswick, if he so desires, that the latter should give him his duchy and accept in exchange the Electorate of Hanover. In a word, let him determine his indemnity as he chooses. If it be at the expense of our enemies, and Holland does not contribute thereto in any respect, we will subscribe to everything, we will guarantee him everything, and we will lay down our arms only when he will be the undisturbed possessor thereof. A secret article is necessary for this. . ."[29]

Hardenberg's instructions were surprisingly in accord with France's wishes, and raised high hopes in Paris when the Committee learned of them through Harnier's loose and friendly tongue. The instructions expressed Prussia's consent to cede her left-bank provinces in so far as she was able under Imperial law, provided, however, that the cession were relegated to a separate and secret article, adequate indemnity were guaranteed, and France renounced all thought of interfering in Polish affairs. Möllendorff's suggestion of a line of demarcation was adopted, and developed to include all northern Germany, not excepting Hanover. If France should fear that Hanover would not maintain its neutrality honestly, or if she should hesitate to benefit so signally such a deadly enemy as the King of England, Hardenberg was authorized to promise, but only verbally, that Prussia, "at the special request of France," would occupy the Electorate "for a time" (*einstweilen*).[30] The intentions of France concerning the future Franco-Imperial peace, the matter of indemnity for the House of Orange, the fate of Belgium, the compensation to be granted Austria, and the influence to be allowed to Prussia at the future Franco-Imperial peace formed other articles of the Prussian envoy's instructions.[31]

At a conference with Barthélemy on March 22, Hardenberg proposed the insertion in the treaty of an article neutralizing northern Germany. The French plenipotentiary protested that this would necessitate the collection of extensive information, which would delay the signing of the treaty; it were far better, he argued, to sign the treaty as it stood, and then make a separate neutrality convention. Hardenberg said that his court had ordered him to insist that the neutrality project should form part and parcel of the treaty proper. No agreement could be reached. The plenipotentiaries separated with a promise from Hardenberg to present his observations on the morrow. The scheduled meeting did not take place, for the arrival of a courier from Berlin prevented the Prussian diplomat from keeping his appointment. The courier brought the order to insert a neutralization

[29] Quoted by Sorel in *RH*, VII, 64, n. 2.   [31] Hüffer, *Europa*, I, 116.
[30] Heigel, *Deutsche Geschichte*, II, 177.

provision in the treaty. Barthélemy wrote to the Committee that Hardenberg had certainly provoked these instructions.[32] Naturally, the Prussian
negotiator was anxious to spare his native Hanover from the tender mercies
of the Revolutionary armies. His notes show that he even favored the
renewal of hostilities should France fail to agree to the proposed neutralization. In insisting on a line of demarcation, however, Hardenberg was
acting perfectly in accord with the wishes of Frederick William.[33]

Harnier, who was favorably inclined toward France, viewed with consternation the possibility of the resumption of hostilities, and the same day
that the courier arrived, he lectured Hardenberg on the danger of prolong-
ing the negotiations. This "Dutch-uncle" talk had a sobering effect upon
Hardenberg, and caused him to comport himself in the most conciliatory
fashion during the next conference with Barthélemy — though his mellowed
attitude did not prevent him from asking the entire suppression of Article
IV of the Committee's project; the division of Article VI into two parts,
one patent and the other secret; the insertion of a very long secret article
concerning indemnities (the terms of which were inconsistent with the
provisions of Article IV); and the rewording of Article IX. The Prussian
plenipotentiary spoke at length about the neutrality plan. The princes of
northern Germany, according to him, would withdraw their contingents
from the army of the Empire and declare themselves neutral. Austria would
be isolated. French traders would be able to cross Hanover without molesta-
tion.[34] Hardenberg urged Barthélemy to recommend the plan to the Committee. He even declared, four days later, that if Barthélemy consented to
his modifications and additions, he would sign the treaty forthwith, for he
was possessed of sufficient powers to do so without referring again to
Berlin.[35]

On March 30 the Committee rendered its decision regarding the modifications proposed by Hardenberg. "To erase Article IV of our project," it
declared, "would be equivalent to reducing the treaty of peace to an armistice. Is one seriously at peace with his neighbor when he retains on the
frontier the same equipment as though he were in the midst of hostilities
. . . ?" The Committee conceded, however, that the article could be relegated to the secret part of the treaty. It even promised a total cancellation
should the King bind himself by a separate agreement to act offensively
against the enemies of France. Regarding Article VI, the Committee refused flatly to change a single word, declaring that all France would disa-
vow it if it did. The secret provision for the compensation of Prussia's

[32] Barthélemy to CPS, *Papiers de Barthélemy*, V, 127–128.

[33] Sorel in *RH*, VII, 319–320.

[34] Barthélemy to CPS, March 23, 1795, *Papiers de Barthélemy*, V, 130–132.

[35] *Idem*, March 27, 1795, *ibid.*, p. 136.

losses, which Hardenberg had demanded as a development of Article VI, was accepted by the Committee, though with the qualification that the indemnity should consist of territory beyond the Rhine. Barthélemy was instructed to specify immediately the particular territories which could form Prussia's compensation if this would not delay the conclusion of the treaty. Regarding the neutralization provision, the Committee announced its disapproval. "In the first place, it would hamper all our military operations. Then, where is the Frenchman who would pardon us for having neutralized a state dependent on England — Hanover? . . . Lastly, it would . . . [render] Article IX . . . without object, for of what use would be the good offices of the King of Prussia . . . if, from this moment, [the states of Germany would gain all the advantages of neutrality] . . . without their intervention and perhaps without their knowledge!" The Committee instructed Barthélemy to exact from Hardenberg a categorical "yes" or "no" as to whether he would accept the Committee's terms, and to send the decision to Paris by the returning courier.[36]

This letter was hardly on its way when there arrived Barthélemy's despatch of March 27 containing Hardenberg's promise to sign the treaty forthwith if France agreed to the neutralization of northern Germany. The Committee immediately regretted its blunt rejection of the scheme, and despatched a second courier to Barthélemy with the order not to communicate the letter of the previous day to the Prussian plenipotentiary until so directed.[37] Late that night still another courier carried to Barthélemy the Committee's authorization to sign the neutralization article and the provision concerning the indemnification of Prussia, and to cross out the fourth article of the French government's project. These concessions were attached to the condition that the treaty should be signed forthwith.[38]

The same day (March 31) Hardenberg brought Barthélemy a project of treaty which incorporated the Prussian ideas with the Committee's plan of March 10; and an extract of a letter from the King. In this letter, the Prussian monarch declared he persisted in regarding the line of demarcation and neutrality as the most important point of the negotiation, and he ordered his plenipotentiary "to maintain a firm tone, holding out the alternative of an equitable peace concluded immediately, with close commercial relations and other bonds which would perhaps result therefrom, and of a continuation of the war. . ." To Frederick William's way of thinking, the Committee's suggestion of armed neutrality, in its despatch of March 10, had paved the way for France's acceptance of the Prussian neutralization scheme, for the latter was a virtual armed neutrality. Hardenberg

[36] CPS to Barthélemy, March 30, 1795, *ibid.*,   [37] March 31, 1795, *ibid.*, p. 146.
pp. 139–142.   [38] *Ibid.*, pp. 146–147.

was ordered to affirm that the King's project did not need the accession of Holland, Sweden, and Denmark to give it consistency, and that an offensive and defensive coalition between Prussia and the said states was at the time impossible because of the former relations of Prussia with certain powers. "It goes without saying, moreover," the letter declared, "that the verbal instructions you have received relative to the promise to occupy Hanover, if it should be required, remain in full force"; and Hardenberg was authorized to stipulate it in the treaty or otherwise.[39]

The treaty project which Hardenberg presented to Barthélemy consisted of twelve patent and three secret articles. Four articles deserve special consideration:[40] Article V provided that French troops might continue to occupy the Prussian left-bank states until the general pacification between France and the German Empire, and that definitive arrangements in regard to the provinces would be postponed until that epoch. The presence of a phrase limiting the French occupation as to time is to be noted. Article XI was somewhat similar to the ninth article of the Committee's project, though it contained important additions. France was to accept Prussia's good offices in favor of those states of the Empire which desired to conclude treaties of separate peace with the Republic and requested the interposition of the King. France would consent not to treat as enemies for three months after the ratification of the treaty those right-bank princes in whose welfare Prussia should declare herself interested. The first secret article provided that if the left bank remained with France at the Franco-Imperial peace, Prussia would concert with the Republic regarding the mode of cession of the Hohenzollern possessions west of the Rhine, in consideration of such indemnity as might be agreed upon. Hardenberg would not admit that the Empire could cede Prussian territory without some action on Prussia's part, though he readily conceded that Prussia could not alienate her own territory (within the Empire) without the Empire's consent. The third secret article traced a line around northern and part of southern Germany behind which no hostile act could be perpetrated, and provided for observers to assure that strict neutrality would be maintained.[41]

This draft was forwarded by Barthélemy to Paris. The Committee rendered its judgment on April 4. It declared it could not accept Article XI, because the provisions contained therein would hamper military operations. As soon as a state saw itself menaced, it would call upon the King of Prussia to mediate peace.[42] Moreover, the system of neutralization was sufficiently

---

[39] *Ibid.*, pp. 149–150.

[40] *Vide* Appendix C for complete outline of this draft.

[41] Enclosed in Barthélemy's letter of March 31, 1795 to CPS, *Papiers de Barthélemy,*

V, 150–153.

[42] This argument had already been made on March 30 (CPS to Barthélemy, *ibid.*, p. 141).

extensive. Regarding the secret articles, the first was adopted with the already-articulated qualification that Prussia's indemnity should be territorial and beyond the Rhine. Article III, Secret, was declared to be acceptable on condition that Prussia should occupy Hanover. Barthélemy was urged to terminate the negotiations.[43]

The same day (April 4) the two negotiators in Basel had a "long but amicable conflict of words." Hardenberg agreed to the insertion of a secret article — in his opinion, superfluous — pledging Prussia not to attack Holland; and to an addition to the secret article relative to the line of demarcation, binding the neutralized states not to furnish further troops to the powers at war with France. However, he refused flatly to accept the wording of Article VI of the Committee's project, concerning occupation of the left bank, declaring that it compromised Prussia. Though it was quite late when the discussion ended, Barthélemy sat down and poured out his heart in a letter to the Committee. "If I do not succeed tomorrow in making your [wording] prevail," he wrote despairingly, "I hope you will not disapprove of my accepting the Prussian expressions." [44]

The next day, April 5, the contest commenced anew. After a long dispute, Hardenberg endorsed the transposition of the phrase, "until the general pacification between France and the German Empire," from the middle to the end of Article V of the Prussian project. However, he would not agree to replace the word "consents" by "is disposed" in the Prussian Article XI, for it would make France, instead of Prussia, appear as the good Samaritan. Neither would Barthélemy approve of Hardenberg's suggestion that the interest of the King of Prussia in the family of the former stadholder should be mentioned in the treaty. "After having exhausted all the means of doing better," the plenipotentiaries decided to sign both the patent and secret articles.[45]

Article I provided for peace and friendly understanding between the French Republic and the King of Prussia in his triple capacity of independent sovereign, Elector of Brandenberg, and Prince of the Empire. Article II provided that hostilities should cease upon ratification of the Treaty, and that neither power should grant aid in any capacity to the other's enemies. Article III forbade the granting of passage to enemies of the other state. These three articles were necessitated by the intricacies of Imperial law, according to which a state could be at war and at peace at the same time. The French wanted peace in all capacities. Article IV required that the French evacuate the Prussian right bank within fifteen days, and that all contributions cease in the cis-Rhenish and trans-Rhenish lands of the King.

[43] *Ibid.*, pp. 160–161.
[44] *Ibid.*, p. 162.

[45] Barthélemy to CPS, April 5, 1795, *ibid.*, p. 163.

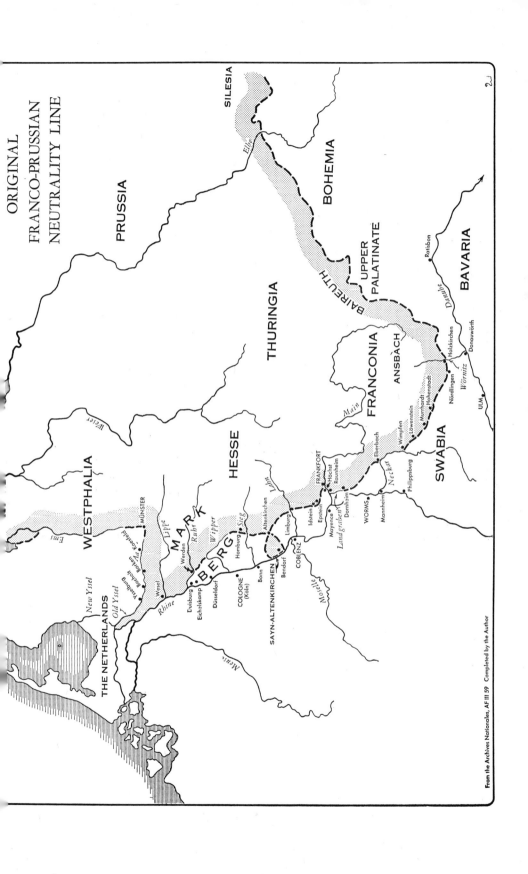

ORIGINAL
FRANCO-PRUSSIAN
NEUTRALITY LINE

PRUSSIA

SILESIA

BOHEMIA

Elbe

BAIREUTH

UPPER
PALATINATE

BAVARIA

Ratisbon

Danube

THURINGIA

FRANCONIA

ANSBACH

Holzkirchen

Donauwörth

Wörnitz

Nördlingen

ULM

Hohenstadt

Murrhardt

Löwenstein

Wimpfen

Main

SWABIA

Eberbach

HESSE

Neckar

Philippsburg

FRANKFORT

Höchst
Raunheim

WESTPHALIA

Weser

Lahn

Idstein
Epstein

Mayence

Dornheim

WORMS

Mannheim

MÜNSTER

Gescher

Beckum

Lippe

Altenkirchen

Landgraben

MARK

Ruhr

Werden

Sieg

Homburg

Limburg

Dülmen

Bocholt

Berkel

Wesel

Wipper

BERG

Bendorf

COBLENZ

Eichelskamp

Duisburg

Düsseldorf

COLOGNE
(Köln)

Bonn

SAYN-ALTENKIRCHEN

Moselle

New Yssel

Old Yssel

Rhine

THE NETHERLANDS

Ems

Meuse

From the Archives Nationales, AF III 59   Completed by the Author

3

Article V is very important, and was destined to engender much strife between the contracting parties. It declared that "the troops of the French Republic will continue to occupy that part of the states of the King of Prussia situated upon the left bank of the Rhine. All definitive arrangements in regard to these provinces will be postponed until the general pacification between France and the German Empire." Article VI provided that a commercial treaty should be concluded later, and that meanwhile prewar commercial relations would be reëstablished. Articles VII–X concerned the cessation of hostilities in northern Germany, the return of sequestrated property, and the exchange of prisoners of war. Article XI declared that France would accept the good offices of the King of Prussia in favor of those princes of the Empire who desired to treat directly with the Republic. Paragraph 2 of this article should be noted well: "The French Republic . . . consents not to treat as enemy country for a period of three months after the ratification of the present treaty those princes and states of the said Empire situated on the right bank of the Rhine in which the King manifests interest." Article XII declared that the exchange of ratifications would take place at Basel within one month. The first secret article engaged the King to undertake no hostile enterprise against the United Provinces, or any other territories occupied by French troops. The second secret article bound the King to concert with France the mode of cession of his left-bank states should his trans-Rhenish lands remain with France at the Franco-Imperial peace. In such case, the King would receive territorial indemnification, for the security of which he would accept the guarantee offered him by the Republic. The third secret article concerned the neutrality of northern Germany. France would not order her troops to penetrate, either by land or sea, that part of Germany situated beyond a designated line. This line was to follow the Ems River, jump to Münster, turn to the west and follow the towns of Koesfeld, Borken, Bocholt and the Aa River to Ysselburg on the Old Yssel. From there the line was to run northwest along the Old Yssel to a point on the New Yssel, and then ascend the Rhine — thus slicing off the segment of Clèves on the right bank of the Rhine. At Duisburg the line was to turn eastward to Werden, and follow the western frontier of Mark and the Wipper River southward, thus excluding most of the Wittelsbach Duchy of Berg from neutrality. From the Wipper the line was to jump to the town of Homburg, then to Altenkirchen — where it would describe a circle to embrace Sayn-Altenkirchen [46] and Bendorf by virtue of Article IV,

[46] A little right-bank state near Coblenz, administered in the name of the Margrave of Ansbach and Baireuth, but which was destined to go to Prussia after his death. The Margrave, in selling Ansbach and Bai- reuth to Prussia, had reserved this little principality for his lifetime — or, as one would say were this a case in private law, the Margrave had conveyed Sayn-Altenkirchen in fee, reserving to himself a life

Secret — and to Limburg on the Lahn. A little stream flows into the Lahn about ten miles above Limburg, and the line was to ascend this stream to Idstein, and jump to Epstein and to Höchst on the Main — enabling Frankfort to be included within the neutral zone. The line was then to hug the banks of the Main River the few miles to Raunheim, and follow the Landgraben to Dornheim. From there it was to go southeast to Eberbach on the Neckar, along this River to the free Imperial city of Wimpfen, then to jump to Löwenstein, Murrhardt, Hohenstadt, Nördlingen, and to Holzkirchen on the Wörnitz north of Donauwörth — thus protecting all of Franconia, where Prussia had the important possessions of Ansbach and Baireuth. The line was to be completed by following the northern boundaries of Bavaria, the Upper Palatinate, and Bohemia, to Silesia. France would consider the territories situated behind this line as neutral, provided that Prussia compelled their rulers to observe strict neutrality, the first manifestation of which should be the recall of their contingents from the army of the Empire. Prussia would guarantee that no armed force would emerge from the neutralized region to attack France. The two contracting parties would concert on the establishment of corps of observation to assure that the line of neutrality would be respected. The fourth secret article provided that Sayn-Altenkirchen and Bendorf should enjoy the same privileges as right-bank Prussian territory. The sixth [47] and last secret article excluded Austria from the benefit of the Prussian good offices and of the three months' armistice provision.[48]

estate. This is apparently the way Hardenberg viewed the situation, for he argued that Sayn-Altenkirchen should be regarded as already incorporated in Prussia (*idem*, March 23, 1795, *ibid.*, pp. 130–132).

[47] The fifth secret article was of no great importance, though it is surprising. It provided that if France acquired Zweibrücken, the Republic should guarantee repayment of the loan made to the Duke of Zweibrücken by the King of Prussia.

[48] The original French text may be consulted in the *Papiers de Barthélemy*, V, 164–168, and in A. de Clercq (ed.), *Recueil des traités de la France* (20 vols. in 21, Paris, 1864–1900), I, 232–236. J. B. M. Duvergier (ed.), *Collection complète des lois, décrets, etc.* (78 vols., Paris, 1824–1878), VIII, 77–78; and G. F. de Martens (ed.), *Recueil des principaux traités d'alliance . . . de l'Europe*, Ser. II (2nd ed. [of Vols. V–VIII by C. de Martens]; 8 vols., Göttingen, 1817–1835), Vol. VI, 45–47, give only the patent articles. An error in Article VI of the secret articles as given by De Clercq renders that article meaningless. It should read, "Les dispositions de l'article 11," and not "de l'article II."

Dumolin, *Précis*, I, 298, asserts that the Treaty of Basel recognized a Prussian protectorate over the Lutheran states of Germany. This is a grossly misleading statement, for, whereas most (not all!) of the territory behind the Line of Demarcation was indeed Lutheran, some Lutheran territory was not included, and the word "Lutheran" is not to be found in the Treaty. The Treaty of Basel was motivated by political and not by religious considerations, though undoubtedly some interaction existed (as always). *Vide infra*, Pt. II, chap. xxvi, n. 21.

3. THE RECEPTION OF THE TREATY OF BASEL

a. General

Such was the Treaty of Basel, the first important[49] chink in the armor of the kings leagued against the regicide Republic. It became the foundation of the German policy of the later Convention and of the Directory. This treaty transformed an enemy into a neutral; the effort of France henceforth was to induce other German states to follow the Prussian example, and then to prevail upon the neutrals to make common cause with France against the latter's hereditary enemy, Austria. This program did not appear so chimerical at the time because of Prussia's need for an ally in the Polish imbroglio. In fact, alliance with France was earnestly considered by the Prussian ministers when, in September 1795, they learned the details of the Austro-Russian Convention of the preceding January.[50] It was expected, moreover, by foreign observers. Even before the Treaty was signed, Lord Henry Spencer wrote to Grenville that he believed alliance with France would follow the signature. Spencer averred that his Prussian Majesty would certainly rather go to war immediately than cede Sandomir and Cracow to Austria;[51] and war against the enemy of France was almost certain to lead to alliance with France against the common enemy. That the Hohenzollern king would rather yield on the Polish question[52] than ally with the

[49] As already mentioned, Tuscany had withdrawn from the war on February 9, 1795. Prussia was therefore not the first to desert the cause of the Allies, though she was the first German state to desert. Many of the states of the Empire were maintaining secret relations with the enemy. During the battle for the Mannheim bridgehead, the Austrian general Wartensleben caught several envoys of the Palatine government who were trying to slip into the enemy camp. They protested vehemently that the Prince-Elector had commissioned them to negotiate regarding the exchange of Palatine prisoners in French hands, and that a prince-elector had a constitutional right to negotiate. Out of consideration for the electoral dignity, the Emperor ordered Wartensleben to yield. The General thereupon despatched an Austrian officer to accompany the Palatine envoys to the French outposts. Merlin-Th. rebuffed their spokesman, a Hofkammerrat (councillor of the exchequer), and his proposals, though the man informed him that "he had other, secret propositions to make."

The Austrian officer noticed that the Hofkammerrat had in his possession a thick packet of written material — material which, however, never left his hands. (Vivenot, *Bas. Fried.*, Pt. I, 51–52. Sorel in *RH*, VI, 46, gives practically the identical citation as authority for a wholly different set of facts. Obviously a wrong citation.) The Mannheim bridgehead was surrendered to the French on December 25, 1794, to save the city from being burned by the Republicans. The Convention grumbled at the leniency of the terms. Carnot replied that Mannheim could have been reduced to ashes, but that the operation would have cost several thousand men (*Moniteur*, XXIII, 91).

[50] Guyot, *Direc.*, pp. 104–105.

[51] March 30, 1795, *Dropmore Papers*, III, 561–562.

[52] Oct. 24, 1795. He accepted the Austro-Russian Convention on condition that he would not be obliged to resume hostilities against France (Guyot, *Direc.*, pp. 104–105).

Republic was little expected, except perhaps by those who realized the magnitude of his hatred for the Revolution,[53] and considered his weak and vacillating nature.[54]

b. By the Committee

The Treaty of Basel did not satisfy the Committee of Public Safety. By its letter of April 11, it censured Barthélemy for having allowed the three months' armistice provision (Article XI of the Prussian draft) to be included despite the Committee's declaration that such a provision would hamper military operations; it announced that it had thought for a while of deferring publication of the agreement until the objectionable paragraph had been canceled; it ridiculed as "absurd" the intimation in the sixth secret article of the Treaty that the Prussian good offices could apply to all the Empire except Austria, and affirmed its intention of interpreting the eleventh article as a vague patent counterpart of the secret article relative to the neutralization of northern Germany. In other words, the Committee decided to restrict the Prussian good offices to northern Germany. An omission on Barthélemy's part also roused the ire of the French government. The royal despatch of March 24 to Hardenberg had declared unqualifiedly that Prussia would occupy Hanover if France exacted it. Barthélemy had failed to exact it, and so the Treaty had been signed without a mention of the Electorate. Hardenberg's note of April 7 to Barthélemy, in which the Prussian plenipotentiary maintained that his government's offer to occupy Hanover was only applicable in case of that state's refusal to accept neutrality,[55] failed to satisfy the Committee. It asked Barthélemy bluntly why he had failed to exact the occupation, and ordered him to provoke a more positive declaration from Hardenberg. The French plenipotentiary was instructed also to express to the Prussian minister the necessity of considering the Treaty of April 5 merely as a preliminary to one of vastly greater importance. He was to say that if the Prussian monarch would concur in the views of France, he could raise himself to unprecedented heights of grandeur and stability, and exercise, conjointly with the Republic, the most useful influence upon all Europe.[56]

c. By the Convention

The Convention seems to have received the Treaty less critically than the

[53] The execution of Louis XVI had made a deep and lasting impression upon Frederick William (Sorel, *Europe*, III, 296) — an impression that the subsequent conduct of the revolutionists did nothing to erase. On January 5, 1794, as mentioned, the Prussian King spoke to Lord Malmesbury about "his invariable abhorrence of the French principles." — Malmesbury to Lord Grenville, *Diar. Corr. Malmesbury*, II, 40.

[54] *Idem*, Feb. 1, 1794, *ibid.*, p. 50.

[55] *Papiers de Barthélemy*, V, 171–172.

[56] CPS to Barthélemy, April 11, 1795, *ibid.*, pp. 173–174.

Committee. Reubell divulged the patent portion on April 10, following a speech in which he had prepared the Convention for relatively moderate terms by pointing out that Prussia also had to be satisfied if the peace were to be durable. Knowing that many members of the Convention were irreconcilably committed to the Rhine boundary, and knowing that the Treaty all but side-stepped the issue, Reubell declared vaguely: "Although you have not expressed your intentions concerning the boundaries of the territory of the Republic, your Committee has believed itself obliged to treat in the sense that until now the nation has appeared to approve." The members of the Convention understood that Reubell was intimating the existence of secret articles, and held their peace. And then came the trump card for a starving people: "The principal end toward which it ["your Committee"] has labored was to reëstablish commercial relations." [57] Reubell's report was received with "lively applause," [58] and four days later, the Convention ratified the Treaty unanimously. "Universal acclamation was prolonged and mixed with cries of *vive la République* several times repeated." [59]

The Convention had good reason to be pleased. The Treaty was equivalent, for it, to a new lease on life. On April 8, Roux had sought to calm the public spirit by rising in the Convention and assuring that body that peace was near. But he knew what was in everyone's mind, and, unable to contribute even hope, he had advanced the unsatisfying argument that England and Germany were just as hungry as was France.[60] Hunger and peace were recognized as the two faces of Janus.[61] Peace was therefore certain to make converts for the government. This fact was rued by Mallet du Pan. It is very possible, he declared, that the nation will think no longer of withdrawing powers from its representatives when they use these powers to secure what the nation wants: peace.[62]

d. By the Man-in-the-Street in France

Mallet's judgment was borne out in the main by the reactions of the French man-in-the-street, but what appears most striking in the police reports on the reception of the Treaty by the Parisians is the extent to which the stomachs of the people had taken over the cerebral functions. The peace

---

[57] Richard (Rp A. N) pointed out in a letter to the CPS that the resumption of commerce with northern Germany would break the virtual monopoly which the Swiss had enjoyed since the start of the war, and which had resulted in excessive prices (April 29, 1795, Aulard, *Actes*, XXII, 536–537).
[58] *Moniteur*, XXIV, 188.
[59] *Ibid.*, p. 215.
[60] *Ibid.*, p. 176.

[61] Audouin, in his observations to the Convention on March 16, 1795, remarked: "I come to the question without speaking of the cries for peace concomitant . . . with the cries of scarcity (*disette*)." — *Ibid.*, XXIII, 709.
[62] A. Michel (ed.), *Correspondance inédite de Mallet du Pan avec la cour de Vienne, 1794–1798* (2 vols., Paris, 1884), I, 173.

and its terms were viewed solely in their relation to the question of sub-sistence. The ideals and ideas of the Revolution had succumbed to the gnaw-ing, nauseating pangs of hunger.

"Down with your guns!" shouted a crowd of four or five hundred women whom soldiers were trying to disperse from before the doors of bakeries. "We want no more soldiers, since there is no more bread." [63] Whether the women knew yet of the peace at that hour (it was April 10) is not indicated in the report, but in the same day's account we read, "this news [of peace] causes the greatest satisfaction among all citizens, and seems to infuse courage to endure the privations in the hope that this partial peace will shortly procure us a general [peace]." [64] Two days later, the police register reads: "People talked about the treaty of peace made with Prussia; but the penury of [the means of] subsistence causes a general outcry of all citizens." [65] On April 13, the report runs: "Peaceable citizens seek . . . to fortify their courage by announcing . . . that a general peace will soon put an end to our calamities." [66] Other reports go to the essence of France's original quarrel with the Coalition: "Several women curse the Convention, and say it matters little to them whether they have a king if only they have bread." [67] "The coachmen . . . said yesterday among them-selves that if it were intended to cause them to die of hunger, they would send the Republic to the devil." [68] "Some one cried out several times at a baker's door: 'We need a king and princes to be happy.' " [69] And "In the Place du Carrousel, a woman was heard to say to her daughter, 'It is here that your father's blood flowed on August 10. Well, [child,] I will shatter your head on these same stones before I see you die of hunger.' " [70]

From all of which it appears that the starving people — dropping dead on the streets from malnutrition,[71] drowning themselves in the Seine,[72] taking their children to the national foundling-home,[73] too weak to work and ill from starvation,[74] crying out in their agony against the government [75] — cared little for such fine points like (de facto) recognition of the Re-public, and peace with Prussia but not yet with Austria.[76] A general peace

<hr/>

[63] Aulard, *Paris*, I, 650. The women threat-ened to go to the Convention with the can-non belonging to their section (*ibid.*). By decree of March 28, 1795, bread was to be delivered to the door by wagons guarded by two fusileers each ("La distribution du pain à Paris en germinal, an III," under "Documents," *RF*, LX [1911], 64). It was thought that this would make for a more equitable distribution of bread; but nothing, equally divided, is still nothing.

[64] Aulard, *Paris*, I, 649.

[65] *Ibid.*, p. 653.

[66] *Ibid.*, p. 656.

[67] *Ibid.*, p. 665.

[68] *Ibid.*

[69] *Ibid.*, p. 670.

[70] *Ibid.*, p. 661.

[71] *Ibid.*, p. 662.

[72] *Ibid.*, pp. 654–655, 660.

[73] *Ibid.*, p. 649.

[74] *Ibid.*, pp. 654–655.

[75] *Ibid.*, p. 655.

[76] Which can be the only meaning of Art. VI, Secret, of the Treaty of Basel.

was their desire because peace meant bread. The Treaty of Basel was, then, to the public of France, not a triumph because of its partial character, but only a partial triumph. Such treaties were only "the harbingers of the general peace we should have with [all] Europe," was how Napoleon Bonaparte expressed it to his brother Joseph.[77]

e. By Frederick William

What was the attitude of Frederick William toward the Treaty of Basel? He was no more satisfied with it than was the Committee of Public Safety. As brother of the ex-stadholder's wife, he could not bring himself to view with equanimity a treaty which consecrated the absorption of the Netherlands by France. Barthélemy, moreover, had declined to mention in the document the interest taken by the King in the House of Orange.[78] France's treatment of the Prussian left-bank possessions intensified the royal displeasure. Prussia had refused to cede her trans-Rhenish territories in the Treaty, and had secured the postponement of the question of cession until the peace of the Empire, in the hope that the tide would turn against France, and the lands return to their Hohenzollern owner. France took the attitude that the formal cession had been omitted from the Treaty only to humor the German public, and to spare the King from the stigma of being the first to subscribe to the dismemberment of the Empire. The Republic therefore treated the territories as conquered lands, and proceeded to collect for itself the annual revenue of almost a million crowns. This revenue the King needed desperately, hence deprecated the arrangement which, while depriving him of his old revenues, postponed his indemnification to a period dependent on the pleasure of France.[79]

But of course it was useless for him to show his resentment, with France in possession, and there was no trace of such sentiments in the declaration which the Prussian monarch presented to the Ratisbon Diet on May 12, announcing the peace. In this document, his Majesty reminded his coprinces how much he had sacrificed in men and money for them, how Prussia had captured Mayence for the Empire and never been reimbursed, how "the insurrection and plundering" of the Poles had forced the King to fight two wars at the same time, how the Empire had refused to support his army, how England had broken its subsidy treaty, how Thermidor had resulted in the triumph of "reasonable principles" in France — and then he "ask[ed] his contemporaries, and [left] it to posterity to decide, if his conduct were susceptible of reproach, considering that his interest in this

[77] Aug. 12, 1795, A. Chuquet, "Lettres de Bonaparte," *FH*, VI (1911), 127. Specifically, Bonaparte was referring to the separate peace with Spain.

[78] Barthélemy to CPS, April 5, 1795, Arch. N., AF III 76, d. 314.

[79] Sorel, *Europe*, V, 29; Bailleu, *Pr. Frk.*, I, xlix–l.

war was not at all immediate or personal." Followed a vivid recital of the joys of peace, and of his Prussian Majesty's magnanimous provision in the Treaty for extending the bounties of peace to all of Germany — even to all the Allies. "But, whatever turn these grand affairs take, and even if an unfortunate outcome be in store for the Empire's war, his Majesty declares . . . formally that he . . . renounces taking . . . any part in the conflict." And then came another series of justifications, ending with, "it is 'beyond all fear' that one could reproach him." [80] From all of which it is evident that the King was none too happy even though the disbursements had ceased. He was learning that there are higher values in the world than those measurable in reichstaler. This "peace, concluded . . . in scorn of the common interest, cost Frederick William his esteem, and the Prussian monarchy its prestige of glory." [81] But of course the King's uncle, Prince Henry, was delighted; likewise, Möllendorff.[82]

f. By the German Press

Upon the Prussian press devolved the task of rendering the Treaty palatable to the common man in North Germany — or rather, upon the press devolved the task of "whitewashing" the royal signatory of the Treaty. "What has Frederick William done in this war in behalf of our German fatherland?" one editorial runs. "Nothing is easier to answer." The King sacrificed his own comfort and safety at the head of his troops. Prussian blood flowed. Many (Prussian) limbs were mangled or lost "for the *German fatherland.*" "The exploits, the outlays, the patriotic intentions of Frederick William will shine yet after the lapse of centuries in the annals of our *German fatherland*, and everyone must needs say: Indeed, what Frederick William did in this war, he did in behalf of the *German fatherland.*" But not only did he support the fatherland in war, but he it was who, on April 5, enabled "the *sorrowing guardian-angel of Germany* to look smilingly once more upon its brothers." The enemy was occupying more German territory with each campaign, the sources of sustenance were being lost by Prussia, the winter was extraordinarily harsh, commerce was at a standstill, everyone was sighing for peace. "Who cannot see, therefore, how necessary . . . *for Germany* was the peace between Prussia and France? . . . It is immaterial to *us Germans* whether France has a king or a republic, religion or anarchy. We can be peaceful spectators of all that passes in France, and congratulate ourselves

---

[80] *Moniteur*, XXIV, 525, 533–534, 541–542. Dated May 12, 1795.

[81] *Mém. homme d'Etat*, III, 151.

[82] Both these wrote letters of congratulation to Bacher (*Moniteur*, XXIV, 525–526). Bacher (an Alsatian) had spent part of his youth in Berlin, where he received his first lessons in military science and maintained rather close relations with Prince Henry, brother of the then-reigning Frederick II (Sorel in *RH*, V, 273–74).

that we have princes who render similar revolutions unnecessary for us. Truly, a general peace would be desirable, but . . . Prussia's peace with France contains *great and wise plans* which certainly will redound to *Germany's advantage.* Can we say that Frederick William, who coöperated most actively during the entire course of the war, deserted . . . our Emperor in this crisis? This could not be deduced from the generosity of the King.— No, it is plain that the peace Prussia made with France applies . . . to the Emperor, the German Empire, and all the warring powers. . . That is the true purpose of this noble king. Fortunate are we that Frederick William harbors such thoughts about our fatherland! . . . Long live Frederick William, King of the Prussians, Restorer of Our Peace and Order!" [83]

With respect both to this editorial and to Frederick William's declaration to the Diet, above, it will be realized that Article VI, Secret, of the Treaty of Basel belies the pretense that Austria could take advantage of the Treaty, and the Committee's decision to interpret the sixth secret article restrictively belies that claim with respect to the unneutralized portion of Germany. But the pretense constituted good propaganda.

From Möllendorff's quarters a proclamation was issued to the Prussian armies apprizing the troops: "It is peace, comrades! for that is the will of the King, and the welfare of the fatherland requires it. We are not defeated! . . . Never did the enemy see you in flight or in disorder. . . No blush need color your cheeks. . . Long live the memory of Frederick the Great! Long live Field Marshal General Möllendorff!" [84] Apparently Möllendorff did not expect the peace to be received by his army with a superabundance of enthusiasm, and indeed many lowly troopers blushed for shame while their officers celebrated with dance and feast.[85]

But great numbers of hostile pamphlets flooded all of western Europe, and "made the hearts of the Prussians bleed." One brochure in particular, *Syrach,* by one knew not whom, exercised an "unbelievable effect." Everyone read it. Peasants pooled their resources to buy it. It belied the charges of ambition leveled at Austria, and condemned Prussia for deserting the Em-

---

[83] Vivenot, *Bas. Fried.,* Pt. I, 494–497. The italicized phrases were italicized in the original.

Hashagen relates that when the Wesel Theater was reopened — a festive occasion — it was noted that a bust of the goddess of peace was fraternizing with a bust of Frederick William. And the festive poem contained these lines (in translation):

"Frederick William! wished his peoples peace,
Wanted their good fortune, and his hands,

In benediction, closed up the Temple of Janus.
Fervent thanks to him! who, during the tempest of war,
Stood fearless and great as peacemaker.
Thank him, [ye] graybeards, children, mothers!
[For] your rescue, thank him, [O] Fatherland."
— *Rheinland,* p. 114.

[84] Vivenot, *Bas. Fried.,* Pt. I, 498–499.
[85] *Ibid.,* p. 493.

pire. In many villages, the Prussians were threatened with violence — even death — should they appear.[86] The Peace of Basel was, then, received roughly by the unshackled press, but the propagandists of the Court of Berlin were extravagant in its praise.

g. By the Rhineland

How did the left bank of the Rhine receive the Treaty of Basel? It was the invasion of the Rhineland, it will be recalled, that had been one of the prime causes of the Empire's declaration of war. And now Prussia had withdrawn from the conflict leaving the question of the left bank still unsolved — or what was worse, partially solved in an adverse manner.[87] On April 8, Hardenberg wrote to the Baron of Albini, minister to the Elector of Mayence: If the Treaty does not contain all the things that my German patriotism and my attachment for your Electoral Prince could wish, it still is a great step toward the pacification of the Empire. "Make sure that Mayence holds out. If it does, I believe for several reasons that the French will soon renounce their designs upon the left bank of the Rhine."[88] To which Albini replied, "I earnestly ask your Excellency: What shall we remaining Germans do who yearn for peace just as ardently [as you do], but who have . . . everything to lose [if] the left bank of the Rhine [is ceded to France]? There can be no peace for us so long as we do not know that France will renounce the Rhine boundary. We must fight like demons, even if no one will help us further. We have no choice but victory or death."[89]

On May 1, Albini observed, "When I consider the unbelievably wretched internal condition of France and of Paris itself, when I ponder that the Convention is not certain of its existence from one day to the next, I should think that this Convention would have far more reason than do we to make peace."[90] Albini meant, of course, a peace without conquests, a peace for the sake of peace.

The Elector of Mayence himself said: "There can be no peace until France withdraws from the Rhineland. 'Peace' and 'Rhine boundary' are two things that cannot coexist." The "unavoidably absent" Trèves Elector was of like mind. The also-absent Elector of Cologne said it was "unthinkable" to cede "one foot of soil" to France. But all three longed for peace, and, not knowing of Prussia's secret commitment with respect to the Rhine

---

[86] Dietrichstein to Thugut, May 20 and June 17, 1795, Vivenot-Zeissberg, *Quellen*, V, 223, 251.

[87] Prussia must, of course, have realized this fully. Still she persisted in viewing the war, not essentially as a Franco-Imperial conflict for the Rhineland, but as a Franco-Austrian contest for Belgium (Bailleu in *HZ*, LXXV, 238).

[88] Vivenot, *Bas. Fried.*, Pt. II, 563–564.

[89] April 15, 1795, *ibid.*, p. 565.

[90] To Hardenberg, *ibid.*, p. 570.

frontier, hoped that an *Imperial* peace might somehow grow out of the Basel agreement.[91]

The populations of the left bank also yearned for peace, but Prussia's defection and her separate treaty caused many a raised eyebrow. The fact that the foreign occupation had been allowed to continue aroused an emotion perhaps akin to resentment, and this emotion, though it could not be aired openly, found its way even into a letter written by one connected with the French-sponsored Bonn District Administration. "I have no liking for the peace with Prussia," wrote notary Falkenstein, "nor have a good many others." [92] The attitude of the Prussian left bank — how the peace caused joy until it was learned that the French were to remain, and then fear that cession to France would follow — will come in for discussion later.[93]

It was naturally among the German left-bank republicans that the Treaty was viewed in its rosiest light. However, high-sounding phrases, such as "War abases the dignity of Man and impedes morality and civilization," took the place of critical appraisal, and need hardly occupy our attention. These German republicans did put forth one point, however, that may constitute food for thought. They said that the Peace of Basel was merely one step in a gradual peaceful revolution in the Rhineland.[94] (Perhaps they did not know what it means, either.)

h. The Internal Crisis and the Treaty

It is indisputable that Prussia, when making the Treaty of Basel, did not capitalize fully the internal political condition of France. The prosecution of the most notorious terrorists by the Thermidorians, and the acute shortage of foodstuffs, had led to repeated insurrections of the turbulent sections of Paris. On March 21, the sections of Montreuil and of the Quinze-Vingts [95] (Faubourg Saint-Antoine) surged in crowds to the Convention to demand "bread and the Constitution of 1793." [96] The Convention was intimidated, and on March 27 and 28, it seriously considered dissolving itself, and convoking the primary assemblies provided for by the Constitution of 1793.[97] On the last day of March, a deputation from the Quinze-Vingts reminded the legislators that "the people know that when they are oppressed, insurrection is the holiest of duties." [98] The next day, 12 *germinal* or April 1, a

---

[91] Hansen, *Quellen*, III, 491–492. The Elector of Mayence would even have accepted the separate-peace principle, at least originally. But the Elector of Cologne soon pointed out how unconstitutional it was (Max Franz to his Ratisbon ambassador, von Karg, May 3, 1795, *ibid*., p. 492, n. 1).

[92] To his friend Wallraf, April 17, 1795, *ibid*., p. 493.

[93] Pt. I, chap. xiv, § 3.

[94] Hashagen, *Rheinland*, pp. 114 *et seqq*.

[95] So called after an institute accommodating three hundred (*quinze-vingts*) blind men, which was known as the "Quinze-Vingts."

[96] Pariset, *La Rév*., pp. 250–253.

[97] Sciout, *Direc*., I, 54, 160.

[98] Dauban, *Paris*, p. 550. Cf. Robespierre's proposed Declaration of Rights, inserted

large crowd again invaded the Convention, demanding bread, the Constitution of 1793, and the liberty of imprisoned patriots.[99] The riot continued on April 2, and General Pichegru, entrusted with the command of the armed forces of Paris, was obliged to fire on the crowd to restore order.[100] The same temper was evident in the provinces. In Amiens, on April 3, a mob of eight or nine hundred men and women broke into the town hall, stamped under foot the emblems of liberty, and also Representative of the People Blaux. As Blaux himself informed the Convention, "they tore off my costume; pulled out a third of my hair; yanked off my shoes and rings; . . . tore my coats, vest, trousers, and shirt to shreds; tried to force me to cry *vive Louis XVII*; threw me to the ground ten times and stamped on me; spat in my face — which they smeared with mud and flour; covered me with wounds and bruises, and strangled me with the scarf from my hat to the point that, when I was rescued, I was no longer breathing." Blaux's agony lasted six hours. The Convention ordered the trial of the malefactors, but such was the popular temper that all were acquitted on the ground that they "had no criminal intent." [101] In Rouen, the populace disarmed the national guard, uprooted the trees of liberty, snatched off tricolor cockades, and demanded a king, peace, and bread. There were riots also at Toulon.[102] It was in times such as these, when the power of the Republican government was hanging by a thread,[103] that Prussia took it upon herself to impart to the Convention the prestige which comes from bringing peace.

"One cannot but be hurt," wrote George III to Lord Grenville on April 22, "that the King of Prussia can have been so ill-advised as to conclude a treaty of peace with the common enemy; but I should not be surprised if, on his hearing how very confused the state of Paris now is, he should decline ratifying this disgraceful measure." [104]

Mallet du Pan also was confounded by Prussia's hasty act. "If the cabinet of Berlin," he wrote to Degelmann (Austrian minister at Basel) on April 28, "had been willing to temporize for six weeks more,[105] instead of pre-

---

verbatim in the Constitution of 1793: "When the government violates the rights of the people, insurrection is for the people and for each portion of the people the most sacred of rights and the most indispensable of duties." — Anderson, *Const's . . . Doc's*, pp. 163, 174.

[99] Dauban, *Paris*, p. 551.

[100] Sorel, *Europe*, IV, 286–287.

[101] Wallon, *Repré.*, III, 400–401.

[102] Sciout, *Direc.*, I, 56.

[103] Wrote Trevor, the British minister to Turin, on March 12, 1795: "Hunger, misery, and despair may overturn a gov-

ernment, but are bad foundations for a Republic." — "Memorandum on the State of France," *Dropmore Papers*, III, 86.

[104] *Dropmore Papers*, III, 57.

[105] Undoubtedly a reference to the riot of 1 *prairial* or May 20, 1795, in which an armed mob broke into the Convention and forced the adoption of several laws. Only one deputy had the courage to resist the entrance of the mob. He was knocked down, kicked, beaten, beheaded — and his head was carried before the president on a pike. This deputy was Féraud (Madelin, *Fr. Rev.*, p. 462), about whom Merlin-Th.

cipitating its treaty with the Convention *at the very instant that the latter was yielding up its power*, . . . the misfortunes of France and of Europe would probably be over." [106] Mallet du Pan thought that if the powers of Europe had let it be known that their granaries would open and peace would be reëstablished as soon as the King were proclaimed, the monarchy would have been restored and the conquered territories returned.[107]

"There is much news to the effect that an explosion is imminent in Paris and in several provinces," wrote General Clerfayt to Thugut on April 9, before the signing of the Treaty was known. "It seems that it has never been more necessary to have firmness and to await events. . . It is apparent that soon we shall be able — should we so desire — to negotiate with advantage, and to secure honorable and advantageous terms." [108] On May 12, the English lady whose letters form *Un séjour en France* reported, "This morning news arrived that the Convention proposed to dissolve. . . We spent two days in these pleasant reveries." [109] And the Emperor (Thugut's draft) wrote to Clerfayt on the seventeenth that "according to the unanimous" reports he had received, "the very existence of the Convention seems lately to be menaced"; and he spoke of the ephemeral nature of agreements with "a government as precarious as that of the so-called Republic." [110]

Hardenberg himself declared later (toward the end of 1795), in a letter to Degelmann not attributable entirely to hindsight, that Prussia had made peace at the wrong time. He added, however, that he had been obliged to negotiate the Treaty because he could not disobey his instructions.[111]

i. Barthélemy Defends His Treaty

On April 16, Barthélemy answered the Committee's attacks of the eleventh

once wrote: "I have the craziest colleague one has ever seen; I am referring to the Representative Féraud, laughingstock of all the army." — To CPS, Dec. 15, 1794, Aulard, *Actes*, XVIII, 746. A little more such craziness and France might have been saner.

[106] H. H. S. Arch., *Schweiz* 197. The italicized words were underscored in the original.

[107] *Inéd. Mallet du Pan*, I, 177, April 22, 1795. Instead, part of Germany, by making a separate peace, took upon itself to provision France. Wrote Clerfayt to the Emperor after the Treaty of Basel: "Much provisions of every kind are passing through Westphalia and are stored at Venloo for transportation to the French army, which will thus be able to dispense

with what the interior of the country should send daily." This of course improved the situation in the interior of France, upon the misery of which the Austrians had been counting for counterrevolution (May 31, 1795, *Thugut, C, W,* p. 141). In June, the Austrians were obliged to take heroic measures to prevent the provisions that they sold to Hamburg from going to France (Thugut to Count Colloredo, June 2, 1795, *Briefe Thugut,* I, 221).

[108] *Thugut, C, W*, pp. 101–102.

[109] P. 272.

[110] *Thugut, C, W*, p. 103.

[111] Hüffer-Luckwaldt, *Quellen*, Pt. II, Vol. I, lxiv.

upon his Treaty. He recalled that he had been ordered to terminate the negotiations immediately, and declared that Hardenberg had been encouraged by the disorders in Paris to refuse to yield on the three months' armistice provision. If a courier had been sent to Berlin to seek permission to omit the provision in question, Barthélemy said, he would perhaps have brought back the order to suspend the negotiations entirely, for the French government seemed to be on the verge of dissolution. Furthermore, the Committee had declared that its acquiescence in the neutrality-line project was conditioned upon Hardenberg's immediate signature of the Treaty.[112]

Barthélemy then defended the armistice provision itself. He declared that Prussia could not pretend to be interested in the welfare of only the northern half of the Empire, and that France had no quarrel, anyway, with the small states of South Germany. Austria, and Austria alone, was her enemy. The provision would enable the entire Empire to withdraw from the war, leaving Austria to bear the full brunt of the French attack. Furthermore, without such an arrangement, the people of southern Germany would rise en masse against the French invaders; now, with it, they would treat them with friendship and fraternity, and supply them with food.[113]

Regarding Hanover, Barthélemy declared that in his opinion Prussia had rendered herself so completely responsible for the behavior of all northern Germany that there was nothing to be feared from any states comprised within the Line of Demarcation.[114] However, to satisfy the Committee, a declaration remitted by Hardenberg to Barthélemy on April 15 was forwarded to Paris. This document formally engaged the King of Prussia to occupy Hanover in case the government of the Electorate refused to conform to the neutralization provisions.[115]

[112] Papiers de Barthélemy, V, 182.   [114] Ibid., p. 184.
[113] Ibid., pp. 182–183.   [115] Ibid., p. 185.

CHAPTER X

THE NEUTRALITY OF NORTHERN GERMANY AND THE QUESTION OF THE LEFT BANK

I. THE REVISED NEUTRALITY TREATY

*W*HILE awaiting the Prussian ratification of the agreement of April 5, the Committee wrote to Barthélemy suggesting that the neutralization provision (Article III, Secret) should be published in order to stimulate French commerce.[1] Hardenberg agreed that it would have to be rendered public in order to be executed, but asked for a postponement so that the dispositions of the various North German states could be ascertained.[2] He was also awaiting further instructions from his court.

When these instructions arrived, Hardenberg drew up a project for a public treaty which conformed with his new orders. The King had found the neutrality line too extended for impecunious Prussia to guarantee, so desired its restriction towards the south. Hardenberg proposed that the Main River should mark the dividing line between the French and Prussian armies. This would offer several incidental advantages to France: ability to surround Mayence completely, to procure foodstuffs from Franconia by river, and to lay contributions on a greater area. Hardenberg's project, moreover, opened up four routes through the neutralized territory — converging upon Frankfort — along which the French might march, and the Austrians retreat.[3]

The French were not adversely disposed toward the new plan, though almost a month passed before its acceptance. The question of whether France should renounce the Rhine as a frontier quite overshadowed it. Hardenberg continually multiplied arguments as to why the Republic should live up

---

[1] April 15. *Papiers de Barthélemy*, V, 179–180.
[2] Barthélemy to CPS, April 19, 1795, *ibid.*, pp. 189–190.
[3] *Idem*, April 23, 1795, *ibid.*, pp. 197–198; April 25, 1795, *ibid.*, pp. 203–204; Sorel, *Europe*, IV, 331.

to its principle of no conquests. The most powerful of these was that Germany would immediately lay down its arms if France distinctly declared that she did not desire to annex the left bank.[4] Goertz, Prussian minister to the Diet, descended to particulars. If, he argued, France, through Frederick William's mediation, returned the Duchy of Zweibrücken to its duke (who was the heir apparent of the Bavaro-Palatine territories), Austria's justification for her designs on Bavaria would be destroyed, and all the states of Germany would cast themselves into the arms of Prussia — and France.[5] Everything depended, according to Prussian reasoning, upon France's renunciation of the German left bank.

The Convention had never pronounced itself upon this subject; some members of the Committee had not yet made up their minds;[6] and the need of the country for peace was progressively growing more urgent.[7] "We are indeed in a terrible state," confessed Merlin of Douai. "Independent of the penury of subsistence from which we always suffer, we lack coin."[8] "The horses are dying of hunger," reported a cartage contractor. "They receive no forage."[9] "We are without horses, without coin, without assignats," the Representatives to the Rhine and Moselle Army wrote in to Paris.[10] "It is cruel, in going through the lines, to hear from the soldier only the cry of 'Bread! Bread!'" ran a letter to Merlin of Thionville from Rivaud, Merlin's colleague on the Rhine.[11] With a hungry, penniless nation and a hungry, penniless army, it finally dawned upon the revolutionists that it was quite anomalous for them to be raising irreconcilable demands, such as that for the natural frontiers. The Committee therefore decided to determine if the Rhine boundary were truly essential to France's welfare. Under the guise of inquiring as to the merit of a design for peace suggested by "some ministers"[12] to the Ratisbon Diet, and as to the advisability of Prussia's propositions to neutralize Mayence and establish the Main as the dividing line be-

[4] Barthélemy to CPS, April 26, 1795, *Papiers de Barthélemy*, V, 206.

[5] Quoted in letter of Merlin-D. to Merlin-Th., May 8, 1795, *Corr. Merlin-Th.*, II, 176.

[6] Take, e.g., the case of Merlin-D. "For my part, I have no opinion yet," he wrote to Merlin-Th. on May 8, 1795. "I am weighing the advantages of the left bank . . . against a very early peace. . . As for myself, I merely seek enlightenment." — *Ibid.*

[7] A. Sorel, "La neutralité du nord de l'Allemagne en 1795," *RH*, XVII (1881), 265.

[8] To Merlin-Th., Aulard, *Actes*, XXIII, 199.

[9] CPS to Rps A. RMo, May 15, 1795, *Corr. Merlin-Th.*, II, 190.

[10] May 11, Aulard, *Actes*, XXIII, 69.

[11] May 22, Bonnal de Ganges, *Repré.*, III, 692.

And still — with men and horses starving — the Committee could not resist the temptation to order sent to Paris two elephants that it proposed to steal from the Netherlands' *Grand Lo*, although these animals consumed each day 50 lb. of bread and 100 lb. of hay (Rps in Holland to CPS, May 11, 1795, Aulard, *Actes*, XXIII, 59). It was March 1798, however, before the elephants actually arrived (G. Robison, *Revelliere-lépeaux, Citizen Director, 1753-1824* [New York, 1938], p. 190).

[12] That the authors were "some ministers" appears later in a letter from Merlin-D. to Merlin-Th., May 15, 1795, Aulard, *Actes*, XXIII, 199. Sorel says the author was Goertz (in *RH*, XVII, 263).

tween the French and Prussian troops, the Representatives to the Rhine and Moselle Army (Cavaignac, Rivaud, and Merlin of Thionville) were consulted on the question of the eastern boundary of France.[13] However, the answers were very slow in forthcoming, and news arrived at Basel that the Emperor was publishing a manifesto denouncing Prussia as a traitor, and urging the states of the Empire to reject the proposed neutrality.[13a] Under such conditions, it was absolutely necessary that the Neutrality Convention should be published, so on May 14, Barthélemy was authorized to sign the revised treaty proposed by Prussia.[14] Three days later this was done (May 17).

The Convention of May 17 reproduced, with changes and additions, the neutralization provisions comprised within the secret articles of the Treaty of April 5. Though the neutrality line, as determined on the latter date, was maintained intact, the King of Prussia engaged himself to force neutrality only on those states which were situated on the right bank of the Main. Four routes through the neutralized region were made available to French and Austrian troops. In the secret articles it was stipulated that though the French troops might march past Frankfort, neither they nor the Austrians could place a garrison in that city. Another secret article remedied the absence in the Treaty of April 5 of a promise by Prussia to occupy Hanover in case that electorate rejected neutrality.[15]

2. REPORTS ON THE QUESTION OF KEEPING THE LEFT BANK

Soon after the Convention of May 17 was signed, the Committee received the long-awaited answer from the Representatives to the Rhine and Moselle Army. The suggested changes in the neutrality line were frowned upon,[16]

[13] Merlin-D. to Merlin-Th., May 8, 1795, *Corr. Merlin-Th.*, II, 175–176; CPS to Rps A. RMo, May 8, *ibid.*, pp. 176–177; Barthélemy to CPS, April 26 and 29, 1795, *ibid.*, pp. 177–178 and 178–180, respectively.

[13a] Hohenlohe had come to see Count Dietrichstein and left in his hands, among other things, copies of the Treaty of Basel, the "Additional Convention" relative to the Line of Demarcation, and Frederick William's declaration to the Empire offering neutrality. Hohenlohe had appealed verbally for Austria's coöperation in the neutrality system (Dietrichstein to Thugut, May 10, 1795, Vivenot-Zeissberg, *Quellen*, V, 202–204).

[14] Sorel in *RH*, XVII, 269–271.

[15] The entire agreement may be found in *Papiers de Barthélemy*, V, 270–272, and in De Clercq, *Traités Fr.*, I, 242–244. De Martens, *Traités Eur.*, Ser. II, Vol. VI, 53–54, gives the patent articles only.

[16] The Representatives pointed out that if passage through the neutral territory were permitted to the Austrians, the French would have to use those routes also to repel the Austrians, and the neutral status of the region would prevent the Republicans from living off the land. But if passage were not permitted, and the Emperor's forces marched through nevertheless, France could enter and live off the country on the ground that the Austrians had already destroyed its neutral condition. To this the Committee replied: "The difficulty . . . of living in a neutral region is, however, common to the enemy. And we may hope that we can easily obtain

but the neutralization of Mayence was highly recommended, provided that a mixed garrison of French and Imperials guarded it.[17] On the question of peace terms and of the Rhine boundary, Merlin of Thionville's individual letter to Merlin of Douai (dated May 12) carried particular weight, owing not only to the former's undoubted ability, but also to the part he had played in the defense of Mayence in 1793.[18]

Merlin commenced with a recital of what he thought France's foreign policy should be. Prussia, he pointed out, was seeking to constitute itself the protector, the pacificator, of the Empire, thinking thereby to restore its faded glory. But to France belonged "this superb role" by virtue of her victories. Merlin was not inclined to play Prussia's game. The Ratisbon plan had been dictated by Prussia, he was sure, and that was no recommendation.

Merlin believed the time was ripe for Austria to absorb Bavaria, and he thought France should acquiesce if the Habsburgs would cede Belgium and abandon the Rhineland princes to their own devices — and to France. "In politics,[19] one should abandon the weaker and league with the stronger." "I say frankly, conclude peace with Austria . . . but do not employ agents from Basel. . . Bacher is completely Prussian. . . The Prussians must be left absolutely in the dark, for the Emperor, by the possession of Bavaria, will become too powerful for them. . . Then war will inevitably break out between them, and we shall have peace. . ."[20]

"Such is my reasoning in the light of the present situation of Europe, and supposing that we had all the means necessary to continue the war with advantage. But, considering now our own condition, here is my per-

---

provisions on the simple credit of the Republic, as was done in the same region during the Seven Years' War." — May 14, 1795, Aulard, *Actes*, XXIII, 168.

[17] Rps A. RMo to CPS, May 11, 1795, *ibid.*, p. 69; Merlin-Th. to CPS, May 16, 1795, *ibid.*, p. 235; *idem*, June 2, 1795, *Corr. Merlin-Th.*, II, 205–208. Wrote the Committee on June 6: "The Committee does not understand your entreaties for the neutralization of Mayence." — To Merlin-Th., *ibid.*, p. 210.

[18] Sybel, *Europe*, III, 438.

[19] Aulard attaches this phrase to the preceding sentence in his *Actes*, XXIII, 111. There are several textual differences, some much more radical, in Reynaud's and Aulard's versions of this letter.

[20] Already the year before, Merlin had indicated to the Committee his belief that the absorption of Bavaria by Austria was on the cards. But he did not think the equilibrium of Europe, upon which the safety of France

depended, would be upset thereby. "Austria has just tossed an archduchess into the bed of old Duke Theodor," he wrote, "and sooner or later she [Austria] will acquire through marriage what she has been denied by arms. As to Prussia, with all the little German states which she defends for her own interest, . . . she will have sufficient means to cope with her rival. . . That is the apple of discord between Prussia and Austria. *In politics, one need not be too assiduous in preferring humanity to his own country. . .* Who cares if powers, crafty out of habit, be thus exposed to . . . war? Who cares if the German lions tear each other to pieces provided that France triumphs?" — Quoted in F. Combes, "Merlin de Thionville et la diplomatie prussienne au bord du Rhin," *RR*, XIII, 361. As to the marriage of "old Duke Theodor," *vide supra*, chap. vii, n. 195. The italicized sentence above must have been underlined in the original script.

sonal opinion. We are marching from trouble to trouble. We are succumbing, so to speak, under the weight of our own victories. Blockaded, up to now, within France itself, we lack everything. Commerce is dead. The assignats, valueless.[21] Our remaining resources will soon be exhausted. We have neither constitution nor government. Royalism is raising its head. Fanaticism [i.e., religion] is lighting its torches. The hopes of traitors who have abandoned their country [i.e., of the *émigrés*] are rising. And yet Europe is at our feet. The world supplicates us for peace when but a single reverse could tear from us in an instant all our former glory. And now I ask you, why did we take up arms? To conquer our liberty, to restore peace, abundance, and happiness. Let us then summon Europe to receive peace, and try to enjoy some of it ourselves. There seems to be a disposition to abandon to us the Bishopric of Spires, Trèves, and Luxemburg to the Meuse — which would become our boundary. Receive that as indemnity and give us peace.

"Give us peace even were we to return to our former boundaries. We would still be great enough, perhaps even greater, since we would have thus proved to the world that we took up arms only [to defend] our liberty. . . That is my opinion. I believe it the only salutary one. May it prevail over the extravagant projects of men who have forgot upon what [flimsy] basis rests the destiny of empires!" [22]

This eloquent and judicious profession of faith,[23] the despatches of

---

[21] Two days before, Merlin-Th. and his colleagues had written to the CPS: "Before long, we shall be giving the entire money-coffer of the paymaster for one crown in coin. . . The reason is too obvious. All the contractors of all the armies go there [Basel] to change [their money]. Thence comes the absolute nullity of the assignat." — May 10, 1795, Aulard, *Actes*, XXIII, 31.

[22] *Corr. Merlin-Th.*, II, 182–185.

[23] Unfortunately this was but a lucid moment in Merlin's career as political firebrand. Merlin had long been advocating the promotion of internecine conflict within Germany so that France could acquire the German territory she coveted. "Our policy should be to let the wolves devour each other," he had written to the Committee on November 21, 1794 (*Corr. Merlin-Th.*, II, 119); and, "What matters it to us that the lions tear each other to pieces so long as the Republic triumphs?" the following December 12 (Aulard, *Actes*, XVIII, 668). On Christmas Day, 1794, he wrote to Paris: "The entire army . . . *is burning to complete its successes in fulfilling the national wish: 'the left bank of*

the Rhine as boundary of the Republic.'" The Committee apparently feared this was not the national wish, for it suppressed the italicized phrases in the version inserted in the *Moniteur* (*Corr. Merlin-Th.*, II, 151). It can be seen from the above assertions of Merlin how far-reaching was the revolution in his mind which produced the letter of May 12.

But this revolution was hardly more than a weekend affair. On May 20, 1795 — only eight days later — Merlin was already weakening. "I do not see how, with the Rhine as our boundary, the Emperor could ever become a threat to the Republic," he declared to the Committee (*Corr. Merlin-Th.*, II, 194). And on May 26: "Vengeance! vengeance! All the left bank of the Rhine! Two hundred thousand soldiers of our native land repeat this cry." — To the Convention, *ibid.*, p. 202.

Merlin's expansionist enthusiasm appears to have struck a responsive chord among the members of the Committee, for on August 26, Merlin-D. wrote to his namesake from Thionville: "I have received . . . your letter

Barthélemy, the moderating effect of the insurrections of *prairial*, the absence of Reubell and Sieyes from the Committee and even from France,[24] all combined to incline the Committee to yield on the question of the Rhine boundary.[25] On May 22, it wrote to Barthélemy that, in insisting on the Rhine as a frontier, it had been acting in accordance with what it believed to be the will of the Convention and of the nation. It did not consider itself competent, however, to answer the question definitively for the Convention, especially in a way which might prolong the war indefinitely. Nevertheless, it feared to suggest abandonment of the fine Rhenish lands. It preferred that the proposition should appear to have come from a foreigner. It therefore requested Barthélemy to send to Paris a proposal, ostensibly made to him, that the French should abandon all the left bank except the Austrian possessions, the Bishopric of Liège, Aix-la-Chapelle, Saarbrücken, Montbéliard, the west-bank portion of the Bishopric of Strasburg, and other fragments of territory.[26]

"What a change I found in the opinions of my colleagues!" Sieyes wrote to Reubell on May 25, upon his (Sieyes') return to Paris. "If necessary, I shall join the majority, but not without groaning every time I see on a map that fine country between the Meuse and the Rhine." [27]

3. THE SELF-INVITED GUEST

On May 17, 1795, Merlin of Thionville, in the company of General in Chief Pichegru, arrived at Hüningen near Basel after an overnight trip from Strasburg. Shortly thereafter arrived Secretary-Interpreter Bacher with a note from Hardenberg inviting Merlin and Pichegru to dinner at Basel.[28] Merlin rejected the invitation. He would leave the soil of France, he declared, only at the "definitive" peace.[29] But Hardenberg could not be so easily turned away.[30] He was puzzled at the inactivity of both the French and Austrian armies,[31] and he feared it might signify the existence of Franco-Austrian negotiations.[32] These fears were fanned into a flame of panic by rumors

---

of 1 *fructidor* [August 18]. . . We all, or almost all, think as you do regarding the left bank of the Rhine; and if the future government [the Directory] does not deviate from our present principles, I say to you that this bank will remain to us." — *Ibid.*, p. 238.

[24] They were in Holland negotiating peace with the Dutch. *Vide* Sciout, *Direc.*, I, 163.

[25] Sorel in *RH*, XVII, 265, 276–277.

[26] CPS to Barthélemy, *Papiers de Barthélemy*, V, 283–284.

[27] Aulard, *Actes*, XXIII, 517.

[28] *Corr. Merlin-Th.*, II, 192. This letter should be dated May 17, as the context shows. It certainly could not have been enclosed in a letter of May 20 if May 28 were the correct date.

[29] Merlin-Th. to CPS, May 20, 1795, *ibid.*

[30] From von Sybel's account, one would think it was Merlin-Th. who sought the meeting. *Vide* his *Europe*, III, 439.

[31] *Vide infra*, Pt. I, chap. xii, § 1.

[32] Barthélemy to CPS, May 20, 1795, *Papiers de Barthélemy*, V, 277.

current everywhere that Thugut had commissioned Count Carletti, the Tuscan ambassador at Paris, to offer that Austria would desert the left-bank princes in return for France's consent to the absorption of Bavaria by Austria.[33]

Count Xavier Carletti had been sent to Paris in 1794 by the Tuscan government (Minister Manfredini) to negotiate a peace with France. The envoy had been warmly received, and in his large (rented) country house was giving sumptuous banquets to the diplomatic corps and the most influential members of the Convention. One of his guests was Boissy d'Anglas, prominent member of a parliamentary group inclined to peace with Austria, with which group Carletti had associated himself.[34] At one of these banquets, Carletti declared categorically that, in return for the assurance of obtaining Bavaria, Austria would forthwith abandon the left bank to France. Carletti could show no mandate from Thugut, but it appeared probable that he knew the intentions of the Vienna government since he represented the Emperor's brother.

Of interest it is to note in passing that Sieyes, who was then assiduously gathering the reins of French diplomacy into his hands, was not averse to Austria's absorption of Bavaria, in itself. His objection was to bringing Austria's boundaries closer to those of France. Sieyes believed that if France ever consented to Austria's acquisition of Bavaria, that consent should be conditioned upon the sacrifice by the Habsburgs of the Breisgau and the Milanese.[35] There was no need, however, for Sieyes to ponder the question. Neither Thugut nor anyone else in Austria had authorized the proposition, which must be attributed to the desire of either Manfredini or Carletti to play the role of pacificator on a grand scale. Nor was authorization even remotely likely, for not only was Thugut obliged, by the Treaty of January 3, 1795 with Russia, to continue the war, but the Austrian helmsman detested Manfredini as a "Jacobin minister"[36] and Carletti as a "most despicable

[33] Sorel in *RH*, XVII, 280.

[34] Count Greppi, "La mission du Comte Carletti à Paris," *RHD (Revue d'histoire diplomatique)*, XV (1901), 351 *et seqq.* This article is based upon the intimate letters of Manfredini and Carletti to Paul Greppi.

[35] Sybel, *Europe*, III, 514–515.

[36] "Gallo [Neapolitan Ambassador to Vienna] asserts that he has information from Naples to the effect that, . . . in case of the birth of a [Tuscan] prince, . . . Manfredini will depart immediately to carry the news to Vienna. Your Excellency can well imagine the sensation that would result at this moment when so many rumors of peace and of secret negotiation are being bruited about, when the King of Prussia is spreading so many calumnies about us, . . . if there arrived at Vienna a person like Manfredini, so discredited . . . in all of Europe for his pacific dreams, for his Jacobin declarations." — To Count Colloredo, Nov. 20, 1794, *Briefe Thugut*, I, 154. On May 4, 1795, Thugut, in sending the Anglo-Austrian subsidy treaty to Count Colloredo for the Emperor's ratification, remarked scornfully that "soon those who suppose me in correspondence with this philosophical and pacificatory general [Manfredini] will be more wrong than ever." — *Ibid.*, p. 207.

man who deceives even the Grand Duke." [37] Lucchesini, who was the first to designate Carletti as the secret go-between of France and Austria, attributed the alleged negotiation to Manfredini's personal ambition; but Manfredini's intimate correspondence shows that he was dominated by a great desire for peace.[38]

Hardenberg tried to extract from Barthélemy information about the rumored parleys, but Barthélemy would tell him nothing because there was nothing to tell. Carletti was wasting a good deal of money on sumptuous banquets — more than tiny Tuscany could afford — and that was indeed a suspicious circumstance;[39] but the Committee was not negotiating with him, and so had not told Barthélemy that it was. Barthélemy's silence was construed as secrecy, and Hardenberg thought it might be easier to milk the mind of a Representative of the Convention than that of a trained diplomat like Barthélemy. Followed a letter from Bacher in which the latter informed Merlin that Hardenberg, unable to induce the Representative to dine with him at Basel, had invited himself to Merlin's at Hüningen.[40]

Merlin naturally ordered a fine dinner prepared. It was the first diplomatic banquet since the Terror,[41] and the Republic must not be found wanting! We do not know what the party ate, but only what they drank, and how much it cost.[42] The cost was sufficient, but it would have been greater had not Barthélemy, who also attended, brought along from his private cellar much good bordeaux, and burgundy, and champagne.[43] In Hardenberg's company were the ministers of Hesse-Cassel, Hesse-Darmstadt, and Württemberg. The list of notables, approximately twenty, included, of course, Bacher and Pichegru.[44]

This dinner is of historical note because of the remarks which did or did not pass between Hardenberg and Merlin on the subject of Bavaria, Austria, and peace. We possess four accounts: Merlin of Thionville's report to the Committee, Hardenberg's report to his king, Hardenberg's memoirs, and Barthélemy's report.[45] The account in Hardenberg's memoirs we may dismiss as untrustworthy; therein, for example, it was Hardenberg who

[37] Thugut to Count Colloredo, Jan. 1, 1795, *ibid.*, p. 166.

[38] Greppi in *RHD*, XV, 351 *et seqq.* Lord High Chamberlain Rosenberg, sent to Florence to hold Tuscany in the Coalition, blamed Manfredini's timidity and love of peace for his continual urging that the Emperor open negotiations with France (to Emperor, Dec. 16, 1794, Vivenot-Zeissberg, *Quellen*, V, 62).

[39] Heigel, *Deutsche Geschichte*, II, 184, n. 4.

[40] *Corr. Merlin-Th.*, II, 193.

[41] Sorel in *RH*, XVII, 284.

[42] Receipted bill in *Corr. Merlin-Th.*, II, 197.

[43] Bacher to Merlin-Th., May 18, 1795, *ibid.*, pp. 197–198.

[44] *Ibid.*, p. 195, note.

[45] Barthélemy's memoirs mention the dinner only to remark that Merlin-Th. wanted the group to drink to the health of the Prussian nation without mentioning the Prussian King — a procedure to which Hardenberg is supposed to have objected strenuously (*Mém. Barthélemy*, p. 127).

suggested that Austria absorb Bavaria [46] — a most unlikely tale. Of the three official reports, it appears to the writer that Hardenberg's is the most credible, for the reasons outlined below.

Merlin reported the meeting as follows: All through the dinner, Hardenberg discoursed upon the protection that France — with Prussia's assistance — should accord to the Empire, and upon the inadvisability of allowing the Emperor to possess himself of Bavaria. Merlin's every response was that he was only a soldier, that one enemy more or less had not inconvenienced France in the past, and that the Committee alone was empowered to hear the Prussian observations. And Merlin recommended to the Committee that since Prussia feared so greatly a Franco-Austrian accord based upon Austria's absorption of Bavaria and France's absorption of the left bank (including Belgium), it might be well to seek to effect just that.[47] It may indeed be that Merlin did show by his facial expression that he was not hostile to the idea.[48] But compare this prosaic narrative with Hardenberg's colorful account.

Merlin — so Hardenberg reported to his king — led the Prussian minister into his bedroom after the dinner, so that he might speak confidentially without being overheard, and insinuated that Carletti was endeavoring to bring about a Franco-Austrian peace, that the Emperor would, with France's consent, establish himself in Bavaria, and that the Empire, faced with a *fait accompli*, would acquiesce; that the Emperor would mediate peace between France and the Empire; that a virtual armistice had been ordered; that France had not yet made up its mind whether it would content itself with the Meuse frontier, and that if Prussia wanted to order the peace, she should propose bases. Involved in the last proposition, but not expressed, was the implied threat that if Prussia did not order the peace — in accord with France, of course — Austria would.[49]

Hardenberg did not accept at its face value everything that Merlin said. "It is very possible," he wrote to his court, "that all these insinuations have as their object only to arouse the jealousy of the King of Prussia" and lead him and those princes who follow him "into offensive connection with France." But he feared that there might be at least a grain of truth in the Carletti tale, and that was too much.[50]

Barthélemy has given us the following version of the dinner discussion — a version in which no mention of Bavaria occurs. If the name of that state did enter into the conversation, it was only casually, for the French am-

---

[46] *Corr. Merlin-Th.*, II, 195, note.

[47] To CPS, May 20, 1795, *ibid.*, pp. 193–194.

[48] *Vide* previous section and n. 20, this chapter. Also, *infra*, Pt. I, chap. xv, § 1.

[49] Quoted from Ranke by Sorel in *RH*, XVII, 284–285.

[50] *Ibid.*, p. 286; *Mém. homme d'Etat*, III, 182.

bassador at Basel wrote to the Committee on May 19, "I went to Hüningen today with Herrn von Hardenberg to dine with Representative of the People Merlin [of Thionville]. They were very glad to see each other and to chat together. The project of neutralizing Mayence on condition that the city be guarded by nought but troops of France and of the circles of the Empire formed part of the discussion, and appears to have met with strong favor on the part of the Prussian minister. He will await your orders to me on this subject before writing to his court." [51] But in his despatch to the Committee the next day, Barthélemy had much to say of Hardenberg's fears respecting Bavaria and Carletti, fears which had had their inception in the Committee's delay in authorizing Barthélemy to sign the Convention of May 17, and which were now apparently aggravated by the dinner.[52]

Since Bavaria is not mentioned in Barthélemy's despatch of the nineteenth and forms so large a part of that of the twentieth, and since the two principals agree that the absorption of Bavaria occupied a prominent place in the discussion, it seems to follow that Merlin spoke to Hardenberg about Bavaria out of Barthélemy's hearing, instead of at table, as Merlin reports. And if Merlin's credibility can be successfully impugned, it may be that Hardenberg's account (to his king) is the most accurate and complete that we possess. This is not the usual view, but, the writer submits, the only logical one.

However that may be, the important point is that Hardenberg, fearful of a Franco-Austrian peace based upon Bavaria's engulfment, decided to depart immediately for Berlin to apprize the King of what was happening. He would have liked to go to Paris also, but that being physically impossible, he sent in his stead Secretary of Legation Gervinus,[53] friend of his college days.[54]

Hardenberg stopped at Mannheim and informed the Duke of Zweibrücken of the contemplated rape of the Wittelsbach patrimony.[55] He asked the Duke to inform the Bavaro-Palatine Elector. Hardenberg of course intended the information to be whispered, but the abbé Salabert, upon whom devolved the task, drew up instead an official note addressed to the Bavarian government. That government forthwith transmitted the note to the Bavarian representative to the Diet,[56] with instructions to lodge a protest. But it was Austria from whom the loudest protest issued. A circular note of Thugut's to all the German courts characterized the stories of secret nego-

[51] To CPS, Papiers de Barthélemy, V, 276.
[52] Ibid., p. 277.
[53] Barthélemy to CPS, May 20, 1795, ibid., p. 278.
[54] Reuss to Thugut, July 5, 1795, Vivenot-Zeissberg, Quellen, V, 274.

[55] The Duke of Zweibrücken, it will be recalled, was the heir apparent to the entire Wittelsbach patrimony (Sorel in RH, XVII, 263).
[56] Sybel, Europe, III, 440.

tiations with Paris as "absurd, childish, and mythical." [57] Hüffer has proved that Thugut was not prevaricating,[58] but von Sybel, basing his case upon a conversation Gervinus had with Sieyes at Paris, was never completely satisfied that there were no negotiations.[59]

4. GERVINUS' MISSION TO PARIS

The instructions of Gervinus directed him to discuss with the Committee the political situation of Europe, the pacification of the Empire, the interests of Prussia and France, and means of establishing on a solid basis the entente between the two states.[60] A Prussian courier accompanied Gervinus, in order that Hardenberg could be informed as soon as possible of the results of the conversations.[61]

Gervinus arrived in Paris on May 25, and was received four days later by the Diplomatic Section of the Committee — which was charged with the foreign correspondence, and was then composed of Sieyes, Merlin of Douai, and Treilhard. Sieyes persisted in his usually extravagant ideas; Merlin was inclined to moderation; Treilhard was silent. Gervinus expressed the desire of his government that Austria should not absorb Bavaria and that the general pacification should be based as far as possible upon the integrity of the Empire. Sieyes replied, "We need to obtain a glorious peace, and to give to Germany at the same time a stable and trustworthy system. . . It seems to me that Prussia is much concerned about the restitution of the Rhenish lands and the interests of the German Empire, which we do not understand at all; it [the Empire] is a chaos which does not present a clear and well-defined picture." To Gervinus' insistence on Prussia's interest in the conservation of the integrity of the Empire, Sieyes interposed the resolutions of the Convention regarding the natural boundaries of France. The Prussian envoy pointed out that the Convention had never voted on the question, and that simple assertions of individual speakers could not bind the whole assembly. Sieyes recognized the validity of this objection, and became more cordial.[62]

Concerning the absorption of Bavaria and the rumored Carletti negotiation, Sieyes would not say categorically that Carletti was not negotiating with France, but only that he, Sieyes, did not think Austria could consider

---

[57] Heigel, *Deutsche Geschichte*, II, 184, n. 4.
[58] H. Hüffer, *Die Politik der deutschen Mächte im Revolutionskriege* (Münster, 1869), chap. vii.
[59] Heigel, *Deutsche Geschichte*, II, 184, n. 4.
[60] Credentials of Gervinus, dated May 20, *Papiers de Barthélemy*, V, 281.
[61] Barthélemy to CPS, May 20, 1795, *ibid.*, pp. 277–278.
[62] Sorel, *Europe*, IV, 341–342.

negotiating at that particular time.[63] The same vagueness was manifest in a conversation Gervinus had with Boissy d'Anglas a few days later. "Up to now," declared Boissy, "our negotiation with Austria has made but little progress." [64] The aim of both French statesmen was, of course, to perpetuate Prussia's nervousness for the sake of the benefits which might possibly accrue therefrom to France. Gervinus gleaned from these conversations that Carletti may have been negotiating for Thugut, but merely unofficially, and that nothing had as yet been accomplished which might constitute cause for apprehension. Gervinus noted also the preponderant influence of the internal crisis, both political and alimentary, upon French foreign policy, and concluded that if Prussia presented a firm front, France could be induced to abandon most of the Rhineland.[65]

5. THE MARANDET-HARNIER CONVERSATIONS

Barthélemy refused the Committee's request to deceive the Convention. It was impossible for him, he declared, to propose the renunciation of the left bank without having people immediately point to him as the author of the suggestion. A discreet third party, who could be safely asked to make the offer, as though on his own initiative, was needed. However, where was an absolutely trustworthy person to be found? Barthélemy decided that the only solution was to try to maneuver the amiably disposed secretary of the Prussian legation, Harnier, into asking his court to make a proposition of the kind desired.[66] He concerted to this end with his own secretary of legation, Marandet, with whom Harnier was accustomed to argue at length about the inadvisability of the extension of France's boundaries to the Rhine.

Barthélemy reported the results in his despatch of May 31. When Harnier referred once again to the question of the Rhine boundary, Marandet, feigning impatience, exclaimed: "You always return to that subject! Do you imagine, anyway, that if the French government were disposed to make sacrifices in this respect, it would hurl itself at the heads of your German princes to restore their territories to them? Do you think, moreover, that we would return within our old limits without conserving divers points absolutely necessary to the security of our frontiers? Since you Prussians are always so eager to speak with us about the left bank of the Rhine, and to remit notes to us, why do you not try to remit one on that subject, based

[63] *Idem* in *RH*, XVII, 290.
[64] Sybel, *Europe*, III, 442.
[65] Hüffer, *Politik Mächte*, p. 181; Sorel in *RH*,

XVII, 291–292.
[66] Barthélemy to CPS, May 27, 1795, *Papiers de Barthélemy*, V, 297–298.

upon what you figure to be in our interest, putting yourselves in our place? I am absolutely ignorant as to whether it will be admitted; I rather imagine that it will not be; however, you will have done all you can to commence negotiations on the subject, and the step will reflect honor upon you in Germany." Then Marandet disclosed, in an offhand manner, what he thought France would insist on keeping. Harnier appeared to be much impressed by the overture, and soon after informed Marandet that he had written a long letter to Haugwitz concerning their conversation, and expected good usage to be made of the proposal.[67]

Harnier's letter of June 8 to the Prussian King and Ministry announced that the French negotiators at Basel (Barthélemy, Bacher, and Marandet), speaking unofficially, that is, as men and not as negotiators, had declared to him: that the French government appeared disposed not to insist on the strict limit of the Rhine, regardless of the former attitude of public opinion in France, but that the public would never tolerate a *status quo ante bellum* arrangement; and that there would be no difficulty in restoring to Germany the three ecclesiastical electorates of Mayence, Trèves, and Cologne, and, in general, the remainder of the left bank also, with the exception of a portion of the Bishopric of Basel, the Alsatian enclaves, some territory in the neighborhood of Landau, the County of Montbéliard, the Principality of Saarbrücken, the Bishopric of Liège, and probably the Imperial City of Aix-la-Chapelle. Barthélemy and Bacher, reported Harnier, gave only hints as to which lands would be returned; the details came from Marandet, with Barthélemy's knowledge and consent.[68]

The results of the overture were soon manifest. On June 28, Alvensleben composed a memoir highly approved by his colleague, Finkenstein. It became the basis of the ministerial advice presented to the King the next day, out of which issued the royal instructions of July 3 to Hardenberg. The latter part of this memoir concerned arrangements for a definitive peace between France and the Empire (including Austria) in case the Diet authorized the Prussian good offices in favor of the Empire. The basis of the negotiation was to be the *status quo ante bellum*, but with the oral reservation that France might have certain territories necessary to the security of her frontiers. If France limited her demands to what was enumerated, Prussia would intercede with the other German states to procure the abandonment of the aforesaid lands to the Republic. The conquered lands to be thus abandoned to France were Nassau-Saarbrücken, Montbéliard, the Palatinate, and the part of Zweibrücken between the Lauter and the Queich. Belgium and Holland

---

[67] Barthélemy to CPS, May 31, 1795, *ibid.*, p. 305. [68] Bailleu, *Pr. Frk.*, I, 5–7.

were not mentioned, though it was specified that France was to indemnify the ex-stadholder in some way.[69]

6. VIEWS OF SIEYES AND BARTHÉLEMY

In the meantime, however, the composition of the Committee had changed. Reubell had reëntered,[70] and with Sieyes and Treilhard, composed the Diplomatic Section. Reubell's attitude respecting the Rhine frontier was the product of two considerations. The annexation of Mayence by the Convention in 1793 had been, in large part, his handiwork; and as an Alsatian, he was convinced that the only way to protect his native province from periodic German invasion was to annex the remainder of the left bank.[71] Sieyes also desired the annexation of the entire left bank, though for him the Rhine boundary was insufficient. He desired the establishment of dependent republics beyond the River as outposts of republican propaganda and military defense. His was a grandiose plan of rejecting Prussia and Austria to the east to hold Russia in check, while France exercised hegemony in a reorganized Germany.[72] "None of the former Jacobins was ever so dangerous to Europe as the Abbé Siéyès may possibly become," wrote the British agent Trevor. "Because he was not noble, he destroyed the nobility; because he was not at the head of the Church, he destroyed the clergy; because he is not King, he wishes to overturn all kings, and all governments which are not founded on his system."[73] Treilhard, the third member of the Section, adopted the viewpoint of his two colleagues in so far as the annexation of the left bank was concerned. Of the thirteen other members of the Committee, almost a dozen were undecided or hostile to the Rhine-boundary idea.[74] However, the Committee, directed by its Diplomatic Section, wrote to Barthélemy on June 26 to bear in mind that it still desired the Rhine as a boundary.[75]

Barthélemy believed that Hardenberg would frighten his court into immediate alliance with France, and that in perhaps a month and a half, Austria would be obliged to sue for peace and renounce all her designs on Bavaria. However, this glorious prospect was dependent, in Barthélemy's opinion, on France's renunciation of the left bank, for Prussia would never dare to unite with the Republic if the Committee insisted on despoiling

[69] *Ibid.*, pp. 10–11.
[70] Guillaume, *Etudes rév.*, Ser. II, p. 243.
[71] Guyot, *Direc.*, p. 118. On December 4, 1791, Reubell wrote to the deputies of the Haut-Rhin: "It is the land of your nativity which is the most menaced." — *Ibid.*
[72] *Ibid.*, p. 119; Bourgeois, *Manuel*, II, 141 *et seqq.*
[73] March 12, 1795, *Dropmore Papers*, III, 86.
[74] Sorel, *Europe*, IV, 355.
[75] Arch. A. E., *Allemagne* 669, f. 169. This despatch, which is not included in the *Pa-*

the states of the Empire.[76] Now that the Committee had decided to keep the left bank, the French plenipotentiary at Basel saw great obstacles in the way of the long-hoped-for general peace of the Empire. Not so with the visionaries of the Committee; not so, especially, with Sieyes. The despatch of June 26, reminding Barthélemy that the left bank was still desired, betrayed the identity of its author by the extravagance of its outlines: The annexation of Bavaria by Austria was truly contrary to Prussia's interests, but "would it not be possible to give more than proportional accessions to Prussia, either by cessions of Austrian territory, or by the secularization of some bishoprics, or by the occupation of Hanover, or by the formation of a new Germanic league which would assure to Prussia a great preponderance? The King of Prussia could render his Westphalian provinces contiguous to the remainder of his possessions. By means of several canals he could connect his Baltic commerce with that of the North Sea, and become not only a very imposing territorial power, but also a maritime power. Leagued with Denmark and Sweden, he could counterbalance Russia on the side of the sea, and leagued with Austria, he could hold it [Russia] in check on the continental side. The remainder of Germany, forming a new federation constituted more soundly and vigorously than that erected by chance in the Gothic ages, and guaranteed by the Republic, could hold the balance between Prussia and Austria. Poland could regain its independence, guaranteed by Prussia and Austria. A king of the House of Prussia could perhaps occupy the throne [of Poland]." [77]

These official reveries did not strike a responsive chord in Barthélemy. Trained in the school of Vergennes, he could not sanction the overthrow of an organization (the Empire) which by its very weakness was a source of strength to France. Why does Austria want Bavaria? he wrote to the Committee. To consolidate her power in Germany. Do you believe she will turn toward the east if she obtains this superb province? No! She will expand in the Empire and in Italy. To win Prussia's consent to Austria's acquisition of Bavaria, you must allow Prussia to augment its strength proportionally. This augmentation can only be at the expense of its neighbors. The small states will disappear from Germany; France will lose her clients.

---

piers de Barthélemy or in Aulard, Actes, is reproduced with some omissions in A. Sorel, "Le Comité de Salut Public et la question de la rive gauche du Rhin en 1795," RH, XVIII (1882), 280–283.

[76] Barthélemy to CPS, May 20, 1795, Papiers de Barthélemy, V, 278.

[77] CPS to Barthélemy, June 26, 1795, Arch. A. E., Allemagne 669, f. 169. Interesting in this connection are some of Barère's remarks concerning Sieyes: "He was not a statesman. . . . He was in politics what a doctor of the Sorbonne is in theology, a subtle arguer and obscure theorist. . . He endured no amendments to his systems or explanation of his obscurities. . . 'I will not talk to you because you do not understand me,' he often said." — Mem. Barère, IV, 351, 359.

Europe and liberty will be menaced.[78] Two months later, Barthélemy had developed this thesis yet further: "Far from weakening these [small German] states, we should endeavor to give them more consistency; far from its being in our interest to aid the two principal powers of Germany to extend their usurpations, we ought to desire that it were possible to partition among many small sovereigns all the countries [at present] in subjection to Austria and Prussia." [79]

[78] Sorel, *Europe*, IV, 363–364. July 6, 1795.   [79] Arch. A. E., *Allemagne* 669, ff. 299–300.

CHAPTER XI

FRANCE AND HESSE–CASSEL MAKE PEACE
AUGUST 28, 1795

*T*HE first German state to follow Prussia's example in making a separate peace with France was Hesse-Cassel. Truly Hesse-Darmstadt and Hesse-Homburg had preceded it in pacific declarations (February 1795),[1] but Hesse-Cassel was the first to bring its wishes beyond the stage of words.[2]

On April 19, 1795, there arrived at Basel Baron von Waitz von Eschen, minister of Hesse-Cassel's landgrave. Introduced to Barthélemy the same day by Hardenberg, he announced that he brought full powers to treat for peace with France. Barthélemy immediately asked the Committee for plenary authority to negotiate with Waitz. The French government was pleased. It viewed the prospective defection of Hesse-Cassel as the first fruit of the Treaty of April 5, which, it hoped, would detach the Empire from the Emperor and enable the Republic to bring the war to a triumphant conclusion. It wrote to Barthélemy that treaties presented from time to time to the Convention would produce the happiest effect, and ordered him to work zealously for peace with Hesse-Cassel and Hesse-Darmstadt.[3]

On April 26, the Committee voted Barthélemy full powers to treat with the two landgraves, and the next day forwarded to Basel a project of treaty. This project, dated April 27, consisted of ten articles. As modified by the despatch of April 28, these articles provided, in their principal points, for French occupation of the Hessian left bank until the Franco-Imperial peace, when its fate would be definitively settled (Article IV); indemnification on the right bank for left-bank losses (Article V, to be held secret); reëstablishment of prewar commercial relations (Article VI);[4] delivery to France of

---

[1] Sorel in *RH*, XVII, 257–258.
[2] An unsigned, undated note in the French archives makes a point of this (Arch. A. E.,

Allemagne 669, f. 360).
[3] Arch. A. E., *Allemagne* 669, ff. 78–79.
[4] The CPS instructed Barthélemy on May 24

50,000 sacks of wheat and 5,000 horses as indemnity, or, if resisted as indemnity, then as merchandise to be paid for in two years (Article IX, also to be
held secret, though intended at first to be patent); and delivery to the
French troops, by the Landgraves of both Cassel and Darmstadt, of the grain,
wine, and fodder needed, compensation to be made in a number of years to
be determined later (Article X, likewise to be held secret).[5]

There was no allusion to the good offices of Prussia in this project, and
yet Hardenberg had written a letter to Barthélemy recommending the interests of Hesse-Cassel. Waitz urgently requested that the treaty should
mention the good offices of Prussia. Barthélemy refused, though he wrote
to the Committee that he saw no grave objection to such a mention. Bacher
and Marandet insinuated to Waitz that there was no need for Prussia's
good offices.[6] The Hessian minister informed Hardenberg that the French
were refusing to acknowledge Prussia's intervention, whereupon the Prussian plenipotentiary told Barthélemy that nothing could have as beneficent
an effect at Berlin as a reference to the Prussian good offices.[7] The French
eventually yielded.[8]

In his report to the King on June 6, Hardenberg speculated as to the
causes of the French objections. He concluded that the objections might have
been due either to "consideration for the Court of Vienna, or . . . to a plan
to detach . . . the states of the Empire from connection with their head,
and to attach them with Prussia to the French government, rather than to
Prussia itself. These last views appear to be those of the Committee of
Public Safety, which undoubtedly prefers treaties of separate peace [9] with
the preponderant princes of the Empire, a schism in Germany, and the overthrow of the Germanic constitution, to a general peace with the entire
body." [10]

Hardenberg had not judged baldly. Assuredly France was not inter-

---

to omit an article to this effect if the prewar
relations were to the disadvantage of France
(Arch. A. E., *Allemagne* 669, f. 97). Barthélemy responded that he knew of no prewar arrangements contrary either to the interests or to the dignity of the Republic
(May 28, Arch. A. E., *Allemagne* 669, f.
103).
[5] Arch. A. E., *Allemagne* 669, ff. 79–81.
[6] Hardenberg to the King, Oct. 13, 1795,
Bailleu, *Pr. Frk.*, I, 26–27.
[7] Barthélemy to CPS, May 18, 1795, Arch. A.
E., *Allemagne* 669, f. 88.
[8] The Committee's note of August 6, 1795 to
Barthélemy authorized the latter to make
mention of the Prussian good offices if he saw
fit, in order to please Hardenberg (Arch. A.

E., *Allemagne* 669, f. 234). *Vide* the preamble of the completed treaty in De Clercq,
Traités Fr., I, 264.
[9] *Vide* the speech of Cambacérès, in the name
of the CPS, to the Convention, March 3,
1795: "A single negotiation for a general
peace is impossible . . . [because] designs
and wishes are so contrary. It is then only
by treaties of separate peace that we can arrive at a general peace." — *Moniteur*, XXIII,
596–597. In the discussion which followed,
the principle of the separate peace was quite
generally accepted. *Vide*, e.g., the remarks of
Roux and of Audouin (*ibid.*, pp. 682 and
709, respectively).
[10] Bailleu, *Pr. Frk.*, I, 5.

FRANCE AND HESSE-CASSEL MAKE PEACE, AUGUST 28, 1795

ested in raising up a rival within Germany, and it was rather naïve of the Prussian plenipotentiary to have imagined that the Republic ever intended to play Don Quixote. The aim of French politics, as interpreted by one of its most moderate oracles (Barthélemy), was to "encourage the most noted princes of the Empire . . . to unite under the Prussian banner in a confederation against the House of Austria — which is the object we should never lose from sight, being the means of enabling France to play a role in the affairs of the Empire." [11]

With the Committee's project of April 27 as a basis, Barthélemy, after much discussion with Waitz, drew up a new treaty project in formal fashion, and sent it to the Committee for approval. One of the criticisms advanced by that body is very curious, and betrays clearly the policy of the French government as then constituted: Barthélemy should not say, "All definitive arrangements respecting these territories [left-bank possessions of Hesse-Cassel] will be postponed until the general pacification between the French Republic and the German Empire," but "postponed until the pacification between the French Republic and the parts of Germany still at war therewith." [12] The Committee made the same objection to Article II of his secret articles. Barthélemy responded that the arrangements between Hesse-Cassel and France had nothing whatsoever to do with the other states of the Empire as states, but only with them as component parts of the Empire. [13] Another criticism of the Committee's related to Article I, Secret, of Barthélemy's project. Barthélemy had not insisted that Hesse-Cassel should abrogate before its expiration (April 10, 1796) the subsidy treaty concluded with England early in the war — an arrangement whereby Hessian troops were hired to Britian at so much per head. [14] The Committee urged Barthélemy to try to secure the immediate withdrawal of the mercenaries, for it was not inclined to make peace with Hesse while Hessian troops were making war on France. This was an unpleasant order, for the subsidy treaty had been legally concluded. However, the Committee affixed a proviso: If nullification of the agreement were impossible, the first secret

---

[11] Barthélemy to CPS, July 16, 1795, Arch. A. E., *Allemagne* 669, f. 191.

[12] Arch. A. E., *Allemagne* 669, ff. 93–94. It would certainly be an error to deduce from these phrases a reluctance on the part of the Committee to recognize the existence of the Empire, though a Francophobe might read most anything into them. Probably all that they signify is that the Committee desired to conclude treaties of separate peace with the individual states of the Empire, and no treaty at all with the Empire as a whole, simply because, by such an arrangement, the bar-

gaining power of the German states would be much reduced.

[13] CPS to Barthélemy, May 24, 1795; Barthélemy to CPS, May 28, 1795: Arch. A. E., *Allemagne* 669, ff. 97 *et seqq.*

[14] Original treaty for 8,000 men, April 10, 1793, De Martens, *Traités Eur.*, Ser. II, Vol. V, 124 *et seqq.* Supplementary agreement for 4,000 men, August 23, 1793, *ibid.*, pp. 141 *et seqq.* Baden had a similar treaty, though it provided for a much smaller force (*Pol. Corr. Karl Fr.*, II, 62 *et seqq.*).

article (permitting the treaty to run until its expiration) should neverthe-less be omitted,[15] and the second secret article should forbid the renewal of the agreement if war between France and England were still going on at its expiration.[16] Barthélemy replied that the troops were already prisoners in France, and that it was to France's advantage that England should continue to pay the subsidies to Hesse-Cassel.[17] Incidentally, Barthélemy later ad-mitted to the Committee that his statement was false that the Hessian mercenaries were already prisoners in France.[18]

The treaty of peace was signed on August 28, 1795. In its principal provisions it followed, *mutatis mutandis*, the Franco-Prussian Treaty of April 5. The instrument commenced: "The French Republic, having wel-comed the good offices of the King of Prussia, etc." Article III pledged Hesse-Cassel not to prolong or renew its subsidy treaties with England so long as France and Britain should be at war. Article V authorized France to continue to occupy the left-bank possessions of Hesse-Cassel until their fate should be decided by the pacification "between the French Republic and the parts of Germany yet at war therewith." Article VI reestablished prewar commercial relations. Article VIII provided for the return of prisoners of war, exclusive of Hessians captured while in the pay of England. The secret articles, of which there were four, dealt with indemnification by seculariza-tion or otherwise on the right bank, and Hessian mercenaries. No further recruits were to be furnished to the Hessian Corps in English pay on the basis of the then-existing subsidy treaties.[19]

These terms were very fair to both parties. The omission of all demands for grain, wine, cattle, horses, etc., is to be noted. To be sure, Hesse-Cassel was situated behind the Line of Demarcation, and had withdrawn its con-tingent. It was therefore neutral, and since this neutrality was guaranteed by Prussia, there would have been no means of enforcing such demands.

[15] It really had no purpose, for it was permis-sive of what would have happened anyway. Besides, the succeeding article really said the same thing in other words. The wording of the latter article was probably preferred be-cause it "forbade" where the first "permitted."

[16] Arch. A. E., *Allemagne* 669, ff. 94, 97.

[17] Barthélemy to CPS, May 28, 1795, Arch. A. E., *Allemagne* 669, f. 103.

[18] July 28, 1795, Arch. A. E., *Allemagne* 669, f. 200. His admission came in response to a letter from the CPS demanding that he clear up contradictions regarding the number of Hessian troops in English pay, and the time when the subsidy treaty would expire. It ap-pears that Barthélemy, in his desire not to impede the negotiations, was not careful al-ways to adhere to the truth, but told the CPS what he knew would please its ears. And that was not always the same thing (Arch. A. E., *Allemagne* 669, f. 199, July 24, 1795). But Barthélemy managed to squirm out of his predicament — or at any rate, the CPS decided to accept his lame explanations (CPS to Barthélemy, Aug. 6, 1795, Arch. A. E., *Allemagne* 669, f. 235).

[19] De Clercq, *Traités Fr.*, I, 264–266. Both pat-ent and secret articles are given in Fain, *Ms. de l'an III*, pp. 421–445, but the secret articles are erroneously dated 18 *fructidor*, III (Sep-tember 4, 1795), instead of 11 *fructidor* (August 28). De Martens, *Traités Eur.*, Ser. II, Vol. VI, 130–132, gives only the patent articles.

Nevertheless, the Committee had instructed Barthélemy to make the attempt.[20]

Barthélemy was a wise negotiator. His treaties with Prussia and Hesse-Cassel left no rancor in the hearts of the pacified states. Bonaparte later followed his example in dealing with Austria at Leoben. Had not the little Corsican repudiated later the principle of moderation, there would probably never have been a Waterloo. But there would never have been a Napoleonic Empire either, and what Frenchman is there who would not exchange the just and durable peace of Barthélemy for a peace of glory, a peace *à la Bonaparte*? It is not Barthélemy's bones, be it noted, which lie enshrined within the granite sarcophagus at the Invalides.

[20] *Vide supra*, treaty project of the Committee, dated April 27.

The Convention ratified the Treaty on September 4, and the Commission of Foreign Affairs so informed Barthélemy (Arch. A. E., *Allemagne* 669, f. 315). In his reply, Barthélemy declared that Waitz was speaking very frankly of the thousand louis d'or which the French government ought to present him (Waitz) for signing the Treaty. Such gifts were customary, explained Barthélemy; and, in view of the penury of his government, he offered to place at its disposal some of the gifts he had himself received in the past (Sept. 23, 1795, Arch. A.

E., *Allemagne* 669, f. 315). The Commission of Foreign Affairs replied that it would send Waitz some porcelain (Sept. 27, 1795, Arch. A. E., *Allemagne* 669, f. 315).

The ratifications were not exchanged until November 7, so it might be the secret articles of this treaty (the archives speak of no other treaty having been negotiated) which in October met with an accident rendering them unintelligible. Another copy had to be procured from Basel, and the Committee was very anxious that Hesse-Cassel should not begin to suspect France's good faith (CPS to Barthélemy, Oct. 18, 1795, Arch. A. E., *Allemagne* 670, f. 12).

CHAPTER XII

THE WAR AND THE LINE OF DEMARCATION

I. THE MILITARY SITUATION

APRIL—SEPTEMBER 1795

*T*HE Duke of Saxe-Teschen, whose appointment as Imperial field marshal in March 1794 had raised high hopes,[1] experienced nothing but reverses,[2] and he was replaced by General Clerfayt on April 2, 1795.[3] The new appointee, who was presently awarded a marshal's baton,[4] had a reputation as a doer of great deeds, and was expected immediately to take the offensive and relieve the besieged fortresses of Luxemburg and Mayence.[5] But all he did was procrastinate[6] and talk politics with the Prussians.[7] On

[1] He was the relative or friend of almost every princely house of Germany (uncle of the Emperor and of the Elector of Saxony, brother of the Trèves Elector, etc.), and it was thought that opinion would unite behind him (Vivenot, *Sachsen-Teschen*, I, 51–52).

[2] *Ibid.*, p. 53.

[3] Heigel, *Deutsche Geschichte*, II, 195; but the citation in his n. 2 is erroneous. Clerfayt was not made Imperial field marshal — that was beyond the Emperor's power. It is true that when Coburg became Imperial field marshal at the start of the war, it was the Emperor who had appointed him, but that was due to a special dispensation granted by the Diet. The regular procedure for the appointment of the supreme commander of the Army of the Empire, and of its general staff, and generals above the fourth rank, was as follows: The Diet nominated, the Emperor approved, and then the Diet — not the Emperor — appointed (*Krieg g. Rev.*, I, 121). Bacher saw in this placing of an Austrian commander over the troops of the Empire

the germ of future unrest in Germany — something which a warring France would welcome. Wrote he: "There will be lively objections, but the Court of Vienna can consult neither the proprieties nor the laws of the Empire. It must either cross the Rhine or retreat behind the Danube. There is no middle course." — To Rps A. RMo, April 27, 1795, reproduced at length in L. de Gouvion Saint-Cyr, *Mémoires sur les campagnes des Armées du Rhin et de Rhin-et-Moselle de 1792 jusqu'à la paix de Campo-Formio* (4 vols., Paris, 1829), I, 565–566.

[4] Dietrichstein to Thugut, April 30, 1795; Emperor to Clerfayt, May 3, 1795: *Thugut, C, W*, p. 122.

[5] Clerfayt to Emperor, March 30, 1795, *ibid.*, pp. 86–87; Emperor to Clerfayt, April 10, *ibid.*, p. 96; *idem*, May 3, *ibid.*, pp. 122–123 *et passim*.

[6] Emperor to Clerfayt, June 10, 1795, *ibid.*, pp. 149–150.

[7] Thugut to Count Colloredo, May 24, 1795, *Briefe Thugut*, I, 218.

June 8, Luxemburg was lost, and Clerfayt, intrenched on the right bank, seemed merely to be resting. Likewise the French, but they were in almost complete possession of what they wanted, viz., the left bank. People in England were saying either that the Marshal must have fallen under the influence of partisans of peace who had persuaded him that the orders of his court to advance were merely a matter of form, to keep England contented;[8] or that Clerfayt must have received secret orders to remain on the defensive until the peace negotiations instituted by the Diet had turned out one way or the other.[9] The most general rumor, in Europe as a whole, was that a secret armistice existed between the two armies.[10] But the causes of the mutual vacation from slaughter have other and more probable explanations.

Aubry, repentant regicide and advocate of France's return to her old boundaries, was on the Committee from April 4 to August 2, 1795. Possessed of military experience, he had been placed at the head of the Military Topographic Bureau, which position enabled him to oppose the passage of the Rhine by the French troops — a passage ordered by the Committee upon the fall of Luxemburg, but which would be unnecessary if France were willing to make a *status quo ante bellum* peace.[11] Pichegru, commander in chief of the now-unified Rhine and Moselle Army,[12] was comporting himself in a most unorthodox manner, which worked in well with Aubry's designs. When the Committee decided that the General should violate Swiss neutrality,[13] the Swiss immediately knew of the plan;[14] and when the scheme was given up in favor of a descent farther north, Pichegru could not seem to complete his preparations. The conqueror of Holland was, shocking as that might seem, in clandestine communication with Condé,[15] whose corps of *émigrés* formed part of Wurmser's army. Pichegru was probably sparing his troops for a descent on Paris.[16] This would explain why he first left unanswered the order to act,[17] and later pleaded lack of facilities for a trans-Rhenish campaign[18] — though everyone[19] knew

[8] Starhemberg to Thugut, June 19, 1795, Vivenot-Zeissberg, *Quellen*, V, 254.

[9] *Idem*, June 23, 1795, *ibid.*, p. 260.

[10] Vivenot, *Bas. Fried.*, Pt. II, 331–332.

[11] Fain, *Ms. l'an III*, p. 282; Guillaume, *Etudes rév.*, Ser. II, pp. 240–245.

[12] *Vide supra*, chap. vii, n. 136.

[13] Barthélemy, in his *Mémoires*, indicates his belief that it was Merlin-Th. who had suggested this base project to the CPS (p. 127).

[14] Fain, *Ms. l'an III*, pp. 283–284.

[15] Names were never used in the communications, but the actuality of the discussions is not a matter of speculation. H. von Zeissberg publishes many revealing documents in his *Pichegru und Condé in den Jahren 1795 und 1796*, Vienna, 1908.

[16] Pariset, *La Rév.*, p. 272.

[17] CPS to Merlin-Th., June 24, 1795, *Corr. Merlin-Th.*, II, 219.

[18] Pichegru to CPS, July 13, 1795, *ibid.*, p. 228.

[19] Except Aubry, who also was suspected — with cause — of treasonable thoughts. *Vide* Merlin-D. to Merlin-Th., July 26, 1795, *Corr. Merlin-Th.*, II, 229–230 and note.

that the Rhine had been crossed many times before under equally adverse conditions. [20]

Clerfayt, on his part, was really weighed down with an imposing array of ills, physical and mental. Old wounds and illness on the one hand, the loss of his native Flanders and all his property on the other, plus — for good measure — a misfortune in his family,[21] apprehension that the Prussian army would actively join the French,[22] fear that the German states would withdraw their contingents from his army [23] as Hesse-Cassel had already done without even giving notice,[24] anxiety that the neutrality line would interfere with his service of supply [25] — these all combined to transform the impetuous conqueror into a trembling old man. The result of all these intrigues, inhibitions, and illnesses was a virtual armistice.

The Emperor resolved the problem of Clerfayt's inactivity [26] by withdrawing from his command the mobile Austrian troops, and placing them under Wurmser as an "offensive" army. The Imperials, far superior in numbers but lethargic like their general, were left to Clerfayt as a "defensive" army, and he was ordered to support Wurmser's operations.[27] Clerfayt declared that the troops he was giving up were the only ones that could be counted upon. He expressed "displeasure at being relegated to a sort of inactivity," and requested permission to resign.[28] It was denied.[29] This division of the army into two parts was a great tactical blunder, and if not for the aforesaid strange behavior of General Pichegru — behavior ascribed

[20] Under any circumstances, the French army would have lived off the country it occupied. As Pichegru himself confessed, the lot of the troops would have been better on the right bank (to CPS, *ibid.*, p. 228).

[21] Vivenot, *Bas. Fried.*, Pt. I, 299.

[22] Heigel, *Deutsche Geschichte*, II, 195.

[23] Emperor to Clerfayt, June 27 and July 18, 1795, *Thugut, C, W*, pp. 157, 168.

[24] Clerfayt to Emperor, May 10, 1795, *ibid.*, p. 130.

[25] *Idem*, May 15 and June 15, 1795, *ibid.*, pp. 131, 153; Emperor to Clerfayt, June 27, 1795, *ibid.*, p. 156. That supply was already sadly impaired. Part of the impairment was due to the great financial burden of the war. "Your Majesty orders me to use severity toward the contractors," wrote Clerfayt to the Emperor. "Wimmer [not Wurmser, as Sorel has it! (*RH*, XVII, 62)] is the sole one charged with this burden; he has no more credit because there is owing to him about 1,800,000 florins; and I have no money to give him." — May 31, 1795, *Thugut, C, W*, p. 139. To be exact, Clerfayt's money chest contained just 25 florins when Lehrbach visited him a few days later (Lehrbach to Thugut, June 6, 1795, Vivenot-Zeissberg, *Quellen*, V, 234). This penury, plus the general unrest consequent upon Prussia's breach of the Coalition, plus downright disloyalty and the effort of Prussia to buy up all available provisions to sell them to France, threatened to suspend the operations of the Austrian army (Thugut to L. Cobenzl, May 27, 1795, *ibid.*, p. 225).

[26] Dietrichstein placed a goodly portion of the blame for Clerfayt's timidity and indecision upon the shoulders of Moriz Gomez, Clerfayt's chief of staff (to Thugut, Sept. 21, 1795, *Thugut, C, W*, p. 180). *Vide* Gomez to Thugut, Oct. 14, 1795, *ibid.*, p. 284.

[27] Emperor to Clerfayt, July 30, 1795, *ibid.*, p. 180.

[28] Clerfayt to Emperor, Aug. 12, 1795, *ibid.*, p. 184.

[29] Emperor to Clerfayt, Aug. 20, 1795, *ibid.*, pp. 187–189. Another general would not know the terrain; a new appointment would further delay operations (*ibid.*).

by Georges Lefebvre, in the first edition of his *Révolution française*, to "either treason or incapacity," and in his second edition [30] categorically to treason [31] — this story would have had a far different ending.

The campaign commenced on the night of September 5–6, when Jourdan crossed the Rhine into the neutralized region (!) and took possession of the mountainous Eichelskamp.[32] The Prussians protested weakly, but did nothing. Previously Clerfayt had desired to possess himself of this position, but refrained when the Prussians informed him it was within the Line of Demarcation [33] — although Clerfayt had received from his government no indication that the very existence of the Line would be at all recognized. Another French corps crossed the Rhine at Düsseldorf, which was surrendered by the Palatine minister Hompesch without the firing of a single shot. This capture netted the starving French abundant supplies and 353 cannon.[34]

The Bavaro-Palatinate had decided it would like to be neutral, which was probably the cause of the surrender of Düsseldorf. Thugut feared a repeat performance at Mannheim. Protests were made to Munich, and Wurmser was ordered to seize Mannheim by surprise, either by ruse or by

---

[30] P. 441 of 2nd ed., p. 280 of 1st ed. — both in the *Peuples et civilisations* series of L. Halphen and P. Sagnac (Vol. XIII). All other references to Lefebvre's book in this monograph are to his 2nd edition.

[31] Cf. *Mém. Saint-Cyr*, II, 266: "I see only blunders where [others] . . . perceive treason. As I view it, their error comes from supposing a great warrior incapable of such grave mistakes. But those who know the difficulties of the art of war realize that the most clever can make them [i.e., mistakes], and I confess that Pichegru has never appeared to me more than a mediocre general. . . . Having been then in contact with him, having been witness to his embarrassments and his anxieties, having been able to appreciate several of his steps and to judge that in reality they were dictated by the desire to avoid a reverse, I have full grounds for believing that the thought of betrayal, though in his mind, did not at all direct, as yet, his military actions."

[32] Eichelskamp formed part of the Duchy of Berg, a possession of the Elector Palatine. The Elector had not withdrawn his contingent from the Imperial army. France took the position that mere geographical location behind the neutrality line did not render a state neutral if its contingent was still fighting against France. *Ergo*, it was no violation of the Treaty to cross at Eichelskamp (Jourdan to CPS, Sept. 10, 1795, Arch. A. E., *Allemagne* 669, f. 321). The French had other arguments too. The movement of the French troops was in the direction of the Cologne-Frankfort route by way of Friedberg, Wetzlar, and Siegen — one of the four routes opened through the neutralized region by agreement with Prussia. And the Austrian troops were accused of having violated the line first by going from Elberfeld to Schwelm (Arch. A. E., *Allemagne* 669, f. 376).

[33] Heigel, *Deutsche Geschichte*, II, 196. According to the Prussian prince Hohenlohe-Ingelfingen, Clerfayt gave his word of honor that he would not violate the neutrality line. Clerfayt later denied this emphatically (*Thugut, C, W*, p. 309 and note). On October 12, the Austrian wounded lay bleeding for three hours, their wounds undressed, before the gates of Frankfort, because the Prussians would not admit them. We are neutral, said the Prussians; yet they allegedly admitted French soldiers who were bodily whole and hence a greater menace to neutrality (*ibid.*, p. 310).

[34] Heigel, *Deutsche Geschichte*, II, 196. "Treason," said Francis II (Hansen, *Quellen*, III, 613).

force, to prevent its delivery to the French.[35] If the Palatine government should conspire with the French to set up a "pretended neutrality," Wurmser was to treat the Palatinate as enemy country.[36] If a certain rumor — that Mannheim had already been surrendered to the French — was indeed true, requisitions for the support of the army were to be levied in the Palatinate without compensation, though useless devastation was to be avoided.[37] Thugut cautioned circumspection, however. He did not want "needlessly to manufacture new enemies, and to complicate, more and more, matters which are already only too confused." Wurmser should confine himself for the time being to mere observation.[38]

There was indeed a good deal to be observed. Recum, a Palatine merchant who had been in unbroken correspondence with Merlin of Thionville, crossed over to the left bank twice in six days. Once he returned with a French officer, and an interview was held with the Duke of Zweibrücken (the heir apparent to the entire Wittelsbach patrimony, it will be recalled) and with Minister Oberndorff — meetings from which the Austrian general stationed in Mannheim, Kospoth, was rigorously excluded. On the night of September 17–18, the abbé Salabert departed from Munich with definite propositions.[39] Wurmser, who knew all this through informers on the left bank and in Mannheim, ordered Kospoth to resist all negotiations tending toward a capitulation,[40] but since Kospoth had only one battalion of Austrians to the Palatinate's ten thousand men, his words carried no weight. On the eighteenth, Wurmser ordered Kospoth to seize by force one of the gates to the fortress, and to hold it until the arrival of a relief force rushing to the city's assistance. But before Kospoth received the last-named order, the Palatine government had induced him to withdraw from Mannheim at the same time that the French forces crossed the Rhine. He was already outside the gates when the vanguard of the relief force appeared. It was no longer possible to pretend that the city was bowing to overwhelming force. To be accurate, it could not have claimed this even had the Austrian army not appeared, for the French were just bluffing. "[We shall] pass this first river [the Rhine] at Mannheim if that fortress surrenders to the summons which is to be made to it, or, if it doesn't, at Oppenheim," wrote the Committee to Gillet, Representative to the Sambre and

[35] Emperor to Wurmser, Sept. 25, 1795, Thugut, C, W, pp. 235–236, 238.

[36] Ibid., pp. 238–239.

[37] Thugut to Wurmser, Sept. 25, 1795, ibid., pp. 240–241.

[38] Emperor to Wurmser, Sept. 25, 1795, ibid., p. 235.

[39] There is evidence that as early as August 24,

Oberndorff had received carte blanche from the Elector to deliver Mannheim to the French in return for the neutrality of the Palatinate (Dietrichstein to Thugut, Oct. 18–19, 1795, ibid., p. 328).

[40] Wurmser to Emperor, Sept. 17, 1795, Vivenot-Zeissberg, Quellen, V, 389–390, and note on 389.

Meuse Army.[41] But the city was more than willing to believe it was necessary to surrender. It wanted to surrender! The garrison trained its guns upon the advancing relief army of Austrians — and admitted the French! [42] (September 20, 1795.) Vivenot asserts that "documents in the *Kriegs- und Staatsarchive* establish indubitably that Prussian agents had their hands in the Düsseldorffer [and] . . . Mannheimer treason." [43]

Treason it was indeed, and of the most flagrant sort, though the Elector disavowed responsibility; he had not ordered the surrender, he averred. But, wrote Wurmser, there has been too much "equivocal dealing between the regency of this city and the French . . . for a long time to render admissible a different interpretation," and he announced that he had disarmed the Palatine garrison (which had, by the terms of the capitulation, also marched out of the city). He was not going to have a potential enemy in his rear, he said.[44] The garrison protested loudly that its honor was being impugned. What honor? queried Wurmser, and continued the disarmament. Thugut agreed that this was the proper course to pursue. "The protests of the Palatine general Deroy [45] require no answer," ran the Emperor's despatch (Thugut's draft) of October 7. Thugut agreed also with Wurmser's suggestion that Mannheim and other (future) traitors be taught a lesson by the recapture of Mannheim through bombardment and other ways not so comfortable for its inhabitants; [46] and the order was repeated to requisition supplies in the Palatinate except in localities which had manifested their favorable disposition.[47] Wurmser thought that the prospect of being disarmed and bombarded would serve to "stop in time this avalanche of partial pacifications which threatens to crush the Germanic constitution." [48]

As to Wurmser's levying of requisitions, an interesting counterfact should be mentioned. On September 20, Merlin of Thionville and Rivaud wrote to the Committee that "Wurmser was advancing with ten thousand men by

[41] Sept. 21, 1795, Aulard, *Actes*, XXVII, 599. For verification, *vide* also CPS to Rps A. RMo, Sept. 22, 1795, *ibid.*, p. 626; Sept. 23, *ibid.*, p. 639.

[42] Sorel, *Europe*, IV, 426, erroneously says that the French "bombarded Mannheim and it capitulated." Fain, *Ms. l'an III*, p. 285, erroneously says that the French crossed the Rhine at Oppenheim. The latter city is twenty-five miles farther north.

[43] *Thugut, C, W*, p. 225, note. Consider in this connection the evasiveness of the Bavaro-Palatine Elector when, in March 1793, he was requested by the Emperor — and by Prussia! — to accept a garrison for Mannheim. Perhaps the Elector could be treasonable on his own account (P. Cobenzl to

Reuss, March 16, 1793, Vivenot-Zeissberg, *Quellen*, II, 503).

[44] Wurmser to Thugut, Sept. 28, 1795, *Thugut, C, W*, p. 250.

[45] Deroy had engaged in correspondence with Merlin-Th. the previous June. The latter had informed him of Luxemburg's fall (Merlin-Th. to Deroy, *Corr. Merlin-Th.*, II, 212).

[46] On November 22, 1795, Wurmser recaptured Mannheim after two months of bombardment and near-starvation (Vivenot, *Bas. Fried.*, Pt. II, 498). *Vide* next chapter, § 5.

[47] Emperor to Wurmser, *Thugut, C, W*, pp. 276–277.

[48] Wurmser to Thugut, Sept. 28, 1795, *ibid.*, p. 251.

forced marches. . . This circumstance obliged us, when consenting to the neutrality of the . . . Prince Palatine, . . . to agree that no requisitions whatsoever would be levied." [49] Here we have indeed an inversion of the natural order of things. It is the enemy that spares the citizen's goods, and the fellow national who seizes them. Or does this case call for a redefinition of the word "enemy"?

That France levied no requisitions in the Palatinate is, however, a statement as misleading as it is true. One must dismiss definitively from mind the picture of the virtuous invaders bleeding the folks back home so they could keep their plighted word to the Palatine authorities. The French found in the fortress a wealth of Austrian supplies: more than 6,000 cwt. of sifted flour, 400 sacks of oats, and some fodder (also much barrack-baggage, more than 200 cannon, and munitions in proportion). And when that would be gone, there were "the fertile lands of Hesse-Darmstadt, Württemberg, etc." which could be invaded, said the Representatives Merlin of Thionville and Rivaud. [50]

The capture of Mannheim was a source of great joy to the French, who thought it signified that, now that Austria had lost the help of North Germany, she could easily be crushed. "This event is of major consequence from all points of view, and prepares us for decisive successes," wrote the Committee. "This is the moment . . . to enflame the hearts, electrify the spirits, stimulate the powers; in a word, to employ all means to bring this campaign to a glorious end." [51] "The passage of the Rhine at Mannheim decides absolutely the outcome of the campaign," exulted Joubert, Representative [52] to the Sambre and Meuse Army. "Soon we shall be able to embrace you." [53] "Grand and important news," declared Barthélemy. "I immediately informed Herrn von Hardenberg and the ministers of the Elector Palatine and Duke of Zweibrücken, who are here." And Barthélemy declared that the capture of Mannheim would "decide the pacification of Germany." [54] Note that Barthélemy spoke of informing Hardenberg in the same tone that he used with respect to the Wittelsbach ministers, as though Hardenberg also was a party to the capture, as Vivenot asserts he was indeed. And Merlin of Thionville, who arranged the treason, wrote to the Committee, "I have reason to hope that it [Mannheim] will serve us as a bridgehead to march against the enemy's center. . . Acceptance of the Con-

[49] Sept. 20, 1795, Aulard, *Actes*, XXVII, 576.
[50] *Ibid.*, pp. 576–577.
[51] To Rps A. RMo, Sept. 24, 1795, *ibid.*, p. 657.
[52] And not "General," as in Heigel, *Deutsche Geschichte*, II, 199. *Vide* Aulard, *Actes*, XXVII, 609–611, 611–613, 633, *et passim*. There was, however, a General Joubert.

[53] To his colleagues, *Corr. Merlin-Th.*, II, 260. Heigel, *Deutsche Geschichte*, II, 199, n. 4, erroneously cites in this connection *Thugut, C, W*, p. 230. His n. 4 should be: *Ebenda*; and n. 5: *Thugut, C, W*, p. 232.
[54] Sept. 28, 1795, *Corr. Merlin-Th.*, II, 260.

stitution by the army, striking victories, . . . and we shall have peace and the end of the Revolution." [55]

Striking victories with an empty treasury! Striking victories with empty granaries! Striking victories with empty stalls where horses earmarked for the cavalry and transport services should have been pawing the ground! The principal problem was the last, the lack of horses. Joubert decided to requisition 600 in the Duchy of Berg, and 400 in parts of Trèves, Cologne, and Neuwied. But the country was very sterile, and it was "only with infinite pains, and by violent and distressing means" that even these few could be obtained. Rye and wheat were procured by contracting for them at Cologne, and paying with requisitions of coin levied on the right bank.[56] Fingerling, a banker of Frankfort, and one Mülens of Coblenz contracted to deliver flour, oats, and hay to the French, payment to come from contributions; and Mülens is said to have sent to the French under Prussian escort a load of requisitioned silver.[57] A land tax of 10,000,000 livres was imposed on the left bank, also for the support of the army,[58] When 800,000 livres was exacted from the Duchy of Berg, the Committee of Public Safety complained that "this sum appears moderate to us, considering the circumstances." [59]

The Committee did not want moderation. "The time for gentleness is past. . . Reject indulgence which would be prejudicial to the interests of our country. . . Raise [the impositions] to the highest point possible without exposing us to the risk of nonpayment under pretext of their exorbitance. . . The war should support the war. We think it incumbent upon the country we have just invaded to indemnify us for the immense outlays their conquest has cost us. The contributions they can furnish should, . . . it seems to us, be proportionate to the dangers we have just run, and to the army's extreme need for provisions of every sort. . . We must, we absolutely must deprive our enemies of the resources they might find some day in these regions, and procure for ourselves what we lack. The English have closed the sea to us. Well, let the earth supply for the time being what is denied to us by the other element. Although we have no reason to fear that we shall be forced back across the Rhine, let us cast into the interior of . . . the Republic everything not indispensable to the daily needs of the army. . . Send to France all the provisions not indispensable to the inhabitants of the states subject to the princes of the Empire; empty absolutely of supplies of

[55] Sept. 11, 1795, Aulard, *Actes*, XXVII, 334–335.
[56] Joubert to CPS, Sept. 20, 1795, *ibid.*, pp. 574–575.
[57] Dietrichstein to Thugut, Oct. 18–19, 1795, *Thugut, C, W*, pp. 313–314.
[58] Meynard, Rp AA. NSMeu, to CPS, Sept. 20, 1795, Aulard, *Actes*, XXVII, 578.
[59] To Gillet, Rp A. SMeu, Sept. 21, 1795, *ibid.*, p. 599.

every kind the hereditary lands of the House of Austria; that is our plan. Nothing should stop us. Therein lies glory and peace!" [60]

This disgraceful policy would not have been so bad, considering that war is war, had the French not preceded their arrival with proclamations guaranteeing respect for persons and property. The inhabitants "awaited vindicators of the Rights of Man, . . . philosophers of a sort — and they found soldiers, unexcelled indeed in boldness, dexterity, and perseverance, . . . but in whose dictionary of war the word discipline did not exist — wild, noisy, restless . . . [folk whose philosophy was] 'Might makes right, and everything belongs to the brave!' " [61]

The surrender of Mannheim placed the Austrian armies in danger of being cut off, one from the other. And of course, instead of going to meet the enemy, "Fabius" [62] Clerfayt was still delaying.[63] The French ranged far and wide over the right bank without meeting resistance worthy of the name, and the Prussian general Prince Hohenlohe-Ingelfingen, in Frankfort, declared (in sarcasm) that he would be forced to cover Clerfayt's rear.[64] Finally the Emperor, at his wit's end, "enjoin[ed Clerfayt] in the most express manner and under penalty of being regarded as disobedient, not to leave the Lahn under any pretext whatsoever"; [65] Clerfayt, he said, would be held personally responsible to Emperor and Empire if the French captured Ehrenbreitstein without his, Clerfayt's, having fought them "more than once, if necessary, with all the energy and stubbornness that the crisis demands." [66]

The political repercussions of the gloomy military outlook were not long in manifesting themselves. The Saxon Elector, pretending that his state was in danger, invoked an old Imperial Resolution (*Reichsbeschluss*) of April 14, 1734, permitting a state of the Empire, when in danger, to call its military forces home.[67] The Saxon troops departed secretly without waiting for Clerfayt's order. Clerfayt received the information by courier from their commander at 11:00 P.M., and immediately forbade the withdrawal to continue.[68] But the contingent was too large and powerful for Clerfayt to be

[60] To Rps AA. NSMeu, Sept. 21, 1795; and to Joubert, Sept. 21: *ibid.*, pp. 597–598 (two reports combined).

[61] Heigel, *Deutsche Geschichte*, II, 196–197.

[62] Expression used by Dietrichstein (to Thugut, P.S. of Oct. 22, 1795, *Thugut*, C, W, p. 340).

[63] But cf. Dietrichstein to Thugut, Oct. 18–19, 1795: "He [General Jourdan] praised Clerfayt for his prompt retreat . . . behind the Lahn, saying that otherwise the destruction of our army would have been inevitable." — *Ibid.*, p. 308.

[64] Sept. 23, 1795, *ibid.*, p. 229. And so indeed

did he maintain to have done (Dietrichstein to Thugut, Oct. 18–19, 1795, *ibid.*, p. 306).

[65] Emperor to Clerfayt, Sept. 23 (*vide* Vivenot's errata), 1795, *ibid.*, p. 232.

[66] Sept. 25, 1795, *ibid.*, p. 233.

[67] Lindt (Saxon commander) to Clerfayt, Oct. 2, 1794, and enclosure: *ibid.*, pp. 265–267. The Hesse-Casseler contingent had been called home on the same pretext (Clerfayt to Emperor, May 10, 1795, *ibid.*, p. 130).

[68] Clerfayt to Lindt, Oct. 2, 1795, *ibid.*, pp. 267–268.

able to force it to remain, as he had been authorized to do but cautioned not to try.[69] Needless to say, the Saxons continued on their way. For a while it had appeared that they would not desert the Empire. When the Prussian contingent was recalled after the Treaty of Basel, the Saxons, who had formed a military unit with the Prussians, separated themselves from the latter and repaired to the Imperial camp. What was responsible for the later defection? According to Vivenot, the answer is: pressure from Berlin.[70]

Dietrichstein attributed to Prussian machinations a selected list of other infamies. Said he, "It is certain that it is the Prussians who induced the French to cross the Rhine . . . by promising them Mannheim and Mayence and Ehrenbreitstein by treason, and the pacification of the Empire as a prompt consequence of their operation.[71] All the French generals and officers have proclaimed it publicly." [72] According to Dietrichstein, the Prussians received four millions for the Eichelskamp accommodation.[73] It is indisputable that Prussia was anxious to promote peace, and that she regarded the abasement of Austria as a means thereto. It is indisputable also that the Prussian Court was not particularly selective as to the means employed to attain this truly noble aim. But it was not necessary to bribe Frederick William. All that was necessary was that his honor should not appear to be compromised. A show of resistance, or even a protest — as at Eichelskamp — sufficed for that.

Up to the twenty-fourth of September, it appeared that the hopes of France and Prussia were about to be realized. Austria, the necessary pivot of the Coalition, seemed to have neither the will nor the vigor to resist the wide-ranging Republican forces. The petty princes of Germany were seized with panic. The Landgrave of Darmstadt fled to Weimar and the Margrave of Baden to Ulm.[74] But the events of the twenty-fourth had a sequel which presently upset all calculations.

The Austrians had stored a mountain of supplies at Heidelberg. If the French could possess themselves of these stores, a body blow would be dealt to Austria, and the needy Republicans would have gained the wherewithal for victory. A small force under Pichegru's personal leadership — only 15,000 men — dashed toward Heidelberg. The way was barred by 4,000 Austrians. The two forces clashed at the little town of Handschuhsheim, and after a bloody encounter lasting twelve hours, the French retreated.[75] Did the 4,000 defeat the 15,000, or was the retreat a product of

[69] Emperor to Clerfayt, June 27 and July 18, 1795, *ibid.*, pp. 157–158, 168–169.
[70] *Ibid.*, p. 293, note.
[71] The same conviction is to be found in Thugut's letter to L. Cobenzl, Sept. 6, 1795, Vivenot-Zeissberg, *Quellen*, V, 347.
[72] To Thugut, Oct. 18, 1795, *ibid.*, p. 301.
[73] *Thugut, C, W*, p. 311.
[74] Sorel, *Europe*, IV, 426–427; Guyot, *Direc.*, p. 110.
[75] Vivenot, *Bas. Fried.*, Pt. II, 495.

Pichegru's nascent treason? Vivenot vigorously rejects the theory of treason. He regards it as a subtle invention on the part of French historiographers to explain away the series of defeats which overwhelmed French arms after Handschuhsheim — as a foul plot to dull the lustre of Austrian achievement.[76] However that may be, September belonged to France, but October was Austria's own.

2. THE LINE OF DEMARCATION IN PRACTICE

"The three months' period provided for by Article XI of the Treaty of 16 *germinal* [April 5] having elapsed," Barthélemy had written to the Committee on July 18, "we could consider the Line of Demarcation as no longer valid when we cross the Rhine, for it is only the Landgrave of Hesse-Cassel who has really fulfilled the conditions by withdrawing his contingent.

"When we cross the Rhine, our needs will be great. We shall have many things to ask of the princes of Germany. Austria is at present hastening to exhaust them as much as she can; we shall finish crushing them, and thereby we shall serve it [Austria] and facilitate for it the means of making its projects succeed."[77]

Barthélemy saw more clearly than many Frenchmen of his time, but the instructions of the Committee to General Jourdan in regard to the Line of Demarcation show that that body was not totally devoid of political sense. These instructions were prompted by a letter from the General, inquiring how he should treat the territory beyond the line in question. Only those states behind the Line are neutral, the Committee replied, which have withdrawn their contingents.[78] If hostile troops (i.e., troops hostile to France) occupy a region which wishes to become neutral, it is still enemy country, though the generous French nation will view it in a more favorable light than occupied states devoted to Austria. In enemy country, contributions in kind may be exacted; in neutral territory they should be paid for in current coin. Avoid as much as possible entering the territories behind the

[76] *Ibid.*, p. 497, note.
[77] *Papiers de Barthélemy*, V, 377.
[78] Thus, Joubert (Rp A. SMeu) imposed contributions upon the right-bank estates of the Nassau-Orange House. The bailiffs presented a request of Frederick William's that the lands be treated as neutral territory, but Joubert refused because the contingent of the state had not been withdrawn (Joubert to CPS, Sept. 24, 1795, Aulard, *Actes*, XXVII, 663). But it was indeed carrying matters to an extreme when the Committee wanted to deny neutrality to Hesse-Cassel, which had

not only withdrawn its contingent, but signed a peace with France. "The Landgrave of Hesse-Cassel is outside the Treaty of Basel," wrote the Committee to Barthélemy, "because he did not withdraw his contingent in time." To which Barthélemy replied: "I pray you to recall that the Landgrave of Hesse withdrew his contingent even before the ratifications of the Treaty of Basel were exchanged." — Oct. 27, 1795, *Papiers de Barthélemy*, V, 491. An inconvenient memory that man Barthélemy had.

Line of Demarcation, limiting yourself to the four passages mentioned in the Convention of May 17.[79] Two months later, however, the Committee had changed its mind, and at a meeting on October 10 between Prince Hohenlohe-Ingelfingen and General Jourdan, the latter declared that his government had definitely commanded him to proceed against those states which had not withdrawn their contingents, even if such states were behind the Line of Demarcation.[80]

On October 3, Joubert complained to Barthélemy that the government had, on the one hand, ordered him to draw subsistence for his army from the recently conquered territory on the right bank, while on the other hand it had exacted that the Line of Demarcation be respected. However, as the French had advanced during the month of September, a constantly increasing number of states within the Line had decided to withdraw their contingents, so that the recognizedly neutral area had progressively expanded. This threatened to check the advance of the French army, said the Representative. Joubert suggested that an agreement between the Republic and Frederick William should permit the French troops to levy supplies of foodstuffs and forage in the neutral area upon the delivery of government debentures.[81]

The Committee found a slightly different solution. Declaring that it was necessary to act decisively and without fear of consequences, it ordered Joubert, on October 8, to draw the necessary subsistence from the neutralized region, and to promise that the requisitions would be returned later in kind, or paid for in coin, as soon as provisions or money should have arrived from the nonneutralized area.[82]

The Committee behaved in a similarly vigorous manner in regard to positions within the neutrality line, the possession of which it deemed necessary to the military operations of the French troops. The brilliant commencement of the autumn campaign of 1795 was due partly to Jourdan's crossing of the Rhine at Eichelskamp, within the Line of Demarcation.[83] The case of Frankfort-on-the-Main affords another example. This former seat of the Imperial Diet was being guarded by General Hohenlohe-Ingelfingen and his Prussian troops in accordance with the Neutrality Convention of May 17. However, Frankfort had not withdrawn its contingent from the army of the Empire, though it had asked for the Prussian good offices with a view to a separate peace with France, and had given Hardenberg a good-will message for the Republic's ambassador at Basel.[84] But because

[79] Aug. 6, 1795, Arch. A. E., *Allemagne* 669, f. 230.

[80] Bailleu, *Pr. Frk.*, I, xx.

[81] Arch. A. E., *Allemagne* 669, ff. 361–362.

[82] Annex to despatch of Oct. 7, 1795 of CPS

to Barthélemy, *Papiers de Barthélemy*, V, 469.

[83] Heigel, *Deutsche Geschichte*, II, 196.

[84] Barthélemy to CPS, Sept. 21, 1795, Arch. A. E., *Allemagne* 669, ff. 310–311.

Frankfort's contingent was still fighting the Republic, Jourdan was ordered to write to Hohenlohe "in the tone of amity which should exist between the two governments, but with the firmness which accompanies right," recalling to him the treaty of May 17, and explaining that France was entitled to occupy the city. Hohenlohe was to be invited to evacuate Frankfort, and to signify his decision the same day. If the response were not favorable, or if it were dilatory, "which amounts to the same thing," Jourdan was to send a new despatch, announcing that if Frankfort were not evacuated within twenty-four hours, the French would enter by force and hold Hohenlohe responsible for his "unjust and unlawful resistance to the law of nations." [85]

Relations between Prussia and France were already at the breaking-point. A Prussian hussar had killed a French officer for saying Frederick William was a knave (or beggar: *un gueux*). At Höchst and Weilburg the French fired on the Prussians. At Eschborn, fifteen Prussians were locked in a barn overnight, then told to go tell their King and Prince Hohenlohe that they (King and Prince) were ———. A last item merits quotation: "A horse was stolen from a Prussian officer, and he presented himself before a French officer to demand it. The Prussian gave his word of honor that the horse belonged to him, to which the Frenchman replied: 'Your King and your Prince have no honor, and I'm not sure you have any. I'll keep the horse.' " [86]

On October 11, the French demanded of Frankfort 1,000 oxen and 50,000 cwt. of wheat, and threatened to take action if these supplies were not forthcoming within seven days. Hohenlohe did not know what to do. He formally forbade the city to comply but insinuated that compliance might really be necessary.[87]

However, he did stand firm on the question of evacuating Frankfort.[88] We shall never know whether the French would have carried out their threat to storm the city, for the advance of the Austrians under Clerfayt (!) transferred the theater of the war elsewhere. Furthermore, the imminence of the Third Polish Partition presently caused Frederick William to desire the presence of his troops farther east, where he could more effectively menace Austria; [89] and on October 24, Prince Hohenlohe received the order

[85] CPS to Joubert, Oct. 8, 1795, *Papiers de Barthélemy*, V, 469–470.
[86] Dietrichstein to Thugut, Oct. 18–19, 1795, *Thugut, C, W*, p. 316.
[87] *Ibid.*, p. 313.
[88] Contrary to Dietrichstein's prognostication. "It is certain," Dietrichstein had written to Thugut, "that the Prussians will let [the

French occupy Frankfort], exacting payment for the accommodation, as they have exacted, according to the French, four millions for the passage at Eichelskamp." — Oct. 18–19, 1795, *ibid.*, p. 311.
[89] Bailleu, *Pr. Frk.*, I, xxi for the Prussian viewpoint; Vivenot, *Bas. Fried.*, Pt. II, 503 for the Austrian.

to withdraw to the Hohenzollern possessions in Franconia,[90] within striking distance of Bohemia.[91]

Clerfayt, in advancing, disregarded completely the line of neutrality,[92] the Emperor having instructed him on May 21 "not to pay any attention to whatever the Prussians might say to you respecting neutralities, lines of demarcation, projects of pacification, and other things of that sort. . . You will not even undertake to transmit the insinuations and messages [to Vienna]. . . I repeat to you, my dear Marshal, do not listen to any proposition of the Prussians, and continue your operations." [93] French and Austrians alike were publicly manifesting their contempt for the weak Prussian monarch. "Herr Hardenberg was almost forced to agree," wrote Barthélemy on October 27, 1795, "that this line, having been respected by no one, no longer has any significance." [94] Merlin of Thionville and his colleagues, who had thought that war would "inevitably" result between Prussia and Austria in consequence of the neutrality provisions, and that France's task was but to hasten the moment of rupture, saw themselves cruelly deceived by their own wishful thinking.[95] Frederick the Great's successor had milk in his veins.

Not only did the French and Austrians violate the neutrality line, but also the English.[96] They landed troops at Cuxhaven and the fort of Ritzebüttel at the mouth of the Elbe, to intercept ships bringing provisions from Hamburg to France.[97] The blockade was not complete, for about twenty French-bound ships did get through between April 13 and 25. However, there were many more which lagged back for fear of being seized. Many of these were of Dutch nationality,[98] which brings up a new problem.

When the Treaty of Basel was signed, there were in Dutch ports nine or ten Prussian ships which had been seized by the French as prizes of war when they invaded Holland. The French regarded these ships as legally

[90] The King to Hardenberg, Oct. 26, 1795, Bailleu, *Pr. Frk.*, I, 30.

[91] Vivenot, *Bas. Fried.*, Pt. II, 503. Before Hohenlohe's withdrawal to Franconia, one Zwanziger of Nuremberg — a democratic and restless soul, anti-Imperial deputy of the Franconian Circle, and archintriguer to whom Director Carnot will entrust a mission — induced Hohenlohe to promise his *personal* protection to Franconia, Hohenlohe being the ruler of vast estates in the Circle. From September 15 to 19, Zwanziger engaged in negotiations for the neutrality of Franconia (Dietrichstein to Thugut, Oct. 18–19, 1795, *Thugut, C, W*, p. 312). The withdrawal of the Prussian army to Ansbach and Baireuth must have allayed Zwanziger's fears, for he ceased his importunities for the time being.

[92] The King to Hardenberg, Oct. 26, 1795, Bailleu, *Pr. Frk.*, I, 30. Barthélemy complained to Joubert that the Prince of Hohenlohe remembered the Line of Demarcation only when the French wished to cross it, and never when the Austrians violated it (Arch. A. E., *Allemagne* 669, f. 363).

[93] *Thugut, C, W*, pp. 133–135. The draft of his Majesty's letter is in Thugut's hand.

[94] To CPS, *Papiers de Barthélemy*, V, 490.

[95] *Corr. Merlin-Th.*, II, 182.

[96] Langwerth von Simmern, *Oestr. Reich fr. Rev.*, II, 197.

[97] *Papiers de Barthélemy*, V, 202.

[98] Cochon (Rp in Holland) to CPS, May 7, 1795, Aulard, *Actes*, XXII, 761.

theirs, maintaining that Article VII, which declared that the theater of the war would be removed from North Germany, was inapplicable — and this thesis appears correct enough. But there were many more than nine or ten Dutch ships in Prussian ports, and it was feared that Prussia would seize these in reprisal if the Prussian ships were not restored. Moreover, France was expecting to break the famine — her own and Holland's — with meat and wheat from northern Germany, and it would not do to irritate a monarch who was in a position to stop the flow of these life-giving commodities. A large quantity of grain, it seems, had been purchased at Hamburg, Danzig, and Copenhagen, and it was expected that some eighty Dutch ships would transport it to France and Holland. It seems also that the Dutch ships were not doing this, whether from ill will or from fear of the English fleet, the French could never quite decide.[99] They took no chances of angering Prussia, however, and restored the Prussian ships as a token of friendship, maintaining nevertheless that they had a legal right to keep them.[100]

Meanwhile, the question of Cuxhaven and Ritzebüttel had been aggravated. News had arrived that troops from Brunswick had occupied Bremen to prevent it from trading with France, and that instead of ousting them, the Prussian King had reacted in a most incomprehensible manner — a manner which can be explained only on the theory that the Peace of Basel irked his Majesty — for from the Berlin Ministry emerged the following: "This is one of those cases where, in an Imperial war, each state should consent, for the safe prosecution of military operations aiming at the defense of the common fatherland, to receive the necessary troops in its cities. . . An Imperial city for which this sad war has become a favorable occasion to engage in advantageous commerce cannot claim to be free of the embarrassments which are its consequence. It ought not claim to be able to continue to trade freely with the enemy of the Empire, to enjoy all the advantages and protection without also incurring the charges." [101] To Barthélemy's protests regarding events in Bremen, Hardenberg replied that the Elector of Hanover was Duke of Bremen, that the city was contesting some of his rights, and that the dispute had nothing to do with the neutrality of northern Germany.[102]

The Committee was beside itself with rage. It threatened to take military action against Hanover should Prussia fail to compel the evacuation of Cuxhaven,[103] and it sent in a refutation of Hanover's claims in regard to

[99] *Ibid.*, Rps in Holland to CPS, May 11, 1795, *ibid.*, XXIII, 57.

[100] Decree of May 15, 1795, *ibid.*, p. 189.

[101] *Papiers de Barthélemy*, V, 320.

[102] Barthélemy to CPS, June 23, 1795, *ibid.*, p. 348.

[103] CPS to Barthélemy, May 31, 1795, *ibid.*, p. 304. "As much as we persist in believing that the premier ally of the most powerful republic in the world should be the most

Bremen.[104] Frederick William was cowed, and asked the Hanoverian Ministry to renounce, voluntarily but categorically, all hostile intention toward France and Holland. At first the Hanoverians resisted, though Prussia had sent one of her best Francophile diplomats, Baron von Dohm,[105] to help them make up their minds. The presence of von Dohm, however, seems to have had some effect. The English troops at Cuxhaven and Ritzebüttel returned voluntarily to their ships.[106] But George III could not shake off his moral obligations as prince of the Empire as lightly as could his royal Prussian brother, and when a minute of his cabinet recommended withdrawing the British cavalry from the Continent, he replied that the minute "so clearly shows that this country means to leave the German Empire to shift for itself that I cannot, till I have maturely weighed the situation in which every German Prince is placed by this change, give a decided answer as to the step that I shall think best to take as Elector." [107] But without allies in northwestern Europe — now that both Holland and Prussia had made peace with France — there was little that George could do. On September 19, Hardenberg announced to Barthélemy that all troops had been withdrawn from Hanover.[108] Approximately one week later, Caillard apprized the Committee that the Regency of Hanover had asked for permission to accede to the neutrality of northern Germany.[109]

The advantages of such neutrality had long been realized in England. Already on April 22, 1795, William Pitt had advocated it as a means of "saving expense, avoiding unpopularity, and obtaining disposable force." [110] That it was not accepted before is a tribute to the integrity of the Anglo-Hanoverians. The arrangement was, after all, plainly unconstitutional, for the Empire was still at war.

---

powerful monarchy of Europe," wrote the Committee to Barthélemy, "just that much are we determined to exact the execution of engagements entered into with us and not to let ourselves be made sport of." — *Ibid.*
[104] CPS to Barthélemy, June 30, 1795, *ibid.*, p. 364.
[105] It was von Dohm, it will be recalled, whom Mettra and Mandrillon had approached.

Vide supra, chap. i, § 4f.
[106] Langwerth von Simmern, *Oestr. Reich fr. Rev.*, II, 197.
[107] To Lord Grenville, Sept. 10, 1795, *Dropmore Papers*, III, 134.
[108] *Papiers de Barthélemy*, V, 459.
[109] Arch. N., AF III 76, d. 315, Sept. 28, 1795.
[110] William Pitt to Lord Grenville, *Dropmore Papers*, III, 58.

CHAPTER XIII

FRANCE, PRUSSIA, AND THE PEACE
OF GERMANY

I. THE QUESTION OF FRANCO-PRUSSIAN ALLIANCE

THE national policy of France, as it developed in the seventeenth century and continued throughout the first half of the eighteenth, rested upon opposition to the other great states of Europe (England, Austria, and, in the eighteenth century, Russia). This opposition prompted France to ally habitually with second- and third-rate states against the powerful ones. To combat England, she allied with Spain and Holland; to combat Russia, with Sweden, Poland, and Turkey; to combat Austria, with the small states of Germany, especially Prussia and Bavaria. The Treaty of Versailles (1756) was a repudiation of this time-honored system; but with the Revolution, the old policy was resumed.[1]

Especially after the Peace of April 5 did the French renew their offers to ally with Prussia. The Prussians saw in these fervent solicitations only an effort on the part of France to induce another state to fight her battles, hence declined *until the remainder of the continent should also have made peace with the Republic.*[2] This proposition did not satisfy the French. On April 22, the Committee of Public Safety complained to Barthélemy that it could not understand the Prussian reasoning. It seemed to the Committee that alliance between Prussia and the Republic would be the most effective means, not only of reëstablishing but even of commanding peace; that the union of the two states would produce an irresistible force, procure satisfaction to the princes of the Empire — especially the lay princes — and render it beyond the power of the Archduke-Emperor to trouble henceforth the repose of Europe.[3]

All to no avail! The King was somewhat crafty too. "Regarding closer connections between us and France . . . ," he wrote to Hardenberg on

[1] Bailleu, *Pr. Frk.*, I, ix–x.
[2] Barthélemy to CPS, April 11, 1795, *Papiers*
de Barthélemy, V, 184.
[3] *Ibid.*, p. 194.

April 27, "you will be careful to reject each such proposition as impossible before the general pacification. However, in the present complicated circumstances, it is necessary that we should not cause the French to lose hope [of alliance] at some future date. . . [We should appear] only to postpone and suspend the relations in question until the epoch mentioned."[4]

On September 10, 1795, were drawn up the instructions of Caillard, newly appointed Minister Plenipotentiary of the French Republic to the King of Prussia. These instructions declared that there were only two possible political combinations for France: (1) alliance with Turkey, Sweden, Denmark, Prussia, other German states, and Poland (when restored); and (2) alliance with Austria, England, and Russia. In either case, France's bonds with Spain, Switzerland, and the republics of Italy could be preserved intact. The first alternative was declared preferable because of the inconveniences of alliance with Austria, as proved by experience; the impossibility of contracting solid engagements with Russia; the grave error of even thinking of attaching England to France's interests; and the harm to French commerce in the Levant, and to the prosperity of southern France, should the Republic abandon Constantinople and the Ottoman Empire to the aggressive spirit of Russia and Austria.[5]

The instructions suggested also that Prussia renew Frederick the Great's "untimely abandoned" League of Princes, so as to prevent Austria from securing Bavaria. "We must confess, however, that this union of Prussia with the princes of Germany to combat the overflowing of Austrian ambition would still be ineffective without the concurrence, and a fortiori, against the will, of France. Thus, in the combinations which are most conducive to the security and prosperity of Prussia, logic, necessity, and the force of things conduct it irresistibly to the system of the French Republic."[6]

2. ARMISTICE AND SEPARATE PEACE

Alliance with Prussia and the minor states of Germany being the supreme goal envisaged by Caillard's instructions, it would seem to follow that, where alliance was not obtainable, friendly relations would be regarded as the next highest good. Such indeed was the case where Prussia was concerned, but with respect to the smaller states of South Germany whose offensive power was meager, the rights attached to a state of war were regarded as too important to forego. Later — under the Directory — the

---

[4] Bailleu, *Pr. Frk.*, I, 3.
[5] Arch. A. E., *Prusse* Supp. 10, f. 270. Folios 200–299 in this volume are duplicated by error. The document cited above is to be found in the first series of numbers.
[6] Arch. A. E., *Prusse* Supp. 10, ff. 272–273.

privileges of war would be continued under the forms of peace. How the Convention treated the problem will appear presently.

On September 20, 1795, Hardenberg informed Barthélemy that Württemberg desired to conclude a separate peace,[7] and five days later, Reubell, Merlin of Thionville, and Rivaud concluded a one month's armistice with Abel, Württemberger counsellor of legation and plenipotentiary. The French Representatives, in the document, excused themselves for violating France's no-armistice policy by (1) explaining that Württemberg's hostility had been due only to her obedience to the laws of the Empire, and (2) requiring that a peace treaty should be signed before the month had elapsed, or the war would recommence. Secret articles granted France free passage through Württemberg, except through two passes of the Black Forest which the Duke should defend against all belligerents. If these passes were forced by the Germans, however, the French could follow the enemy through them undisturbed. French troops were to be free to exact the necessary means of transport (Article I). The Duke promised to furnish the French army 50,000 *maldres*[8] of grain (to be deposited in indicated storehouses the moment French troops should enter the Duchy), 40,000 cwt. of hay, and a like quantity of straw. The whole was to be paid for later, in coin, at the price and on the terms to be agreed upon in the definitive Franco-Württemberger peace (Article II).[9]

"You will readily recognize that this pretended armistice is only a means of procuring subsistence for our army in a regular manner," the Representatives wrote to the Committee;[10] but that body was not impressed. It had been led by the letters of the Representatives themselves to expect something different. On September 22, the latter had written to Barthélemy that "we believe it our duty . . . to let you know that though the partial agreements which the Republic is able to make with the princes of Germany have the advantage of preparing a general peace at a future time, they have the present inconvenience of depriving the army of all the resources it could find in the possessions of these princes according as it occupies them."[11] On September 24, a letter of Reubell to the Committee had manifested a disposition absolutely contrary to a suspension of hostilities. This letter had made the Committee feel "that it would be infinitely dangerous for us to

[7] Barthélemy to CPS, Sept. 21, 1795, Arch. A. E., *Allemagne* 669, ff. 310–311. It was the estates of the Duchy which had prompted the Duke to institute overtures (Barthélemy to Merlin-Th., *Corr. Merlin-Th.*, II, 193).

[8] A *maldre* was 16 bushels (P. Larousse, *Grand dictionnaire universel du xix⁰ siècle* [15 vols., Paris, 1866–1876], s.v. "maldre").

[9] G. W. Vreede, *La Souabe après la Paix de Bâle. Recueil de documents diplomatiques et parlementaires concernant les négociations avec la République Française . . .* (Utrecht, 1879), p. 2.

[10] Reubell to CPS, Sept. 25, 1795, Aulard, *Actes*, XXVII, 676.

[11] Arch. A. E., *Allemagne* 669, f. 326.

allow ourselves to be hemmed in by our treaties with the princes of Germany; that the separate peace would reduce us to die of hunger and to retreat, and would render us the laughingstock of the Germans. . . What, anyway, gives the Duke of Württemberg a title to obtain this armistice? Did he speak of peace while we were on the left bank? No. He waited until we were on the Main and the Neckar." The Committee then discussed the amount of supplies to be delivered to the French army on entering Württemberg, and queried how the Duke could have offered so little. "Certainly we shall not limit ourselves to such a small contribution in provisions. Certainly instead of paying for the supplies which we take, we will exact several millions to recoup ourselves for the expenses of the war.[12] . . . The Committee has determined not to ratify the armistice. . . As to the deliveries already made, they will be deducted from the contributions to which the inhabitants of the Duchy will be subjected. . . Desiring as we do to establish our winter quarters beyond the Duchy of Württemberg, you can see how burdensome and even baleful an armistice, were it only for a month, might be. . . "[13] On October 1, the Committee sent a copy of this letter to Barthélemy to leave no doubt in his mind as to its firm resolution to reject every armistice proposal.[14]

A week later, the Emperor, in consequence of the widespread rumors of a Franco-Württemberger separate peace, cautioned Wurmser not to allow Württemberg to withdraw the entire Swabian Circle's contingent. Nor should he permit the recall even of the Württemberger contingent itself. A close secret watch should be maintained upon all troops to prevent their defection.[15] And the Emperor asked Wurmser to consider what part of Württemberg it would be necessary for Austria to occupy in order to assure passage and supply.[16]

The Emperor's worry was gratuitous. The peace negotiation followed the fate of the armistice. It also died a-borning.[17] The small states of Germany had ceased to be potential allies of France and become supply depots on the road to Vienna. If they would be friendly depots, so much the better. But

---

[12] Cf. CPS to Rps A. RMo, May 15, 1795: "It is a general principle of war that armies should live at the expense of enemy country. . . . When you shall have passed the Rhine, heavy contributions should be imposed, both in provisions and in coin. . . Requisitioning [of provisions] is slow, difficult, and often insufficient. You will avoid its inconveniences by levying contributions in coin, which will be employed to pay for purchases of provisions. . . Forage should be paid for uniquely in [assignats] . . .; it is not something which can be hidden, and when it can be found in return for coin, it should be possible to find it in return for assignats." — Corr. Merlin-Th., II, 190.

[13] CPS to Reubell, Merlin-Th., and Rivaud, Sept. 28, 1795, Arch. A. E., Allemagne 669, f. 382.

[14] Arch. A. E., Allemagne 669, f. 381.

[15] Oct. 7, 1795, Thugut, C, W, p. 275.

[16] Sept. 25, 1795, ibid., pp. 235–236.

[17] Pol. Corr. Karl Fr., II, 343, n. 2.

provision the French armies they must, and all the good offices of all the Hohenzollern tribe would avail not a jot or tittle to alleviate the crushing load. However, the full blossoming of this story belongs, as indicated, to the Directorial era.

3. GOOD OFFICES

Caillard's instructions devoted much space to the question of Prussia's good offices: "Faithful to the Treaty we have ere now concluded with her at Basel, we will receive with the greatest consideration all those who avail themselves of her intervention with respect to us; we will accord everything compatible with the interest and dignity of the Republic; and in giving them peace, far from disparaging the value of the intervention of the King of Prussia, we will neglect no occasion to inform them of the full value we attach to his good offices in order to conserve *in toto* the gratitude which they owe him for so important a service."[18]

Hardenberg reported to his court in October that France's actions were not at all in conformity with her words. He was very dissatisfied with the manner in which the French were treating the peace negotiations of the individual states of the Empire. Never did Barthélemy speak to him of them unless he (Hardenberg) broached the subject himself, and never did the French plenipotentiary give a written answer to the notes Hardenberg sent to support the negotiations. "The French system," wrote the Prussian minister, "is to make individual treaties of peace without any intervention; to isolate, to divide, the states of the Empire; to make arrangements with them regarding the cessions they require. . . They [the French] trouble themselves little about the general pacification of the German Empire, to which these provisional arrangements are deferred."[19] In the same despatch, Hardenberg announced that all that had resulted from Prussia's intercession in favor of the princes of Ysenburg and of Hohenzollern was a statement that the French would manifest all the consideration "which the operations and needs of the army permitted."[20]

Article XV of the Franco-Spanish Treaty of Basel (July 23, 1795) had stipulated that his Catholic Majesty might mediate peace between France on the one hand and Portugal and the states of Italy on the other. Hardenberg declared to Barthélemy that the Prussian King expected to be recognized, in like manner, as mediator for the states of Germany. The Committee of Public Safety responded that Austria would never consent to Prussian

[18] Arch. A. E., *Prusse* Supp. 10, ff. 272–273.   [20] *Ibid.*, p. 25, Oct. 13, 1795.
[19] Oct. 13, 1795, Bailleu, *Pr. Frk.*, I, 26–27.

mediation, and that, besides, Prussia was too interested as co-state and as partial possessor of the left bank to fulfil this function impartially.[21] We desire no formal mediation, the Committee had declared to Barthélemy on August 6, for it would not leave us free to act as we please. We wish to limit the activity of the King of Prussia to simple good offices. We are inclined to lend much importance to the King's good offices, and to yield to them in whatsoever does not prejudice the interest or dignity of the Republic. We want the states of the Empire to be indebted to Prussia, at least in part, for their treaties of peace.[22] And in execution of these instructions, when Hardenberg next broached the subject of mediation to Barthélemy, the latter evasively replied that an offer of mediation would only draw from the Committee a condemnation of what was going on in Hanover — events which the Prussian King should have opposed, according to Barthélemy.[23]

There was one sort of good offices which the Committee would absolutely not tolerate, and for an example of this we must turn back the calendar a few months. In the spring of 1795, Baden was threatened with invasion by the French, and the Margrave asked for the Prussian good offices to save his lands from being treated as enemy country.[24] To Hardenberg's presentation of the Margrave's request were added the words: "until such time as he could treat either conjointly with the Empire, or separately, for his peace with the French Republic." [25] The Committee of Public Safety pointed out that Article XI had been inserted in the Treaty of April 5 to facilitate the conclusion of treaties of separate peace. Were requests such as Baden's admitted, the Committee argued, as soon as the French crossed the Rhine, all the states of the Empire not protected by the neutrality line would claim the intervention of the King [26] to assure that they would not be treated according to the rules of war; perhaps, even, they would contest the passage of the French troops.[27] On June 28, the Committee pointed out that Article XI was not intended to extend the line of neutrality, but only to prepare peace; that Hardenberg was interpreting the phrase "not to treat as enemy country" as meaning "to treat as neutral country." The Committee declared that the two expressions were widely divergent in sense, and that it was in the interest of Prussia, as well as of France, that the French troops should not be reduced to a simple passage through the South German states in which the King had declared his interest. However, to manifest the kindly disposition

[21] Report of Hardenberg to the King, Aug. 13, 1795, *ibid.*, pp. 14–15.

[22] Arch. A. E., *Allemagne* 671, f. 51.

[23] Barthélemy to CPS, Aug. 11, 1795, Arch. A. E., *Allemagne* 669, ff. 232–233.

[24] Baden was of course not within the neutralized region.

[25] Hardenberg to Barthélemy, May 24, 1795, *Papiers de Barthélemy*, V, 316.

[26] *Vide* CPS to Barthélemy, March 30, 1795, *ibid.*, p. 141.

[27] *Idem*, June 16, 1795, *Pol. Corr. Karl Fr.*, II, 329–330.

of the Republic for Prussia, the Committee promised not to treat as enemy country the lands mentioned in Hardenberg's note.[28] And on September 30, the Badenese aulic councillor, Reitzenstein, was granted full powers by the Baden government to treat for peace with France with the assistance of the Prussian good offices.[29] The result was disastrous — for Baden.[30]

4. THE RATISBON DIET AND PEACE

One of the Committee's objections to Baden's mode of asking for the Prussian good offices has been reserved for special consideration because it shades into another subject: that of the Ratisbon Diet's overture for a Franco-Imperial peace.

The objection in question concerned the last four words of the phrase, "until such time as he [the Margrave] could treat . . . conjointly with the Empire. . ." These four words, declared the Committee, were equivalent to "conjointly with the Emperor," and as such inadmissible. The states of Germany would have to treat with France singly, or together with Prussia, for the Prussian good offices to avail.[31]

This attitude on the part of France was destined to produce an interesting situation. It will be recalled that when Frederick William, with many excuses, informed the Diet about the Treaty of Basel, he invited the states of the Empire to avail themselves of the Prussian good offices for the settlement of their quarrel with France.[32] On July 3, the Diet rendered its *Conclusum*. This document, while it censured Prussia and Hesse-Cassel for breaking the united front, yet declared that "the constant wish and formal resolution of the Diet are still[33] for a perfect and unalterable union between all the states of the Empire with their supreme head for the conclusion of a durable general peace by constitutional means, and for the reestablishment through this peace as soon as possible of the integrity of the territory of the Empire."[34] And it requested the intervention and coöpera-

[28] *Idem, Papiers de Barthélemy*, V, 361–362.
[29] *Pol. Corr. Karl Fr.*, II, 352.
[30] The Franco-Badenese armistice and treaty are discussed in Pt. II, chap. ix, § 2; chap. xiii, § 3.
[31] CPS to Barthélemy, June 16, 1795, *Pol. Corr. Karl Fr.*, II, 329–330.
[32] May 12, 1795. *Supra*, chap. ix, § 3e. Thugut did his best to thwart the Prussian scheme. It was largely Thugut's despatch of Count von Lehrbach to the various courts of southwest Germany that held the states south and

west of the neutrality line true to the Emperor. Thugut, of course, would have liked to attach them to his plan for vigorous prosecution of the war, but he was grateful for the lesser boon of foiling Prussia's unconstitutional interference with the Emperor's prerogative in foreign affairs (Hansen, *Quellen*, III, 493).
[33] A reference to the *Reichsgutachten* of December 22, 1794.
[34] French translation. Arch. A. E., *Allemagne* 669, ff. 339–341.

tion of the King of Prussia in the work of pacifying the Empire[35] — a task which Frederick William viewed with joyous anticipation.[36]

The Diet's reference to the integrity of the Empire is interesting but natural; Prussia had not imparted to that body knowledge of the secret articles, and it was in those articles that the future cession of the left bank was intimated. The suggestion of Prussian good offices was not inserted expressly to please Thugut. As that minister wrote to Louis Cobenzl at St. Petersburg, it "would constitute approbation of the [Prussian] King's abandonment of the . . . Empire, . . . recompense by a mark of confidence . . . an act of veritable felony, . . . subvert all rules, completely annihilate the Imperial authority, deliver Germany over to the arbitrary arrangements of perfidious collusion between the brigands of France and Prussia."[37] But the Diet's *Conclusum* did contain an ameliorating clause to placate the Emperor: the reference to the union of the states with their supreme head for the conclusion of peace. However, this rallying of the states about their supreme head for any purpose whatsoever was exactly what France did not want — what she was determined not to tolerate — and what she did not tolerate.

But the Emperor, that "supreme head," was equally determined that the overture should come to nought. The military situation in the summer of 1795 was too favorable to France. Luxemburg had fallen on June 8, and Clerfayt had proved himself too adept at retreat and proscrastination. Still the situation was not without its redeeming features. Clerfayt's army was rested and, for the first time since the *levée en masse* had been instituted in France, the Imperial army was more numerous than the French[38] (though still sadly lacking in engineers and staff).[39] On May 4 a subsidy treaty had been concluded between England and Austria, relieving the financial stringency which had up to now limited the military efforts of the Vienna government.[40] Russia had, by its treaty of January 3, 1795, agreed to hold Prussia in check, and compel her to accept the portion of Poland allotted to her by the two Imperial Courts. There was no reason to rush pell-mell into peace negotiations just because Prussia had given a nod, and the Diet was weak.

Of course, it would not have been politic for Austria to inform the Diet that this was her view of the situation. Such a confession would have thrown

[35] Note remitted by Hardenberg to Barthélemy, July 24, 1795, *Papiers de Barthélemy*, V, 389.
[36] Hardenberg to Merlin-Th., July 21, 1795, *Corr. Merlin-Th.*, II, 229.
[37] May 27, 1795, Vivenot-Zeissberg, *Quellen*, V, 225.
[38] Pariset, *La Rév.*, p. 272.
[39] Dietrichstein to Thugut, April 30, 1795,

Vivenot-Zeissberg, *Quellen*, V, 190.
[40] Hüffer, *Europa*, I, 192. On May 20, this was changed into an actual alliance between the two powers (Sybel, *Europe*, III, 444). And on September 28, it was broadened into a Triple Alliance between Austria, Russia, and England (Hüffer, *Europa*, I, 192).

the peace-hungry Empire into the arms of Prussia. It was necessary to pretend to coöperate. Especially were tact and diplomacy necessary with respect to the question of Prussia's good offices. The Diet's *Conclusum* was therefore ratified by the Emperor, but the decree of ratification declared that the Empire possessed sufficient authority and power to make peace without the assistance of anyone. Since, however — the decree ran — the Diet had expressed the desire for Prussia's assistance, the Emperor consented on condition that Prussia agreed to take as its rule of action the bases established by the Diet [41] and that the Hohenzollern coöperation should not prejudice the rights of the head of the Empire and the deputies thereof.[42]

Thugut thought this was a master stroke, for in the Treaty of Basel Prussia had implicitly agreed to France's acquisition of the Rhineland. Thugut of course did not know this, but he had his suspicions. The crafty Prussians were, however, not to be so easily outdone. They insinuated confidentially to the lesser German princes that they (the Prussians) would gladly employ their good offices to procure for the princes the recovery of their left-bank possessions.[43] The French government protested against these insinuations, but Frederick William replied that this manifestation of his patriotism was necessary to induce the states to detach themselves from Austria, and to have recourse to his intervention. Besides — added the Prussian King — if the Committee continued to insist upon annexing the Rhineland, peace with the Empire would be indefinitely delayed.[44]

Frederick William went even further. To gain the good will of the Empire, he — or, rather, Hardenberg, who was now back in Basel — suggested that a general Franco-Imperial armistice based on the *status quo* should be concluded; that no further contributions or requisitions should be levied on German territory occupied by French troops; that Frankfort-on-the-Main should be the seat of the proposed negotiations; [45] and that France should, as soon as possible, send a plenipotentiary to treat with the Imperial Commissioner and the deputation about to be named by the Empire.[46] (This deputation was actually named on August 21.) [47]

[41] *Ibid.*
[42] Sorel in *RH*, XVII, 300.
[43] The King to Hardenberg, July 10, 1795, *Papiers de Barthélemy*, V, 399.
[44] *Ibid.*
[45] In this connection, the following document is of rare interest: "If Ambassador Barthélemy arrives with a passport from the Court, Ministry, or Minister Degelmann, he must be allowed to pass. Any other passport, even Prussian, can avail him nothing. . . We have found a patent of his Majesty the Emperor's, forbidding passage to all French envoys. . .

He [Barthélemy] has the choice to return; . . . if he refuses, . . . arrest him. . . Avoid everything which might make a scene or cause useless gatherings. . . I do not think he'll come, for it is said the congress will not be in Frankfort." — Marshal Clerfayt to Alvinczy, June 16, 1795, Vivenot-Zeissberg, *Quellen*, V, 242.
[46] *Papiers de Barthélemy*, V, 390.
[47] Hüffer, *Europa*, I, 191. The drawing up of the Imperial instructions was completed on October 7 (*ibid.*).

The Committee rejected the suggestion of an armistice during the proposed negotiations. Its reasons were fourfold. The princes of the Empire, delivered from the fear of invasion, would prolong the negotiations with innumerable difficulties drawn from the "labyrinth of the German constitution"; Austria would send reinforcements to Italy; the French troops would desire to return to their homes; lastly, the continuation of hostilities was conducive to the negotiation of treaties of separate peace.[48] Barthélemy added another reason. An armistice with the Empire would necessarily include the Emperor, and the Committee could not countenance the thought of an armistice with Austria.[49] It should be noted that Caillard's instructions also ordered the rejection of all armistice proposals.[50] Just why the Prussians thought France would grant an armistice to the Empire when she had refused one to them is difficult to explain except on the basis of wishful thinking. It had been Prussia's theory that she was making the Treaty of Basel not only for herself, but for all her co-states (Austria of course excepted), and Frederick William was burning with a desire to procure for the Empire something that it could not have obtained by itself — in order to justify his defection, as it were. But the Republic, which was being asked to sacrifice this "something," declined.

"France distrusts Prussia," Hardenberg wrote to his king toward the end of August. "She does not favor its good offices, either for the Empire as a whole, or even for the states of the Empire individually."[51] Interesting it is to consider, in connection with Hardenberg's observation, a document in the Archives des Affaires Etrangères. This document, signed by Barthélemy, but with the signature crossed out in different-colored ink, once read: "The French government sees with pleasure that the German Empire, fatigued by a war the cause of which becomes every day more foreign to it, has asked for the good offices of his Prussian Majesty. . ." The words, "the good offices," are deleted, and above is written, "the intervention and cooperation."[52]

Hardenberg's disillusionment was shared by his king. On August 25, Frederick William ordered the following note despatched to Hardenberg: Considering the meager likelihood of an advantageous peace, and my wish not further to embitter Austria, I do not desire the title of mediator, either of the peace treaty between France and the Empire, or of treaties between France and the individual states of Germany. I am interested only in maintaining my due influence in the Empire, and in retrieving my left-bank

[48] CPS to Barthélemy, Aug. 6, 1795, Arch. A. E., *Allemagne* 669, f. 227.
[49] Langwerth von Simmern, *Oestr. Reich fr. Rev.*, II, 198.
[50] Bailleu, *Pr. Frk.*, I, 21–22.
[51] *Ibid.*, p. 17, Aug. 26, 1795.
[52] Aug. 10, 1795, Arch. A. E., *Allemagne* 671, f. 58.

states [53] as soon as possible.[54] Thus vanished the hope of a Franco-Imperial peace through the good offices of Prussia. There remains to be considered, however, an ephemeral revival of Danish mediation.

5. THE DANISH MEDIATION

The Emperor had never intended to let the King of Prussia mediate the peace. For that matter, neither did he intend that anyone else should mediate it. In fact, there was to be no peace — yet. The request below for Danish mediation was a play to amuse the restless Diet. "Our secret interest is to draw things out and to seek means of temporizing within the forms and in the confused medley of the Germanic constitutions," wrote Thugut to Count Colloredo.[55] This attitude was no secret to Prussia. "Whether, on the whole, anything real will come of it," wrote Goertz to Frederick William from Ratisbon, "depends upon whether France will grant reasonable terms." If she should, said the Prussian minister, the states of the Empire would immediately accept them, and Austria, "truly *de mauvaise grâce*," would have to consent.[56]

Toward the end of July 1795, Baron von Ludolph, the new Austrian minister to Denmark, was ordered to sound von Bernstorff on the subject of mediation. Austria, Ludolph was instructed to say, had not yet decided to make peace on its own account, and desired therefore a neutral mediator to give effect to the Diet's *Conclusum* in favor of peace. Similar overtures were made to the Danish envoy in Vienna.[57] Denmark was asked to procure an armistice, during which she could mediate the peace at a congress to be held in Augsburg.[58]

Bernstorff welcomed the opportunity at last to be someone important, and in due time, a note was sent to France by the Danish government.

[53] Aug. 25, 1795, Bailleu, *Pr. Frk.*, I, 15–16. This was a far cry from the position of virtual *Gegenkaiser* which Frederick William had occupied in the days immediately following the Treaty of April 5 (Wahl, *Staatensystems*, p. 67). It was just one month later that Reitzenstein wrote: "Now even Herr von Hardenberg, who has always held out the most hope, doubts no longer that the French will have the Rhine as a frontier." — To Lord High Chamberlain Edelsheim of Baden, Sept. 25, 1795, *Pol. Corr. Karl Fr.*, II, 342.

[54] The King may not have been thinking only of taxes lost. Observed Elgin to Lord Grenville some two years later: "Where the French armies have been, the minds of the inhabi-

tants are much corrupted," and "the Revolution has approached too near them [the Prussian left-bank provinces] for the King not to insist upon giving them up and obtaining indemnification on the right bank." — March 10 and Feb. 20, 1798, P. R. O., F. O. 64, 48. The King probably wanted his subjects back before their minds should have become so tainted that there was danger the virus would spread to his other provinces.

[55] May 14, 1795, *Briefe Thugut*, I, 213.

[56] Quoted in Heigel, *Deutsche Geschichte*, II, 194.

[57] Sorel in *RH*, XVII, 301.

[58] Hüffer-Luckwaldt, *Quellen*, Pt. II, Vol. I, lxxxiii.

Meanwhile, however, several considerations had served to render the French more intractable. The treaty with Spain had improved the international position of the Republic. The Vendée had been subdued. Some successes had been scored in the sea war against England. The party of the natural frontiers had gained the ascendancy.[59] The result was that, on October 13, the Danish proposals were impolitely and abruptly rejected. The Committee would consent to a congress, it declared, only after the conclusion of peace, when there was no longer question of anything but arrangements concerning that peace, and of means of securing all possible advantage therefrom.[60]

Only a week before, the Diet had finally drawn up a *Schema Sessionis*, or instructions for the guidance of the Imperial peace deputation — a group consisting of the appointees of Austria, the Bavaro-Palatinate, Mayence, Baden, Saxony, Hanover, and four lesser states and cities.[61] It is to be noted that Prussia was not represented thereon. This was certainly due to Austria's influence, but as it turned out, the precaution was unnecessary. The Diet was requesting peace, and, as Mallet du Pan phrased it, the Committee confused "peace" with "submission." [62] For abject submission, even the Diet (some members excepted) was not ready — at least not any longer, for as indicated, September 24, 1795 had witnessed a turn in the fortunes of war in favor of the Emperor and Empire.[63] Wurmser, disgraced in 1793 for the disastrous defeats of December of that year, had set the pace for a new era of victory for Austria.

Great was the joy in the districts liberated from the French, and the white-coated Austrians were met by deputations of white-robed girls who threw themselves upon the soldiers' necks and smothered them with kisses of gratitude. Flowers were scattered, wreaths were hung, a poem was dedicated to the victorious host.[64] "Our successes have caused very great satisfaction in all these regions," reported Clerfayt; and he added, "I am informed that the minister of Mayence, Albini, was . . . on the point of requesting the protection of the King of Prussia to compel the acceleration of peace." [65] "We are loved, . . . we are triumphant; the Empire, despite the obstructions erected by the Prussians, owes its safety to us," exulted Dietrichstein.[66] "Hate against the Prussians and French, enthusiasm for us, is now at its zenith in

[59] Heigel, *Deutsche Geschichte*, II, 194.
[60] Hüffer-Luckwaldt, *Quellen*, Pt. II, Vol. 1, lxxxiii; A. C. Thibaudeau, *Mémoires sur la Convention et le Directoire* (2 vols., Paris, 1824), II, 117–118.
[61] Hüffer, *Europa*, I, 191.
[62] *Mém. corr.*, I, 330, Oct. 11, 1795.
[63] In August, the Emperor had approved a resolution of the Diet which urgently requested peace on the basis of the integrity of the

Empire (Lefebvre, *Fr. Rev.*, p. 441). With integrity insisted upon in the bleak days preceding Handschuhsheim, there was little chance that it would be dispensed with after that.
[64] Vivenot, *Bas. Fried.*, Pt. II, 501.
[65] To Emperor, Oct. 16, 1795, *Thugut, C, W*, pp. 293–294.
[66] To Thugut, Oct. 18, 1795, *ibid.*, p. 315.

all this region. We could make a revolution there if we wished." But Dietrichstein, like Clerfayt, was obliged to add something respecting Albini: "Albini . . . excels only in treasons; his elector has dared, through him, to invite, one by one, all the deputies of the circles, to induce the anterior circles to address themselves to him to compel the Emperor to make peace, and if his Majesty should refuse, himself to make peace with France. . . . Albini was on the point of going to Basel with Secretary of Legation Ott, . . . but Hardenberg wrote from Basel that peace prospects were not bright — that we [the Austrians] were retarding them." [67] Most interesting, however, is Dietrichstein's statement that he believed the Electors of Saxony, Hanover, the Palatinate, Cologne, "even Brandenburg," were ashamed of their conduct and "beginning to fear us." [68] However, a few days later Dietrichstein reported that the Bavaro-Palatine Elector had threatened to make a separate peace with France if Austria showed herself severe with Mannheim. "I imagine all our success will make him think that over twice," declared Dietrichstein,[69] and 21,105 projectiles were shot into the city. It surrendered — the third that was not in ashes — on November 22.[70] A grim lesson had been taught to traitors, but the last page of that lesson belongs to the period of the Executive Directory, for the Convention had ceased to exist on October 26, 1795.

[67] Same report, *ibid.*, pp. 318, 322–323.
[68] *Ibid.*, p. 324.

[69] To Thugut, Oct. 21, 1795, *ibid.*, p. 334.
[70] Vivenot, *Bas. Fried.*, Pt. II, 498.

CHAPTER XIV

THE LEFT BANK AFTER THE TREATY OF BASEL

I. IN GENERAL

*I*T will be recalled that, during the negotiation of the Treaty of April 5, Hardenberg had insisted that nowhere in the Treaty should the cession of the left bank be mentioned. One reason for his attitude was that he had hoped the cession could somehow be avoided. In April 1795, the extension of France's boundaries to the Rhine had not yet become a national dogma. An important segment of French opinion known as the party of the *anciennes limites* (former boundaries) was opposed to expansion. Most Prussians expected, therefore, that France would refrain from insisting upon a cession of territory which would, in all likelihood, sow the seeds of discord for all time.[1]

On April 10, 1795, Hardenberg wrote to the King that it seemed to him more and more probable that the French would eventually renounce the left bank of the Rhine.[2] In his reply ten days later, the King mentioned the moderate tendencies then prevalent in France, and the possibility that the French would give up their designs on the Rhineland;[3] and his instructions to Hardenberg on April 27 and May 3 set the renunciation of the left bank by France as the goal for which the Minister should strive the hardest.[4] But while King and Minister were very anxious for the Rhineland to return to the Empire, it is interesting to note that, were it ever to come to a choice, they preferred the Committee to the Emperor as the ruler of the left bank. Hardenberg's despatch of April 20 expressed the fear that, considering the weakened state of France, Austria would conquer the left bank.[5] That

---

[1] Bailleu, *Pr. Frk.*, I, xi.
[2] *Ibid.*, p. 1.
[3] April 20, 1795, *ibid.*
[4] *Ibid.*, p. 3.
[5] *Ibid.*, pp. 1–2. Marshal Clerfayt and General

Wurmser, with their Austro-Imperial forces, did conquer all the region between the Rhine and lower Moselle during the latter part of 1795 (Vivenot, *Bas. Fried.*, Pt. II, 497).

would be worse than having France there! This attitude explains why the revolutionists were able to run amuck in the Empire. Their victims hated and feared each other more than they did the declared enemy.

2. THE LEFT-BANK ÉMIGRÉ PROBLEM

We have seen how *émigrés* had been created on the left bank out of all absent persons, and that Roberjot and Dubois, on March 24, 1795, had endeavored to bring a little reason into the emigration regulations for the northern Rhineland. The Representatives, it will be recalled, had drawn a distinction (loosely speaking) between political, religious, and aristocratically minded *émigrés* on the one hand, and, on the other, those whose physical bodies were indeed outside the country but whose sentiments were either friendly or indifferent to the French occupation, and whose interests were not intrinsically antagonistic to those of France. The latter group might return within forty days and receive their property back.[6]

This decree had an important effect, in so far as the second class above was concerned. Very many *émigrés* returned and received their property back within the next few months. Dubois reported on April 20 that already almost all of the Aix emigrants had returned. On April 16, in Cologne, the sale of emigrants' furniture was suddenly discontinued, and a far milder emigration decree — that prevailing in the Brabant — was introduced. It took only a few weeks for all the Crefeld emigrants to be back under their own roofs.[7]

This was all very fine for those belonging to group "two," above. But what about group "one"? What, particularly, about group "one" in the Prussian territories?

On April 24, Hardenberg remitted a note to Barthélemy, with a formal complaint against the measures of rigor being perpetrated in the Rhineland, in so far as they applied to Meurs, Clèves, and Gelderland. Some of the inhabitants had left the Prussian left-bank states, he declared, to take refuge in the right-bank portion of the King's domains; others — such as the members of the colleges of the provinces, who had removed to the right bank on the express command of the monarch — had left in order to continue the official functions with which they were invested. Both classes of persons had been dubbed *émigrés*. Hardenberg argued that since the status of the provinces would not be determined until the definitive peace with the Empire (according to Article V of the Treaty of April 5), the *status quo* should be maintained in good faith, domanial and individual property should be

---

[6] *Supra*, chap. vii, § 3.   [7] Hansen, *Quellen*, III, 452, n. 1.

respected, and *émigrés* should not be created for the simple act of going to another part of the same kingdom.[8]

The attitude of Roberjot and Dubois is in this respect very interesting, and displays in bold outline the error of those who think to find the German policy of the Convention in the acts of the Paris government alone. On March 24 (the very day of the above-quoted decree), the Committee informed the Representatives that persons who had absented themselves from the Prussian left bank either before or after the entry of the French troops were not to be considered as *émigrés*.[9] Result? Nothing. The Representatives could not or would not regard the order from Paris as anything but a mere expression of opinion, to be accepted or rejected as they saw fit. The Committee repeated its order a month later (April 21);[10] but it was only on April 30 that a decree of Dubois "temporarily" authorized the return, with full enjoyment of their real and personal property, of those inhabitants of the Prussian left bank who had moved to the right-bank states of the King.[11]

In *thermidor* of the Year III (July–August 1795), Roberjot rendered account to the Convention of his mission in the conquered territory. "We likewise believed it to be our duty," he said, "to direct public opinion and to regulate the conduct of the administrations by promulgating a decree on the 4 *germinal* [March 24] which designated those who should be considered as *émigrés*. One must have crossed these lands and heard the reasons given for the absence of some of the inhabitants to be able to judge of the necessity and importance of decrees on the question of emigration."[12] These vague expressions should not, however, cause one to forget that the whole purpose of applying the emigration laws to the conquered territories was to benefit the position of the French *fiscus*, and if one made too many exceptions, the whole purpose would be lost. Therefrom, the resistance of the Representatives to the Committee's orders.

3. GLOOM SETTLES ON THE PRUSSIAN LEFT BANK

Prussia's protests regarding the treatment of her left-bank possessions were so insistent that Dubois felt himself obliged, when promulgating the decree of April 30 cancelling the indiscriminate creation of *émigrés*, to announce a respite in the levy of contributions in Gelderland, Meurs, and Clèves, and to order that no requisitions in excess of the indispensable needs of the army should be levied there.[13] Nothing could have been farther from the Committee's intentions. "The spirit of Article V of the Treaty of Peace con-

[8] Arch. N., AF III 76, d. 314, March 24, 1795.   [11] *Ibid.*, pp. 229–230.
[9] *Papiers de Barthélemy*, V, 194.   [12] Arch. A. E., *Allemagne* 669, f. 253.
[10] *Ibid.*, pp. 194–195.   [13] *Papiers de Barthélemy*, V, 229.

cluded the 16 *germinal* [April 5] between the Republic and the King of Prussia," it wrote to Dubois on May 7, "is that, until the general pacification, the states of Clèves, Meurs, and Gelderland, conquered from the Prussian government, ought to remain in the same condition they were in before the Treaty. . . Thus, there exists no doubt that these lands ought to remain subject to requisitions and contributions, as before the Peace; however, all the moderation necessitated by the good understanding between the Republic and Prussia should be exercised. . . Of the three provisions of your . . . decree [of April 30], only the third, i.e., the one concerning absent persons, should be definitively maintained. We leave it to your prudence to manifest all the consideration necessary to avoid arousing discontent while you employ the measures incidental to the reëstablishment of requisitions and contributions." [14] This was, of course, an order to violate Article IV of the Treaty of April 5, which guaranteed all the Prussian territory (which included the Prussian left bank) against contributions. Incidentally, the Committee also affirmed that there was "no doubt that the assignats should continue to circulate, and that you should repress severely every obstacle which it is sought to oppose thereto." [15] It appears that a good deal of repressing was going to be necessary, for, as Dubois had written to Paris, "the inhabitants of the states of Gelderland, Clèves, and Meurs regard themselves as, from this time forward, returned to the Prussians; . . . they refuse absolutely to accept the assignats; . . . this example is very baleful for the entire region." [16]

It would be an injustice to the Committee should we fail to point out that necessity compelled it to violate the above Article IV. Indeed, the violation did not last. In the early days of June, when Reubell was presiding over the Committee, that body, in deciding that a new contribution should be levied on the left bank north of the Moselle, stipulated that the heretofore-Prussian territories should be exempted.[17] How ill the Republic could afford such generosity will appear from the following.

On June 13, Pérès, newly arrived Representative to the Sambre and Meuse Army, decreed a contribution of 22,000,000 livres for the area under his jurisdiction, to be paid in coin, or in assignats at the rate of exchange prevailing on the Amsterdam Bourse. Inasmuch as hardly an eighth of the previous contribution of 8,000,000 (originally 25,000,000, but reduced) had been paid, Pérès really decreed the payment of a total of well-nigh 30,000,000 livres. The protests were immediate and loud. The Central Administration at Aix accused Pérès of having acted before he had become acquainted with

[14] *Ibid.*, p. 230.
[15] *Ibid.*
[16] To CPS, April 30, Hansen, *Quellen*, III, 497,

n. 1.
[17] June 4, 1795, *ibid.*, p. 532.

the potentialities of the region, and without having asked the opinion of the local constituted authorities. Pérès wrote the Committee that the Aix administration was going to repair to Paris to protest, but that he thought he could obtain the money if he did not yield.[18]

The Committee advised Pérès to hold firm. However, when several district administrations and the National Agent to Bonn voted to join in the march on Paris, the Committee weakened, and sought advice from the experienced Gillet and Roberjot. Gillet wrote: Cut the amount down considerably. Roberjot replied: These people are in the grip of deep despair; you promised them no more contributions; either keep your promise or you will have your troops in the midst of enemies instead of among brothers.[19] But the Aix deputies, having arrived in Paris, surprisingly offered to pay, in composition for Pérès' imposition, 10,000,000 in provisions. Meanwhile, Dubois, present on the local scene, had cut the 22,000,000 to 3,000,000 in coin, and 19,000,000 in agricultural products (July 15).[20] The very next day, the Committee, accepting the Aix deputies' offer, decreed the above 10,000,000 in (army) provisions, and again stipulated that the Prussian left bank was to be exempt.[21] Subsequently, to be sure that matters were sufficiently complicated and incomprehensible, it also approved Dubois' action.[22] This restored the 22,000,000-livre levy which the Committee had recognized as excessive by reducing it.

However, it did not really matter. The 10,000,000 itself was too far above the ability of the ravaged country to pay — especially with the Prussian territory exempted — to constitute any more than a mere figure on paper. But the Committee did not go back on its word with respect to the Prussian territory. How the Directory will view this act of alleviation is another story.[23]

Frederick William seems to have felt a genuine concern for the welfare of his left-bank states. It was probably a selfish concern. It was not absolutely certain that the region would not be returned to him some day. Especially was he grieved when the Central Administration at Aix-la-Chapelle, desiring to show favor to the regions in its immediate neighborhood, connived at the ruin of the Prussian territories. On May 8, the King wrote to Hardenberg that he believed the Treaty of April 5 granted him the right to demand that the civil administration of the Prussian left bank should

[18] *Ibid.*, pp. 533–534. Pérès to CPS, June 18, *ibid.*, p. 533.

[19] *Ibid.*, pp. 532–534.

[20] Rp Gillet to Louvet of CPS, Aug. 11, Aulard, *Actes*, XXVI, 328. Hansen thinks it was cut to 3,000,000 in agricultural products, which is wrong (*Quellen*, III, 532–538).

[21] July 16, 1795, Aulard, *Actes*, XXV, 462.

[22] Gillet to Louvet, Aug. 11, Aulard, *Actes*, XXVI, 328.

[23] "The favor accorded them . . . singles them out . . . in the collection of the new imposition. . ." — *Infra*, Pt. II, chap. v, § 1.

be committed to persons of his own choosing; that this was the only means of tranquillizing the people and of preventing them from committing reprisals against the French for their excesses.[24] The King renounced, however, all thought of collecting any part of the revenues of his left-bank states, desiring only, so he declared, to prevent further injustices and the total ruin of his subjects. His wish was to send two persons selected by himself to place the provinces on a tolerable interimistic footing.[25]

This request was forwarded to Paris by Barthélemy on May 22, with the Ambassador's own reflection that "if we grant the wish . . . for a provisional Prussian administration, from that instant the King of Prussia will send wheat into these territories to feed the inhabitants. . . Without doubt . . . we would be able to obtain grain for ourselves [also]."[26] Barthélemy suggested the generalization of the measure so as to include the whole Rhineland, in the hope that the left-bank rulers, who would thus be recalled, would shower the region with provisions.[27]

The Committee rendered its decision on June 4. The despatch to Barthélemy which embodied the answer was drawn up with revolutionary abruptness:

Our response will be simple.

In the discussions which preceded the Treaty of Peace of 16 *germinal* [April 5], the King of Prussia formally demanded that the civil administration of the states in question should be conserved to him until the definitive arrangements relative to the left bank of the Rhine had been made.

We rejected the proposition.

The King of Prussia did not return thereto.

In this state of affairs the peace was signed.

Certainly there can be no doubt in anyone's mind that the civil administration of the states of Gelderland, Meurs, and Clèves should remain in the hands of the French Republic.[28]

The abruptness of the reply could not destroy the desire of the suffering populations of the Prussian left bank to be freed from their "liberators." The news of the Treaty of April 5 — at first received with great joy (as mentioned above) [29] — had plunged them into the deepest gloom when they learned the occupation was to continue.[30] City and country protested against union with France. Deputies of the noble estate from Clèves, Meurs, and Gelderland despatched an urgent message to Frederick William affirming

[24] To induce the Republic to yield, the civil servants of the Prussian territories did what they could to place obstacles in the way of the French — aided and abetted by the Prussian government (Hashagen, *Rheinland*, p. 99).

[25] *Papiers de Barthélemy*, V, 290.
[26] Barthélemy to CPS, *ibid.*, p. 285.
[27] *Ibid.*, p. 286.
[28] *Ibid.*, pp. 317–318.
[29] Chap. ix, § 3g.
[30] Hansen, *Quellen*, III, 493.

their undying devotion to his dynasty, and beseeching that the Prussian left bank be not renounced; and they sent two deputations to Berlin to plead their cause personally. Haugwitz and the King gave assurances that there had never been any intention of ceding the provinces, and expressed appreciation of the loyalty of his Majesty's trans-Rhenish subjects.[31]

4. LITTLE FOOD, LESS MONEY, BUT NO DEARTH OF RUMORS

On July 3, as indicated above,[32] the Diet rendered its *Conclusum* in favor of peace, but neither Austria nor France was peace-minded. Austria was not because the seesaw of war had raised her high off the ground and left her dangling helplessly in mid-air; France was not largely because she was penniless and hungry and wanted to eat at her neighbor's table. The Republic must not be condemned too much for this, for both the Rhine[33] armies were in desperate straits. North of the Moselle, the left bank, sole support of the Sambre and Meuse Army for eight months, was so exhausted that "vigorous and extraordinary measures" had to be used to procure the barest of subsistence (and this cost the Republic seven to eight times the value of what it obtained, according to Treasury Agent Hertzog).[34] In the domain of the Rhine and Moselle Army, things were quite as bad. Wrote Representatives Merlin of Thionville, Cavaignac, and Rivaud, "We, here, are without resources and in the most desperate and despairing state. . . All the coffers are empty. In the name of our fatherland, answer us, and come to the aid of our defenders."[35] On May 15, Merlin of Douai replied in a personal note already once quoted in part: "We are indeed in a terrible state. Independent of the penury of subsistence from which we always suffer, we lack coin. . ."[36] And the Committee answered: "It is a general principle of war that armies should live at the expense of enemy country. . . Make the [Rhineland] . . . furnish all possible subsistence. When you will have crossed the Rhine, heavy contributions should be imposed, both in provisions and in coin. . ."[37]

Something, indeed had to be done, and done quickly.[38] The troops were getting out of hand. In Aix-la-Chapelle and Trèves, soldiers repeatedly

---

[31] Hashagen, *Rheinland*, pp. 97–98.

[32] Chap. xiii, § 4.

[33] Technically, of course, the Sambre and Meuse Army was not a Rhine Army. Actually, however, it had become one by turning southeast after Austria's evacuation of Belgium, and remaining on the left bank of the Rhine.

[34] Hansen, *Quellen*, III, 476, n. 2.

[35] *Ibid.*, p. 517, n. 1.

[36] *Supra*, chap. x, § 1. Addressed to Merlin-Th.

[37] Aulard, *Actes*, XXIII, 197–198. Rivaud wrote repeatedly in June and July of the "alarming distress," and told how the army on the middle Rhine kept alive by plainly seizing food from the local populations, without paying therefor: the troops had no money with which they could pay (Hansen, *Quellen*, III, 538).

[38] The crossing of the Rhine had been contemplated since April (*ibid.*, p. 613).

robbed farmers going to market of their produce because no one would sell the troops anything for assignats. There were similar occurrences in Cologne. A soldier was killed at Aix for trying to steal butter and vegetables. A spirit of pillage understandably possessed the troops.[39] In Trèves, almost every night without exception, the French soldiers in the Palace-hospital would swarm into the gardens of the inhabitants, steal the produce, and return to their beds. As many as nine soldiers were said to have been beaten to death in gardens. At Kürenz and Euren, there were clashes between soldiers and the owners of plundered cherry trees. On July 25, the inhabitants were forbidden to go out of their houses with guns, and they were further forbidden to beat Frenchmen.[40]

July 27, 1795, was the anniversary of Robespierre's fall. An imposing celebration was scheduled at Aix-la-Chapelle. Representative Meynard made a speech to the assembled troops, and ended with the usual *"Vive la République."* But the troops did not *vive* back. They were dissatisfied. The food they received was insufficient; the money they received could not be used to buy victuals to supplement their diet. The unrest increased when, at a ball the same night, there were angry words between Meynard and the officers. On July 29, on orders from Meynard, the soldiers' already meager bread rations were reduced. The reduction was probably due to scarcity, but some of the troops considered it an act of punishment. They complained to Meynard that they could not subsist on so little bread. Meynard ordered two ounces of biscuits added. This would have availed little. The soldiers rejected the bread altogether, and added menaces to their complaints. Meynard ordered the arrest of a corporal of the grenadiers who had "insulted and threatened the national representation." This was the spark which set off the real conflagration. All day long the rioting raged. There were several wounded, but no fatalities — at least, not until the court-martial handed down its verdict: six to be shot; eleven to serve two years' imprisonment. *Vive la République.*[41]

It seems that the Germans of the left bank, and some of the right, based real hope of peace on this destitution of the French armies, and indeed their reasoning was not too farfetched. With no money to buy food, the French had no money to procure boats to cross the Rhine, either. But they wanted desperately to cross, and demanded 200,000 livres of the Cologne Senate, on account of Cologne's share of past unpaid contributions. The Senate manifested much zeal, but produced no money. Next day three Representatives, Gillet, Joubert, and Dubois, summoned the merchants and bankers of the city, and renewed the demand. Again much show of zeal, but no money.

[39] *Ibid.*, p. 548, n. 4.   562, n. 1.
[40] Müller's *Tagebuch*, in Hansen, *Quellen*, III,   [41] *Journal du canonnier Bricard*, pp. 163–171.

Then Representative Meynard cut down the amount asked to 100,000 livres, and approached the clerical deputies. The clergy demanded the redress of their grievances: specifically, a reapportionment in their favor of the contributions,[42] and the return of certain church property. Meynard agreed. The clergy produced the 100,000 livres. (It was with 61,800 livres of this money that the French crossed the Rhine at Eichelskamp and Düsseldorff on the night of September 5–6.) [43]

Other hopes of peace were based on the Prussian-intervention provisions of the Treaty of April 5, embroidered with rumors coming from Paris [44] and from Switzerland. According to one report, dated at Basel, July 22, Hardenberg was momentarily expected there. He would immediately commence negotiations with Barthélemy for peace between France and the entire Empire. An armistice would probably be the first fruit. The report was published by a Cologne paper,[45] which followed it a few days later with this: "Several letters from Bonn affirm that Representative Dubois has informed the [district] administration there that the conflict between the French Republic and the German Empire has by this time been fully terminated. The conditions of peace themselves are very anxiously awaited." [46] Representative Meynard, in belying this rumor, took the opportunity to lay to rest yet another — that the Committee had announced its opposition to the annexation of the Meuse-to-Rhine region.[47]

One wild tale which certainly had its origin in wishful thinking of a very fundamental and functional sort had the Prince-Elector of Cologne shipping 72,000 bushels of grain to Frankfort for delivery to his subjects upon France's expected withdrawal from the left bank. Another story had the Prince-Elector of Trèves ready to distribute 2,000 taler and 2,000 gulden to the poor and the clergy of his territory. And food was fed to these rumors by the order of Prince-Elector Max Franz of Cologne to certain of his superior officials that they gather near the yet-occupied Electorate so as

[42] In the course of 1795, various summary regulations had established the rule that, in contributions, the clergy would be assessed six tenths; the nobility, three tenths; and the third estate, one tenth (Hansen, *Quellen*, III, 291, n. 2). Truly, on April 5, 1795, the Central Administration at Aix had decreed that there should be equality in taxation between the three estates (*ibid.*, p. 427, n. 1). But that was theory, not practice (*ibid.*, p. 622, n. 1).

[43] Meynard to CPS, Aug. 24, 1795, *ibid.*, pp. 598–599. Meynard learned from this experience what real poverty meant, and he unfolded to the Committee a plan for establish-

ing an emergency fund of 200,000 to 300,000 livres: One could levy, upon those religious houses which had emigrated and returned, an emergency contribution based on the privilege of reëntering into possession of their own property (*ibid.*, p. 600).

[44] Sent in by Dumont, one of Cologne's burgomasters, from Paris, *ibid.*, pp. 494, 561. *Vide infra*, n. 67, this chapter.

[45] *Stadtkölnische Kurier*, Aug. 8, Hansen, *Quellen*, III, 561, n. 1.

[46] Aug. 12, *ibid.*, p. 592, n. 3.

[47] To Central Administration at Aix, Aug. 15, *ibid.*, p. 592.

to be close at hand when the French should leave. Max Franz also ordered to be adapted to Cologne's needs the decree released by the Prince-Elector of Mayence when that prince recovered his lost "Key of Germany" in 1793.[48] And then there was the unheralded presence of numerous bailiffs and other officials of the former rulers who infiltrated the administrative services of the Rhineland, and insinuated that return to the Empire was imminent.[49]

Needless to say, all these facts and fancies created a state of tension in the Rhineland, heightened by overbold news items unfavorable to French arms.[50] Caselli, National Agent to the Central Administration at Aix-la-Chapelle, tried to quiet the frayed nerves by a circular letter addressed to the National Agents to the district administrations. One of these letters, found by the present writer in the Prussian archives, was arranged in parallel columns of German and French, the latter of vicious orthography. It reads:

Persons corrupted by the poisonous breath of servitude are overrunning the country. They are seeking to persuade the credulous inhabitants that the territory conquered by our prodigious bravery will have its arrogant masters as its rulers again. They go further: They affirm that the Electors, those shades of pretended sovereign power, will accord indemnities to all citizens who have suffered losses; they pretend, those impudent liars, to feel compassion, whereas they have compassion only for themselves. They are asking the agriculturist, the artisan, [and] all simple men, for a list of the losses they have suffered, whether in furniture, domesticated animals, vegetables, etc. They are promising them, with that perfidy akin to slavery, an indemnity equal to the said losses. They are promising, and they have neither means, nor good faith - - - - [sic]. The knaves! they are talking thus only to discourage the people, whom we have ranged under our aegis. . .

The English and Austrians are then declared to be responsible, and the peasants are advised to seize those who try to seduce them. If they (the peasants) have any wrongs which need redressing, let them appeal to the courts, the decisions of which will restore security and confidence.[51]

Merlin of Thionville also released a proclamation, but not for two months, and it was typically Merlinian: "We, Representative of the French People

[48] Ibid., p. 521, n. 1. The projected electoral decree forgave acts performed under duress, restored sequestered property, and provided for a commission to investigate the loyalty of those who had served under the French (ibid., pp. 547–548).

[49] Merlin-Th., "Proclamation to the Peoples of the Left Bank of the Rhine," September 1795, ibid., p. 593, n. 2.

[50] The editor of the Cologne Welt- und Staats-both wrote in his paper that some French

troops had crossed the Rhine at Weil and met with such a reception that no more crossed. Pichegru ordered the editor arrested and conducted on a tour of the Rhineland to convince him that the military situation was not unfavorable to France. The editor was obliged to write a retraction, and pay one third the cost of his enforced excursion (ibid., pp. 548–549).

[51] Arch. A. E., Prusse Supp. 10, f. 242, July 5, 1795.

and Commissioner[52] to the Armies of the Republic, authorized by the National Convention, do declare in the name of the Republic that these rumors are the effect of malevolence, that the French nation, always generous and just, will never abandon peoples who have shown themselves so worthy of liberty. . . [An] investigation will be conducted among the bailiffs and former municipal officers, . . . and justice will be done [the guilty] . . . according to the rigor of the laws."[53]

5. THE ESSAY CONTEST

It will be recalled[54] that Merlin of Thionville, on May 12, 1795, advocated renunciation of the left bank, and that Sieyes, on his return from Holland, indicated that the sentiment toward renunciation was quite general, and that he would (reluctantly) join the majority. It was this willingness of the French to renounce, after they had instigated many Mayençais to treason, which so agitated ex-Professor A. J. Hofmann, president of the Paris Club of Mayence Patriots.[55] Merlin, especially, had promised the Mayençais quislings that France would never lay down its arms until the freedom of Mayence had been assured; and when the Prussians were already encircling the city, Merlin had pressed the Mayençais for a vote on union with France — and obtained it.

In July 1795, minds at Paris were still undecided whether to keep or to renounce, and Hofmann tried to influence the decision by influencing Merlin, whose opinion was much respected. Now, as it happens, Merlin had held firmly to his May 12 decision just eight days, and fourteen days later was his old reckless self once more.[56] But much damage had already been done, and Hofmann hoped to undo at least part of it. On July 21, he wrote to Merlin a very bitter letter. Morally, he said, Merlin was bound to advocate French absorption of Mayence after having enticed him (Hofmann) into an act which had cost him his fortune, his station in life, and his health. Politically, he said, Merlin's position — that keeping the Rhineland would be injurious to France's interests — was untenable. He asked Merlin if the sale and purchase of human flesh entered into his calculations, as it had in those of his (France's) kings. "Answer my questions . . . as friend to friend and I will say to the enemies of the French . . . that

[52] It seems silly to have to remind Merlin that since April 11, 1793, he was no longer "Commissioner" but "Representative on Mission."

[53] Hansen, *Quellen*, III, 593, n. 2.

[54] *Supra*, Chap. x, § 2.

[55] Hofmann had escaped from Mayence after its capitulation by attaching himself to Merlin of Thionville's party. He had been given employment at Paris as head of the Alien Office in the Ministry of Police. He was on a mission to England during 1794 and part of 1795 (Hansen, *Quellen*, III, 554, n. 1).

[56] *Vide supra*, chap. x, n. 23.

there is yet one of them [i.e., one Frenchman] who does not partake of their perfidy." [57]

One of Hofmann's questions concerned the ideas expressed in a pamphlet published by General Miranda on July 2, 1795. Miranda, it will be recalled, had published anonymously, on February 25, a little work on the Rhine-boundary question which was highly esteemed.[58] His latest contribution elucidated his plan of a frontier reinforced with several new forts and re-quiring, for its effectiveness, the annexation only of the region between the Moselle and Saar, up to Conz. Miranda declared that annexation of the left bank, in whole or in part, would create unrest in the Empire and in Europe, and he warned France to renounce the "vain glory of having extended the boundaries of France." [59]

A few voices in France were yet raised in July 1795 in favor of an inde-pendent republic (or republics) on the left bank, with local option as to exact form of government; [60] and one can see from Hofmann's letter that this would not have been to him an unwelcome alternative. It was the true wish of those two other German republicans, Franz Theodor Biergans [61] and the already-mentioned [62] Johann Baptist Geich,[63] who, while crusading

---

[57] *Corr. Merlin-Th.*, II, 60.

[58] *Vide supra*, chap. vii, § 6.

[59] *Opinion du général Miranda sur la situa-tion actuelle de la France et sur les remèdes convenables à ses maux* (Paris, 1795), in Hansen, *Quellen*, III, 574, n. 2.

[60] So wrote J. N. Dumont to Cologne Senate, July 14, 1795, *ibid.*, p. 561.

[61] Born in 1768, of wealthy parents, at Alden-hoven, near Jülich. Through the influence of his mother, he entered the monastery of Schwarzenbroich, in the neighborhood of the Netherlands. Leaving the monastery, he joined the Austrian army and fought the Turks at Belgrade, then deserted. The vicar-general of Cologne secured his reëntrance to Schwarzenbroich. Here, Biergans wrote a poem urging the revolting Belgians to sub-mit to Austria. He became a priest in 1793, and when the French armies came in 1794 and dissolved, sacked, and destroyed the monastery, he was freed of his vows. He became a political propagandist, publishing the *Brutus oder der Tyrannenfeind* in Cologne and Aix. This pro-French thrice-monthly paper, extremely dull and in bad taste, attacked the Cologne Senate so vicious-ly and coarsely that Cologne secured Bier-gans' arrest. Biergans himself had supplied the handle: he published anonymously a

pro-Austrian poem, probably the one men-tioned above. He was treated very badly in the Cologne prison, being housed with the worst criminals. Freed by the French National Agent, Biergans went to Aix, where he published *Brutus der Freie*, of slight political import, for a few months. Biergans' activity as publicist ended in May 1796 (*ibid.*, I, 588 *et seqq.*; III, 16 *, 724, 780).

[62] Chap. i, § 2m, and n. 160.

[63] Born, or rather baptized, on May 15, 1767, in Cologne, Geich was the son of a master tailor. He received his Bachelor of Arts degree from the University of Cologne, studied theology, and became a priest in 1790. As catechist at a Cologne college, he became personally acquainted with several Bonn professors holding advanced princi-ples, among them Eulogius Schneider. This connection it was, plus Geich's own ad-vanced principles, that kept him from get-ting a university post. Turning to the field of publicity, he put out the *Pharos für Aeonen* ("Beacon for Æons") from January to August 1794. In February 1795, he sup-ported the Bonn District Administration in a pamphlet directed at Cologne. Not long after, he went to Paris to take a normal school course, thinking to become a teacher

for annexation of the Rhineland to France, would much have preferred that France should merely constitute herself protectress of an independent German republic. However, the small number of German republicans, especially between the Meuse and Rhine, and the great influence of the nobles and clergy there, seemed to render formation of such a republic impossible.[64]

Portiez of the Oise, in his report to the Convention (August 14) on his mission to the conquered left bank, rejected the idea of an independent republic because, said he, a civil war would break out when the French withdrew. And since return of the region to its tyrants was unthinkable, there was no other course than annexation. Besides, it was contrary to the integrity of the nation to refuse an annexation sought in the name of the people. This report was greeted with great applause, and ordered printed and widely disseminated.[65] This, certainly, was to Hofmann's liking.

August 1795 witnessed the publication also of Roberjot's report on the left bank, written in consequence of the mission entrusted to him the preceding *ventôse* (February–March 1795). Roberjot, too, pronounced himself for annexation, because, said he, such was the desire of the majority of the inhabitants:

They want to associate themselves with the French to partake of their future prosperity. Exceedingly perspicacious respecting the advantages . . . of reunion, calculating the effects of liberty of commerce and the consequences of the encouragement rendered to industry and the arts, they are convinced that they have all to gain by being French.[66]

It was this custom of presenting the wish of the speaker as the wish of the people, which so irked the "Paris-domiciled" [67] burgomaster of Cologne, J. N. Dumont: "It is amazing," wrote he, ". . . that . . . the possible wish of the Belgians and Liégeois to be united with France is always regarded as if it were the wish of the Rhinelanders, who certainly did not give and could not give the mandate to make this declaration. In accordance with

---

consecrated to French absorption of the Rhineland. The school closed. Geich could not go back to Cologne, so went to Bonn, to establish a newspaper dedicated to annexation. He gave it the name of a former newspaper not published since 1794, the Bonn *Intelligenzblatt* — to appear twice every *décade*. The Bonn government agreed to subsidize it. Geich also established a *Dekadenschrift*. The former paper lasted until July 1796; the latter, only until November 1795 (*ibid.*, I, 508; III, 22 *, 28–29, 566–70, 780).

[64] *Ibid.*, pp. 568–569.

[65] *Ibid.*, p. 592, n. 3.

[66] "Rapport fait à la Convention nationale par Roberjot sur sa mission dans les pays conquis par les armées du Nord et de Sambre-et-Meuse, thermidor, an III," *Moniteur*, XXV, 634 (Sept. 4, 1795).

[67] Having come to Paris to protest against subordination to the authority of Bonn, and against the contributions, Dumont remained to protest against almost everything — well-nigh daily. There was, indeed, no dearth of acts demanding censure, and Dumont was brilliant in criticism.

preconceived principles, people certainly have the right, in legal and orderly assembly, . . . to declare their will; and when, where, were these [people] . . . assembled? . . . Who can take upon himself to express the unheard, unasked will? Certainly not France's officials on the recommendation and entreaty of some disaffected persons. There are disaffected persons everywhere. . ." [68]

Dumont must have been exceedingly interested in the second of two reasons for annexation reported by private letters from Paris as being of great moment to many persons in the capital. The two reasons were: (1) it was patently not in France's interest to yield the natural barrier of the Rhine because, without that barrier, the Republic could not consolidate its position; (2) France had promised freedom to the Meuse-to-Rhine region, and could not return it to its former owners without breaking its word, or, at least, without having first obtained the inhabitants' consent.[69] It was just this little matter of consent that riled the Burgomaster of Cologne, and he must certainly have remarked to himself: no consent necessary to be annexed; only not to be annexed.

Incidentally — and Professor Hofmann would certainly support this affirmation with jutting jaw — the Meuse-to-Rhine region was not the only district to which France had offered freedom, and was under obligation to honor her word.

On August 7 there appeared, in P. L. Roederer and Corrancier's *Journal de Paris*, an offer of 4,000 and 2,000 francs, respectively, for the two best essays on "Is It in the Interest of the French Republic to Extend Its Boundaries to the Banks of the Rhine?" [70] This was too much for Hofmann — to present as a moot question a matter whose decision was sealed by his dis-

---

[68] To Cologne Senate, Aug. 18, Hansen, *Quellen*, III, 577, n. 2. "You have not the slightest idea how many members of the Convention there are who naïvely believe that these regions are asking for annexation, whereas everyone in Germany knows the contrary to be true. They [the French] rely upon the claims and entreaties of the German *émigrés* who are here, and who give out their opinions and their desires as those of the inhabitants. It is almost as though the [French] *émigrés* would advance their opinions and wishes as the voice of the French nation, for they also want, not only to return, but to overthrow the present constitution of their country." — Gervinus to Hardenberg, Oct. 14, 1795, Bailleu, *Pr. Frk.*, I, 411–412.

[69] *Stadtkölnische Kurier*, Aug. 14, Hansen,

Quellen, III, 592, n. 3.

[70] The identity of the donor of the prize money was not divulged, and many writers have set down their speculations as fact. Hansen, after much research, believes he has found the answer. It was, says he, almost certainly Johann Georg Friedrich List of Basel, an ex-councillor to the Palatine exchequer and member of the Illuminati, who had fled to Switzerland in 1787 to escape prosecution by Elector Karl Theodor. A document in the Mayence archives, cited by Hansen, indicates that List paid both the prize money and the cost of publishing thirty of the essays. In Basel, List served as a business executive and unpaid agent of France (*Quellen*, III, 586, n. 3; *vide*, also, *infra*, Pt. II, chap. viii).

grace and exile two years before. He wrote an open letter to the *Journal*. Unless, said he, the proposed question meant to weigh the merits of an- nexation as against those of a system of dependent republics, such a question must have been proposed by an imbecile. It was equivalent, he said, to asking if one should close his door when he goes to sleep, so as to exclude possible disturbers. Or it was proposed by an ignoramus, or a dupe — and Hofmann railed on, casting aspersions as he went. Finally, he offered a prize of 4,000 livres to anyone who could prove that it was *not* in the interest of the French Republic either to extend its boundaries to the Rhine, or to form a separate republic on the left bank, under French protection.[71]

The *Journal* published Hofmann's letter, treating it with cold irony. In the course of his reply, Roederer expressed his belief that the Belgian and Dutch Netherlands should be free and independent under French protection. The left bank of the Rhine he mentioned not at all.[72]

Hofmann immediately sent in a reply, but Roederer's partner, Corrancier, declined to publish it. Roederer did, however, reply personally, but with no reference to the issue at hand. So Hofmann published a pamphlet "Con- cerning the New Boundaries of the French Republic, by Citizen Hofmann, in Reply to Citizen Roederer." Therein Hofmann says: France annexed the free Rheno-Germans in 1793. How can she now ask — as the essay-question does — if it is in her interest to annex them? That should have been deter- mined first. He makes a plea for a system of politics based on morality. France is bound by her word, he says, whether she now thinks annexation is in her interest or not. But he maintains that it *is* in her interest. Only the Rhine affords France a satisfactory eastern frontier.[73]

Quite aside from the vitriolic attacks of Hofmann, the contest did not have easy sledding. The *Moniteur* did not want to announce the competi- tion at all, suspecting that the *émigrés* were behind it. This paper published a glowing account of the natural wealth of the Rhineland, "which has re- ceived as a gift from Nature all the products which she has denied us. . . That is the country concerning which we are asked if it is to our advantage to retain it." [74] Apparently the *Moniteur* also thought a well-intentioned patriot would have phrased the question: "Is It Not in the Interest, etc.?" or "Why It Is in the Interest, etc." Two days later the objection to the title was repeated.[75] G. W. Böhmer,[76] who will be remembered as one of the Mayence triumvirate of Custine, Böhmer, and Dorsch — thereupon wrote

[71] Hofmann's masterpiece in violence is re- produced in Hansen, *Quellen*, III, 586–588.
[72] *Ibid.*, pp. 588–589.
[73] *Ibid.*, pp. 589–591.
[74] *Moniteur*, XXV, 441.
[75] *Ibid.*, p. 461.
[76] Böhmer had tried to escape from Mayence after its capitulation in 1793, but was cap- tured and imprisoned in Ehrenbreitstein and Erfurt. He was exchanged on Febru- ary 12, 1795 (Hansen, *Quellen*, III, 554, n. 1).

to the *Moniteur* as "ex-Deputy to the Rheno-German National Convention," defending the patriotism of the sponsor, his friend, whom he described as a merchant of the left bank of the Rhine who would be sorely grieved to be classed with aristocrats. He said the phraseology of the question had already undergone revision, and that this form had been finally agreed upon to assure the greatest impartiality. Besides, it was "morally impossible" to prove that it was not in France's interest to keep the Rhineland.[77] In other words, the question was merely rhetorical, hence not politically objectionable.

There were fifty-six contestants, and the essays were overwhelmingly — though not unanimously — in favor of annexing the Rhineland. Because of the unexpectedly large number of entries, the number of prizes was increased to two first prizes of 4,000 francs each, and eleven second prizes of 1,000 francs each. The two first prizes were awarded to Théremin and Tainturier.[78] Théremin was a former Berliner, sometime counsellor to the Prussian legation in London.[79] Descendant of a Huguenot family which had settled in Prussia, the democratic principles of the Revolution had attracted him back to the old *patrie*.[80] He had secured employment in the diplomatic bureaus of the Committee, bought *émigré* possessions in Lyons, and earned fame (or rather notoriety) by a pamphlet very insulting to England and Austria.[81] We shall soon hear of him again. Tainturier was a civil judge of Liège, and captain of the Eighty-Seventh Brigade. Tainturier was not important.

The arguments of the essayists were principally economic, but political, strategic, sentimental, and even artistic considerations were not entirely neglected. The following analysis will give some idea as to the species of arguments which it was thought would provide a general appeal. It must be repeated, however, that — generally speaking — only those persons contributed essays who desired the annexation of the left bank; the indifferent

---

[77] *Moniteur*, XXV, 518.

[78] Eleven second prizes were given, one of the recipients of which we know very well (Dorsch) and another of whom (Derché) attained some distinction later as secretary-general of Bonnier and Treilhard in their negotiations with Malmesbury after Fructidor. In 1795, Derché was an employee of the Committee in the Section of Foreign Affairs.

The principal essays were published soon after (in 1796) by G. G. Böhmer (i.e., G. W. Böhmer) as *La rive gauche du Rhin, limite de la République française, ou Recueil de plusieurs dissertations jugées dignes des prix proposés par un négociant de la rive gauche du Rhin*, Paris, Year IV. The frontispiece of the compilation bears the interesting inscription: "The descendants of the Gauls, having become their own masters once more, resume their former frontiers. Their interest dictates that they should keep them, and their courage will know how to guarantee them." The frontispiece before the second *cahier* represents the commercial advantages of the left bank to France.

[79] *Thugut, C, W*, p. 246.

[80] Sorel in *RH*, XIX, 27. The Constituent Assembly had called the Huguenots back to France (Hansen, *Quellen*, I, 663, n. 2).

[81] *Thugut, C, W*, pp. 241, 280.

or hostilely inclined were mostly silent. Thus, these essays may not be taken as indicative of the public opinion of France.

The left bank, according to the essays, was very rich in products of the soil. It yielded fruits, vegetables, grain, wines, and tobacco. It had rich pasture lands upon which grazed fine herds of horses, cattle, and sheep. Nor was it lacking in those agricultural products which served as industrial raw materials, e.g., hemp, flax, madder (a plant with yellow flowers, from which dyes were made), coleseed (a species of cabbage, from the seeds of which a lamp oil was extracted), and forests.[82] The annexation of the left bank would result in the introduction into France of several plants of whose very existence Frenchmen were ignorant — or which were at least very rare in the Republic.[83] The Germans of the Rhineland would teach the French better ways of raising and conserving grains and vegetables.[84] From the point of view of agriculture, the annexation would be very advantageous to France.

The subsoil, continued the essays, was not less productive than the surface. Gold, silver, mercury, tin, copper, lead, calamine (native zinc carbonate), alum, salt, mineral waters, amethysts, agates, marble, quartz, cornelian stone (a semitransparent quartz used for seals, etc.), slate, coal, and peat were found in abundance.[85]

The industrial life of the left bank was described as very active. Meurs had soap and starch factories. Meisenheim and Andernach had glassworks. Mayence and Frankental manufactured — in addition to glass — porcelain, and gold and silver thread. Crefeld produced velvets and silks, stockings and handkerchiefs. The list of products was completed with a mention of serges, plushes, linen, woollen and cotton goods, ribbons, floss silk, paper, and beer.[86]

The commerce of the left bank also attracted the attention of the essayists. The annexation of this region, they said, would supply France with a larger market in which to dispose of her silks, books, wines, perfumes, watches, and dried fruits.[87] It would render possible the abolition of a thousand onerous tolls, thus reducing prices and stimulating intercourse.[88] To require Prussia to abandon its left-bank states would be to deprive it of the power of closing the Rhine to navigation at will.[89] The possession of the left bank from Basel to the sea would enable France to connect the Rhone with the Rhine by canals, with resultant gains to commerce.[90] The navigation of the Rhine, Moselle, and Meuse could be improved.[91]

In the realm of finance, also, great benefits were to be expected from an-

[82] Böhmer, Rive gauche, pp. 33, 43–44.
[83] Ibid., p. 141.
[84] Ibid.
[85] Ibid., pp. 43–45.
[86] Ibid.
[87] Ibid., pp. 141–142.
[88] Ibid.
[89] Ibid., p. 32.
[90] Ibid., p. 33.
[91] Ibid., p. 41.

nexation. The staggering total of assignats hypothecated upon the national domain of France rendered highly desirable the increase of the security in order to decrease the amount of the mortgage upon each unit of the national domain.[92] The acquisition of the property of the clergy on the left bank would serve to increase the security of the assignats by 3,000,000,000 livres.[93] And if one took into account also the former princely domains on the left bank, this figure might well be set considerably higher.[94]

Some essayists directed attention to the left-bank populations themselves: The annexation of the left bank, by adding over two million inhabitants to the population of France,[95] would decrease the amount of taxes to be paid by each French taxpayer.[96] It would recoup France for the loss of manpower suffered in her depopulating revolution.[97] It would supply the French army with needed troops. If one soldier could be obtained from each 100 inhabitants of the left bank, there would be over 20,000 men capable of bearing arms. If the proportion of soldiers to inhabitants were the same as that maintained in France when the Republic was defending its liberty, over 70,000 men could be drawn from the left bank.[98] The acquisition of the Rhineland would thus augment the power of France to such an extent that any coalition, to be effective, would have to consist of all Europe.[99]

It was recognized that the left bank would need to be defended against "enterprising" neighbors, and that constant occupation of the region by troops would be an inevitable concomitant of the projected annexation. That entailed expense. However, "it has been demonstrated that 25,000 men . . . are able to subsist [upon the left bank] without the conquered country's perceiving their presence. The Palatinate . . . and the Electorate of Cologne, with the superfluity of their abundant crops, . . . the Electorate of Trèves and the Duchy of Luxemburg with their oats, wines, and forests, could nourish an army ten times more numerous, without exposing themselves on that account to penury or to an excessive rise in the price of provisions or of the products of industry."[100] Another essayist suggested that the

[92] Ibid., p. 54.

[93] Ibid., p. 34.

[94] Dorsch set the value of the ecclesiastical and national domains of the left bank at 2,000,000,000 livres (ibid., p 67). But this estimate is probably too conservative.

[95] Ibid., pp. 63–64. Roberjot's report to the Convention in thermidor, Year III (July-August 1795), concerning his mission in the conquered left-bank territories, declared that the population of the region between the Meuse and the Rhine was 1,807,000 (Arch. A. E., Allemagne 669, f. 255). The population of the entire Empire was 27,000,-

000. This included, of course, Belgium, Luxemburg, Liechtenstein, and Savoy (Krieg g. Rev., I, 66). If Roberjot's figures are correct, Dorsch's figure of 2,212,800 for the entire left bank would be conservative, but Hansen (Quellen, III, 556, n. 1) thinks it is "very high."

[96] Böhmer, Rive gauche, p. 34.

[97] Ibid., p. 118.

[98] Ibid., p. 64.

[99] Ibid., p. 123. The revolutionist delighted in hyperboles.

[100] Ibid., pp. 136–137.

left bank could serve as a guarantee for the subsistence of all the defenders of France — which is advancing yet one step farther.[101]

As might have been expected, the Rhine boundary was proclaimed to be, not merely of value to the defense of the Republic, but indispensable. Without it, France could never enjoy tranquillity and security.[102] It was the equivalent of several fortresses in defensive value.[103] It was — so it was maintained — a more formidable boundary than the Meuse, for the latter was dominated on the right by heights, and crossed by several stone bridges; besides, the Meuse could be forded at certain times of the year.[104] The Rhine was so wide that it could be defended as the ocean shore was defended — by coast guards alone.[105] If the Rhine were France's boundary, a large standing army would not be necessary, for there would be time to raise troops while the "Rhine coast guards" staved off the attacks, at least temporarily.[106] Moreover, this boundary would facilitate the exclusion of the *émigrés* and help prevent illicit importation and exportation.[107]

Turning to the realm of international relations, the acquisition of the Rhineland by France was declared to be necessary to counterbalance the added strength accruing to the partitioners of Poland from their crime.[108] The acquisition was necessary also to bring humiliation upon France's ancient rival, the House of Habsburg: "It is high time that we deprive it of . . . [its] preponderance in the Empire." Prussian ambition, also, should be stopped at the Rhine.[109] The possession of the left bank would force the small right-bank states, the flourishing cities on the Main and Lahn, and all wishing to use the Rhine, to maintain harmonious relations with the French Republic.[110] The retention of its acquisitions by France would advance the general civilization of Germany by destroying the old forms. "The German constitution has . . . lasted too long for the welfare of that precious portion of the human species which inhabits Germany" (Théremin).[111]

There remain but a few miscellaneous arguments. The left bank should be retained because it can be retained with impunity.[112] The Empire would make peace even if these territories were not restored. Europe was too little in accord to continue the war.[113] The coalesced princes of Europe had forced peace-loving France to fight; France had proved to be the victor; who could say that she should relinquish her conquests?[114] If the Republic re-

[101] *Ibid.*, p. 55.
[102] *Ibid.*, p. 31.
[103] *Ibid.*, p. 15.
[104] *Ibid.*, p. 31.
[105] *Ibid.*, pp. 40–41.
[106] *Ibid.*, p. 41.
[107] *Ibid.*, p. 53.
[108] *Ibid.*, pp. 17–18.
[109] *Ibid.*, p. 32.
[110] *Ibid.*, p. 52.
[111] *Ibid.*, p. 19.
[112] *Ibid.*, pp. 19–20.
[113] *Ibid.*, pp. 15–16.
[114] *Ibid.*, p. 9.

turned the left bank, her generosity would be mistaken for weakness, thus endangering the safety of the state. Machiavelli had pointed out that men attack more readily those who make themselves loved than those who make themselves feared.[115] The extension of France's boundaries to the Rhine would add to her glory, and "glory is in politics what credit is in finance." [116] The Rhine had been the boundary of Gaul.[117] The left bank abounded in majestic scenery of great interest to the artist,[118] and in famous men.[119] Lastly, prudence and the security of the state forbade that one should be so overconfident as deliberately to strengthen those who might at any time become his enemies.[120]

This enumeration can be compared with the following excerpt from Roberjot's report on the conquered left bank:

Region between the Meuse and the Rhine.

Clèves: Grains; linen industry important; hides made into leather. Size (including Meurs, which is an enclave of Gelderland): 36 square leagues. Population: 60,000.

Gelderland: Very fertile, except for some heathy regions; linen industry; embossing of cloth. Size: 36 square leagues. Population: 280,000.

Jülich: Extremely fertile; cloth and brass needles manufactured; many foundries, forges; much coal. Size: 130 square leagues. Population: 280,000.

Electorate of Cologne: Most fertile; cloth manufactured. Size: 57 square leagues. Population: 160,000.

. . . .

Electorate of Trèves: Not much grain but much wine. Many foundries and forges; slate and marble. Size: 160 square leagues. Population: 130,000.

Left-bank portion of the Palatinate, Zweibrücken, Bishoprics of Worms and Spires, Electorate of Mayence, etc.: Very fertile; good quality iron ore; rich in mercury. Size: 400 square leagues. Population: 560,000.[121]

It is apparent that the contestants had an intimate knowledge of the Rhineland and its resources.

As mentioned, not all the essays were in favor of annexation. There was one negative entry which created, according to its author, much impression at Paris.[122] It was the last entry to come in, and was the contribution of Burgomaster Dumont of Cologne, who feared that the antiannexationists would not be represented at all unless he represented them himself.

---

[115] Ibid., pp. 9–11.
[116] Ibid., pp. 123–124.
[117] Ibid., p. 32.
[118] Ibid., p. 142. A rather trivial argument.
[119] Ibid., p. 143. Evidently there were not enough candidates for the Hall of Fame living on the banks of the Loire and the Seine. Or perhaps the revolutionists preferred exotic products. Cf. the Legislative Assembly's adoption of famous foreigners in August 1792 (supra, chap. iv, § 2c).
[120] Böhmer, Rive gauche, pp. 9–10.
[121] Arch. A. E., Allemagne 669, f. 256.
[122] Hansen, Quellen, III, 637.

Written under the appellation, "An Inhabitant of the Left Bank of the Rhine," this brilliant sixteen-page essay in octavo makes the following points. (1) Justice takes precedence over self-interest, even in the case of states. It is in one's interest to do what is just, but it is not always just to do what is in one's interest. France promised "no conquests." The left-bank inhabitants relied upon these promises and let them (the promises) influence their actions.[123] Justice demands that France honor her word. (2) An adoptive child always yearns for its true mother. So it is with states. You cannot tear people away from their customs without rendering them unhappy. Nor do people want their identity effaced. You may be able to offer them much, but you can keep your palaces; they are satisfied with their cottages. (3) You say Nature set the Rhine as the boundary of France. Assuming for the moment the validity of this proposition, was that not the case also when you renounced conquests? Yet you renounced them. Again, if Nature sets bounds for a stronger state, does she not do so likewise for a weaker? Perhaps it is the weaker states that should extend their bounds at the expense of the stronger. What would you say to that? And what would you say if a terrestrial convulsion changed your bounds? Would you be willing to yield territory to your neighbors? It is clear that the only line of demarcation which Nature has traced is that of Justice. Any other line leads to war and desolation. (4) You want the conquered territory to redeem your assignats. It is unworthy of you to be thus baited. When you created the assignats, you intended to pay for them yourself. You had adequate security — security of a sort without which no other security has any worth at all. Your security is your national honor. If you violate your word, who is going to have faith in your bills of exchange? You promised "no conquests." Stick to it. Therein will lie your true glory.[124]

6. THE VOTE UPON THE BOUNDARIES OF THE REPUBLIC

Roberjot's report on the left bank addressed the following statement to the Convention: "You have made this people hope for annexation. . . The Representatives of the People, who knew your intentions, have heralded it [the annexation] loudly. Your committees of government recommended that [the Representatives] incline minds, dispose sentiments — in short, that they act as if [the region] would one day be united with France."[125] And still neither Convention nor Committee knew for certain what it

---

[123] Therefore — in legal parlance — France was estopped from denying her promises.

[124] *Denkschrift des Kölner Bürgermeisters J. N. Dumont über die Frage der Rheingrenze,*

Sept. 28, 1795, *ibid.,* pp. 629–636.

[125] Dated *thermidor,* III (July 19–August 17, 1796); published in August.

wanted. The indecision of February and March 1795 [126] still obtained. Indeed, Reubell, Sieyes, and (after September 1) Cambacérès [127] were members of the Committee,[128] and their views were never hidden under a bushel; still there were so many factors to be considered.

Aubry (after August 2 no longer on the Committee) had raised doubts as to the military feasibility of the Rhine frontier. Barthélemy had attacked its political advisability. The public was impatient with any impediment to peace.[129] The economic and political situations were explosive. The assignats had sunk to one-half per cent of their face value.[130] The increase of the bread ration to one pound was insistently demanded.[131] Preferences in the distribution of bread and meat were protested [132] and the gatherings incident to these distributions were "little moderate" in their remarks about the Convenion.[133] The troops lacked shirts and shoes, and, like the civilians, bread [134] — despite an abundant harvest.[135] The horses lacked oats and hay, when there were horses to possess a lack: many cavalrymen were without mounts.[136] The royalists were restive.[137] Popular discontent with the Convention had increased to nausea because of a law requiring that, under a new constitution soon to take effect, two thirds of the new legislators would have to be chosen from among former Convention members.[138] A battle of pens and printing presses covered the walls of Paris with placards, appeals, and provocations.[139]

The Rhine-boundary advocates were cowed, though there were many persuasive controversialists among their number. In the Convention, or on mission, or on the Committee, those in favor of absorbing the Rhineland were Sieyes, Reubell, Cambacérès, Carnot, Jean Debry, Tallien, Roberjot, Portiez of the Oise, Gillet, Chénier, and, aside from momentary hesitations, the two Merlins. Against, were Aubry, Barras, Fréron, and usually, though not always, Boissy d'Anglas.[140]

Albert Sorel declares in his *Bonaparte et Hoche en 1797* that the Committee of the Year III identified the establishment of a Republic in France with the conquest of the natural boundaries.[141] Aside from the fact that

[126] *Vide supra*, chap. vii, § 6.

[127] The views of Reubell and Sieyes need no reference. For Cambacérès, *vide* his March 3, 1795 report to the Convention, *Moniteur*, XXIII, 597.

[128] Guillaume, *Etudes rév.*, Ser. II, p. 215.

[129] Sorel in *RH*, XVIII, 290.

[130] Heigel, *Deutsche Geschichte*, II, 197.

[131] Aulard, *Paris*, II, 246.

[132] *Ibid.*, p. 238.

[133] *Ibid.*, p. 235.

[134] Heigel, *Deutsche Geschichte*, II, 197.

[135] Aulard, *Paris*, II, 235.

[136] Heigel, *Deutsche Geschichte*, II, 197.

[137] *Mém. corr. Mallet du Pan*, II, 182. "Carletti said recently to a person of my acquaintance that he saw [about him] only royalists." — *Inéd. Mallet du Pan*, I, 284.

[138] *Vide* next chapter, § 7.

[139] *Inéd. Mallet du Pan*, I, 304.

[140] On January 30, 1795, for example, Boissy, speaking for the Committee, strongly recommended the Rhine boundary (*Moniteur*, XXIII, 343). General authority for this paragraph: Sorel in *RH*, XVIII, 275.

[141] Paris, 1896; p. 2.

there was no single Committee of the Year III — its membership being changed by fourths every month [142] — the following two documents show how inaccurate is bound to be any attempt to formulate a system from the fluctuating ideas of the Committee.

The first document is a memoir of Boissy d'Anglas', which was sent by the Committee to Barthélemy to direct its ambassador's conduct; the second, the Committee's instructions of September 10 to Caillard.

Boissy's memoir declared that for France "to retain all [her conquests] would be to perpetuate the war; to return all would be dupery. To unite to France what is necessary for her tranquillity, and to renounce what would be only a litigious superfluity is the counsel of wisdom. . . This magnificent project [i.e., the acquisition of the left bank], which appeared a chimera in the glorious days of Louis XIV, [has been realized] . . . ; [but] by what right could France, which ought to be giving lessons in philosophy to the world, and which has proclaimed herself the enemy of all oppression, by what right could she despoil of their lands five or six petty sovereigns who never had the will to make war against her, who were engaged only in self-defense, and from whom she has nothing to fear? . . . I demand of it [i.e., of the Committee], then, if it would not be more reasonable and more advantageous to the nation that it represents, and much wiser politics, to separate the interests of the *Corps Germanique* from those of the House of Austria; to accord to the one the peace which it seeks and the integrity of territory which it claims, in order to be more surely able to deprive the other of all hope of recovering the states it has deserved to lose, and to reduce its power to the point of weakness demanded by the public tranquillity. By this means, the odium of an unjust spoliation and the reproach of inconsistency with respect to principles professed would be avoided, . . . the attachment of the Empire [for France], which [Empire] France ought to protect rather than dismember, would be reëstablished, . . . the bonds of alliance with the Court of Berlin would be strengthened. . ." Moreover, the too-eccentric Rhine boundary would be replaced by the Meuse, thus presenting a more easily defensible frontier. Lastly, Belgium and Luxemburg would be no mean acquisitions, being fertile, industrious, wealthy, populous, well stocked with animals, and rich in wood and (in Luxemburg) iron.[143]

[142] Guillaume, *Etudes rév.*, Ser. II, no. 4, pp. 238–246.

[143] "Mémoire sur les limites futures de la République fr. presenté au Comité de Salut Public par Boissy d'Anglas, et envoyé à M. Barthélemy pour sa direction. . . ," H. H. S. Arch., *Schweiz* 197. This document is not itself dated, but it bears the notation: "Bⁿ Degelmann 13–8bre 1795." This seem-

ingly could mean only October 13, 1795, the *Octo* being rendered by 8. Certainly *août*, the eighth month, has no terminal *bre*. However, the document is probably from the month of August. A semiweekly leaflet printed in French in London, a few sheets of which are in the French archives (Arch. A. E., *Allemagne* 669, ff. 236–239), reproduces the memoir in its num-

The instructions of the Commitee to Caillard betray the same indecision. Caillard was given no definite order regarding the future disposition of the Rhineland, for "the complete solution is connected with events more or less subject to a certain degree of incertitude. He [Caillard] will be careful to leave this matter vague until further order — in a manner, however, not to give the impression . . . [that we are disposed] to return to our former limits. But while always weighing his reasons in accordance with the hypothesis that we will conserve the Rhine frontier, he will receive carefully the objections which will be made to him; he will weigh them, discuss them, and send them in to us, accompanied by his own reflections, in order that we can balance some by others and judge with a full knowledge of the facts before us." [144]

From all of which it appears that the only generalization possible is that the Committee was, at this time (September 1795), favorably disposed toward the Rhine frontier. A *sine qua non*, the Rhine boundary was not, but could become if the personnel of the Committee, the military outlook, and the internal situation concurred to render its attainment feasible. The personnel and the military situation were satisfactory in September, but the internal situation was fast approaching a climax, and the expansionists were therefore wavering in their allegiance.

On September 30, discussion commenced in the Convention on the question of what were the boundaries of the Republic. This was just two days after J. N. Dumont's essay struck an incredulous Paris. The mass of contest essays did not appear in print until 1796, but the summer months had been filled with essays that did appear; and there had been the official reports of Portiez of the Oise and of Roberjot. Also, Reubell had reported to the Committee on a conversation he had had on the selfsame subject with Secretary of Legation Laquiante.[145] All in all, the soil had been well prepared for the crucial debate.

Merlin of Douai opened the discussion. His report contained a reminder that, in 1792 and 1793, many communities and regions in the Austrian Netherlands had requested annexation, and been annexed between March 1 and 23, 1793.[146] Armand remarked that the Belgian elections had taken

---

bers of September 1, 4, and 8. The memoir must therefore be dated prior to September.

[144] Arch. A. E., *Prusse* Supp. 10, f. 275.

[145] Quoted by Sorel in *RH*, XVIII, 317–319.

[146] Such were Ghent, Bruges, Brussels, the Principality of Salm, the Marquisate of Franchimont, the County of Hennegau, Hainault (annexed as the *département* of Jemappes), and many other places (Hansen, *Quellen*, II, 785). A deputation from Liège was in the French capital to request that the Bishopric of Liège be made into a French *département* when the tide of war turned (*ibid.*). It was annexed, however, on May 8 — i.e., completely; part had been annexed on March 2 and 4 (*Moniteur*, XXVI, 84).

place in the presence of armed troops,[147] so could not be called a free expression of the will of the inhabitants. Lesage added that he had heard on all sides that the requests for annexation had been exacted by "cruelly revolutionary" means. Merlin assured the Convention that everywhere the vote for union with France had been accompanied by "gaiety." He said the Belgians and Liègeois were worthy of liberty, but that that liberty had to be by union with France, for a separate republic would redound to England's advantage. And then Merlin had the shamefacedness — after what J. N. Dumont had written on the subject — to exalt the advantages the assignats would receive from the confiscation of property in the Belgian Netherlands.[148]

Merlin noted parenthetically that, of course, his arguments could be applied to all the conquered territory; but there was a difference, he said. The treaties of peace with Prussia and Hesse-Cassel had deferred the question of the fate of the German left bank to the Franco-Imperial peace. The disposition of this region was therefore a matter for diplomacy. But there were no strings attached to the Belgian Netherlands. There, France need consult only the rights of the populations and her own interest. The populations had a right to be French, and France's interest required them to be French — so French they could be if the National Convention would so order.

Did Merlin mean to say here that the fate of the German left bank might really be a matter for negotiation? Unlikely! Merlin said: "Assuredly there is none amongst us who does not hold constantly to that great truth: . . . that the consolidation of the Republic and the repose of Europe are intrinsically bound up with the extension of our territory to the Rhine. . . But we respect treaties."[149] The proper interpretation seems to be: France would have the left bank, but she would have it with the ceremonial trappings of diplomacy. She was willing to adopt a procedure that would give her more than the bare title of possession, which would be the sole fruit of unilateral action. But she did not consider that she was yielding anything. And thus did the Convention understand Merlin's remarks.

But Merlin had a problem. Luxemburg and Limburg had not asked for annexation as had the Belgian region. Indeed, they had sent petitions, but France, according to Merlin, could honor only "deliberations legally con-

---

[147] The *modus operandi* of the Belgian elections has been thus described: "Convoking of the inhabitants in a church surrounded by, or filled with, troops; a harangue by the French Commissioner; applause by the Clubists; immediate vote by acclamation, which has the advantage of permitting the identification of persons; opening of a register of protest which no one dares to sign." — Chuquet, *Guerres Rév.*, IV, 231. The potentialities of taking aye votes by acclamation, and recording nay votes in a register at the point of a bayonet, will be appreciated by all.

[148] For this and the next three paragraphs, *Moniteur*, XXVI, 44, 84–96, 98–103, 106–112, 121–123.

[149] *Ibid.*, p. 89.

ducted in primary assemblies." Merlin made so bold as to suggest that "the French Republic could and should retain, by right of conquest, or acquire by treaties, regions which were *à sa convenance*, without consulting the inhabitants."

Boissy d'Anglas asked that Carnot's opinion be heard as to the military advisability of the frontier which would result from the annexation of the Austrian Netherlands. Carnot divided his reply (October 1) into two sections. The annexation of the *right* bank of the Meuse, he said, would give France the fortress of Luxemburg,[150] which the Austrians had been using as a key to the invasion of France, and which, in French hands, would become the key for the invasion of the Empire. If France had the key, no prince would attack her from that side, for that would result only in invasion of his own soil.

Regarding annexation of the *left* bank of the Meuse — i.e., Belgium, this, said Carnot, would add to France's barrier of fortresses a second barrier, viz., the Meuse River itself. He advised against destruction of the fortresses, "since they cover us not only on the side of Belgium but also on that of the sea." And then he showed what value he attached to fortresses as compared with a simple river-line by extolling the Meuse River barrier because of the fortresses which covered it and tended to prevent passage by an enemy. In conjunction with the fortresses, he said, the Meuse was a "very respectable" barrier, and worth "three years." By this Carnot meant that, with the Meuse frontier and its strong points in France's hands, it would take three years of military reverses to reduce France to the military position she now was in, not possessing that frontier.[151]

Throughout the debate, one of the weightiest arguments was how the Roman Senate would have acted in like circumstances. Lesage ventured to suggest that it was victory which had brought about Rome's ruin. The warning passed unheeded. On October 1, the Convention voted that Belgium, Liège, and Luxemburg should thenceforth constitute part and parcel of France. However, since part of Belgium had already been annexed in 1793 — annexed and then lost — the Decree of October 1 merely provided for the execution of the former decrees, with the proviso that, where there

---

[150] "Luxemburg" itself signifies "little fortress" (from the Teutonic *Lucilin-burhuc*). For sixteen centuries, until its dismantlement in 1867, Luxemburg was one of the strongest fortresses in Europe (Sir Harry Luke, *In the Margin of History* [New York, i.e., London, 1933], p. 105). Luxemburg was the strongest fortress in Europe after Gibraltar, according to Carnot (*Moniteur*, XXVI, 121).

[151] *Ibid*. Roberjot, in his report on the left bank, compares the Rhine and Meuse frontiers. The Rhine has a faster current; it is ordinarily twice as wide; its depth is greater; it is more difficult to navigate or cross; its banks are sometimes steep, though not always. And Roberjot concludes that the Rhine would make a more advantageous boundary for France than the Meuse (*ibid.*, XXV, 626).

were none such, the new decree would apply.[152] The Belgian Netherlands were locked securely within the embrace of France, but one arm was left free to welcome the Rhineland.

7. THE REORGANIZATION OF THE LEFT BANK

The kaleidoscope of governmental changes on the left bank south of the Moselle presented, after Basel, one last picture before the Convention yielded to the Directory.

On May 27, 1795, the region south of the Moselle, with the exception of Trèves and Coblenz, was detached from the Central Administration at Aix.[153] On Representatives Merlin of Thionville and Rivaud[154] devolved the task of organizing this region, which was a virtual desert as a result of the plundering of French troops, the activities of the Agency of Evacuation, and the kind attentions of Bourbotte and company.[155]

Merlin and Rivaud sent two expert administrators, Bella of National Domains and Kolb of Forests, on an inspection tour, and these reported that the country was swarming with multitudes of incapable and not always honest agents whose functions overlapped and clashed to such an extent that economic stability was out of the question.[156]

On the basis of this report, the two Representatives created (August 9) a new administration for the region between the Rhine and Moselle, including therein Trèves and Coblenz. In form, this administration was tripartite: a Central Commission of five to oversee the assessment of taxes and contributions, to supervise the policing of roads and rivers, and to exercise a check upon the police themselves; an Agency of Domains and Contributions (or Taxes) to administer the industries and properties confiscated by the Republic, to collect taxes and contributions, and to keep in repair the highways of commerce; and a rudimentary form of justiciary. Bella was appointed Director-General of Domains and Contributions.[157]

The Committee of Public Safety approved the appointment of Bella at the same time that it approved the new government with Trèves and Coblenz, and their territories on both banks of the Moselle, included.[158] Of

---

[152] *Ibid.*, XXVI, 122.

[153] Hansen, *Quellen*, III, 489, n. 3.

[154] The Féraud here, in Sagnac, *Rhin fr.*, p. 113, is an inadvertence. His footnote is correct.

[155] When Luxemburg fell to the French on June 6, 1795, Representative Talot wrote to the CPS: "If you . . . deliver . . . this country over to . . . those who have ravaged and desolated the region of Trèves and the Palatinate, you will render execrable the French name." — Hansen, *Quellen*, III, 531.

[156] Report accompanies letter of Merlin-Th. and Rivaud to CPS, Aug. 9, 1795, Arch. N., AF III 244, d. 2089.

[157] *Ibid.*, reproduced in Hansen, *Quellen*, III, 583–585. Note that his archive citation is not correct.

[158] Aug. 25, 1795, *ibid.*, p. 583 and n. 2. But

course, the Representatives had recommended that government in terms which they knew would be understood in Paris: All the expenses would be charged to the inhabitants and all the revenues would redound to the benefit of France.[159]

The new plan could not be completely carried out, however, for the changing fortunes of war and the treasonable conduct of Pichegru returned a victorious Austrian army to the left bank of the Rhine in October. On October 18, the entire region was divided into six districts, with the capital at Kreuznach half way between the Moselle and Rhine; but only the area north of the Nahe could be organized because only that was beyond the theater of conflict.[160]

Regarding the area between the Meuse and Rhine, a rumor was rife in August 1795 that a fundamental reorganization of the government there was being considered. Representative Meynard pleaded against it. Great strides had been made, he said, in improving the regulations concerning contributions, provisioning of the army, roads, forests, and national domains, and any changes would destroy their unity.[161] The Convention ended without the rumored upheaval, but reorganization was apparently a crying need, for in May 1795 Roberjot had observed to Carnot: "The organization

---

in October 1795, as a result of the efforts of one of the members of the Central Administration at Aix (Hetzrodt), Trèves and Coblenz were once more attached to the Aix government (*ibid.*, p. 1014, n. 2). Thus, Coblenz, crushed by the heavy contributions imposed by Bourbotte — because, allegedly, he wanted to reclaim the coin the French *émigrés* had spent there, and to cleanse the city of the political stain incident to its hospitality to the *émigrés* — became subject to Pérès' contribution of June 13. In figures, this meant that, to Bourbotte's 4,000,000 livres, was added 4,000,000 from Pérès. Now Pérès' 22,000,000 on the entire Sambre-and-Meuse-Army region was cut down drastically on July 16. Therefore, Coblenz reckoned that the Pérèsian 4,000,000 should have been reduced in the same proportion to 1,280,000. Coblenz had paid in, in both contributions, 1,627,000 livres in coin. It wanted 427,000 livres back, and to have Bourbotte's contribution declared null and void. Instead, it said, it was being threatened by Treasury Agent Hertzog with execution on behalf of Bourbotte's levy.

The city pointed out that Bourbotte's reasons, given above, were sheer nonsense. One might as well say that France would be justified in levying contributions on Switzerland, for Switzerland, also, had sold much to Frenchmen for coin. It was pointed out, also, that a decree of the Committee of July 18, 1794, had limited military impositions to two, or at most, three times the ordinary taxes.

The Committee deputed Gillet to investigate (Hansen, *Quellen*, III, 291, 532, 550–551, 616–623). But the investigation netted nothing. Under the Directory, the city was still being dunned in Bourbotte's memory (*vide infra*, Pt. II, chap. v, § 1). Bourbotte, it might be parenthetically recalled, was now no longer in the realm of the living: extremist that he was, he had participated in the riot of Prairial (May 20, 1795). One might be tempted to remark that though this extremist's body lay a-moldering in his grave, his extreme acts went marching on with the government's approval.

[159] Hansen, *Quellen*, III, 583, n. 2.
[160] *Ibid.*, pp. 584–585.
[161] To CPS, Aug. 3, 1795, *ibid.*, p. 584, n. 1.

of this region, administratively speaking, has never been completed," [162] and Gillet had written on August 11 that "there has never been an established plan for the government of the conquered country." [163]

It might be mentioned for the record that the District Administration of Blankenheim had ceased to exist after May 27. Part of its territory was, on that date, attached to Trèves, part to Coblenz.[164] And with the annexation of Belgium, Liège, and Luxemburg on October 1, 1795, the non-German districts were removed from under the Central Administration at Aix. Thenceforth, there were only the Districts of Aix, Bonn, Geldern, Coblenz, and Trèves.[165]

[162] Hansen, *Quellen*, III, 533, n. 2.
[163] *Ibid.*, p. 536, n. 4.
[164] *Ibid.*, p. 533, n. 2. The Blankenheim District Administration is noteworthy for us because, on March 28, 1795, it sent to the cantonal administration of the Blankenheim District (the Eifel region from Prüm to Coblenz) two draft petitions for annexation to France, with the request that the cantonal administration find out how people felt about union with France. But it is likely that Blankenheim was merely seeking amelioration of the charges of war (*ibid.*, pp. 459–462).
[165] *Ibid.*, p. 655, n. 1.

CHAPTER XV

THE LATE THERMIDORIANS AND AUSTRIA

I. THE KROCH—MERLIN OF THIONVILLE PARLEY

*W*HILE France, confident of victory, was delineating her northern boundary by unilateral, legislative act, instead of by agreement with her neighbors, as is the custom, Austrian arms, having reached their lowest ebb, were slowly climbing back, higher and higher up the rocky crags that form the shoreline of military glory. It was an unexpected turn. For three years France had conquered, conquered, conquered, always against incredible odds, and her entire diplomacy was based upon the expectation that this situation would continue. To the mind of the revolutionist in Paris, his place in the diplomatic scheme was to pull the strings while the defeated sovereigns of Europe danced to the tune of the Marseillaise.

The Habsburgs wanted Bavaria. Everyone knew that. But it was for France to make the arrangements, to determine the conditions. Already in June 1795, in conversations during the Austrian evacuation of Luxemburg, Merlin of Thionville had offered Bavaria to Austria through Captain Kroch, adjutant to Marshal Bender, the Austrian commander at Luxemburg. The offer was made in storybook fashion.

While the French and Austrian generals were walking in the garden of the building where they had just dined together,[1] Merlin drew Kroch into a side path and declared that his government was convinced of Austria's integrity and wished, not only to be reconciled to her, but to do anything conducive to the establishment of lasting peace, friendship, and confidence. However, declared Merlin, the ordinary channels of negotiation were inadvisable in such a case, for Basel had "sold itself out to Prussia," and Bar-

---

[1] According to Fain, *Ms. l'an* III, p. 279, Merlin had given the dinner; but the date was not June 5 as Fain has it, nor is June 5 the 16 *prairial*, as Fain says. Nor was the presently-to-be-described overture made to an inebriated Bender but to his sober adjutant.

thélemy was a friend of the Prussians; moreover, hardly a step could be taken at Basel before the secret would be compromised and innumerable intrigues and obstacles would spring up. But if Kroch presented propositions to him, Merlin, the latter could forward them directly to the Committee, whose present members were his friends. And Merlin proceeded to say that he was convinced that France would, in return for the cession of the Belgian Netherlands, permit Austria to possess herself of Bavaria — and an army of 100,000 men could be established to overawe possible objectors. The above version is from Marshal Bender's report to the Emperor;[2] Merlin reported to the Committee that he had offered Bavaria to Austria in return for Austria's abandonment of the Empire.[3] France, said Merlin (Bender's report), had indeed concluded peace with Prussia, but not from inclination; it had been necessary in order to split the Coalition.[4] "I said much ill about the Prussians," Merlin's account confesses, "[and Kroch] said more."[5]

How was the overture received at Paris? Merlin did not report it to Paris for three months;[6] that is how important he regarded it. And he wrote to Barthélemy: "It is a letter from Herrn von Bender himself that I am sending you, for Hardenberg to read. . . I said to him much ill about the Prussians (for whom you know my esteem); he said more, and confirmed me in the idea that if France, without intermeddling, was willing to see Bavaria occupied by the Emperor, the Emperor would abandon the Electors."[7]

How was the overture received at Vienna? Thugut wrote to Count Colloredo: "It would be the most unpardonable weakness to pay the least attention to such reveries." France was "infinitely embarrassed . . . in its interior," and seeking merely "to sow dissension and distrust." Kroch "perhaps had zeal but little intelligence." Merlin must have "regaled himself at meeting such a dupe." If Austria were foolish enough to fall in with such a scheme and occupy Bavaria, Prussia, reinforced with all the Empire, would order the Emperor to leave within twenty-four hours, and Russia would allow Turkey to attack Austria in the rear. "Then Herr Kroch would go to implore help from his friend Merlin — and would find that Citizen Merlin and his associates had meanwhile been guillotined." Bender should be told to order Kroch not to speak of his conversation with Merlin "to anyone whomsoever without any exception." If the secret could not be kept, "it would be indispensable for us to anticipate trouble by being the first to communicate the whole adventure both to St. Petersburg and Lon-

[2] June 24, 1795, Vivenot-Zeissberg, *Quellen*, V, 261–262.
[3] Sept. 11, 1795, *Corr. Merlin-Th.*, II, 251.
[4] Vivenot-Zeissberg, *Quellen*, V, 262.
[5] *Corr. Merlin-Th.*, II, 251.
[6] Sept. 11, 1795, *ibid.*
[7] *Ibid.*, p. 248. Reference here is, of course, to the Electors of Mayence, Trèves, Cologne, and probably also of the Rhenish Palatinate.

don." [8] On July 6, the Emperor wrote to Bender: "The peace proposal you sent me, being but the lengthy prattle of an unimportant French commissioner, merits no attention at all." [9]

Such was the Kroch–Merlin of Thionville parley, of significance only to show the attitude of Austria toward propositions essentially the same as those carried by Théremin to Basel the following September. As a concession to chronology, however, a section must first be devoted to a charming but unhappy girl of seventeen, a girl into whose young life had been crowded more contact with brutality than ever human soul should be asked to endure. Father, mother, aunt torn from her tender side and butchered! Her young brother virtually tortured to death and she forbidden to see him! Sad is this commentary upon the moral state of those in power, and every lover of France, every thinker who sees in the French Revolution the harbinger of modern liberalism, must apologize for this episode if he would retain his self-respect as a human being.

2. PRINCESS MARIE THÉRÈSE CHARLOTTE

(MADAME ROYALE)

During the Republic's negotiations with Spain in May and June of 1795, the Spanish plenipotentiary insisted that Madame Royale (Louis XVI's daughter) and her young brother should be surrendered to the Spanish Bourbons. He argued that inasmuch as the execution of Louis XVI was the cause of the Franco-Spanish conflict, the termination of that struggle should be marked by the surrender to Spain of Louis XVI's son.[10] Barthélemy, the French negotiator, had been authorized to promise that the young prince — his sister too, certainly — would be surrendered at the general peace, but Spain was unwilling to wait; and presently the Committee withdrew even this concession. It would have been dangerous to the Republic to supply the royalists with a rallying point, and it is indeed surprising that such a promise should ever have been considered. Barthélemy was ordered to try to evade the question.[11]

Evade the question! To Spain, the release of the children was a *sine qua non*, a holy "duty [to an unfortunate mother], a religion, a cult, a fanaticism, if you wish. . . If we had our choice between the children of Louis

[8] July 5, 1795, *Briefe Thugut*, I, 236–238.

[9] Vivenot-Zeissberg, *Quellen*, V, 279.

[10] Fain, *Ms. l'an III*, p. 210. This son was Louis Charles, the second dauphin, known as the Duke of Normandie until the death of his older brother in 1789. Louis Charles had been born on March 27, 1785; his older brother, on October 22, 1781 (M. Tourneux, *Bibliographie de l'histoire de Paris pendant la Révolution française* [5 vols., Paris, 1890–1913], IV, 100–101, 132).

[11] Fain, *Ms. l'an III*, pp. 210–212.

XVI and the offer of some *départements* along our frontier, we would ask for the children of Louis XVI." So spoke the Spanish negotiator.[12] No compromise was possible. Did France cut the Gordian knot?

Young Louis was being subjected to a regime which was equivalent to a sentence of death. And what a death! A few quotations from a soul-searing account will suffice to tell.

Simon [the jailer] was awakened in the night, and heard the child praying as he knelt by his bedside. "I'll teach you," he cried, "to whine your paternosters," and pouring a pail of cold water over his body and his bed, he compelled him by blows from an iron-heeled shoe to pass the rest of the winter night in the wet, cold bed. . . Robespierre decreed that there was no need of any special jailer . . . and the Municipality thereupon caused the Prince to be [nailed] up in a little cell . . . [for] six months. . . Once a day his food — a small piece of meat, some bread and water — was pushed through the lattice of the door. . . Two or three times in the night . . . the child . . . [was] compelled . . . to show himself at the lattice. He . . . received no water to wash himself, no change of clothes or bedding; not even the excrements were removed from the ever closed and unaired cell. . . On the [eleventh] of Thermidor, . . . [a new] jailer of the two royal children . . . caused the door to be broken open. . . In this poisoned atmosphere, a pale and emaciated child, with matted hair, lay upon a filthy lair, clothed with half rotten rags, his head covered with an eruption, his neck with festering sores, and his whole body with swarms of vermin. His eyes were widely opened, but dim and without expression; his back was curved, and all his joints were swelled, or sore and bloody. . . To the terrified questions of [the jailer,] the boy . . . sighed out at last, "I wish to die." . . . He was bathed, put into a clean bed, and provided with fresh clothing. . . But . . . the government committees . . . obstinate[ly manifested] their disinclination to permit any essential improvement in his condition. . . The request to be allowed to take walks in the garden was . . . refused. . . [The jailer's company] was only allowed . . . during meal times. . . On the 3rd of May, [1795,] . . . the little Capet was [reported] ill. . . No answer. . . On the 4th, . . . he was [reported] seriously ill. Still no answer. On the 5th, . . . his life was [reported] in danger. The Committee . . . sent the famuos surgeon Dessault. . . A city Commissioner . . . said, "The boy is lost, is he not?" — "I fear so; perhaps there are some people who hope so," [replied the doctor]. On the following day Dessault died after an illness of three hours[!]. . . The Committee allowed five days to pass before appointing a successor. . . On the eighth of June all the symptoms of approaching dissolution increased. . . When [the jailer] asked him whether he was in pain he answered, "yes," but said that the music above was so beautiful, and then suddenly cried in a loud voice: "I hear the voice of my mother; I wonder whether my sister heard the music too." Then followed a long silence and then a joyful cry "I will tell you," and he turned to [the jailer] who was

[12] *Ibid.*, p. 212.

bending over him to listen. But . . . the boy had ceased to breathe and the sacrifice was completed.[13]

The body was opened for a post-mortem. The report of the examining physicians declared that death had been due to scrofula of long standing.[14] It may indeed be true that the child was scrofulous — the first dauphin's death had been due to scrofula — but inasmuch as the young king was suffering from rickets also,[15] it is not certain which disease claimed his life. Rickets would have been the fault of those who controlled his diet; scrofula of his royal inheritance. Not that the exact nature of either of these diseases was understood at that early date, but the factor of heredity in scrofula had been recognized. So the post-mortem report omitted all mention of rickets. Was not the government seeking, by this means, to absolve itself from responsibility for the lad's death, not only for the benefit of critics at home, but for those on foreign thrones? It is indeed possible that if the post-mortem had been performed upon the defunct consciences of the authors of this crime, *there* would have been found a *worse* case of scrofula than that attributed to the unfortunate child.

Propriety demanded that Spain should be informed officially and completely of the demise of the prince whose possession she had been seeking so insistently. But the revolutionists wished to treat the death as a matter of no real importance, so merely added a postscript to a despatch for Barthélemy: "In the Convention this morning was announced the news of the death of the son of Capet,[16] which was learned with indifference, and of the

[13] Sybel, *Fr. Rev.*, IV, 321–326. Sybel's account of the Dauphin's death accords substantially with that in A. Thiers, *The History of the French Revolution* (tr. from the French by F. Shoberl; 5 vols., London, 1854), IV, 624–652. Thiers' account is of course much fuller, but the words placed in the child's mouth, though similar, are not identical in the two works. Sybel gives no authority, but Thiers cites Alison.

[14] Fain, *Ms. l'an III*, pp. 430–433 reproduces the report *in toto*.

[15] Pariset, *La Rév.*, p. 287.

[16] Regarding the dispute whether the lad in the Temple was a changeling, von Sybel points out that since Spain hesitated to make peace so long as Louis XVII was incarcerated, the CPS would have been only too glad to admit that the prisoner was a changeling — if he had been (*Fr. Rev.*, IV, 326, note). Thugut did his part to raise doubts as to the identity of the little occupant of the Temple. Desiring to partition

France, he thought it advisable not to recognize Louis XVIII as king. But he had to give a reason which could be publicly avowed. So he declared there was "no true legal certitude of the death of Louis XVI's son." — Thugut to Starhemberg, July 11, 1795, Vivenot-Zeissberg, *Quellen*, V, 289.

There are two recent books on the subject. One, arguing from interruption in the young king's laundry schedule, testimony concerning the later discovery of a lime-covered child's skeleton, and other points, concludes that Louis XVII died in the Temple in January 1794, and that the child who passed away on June 8, 1795, was another person, perhaps introduced into the Temple by the washerwoman, herself later imprisoned. This hypothesis would reconcile the various conflicting accounts of eyewitnesses and relatives (L. Hastier, *La Double mort de Louis XVII* [Paris, 1951]). The other book also concludes that the son of Louis XVI died in the Temple, but this

capitulation of Luxemburg, which was received with the liveliest transports."[17] The Almighty Father, with the aid of certain demons in human form, had cut the Gordian knot. The heir to the throne — the King, in many eyes — no longer existed for Spain to demand. And since Monarchy in France denied the right of succession to females,[18] the remaining child of Louis XVI, being but a girl, could be surrendered without danger.

But surrendered to whom? That was another question. And in return for what? That was still another. France had no intention of yielding to impotent Spain a princess whose Habsburg blood could be used to extract concessions from Austria. But Thugut did not want Madame Royale. Her presence "could be only embarrassing. What would we do with her? . . . And then all the Bourbons who are yet in France . . . would for some time at least also be a charge on his Majesty . . . at a time when no expense can be regarded with indifference." Thugut had learned of the project of exchange through the French newspapers, and advised that the Emperor should pretend not to lend credence to the information on the ground that newspaper accounts were proverbially unworthy of attention.[19]

But there were Habsburg relatives who were anxious to give a home to the poor little orphan. The Queen of Naples, Marie Caroline, sister of Marie Antoinette, wished to take the girl as one of her own children.[20] Louis XVIII ordered the Prince of Condé to receive his niece in his name, explaining to the Emperor that he had an "ardent desire to possess all that remains of what I had that was the dearest in the world to me." [21] It is true that Louis XVIII soon changed this magnanimous offer to an insistence to see and speak with Madame Royale,[22] after which his representative would conduct

book kills him only once (M. Garçon, *Louis XVII ou la fausse énigme* [Paris, 1952]).

[17] Fain, *Ms. l'an III*, p. 216.

[18] The expression "Salic Law" is here intentionally avoided, for that law, forbidding women to inherit land (chap. 59, par. 5), had nothing whatsoever to do with succession to the throne of France. *Vide* C. Pfister (Sorbonne) and K. A. Eckhardt (Gottingen), in *Encyc. Brit.*, *s.v.* "Salic Law"; *Webster's New International Dictionary of the English Language* (2nd ed., unabridged; Springfield, Mass., 1954), *s.v.* "Salic law."

[19] Thugut to Count Colloredo, July 15, 1795, *Briefe Thugut*, I, 241–242.

[20] To Emperor, July 18, 1795, Vivenot-Zeissberg, *Quellen*, V, 298; to Empress, Aug. 11, 1795, *ibid.*, p. 325.

[21] July 27, 1795, *ibid.*, pp. 303–304.

[22] Louis informed the Emperor in no uncertain terms that he was much concerned about seeing Mme. Royale *first*. He asserted that he wished to learn from his niece what Louis XVI, Marie Antoinette, and Mme. Elisabeth might have imparted to her as personal messages for him; but it is difficult to comprehend why, for that, it was essential for Louis XVIII to have seen the child before the Emperor did (Aug. 21, 1795, *ibid.*, pp. 333–334). A report to Lord Grenville from Lord Macartney in Verona explains as follows Louis XVIII's desire to see his niece first: Louis feared that Navarre would try to break away from the French Crown and proclaim Mme. Royale as queen, for the estates of Navarre recognized female succession, and had never confirmed an edict of Louis XIII altering that order. Louis therefore wanted Mme. Royale to marry the Duke of Angoulême (Artois' son) to assure the unity of France. It was

the girl to Rome, where his aunts had generously offered to provide for the child's needs, "not with splendor . . . but with decency."[23]

It remained for M. Carletti, minister of another relative, to create the greatest stir. As soon as Carletti heard that the liberation of the princess was under consideration, he, "as the sole foreign envoy who represents at this moment in Paris a prince of the House of Austria," decided to risk a *démarche* in her favor. Declaring that he was acting without the authorization of his court, and for himself alone, he asked the Committee (by letter) "if the Republican Government would not be very pleased if Tuscany requested the liberty of the daughter of Louis XVI, and relieved it of this difficult trust." And he sought permission to present his homage to the "illustrious prisoner."[24] Three days passed — three days without an answer. Perhaps, thought the Italian minister, I should not have said I was acting for myself and without authorization. Carletti thereupon wrote a second letter explaining that though he was acting without express orders, he was yet doing so as the minister of the Grand Duke of Tuscany. The Convention felt obliged to answer, but that answer afforded little in the way of consolation: "The Republic has a rule not to meddle in the internal affairs of neutrals, and expects reciprocity."[25] Then Carletti sought the aid of two influential deputies whose names are yet unknown. This effort also was in vain.[26] A third *démarche*, with quite unforeseen consequences, was made under the Directory. But that story will be told in its proper place.

On June 30, Treilhard, speaking in the name of the Committees of Public Safety and General Security, declared to the Convention that the Republic was already sufficiently consolidated so that it no longer needed to retain the daughter of the last king, or the other members of the royal family.[27] He proposed that Madame Royale be exchanged for the deputies and minister of war delivered over to the Austrians by Dumouriez,[28] and for Sémonville and Maret, arrested shortly thereafter in Switzerland. The

---

to ascertain the degree of her education and the state of her health that Louis wished so much to see Mme. Royale first (Sept. 27, 1795, A. Lebon, *L'Angleterre et l'émigration française de 1794 à 1801* [Paris, 1882], p. 342). Louis XVIII did not see his niece until June 3, 1799 (Lenotre, *Dtr. Louis XVI*, pp. 332–333), for reasons which are beyond the purview of this work.

[23] *Ibid.*

[24] Authority for this sentence alone: Greppi in *RHD*, XV, 351 *et seqq.*

[25] Fain, *Ms. l'an III*, pp. 216–217.

[26] Greppi in *RHD*, XV, 351 *et seqq.*

[27] Madame Royale was the only surviving member of the immediate royal family in France. The King had been executed January 21, 1793; the Queen, October 16, 1793; the King's sister, Elisabeth, May 10, 1794.

[28] Also for the deputy Drouet, captured while with the Army of the North (Thibaudeau, *Mém. Conv. Direc.*, II, 39–40). Drouet and the four betrayed by Dumouriez make the five deputies about whom the documents speak in a way which has led many historians to believe that Dumouriez turned five deputies over to the Austrians. *Vide.*, e.g., Guyot, *Direc.*, p. 125.

project was adopted unanimously.[29] At first General Pichegru was charged with the execution of the decree, and there was much intercourse between the French and Austrian camps.[30] But on August 14, Bacher was ordered to attend to the matter. The exchange was to be a condition precedent and *sine qua non* to the further exchange of military personnel with Austria.[31]

Neither Emperor Francis nor Louis XVIII was pleased with the conditions attached to the French offer of exchange. "Nothing is more insolent . . . than the species of parallel that the rebels dare to draw between my niece and scoundrels," wrote Louis to the Emperor.[32] "In any other circumstances," ran a letter from the Emperor to Clerfayt, "the conditions . . . would be regarded as absolutely inadmissible." It was only regard for his relative and the Bourbon princes and princesses, he declared, which prompted him to accede.[33]

But the negotiation, thus commenced for the second time,[34] was destined to suffer many delays, for great were the difficulties to be surmounted. The Princess must not come personally into contact with the regicides with whom she was to be exchanged.[35] She must be granted all possible considera-

---

[29] *Moniteur*, XXV, 115–116.

[30] Fain, *Ms. l'an III*, p. 279.

[31] Sorel in *RH*, XVIII, 312. This unyielding attitude right at the outset of the negotiation was the result of a previous, unsuccessful effort on the part of Bacher to secure the exchange of the deputies and minister betrayed by Dumouriez. The Vienna government then took the attitude that these men were not prisoners of war, hence not exchangeable with soldiers captured in battle. Austria was willing, however, in case of a general exchange of nationals, to make a special agreement which would include the deputies and Beurnonville (Gresselberg to Saxe-Teschen, Basel, Feb. 24, 1795, sent to Thugut by Degelmann on Feb. 26, 1795, Vivenot-Zeissberg, *Quellen*, V, 105–106 and note). It will be recalled (*vide supra*, chap. iii, § 1) that France, who now wanted to assimilate Beurnonville and the deputies to ordinary prisoners of war, had protested at the time of their betrayal by Dumouriez that the five men could in no wise be regarded as prisoners of war, hence should be returned.

[32] July 27, 1795, Vivenot-Zeissberg, *Quellen*, V, 303.

[33] July 30, 1795, *Thugut, C, W*, p. 180.

[34] *Vide supra*, chap. iii, § 4.

[35] Especially was this true with respect to one of the prisoners, Drouet, sometime postmaster of Sainte-Menehould. It was essential that Madame Royale should under no circumstances chance upon this wretch, for sight of him might recall one of the terrors of her childhood.

To facilitate the escape of the royal family in June 1791, loyal troops had been stationed at certain towns along the projected line of flight. Thirty dragoons and their horses had been quartered in Sainte-Menehould, at a tavern but fifty paces from Drouet's stables. Drouet was furious that the horses had not been put up with him, and swore that he would remember it. These thirty dragoons were present without the concurrence of the *municipalité*, which fact rendered them suspect. And when a heavy berlin drew up, and the dragoons forgot themselves for a moment and saluted its occupants, suspicions rose higher. Postmaster Drouet thought he recognized the King, and galloped by side roads to Varennes, arriving ahead of the berlin. He roused the populace, blocked the bridge, and obliged the party to show its passports. These were found satisfactory — they had been made out in others' names — and Pultier, municipal officer of Varennes, was about to allow the berlin to proceed, when Drouet, in a rage, insisted that here was the royal family, and that the Varennois would be guilty of treason if they let the

tion by the French. Gaping crowds must not be permitted to make of her an object of curiosity; the strictest secrecy must be observed. Some French-speaking companions must accompany her. The place of exchange must be as close as possible so as not to tire the Princess by needless travel, yet there must be no danger from military operations. The drawing-up of an official report of the exchange was the desire of Bacher; a simple receipt was suggested by Degelmann, who was anxious to get away from ceremony, and from documents which succeeding generations might misinterpret. The disposition of the Bourbon princes and princesses [36] had to be decided, since their property and personal liberty to come and go as they pleased had already been restored. All difficulties were finally ironed out with the assistance of Bourcard, Basel burgomaster, who acted as intermediary between Bacher and Degelmann; but so much time elapsed during the process that the exchange could not take place under the Convention.[37]

It must not be thought that Bacher showed himself a hard negotiator. In fact, his moderation was so marked that Degelmann suspected it was part of a plan to approach Austria on the subject of peace; [38] and indeed it did appear from certain expressions of Bacher's that the Committee hoped the exchange would provide an occasion for peace negotiations.[39]

It was quite in line with France's effort to placate Austria that, pending the exchange, the lot of the hapless occupant of the Temple was made less rigorous. She was granted "two morning gowns of colored taffeta, and two of pekin and cotonnade with a lining of Florence taffeta, six pairs of colored silk stockings, six pairs of shoes, two dozen Chemises of the finest Dutch linen, and a green silk gown"; also "paper, pencils, Indian-ink, and brushes." Two books were procured for her from a library. Lastly, she was

---

King and his party escape to a foreign country. It was agreed, therefore, to detain the group until morning. In the morning, Louis was recognized by another person and admitted his identity. The mob then forced the royal family to return to Paris. From Drouet, therefore, flowed all Madame Royale's tribulations (G. Lenotre [pseud. for L. L. T. Gosselin], *Le drame de Varennes, juin 1791* [Paris, 1905], pp. 74–118).

It may seem strange to some that Drouet succeeded almost single-handedly in holding up the royal party, and this point does indeed require elucidation. Under the old regime, postmasters were *de facto* administrative officials of a sort. Holding in their hands the channels of information and of travel, they possessed a certain amount of power; and from power flows a quasi-

authority. This authority was tacitly recognized by the public (G. Laurent, "A propos de Drouet, l'homme de Varennes," *AHRF*, XXI [1949], 247). It is curious to consider, however, that the "authority" of Drouet, which — in the last analysis — flowed from the monarchy, should have been used against the monarch himself.

[36] The wife and children of Philippe Egalité, the Duchess of Bourbon, and the Prince of Conti (Lenotre, *Dtr. Louis XVI*, p. 55, note).

[37] Degelmann to Thugut, Sept. 18, 1795, Vivenot-Zeissberg, *Quellen*, V, 381–382; enclosure: Burckhardt to Degelmann, Sept. 14, *ibid.*, pp. 382–383.

[38] Degelmann to Thugut, Sept. 8, 1795, *ibid.*, p. 354.

[39] *Idem.*, Aug. 23, 1795, *ibid.*, p. 336.

allowed a companion to live with her in the Temple — Mme. Hillaire Chanterenne, whom the delighted girl soon nicknamed Renète. Madame Royale was ignorant of the death of her mother, brother, and aunt, and Renète had strict instructions not to enlighten her. Without this burden to crush her soul, the poor child became cheerful and even gay. Soon she was permitted to walk in the garden and to receive visitors.[40] Among her callers were Mme. de Mackau, one of the four assistant governesses of the royal children before the Revolution; Mme. Laurent, Madame Royale's old nurse; and the Tourzel mother and daughters. Mme. de Tourzel was a former governess of the royal children, and her daughter Pauline was of Madame Royale's age. The Tourzels came three times a week, but never dined in the Tower.[41] It was they who informed the ill-starred princess of her bereavements, though the poor child continued to hope against hope that her brother was not dead.[42] This mother and daughters it was who were selected — tentatively — to accompany Madame Royale to Austria. The final arrangements (and the heartbreak which accompanied them) belong, as indicated, to the Directory.

3. THE THÉREMIN MISSION

On September 25, 1795, there arrived in Basel one of the winners of the essay contest on the advantages of annexing the Rhineland. It was Théremin, the former Prussian, and like all Prussians, there was peace on his lips. He had intended to carry pacific proposals to Schlik, Austrian Ambassador to the Electorate of Mayence and to the Franconian Circle, but Degelmann, the Emperor's minister to Switzerland, was smarting so under Austria's defeats of early September that Théremin decided he would do well to concentrate on him.[43] And indeed, Degelmann did report faithfully everything that Théremin said, even the delicate compliment for his "Excellency [Thugut], of whom many members of the Convention speak with great respect." [44]

Théremin declared that he was acquainted with various members of the Convention, especially Sieyes and Boissy d'Anglas; that he had not been officially commissioned to make peace proposals, but had determined, with the permission of various members of the Convention, to inform the first Austrian minister he met on his way to Germany of the pacific inclinations of the Convention toward Austria, and of its willingness to allow the Habs-

[40] Lenotre, *Dtr. Louis XVI*, p. 73.
[41] Aulard, *Paris*, II, 243–244.
[42] Lenotre, *Dtr. Louis XVI*, pp. 74–75.

[43] Sorel in *RH*, XIX, 41.
[44] Sept. 25, 1795, *Thugut, C, W*, p. 242.

burgs to possess themselves of Bavaria in return for Austria's consent to France's retention of the left bank.[45] The latter point — retention of the left bank — was a *sine qua non* in the Committee's eyes, Théremin intimated.[46]

Degelmann's reply was of the sort an Austrian would reserve for one who was not only a Prussian or a Frenchman, but both! The Austrian monarchy, he said, was founded on honesty, candor, directness; and this probity was not a veneer. Political morality was the bond which held together not only individual governments but human society. If France wished to negotiate with the House of Habsburg, she had to profess similar principles.[47]

The French government had changed entirely for the better, replied Théremin; and he set about canonizing Sieyes and Boissy. Their homes were simple and poverty-stricken. Sieyes was not ashamed to confess he had no servants. Both men were moderate, talented, energetic, firm, fair. " 'We have never had any idea,' Sieyes said to me a few days before my departure, 'of making peace with Prussia to the detriment of Austria.' " And in leaving Degelmann, Théremin declared: "France wants to make peace with Austria, . . . but no evasions! a simple, definite answer!" [48]

Degelmann was of the opinion — and he so reported to Thugut — that Théremin' propositions were either official overtures or an official trap concerted between France and Prussia to compromise Austria in the eyes of the Empire.[49] The overtures were indeed official, for Théremin had been commissioned by the Committee of Public Safety.[50]

On September 29, Théremin paid Degelmann a second visit. He declared that Sieyes and Boissy desired the immediate commencement of negotiations, because they would soon cease to be deputies, and could not be positive of reëlection. He said that if the Austrian government wished him to obtain the authorization of the Committee, he would do so forthwith, and he offered to journey to Vienna should the Habsburg Court so desire. Théremin presented Degelmann with a scheme for an armistice, which, if accepted, could be followed by peace negotiations, either with Barthélemy or with Théremin himself.[51] Théremin later averred to Degelmann that the idea of an armistice was personal to him; [52] that when he had last been in Paris, he had discussed

[45] Not "right" bank as in Sybel, *Europe*, III, 521.

[46] Authority for this sentence alone: Sorel's quotation of Théremin's report to Boissy d'Anglas, Sept. 25, 1795, *RH*, XIX, 43.

[47] Degelmann to Thugut, Sept. 25, 1795, *Thugut, C, W*, p. 242.

[48] *Ibid.*, pp. 242–245.

[49] *Ibid.*, pp. 245–246.

[50] Report of Delacroix to Dir., Nov. 13, 1795, Arch. A. E., *Autriche* Supp. 25, f. 29.

[51] Degelmann to Thugut, Sept. 30, 1795, *Thugut, C, W*, pp. 257–259.

[52] He had not presented it in that light (Degelmann to Thugut, Oct. 23, 1795, *ibid.*, p. 345).

the subject with Sieyes and Boissy, and that they had declared France would never agree to an armistice with a state with which she was at war.[53] Degelmann attributed the change of heart to the Austrian victory of October 12 between Mayence and Frankfort,[54] which had rendered the military situation less favorable to the French. An armistice crystallizes the *status quo*, and a *status quo* of defeat was not to the liking of Sieyes and Boissy. And, of course, allergy for armistices was a chronic weakness of France.

In each of his meetings with Degelmann, Théremin urged speed lest it should be too late. "Events in France," the Austrian minister wrote to Vienna, "explain Théremin's haste regarding his proposal."[55] But Thugut did not consider the matter so urgent. Austria desires the conclusion of peace on just and honorable conditions, he declared to Degelmann, but such a thing must not be done precipitately. The passage of the Rhine by the French has introduced complications; thus the moment for the conclusion of a stable peace, or even of an armistice, does not seem propitious. However, after the end of the campaign has resulted in a greater degree of calm, Austria will welcome propositions aiming to prevent the further effusion of human blood.[56] Degelmann was instructed to break off the negotiations with Théremin.[57]

On November 3, Théremin sent Degelmann another armistice proposal — through one Herrn Hilscher, a former Leipzig professor who had been exiled because of his democratic principles. This proposal had admittedly been authorized by the Committee.[58] However, there was little likelihood that it would be accepted, for the closing days of October witnessed several brilliant victories at France's expense. The fourteen-months-old blockade of Mayence was terminated, and into the hands of Austria fell 138 cannon, 250 munition wagons, and important supplies both of powder and of food.[59] Furthermore, on October 26, the Convention had given way to the Directory, and Herr Hilscher had ceased to represent a living government. It is true that the Committee of Public Safety's life continued beyond the Convention's. But it continued only until the Directory was ready to take over the reins, and that was on November 2.[60] Another negotiation, or attempted negotiation, just missed the November 2 deadline, and that will be considered in the next section, together with another torso — for torsos they both were, as will presently appear.

[53] Théremin to Degelmann, Oct. 18, 1795, *ibid.*, p. 299.

[54] Degelmann to Thugut, Oct. 23, 1795, *ibid.*, p. 345.

[55] Oct. 10, 1795, *ibid.*, p. 281.

[56] Oct. 11, 1795, *ibid.*, pp. 282–283.

[57] Thugut to Degelmann, Oct. 31, 1795, *ibid.*, p. 352.

[58] Degelmann to Thugut, *ibid.*, p. 355; enclosure, *ibid.*, pp. 358–359.

[59] Heigel, *Deutsche Geschichte*, II, 200.

[60] A. Debidour (ed.), *Recueil des actes du Directoire Exécutif* (4 vols., Paris, 1910–1917), I, 1.

4. VON ANDLAU AND DE RAYNEVAL

On November 1, 1795, one von Andlau, young and not inspiring confidence, informed Degelmann that an agent of the Convention, Maugeot, had commissioned him to ask for a safe-conduct for someone who wished to repair to Vienna with propositions of peace.

Maugeot had formerly been in the Austrian military service, and knew Bacher. But Degelmann informed von Andlau that he would have to procure written authority from the government at Paris before his request could even be considered. "I knew I should receive such an answer," the young man replied; and with that he lapsed back into obscurity.[61]

De Rayneval's overture, it seems, did not even progress that far. De Rayneval, the brother of Gérard de Rayneval,[62] wrote a letter to Thugut asking him to send a negotiator to some frontier town with propositions of peace. The negotiator could pretend to be a merchant, and the strictest secrecy would be maintained. It seems that this letter was never despatched.[63]

In the weeks preceding the end of the Convention, the government and "free-lance diplomats" of France struck out in all directions in a frantic effort to capture the laurels of pacificator before the advent of the new government should have relegated them to possible obscurity. Von Andlau and De Rayneval were mere manifestations of what might be termed a negotiation-panic. This, like other panics, netted nothing. Or, more strictly speaking, it yielded less than nothing, for it brought to the fore Claude Pierre, the "Marquis" de Poteratz, of whom too much anon.

5. BOISSY D'ANGLAS AND POTERATZ

Boissy d'Anglas appeared often upon the stage during the stirring drama of the Convention, and played his part nobly and well. Sometimes his beliefs were exaggerated or erroneous,[64] but they were always honest convictions, and subject to change by the first fair argument that could be adduced. But this upright man chose as his political mentor a person to whom the same adjective would never have been applied except in jest, to wit, the afore-mentioned "Marquis" de Poteratz. This pseudo marquis (no official document grants him the title) had entered the army as a volunteer in 1752, and reached the rank of major by 1785, when he was pensioned. He had fought in six campaigns, and been wounded (once), but never received the Cross of Saint-Louis. Ever since his youth, Poteratz had been involved

---

[61] Degelmann to Thugut, Nov. 3, 1795, *Thugut, C, W*, pp. 357–358.
[62] *Vide supra*, chap. viii, § 1a.

[63] Sorel in *RH*, XIX, 26–27.
[64] Some of his enemies called him Boissy Famine (*Mem. Barère*, II, 115).

in "shady" transactions, and more than once was a guest in the Bastille. He was there in 1789, though not on July 14, for he was not one of the seven wretches "rescued" on that historic day.[65] Soon after his release, he wormed his way into Dumouriez' confidence. He also made friends with Barère and Hérault de Séchelles, through whom he obtained a position procuring supplies for the army. Constitutionally unable to tread the straight and narrow path, the "Marquis" was presently behind bars again — this time for speculating in supplies. He was released after Thermidor.[66]

Obser has sketched with deft pen a colorful word-portrait of this rascal: "The type of political adventurer so often found under the old regime, as clever as he was conscienceless, accustomed to take money where he could find it, restlessly occupied with audacious intrigues and fantastic projects, consumed with the ambitious endeavor to play a role in public life, Pierre Claude de Poterat[z] . . . , like so many other unclean elements, owed his rise to the Revolution." [67]

The miracle was that a distinguished, witty, honest admirer of modern philosophy [68] like Boissy should have consented to link his name with such scum as the "Marquis," but revolution makes strange bedfellows, and the affable scoundrel did know how to win friends and influence people. It was not long before Boissy was introducing Poteratz to the Committee, and reading his interminable memoirs.

Thus, since Boissy exercised much influence upon the German policy of the Republic, and Poteratz exercised much influence upon Boissy,[69] it is important to examine some typical memoirs of Poteratz'. The two summarized below, the first of which has not hitherto seen the light of day,[70] were remitted to Boissy d'Anglas on July 12 and 21, 1795, respectively.

The first memoir asserted that the only way the various neighbors of France could be forced to consent to their own spoliation — the only way, in other words, that France could acquire the three ecclesiastical electorates,

[65] A. Bégis, "Noms des prisonniers de la Bastille délivrés le 14 juillet," according to the jail book of the Bastille, in P. Cottin (ed.), Revue rétrospective; recueil de pièces intéressantes et de citations curieuses (20 vols. in 2 ser., Paris, 1885–1894), Ser. I, Vol. I, 21. Sorel states incorrectly that the Revolution rescued Poteratz from the Bastille (in RH, XVIII, 291). Undoubtedly, Sorel has lent credence to the statement in Mém. homme d'Etat, III, 79: "Poterat[z] . . . boasted that he was one of the seven prisoners found in the Bastille on July 14."

[66] Guyot, Direc., p. 134 and n. 2; Debidour, Recueil, I, 137, n. 2.

[67] K. Obser, "Der Marquis von Poterat und die revolutionäre Propaganda am Oberrhein im Jahre 1796," ZGOR (Zeitschrift für die Geschichte des Oberrheins), n. F., VII (1892), 385.

[68] Trevor, British minister to Turin, in "Memorandum on the State of France," Dropmore Papers, III, 86.

[69] Perhaps Boissy had two mentors. Sandoz wrote of him on March 14, 1796, "He is an honest man who is allowing himself to be deceived by the paradoxes of the abbé Sieyes." — To the King, G. S. Arch., R XI Frankreich 89, fasc. 346, p. 189.

[70] The second is reproduced in large part by Sorel in RH, XVIII, 293–296.

and Clèves, Gelderland, Maestricht, Brabant, Dutch Flanders, part of
Zeeland, etc. — was to make an accord with Austria. With Austria and
France agreed, the other states would not dare to protest, and France would
be able to dictate a stable, useful, and honorable peace respecting Germany
and Italy. It might truly be difficut to reach such an accord, but with
adroitness and *money*,[71] success would by no means be impossible. Poteratz
confessed he had always distrusted "the frightfully Machiavellian principles"
of the Berlin cabinet, whose promises were worthless unless force were at
hand to compel their fulfillment.

After making peace with Austria, France could "unleash against it
[England] that terrible pack of turbulent and victory-accustomed men who
abound in the armies, and who would be very embarrassing indeed if they
were suddenly [disbanded], for, having lost the habit of work, they would
become extremely difficult to keep within bounds, and yet more dangerous
to the public tranquillity." [72] This fear of the return of the French armies
should be noted well. It was an element which contributed to the continuation of the war far beyond the time when it (the war) could have been of
any possible benefit to France.

The other memoir bore the same title. (*Vide* note last cited.) After painting a sad picture of the internal and external condition of France, Poteratz
declared that the panacea for France's ills was to negotiate simultaneously,
but separately, with all the enemies of France; to sow discord among them; [73]
to promise them what they demanded, and grant them what one pleased;
to lavish money on the cabinets; to deceive everyone if France's interest
demanded it.

If there was to be yet another dismemberment of Poland (the Third
Partition did not actually take place until October 24, 1795), since France
could not prevent it, "she should at least be given, directly or indirectly, a
portion — or take it by force if it were not given to her with good grace."
This would enable part of Poland to serve — as the ecclesiastical states of
Germany were expected to serve — for compensations.

After considering the various possible indemnities of German princes
who would lose territory by the cession of the left bank to France, and after
discussing the German constitution, Poteratz suddenly realized that "all
these internal arrangements are as nothing to the Republic; it should manage

[71] For bribery, of course.

[72] "Mémoire sur les moyens de procurer promptement la paix à la France en traitant avec la cour de Vienne," remitted to Boissy d'Anglas for the Committee on July 12, 1795, Arch. A. E. *Autriche* 364, ff. 156–157.

[73] However, Poteratz was not the only modern Machiavelli. Cf. Alvensleben's memoir to the Prussian King and Ministry, dated June 28, 1795, and approved, especially by Fin-kenstein: "The role of his Excellency, Mr. Hardenberg . . . [shall be] to try to arouse hatred between the two nations [France and Austria]." — Bailleu, *Pr. Frk.*, I, 10.

things in such a way that it can conserve its natural limits. That is the essential point."

The mode of accomplishing this, aside from the general panacean measures quoted above, was to foster the formation of a league of armed neutrality between the Danes, Swedes, republics of Italy — and Prussians, if they were willing to join. The King of Prussia should be urged to invade Bohemia and to threaten Frankfort. If he hesitated to do so, that was proof that he had been won over by England, and was treating with Russia and Austria. Another possible means was to negotiate with Austria. If an arrangement reciprocally advantageous to the two states were made, they would become faithful friends — as faithful as they were anxious that the treaty should endure.

Poteratz presented a list of the military and financial advantages of the left bank to France. All of the arguments we have heard before, except two: Not many places along the Rhine frontier would have to be fortified, for there are no open spaces between Mayence and Nijmwegen. By conserving *both* banks of the Rhine, Wahal, and lower Meuse, France would conserve all the means of offense and defense, while the enemy would have none to utilize against France.

Poteratz ended this memoir with a statement of the conditions under which he would agree to initiate negotiations with Vienna. These were, briefly, personal security for his acts, responsibility only to the Commission of Foreign Affairs, and permission to offer recompense to those who had lost considerably by the French Revolution and would render service to France.[74]

6. THE POTERATZ MISSION TO VIENNA

The Committee of Public Safety did see fit to send Poteratz to Vienna.[75] However, to understand the negotiation with which he was charged, the life of the Austrian helmsman, Thugut, must first be scrutinized.

Louis XV had been accustomed to maintain, at the various courts of Europe, secret agents whose function it was to induce officials to sell their secrets to France. A certain Barth had arrived at Vienna in 1766 on such a mission, and Thugut, then junior court secretary and court interpreter,

[74] Arch. A. E., *Autriche* 364, ff. 158–161. As will appear in the next section, Poteratz had Thugut in mind.

[75] Sorel shrewdly remarks: "Until then, the diplomacy of the Committee of the Year III was violent, . . . haughty, sometimes wily, often arrogant, . . . [but] it had at least recoiled from despicable means and unavowable combinations. . . Sieyes had traced the plan of the diplomacy of the future. Poteratz was to place at the disposal of his ideas the arsenal of the intrigues of the past. He [Poteratz] showed how the grand design of the Republic could be realized by the means of corruption of the old regime. He forms thus the transition between the Committee of the Year III and the Directory." — In *RH*, XVIII, 291.

readily agreed to maintain a secret correspondence with the French government. Louis XV found this correspondence of value, and conferred upon
Thugut a pension and the brevet of lieutenant colonel in 1768. Shortly thereafter, the young Austrian was granted a yearly income of 13,000 livres, and
promised an asylum in France in case of need. In 1769, the Austrian government named Thugut chargé d'affaires at Constantinople, and as such he
continued to correspond with Versailles under the name of M. Freund.
Thugut's double rôle ended in 1774, with the death of Louis XV. The new
king was no friend of corruption, and neither was the new minister of
foreign affairs, Vergennes (though Vergennes was initiated into the secret).
Thugut, also, desired to put an end to his double rôle. Saint-Priest, French
Ambassador to Constantinople, recalled to his government the promises
which had been made to Thugut; he declared that the Austrian agent was
about to be recalled from Constantinople, and desired to come to France
and enter the service of the Queen. In 1777, Thugut, on leave, went to Paris,
and Louis XVI promised him the brevet of brigadier general in case a war
should break out. In 1780, Thugut's French pension was changed into a
life annuity of 13,000 livres. Three years later, Thugut secured a mission to
Paris, and remained in the French capital for four years. There he made
many close acquaintances: Mirabeau, Augeard (private secretary to the
Queen), Lafayette, and Poteratz.[76]

It must be admitted, in justice to Thugut, that his communications with
France were of little real importance, and that of his two employers, he
served the Emperor the better. His services to the Habsburg ruler earned
him the title of Baron of the Empire as early as 1774.

The Revolution and the downfall of the monarchy put an abrupt end to
Thugut's relations with France. Moreover, the secret of his treason was
discovered by the revolutionists during an inventory of the documents
found in the Tuileries on November 20, 1792. In the *armoire de fer* (iron
safe), a secret cabinet built in the wall by Gamain, the locksmith, at Louis
XVI's order,[77] Soulavie uncovered Saint-Priest's correspondence. This correspondence the Committee of Public Safety decided to use to force Thugut
to make peace on France's terms. It was thought that fear of the skeleton
in his closet would render the Austrian minister docile.[78]

[76] H. Zeissberg in *Allgemeine deutsche Biographie, s.v.* "Thugut"; Sorel in *RH*, XVII,
38 *et seqq.*

[77] Mathiez, *Fr. Rev.*, p. 257. Louis XVI forged
the door himself, Gamain putting on the
hinges and lock. The iron safe was located
behind a panel along a dark passageway
(*Diary* of Gouv. Morris, II, 580, n. 2).

[78] Guyot, *Direc.*, p. 175, n. 1 *et passim.* Cf.

Langwerth von Simmern, *Oestr. Reich fr.
Rev*, I, 346: "The stories circulated at that
time by the French, that Thugut was
bribed in Constantinople, are manifestly so
unsubstantiated that we do not even need
to take notice of them here." It might have
been worth while if Langwerth von Simmern had taken notice of them, and had
perhaps even run them down to their ori-

In *vendémiaire*, Year IV (September-October 1795), Poteratz arrived at Vienna. Thugut did not dare expel him because he feared the secret would leak out. He also was curious as to what Poteratz had to say. Poteratz commenced by asking Thugut whether he would speak as the Baron of Thugut, or as the Minister of the Emperor, adding that he had certain things to say to the Baron which the Minister could never hear. Thugut remained silent a long while, then smiled, and said he would speak as Poteratz' old friend, the Baron of Thugut. In the course of the conversation, however, the Baron demanded "how it was possible that I was charged with so contemptible a mission," and let loose a fearful tirade at the government of France.[79]

Poteratz reported to Boissy that he had told Thugut he was authorized to say that France invited the Emperor to choose and take possession of any territories he wanted, provided they were contiguous to the mass of his hereditary states, at a distance from France, and not allies of the latter.[80] The French agent was alluding to Bavaria, of course.

Thugut declared to Poteratz that he loved France, which love had caused him to invest all his money there;[81] and that his money had been completely lost. Poteratz answered, "You need only speak, and all your money will be returned." Thugut replied, "But what will I do with your paper?" "I [Poteratz] assured him that he had misunderstood me; that since he had invested coin, it was likewise in coin that I intended he should be repaid. . . He answered me very affectionately: 'It is not yet the time.' "[82]

Thugut sent Blumendorf, former secretary of the Austrian embassy at Paris, to see Poteratz, to mask, so Thugut explained, the object of the French agent's visit, which people were beginning to notice. Poteratz assured Blumendorf of his good intentions toward the Baron, and promised to re-double his circumspection so as to remove all legitimate causes of suspicion, "fully resolved, however," he wrote to Boissy, "not to lose a single chance to create and vivify them, for according to my principles, in politics as in war, one should always do what his enemy fears. Judged by this standard, my success has far exceeded my hopes, though outwardly my conduct is worthy of praise, and beyond all reproach on the part of the Baron."[83]

Thugut soon asked Poteratz to return to Paris for powers and instructions, arguing that whatever the French agent did, he might be disavowed by

---

gin in the documents, and then reconciled these documents with the subsequent history of Thugut.

[79] Poteratz to Boissy d'Anglas, Oct. 5, 1795, Arch. A. E., *Autriche* Supp. 25, ff. 6–7.

[80] Hüffer-Luckwaldt, *Quellen*, Pt. II, Vol. I, 8–9, Oct. 9, 1795.

[81] He probably feared to invest his French income in Austria lest it be queried by what sleight of hand he had managed to invest more than his entire salary.

[82] Hüffer-Luckwaldt, *Quellen*, Pt. II, Vol. I, 7.

[83] *Ibid.*, p. 6, Oct. 9, 1795.

the Committee. Thugut declared that he had himself received a letter from
the Committee that very morning, about which Poteratz knew nothing.[84]
In reality, the Austrian minister was merely trying to rid himself of the inconvenient visitor. He succeeded, and the Convention came to an end without further prosecution of the blackmail scheme. But the showdown had
only been postponed, and the "negotiations" of Poteratz form one of the
most "intriguing" episodes of the Directorial period.

7. THE POLITICAL AND MILITARY SITUATION ON THE EVE
OF THE DIRECTORY

As mentioned above, the minor engagement at Handschuhsheim on September 24, 1795, marked the turning point of the autumn campaign — a campaign which, for France, had come in like a lion and was going out like a
lion in reverse. Jourdan was forced back to the Lahn; the right-bank
blockade of Mayence was ended, and — to repeat what has already been
anticipatorily mentioned — the intricate system of fortifications before Mayence on the left bank was stormed by the Imperial troops of Clerfayt and
captured; Mannheim was besieged by Wurmser (and later captured); a
goodly part of the Rhineland was rewon.[85] If Clerfayt had not relapsed into
his habit of "excessive prudence"[86] — if it had not been necessary "to go
down on one's knees before him twenty times to induce him to take one
step forward"[87] — the autumn campaign of 1795 might have marked the
end of the French Revolution. Indeed, the Revolution came precariously
close to liquidation anyway.

When the Convention was elected in 1792, it was supposed to formulate
a constitution for France, and dissolve. It did formulate a constitution —
several of them, in fact — but it hesitated to give up its power. Some of its
members felt that its continued existence was necessary to the preservation
of the Republic and of their own lives. An election might sweep into office
the relatives and friends of *émigrés* and priests, who would forthwith call
back the Bourbons, and wreak vengeance upon the Conventionals for their
crimes. Finally, however, a new constitution was made (Constitution of the
Year III) and presented to the vote of the people; but with it — as a rider,
so to speak — was the above-mentioned[88] law providing that two thirds of
the legislators of the new government should be selected from among the
former members of the Convention. The moderate bourgeois and royalist
sections of Paris armed to resist this so-called "Law of the Two Thirds."

[84] Poteratz to Boissy d'Anglas, Oct. 13, 1795,   [87] Thugut to Count Colloredo, Nov. 18, 1795,
ibid., p. 10.   *Briefe Thugut*, I, 282.
[85] Heigel, *Deutsche Geschichte*, II, 200–201.   [88] Chap. xiv, § 6.
[86] *Mém. Saint-Cyr*, II, 284.

The Convention deputed Barras to defend it. The result was the riot of 13 *vendémiaire*, III (October 5, 1795), in which a "whiff of grape-shot" from Barras' assistant, Bonaparte, crushed the dissentient element.[89]

Barras pretends in his memoirs that the suppression of the insurrection of Vendémiaire was a measure of national defense — to save France from being partitioned by the foreign enemy.[90] Perhaps he expects one even to believe it was a peace measure, for he quotes P. F. Réal to the effect that "if colorless men, without spirit, if friends of nobles . . . and priests, if protectors of *émigrés*, if *émigrés* themselves are borne to this sublime magistracy,[91] the foreign war will resume its baleful activity." [92] This, of course, is sheer nonsense, for if it were the Convention which stood for peace, why should its members — many of them regicides who dreaded the return of the *émigrés* [93] — have voted to exclude from public office all *émigrés* and relatives of *émigrés* until the general peace? [94] Does not the postponement till the general peace of an event which might sound the death knell of many a Conventional justify the assumption that it was not intended that the era of general peace should ever arrive?

There are indeed those who maintain that "general peace" was used by the victors of Vendémiaire as a euphonious equivalent of "doomsday." Is this point of view defensible? Does not the "negotiation-panic" of autumn, 1795, belie such a theory? The answer to the latter question is "not necessarily." Peace with some of the coalesced powers would not be the same as general peace so long as one enemy remained. And we have no evidence that it was contemplated to come to terms with all the Republic's enemies. In fact, we know that many of the revolutionists favored retaining permanently at least one foe, England or Austria usually being singled out for this honor, though Russia was not entirely neglected.

It is not at all unlikely, then, that the retiring Conventionals had no intention of ever being confronted with a general peace. The same can be said of the new government, by virtue of the Law of the Two Thirds. A purely domestic matter — the personal safety of a few hundred regicides — thus bade fair to trap Europe in the abyss of war. How inauspicious a start for the new government! How unfortunate for the peace-loving moderates of France, and for a war-weary continent!

---

[89] Pariset, *La Rév.*, pp. 285–292; Sciout, *Direc.*, I, chaps. vii–viii.

[90] *Mém. Barras*, I, 260. Or is it Saint-Albin speaking?

[91] The Council of Five Hundred and Council of Ancients — the bicameral legislature provided for by the new constitution (Duguit and Monnier, *Const. et lois*, p. 86 [*Titre*

V, art. 44]).

[92] "Essai sur les journées du 13 et 14 vendémiaire," quoted in *Mém. Barras*, I, 276.

[93] Four fifths of them could not "return," for they had never left France (Sciout, *Direc.*, I, 411).

[94] Law of Oct. 25, 1795, *Moniteur*, XXVI, 332.

CHAPTER XVI

CONCLUDING REMARKS — CONVENTION

*W*HAT was the German policy of the Convention, as portrayed in the foregoing pages? The question is not easily answered. The German policy of the Convention was like the alphabet, which defies description except as the sum total of its component parts. We have, then, a series of German policies. There was the policy of the newly created Convention, whose first cry blended with the shouts of exultation as the Prussians turned about after Valmy; the policy of the First Committee of Public Safety, born of bitter defeat and treason; the policy of the Great Committee, conceived in despair and suckled on patriotic frenzy; and the policy of the Thermidorians, hunted men whose ruling passion was fear of the block.

But this is an oversimplification of a very complicated situation. Each member of the Convention had his personal opinion as to what France's German policy should be, and that opinion was not always the same, but varied with circumstances. Came news of a defeat, and he worried lest the integrity of French soil should not be respected; followed news of a victory, and usually he saw no reason why Liberty, Equality, and Fraternity should not presently conquer the Universe, or Europe, or at least the left bank of the Rhine. It was not only the radicals who wavered thus. Staunch moderates like Boissy d'Anglas were equally vacillatory. And the policy of the Convention followed the opinions of its members, swaying to and fro with the military fortunes of its armies.

Then we must take account of the Provisional Executive Council or Ministry. Each minister had his personal policy, and the views of the minister of foreign affairs did not necessarily prevail in the Council. For example, Danton, as minister of justice in the autumn of 1792, controlled foreign policy more completely than he did justice.

After the creation of the Committee of Public Safety, a further complicating element was introduced. The Committee was superior to the ministers, yet the policies of the two sometimes clashed, and we have the phenomenon of contradictory orders — until the Committee acted to suspend the objectionable ministerial decree. Nor was the will of the Committee itself a simple fact to be determined by the counting of noses. Danton ruled the First Committee, and Robespierre, the Great Committee, by personal influence; and the requirement of a two-thirds vote was often little more than a mere technicality.

By the summer of 1794, the Ministry had dropped completely out of the picture, but the situation with respect to the Committee became yet more confused when the Thermidorians provided for the renewal of the Committee monthly by fourths. Thereafter, one must reckon not only with fluctuations in policy of the individual members of the Committee, but with fluctuations in membership. Also, after Thermidor, the Convention was no longer a rubber stamp to register the Committee's will, and parliamentary debates become of increased importance as gauges of France's German policy.

Should mention of the Republic's generals be omitted, it would be a major error, for they often had their own policies which coincided little with the Paris government's policy — or should we more realistically say "policies"? The independence of Dumouriez and Custine and Pichegru will readily be recalled. Custine went so far as to imprison the commissioners of the minister of war. He would "never make a god out of an imbecile, even if the latter were a minister," he said.[1]

Then there were the Representatives on Mission, who often bent the Paris government's policy into shapes which accorded with their own wills — shapes directly antithetic to their orders from the capital. It was not the ingenious Merlin of Thionville who was most guilty in this respect, but the Representatives Roberjot and Dubois. Merlin had a different way of making his policy prevail. He wrote to his friend, Merlin of Douai of the Committee of Public Safety, and the latter changed the minds of his colleagues on the Committee to correspond with Merlin of Thionville's.

Lastly, there was the policy of the Republic's diplomatic representatives abroad, principally of Barthélemy, who forced the foreign policy of France into a mold consonant with his own ideas.

These, then, are the elements which constitute the German policy of the Convention — the official German policy. Or are we drawing a distinction where none really exists? In revolutionary times it is not always certain which is the true government — the silk-scarved, illegally elected deputy or the mud-bespattered, perhaps blood-bespattered source of the deputy's power; the bemedalled, epauletted officer or the underpaid, ill-clothed private who wins his medals for him. Why are not the groans of the soldier home on furlough, the extravagant proposals of the Jacobin Club, the

[1] Sybel, *Europe*, II, 341, n. 1; 342.

angry protests of the wineshop, café, and street as much a part of the policy of France as the machinations of an Aubry, or the intrigues of a Dumouriez or a Pichegru? And how can we deny the right of the moderate element crushed at Vendémiaire to at least as much standing as we grant the ultra-radical Jacobin Club and street? It is clear that a true picture of the German policy of France must deal with more than laws and decrees and official documents. It must deal with men, all brands of men, washed and un-washed, for therein, in the last analysis, lies the policy of a nation.

Obviously, it would be impossible to comprise within this analysis all the preceding factors without reproducing the foregoing volume. It will there-fore be necessary to speak in somewhat general terms. Two factors stand out as especially constant elements in the Convention's German policy. They are friendship for Prussia, and desire to give the Republic the ancient bounds of Gaul. Neither factor enjoyed uninterrupted favor throughout the life of the Convention, but deviations were always followed by a return to the norm. The reason was grounded deep in French history. Alliance with the enemies of the Habsburgs had constituted the pivot of France's German policy ever since Emperor Charles V threatened the very existence of France with the German and Spanish jaws of his dynastic pincers. True, France was hostile to her trans-Rhenish neighbors before this, but her hostility did not approach in sustained bitterness the life-and-death struggle of the six-teenth and seventeenth centuries. Previous policy was largely concerned with the series of nibbles by which France sought to gnaw away the undue ad-vantage gained by Louis the German at Mersen in 870 — by which she hoped some day to plant the fleur de lys on the banks of the magnificent stream which divided Gaul from Germany in Caesar's time.

France's friendship for Prussia was not the result solely of utilitarian motives, as some Germans would have us believe. Indeed, it was conditioned to some extent by the principle of *divide et impera*, but it would be unjust to a great nation to neglect her virtues and see only her sordid side. France has always been liberal in thought. Catholic? yes; but her Catholicism did not prevent her from allying with the German Protestants to combat a fellow Catholic. Nor did it prevent her from becoming the cradle of a most un-Catholic philosophy. France sympathized with the striving of Prussia against constituted authority as represented by the Emperor, the Catholic Emperor. She exalted the Hohenzollern king who appreciated her own iconoclastic idol, Voltaire, and who spoke French and thought French and loved France. Jefferson's epigram, "Every man has two countries: his own, and France," was never more applicable than in the case of Frederick the Great. That monarch may have combated France in the Seven Years' War, but that was the fault of France. Why had she allied with the enemy of her friend? France fully expected the land of the late philosopher-king to view her Revolution as the bloom, the flower, of philosophy. Indeed, the Revolution did have many sympathizers on the banks of the Spree and the Havel, not only among *hoi polloi* but also among the educated and blue-blooded official classes. Friendship for Prussia was one of the most sincere as well as the most useful of the Convention's policies.

If Prussia had agreed to ally with France, as the Republic desired, the German policy of the Convention would have been much simplified. But without ever definitively refusing, the Prussians continually postponed discussion of the subject, alleging first one reason, then another. France felt thwarted, and began to cast about for other possible friends in Germany. There were none of military consequence save Austria! The tribune, the wineshop, the street shuddered at the thought. Would it be necessary, however, actually to become reconciled to Austria? If negotiations, however tenuous, were commenced with that power, Prussia would surely hear of them and fly into France's arms. This hypothesis prompted most of the overtures made to Austria during the Convention, and there were many.

Aside from immediate military and commercial benefits consequent upon Prussia's withdrawal from the Coalition, aside also from the prospect that Prussia would join France in armed conflict against Austria, what exactly did France expect to gain by her friendship with Prussia? Renunciation by Prussia of her left-bank territories (Clèves, Meurs, and Upper Gelderland) in return for compensation on the right bank; Prussia's aid in inducing the Empire to relinquish the Rhineland at the end of the war; and the assurance of prolonged peace for the Republic by the erection within Germany of a formidable rival to the House of Habsburg.

A glance at the map of Europe in 1792 will show how much more extensive were the Habsburg possessions than the Hohenzollern — reckoning both Imperial and extra-Imperial territories. If Prussia possessed exactly the same resources in men and money as Austria, France would be able to control Germany by shifting her influence from one to the other as circumstances required. The Committee seems at isolated intervals to have appreciated the wisdom of such a policy, but too often we find it acting as though it had never heard of it. Possessed of but a modicum of political experience, the French government failed fully to appreciate that statesmanship involves planning for all the eventualities of a perhaps distant future, and adhering to that plan with inflexible will in the face of temptations offering present advantage. The Committee, interested mainly in procuring *now* an ally against Austria — as strong an ally as possible — sought to lure Prussia into alliance with France by offering to help build the Hohenzollern state into the most powerful unit of Germany. Barthélemy, more perspicacious, saw the dangers in this policy. He did not even favor building Prussia up to equal strength with Austria. France, he cautioned, should further the breakdown of the large units of Germany into small ones instead of help-ing large units to become larger.[2] The strongest bond France should approve, he believed, was a Prussian-led *confederation* of German princes hostile to Austria, inasmuch as a confederation was inherently weak and would not constitute a bar to French influence in the Empire. It seems that the Com-mittee adopted this viewpoint when it composed the instructions to Caillard, its plenipotentiary to Berlin, in September 1795, for Caillard was ordered to work for the reconstitution of Frederick II's League of Princes to prevent Austria from absorbing Bavaria. But the total lack of consistency in the Com-mittee's policy appears again two weeks later when France offered Bavaria to Austria through Théremin.

Looking at French policy retrospectively, we can see how right was Bar-thélemy in opposing the building up of nuclei of future resistance to France. Certainly it was a French God Who had parcelled Germany out among hun-dreds of mutually hostile princes. The failure of France to realize the good fortune she enjoyed contributed largely to the dismal days of 1870 and 1914 and 1940.

As a rule, then, the Committee desired to see Prussia "the most powerful monarchy in Europe." What lands was it willing for Prussia to annex in order that this very desirable(?) end should be attained — first, assuming that Prussia would merely be friends with France; and secondly, that Prus-sia would ally with France? In default of alliance, the Republic favored the secularization in Prussia's behalf of a bishopric or two on the right bank of the Rhine. This would constitute mere indemnification for the loss of Clèves, Meurs, and Upper Gelderland. But if Prussia agreed to alliance, France would not begrudge Hanover to Frederick William, in addition to any ecclesiastical territory that monarch might covet. Or Frederick Wil-liam might have Brunswick, and let Duke Ferdinand have Hanover. It mattered little to the Committee what territories Prussia chose, so long as they were on the right bank of the Rhine, and the property of ecclesiastical or hostile princes.

Not hostile territory, and therefore not legitimate booty for Prussia, was Poland. In fact, the Republic regarded the Polish partitions as the carving up of a friend — and clenched her teeth in sullen anger as her potential ally smacked his lips and reached out his knife for more. It was only by pre-tending to herself that Russia was the real villain that France was able to

---

[2] Cf. the words of one of Böhmer's essayists: "God forbid that we should be so overcon-fident as to deliberately strengthen those who might at any time become our enemies." — *Supra*, chap. xiv, § 5.

continue cooing in Frederick William's ear. Sieyes even went so far as to suggest that a Hohenzollern king could become sovereign of a reconstituted Poland — as if Prussia were interested in the restoration of Poland!

It might be illuminating to inquire why *France* was so interested. Undoubtedly there was much sympathy with Poland because that country was, in effect, the little fellow who was being martyred by the neighborhood bullies. However, it would be a gross error to neglect the factor of so-called checkerboard diplomacy by which contiguous states are natural enemies; alternate states, natural friends. According to this principle, France and Poland were destined by their very location to be friends; France and the Empire and Russia, enemies. Poland was therefore a "natural" ally of France against the Emperor, and as such, necessarily an object of French solicitude.

It could be argued that sympathy for Poland cannot have played a major share in the Convention's German policy, or it would have been easier for France to come to an arrangement with Austria than with Prussia.[3] Maria Theresa had participated in the First Partition of Poland with obvious regret, and had taken no part in the Second Partition. But Austria nurtured designs in the West at the expense of France's friend, Bavaria, and at the expense of France herself. The Republic, on the other hand, coveted that Austrian province — Belgium — which Austria wanted to give to the Wittelsbachs in exchange for their ancient patrimony. Belgium was populous and wealthy — very wealthy; part of its inhabitants spoke French; Belgium had formed part of Roman Gaul, the prototype of France; Belgium would be easily defensible against its former, distant ruler — all these things rendered Belgium a choice morsel in French eyes. We may say, then, that the Republic was not less interested in Poland; merely more interested in other things.

As indicated, the usual Revolutionary policy of shunning Austria in favor of Prussia was not invariable or universal. Danton, as head of the First Committee, tried to negotiate peace with both powers; the Great Committee shunned both at first, then sounded Prussia, and finally negotiated in all seriousness with Austria; the early Thermidorians, nervously excited after their *coup d'état*, shied away from both powers like the early Robespierrists, but presently engaged in unofficial parleys with both Prussia and Austria, then in official parleys with Prussia (Treaty of Basel), and finally in official parleys with Austria (through Théremin and Poteratz). In the Convention there existed a group of deputies with a predilection for Austria, the most

[3] Indeed, five Polish deputies who were refugees in France recommended to the French government that Austria's jealousy of the Prussian and Russian shares of the Polish partitions be utilized to secure Austrian aid for the resurrection of Poland (Oct. 10, 1795, Arch. N., AF III 74, d. 301).

prominent of whom was perhaps Boissy d'Anglas; and they possessed considerable influence. Among the masses, the more moderately inclined were not unfavorably disposed to Austria, especially after the Treaty of Basel, when it was realized that only a *general peace* would fill the empty bread basket. The royalists, of increasing influence during the later Convention until Vendémiaire, were pro-Austrian, and so were many of the wealthy bourgeois. All in all, there was a fairly strong branch of public opinion open to reconciliation to Austria. How, then, does it happen that France and Austria were unable to reach an accord, like France and Prussia? Did not France and Prussia have differences too, just as difficult of solution as the dispute over Belgium? Was there any real, any vital, difference in the relation of these two powers with respect to France?

Let us consider first questions of territorial adjustment. At Basel, France had demanded of Prussia Clèves, Meurs, and Upper Gelderland. In her conversations with Austria, she demanded the Austrian Netherlands, i.e., Belgium and Luxemburg. The Republic was indeed asking more of Austria than she had of Prussia, both in population and in taxable wealth, but it is unlikely that Belgium was the principal obstacle to a settlement. The Archduke of Austria, as Emperor, was sworn to defend the Empire and the Imperial constitution, and the Republic was demanding that Francis II allow her to annex the entire left bank of the Rhine. Now, the left bank included the possessions of many lesser German princes, several of them electors, and Austria's compliance with this request would have constituted a bad blow to the whole Imperial structure, and perhaps have cost the Habsburgs the Imperial crown. The same demand had been made upon Prussia at Basel, but Frederick William — possibly pleased with the dynastic advantages such a blow would offer — sloughed off all responsibility upon his coprinces. The Emperor, vitally concerned, could not afford to indulge in similar tactics. Another difference was that Prussia's interest in the French monarchy was merely academic. The blood of Austria's gallant Maria Theresa flowed in the veins of France's martyred queen and dauphin and little princess. The reëstablishment of the monarchy was for a Habsburg a living issue, a personal issue. Then there was the religious question: When the revolutionists attacked the Catholic Church, they were attacking the Emperor's own church. Frederick William was a Calvinist,[4] and cannot have felt a personal pang, as Francis undoubtedly did, at each instance of mistreatment of the Catholic clergy. Further, Prussia had glutted her appe-

---

[4] It is explained *supra* (Pt. I, chap. iv, n. 134) how a Lutheran people came to have a Calvinist prince. Actually, the King was an occultist, and too busy communing with the shade of Jesus (!) to be concerned with His earthly subordinates. Moses and Caesar, too, visited the gullible monarch (*Biog. univ.* [Michaud], *s.v.* "Frédéric-Guillaume II").

tite for territory by her depredations in the East; Austria's compensation for the expenses of the war and the aggrandizement of Prussia was supposed to be at the expense of France — which rendered Austria less conciliatory. Again, Hamburg was one of the principal channels, if not *the* principal channel, for sea-borne trade between France and Germany (in fact, between France and all northern Europe), and Hamburg was potentially under the actual physical control of the Prussian King in his capacity of alternate Director of the Lower Saxon Circle. This inclined France to humor Prussia, and to yield on points which Austria never could have induced her to concede. Lastly, the long struggle between Bourbons and Habsburgs had decided that Austria should be singled out as *the* one continental enemy which the revolutionists desired to preserve for reasons of internal politics. A foreign enemy would keep the minds of the people from their governors' actions and would postpone the return of the *émigrés*. Austria was the hereditary enemy of France, hence a more satisfactory foe than the traditionally friendly Prussia could ever be.[5]

A word of caution must be added concerning France's policy of friendship for Prussia. Sometimes the term "Prussia" implicitly includes the small states of Germany; sometimes it does not. In other words, sometimes the Republic regarded the small states as mere satellites of Prussia. Sometimes it planned an independent role for them. They were to remain within the existing Empire[6] but to serve as a counterpoise to keep Austria and Prussia in balance, so to speak. To this end, every effort was made to evade the Prussian-good-offices provision of the Treaty of Basel. It was insinuated that Prussia's good offices were unnecessary, France being sufficiently friendly inclined without any intervention whatsoever. By thus seeking to bind the small states directly to France, instead of to France through Prussia, the Committee frustrated Frederick William's hope of being regarded as the hero-pacificator of Germany.

France's attitude toward the peace negotiations of the small states was a plain violation of the intentions of the Treaty of Basel, but that document did not represent the Committee's wishes anyway. The theory of the separate peace had turned out to mean starvation for the French troops, who were accustomed to live at the expense of the (now-fast-disappearing) enemy. And neutrality meant only starvation spelled another way. Likewise, armistice. The Committee seems to have foreseen at least some of these difficulties when it informed Barthélemy at the inception of the Basel negotiations that

---

[5] Louis Gottschalk has suggested the following additional point: "Prussia had little to gain by an Austrian victory or to lose by a French victory; but to Austria the outcome was vital."

[6] Below will be discussed Sieyes' plan for detaching the small states from their political union with Austria and Prussia.

"no suspension of hostilities, no armistice, no neutrality of the states of the Empire before the definitive pacification, accords with the interests of France." But Prussia had been unwilling to make peace on other terms. The only solution, therefore, was to sign the peace and violate the terms. At least, that is what was done. The small states of Germany, whose attachment France really desired, by dint of circumstances lost their favored position as eventual allies, and became simply purveyors-extraordinary to the famished French troops trudging the long and weary road to Vienna. Economic motives had caused a virtual reversal of the Convention's policy with respect to the small states of Germany.

A contradiction in the Committee's policy must be pointed out here. The Committee frowned upon the separate peace because it was "economically" fatal to France. It favored the separate peace because it was politically advantageous to France. The French government wished to make peace with Germany by making individual treaties with all the component states of the Empire, and no treaty at all with the Empire as a whole. By this means it would be able to overawe and overwhelm the German princelets. But these separate-peace treaties must not be made until Austria was conquered, else France could not make use of the rights of war to provision the troops conquering Austria. Still these treaties must not all be postponed till the conquest of Austria, for then there would be a demand for a congress, and in union there is strength. The riddle was not solved under the Convention, but the Directory did find an answer which will be supplied in Part II.

Meanwhile, Frederick William fretted and fumed — until he finally realized that the provisions of the Treaty of Basel relating to the small states were not worth the paper on which they were written, that there was no use wasting further paper in remitting protests to Barthélemy. France was friendly to Prussia, it is true, but Frederick William was only the star performer of the show. And when his performance had turned out to be not sufficiently profitable, the producer had decided to take up contributions from the supporting cast. That cooled the ardor of the star, but the show went on.

The second quite constant element in the Convention's German policy concerns the left bank of the Rhine (as indicated). There were many reasons why a nation — any nation — should desire to possess the left bank. For France there were these general reasons, and many special ones besides: The French army could be provisioned there without cost. Cash contributions imposed on the Rhineland could fill the void euphemistically dubbed the French treasury. The possessions of privileged persons in the region could serve as security for some of the Republic's assignats. The Rhineland would

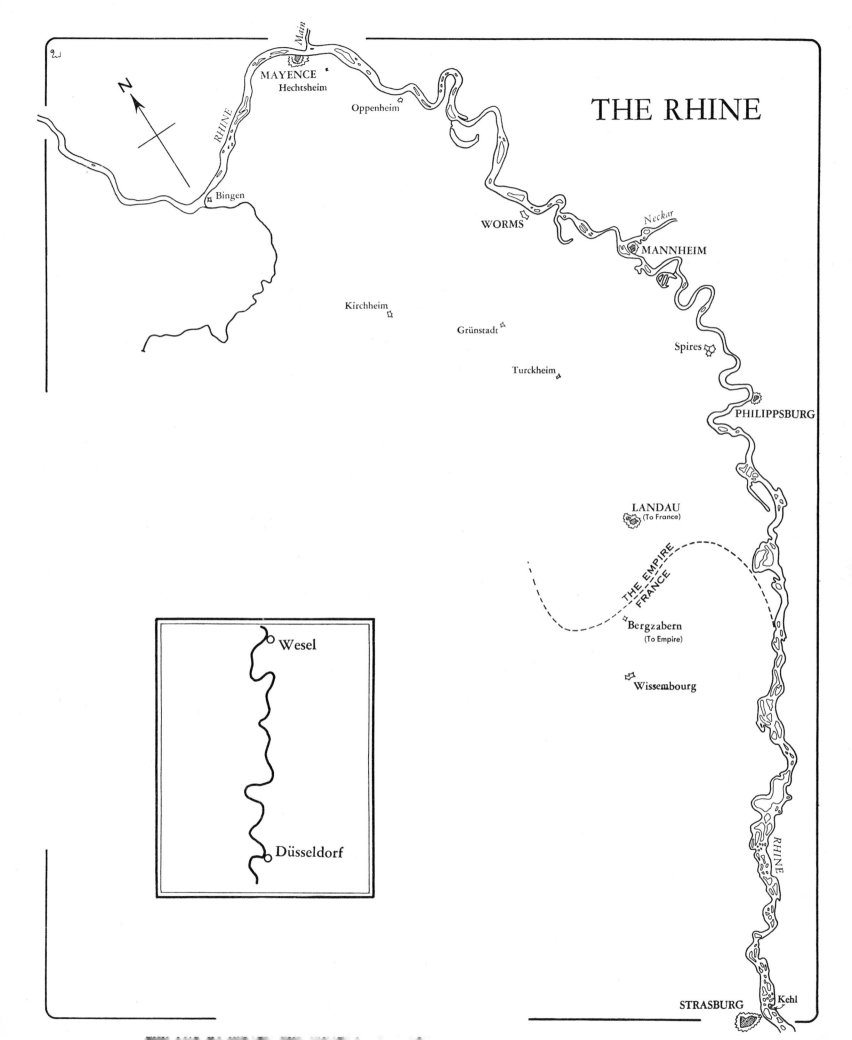

THE RHINE

N

RHINE

Main

MAYENCE
Hechtsheim

Oppenheim

Bingen

Kirchheim

Grünstadt

Turckheim

WORMS

Neckar

MANNHEIM

Spires

PHILIPPSBURG

LANDAU
(To France)

THE EMPIRE
FRANCE

Bergzabern
(To Empire)

Wissembourg

RHINE

Wesel

Düsseldorf

STRASBURG

Kehl

offer some tangible return for the blood and money expended on its conquest. Raw materials, both of the soil and subsoil, were plentiful there, and the horses which grazed on its grassy slopes could provide fine mounts for the French cavalry. The left bank possessed many industries which could complement those of France, and France could learn their processes. Commerce would profit greatly by annexation. Paris would become more nearly the geographical center of France, and would no longer be so close to the frontier. The additional territory would assist in restoring the European balance upset by the Polish partitions, and help to break what Barère called the "commercial tyranny" of England.[7] "Possession [was] nine points of the law," and a goodly part of the Rhineland was in French hands. Patriotism — the desire to extend the power and area of the *patrie* — demanded annexation, especially since Roman Gaul extended to the Rhine. Nature intended states to be bounded by natural barriers — seas, mountains, and great rivers such as the Rhine. Lastly, the Rhine constituted a formidable bulwark against Germanic invasions. In other words, it was a good — yea, the very best — military frontier.

Two of these arguments call for special consideration, the historical and the military. First as to the historical: True it is that Roman Gaul extended to the Rhine, but the matter is not so simple. There were Germans on the Roman side of the River; had been for years. Indeed they were not indigenous, having moved in upon the "autochthonous" Celts. But is any people indigenous?[8] The German infiltration seems to have been a continuing process having its roots in time immemorial, but in the fifth century of our era the trickle became a flood engulfing all of western Europe. Some of the invaders established an empire which included France and part of modern Germany. Then this Empire was divided into three. The left bank of the Rhine formed part of a state wedged in between the nucleus of modern France and the nucleus of modern Germany. Presently this central state was itself partitioned, and in the process, the progenitor of France saw the left bank of the Rhine, an integral part of old Gaul, become part of Germany. Of course, its inhabitants had become thoroughly Germanized if they were not German originally, but the valleys and rivers did not know that. They were still Celtic or French. That was how France viewed the matter, and she saw nothing wrong in trying to regain the Rhineland. In fact, it was a national duty, and both Monarchy and Republic felt its urge. But the Ger-

---

[7] To Conv., Aug. 1, 1793, *Brochures pol.*, LXIII, no. 7, p. 24.

[8] Actually, few if any races on earth today are indigenous. But some are, so to speak, more indigenous than others. It seems that if we go back far enough, we find that no nation has moral title to its lands. Each is merely a squatter who has acquired bare legal title by that agreement among thieves known in International Law as the Doctrine of Immemorial Prescription.

mans have regarded the French version of the *"Drang nach Osten"* as an encroachment on German territory, and wax patriotic over France's wickedness.[9]

Intrinsically, it is difficult to say which side is right. When two children fight over a plum, it is often right to deprive them both of it. Certainly it is good discipline. Historically we have two precedents for an independent state between France and Germany: Lothair's Middle Kingdom, 843–870; and Charles the Bold's more restricted, embryonic copy, 1467–1477.[10] Therein may lie the hope of western Europe for a solution of what has come to be known as the "Rhine problem."

The second reason adduced by France for desiring the left bank of the Rhine was that the Rhine River would guarantee France against Germanic invasions. Let us look at this argument from various points of view.

First as to the thesis itself: Did the Rhine River keep the Germans out of Gaul in the declining years of the Roman Empire? Did the Rhine River keep Louis XIII and Louis XIV out of Germany? Is a river a bulwark, or is it a boulevard, a highway, where points of friction are especially profuse?

Of course the Rhine is a boulevard par excellence. Regarding its potentialities as a bulwark, let us look at the experiences of the French and their enemies during the period treated in this monograph — both before and after October 26, 1795. First, we must draw a distinction between the Upper Rhine in the neighborhood of the Breisgau and Alsace, and the remainder of the River. Austrians and French agree that the Rhine is a true defensive frontier in the south. Wrote General Wurmser to Thugut, "the passage of the Rhine is always very difficult in that region."[11] Declared Carnot, the Upper Rhine presents great difficulties to the aggressor.[12] Explains Saint-Cyr in his *Mémoires*, "The (Rhine) River, in the *départements* of the Haut- and Bas-Rhin, presents difficulties in crossing which do not exist elsewhere. It is dotted with a multitude of islands and of sand banks, which render navigation very difficult. There are few points on the right bank upon which one can land directly. One is almost everywhere obliged to disembark on several islands, in order then to force a passage to the opposite bank; this doubles the obstacles. Also, there are few points where one is able to establish pontoon bridges, and yet less, hanging bridges."[13] Saint-Cyr might have added that the Upper Rhine has a crosswise current which varies from

[9] *Vide* A. Tellkampf (ed.), *Die Franzosen in Deutschland*, Hanover, 1864. Consists of excerpts from various German histories to the effect that ever since France's seizure of the Three Bishoprics (Metz, Toul, Verdun), France has been encroaching on German territory.

[10] Hoche is said also to have contemplated the formation of some sort of Middle Kingdom, as will appear in Pt. II, chap. xxviii, n. 113.

[11] Sept. 16, 1795, *Thugut, C, W,* p. 213.

[12] *Mém. sur Carnot,* I, 478.

[13] III, 35.

left to right and right to left, depending upon the location. This serves as an additional hurdle, for an army intending to cross the River has to choose from a limited number of possible routes.[14]

However, at times, even the southern reaches of the Rhine yield up their defensive qualities. On November 13, 1793, Rivalz informed Deforgues that it had recently rained heavily, "swell[ing] the Rhine, and dissipat[ing] fears that the enemy would seek to cross near here [Basel]."[15] Three years later, almost to the day (November 12, 1796), Desaix wrote to Moreau: "I have just come from Kehl, my general . . . Our means of defense are departing every day in an astonishing manner by the prodigious decline in the level of the stream. Our islands are no more, and we are at the mercy of the enemy."[16] It should not be assumed that this decline is peculiar to the month of November. On the night of April 19–20, 1797, the French wished, according to long-prepared plans, to cross the River to Kehl, but the level of the stream had unaccountably sunk so low that the Mabile Arm of the River was dry.[17] By and large, however, the Upper Rhine forms a good military frontier.

With respect to the remainder of the River, this is far from true. The Rhine is not very difficult to cross, even in the face of a numerous or well-intrenched enemy.[18] Wrote Dumouriez, the conqueror of Belgium: "The famous barrier of the Rhine is good only on the map."[19] And Bonaparte, whose authority cannot be doubted, said: "Never, since history retraces military operations for us, has a river succeeded in constituting a real obstacle. If Moreau wants to cross the Rhine, he crosses it."[20] Cochon, member of the Convention on mission in Holland, sent the following despatch to Merlin of Douai: "If we were wise, we would renounce this barrier of the Rhine, which, moreover, is not so good as is maintained by overexcited persons who know nothing about it. . . . I have not met a single well-informed military man who does not think it would be much more difficult and much more costly to hold than our old boundaries [with rectifications]."[21] Talleyrand,

[14] Poteratz, "Copy of the Propositions . . . Made to Me by Several *Emigrés*," June 1, 1796, Arch. A. E., *Autriche* 365, f. 216.
[15] *Papiers de Barthélemy*, III, 222.
[16] *Mém. Saint-Cyr*, IV, "Pièces justificatives," no. 10 (p. 242). Kehl is at the confluence of the Rhine and Kinzig, within the very acute angle formed by these two rivers.
[17] *Guerres Rév. Emp.*, IV, 365.
[18] "The French succeeded in crossing the Rhine in the face of a much more numerous enemy." — *Guerres Rév. Emp.*, II, 475. "Hoche boldly crossed the Rhine in the presence of the Austrians entrenched on the right bank, and won over them [a] brilliant victory." — Michelet, *Œuv. compl.*, XXXIX (Pt. II: *Les soldats de la Révolution*), 401. "It would be easy for General Wurmser . . . to pass the but-weakly-held Rhine." — Wurmser's "Gedanken über die Eroberung der Provinz Elsass," Vivenot-Zeissberg, *Quellen*, III, 38.
[19] *De la République, ou Coupe d'œil politique sur l'avenir de la France* (1797), quoted in *Mém. sur Carnot*, II, 133, n. 1.
[20] To Dir., April 16, 1797, *Corr. Napo.*, II, 641.
[21] Sorel in *RH*, XVII, 267, April 10, 1795.

the Directory's second minister of foreign affairs, expressed himself thus: "The Rhine, which in several parts of its course winds about, which is in many places studded with islands, is not at all preferable as a frontier to a fortified military line." [22] That the Rhine is too eccentric for a military boundary was the view also of Boissy d'Anglas.[23] Said Tallien, "Several generals and a number of French engineers maintain that the extension of our frontiers to the banks of the Meuse or Rhine would be dangerous because it would lengthen our line of defense without giving us proportional means of rebuffing these attacks." [24] And Lesage of Eure-et-Loir wrote, "The line from Landau to Sedan, says Lloyd, one of the foremost writers on the art of war, is very strong by art and by Nature. It has good forts and the country in front of it is difficult because of mountains and narrow defiles. It appears to me impossible that an enemy could approach with any chance of success." [25]

Here we have, then, on the best authority, that a line of forts constitutes a far better military frontier than the meandering stream which offers in its numerous convolutions a paradise of potential pincers movements to the most mediocre general. If France had her heart set on the Rhine boundary, her only solution was to possess, in addition, a line of forts on the right bank. This was necessarily involved in Brissot's plan to reinforce the natural frontiers with a cordon of small independent republics beyond those frontiers — a design adopted by Sieyes and transmitted by him to Revellière-Lépeaux, Barras, and Bonaparte.[26] Of course it was contemplated that those independent republics would have French garrisons to protect them. Right-bank garrisons must have been contemplated also by Poteratz when he recommended to Boissy that France conserve both banks of the Rhine.[27] And indeed, a forthright demand for right-bank forts was made later — under the Directory.

One of the fondest hopes of the revolutionists was so to reorganize the Empire that it would be forever harmless to France. Some of their plans — in so far as they relate to Franco-Prussian friendship and the left bank of the Rhine — have already been discussed. But others contain new elements that require independent treatment. One of Sieyes' grand designs was that Austria should be allowed Bavaria; Prussia should be allowed proportional gains at the expense of the ecclesiastical states, Hanover, or Austria; and the remainder of the Empire should be formed into a separate confederation

[22] To Bonaparte, Feb. 21, 1798, G. Pallain, *Le ministère de Talleyrand sous le Directoire* (Paris, 1891), p. 199.

[23] Memoir to Conv., Sept. 1, 4, 8, 1795, Arch. A. E., *Allemagne* 669, ff. 236–239.

[24] To Conv., Sept. 30, 1795, *Moniteur*, XXVI, 96.

[25] *Ibid.*, p. 98.

[26] Guyot, *Direc.*, p. 119.

[27] Chap. xv, § 5, *supra*.

guaranteed by France. This new German Empire would then hold the balance between the two other German powers.[28] During the Basel negotiations, Merlin of Thionville presented a Prussian minister in Frankfort with a peace plan purporting to come from the Committee. Article V demanded that four of the southwestern circles of Germany (Upper Rhenish, Electoral Rhenish, Swabian, Franconian) be formed into an independent republic to serve as "a buffer between [France] and the monarchies dangerous to its liberty." France promised "to respect forever the independence of the federal German Republic which it demands as a neighbor." The plan of course provided that the Rhine should be the boundary of France (Article IX).[29]

The Committee often expressed itself as desirous of remolding the Empire at the expense of Habsburg influence, on the lines set down at Westphalia. But such a thoroughgoing reorganization as that suggested by either Sieyes or Merlin was perhaps more than necessary for France's security. Aulard, in his article "La paix future d'après la Révolution française et Kant" ("The Future Peace According to the French Revolution and Kant"), offers a suggestion that would probably have satisfied the Committee (and the Empire), but hardly the Emperor — viz., that the "presidency" of Germany should alternate between the states of the Empire.[30] The preference granted the Habsburgs in the Imperial Electoral College was indeed as little a part of the German constitution as the preinstruction of delegates in our own Electoral College. However, when the lot should once have fallen on Prussia to preside, it probably never would have fallen off, for the Hohenzollerns aspired to the Imperial office with Prussian thoroughness.

A semihumorous aura surrounds the French plans to reorganize the Empire when we know that the Allies were planning to reorganize France. France should be divided into several confederate republics, Philipp Cobenzl suggested on the very day of the cannonade of Valmy.[31] And a map printed in London, and found on a Neapolitan galley, represented Allied plans for France's future as follows (according to Barère's memoirs): Alsace, Lorraine, and the Free County of Burgundy to Austria; Flanders and the land contiguous to the Meuse and Moselle, to Prussia; the seacoast from old Aquitaine to Belgium, to Britain; Roussillon and Navarre to Spain; and southern France to the House of Savoy.[32] The historical basis for assigning Alsace, Lorraine, and the Free County of Burgundy to the House of Habs-

---

[28] This plan for a tripartite division of Germany reappeared on Talleyrand's lips about a decade later (Sorel in *RH*, XVIII, 285–286).

[29] *Propositions de paix du Comité de Salut Public de la République française au Corps germanique,* quoted in Vivenot, *Bas. Fried.,* Pt. I, 253, n. 1.

[30] *RF,* LXVIII (1915), 117.

[31] To Spielmann, Sept. 20, 1792, Vivenot-Zeissberg, *Quellen,* II, 218.

[32] *Mem. Barère,* II, 131–132.

burg-Lorraine is clear;[33] also the reason for assigning western France to the English successors of the Norman dukes.

In the early days of the Revolution, thinkers of every land speculated whether the French Revolution did not signify the dawn of a new era in international relations — an era free from antagonisms, and strivings for power, and wars.[34] They reasoned thus: Wars are the sport of kings, and this sport is loathed by those upon whom devolve its actual burdens. If the Revolution should encompass the earth, kings would disappear, and peoples of all races and creeds would live together in sweet humility. This idea that war is due to the machinations and heartlessness of kings, and that republics are by their very nature inclined to peace, appears in an anonymous pamphlet of the Year I in the Bibliothèque Nationale, *Le rêve d'un homme de bien réalisé, ou Possibilité de la paix générale et perpétuelle* ("The Dream of a Righteous Man Come True, or Possibility of General and Permanent Peace");[35] in Kant's *Perpetual Peace*;[36] in Merlin of Thionville's (the Committee's?) peace plan; and in many other places. It was this idea which served as the justification for much of the early revolutionary propaganda. If all France's neighbors were republics, no one would ever wish to attack her. Thence Brissot's cordon of republics; thence Valence's propositions to Reuss and Lucchesini;[37] thence Article V of Merlin's(?) peace plan — all of which expressed France's wish to be surrounded by free peoples.

For a time it was contemplated that the French Convention should serve as the legislature of the free civilized world,[38] that is, that free men the world over should unite with France to form one state,[39] or at least a fed-

[33] Introduction, § 2e. Austria seems to have reserved her ambitions for cases where she possessed a historical claim. Bavaria, for example, was once the same state as Austria — or rather, Austria was the east march of Bavaria. *Vide* Map 62–63 of W. R. Shepherd, *Historical Atlas*, 4th ed., rev., New York, 1924.

[34] Wrote Condorcet in his *Tableau des progrès de l'esprit humain*: "Nations should seek security and not power." — Quoted in A. Aulard, "Condorcet et la Société des Nations," *RF*, LXXI (1918), 358.

[35] Quoted by Mirkine-Guetzévitch in *RF*, LXXXIV, 327–334. The first half of this title (*Le rêve . . . réalisé*) has the following origin. Under the Regency in France, one *abbé* de Saint-Pierre proposed a confederation of the princes of Europe, an international court, and the outlawry of war. The Regent, upon hearing of the plan, remarked: "C'est le rêve d'un homme de

bien" (That's the dream of a righteous man). The pamphlet of the Year I discusses the question whether this dream could be realized.

[36] *Vide supra*, chap. i, n. 16.

[37] *Vide supra*, chap. i, § 4f.

[38] The idea behind the plan was this: The French Revolution was the product not only of France but of all nations; however, it was "the glory of France to have performed the work of the human race at the price of her own blood" (Louis Blanc, quoted in G. P. Gooch, *History and Historians in the Nineteenth Century* [London and New York, 1913], p. 229). This service gave the French the right and the ability to represent all men.

[39] This is the idea behind Cloots's "State of United Individuals," his "Universal Republic," in which states would be wiped out, and only the State and individuals would remain. Cloots thought to bring about this

eral union, with peace and the general good as its supreme goal.[40] This was the hope of Kant.[41] The French offer of citizenship to liberals and scientists of every nation, and the great consideration accorded foreigners, were steps in the same direction.

It is to be noted that this philosophy was not entirely new. In Cicero and the early Christian writings is found the concept that the human race forms but one and the same society.[42] The contribution of the French Revolution was that sovereignty resides in the universality of the human race.[43]

When once this and related ideas were thoroughly assimilated by the French, they realized how utterly lacking in legality were measures aimed by nation against nation, and in a burst of generosity, renounced war as an instrument of aggrandizement, reserving recourse to force only for the vindication of a just right.[44] But France's enemies ascribed her nobility and good sense to weakness,[45] and when the revolutionists were so foolish as to declare war on Austria for considerations of domestic policy, Austria and Prussia pitted their lust for territory against the French idealism. Now, idealism, embittered, is a bitter foe indeed, and the enlightened propaganda that once aspired to introduce a better world became the instrument of a lust for conquest as insatiable as that which ever emerged from a royal chancellery. Reaction followed also toward the foreigners in France's midst. They were regarded as foreign spies in league with the hated kings, and not a few of them, among them many Germans, were executed.

It is true that Danton and Robespierre and the Thermidorians sought to put a check to revolutionary propaganda, and even renounced its use entirely, but influential individuals who favored the establishment of dependent republics around France — Sieyes, Revellière-Lépeaux, Barras, Bonaparte,

---

end by annexing to France the rest of the world.

In the above-quoted *Rêve*, *RF*, LXXXIV, 330–331, is suggested a European Convention to which each state would send one or more deputies. Another plan, this by one Delaunay, *Plan d'une pacification générale en Europe* ("Design for a General Peace in Europe"), dated Year II, provided for two European confederations, an east and a west (*ibid.*, p. 334).

[40] Condorcet pointed out, in his "D'influence de la Révolution d'Amérique sur l'Europe" that mere pacifism cannot assure peace. One must have an international organization, and then peace will flow therefrom (Mirkine-Guetzévitch in *RF*, LXXXIV, 326) as water from a brimming pitcher. If one leaves a pitcher dry, he ought not expect

to pour out water.

[41] *Vide* his *Perpetual Peace*. The idea appeared again a half century later in Mazzini's plan for a "Solidarity of Republics," whose pledge read: "I believe in the solidarity of Humanity, the duty of nation toward nation, and the duty of every individual in every nation not only to his nation but to the world." — Quoted in W. F. Galpin (ed.), "Letters Concerning the 'Universal Republic,'" *AHR*, XXXIV (1928–29), 786.

[42] Aulard in *RF*, LXVIII, 104.

[43] Carnot combated this theory, for then France would be only part of a sovereign (Aulard in *RF*, LXIX, 70).

[44] *Moniteur*, IV, 432. *Vide* Mirkine-Guetzévitch in *RF*, LXXXII, 260.

[45] *Ibid.*, p. 262.

Hoche — saw in propaganda a legitimate means to a desirable end, and kept the system alive. Propaganda, moreover, continued to be utilized openly as a war measure right through the Revolution, and French generals in Germany regularly issued revolutionary proclamations, and, in their levying of contributions, tended to spare the poor and overburden the privileged classes. Especially was this the custom on the left bank of the Rhine. But all classes were bled so mercilessly for the support of the French troops that the favor to the poor was only relative. To the German farmer whose horses were driven off, to the merchant whose stock was seized, to the village priest who lost his silver relics and perhaps his life to the invaders, there was little doubt that the Revolution was a *French* Revolution, and not a human revolution with French troops as ministering angels.

Partly as a result of Europe's interference in the internal affairs of France, partly because those of low character were quickest to seize the opportunities for power offered by the disorganization of the French state, partly because hunger and other physical wants are more potent factors than reason in determining action, and partly because a multitude of German quislings egged the French on to conquer, the glorious self-denying principles of 1789 were largely forgotten and relations with Germany reverted to the system prevailing before D'Argenson and Vergennes — with new red, white, and blue trimmings, to be sure. The rich Rhine valley became once more the Promised Land, and Nature, the only God whose dictates the revolutionists recognized, beckoned them to enter and take possession. Dutiful sons of Nature, they could not refuse.